THE ARCHAEOLOGY AND ANTHROPOLOGY OF LANDSCAPE

The study of landscape has become increasingly important in archaeology, anthropology and geography. Researchers have raised their perspective beyond that of the individual site or settlement to address the ways in which social process and cultural meanings are shaped by and leave their mark upon the landscape.

The Archaeology and Anthropology of Landscape contains twenty-eight thematic chapters based on contributions to the third World Archaeological Congress held in New Delhi in 1994. Contributors from the British Isles, Scandinavia, North and South America, India, Australia and the Pacific demonstrate the value of cross-disciplinary research in the fields of archaeology, anthropology and geography. They investigate how the meaning of landscapes has either been retained or transformed over time. They also explore how and why different communities sharing the same environment have different perceptions of their surroundings, especially where one is a colonising power.

This book provides new and varied case studies of landscape and environment from five continents and will be of interest to all concerned with the theoretical debates as well as the policy-making issues concerning development and the management of heritage.

Peter J. Ucko is Director of the Institute of Archaeology, University College London. **Robert Layton** is Professor of Anthropology at the University of Durham.

ONE WORLD ARCHAEOLOGY
Series Editor: P. J. Ucko

THE ARCHAEOLOGY AND ANTHROPOLOGY OF LANDSCAPE

Shaping your landscape

Edited by

Peter J. Ucko and Robert Layton

London and New York

First published 1999
by Routledge
2 Park Square, Milton Park, Abingdon, Oxon, OX14 4RN

Simultaneously published in the USA and Canada
by Routledge
711 Third Avenue, New York, NY 10017

First issued in paperback 2011

Typeset in Bembo by The Florence Group, Stoodleigh, Devon

British Library Cataloguing in Publication Data
A catalogue record for this book is available from the British Library.

Library of Congress Cataloging in Publication Data
The archaeology and anthropology of landscape : shaping your
landscape / edited by Peter J. Ucko and Robert Layton.
– (One World Archaeology)
Papers presented at the third World Archaeological Congress,
held in New Delhi, India, Dec. 1994
Includes bibliographical references and index
(hardbound : alk. paper)
1. Landscape assessment – Cross-cultural studies – Congresses.
2. Landscape archaeology – Congresses. I. Ucko, Peter J.
II. Layton, Robert. III. World Archaeological Congress
(3rd: 1994: New Delhi, India) IV. Series.
GF90.A73 1994
304.2–dc21   98–20323

ISBN13: 978-0-415-11767-8 (hbk)
ISBN13: 978-0-415-51496-5 (pbk)

Contents

List of figures

List of tables

List of contributors

Nilu Abeyaratne, School of Anthropology and Archaeology, James Cook University of North Queensland, Townsville, Queensland 4811, Australia.

John Allison, 412 NW 7th Street, Corvallis, OR 97330, USA.

Fisi Andoque, Andoque People, Colombian Amazon, Colombia.

Mónica Espinosa Arango, Department of Anthropology, National University of Colombia, Bogotá (currently, c/o Department of Anthropology, University of Massachusetts, Amherst, USA).

William S. Ayres, Department of Anthropology, University of Oregon, Eugene, OR 97403, USA.

John C. Barrett, Department of Archaeology and Prehistory, University of Sheffield S10 2TN, UK.

Tim Bayliss-Smith, Department of Geography, Downing Place, Cambridge University, Cambridge CB2 3EN, UK.

Barbara Bender, Department of Anthropology, University College London, Gower Street, London WC1H 0PY, UK.

Jaromír Benes, Museum Prachatice and Faculty of Biology, University of South Bohemia, Ceske Budejovice (Czech Republic).

Ashish Chadha, 42-B, Southern Avenue, Calcutta 700 029, India.

Gabriel Cooney, Department of Archaeology, University College Dublin, Belfield, Dublin 4, Ireland.

Timothy Darvill, School of Conservation Sciences, Bournemouth University, Fern Barrow, Poole, Dorset BH12 5DD, UK.

Christopher Evans, Cambridge Archaeological Unit, Department of Archaeology, Cambridge University, Downing Street, Cambridge CB2 3DZ, UK.

Graham Fairclough, English Heritage, 23 Saville Row, London
W1X 1AB, UK.

Andrew Fleming, Department of Archaeology, University of Wales, Lampeter,
Dyfed SA48 7ED, Wales, UK.

Richard Fullagar, Anthropology Division, Australian Museum, PO Box A285,
Sydney South 2000, Australia.

Almudena Hernando Gonzalo, Departamento de Prehistoria, Universidad
Complutense, E-28040 Madrid, Spain.

Lesley Head, School of Geosciences, University of Woolongong,
Woolongong 2522, Australia.

Galina Kharyuchi, Laboratory for the Ethnography and Ethnolinguistics
of the Yamal Peninsula, Salekhard 626600, Yamalo-Nenets Autonomous
Okrug, Russia.

John Kinahan, Namibia Archaeological Trust, c/o PO Box 22407,
Windhoek, Namibia and Department of African Archaeology, Institute of
Archaeology and Ancient History, Uppsala University, S75310 Uppsala,
Sweden.

Sunil Kumar, Department of History, University of Delhi, Delhi 110007,
India.

Nayanjot Lahiri, Department of History, University of Delhi, Delhi 110007,
India.

Robert Layton, Department of Anthropology, University of Durham, 43 Old
Elvet, Durham DH1 3NH, UK.

Lyudmila Lipatova, Yamalo-Nenets District Regional Museum, ul. Titova 5,
Salekhard 626600, Yamalo-Nenets Autonomous Okrug, Russia.

James McGlade, Institute of Archaeology, University College London, 31–4
Gordon Square, London WC1H 0PY, UK.

Rufino Mauricio, Historic Preservation Office, Federated States of Micronesia,
Pohnpei.

Inga-Maria Mulk, Ajtte Swedish Sámi and Mountain Museum, S-96223,
Jokkmokk, Sweden.

Mike Parker Pearson, Department of Archaeology & Prehistory, University of
Sheffield S10 2TN, UK.

Ramilisonina, Institut de Civilisation, Musée d'Art et d'Archéologie,
Antanarivo, Madagascar.

Retsihisatse, Analamahery, Andalatanosy, Ambovombe 604, Madagascar.

David Roe, School of Anthropology and Archaeology, James Cook University of North Queensland, Townsville, Queensland 4811, Australia.

Robin Sim, Division of Archaeology and Natural History, Research School of Pacific and Asian Studies, Australian National University, Canberra ACT 0200, Australia.

Upinder Singh, St Stephen's College, University of Delhi, Delhi 110 007, India.

Claire Smith, Department of Archaeology, School of Humanities, Flinders University, Adelaide, Australia.

Veronica Strang, Department of Archaeology, University of Wales, Lampeter, Dyfed SA48 7ED, Wales, UK.

Jerry Taki, Cultural Centre, Erromango, Vanuatu.

Peter J. Ucko, Institute of Archaeology, University College London, 31–4 Gordon Square, London WC1H 0PY, UK.

Darrell West, Aboriginal Heritage Office, Forestry Tasmania, PO Box 180, Launceston, Tasmania 7249, Australia.

Mats Widgren, Department of Human Geography, Stockholm University, S-106 91 Stockholm, Sweden.

Marek Zvelebil, Department of Archaeology and Prehistory, University of Sheffield S10 2TN. UK.

Preface

The third World Archaeological Congress (WAC 3) was held in New Delhi, India, in December 1994. Its academic sessions lasted for five days, some of which were marred by administrative problems within an overly politically fraught atmosphere (and see, e.g., Golson 1995; Hassan 1995; Sawday 1995; Quinn 1999). Happily, the sessions in 'Theme 12: The Frontiers of Landscape Archaeology: time, space and humanity' (originally to be organised by M.K. Dhavalikar, D. Austin, A. Fleming and P.J. Ucko), which form the basis of this book, ran smoothly in the advertised meeting room, and happened more or less on time.

What follow are some of the papers presented in 1994, completely rewritten and updated by their authors for publication as chapters for this book, as well as some specially commissioned new contributions; inevitably – for reasons of space as much as anything else – many of the original 1994 papers have had to be excluded from this volume. Nevertheless, the book maintains much of the original intention of its advertised sub-themes: discussion of new approaches to landscape studies, especially as 'a form of social and environmental enquiry'; landscapes in the context of social power and the exercise of political control; and the management and conservation of landscapes. Above all we have been concerned to keep to the spirit of the 1993 announcement of the WAC 3 landscape theme, which stressed – 'possessing your landscape' – that it would also focus on the way in which 'communities understand and express their relationships with their landscapes', and to this end we have included detailed case studies from many different parts of the world.

We thank David Austin, Gabriel Cooney and Andrew Fleming for trying to assist at various times in this whole venture. David Austin was involved first in the UK, then in India and again, subsequently, in the UK. Above all we thank the authors of the following pages for their patience in what has proved to be a very long gestation process.

P.J. Ucko, London
R. Layton, Durham

References

Golson, J. 1995. What went wrong with WAC 3 and an attempt to understand why. *Australian Archaeology* 41, 48–54.

Hassan, F. 1995. The World Archaeological Congress in India: politicizing the past. *Antiquity* 69, 874–7.

Quinn, M. 1999. The séance of 27 August 1889 and the problem of historical consciousness. In *Back from the Edge: archaeology in history*, P. Funari, M. Hall and S. Jones (eds). London: Routledge.

Sawday, J. 1995. Site of debate. *The Times Higher Educational Supplement* 13 January, 16–17.

1   *Introduction: gazing on the landscape and encountering the environment*

ROBERT LAYTON AND PETER J. UCKO

Interest in landscape transcends many traditional academic divisions and disciplines. Use of the term is becoming wider and wider. Rowlands, for example, has recently entitled a discussion of modern economics in the Cameroon 'Looking at financial landscapes' (Rowlands 1996). In this Introduction we review recent ways in which archaeologists and anthropologists have made use of the concept of landscape and show how these uses relate to issues addressed by contributors to the volume.

Landscapes are particular ways of expressing conceptions of the world and they are also a means of referring to physical entities. The same physical landscape can be seen in many different ways by different people, often at the same time (as is shown by, e.g. Franklin and Bunte 1997; Pokotylo and Brass 1997). There is much recent writing on the subject of landscape which has established, in sensitive and wide-ranging discussions, that the term may refer both to an environment, generally one shaped by human action, and to a representation (particularly a painting) which signifies the meanings attributed to such a setting (Olwig 1993: 307, 312; see also Penning-Rowsell and Lowenthal 1986; Bender 1993; Hirsch 1995). Even advertisers can wax lyrical on the subject. ESSO has recently endorsed the view that 'landscape is undoubtedly one of the most popular and universally loved themes in the history of Western art'. The matter is further complicated by the fact that, while landscape painting is clearly a mode of representation that signifies ideas and values about its subject matter, the construction of monuments, ornamental lakes and groves turns the land itself into a signifier, a process that Olwig calls 'the colonisation of nature by landscape' (Olwig 1993: 332). These multiple senses give rise to what Gosden and Head call landscape's 'useful ambiguity': 'Landscape encompasses both the conceptual and the physical' (Gosden and Head 1994: 113). While such ambiguity may sometimes be useful, it can also obscure the different orientations that writers can draw upon when they use the term landscape. One approach equates landscape with an environment that has an existence independent of those who live in it, as the following definition illustrates: 'In general, the physical environment describes the characteristics of a landscape (e.g. climate, geography) which have not been markedly changed by human impact' (Crystal 1990: 412). Another insists that 'a landscape is a cultural image, a pictorial way of representing, structuring or symbolising surroundings' (Daniels and Cosgrove 1988: 1). While Ingold has argued for a single definition of landscape, Olwig shows that it is fruitless to argue over which of the two orientations cited above is correct; both are established usages (Ingold 1993: 153–7; Olwig 1993: 339–40). In fact, while Ingold argues that 'the landscape is the world as it is known to those who dwell therein' (Ingold 1993: 156), he also defines landscape as 'a pattern of activities "collapsed" into an array of features', an external form created by a pattern of human activities which remains visible to archaeologists after its creators have disappeared (Ingold 1993: 162).

The two definitions correspond to two of the principal themes in this volume and can be characterised in terms of the Weberian distinction between explanation and understanding. According to Weber (1947: 79ff), explanation depended on recording statistical regularities in human behaviour that could then be explained in terms of sociological laws, while under-standing depended on observation of meaningful interaction, in order to discover the meanings specific to that time and place which actors attributed to their own and others' behaviour. An ecological approach explains behaviour as a response to external causes, while a cultural approach aims to understand behaviour as meaningful. While contributors to this volume iden-tify external causes of behaviour in both natural and social environments, the first approach treats landscape as an object external to perception but capable of description. The second approach regards landscape as the expression of an idea, which the analyst must try to understand and, as far as possible, translate into the terms of his or her own discourse (for a review of similar debates in psychology, see Stokols and Shumaker 1981).

Explanation

Several contributors to this volume explain patterns of social behaviour in terms of adaptations to the natural environment. Abeyaratne (Chapter 10) argues that the ecology of Sri Lanka's Dry Zone constrains levels of produc-tivity; Smith, Strang, Layton, and Fullagar and Head all explore aspects of Australian Aboriginal social behaviour as adaptations to the savannah zone of northern Australia (Chapters 14, 15, 16 and 22), and Kharyuchi and Lipatova (Chapter 20) describe how the Nenets have adapted to the Gydan Peninsula of Siberia. Widgren, Abeyaratne and Chadha explain how relations of power in the social environment constrain or enable social strategies (Chapters 7, 10 and 11).

Understanding

The idea of landscape as an ideologically motivated representation of the world is particularly associated with the work of Cosgrove and Olwig (e.g. Cosgrove 1984; Olwig 1993, 1996). They trace the origin of the modern concept of landscape to a genre of painting patronised by a new mercantile class. Anthropologists and archaeologists have developed this approach by arguing that other cultural traditions have also constructed 'landscapes', expressed in oral tradition and in the construction of monuments, that reveal other assertions of power or right to the land (Bender 1993; Hirsch and O'Hanlon 1995). In the contributions by Evans and Hernando (Chapters 28 and 18), the study of landscape is seen to require learning to read landscapes constructed in the idiom of another culture and translating those readings for an academic audience. The problem of rereading landscapes created in prehistoric times poses particular problems that are discussed later in this Introduction.

The impact of postmodernism

Postmodernism challenges the neat distinction between explanation and understanding, and it is questionable whether either archaeology or anthropology has fully come to terms with the challenge. It has become impossible to deny that our own explanations are culturally constructed; even if they refer to an independent reality, they enable knowledge of the world not as it is, but merely as we represent it to ourselves. From the thoroughgoing postmodernist perspective, there is no environment, only landscape (see Table 1.1). Thus Bender and Hirsch, following Cosgrove, have pointed out that the current western notion of landscape draws upon an Enlightenment notion of the land

Table 1.1 Landscape and environment: the modernist and post-modernist positions

Landscape	Environment
interaction with interpretation representation } 'gaze upon'	explanation cause or constraint } 'bump into'
consequence meaningful action	adaptation
Modernist representation emic (local) beliefs them/arts	etic (universal) theories us/science
Postmodernist representation their interpretation	our interpretation

viewed by a seemingly disengaged observer (Bender 1993: 1; Hirsch 1995: 2), originally the landlord of the age of enclosures (Cosgrove 1984) but sometimes today the academic researcher (Thomas 1993a: 25). Any view may be contested and 'even in the most scientific of Western worlds, past and future will be mythologised' (Bender 1993: 2). Mulk and Bayliss-Smith's contribution to this volume shows how interpretations of archaeological material may be politically motivated (Chapter 24).

The argument that the Enlightenment's 'objectivity' was compromised from the start by its implication in methods of social control was memorably expressed in Foucault's discussion of Bentham's Panopticon (Foucault 1977: 195ff). Foucault associates the Enlightenment with the transition of methods of social control from the public display of punishment to more insidious control, from torture to discipline. Excruciating public execution was the tool of kings, used to punish the disloyalty of lawbreakers. Surveillance and discipline are the tools of the modern state first developed in the Prussian army, to straighten those who deviate from the common good. The chilling rationalism of the Panopticon placed prisoners (or factory employees, or hospital patients) in cells around a central tower, from which they could be subjected to surveillance by an unseen warden (Foucault 1977: Plates 3 and 6). Implicitly, the Cartesian 'I' which exists separately from its sensory experiences is not a disinterested observer but a political agent who gazes on those under his surveillance. The Renaissance technique for plotting a three-dimensional landscape, transforming and framing it into a two-dimensional painting available for inspection, invites the inference that landscape painting also had a political dimension. This inference is supported when we learn that those who promoted the enclosures also strove to erase the peasant society of the dispossessed by replacing it with a romantic image of wild, untouched nature, while those who opposed enclosure contrasted the benign, 'unimproved' landscape of the past with the regimented and fenced landscape that had replaced it (Daniels 1988: 70–2; Olwig 1993: 322, 333; Prince 1988; compare Bender 1993: 2, 10 and Barrett this volume Chapter 2). Maps can also be said to order and control the landscape (Harley 1988: 279; Bender this volume Chapter 3, and see Tanner in press for the way in which maps differ from landscapes).

The Enlightenment provided the grounds for treating western knowledge as globally valid, opposing it to the local knowledge of indigenous cultures. This tendency is graphically conveyed in Adam's breathtaking claim that 'a good test case of art for art's sake is landscape painting. Generally speaking it is very rare in primitive art' (Adam 1963: 48). The same tendency can be seen in some contributions to the present volume, such as Hernando, and Arango and Andoque (Chapters 18 and 17). In the latter case, however, it is the indigenous author Fisi Andoque who writes 'we, the Andoque people, think that the world is limited to only what is directly known to us'. Fisi Andoque's remark recalls the Inuit witness's refusal to take the oath during the hearings into the James Bay hydro-electric scheme on the grounds that he could not tell 'the truth, the whole truth and nothing but the truth', he could only say what he knew (Clifford 1988: 8). Among contributors to this volume, Barrett (Chapter 2) writes of the way in which legitimacy was denied to local knowledge in England during the eighteenth century, while Chadha (Chapter 11) describes how the local knowledge of Indian 'tribals' has been marginalised in the name of 'progress'. McGlade (Chapter 29) reviews ways of integrating local and scientific knowledge in the management of cultural landscapes. The error lies in claiming that our elaborate techniques of investigation and wider experience render our knowledge transparent and universal, as opposed to accepting, like the Inuit and Andoque, that it is mediated and limited. Barrett writes in this volume of the archaeologist's tendency to privilege the moment of creation as the 'date' for a reused and reinterpreted artefact, while Fairclough (Chapter 9) criticises the 'time-sliced' approach to repair and reconstruction. Both are consequences of a conceptual 'lens' in archaeology which represents the world as a linear chronology and explains phenomena with reference to their origins. Allison and McGlade both highlight the political dimension of 'heritage management' in the United States and Europe respectively (Chapters 19 and 29). Fleming (Chapter 5) considers how changes in the English landscape of Swaledale can be differently represented when observed from different political perspectives.

Writing as oppression

During Lévi-Strauss's fieldwork among the Nambikwara of Brazil, the leader of the band with whom he was travelling realised that note-taking gave the anthropologist an important source of power. Wanting to impress the other members of the band, the leader pretended to be able to read and write. Lévi-Strauss was prompted to speculate about what it was that writing had made possible, developing as it did after such important events as the origin of farming. He concludes that writing was invented to facilitate slavery in early empires; the 'disinterested' writing of intellectuals was a secondary development (Lévi-Strauss 1973: 296–9). Derrida took issue with the claim that any writing could be disinterested. The very act of characterising the Nambikwara as different to Europeans was a form of oppression. The violence of anthropology occurs at 'the moment when the [cultural] space is shaped and reoriented by the gaze of the foreigner' (Derrida 1976: 113). The colonial act of 'discovering' and renaming places is an example of such oppression. So too is the rereading as wild or barren of a landscape that, to its indigenous inhabitants, is filled with tradition. This is exemplified by Cooney, Strang, and Allison in their respective contributions (Chapters 4, 15, and 19) and, perhaps most explicitly, by Mulk and Bayliss-Smith in Chapter 24, where it is shown how Scandinavian colonialism continues in its attempt to freeze the indigenous people into a single, unchanging pattern of nomadic reindeer-herding. Competing readings may put the researcher at odds with the local inhabitants. Sim and West (Chapter 27) describe a case where such opposition was transformed into co-operation. Evans (Chapter 28) records the negotiation of interpretations that took place between shamans and archaeologists among the ruins of former settlements in the Himalayas, while Fullagar and Head (Chapter 22) discuss ways in which archaeological and indigenous interpretations can be reconciled. Ayres and Mauricio (Chapter 21) look at the additional problems that arise where the control of indigenous knowledge confers power, while Bender (Chapter 3) documents ways in which indigenous people have subverted the 'Western gaze'.

It has become increasingly common in anthropology to try to overcome the oppression created by academic writing by dispelling the illusion of objective observation. Anthropologists describe their anxieties in the field and their struggles with informants. Discussions with members of the community are presented in the text, so that the people with whom one worked are transformed from objects of research into active subjects participating in an intercultural discourse. In this volume, several chapters are jointly authored by a member of the community studied (Arango and Andoque, Ayres and Mauricio, Mulk and Bayliss-Smith, Parker Pearson, Ramilisonina and Retsihisatse, Roe and Taki).

Is there a world out there?

There is an unfortunate tendency in some postmodernist literature to confuse the proposition that we can never know the world as it is but only through our representations of it (Thomas 1993a: 23, 28) with either or both of the claims that there is no (meaningful) world external to consciousness, or that meaning can make no reference to the world, since the meaning of words is defined only in relation to other words. These other claims originate in the work of Derrida. Saussure had argued that the association of sound and meaning was created entirely by cultural convention. The meaning of each linguistic sign is determined by its position in the total language, in opposition to other signs. Language, for Saussure, was a property of what Durkheim called the 'collective consciousness', which outlived and transcended individual members of the community (Saussure 1959).

Derrida took half of the Saussurian theory of meaning, but threw out the notion of a durable, shared language. For Derrida, there is no collective consciousness. Current meanings are established by usage, in juxtaposition to the meanings that preceded them. Because meanings are defined in a dictionary-like sense, in opposition to other meanings within the structure of language, the world itself has no meaning. There is no 'transcendental signified'. As language changes, so it becomes impossible to recover the meanings that people intended in the past (Derrida 1976: 49–60). Derrida's notion of speech as a negotiated process is probably accurate, as the constant revision of dictionaries suggests. Both Cooney's and Strang's chapters in this volume show how a single environment may be construed as two quite different landscapes by the indigenous and colonising people who rely upon it. It would be difficult to argue that these environments contained any 'natural' meanings. What Derrida fails to explain is the process by which intersubjective understanding is achieved during daily social interaction. A complete theory of communication therefore also needs to take account of the American theorists Peirce and Morris, as well as Saussure. According to these writers, signs can be classified according to the way in which they denote or refer to objects in the environment (Peirce 1931; Morris 1938: esp. 24, 47). Those who interact in a particular setting can become aware of each others' subjective intentions by identifying the references they make in the course of communicating (Rommetveit 1987: 86; cf. Olwig 1993: 319–20; Layton 1995: 215–16, 1997: 125–8).

	denotation		*signification*	
object	←	sound/picture	→	idea

In this volume, Fairclough (Chapter 9) cites physical transformations to the environment such as soil changes caused by human action, but also writes of the problem of defining a landscape for management purposes. Landscape 'is created in perception, [and] does not in a real sense exist as a material object'. Ayres and Mauricio (Chapter 21), however, describe landscape as situated on the interface between the physical and cognitive. They stress how really effective environmental and cultural conservation can result only when based on concepts of indigenous landscapes together with the archaeological evidence of subsistence and settlement patterns. Beneš and Zvelebil (Chapter 6) quote Vidal de la Blanche's (1902) somewhat earlier remark that 'landscape itself is an imprint left by the image of its people'. Landscape inextricably combines referents and signifiers.

The theory that meaning is established and changes through usage is central to the work of Bourdieu and Giddens, as well as that of Derrida. Bourdieu defined *habitus* as a set of principles enabling people to cope with unforeseen and ever-changing situations (Bourdieu 1977: 72). In order to explain how a community's *habitus* could come into being in the absence of a collective consciousness, he interpreted it as a set of strategies that had been shaped by past circumstances, handed down in sayings and popular wisdom. Over time, individuals gain material wealth and a reputation (symbolic capital) as a result of their success in using strategies drawn from the *habitus* (compare Giddens's concept of 'practical consciousness' (Giddens 1984: 90)). Several contributors to this volume interpret the genesis of meaning in similar ways. Abeyaratne relies explicitly on Bourdieu. Barrett (Chapter 2) writes, 'Inhabiting a landscape involves understanding that landscape, with reference not to ahistorical principles but to earlier experiences'; Smith (Chapter 14) states, 'Social landscapes are both "transformed" and "transforming"'. Strang (Chapter 15) describes how the pastoral (colonial) landscape of Cape York becomes sedimented as a history of individuals battling against a hostile environment, whereas for the indigenous people it is affiliation by birth and descent to the ancestral beings and the places they formed that gives meaning to people's place in the landscape. Quoting Bender (1993: 1), Strang argues that landscapes are created by people through their engagement with the world around them; Gosden and Head similarly argued that the idea of a 'social landscape' reverses the concept of environmental determinism, and treats the environment as a space in which human skills are deployed. Material settings are therefore not external to social being, but constructed through past human action (Gosden and Head 1994: 113, 114). Tilley likewise proposed that 'locales are places created and known through common experiences, symbols and meanings' (Tilley 1994: 18). Fullagar and Head (Chapter 22) cite Morphy's observation that landscape is not just the signifier in a sign system, it is the referent, and integral to the message (Morphy 1995: 186).

Barrett (Chapter 2) writes, 'Meaning is not simply produced or stated: it must be recognised through a practical understanding of the world and its interpretation'. The researcher and the people under study can both speak of external constraints that influence behaviour. The environment can, for example, be referred to by indicating the direction of river flow. For the Andoque the west is 'up', while for the Alawa it is from the south that the principal rivers run (see Chapters 17 and 16). When, however, shamanistic encounters or the routes of ancestral beings are anchored by reference to the topography, the culturally relative character of causal theories is thrown into relief. We can easily accept the rationality of orienting oneself in an environment in terms of drainage patterns, but it is harder to accept that places were created by the actions of beings who could transcend the boundary between animal and human existence. It is here that the problem of translation is most acute. Kinahan (Chapter 23) shows how San combine acute observation of weather patterns in the deserts of southern Africa with a culturally specific theory of causality. The problem of translating theories of causation was noted by Quine (1960). He argued that an anthropologist could easily learn statements in a foreign language such as 'there goes a rabbit', since rabbits are objects of shared experience. Quine called this kind of statement an 'observation sentence'. A sentence such as 'neutrinos lack mass' can be understood only if one has learnt the theory of being that justifies it. 'Theoretical sentences' are less anchored to their references than are 'observation sentences' (Quine 1960: 76). Quine contends that theories are always underdetermined by experience. In trying to explain any aspect of how the world works, 'countless alternative theories would be tied for first place' (Quine 1960: 23). Derrida's argument that meaning is created within the shifting structures of culture, and cannot be referred to the environment, is most plausible with regard to theoretical sentences. It can, nonetheless, be countered by the argument that any system of belief, or theory of causation, must at least produce behaviour that is compatible with survival.

Expressions of culture in the environment

Three principal ways in which culture is expressed in the environment are identified by contributors to this volume. Having represented the environment in his or her own terms, usually as an ecological system to which behaviour must adapt, the analyst can identify the strategies that people rely on as they respond to, negotiate with or overcome any perceived constraints. Strategies are not necessarily individual ones, and the analyst can also examine evidence for the social organisation of labour that regulates people's access to resources and transformation of their surroundings. Finally, recalling Olwig's idea of 'the colonisation of nature by landscape' (Olwig 1993: 332), the analyst can attempt to identify other communities' meaningful references to landscape features embedded in monuments.

Human adaptation and transformation of the environment

An analysis that aims at explanation is likely to concentrate on the ways in which people respond to the constraints and opportunities of their environment. This approach treats cultural traits as potentially adaptive. It argues that, regardless of how we perceive the environment, the blind forces of evolution will shape culture. The idea that an innovation can be regarded as the cultural analogue of a genetic mutation has a long history, traceable to the work of the French sociologist Tarde writing at the end of the nineteenth century (Tarde 1969). Boyd and Richerson, and Durham have argued that culture is a body of ideas that are translated into action in a fashion analogous to the process by which genes are translated into bodily form and behaviour (Boyd and Richerson 1985; Durham 1991). The trajectories of human adaptation are a consequence of what Durham termed the 'coevolution' of genes and culture (cf. McGlade this volume Chapter 29).

If the postmodern insight, that Darwinian theory is a representation of interaction between organisms and their environment that draws heavily on the style of analysis used in market economics, is put to one side, the theory is useful, and is used by several contributors. In seeking to explain why culture became so important in human evolution, writers working within the neo-Darwinian paradigm have pointed out several differences between cultural and genetic evolution (see, for example, Cavalli-Sforza and Feldman 1981; Boyd and Richerson 1985; Durham 1991). These authors argue that culture has a potential advantage in allowing new patterns of behaviour to be transmitted more rapidly (within the span of one generation) and more widely (beyond the parent–child relationship) than would be possible through the natural selection of random genetic variation. If transmission from parent to child were the only mode of transmission for cultural traits, culture would follow the same lines as genetic transmission. The significance of cultural inheritance increases when traits can be transmitted horizontally (between members of the same generation) and obliquely (between generations, but not to the transmitter's own children). A single teacher can transmit to many pupils.

This approach responds to the questions posed by postmodernism by arguing that the way in which people attribute meaning to the world, or model causation, is incidental to the objective consequences of behaviour. The fact that the writers' own theories about how behaviour is shaped are specific to western culture, and that no more than provisional knowledge can be accepted, has in fact been acknowledged from the Enlightenment onwards (cf. Gower 1997). It is recognised that, whereas all genetic mutations occur at random, a cultural innovation may be devised in response to a perceived problem. Humans are, however, rarely perfectly informed. Errors in assessing the innovation, or lack of information about the environment, may render the response to a perceived problem inappropriate (Cavalli-Sforza and Feldman 1981: 342). Even when those adopting cultural traits have no effective means of judging their consequences, the capacity of culture to generate new variants, and to transmit them rapidly and widely, may give culture an advantage over genetic evolution by speeding up the rate at which random variants are subject to selection (Boyd and Richerson 1985: 199).

Odling-Smee (1988, 1995) and McGlade (this volume Chapter 29) have pointed out that organisms are not just subject to natural selection pressures in environments, they also change their environment by constructing nests, burrows and trails, by influencing its humidity, pH and temperature. They therefore must modify at least some of the selection pressures that bear upon succeeding generations. Culture amplifies the capacity of human beings to modify their environments and therefore enhances the process of niche-construction, but culture is not exempt from the effects of natural selection.

Ayres and Mauricio (this volume Chapter 21) follow other writers on the Pacific in describing the introduction of plants and animals to Pacific Islands as 'transporting landscapes' (cf. Gosden and Head 1994: 114). Kumar's detailed and unusual analysis of the history of human interaction with a reservoir on the outskirts of Delhi traces the way in which a human modification to the environment influences subsequent behaviour (Chapter 12). Beneš and Zvelebil demonstrate that the Czech landscape is not a passive recipient of human activities, and show how antecedent use influences successive behaviour. Initial forest clearance is followed not by full regeneration but by a more open mosaic; episodes of erosion coincide with change in both climate and land use (Chapter 6). Fleming plots the traces of earlier land-use patterns in Swaledale left in field names and boundaries (Chapter 5).

Social strategies which co-ordinate or coerce action

Widgren (Chapter 7) shows that the survival and later abandonment of small farms in parts of southern Sweden cannot be explained solely in terms of the actions of those who worked them. To survive, the farms had to be part of a wider social network, sustained by the power of landlords. Once that social network had broken down, the farms ceased to be viable. Strang (Chapter 15) contrasts the traditionally self-sufficient indigenous economy of Cape York with the pastoral economy that survives as an outpost tenuously connected to urban Australian society. The fencing of paddocks, sinking of bores and construction of mustering camps are all assertions of power that depend entirely on the success of selling cattle in distant markets. Smith and Layton (Chapters 14 and 16) also show how contemporary Aboriginal culture in northern Australia has been sustained in the face of the predation of colonists and their pastoral economy. The community studied by Smith has been displaced from its traditional country, while that described by Layton has managed to remain within it. Allison describes the increasing constraints placed on native American land use in the state of Oregon and their concerted efforts to resist attempts to dispossess them (Chapter 19). Evidence of the co-ordination of action in the past can be found in estates (Fairclough, Chapter 9) and forts (Evans, Chapter 29)

Reading the landscape

Reading the landscape as an expression of meanings negotiated in past or present cultures will depend on identifying a community's references to external features that we also can perceive. The opportunities for achieving this differ for anthropology and archaeology.

Schutz developed the phenomenological approach to interpretation in the 1930s (Schutz 1972). Meaning, he argued, is that which individuals attach to their own acts. Awareness and meaning are obtained by 'reflecting' back, or casting a retrospective glance upon lived experience (*Erlebnisse*) as it carries us forward. Such subjective activity differs even between individuals who frequently come into contact, but more so between people separated in time or space. Schutz used the term 'intersubjectivity' to describe the condition in which we experience the world as something whose significance we share with others (Schutz 1972: 139). To intuit the subjective meanings another person attributes to the world, we try to imagine the 'project' in which the other is engaged by matching it with one in which we have participated. Yet, to the extent that our previous experiences differ, we can never fully achieve intersubjective understanding. 'I ascribe to you an environment which has already been interpreted from my subjective standpoint' (Schutz 1972: 105).

What Eco calls communicative discourse (Eco 1990: 40–1, 53) occurs in face-to-face, spoken interaction of the sort practised during anthropological fieldwork. Participant observation can be considered as a technique for achieving the intersubjective understanding advocated by Schutz across cultural boundaries. The basic limitation of fieldwork is the extent to which the anthropologist can, in a matter of months, participate in a flow

of significations in which the lived experience of indigenous people within
their landscape extends, via contemporary racism, back to the violent disruption of colonialism and further into the past. The retrospective glance cast
by indigenous peoples upon their own experience (including encounters with
other anthropologists) draws upon events that occurred long before the arrival
of the fieldworker.

Denied the possibility of participant observation, it can be expected that
the archaeologist will have even greater difficulty than the anthropologist in
attempting to understand the lived experience of another cultural tradition.
Nonetheless, we have argued above that the postmodernist habit of treating
systems of meaning as entirely self-defining is in error. During cultural
communication, reference is made either to objects or agents (through denotation), or to a broader cultural discourse, which exist outside the message
itself. Meaningful practices may leave their mark on the landscape. Where
an enduring cultural discourse, or *habitus*, is transmitted over successive generations, the patterning of such references becomes sufficiently habitual to be
recognisable to the archaeologist. If references to objects and places become
visible as a recurrent practice the denotative aspects of past communication
may still be apparent. This perhaps allows archaeology to escape from the
closed worlds of postmodernist theory.

Unlike denotation, however, signification can be discovered only through
interaction with members of the cultural tradition. For archaeology, only the
world of references is left. We may attempt to construe the text in terms of
our inferred understanding of the 'possible world' of meaning inhabited by
the performers, but those performers of the past cannot correct our mistakes
(cf. Shanks and Tilley 1987). Purely referential gestures leave the analyst with
an 'empty' system of signification. The desire to fill the empty signs with
meaning almost invariably leads the analyst to create a surrogate discourse.
The analyst may attribute modern values to a prehistoric tradition (religion),
invert modern values to create a system based on magic and superstition, or
import ethnographic meanings drawn from other cultures (shamanism or
totemism).

Two problems for archaeology

A hermeneutic (interpretive) approach to the study of landscapes reveals two
problems for archaeology. The first is that cognitive systems are underdetermined by their environment. Experience is never adequate to determine
which of many possible theories is correct: 'alternatives emerge: experiences
call for changing a theory, but do not indicate just where and how' (Quine
1960: 64). Many possible cultural systems can therefore exist within the same
ecological space, and none could be predicted in its entirety or specificity
from the ecological conditions. Lahiri and Singh (this volume Chapter 13),
for example, conclude that rural perceptions in Ballabgarh do not simply and

mimetically reproduce the formal, physical attributes of the landscape, they actively transform what is given. Wherever actions are predicated on intention or meaning, any explanation of behaviour in terms of the shaping role of the environment will therefore be incomplete. A complete account would have to include a description of the meanings that the actions intended to convey. The construction of monuments, or other meaningful transformations of the landscape, can only partly be analysed through theories of adaptation.

The second difficulty for archaeology is that expressions of cognition or meaning in the environment are often ambiguous. Normally, repeated interaction within a community will clarify the circumstantial or contextual clues that are needed to clarify such ambiguity (cf. Layton 1997). Eco argues that every discourse belongs to a community of knowers who can agree on what constitutes a relevant reading of an ambiguous text (Eco 1990: 38–41). Denied access to the community that created his objects of study, the archaeologist cannot be sure what would constitute an authorised interpretation of a prehistoric monument.

One solution to this problem that appears frequently in the recent archaeological literature on landscape is to adopt a structuralist method, implicitly following Lévi-Strauss's approach to South American mythology (first advanced in Lévi-Strauss 1970). This approach looks for evidence of the structuring of material settings that can be read as signifying universal cognitive oppositions. Such oppositions are, according to Lévi-Strauss, intrinsically generated by the way in which the human mind works and therefore have cross-cultural validity. Once these universal elements have been identified, a bridge has been built allowing access to the specific meanings that characterised ancient cultures.

Thomas (1993a: 32, cf. 1993b), for example, argues that the Neolithic arrives in Britain as a 'package' in which cultural constructions of meaning gave rise to various practices that left material residues in the landscape. These, he proposes, acted as channels for the flow of meaningful action from past into future. As Bourdieu argued, meanings are transmitted from one generation to the next through their manifestations in interpersonal relations, house construction and ritual (Bourdieu 1977). A regular patterning of references to the landscape can be detected in the way in which neolithic monuments are constructed and distributed. Thomas infers that chambered tombs conveyed different messages to those who viewed them from afar, close to or inside and the latter position was conferred only on the most privileged, who had access to its 'hidden, enigmatic contents. . . . If the bodies of the dead were introduced into the chambers whole, and then partly or wholly disordered, it follows that the tomb was less a place of resting than a site of transformation' (Thomas 1993a: 35). Noting the various activities that seem to have been conducted near the tomb entrance, he (Thomas 1993a: 37) infers a structural equivalence between handling goods brought from a distance, the treatment of the newly dead, and communal feasting on freshly slaughtered livestock.

Richards (1996) notes that the late neolithic houses on Orkney have the same cruciform arrangement as the local, contemporary chambered tomb of Maeshowe. The houses, however, have a central hearth and are situated around a public space where pottery, stone and bone artefacts were made whereas the tomb lacked a fireplace. Richards draws on apparently universal meanings to construct a cognitive opposition: people 'dwelled' in the houses, where the central hearth contained the 'life-maintaining fire', whereas the perpetual darkness of the tomb signified its role as 'a residence of the dead' (Richards 1996: 202). Like the surrounding hills, Maeshowe was covered with a grassed mound of clay that 'positions the dead as being below the surface of the humanly inhabited world' (Richards 1996: 202). Twice a year, just before and just after the winter solstice, the winter sun shines through the tomb's entrance passage, marking a time of celebration at the old year's death and the new year's birth. The spectacular reference that the tomb's orientation makes to the winter solstice and the apparent anchoring of the tomb in the surrounding landscape of hills, the parallel organisation of tomb and house, allow Richards to locate inferred symbolism in a specific context. Like Thomas, Richards finds evidence for the incremental social control of knowledge in the construction of high walls around the settlement once people ceased to live there.

Attractive as these interpretations are, the method runs the risk of producing exercises in filling empty semantic systems of the sort alluded to above, a criticism that can be made of Lévi-Strauss's own work. Contributors to the present volume have examined whether or not the specific, intersubjective meanings attributed by a living community to their landscape are accessible. Lahiri and Singh, Ayres and Mauricio, Fullagar and Head, Kinahan, Parker Pearson and his co-authors, and Evans all explore the depth to which contemporary readings of the landscape are consistent with the patterning of archaeological remains, thus exploring the probability that past meanings can be extrapolated from a present cultural context (Chapters 13, 21, 22, 23, 25, 28). Several, particularly Parker Pearson et al. (Chapter 25), conclude that it is the needs of the present rather than time-honoured tradition that shape current perceptions of the importance of the landscape: the 'active creation of pasts for contemporary needs' (Evans 1997: 105). Kinahan (Chapter 23) uses clues from the character of sites, such as accessibility and proximity to water, to try to reduce the ambiguity of Namibian rock art. Contributors' findings reveal clearly that there can be no general rule about the durability of oral tradition. Lahiri and Singh (Chapter 13) consider oral tradition concerning changes in river flow in an area near Delhi to be accurate, but also found evidence for the reinterpretation of medieval religious monuments. Evans (Chapter 28) found the local interpretation of Himalayan ruins (perhaps 500 to 800 years old) convincing, but also found evidence of rapidly changing readings of a series of stone cairns. Frimigacci (1997) found evidence that oral tradition on Uvea records events that occurred in the eleventh century AD (cf. Minthorn 1997). Fullagar and Head (Chapter 22) reconstruct long-term continuity in the cultural significance of sites in northern Australia. They propose that the rock outcrops connected by the travels of ancestral beings in contemporary legend yield a distinctive set of resources (stone, ochre and starch-rich plants) whose use at the local site of Jinmium can be extrapolated into the past through archaeological research. The current form of the legend may constitute a relatively transitory expression, but it maps a durable complex of relationships.

Derrida's concept of meaningful communication as a process in which current usages constantly transform previous ones suggests, however, that meanings are more likely to change than remain constant. Whilst the placing of monuments in the landscape can be considered to be a kind of semantic 'niche construction', political processes are likely to transform the flow of negotiated meaning. Cooney (Chapter 4) interprets the construction of stone circles, barrows and other features close to earlier megalithic tombs in Ireland as symptomatic of such transformations in meaning. Kumar (Chapter 12) uses historical documentation and ethnographic enquiry to show how the significance of a small reservoir on the southern fringes of New Delhi has been transformed since its construction 900 years ago.

Conclusions

Within at least the United Kingdom, landscape studies have recently swept to a commanding position in the practice and teaching of archaeology. Within the last three years, there has been a flurry of activity as new Master's degrees in landscape studies have been introduced at universities up and down the country. Landscape archaeology, it is argued, can be distinguished from the subject matter of other Master's degrees in its practical aspects (laboratory and field techniques, instruction in the recognition of elements of ancient activity in the landscape), its theoretical aspects (which include a history of the 'sub-discipline') and its philosophy and politics. An interdisciplinary research group for the study of cultural landscapes has been proposed, which intends to establish a collaborative research network linking archaeology, palaeo-ecology, environmental science, history, human geography and social anthropology. At least one academic lectureship in 'landscape studies' has been established.

Even the archaeology of the very recent past has received new impetus from the notion of landscape. It has recently been recognised that the 'defence of Britain' during the Second World War transformed the British landscape through the construction of

> over 18,000 concrete pill boxes . . . , together with hundreds of miles of defensive ditches, hundreds of airfields, and tens of thousands of gun emplacements, radar stations, air-raid shelters, tank-traps, bombing decoys, Nissan Huts and other structures great and small.
>
> (Denison 1995: 8)

It is interesting to note that the study of these wartime features combines questioning the relatively few informants still living who remember their construction, with the recording, listing and scheduling of the material remains. The current recognition that these kinds of constructions combine to form a landscape worthy of protection raises all kinds of interesting questions regarding the changing nature of 'visibility'.

It is informative to speculate what wider intellectual developments have contributed to the rise of landscape studies. Perhaps their popularity coincides with the desire to 'populate' the past, rather than to treat it as inhuman, and part of a reality knowable only through the application of scientific archaeological techniques. As we have seen, landscape has also become fertile ground for interdisciplinary enquiry, a means to break free from current academic boundaries and to link the strictly scientific with the historic, ethnographic and even artistic. A recent meeting of the Theoretical Archaeology Group recognised that to study the 'social construction of landscape' requires a variety of different theoretical approaches in order to understand how the landscape has been constructed, conceptualised, manipulated and transformed by societies. As Morphy (1993: 205) has claimed, 'one of the reasons that the concept of landscape is beginning to prove so useful is that it is a concept in between'. If landscape is indeed a new mediation, then it has found surprising outlets. ESSO, for example, is taking 1998 as its opportunity to present (in a 'major' exhibition in the National Gallery of Australia) 'new worlds from old, 19th century Australian and American landscapes', recognising them 'as subjective interpretations rather than objective reflections of a cultural reality'.

Despite the new and widespread popularity of landscape, we need to show caution in case, having created landscape archaeology, its practice swamps other aspects of the discipline. As Cooney (1993: 636) warns, by concentrating on landscape and separating it off from other archaeological evidence such as artefacts, one may lose part of the evidence for human patterns of landscape use. Nor must interest in the research potential of landscape study obscure the fact that discussions about what might constitute a landscape have ramifications far beyond the purely academic. Management of the landscape involves, as we have seen, many different groups of people. Those connected with tourism are by no means the least influential in considering how landscape should be managed and represented. Landscape is also at the very forefront of policy debates concerning the relationship between the diachronic and synchronic, between process and change and the freezing of what is to be displayed and explained to the tourist or public into a static moment. Fascinating examples are coming to light of the varying cultural interpretations of the same landscape being presented as equal but alternative (e.g. Pokotylo and Brass 1997: 156, 165; Potter and Chabot 1997: 50), and of the public being led to understand the character of landscape change (e.g. Yamin 1997: 212).

Development policy interests have caused cultural heritage (of which the cultural landscape is a part) to become a major component of environmental assessments in many parts of the world. Within the UK, English Heritage's Monuments Protection Programme recognises an essential difference between the scheduling and protection of large sites and concentrations of monuments, and work on the scale of 'landscapes' (see Darvill and Fairclough, Chapters 8 and 9, Schofield 1999). The difference is expressed in the reduction of the former to archaeological classes and components, while the latter requires a much wider approach if the sum of all its parts, including its ecological and visual attributes, its geology and topography and its local social values and attributes, are to be captured. The Monuments Protection Programme has provided a comparatively rare opportunity for academic input to be explicitly recognised in the 'real world' of recording and protection undertaken by English Heritage, the Countryside Commission and other organisations that will contribute to the future appearance(s) of our landscape(s). The degree of effort put into consulting the public in the course of this programme is also noteworthy, seeking to associate a wider audience with the affairs of 'their' landscape heritage (see Brisbane and Wood 1996; Countryside Commission 1996; English Heritage 1996).

On a more global scale, the absence of references to the landscape in environmental assessments undertaken by the World Bank is just as striking. A recent publication makes no reference to landscape other than one mention of the need to consult landscape architects. Despite recognising that 'cultural heritage' is 'a record of humanity's relationship to the world, past achievements and discoveries', the whole of the World Bank's discussion is centred on applying vigilance, before and after development activities, to the potential and actual disturbance of sites. The World Bank's policy is in marked contrast to that of UNESCO, which now recognises that a cultural landscape may be one whose significance lies 'in the powerful religious, artistic, or cultural associations of the natural element rather than material culture evidence' (Cleere 1999, and see Ucko 1997: xviii–xxii).

One may well suspect that the World Bank's circumscribed policy stems from recognition of the potential that broader approaches offer to pressure groups who oppose all change. Archaeology has already gained some experience of such developments, and some of its agents have insisted that academic archaeology must learn to formulate criteria that enable judgements to be made on the rarity and aesthetic appeal of sites and monuments, thereby enabling conclusions to be formed as to their expendability. Those cultural landscapes that contain no visible human artefactual remains promise to remain particularly problematic. Even a country such as England, which prides itself on its interest in 'heritage', favours 'reconstruction sites' over the actual archaeological site when it turns out that commercial development threatens the urban landscape (see Stone and Planel 1999). As World Heritage legislation begins to affect a country's planning processes (see Evans et al. 1994), so the *Evening Standard* newspaper pronounces, 'London is not a gigantic museum' (*Evening Standard* 14 March 1997; and see Beneš and Zvelebil, this volume Chapter 6, on the importance of change in landscape studies). Our concepts of what constitutes 'landscape' will be immensely important to the quality of life of our descendants, and such concepts must be flexible enough to contain the reality of past and future change.

Acknowledgements

We thank Jane Hubert and Jeremy Tanner for their comments on a draft of this Introduction.

References

Adam, L. 1963. *Primitive Art*. London: Cassell.
Bender, B. 1993. Introduction: landscape − meaning and action. In *Landscape: politics and perspectives*, B. Bender (ed.), 1–17. Oxford: Berg.
Bourdieu, P. 1977. *Outline of a Theory of Practice*. Cambridge: Cambridge University Press.
Boyd, R. and P.J. Richerson 1985. *Culture and the Evolutionary Process*. Chicago: University of Chicago Press.
Brisbane, M. and J. Wood 1996. *A Future for our Past?: an introduction to heritage studies*. London: English Heritage.
Cavalli-Sforza, L.L. and M.W. Feldman 1981. *Cultural Transmission and Evolution: a quantitative approach*. Princeton: Princeton University Press.
Cleere, H. 1999. The World Heritage Convention in the Third World. In *Perspectives on Cultural Resource Managements in Modern Society*, F.P. McManamon and A. Hatton (eds). London: Routledge.
Clifford, J. 1988. *The Predicament of Culture: twentieth-century ethnography, literature and art*. Cambridge, Mass.: Harvard University Press.
Cooney, G. 1993 A sense of place in Irish prehistory. *Antiquity* 67, 632–9.
Cosgrove, D. 1984. *Social Formation and Symbolic Landscape*. London: Croom Helm.
Countryside Commission 1996. *Views from the Past*. Northampton: Countryside Commission Postal Sales.
Crystal, D. (ed.) 1990. *The Cambridge Encyclopedia*. Cambridge: Cambridge University Press.
Daniels, S. 1988. The political iconography of woodland in later Georgian England. In *The Iconography of Landscape*, S. Daniels and D. Cosgrove (eds), 43–82. Cambridge: Cambridge University Press.
Daniels, S. and D. Cosgrove 1988. Introduction: iconography and landscape. In *The Iconography of Landscape*, S. Daniels and D. Cosgrove (eds), 1–10. Cambridge: Cambridge University Press.
Denison, S. 1995 Tracing the relics of wartime defence. *British Archaeology* 3, 8–9.
Derrida, J. 1976. *Of Grammatology*. Baltimore: Johns Hopkins University Press.
Durham, W.H. 1991. *Co-evolution: genes, culture and human diversity*. Stanford: Stanford University Press.
Eco, U. 1990. *The Limits of Interpretation*. Bloomington: Indiana University Press.
English Heritage 1996. *The Monuments Protection Programme 1986–96 in Retrospect*. London: English Heritage.
Evans, C. 1997. Sentimental prehistories: the construction of the fenland past. *Journal of European Archaeology* 5, 10–36.

Evans, D.M., J. Pugh-Smith and J. Samuels 1994. World Heritage sites: beauty contest or planning constraint? *Journal of Planning and Environmental Law* June, 493–576.

Foucault, M. 1977. *Discipline and Punish: the birth of the prison*. London: Penguin.

Franklin, R. and P. Bunte 1997. When sacred land is sacred to three tribes: San Juan Piaute sacred sites and the Hopi-Navajo-Paiute suit to partition the Arizona Navajo Reservation. In *Sacred Sites, Sacred Places*, D.I. Carmichael, J. Hubert, B. Reeves and A. Schanche (eds), 245–58. London: Routledge.

Frimigacci, D. 1997. Puhi, the mythical paramount chief of Uvea and ancient links between Uvea and Tonga. In *Archaeology and Language I: theoretical and methodological orientations*, R. Blench and M. Spriggs (eds), 331–44. London: Routledge.

Giddens, A. 1984. *The Constitution of Society*. Cambridge: Polity Press.

Gosden, C. and L. Head 1994. Landscape – a usefully ambiguous concept. *Archaeology in Oceania* 29, 113–16.

Gower, B. 1997. *Scientific Method: an historical and philosophical introduction*. London: Routledge.

Harley, J.B. 1988. Maps, knowledge and power. In *The Iconography of Landscape*, S. Daniels and D. Cosgrove (eds), 277–312. Cambridge: Cambridge University Press.

Hirsch, E. 1995. Landscape: between place and space. In *The Anthropology of Landscape: perspectives on place and space*, E. Hirsch and M. O'Hanlon (eds), 1–30. Oxford: Oxford University Press.

Hirsch, E. and M. O'Hanlon 1995. *The Anthropology of Landscape: perspectives on place and space*. Oxford: Oxford University Press.

Ingold, T. 1993. The temporality of the landscape. *World Archaeology* 25, 152–74.

Layton, R. 1995. Relating to the country in the Western Desert. In *The Anthropology of Landscape: perspectives on place and space*, E. Hirsch and M. O'Hanlon (eds), 210–31. Oxford: Oxford University Press.

Layton, R. 1997. Representing and translating people's place in the landscape of northern Australia. In *After Writing Culture: epistemology and praxis in contemporary anthropology*, A. James, J. Hockey and A. Dawson (eds), 122–43. London: Routledge.

Lévi-Strauss, C. 1970. *The Raw and the Cooked*. J. and D. Weightman (trans.). London: Cape.

Lévi-Strauss, C. 1973. *Tristes tropiques*. J. and D. Weightman (trans.). London: Cape.

Minthorn, P. 1997. The archaeology of the dammed. *Common Ground* 2, 34–7.

Morphy, H. 1993. Colonialism, history and the construction of place: the politics of landscape in northern Australia. In *Landscape, Politics and Perspectives*, B. Bender (ed.), 205–43. Oxford: Berg.

Morphy, H. 1995. Landscape and the reproduction of the ancestral past. In *The Anthropology of Landscape: perspectives on place and space*, E. Hirsch and M. O'Hanlon (eds), 184–209. Oxford: Oxford University Press.

Morris, C. 1938. *Foundations of the Theory of Signs*. Chicago: University of Chicago Press.

Odling-Smee, J. 1988. Niche constructing phenotypes. In *The Role of Behaviour in Evolution*, H.C. Plotkin (ed.), 73–132. Cambridge, Mass.: M.I.T. Press.

Odling-Smee, J. 1995. Biological evolution and cultural change. In *Survival and Religion*, E. Jones and V. Reynolds (eds), 1–43. New York: Wiley.

Olwig, K.R. 1993. Sexual cosmology: nation and landscape at the conceptual interstices of nature and culture: or, what does landscape really mean? In *Landscape: politics and perspectives*, B. Bender (ed.), 307–43. Oxford: Berg.

Olwig, K.R. 1996. Nature: mapping the ghostly traces of a concept. In *Concepts in Human Geography*. C. Earl, K. Mathewson and M.S. Kenzer (eds), 63–9. Savage, Md.: Rowman & Littlefield.

Peirce, C. 1931. *Collected Papers of Charles Sanders Peirce, Volume II*. Cambridge, Mass.: Harvard University Press.

Penning-Rowsell, E.C. and D. Lowenthal (eds) 1986. *Landscape Meaning and Values*. London: Unwin-Hyman.

Pokotylo, D. and G. Brass 1997. Interpreting cultural resources: Hatzig site. In *Presenting Archaeology to the Public: digging for truths*, J.H. Jameson (ed.), 156–65. Walnut Creek, Calif.: AltaMira.

Potter, P.B. and N.J. Chabot 1997 Locating truths on archaeological sites. In *Presenting Archaeology to the public: digging for truths*, J.H. Jameson (ed.), 45–53. Walnut Creek, Calif.: AltaMira.

Prince, H. 1988. Art and agrarian change, 1710–1815. In *The Iconography of Landscape*, S. Daniels and D. Cosgrove (eds), 98–118. Cambridge: Cambridge University Press.

Quine, W.V.O. 1960. *Word and Object*. Cambridge, Mass.: M.I.T. Press.

Richards, C. 1996. Monuments as landscape: creating the centre of the world in late neolithic Orkney. *World Archaeology* 28, 190–208.

Rommetveit, R. 1987. Meaning, context and control: convergent trends and controversial issues in current social-scientific research on human cognition and communication. *Inquiry* 30, 77–99.

Rowlands, M. 1996. Looking at financial landscapes: a contextual analysis of ROSCAs in Cameroon. In *Money Go Rounds*, S. Ardener and S. Burman (eds), 111–24. Oxford: Berg.

Saussure, F. de 1959. *Course in General Linguistics*. London: Owen.

Schofield, A.J. 1999. Addressing the unknown in archaeological conservation policies: scheduling research and the Monuments Protection Act. In *Perspectives on Cultural Resource Management in Modern Society*, F.P. McManamon and A. Hatton (eds). London: Routledge.

Schutz, A. 1972. *The Phenomenology of the Social World*. London: Heinemann.

Shanks, M. and C. Tilley 1987. *Social Theory and Archaeology*. Cambridge: Polity Press.

Stokols, D. and S.A. Shumaker 1981. People in places: a transactional view of settings. In *Cognition, Social Behaviour and the Environment*, J.H. Harvey (ed.), 441–88. Hillsdale, N.J.: Lawrence Erlbaum.

Stone, P.G. and P. Planel (eds) 1999. *The Constructed Past: experimental archaeology, education and the public*. London: Routledge.

Tanner, J. In press. Action theory and the sociological interpretation of art. *Journal of Material Culture*.

Tarde, G. 1969. *Gabriel Tarde on Communication and Social Influence*. T.N. Clark (ed.). Chicago: Chicago University Press.

Thomas, J. 1993a. The politics of vision and the archaeologies of landscape. In *Landscape: politics and perspectives*, B. Bender (ed.), 19–48. Oxford: Berg.

Thomas, J. 1993b. The hermeneutics of megalithic space. In *Interpretative Archaeology*, C. Tilley (ed.), 73–97. Oxford: Berg.

Tilley, C. 1994. *A Phenomenology of Landscape: places, paths and monuments*. Oxford: Berg.

Tilley, C. 1996. The powers of rocks: topography and monument construction on Bodmin Moor. *World Archaeology* 28, 161–76.

Ucko, P. 1997 Foreword. In *Sacred Sites, Sacred Places*, D.l. Carmichael, J. Hubert, B. Reeves and A. Schanche (eds), xiii–xxiii. London: Routledge.

Vidal de la Blanche, P. 1902. Les conditions géographiques des faits sociaux. *Annales de géographie* 11, 13–23.

Weber, M. 1947. *The Theory of Social and Economic Organisation*. London: Hedge.

Yamin, R.A. 1997 Museum in the making: the Morven project. In *Presenting Archaeology to the Public: digging for truths*, J.H. Jameson (ed.), 205–20. Walnut Creek, Calif.: AltaMira.

2 Chronologies of landscape

John C. Barrett

The practice of archaeology demands our commitment to the view that certain objects are understood only by reference to the human past. These objects are regarded as a residue of the past. What we envisage the past to be, for there are potentially many pasts, is a matter of debate. Similarly debatable is the link between the surviving residue and the particular processes we choose to investigate, be they human actions or such long-term processes as social or economic change. Archaeology's priority to order the residues chronologically is understandable. The residues form part of our contemporary world, but we think of the past as flowing through time in a linear fashion. Relative sequences or absolute dates, once established, present archaeologists with a seemingly straightforward challenge. The processes of the past roll forward in time, leaving behind them a complex material trace that we recover as the factual record of the past. Through the interpretation of the record, we believe that we can identify the processes that created it, and so understand the past. The past is thus the explanation of the archaeological record.

Although the logic is simple, it poses problems for our current understanding of landscape archaeology. It is a logic that introduces the powerful image of an absent origin. By this I mean the record is created by something we cannot see (the past) which necessarily existed prior to the creation of its record. The point is contained in the way in which archaeologists write about the importance of understanding formation processes; this expresses a concern with both the human and the natural making of the material we recover. The material is explained when we answer such questions as: Why was it made in this way? What use did it have? Thus the function of the artefact or of the building is the purpose that lay behind its creation; residual survivals or reuse are out of place and time and are regarded as 'secondary', both in terms of chronology and of importance.

Current dating methods prioritise dates of origination. Artefacts are normally given a single date, which is the date of their production. In this way artefacts represent the traditions and techniques employed at the time of their making. When artefacts are deposited significantly later than this, they are termed survivals and are regarded as residual. We do not, therefore, give a single artefact many dates, even though it may have played a part in many different periods of human activity. (A painting by Titian, for example, is not regarded as a twentieth-century painting, but more people will have seen and appreciated that painting in this century than in any other. We privilege the date of creation over the chronology of appreciation.) Structural remains are similarly dated to their period of construction, and this partly reflects the logic of stratigraphic dating. Material stratified in foundation deposits is normally used to provide the vaguely open-ended date of a *terminus post quem*; only when buildings are sealed as part of a deeply stratified sequence can the end life of the structure be fixed at a *terminus ante quem*. The use-life of buildings is, in fact, notoriously difficult to date. A well-used floor will not accumulate debris, and the foundations of a building whose roof has been maintained over generations will not appear much dissimilar to the foundations of a rapidly abandoned building of similar construction. Such problems are well known in, for example, the study of urban life through the fourth and fifth centuries AD in the western Roman Empire.

Stratigraphic dating and functional ascription both privilege the period and the purposes of construction. A sequence of building activity is normally divided by archaeologists into periods where each begins with a new phase of foundations. Building periods are not divided mid-way in the life of a building but are divided about its structural modifications. What is significant about a building for the occupant is what takes place within it during lengthy periods of stability and maintenance, periods that may leave few archaeological residues. For the archaeologist, on the other hand, the significant moments tend to be those of refurbishment, the cutting of new foundations and thus, possibly, periods of abandonment. In his discussion of archaeological stratigraphy Harris has noted the tendency for plans to be drawings of walls, dug features and only those soil features that are 'monumental in scale' (Harris 1989: 26). The occupied spaces are what is left; we draw the walls, and the floors simply appear.

All these issues may seem no more than subtleties of expression or concerns with the methodological limitations of stratigraphic analysis. However, as I have hinted, they do have a bearing upon recent developments in landscape archaeology. A distinction has recently been drawn between landscape as a 'cultural image, a pictorial way of representing or symbolising surroundings' (Daniels and Cosgrove 1988: 1), and landscape as something that contains, and is the product of, human dwelling. Cosgrove's original argument was to define the moment when landscape became representation (Cosgrove 1984). That moment made a position for the observer who was at once disengaged from and thus outside that landscape, but who could claim that this position secured them the status of a disinterested, objective narrator. That moment occurred in a wider European discourse that also spoke of its control over nature and of land as alienable property, with the subsequent denial of the temporality of the land as the product of human labour. It was a discourse that included the technologies of landscape art, which framed the landscape and, through perspective, placed the observer beyond the frame looking in, and of cartographic representation, where each point on an undulating land surface was mapped onto a single plane. The latter allowed the observer to gaze over that terrain in a single moment. It dislocated time from space because space was no longer experienced as the commitment of time; space was not an area over which one moved to encounter places in turn, because all places appeared at the same moment to the observer who no longer inhabited the surface that contained them. As Thomas has commented, the project that Cosgrove identifies 'can be seen as genealogical, in Foucault's sense of the word . . . , charting the trajectory of particular ways of looking and thinking' (Thomas 1993: 21). Such ways of looking and thinking manifest a power over nature and the labour of others; it is the power of those who stand back from the local and mundane engagements of human dwelling that are now to be objectively described, assessed and administered. The administrative gaze (cf. Bauman 1987) thus manifests itself through a cartographic objectivity along with the production of various catalogues of materials and peoples. Its maps and inventories describe human lives, yet it is these lives as lived to which it pays scant attention. The rights to land based upon the traditional practices of dwelling no longer had validity, and the understandings of land lived through those practices, whilst recorded as the amusing, even diverting, folk tales of a place, were never given any real consequence. To silence these voices was a necessary step in claiming the legitimate authority to speak on their behalf and thus administer in their name. The recognition that the claimed objectivity by which European geography mapped the world was itself situated within programmes of political and economic paternalism has given rise to the 'cartographic anxiety' (Gregory 1994) found in geography and which has now spilled over into archaeology.

Bender has discerned the tendency for archaeologists to look at the changes wrought upon the landscape as something done to the land, a particular 'way of seeing' that fails to give voice to the ways in which 'people understand and engage with their worlds . . . [which] . . . depends upon the specific time and place and historical conditions; it depends upon gender, age, class and religion' (Bender 1992: 735). The alternative is to touch upon the inhabiting of the land, to locate our enquiry among the subjective experiences by which a situated human engagement with the land was lived. Ingold introduces the concept of the taskspace as one that allows us to talk about dwelling in the land where tasks are

> the constitutive acts of dwelling. Every task takes its meaning from its position within an ensemble of tasks, performed in series or in parallel, and usually by many people working together. . . . It is to the entire ensemble of tasks, in their mutual interlocking, that I refer by the concept of taskspace.
>
> (Ingold 1993: 158)

Tasks enfold space and time through temporal rhythms where place and time are occupied together as part of a sequence of movements, where certain communities converge at certain places. Indeed, 'it could be argued that in the resonance of movement and feeling stemming from people's mutually attentive engagement, in shared contexts of practical activity, lies the very foundation of sociality' (Ingold 1993: 160).

Taskspace therefore seems to recognise the creation of the landscape as it was occupied, a creation that was drawn out through time in such a way that our understanding of it cannot be expressed in one moment, but must trace the threads of movement and the temporal rhythms played out as people traversed the land. In this way we seem to watch communities form, work and disperse, which is precisely the sequencing of subjective experiences that the external observer will always fail to observe when treating the landscape as a system of spaces. However, this position has not moved beyond the one long ago established by time-geographers. We may now map time-space, recognise that people moved and that the meanings and perceptions of place will have changed through time, and accept that to understand landscape is to live within it and to 'look about' oneself, but have we radically questioned our position as the privileged observer and avoided the voyeurism that Thomas (1993) has found so troubling? I think not.

It is interesting that Ingold chose to explore his concept of the taskspace via a discourse on a landscape painting, *The Harvesters* by Pieter Bruegel the Elder. He invites us into the scene and asks us to look about in his company. The move is not too intrusive, for we appear to go unnoticed. Ingold is eloquent, inviting us to look afresh at the hills and valley, paths and tracks, the tree, corn and church, and only then at the people. So much of what we see was formed by their labour and the labour of their forebears. In the midday heat most rest from their work. Their tasks register upon us as sound: the snoring sleeper, the muffled sounds of eating and the occasional murmur of the conversation taking place some distance away. Landscape is 'not a totality that you or anyone else can look at, it is rather the world in which we stand in taking up a point of view on our surroundings' (Ingold 1993: 171). But others have also stood in this world and taken up their own point of view. Certainly we write the past, and archaeology is, as Ingold asserts, a form of dwelling; the problem is how we share that dwelling with those lives we study. Dwelling involves understanding, an ability to comprehend and to interpret that grows from expectations about the order, regularities and ironies of life. What gives the occupation of place meaning is not simply the tasks carried out there, which merely 'takes its meaning from its position within an ensemble of tasks, performed in series or in parallel' (Ingold 1993: 158), for such a meaning may be assigned unproblematically by any observer, be it Bruegel, Ingold or ourselves. The subjectivities that should concern us as historians arose as those tasks were executed by people whose own knowledge of how to proceed was reworked by their ability to read each situation. That reading involved carrying past experiences forward in the form of expectations that were either confirmed or challenged in each new engagement. The mutuality of each engagement therefore meant something only by reference to the experiences of past engagements and the desires for the future; it is a meaning of memory and of hope.

Landscape archaeology has tended to follow the same methodological procedures as the rest of the discipline. It has developed a chronological sequence for the remains of settlements, monuments and land divisions whilst establishing the wider environmental contexts within which these various material features were built. In many regions of Britain, for example, it is now possible to produce maps that describe these material features as a sequence of building operations assigned to broad chronological periods. Dating depends upon the finds recovered from primary deposits, and it orders monuments in much the same way that stratigraphic sequences order deposits from the earliest to the latest. If we take as an example the publication of the landscape survey around Stonehenge, we find that monuments and artefact scatters are recorded by date of production and are presented in a sequence of chronological periods running between the Earlier Neolithic, Later Neolithic, Earlier Bronze Age and Later Bronze Age. Represented as a series of maps (Richards 1990: Figs 157–60), the survey shows us a series of static formations, of things 'done to the landscape' at different times. This creates a sequential order in the monuments, but in so doing it directs our attention in a certain way, making our next task that of explaining how each set of monuments came to be etched upon the land surface. In the case of Stonehenge itself, our priorities are also established by the sequential ordering of the material. The major stone settings are assigned to constructional periods II and IIIa. This time of construction is equated with processes of political control: 'an extraordinary period in which, as part of the active constitution and reconstitution of a more restless and competitive society, the stone settings . . . are shuffled and re-shuffled like a pack of cards' (Bender 1992: 751). The problem for interpretation lies in equating continuity in archaeological deposition with continuity in human practices. Building activity at Stonehenge is certainly evidenced in the following periods, characterised as 'a chronologically discrete phase within the second millennium' (Richards 1990: 277), but the structures are slight and the monument seems to slip more ambiguously into the later landscape; the area 'seems to have been more or less abandoned or perhaps avoided' (Bender 1993: 252). This 'more or less' existence for the completed monument expresses more the difficulty of recovering archaeological traces of inhabitation, less the reality that the remarkable structure always demanded to be understood. Perhaps what Bender is trying to capture here is a distinction between an understanding of the place (an understanding situated in a wider network of experience) that we regard as conforming to the original intentions of the builders, and thus expressed most clearly in the moments of its building, and an understanding that was also situated whilst being at the same time a misunderstanding or a forgetting of that original meaning. The latter appears separated by a discontinuity from the original purpose, and we assume that this conforms with archaeological discontinuities which may be defined by either a break in building activity, or by the collapse and demolition of the structure.

Bradley has defined an afterlife for monuments precisely by this discontinuity in their use (1993: 113ff). Taking the Anglo-Saxon palace complex at Yeavering in northern England as his starting point, Bradley rejects the excavator's argument that the reuse of two prehistoric monuments in the early historic period indicates continuity (i.e. an unbroken usage) in this place as a focus for ritual activity (Hope-Taylor 1977). Bradley comments that here, as elsewhere, it is more likely that the earlier monuments are reappropriated, after a period of abandonment, by a particular elite who wished to lay claim to the past in order to promote or protect its own interests (Bradley 1987: 15). Bradley is therefore able to distinguish between the sometimes lengthy continuity in the modification of monuments, periods of disuse and destruction (by ploughing for example), and the reuse of monuments after a hiatus when they became the physical manifestation of a mythical past.

Bender employs a similar approach to the Stonehenge landscape. The monument is situated in a series of 'contested landscapes'. Initially the contestation is for official power when the 'claims on the past were ... an aggressive piecemeal appropriation' of the place through its monumental elaboration. But when that official power vacated the monument, then 'the stark abandonment speaks for an unofficial and unofficiated power' (Bender 1993: 252). From this abdication emerges the conflict between the folk veneration of the place and the attempts of the Church to 'negotiate, trim and adapt' in the face of passive resistance to the new orthodoxy, before confronting superstition directly with attempts at its eradication:

> The more pronounced attempts by the church, in the seventeenth and eighteenth centuries, to impose Christian teachings and Christian marriage, upon the vestigial paganism and easier-going sexual mores of the countryside, were only aspects of a greater intervention in the lives of ordinary people by church and state.
>
> (Bender 1993: 252)

As we know, the history of the contest has continued: English Heritage and the National Trust now act as the guardians of the place and its environs, controlling access to the monument itself.

To describe the landscape as a history of things that have been done to the land results in a cataloguing of the material transformations wrought upon the land. This procedure conforms with current archaeological expectations. To understand the landscape as inhabited demands a significant shift in our perceptions, and it is one that will not carry current methodological procedures with it. To inhabit the landscape is to look about, observe and to make sense of what one sees; it is to interpret. When things are done to the land, they are done knowledgeably, expressing an understanding of what is required at that moment and at that place. Such an understanding draws upon previous experiences as a means of recognising what course of action may be required. Returning to Stonehenge, the meaning or significance of that monument is not to be found in the reasons for its construction (which archaeologists assume are manifest in the act of building) but was emergent through the struggle to interpret the significance of that place within its landscape, a struggle that predated the building of the monument and encompassed the consequences of its construction. Meaning is something recognised by an observer, it is not some quality inherent to the place or the monument. Thus we may ask: how was it possible to think of the landscape in such a way that Stonehenge became possible? What are the consequences of living within and interpreting a landscape in which Stonehenge stands? Such questions open up the meaning of the site of Stonehenge to a number of interpretive possibilities rather than attempting to close down the significance of the place to a single, original meaning.

Meaning is not simply produced or stated: it must be recognised through a practical understanding of the world and its interpretation. This position allows us a brief reconsideration of the contrast that Bender has proposed for the history of the Stonehenge landscape. If the construction of the monument did mark a moment when a particular authority gained hegemony, then we must discover the sources by which that authority achieved its power and the ways in which that authority came to be more widely recognised. The considerable communal effort invested in building the monument certainly expresses a widely held understanding of the significance and meaning of the place, but need this imply the existence of a coercive leadership to establish that meaning? Stonehenge fulfilled the expectations many had come to have of this place, expectations that were sedimented over generations in the routine inhabitation of a landscape. It was those expectations that the monument came both to address and transform (Barrett 1994). But such expectations, whilst finding a common voice through this particular architectural expression, will have been lived out through a diverse range of experiences. This is where the engagements that depend upon gender, age and rank operated, between specific experiences and a common language of expression. It is the ability of the latter to sustain meaning that characterises ideologies.

In the centuries that followed upon the building of the monument, Bender sees the political authority represented by the place withdrawing, presumably to some other location. This withdrawal heralds, in her view, a more fragmented understanding of the place. We must presume that the political ideology in which diverse experiences could each find their place no longer existed. But how did people learn to forget that which had taken centuries to understand? What were the practicalities of such a 'forgetting'? There are two paths that might be suggested. First, that the routine lives that read and understood the Stonehenge landscape were themselves transformed; the site became irrelevant or incomprehensible. Second, that the ideological landscape continued to be reworked in such a way that a reading of its dominant significance shifted in emphasis, away from the site of Stonehenge to a more diverse set of places. Both processes appear to have been at work, with the development of an increasingly enclosed landscape by the end of the second millennium BC and by the development of funerary practices that ultimately created an architecture of burial mounds in the landscape around Stonehenge. And both processes appear related, creating more closed systems of inheritance which were capable of redefining tenurial rights to the land. If, as seems probable, these processes broke with ideas of a larger community and its ritualised identity, then Stonehenge may have lost its specific significance.

But the monument and the funerary mounds remained, as much if not more a part of the iron age landscapes as they are of ours. Archaeological research now expresses our dominant readings of these antiquities, and we may wonder how they were incorporated within an iron age mythology. One change may have been the way in which such monuments had gradually lost their immediacy: no longer linked with mortal history, they transcended it, expressing a feeling of completion, finality and stability to those spectators from whom they were displaced. These elements of the landscape were no longer embedded in the necessary engagements of routine or ritual but may have been looked upon with that reverie reserved for more distant times and places (Smith 1993).

One way of thinking about the contrasting interpretations that I have attempted to outline here is to consider them involving different kinds of chronological reasoning, between chronologies of authorship and origins (by which I will characterise the traditional archaeological obsession) and chronologies of reading and interpretation. The former interpretation is concerned with fixing the moment of creation as if the true significance of the monument or object was also fixed at that time (the time of creation by some author – literally the authoritative voice); the latter explores the chronologies over which certain interpretive strategies may have run (the time over which a common readership might identify itself).

My point is to question the extent to which authorship might impose its own meanings through the texts it creates. Today we are too familiar with the massive accumulation of the means to inflict violence and to exert economic control, which directly threaten the life chances of so many people, to make doubts as to the effectiveness of centralised authority appear realistic. The coercive forces of military might, economic power and bureaucratic surveillance appear effective enough to silence any alternative voice against which they may be directed. If such forms of power had resided in a site such as Stonehenge, then it is possible that 'unofficial' meanings may have taken hold only when such a dominant authority abandoned the place. Origins, centres, authorities – the words seem to converge in the creation of the history of places from which a dominant power was exercised. But if the meaning of the place is recognised by the interpreter, then how can we assume that any single meaning was ever secured? Or if we believe that such dominant meanings did exist, then surely we must try to understand how they were created and how extensive was their reach. If we act as if the meaning of a place was, at any time, self-evident, by not enquiring about how that or any other meaning was both recognised and sustained, then we effectively decontextualise the place. As Smith has written: the irony is that the clarity with which we see place is part of a project of displacement (Smith 1993: 78); and this displacement removes humans from the place, thus putting it beyond interpretation. The significance of the place becomes obvious to us when we decide to disregard the understandings others may have had of it.

A common reading of place may, of course, be enforced, but we must always explore what forces could have ensured the subjugating of the interpreter and their effectiveness over time and space. And if a common reading emerges, not through coercive power but from a commonly held set of principles, then we must understand how those principles were established and sustained, as well as understanding the extent of the community that felt itself bound by them.

The recently expressed desire by some archaeologists to write the history of landscape as inhabited requires a fundamental shift in our thinking. This shift is more than a methodological refinement, and it demands more than the adoption of time-geography to archaeology. The latter simply recognises that people moved through the landscapes we describe, and that such movement may be mapped in terms of allocations of time and space. Inhabiting a landscape involves understanding that landscape, with reference not to ahistorical principles but to earlier experiences or to the cultural expression of some metaphysical order. Experience is therefore carried forward in the practices of inhabiting. The ability to live, the security of knowing how to act, is an expression of the agent's own powers. Such a form of enabling power must be distinguished from the more negative connotations of power as 'power over', which is expressed as 'definite commands and conscious obedience' (Mann 1986: 8).

There are four points of summary. First, the ways in which different forms of social power operate, the spaces they occupy in different fields of social practice, are historical issues that demand investigation. Second, meaning is never secured as the essential quality of the thing itself, rather it is secured only by the expectations through which the thing is identified and interpreted. Meaning is therefore context bound and is a question of historical investigation. Third, an archaeology concerned with agency and human practice cannot take the material residues of the past unambiguously to reflect the form the past took. Instead those residues are all that remain of different conditions of materiality that other people once inhabited; the latter become the object of our attention and interpretive enquiry. We must explore how it was possible, under certain historical conditions, to make sense of these materialities and to act effectively within them. There are two consequences that follow. One is to abandon the reductive reasoning that seeks truth in an original state of being; the second jettisons the belief that history emerges through the ordering of the material residues. History instead emerges through writing about how different ways of occupying the world may have been possible. Fourth, landscape archaeology is not a sub-specialism of the discipline, nor is it a particular method (such as the mapping of material at a certain scale); rather it is central to the archaeological programme as a whole because the history of human life is about ways of inhabiting the world. That inhabitation has always discovered different meanings in the world, and it is this development of the cultural diversity of meaning that marks the trace of human history within the evolution of life.

Acknowledgements

I am grateful to Shannon Fraser for comments on an earlier draft of this chapter and to David Austin for the invitation to contribute to the Landscape Archaeology Symposium at the World Archaeological Congress in New Delhi.

References

Barrett, J.C. 1994. *Fragments from Antiquity*. Oxford: Blackwell.
Bauman, Z. 1987. *Legislators and Interpreters*. Oxford: Polity.
Bender, B. 1992. Theorizing landscape and the prehistoric landscape of Stonehenge. *Man* 27, 735–55.
Bender, B. 1993. Stonehenge – contested landscapes (medieval and present day). In *Landscape: politics and perspectives*, B. Bender (ed.), 245–79. Oxford: Berg.
Bradley, R. 1987. Time regained – the creation of continuity. *Journal of the British Archaeological Association*, 140, 1–17.
Bradley, R. 1993. *Altering the Earth*. Edinburgh: Society of Antiquaries of Scotland.
Cosgrove, D. 1984. *Social Formation and Symbolic Landscape*. London: Croom Helm.
Daniels, S. and D. Cosgrove 1988. Introduction: iconography and landscape. In *The Iconography of Landscape*, D. Cosgrove and S. Daniels (eds), 1-10. Cambridge: Cambridge University Press.
Gregory, D. 1994. *Geographical Imaginations*. Oxford: Blackwell.
Harris, E. 1989 *Principles of Archaeological Stratigraphy*. London: Academic Press.
Hope-Taylor, B. 1977. *Yeavering: an Anglo-British centre of early Northumbria*. London: HMSO.
Ingold, T. 1993. The temporality of the landscape. *World Archaeology* 25, 152–74.
Mann, M. 1986. *The Sources of Social Power, Volume 1*. Cambridge: Cambridge University Press.
Richards, J. 1990. *The Stonehenge Environs Project*. London: English Heritage.
Smith, J. 1993. The lie that blinds: destabilizing the text of landscape. In *Place/Culture/Representation*, J. Duncan and D. Ley (eds), 78–92. London: Routledge.
Thomas, J. 1993. The politics of vision and the archaeologies of landscape. In *Landscape: politics and perspective*, B. Bender (ed.), 19-48. Oxford: Berg.

3 Subverting the Western Gaze: mapping alternative worlds

BARBARA BENDER

Introduction

The 'Western Gaze' succinctly expresses a particular, historically constituted, way of perceiving and experiencing the world. It is a gaze that skims the surface; surveys the land from an ego-centred viewpoint; and invokes an active viewer (the subject) and a passive land (object). This active viewer is equated with 'culture' and the land with 'nature'; and viewer/culture are gendered male, land/nature are gendered female. Finally, the Western Gaze is about control.

An article by Anne Salmond (1992), on western and non-western knowledge metaphors, jolts us into a recognition of how the Western Gaze colours much of what we say and write. We 'chart new territories', 'break new ground', 'open up new horizons', have 'viewpoints', 'overviews', 'landmarks', 'vantage points' and 'ways of looking'. We 'chart' and 'explore', come up against intellectual 'barriers', and operate on 'frontiers'. It amounts, Salmond suggests, to an assumption of 'detached intelligence working to domesticate and master an objectified world' (Salmond 1992: 85).

The Western Gaze informs a great deal of contemporary sociological theory and practice. As a discourse of power and control it can be envisaged, following Gramsci (1971), as a top-down hegemonic discourse. Or, following Foucault (1994), it can be seen as something that permeates the totality of social practice, pervading and reconstituting the body politic.

Maps can be seen as part instrument, part result of this Western Gaze. Turnbull (1989) appropriately entitled his book *Maps are Territories. Science is an Atlas. A portfolio of exhibits.* And in the writings of Harley (1988; 1992a), Monmonier (1991) and Wood (1993) the brooding pervasive power of the western map is stressed.

These authors talk about post-Renaissance maps that cover the surface of the world with a homogeneous Cartesian grid (grip?); that present a bird's eye – *lord's eye* – view of the world; that register a palimpsest of past activities, a narrative of action and event. They talk of maps that are mesmerising

in their apparent exactitude, transparency and scientific neutrality; and it
is precisely this 'transparency' and 'neutrality' that they work to undermine.
Lefebvre (1991: 28) notes the way in which the visual gives an *illusion* of
transparency: 'within the spatial realm the known and the transparent are
one and the same thing', and Wood (1993: 18) notes that when we talk
about the map as 'a transparent window on the world', we fail to note
the framing – the way in which the window isolates one view at the
expense of another. It is not so much the exactitude that has to be questioned (though that too), but exactitude in respect to what, exactitude for
whom and by whom.[1]

These geographers insist that we embed these maps within historically
specific social relations. The invention and refinement of the cartographic
equipment that made for more accurate mapping was part-cause/part-effect
of developing mercantile capitalism (Cosgrove 1984: 140).[2] Cartography
was not just an adjunct to exploration and colonisation, it helped create the
conditions for such enterprises. Equally, it was not just an aid to the establishment and monitoring of different sorts of property and of national and
regional boundaries, but a force in the creation of changing social
configurations (Helgerson 1986). Wood suggests that a focus on maps goes
hand in hand with the emergence of the State and with increasing territoriality, surveillance and control (Wood 1993: 147). And Harley (1992a: 244),
citing Foucault, suggests that the map is 'a spatial panopticon'. Sixteenth- and
seventeenth-century cartography was, he suggests, 'simultaneously a practical
instrument for colonial policy, a visual rhetoric for fashioning European
attitudes towards the Americas and its people, and an analogue for the acquisition, management and reinforcement of colonial power' (Harley 1992b:
528). He and Wood proceed to elucidate the tricks of suppression, enlarge-
ment, projection etc. used to enhance the power of western nations.

It is not my purpose to criticise these deconstructions. The power of
lines on the map, whether in colonial, neo-colonial, or post-Cold War nationalist carve-ups, is all too hauntingly obvious. But I want to question the
all-encompassing power of these maps, and, more generally, the Western Gaze.
Reading these deconstructions, the maps/the Gaze feel like cling-film, there
is a sense of total claustrophobia. But, in reality, they are not so all-pervasive,
and we need perhaps to pause and examine some of the interstices, resistances
and alternative messages. Both claustrophobia and resistance are wonderfully
described in a passage from Borges:

> In that Empire, the Craft of Cartography attained such Perfection
> that the Map of a Single province covered the space of an entire
> City, and the Map of the Empire itself an entire Province. In the
> course of Time, these Extensive maps were found somehow
> wanting, and so the College of Cartographers evolved a Map of
> the Empire that was of the same Scale as the Empire and that
> coincided with it point for point. Less attentive to the Study of

Cartography, succeeding Generations came to judge a map of such Magnitude cumbersome, and, not without Irreverence, they abandoned it to the Rigours of sun and Rain. In the Western Deserts, tattered fragments of the Map are still to be found, Sheltering an occasional Beast or beggar.

(Borges, cited in Turnbull 1989: 2)

The geographers cited above have picked up on one part of Foucault's thesis, the part that examines in great detail the 'continuous and uninterrupted processes which subject our bodies, govern our gestures, dictate our behaviours' (Foucault 1994: 213–14), the part that is about power, surveillance and discipline. But Foucault also discusses resistance. He talks of 'the insurrection of subjugated knowledge', and by this he means both historical knowledge that has been co-opted and submerged in systematised authoritative discourses and other sorts of knowledge which he describes as 'local, discontinuous, disqualified, illegitimate'. These latter contain 'the memory of hostile encounters' (Foucault 1994: 203). In many of his writings, Foucault ferrets away at retrieving historical knowledges that have been gobbled up in scientific discourse and practice. He is, perhaps, more reticent about 'disqualified and unqualified knowledge'. He is pessimistic about its effectiveness, for it is, he suggests, 'particular, local, . . . differential knowledge incapable of unanimity, which owes its force only to the harshness by which it is opposed by everything surrounding it' (Foucault 1994). But sometimes he accepts that it can go further, that it 'disturbs . . . rebounds . . . and on occasion . . . ruptures' (Young 1990: 87).

The geographers cited above have tended to neglect this potential for resistance, although Harley, just before he died, wrote a very interesting paper on the way in which native North American Indians and Meso-American Aztecs both contributed their knowledge to the making of western maps, and used their knowledge to create alternative maps of resistance (Harley 1992b). This chapter attempts to tilt the balance further in that direction. It focuses on local knowledge and resistance, on small subversions. I proceed by way of examples – first from within western contexts and then from 'contact' situations.

There is a final section on non-western indigenous mappings. This is to demonstrate that maps are not simply a response to colonial encounters. There has been some discussion about whether *all* people create maps, mental or material. Does map-making arise only under certain historic conditions? Some anthropologists attempt to make a distinction between mental mapping and practical mastery, and suggest that only the latter is universal (Gow 1995). 'Practical mastery' (m/stery) is part of being-in-the-world and is subject-centred. It depends upon the activities, perceptions and bodily attitudes of the subject. In contrast, mental maps are not subject-centred: the position of places is defined 'absolutely'. (This is not a question of subjectivity v. objectivity, but of being subject-centred v. decentred.) Gell (1985: 279) has argued, persuasively, against any such hard and fast division and suggests that practical mastery and mental mapping go hand-in-hand:

> We . . . locate our bodies in relation to external coordinates which are unaffected as we move about, and it is in relation to these coordinates that we entertain token-indexical beliefs as to our current location in space.

I believe that the examples that follow support this understanding.[3]

Western maps in western contexts

Official maps are undoubtedly part of the panoply of authority. Thus, for example, the British Ordnance Survey map, as the name implies, was initiated under the auspices, and for the use of, the army.[4] There is control over what is and is not on the map, what is highlighted etc. But intention and usage are relatively easily suborned. Of course, places (nuclear installations and the like) can be left out, but there is a tension between selective omission and the quest for – pride in – *comprehensive* coverage, so that potentially disruptive details get included. Moreover, property or landclaims are, by definition, bounded. Bordering the landed estate on an English Ordnance Survey map are the remains of the Common; between the grand boulevards of Paris lies the understated (but thereby, if desired, almost more visible) warren of tenements and slums. There are many writers who insist on focusing attention on the wrong side of the property boundary: on the significance of the vanishing contours of the commonlands or on the disruption of working-class urban districts (Hammond and Hammond 1948; Cobbett 1987; Davis 1990; Pred 1990; Edholm 1993).[5] The official map, then, constrains but is also 'detachable, reversible, susceptible to constant modification. It can be torn, reversed, adapted to any kind of mounting, reworked by an individual, group or social formation . . . it always has multiple entryways' (Deleuze and Guattari, cited in Crouch and Matless 1996).

There is also the possibility of using the controlling over-view of the official map as the starting point for a phenomenological being-in-the-landscape approach. Tilley, for example, does this in his re-evocation of the prehistoric landscape of Bodmin Moor in southwest England in which people meet, walk, celebrate and communicate (Tilley 1994). Interestingly, returning to Anne Salmond's study of knowledge metaphors, there are metaphors that acknowledge this being-in-the-world, metaphors such as: 'taking a particular path', an intellectual 'cul-de-sac', getting lost, 'not seeing the wood for the trees', 'taking a first step', being trapped. These seem to go against the grain of the more pervasive metaphors of control.

These lived-in mapped worlds may be more or less radical. Pred (1990) shows the way in which, at a time during the nineteenth century when the Stockholm authorities were asserting their control over the rapidly expanding

city, renaming the streets, and policing them, the working classes created a
network of alternative, scurrilous, street names and places. More consciously,
Walter Benjamin attempts to subvert the whole notion of the western map
as a means of orientation and as a compendium of scientific knowledge.
Whether in Vienna, or Berlin, or most passionately in Paris, he uses the map
in order to get lost:

> Not to find one's way in a city may well be uninteresting and
> banal. It requires ignorance – nothing more. But to lose oneself
> in a city, as one loses oneself in a forest, that calls for quite a
> different schooling. The signboards and street names, passers-by,
> roofs, kiosks, or bars must speak to the wanderer like a cracking
> twig under his feet in the forest.
>
> (Benjamin 1985: 298)

This is a perfect example of what Gell was talking about, a system of checks
and balances between the subject-centred world and the decentred world.
Benjamin loses himself, and then, through 'practical mastery', finds himself
in relation to significant places, names and passers-by.

Alternatively, Benjamin subverts the authoritative purposes of the official
map, refuses the palimpsest of historical event, and imposes his own history
of jumbled memories, collapsing personal time onto space. He imagines taking
'the general staff's map of a city centre':

> I have evolved a system of signs and on the grey background of
> such maps they would make a colourful show if I clearly marked
> in the houses of my friends and girl friends, the assembly halls of
> various collectives, from the 'debating chambers' of the Youth
> Movement to the gathering places of the Communist youth, the
> hotel and brothel rooms that I knew for one night . . . and the
> graves that I saw filled.
>
> (Benjamin 1985: 295)

At one level, this is no more than the isolated biography of an individual;
but it is also a map of subversion – the Youth Movement, the gathering
place of the Communist youth, the brothel, untimely deaths – plotted/
plotting against the General Staff map.[6] These are places and spaces of political and personal resistance, of memory and action. In and of itself this will
not bring the State to its knees – indeed the Nazis brought about Benjamin's
own untimely death – but it does suggest, quite brilliantly, the dialectic
between lived experience/embodied space and the larger political and cultural
world, and the potential for subversion.

Benjamin's insistence that memory collapses time into space goes against
the western notion of the linear narrative, of biography as sequence, of
maps that chart events and actions as though they were over and done with.
It emphasises flux, change, potential:

> Time . . . thrusts us forward from behind, blows us out through
> the narrow funnel of the present into the future. But space is
> broad, teeming with possibilities, positions, intersections, passages,
> detours, U-turns, dead ends, one-way streets.
>
> (Sontag in Benjamin 1985: 13)

Part of Benjamin's fantasy of alternative ways of mapping have been put
into action in contemporary Britain by organisations such as Common
Ground, which try to get people to draw their own maps: 'authorising' their
version of the world, the places and paths they know as against the grey
anonymity of the official map. In such undertakings the map is as much
performance and process as object. It may become

> a site for struggle as well as celebration, bringing out social differ-
> ence by providing one public imaginative space on which to work.
> Even the most outwardly conciliatory and harmonious of Parish
> Maps might act as a blanket thrown over difference which, in
> covering it, keeps it warm and stewing.
>
> (Crouch and Matless 1996: 253)

In part, Benjamin's fantasy is given academic expression through Giddens's
mapping of people's movement between places, of entrances and exits, back-
stages and fore-ground, in which repetitive time and cyclical time are played
off against time's arrow (Giddens 1985; see also Harvey 1989; Soja 1989;
Pred 1990). Rose (1993: 21) takes Giddens's experiential map a step further
and genders it.

These alternative maps emphasise *agency* – differentiated worlds of experience. It could, I suppose, be suggested that Giddens or Rose is simply mapping
Bourdieu's *habitus*: mapping the everyday places and encounters through which
people are socialised and disciplined; logging the behaviour that creates and
maintains Foucault's structures of surveillance. But, equally, they may be
mapping potential nonconformism, ways of questioning – even undermining
– the accepted way of doing things.

Western maps in contact situations

In this section five contact situations are sketched, five ways of responding
to the western map. Some do little more than register suspicion or fear; some
question; some subvert.

The people of Santa Clara live in shifting settlements on the braided river
course of the Bajo Urumbamba in eastern Peru (Gow 1995). They do not
make maps, but they do, in their mind and in speech, create kinscapes –
'maps' of social relationships – places and traces (old gardens, old house-sites)
that implicate people *vis-à-vis* each other and the land. It is the older people

who tell stories that, as in Benjamin's map and in many of the case studies that follow, are 'memory work', where time collapses into space.[7]

There is, however, an *official* map: the land title map created by government bureaucrats in Lima. The map is very empty. It simply has the boundary lines and co-ordinates. It takes no account of the shifting nature of the river or the settlements. The map shows that Santa Clara now lies outside the community territory.

This abstract western map is part of an alien world that is, by and large, irrelevant to the people of Santa Clara. But it is perceived as powerful, though the power is context specific. In a local context, it may, with caution, *empower*. On very rare occasions, the local map has been used successfully to stave off encroachment by the neighbouring white plantation-owner. On the other hand, the copy in Lima has never been used, any attempt to refer matters to the capital is seen as inherently dangerous. Local people perceive that state intervention rarely works to their advantage. In the larger Peruvian political arena, the map is more likely to dispossess than empower.

My second case study is a curious one. In Lahore, Pakistan, there are, of course, official maps, mainly dating back to the British occupation. Local people, however, have constructed, not on paper but in the form of stories and legends, a different map, one that represents an underground world of tunnels that link the gardens, shrines and forts built by the Mughal princes who governed the area over 250 years ago. Stories tell of an Imperial tunnel that links Lahore to Delhi, and of provincial tunnels connecting Lahore with smaller places to the West. They speak of armies, several men abreast, marching swiftly along the tunnels (far more swiftly, they say, than on the roads of today!), of modest women moving without harassment, of lovers on secret assignations, of princes cunningly escaping from besieged fortresses. The tunnels are also, especially when associated with rivers, places of danger where demons lurk.

During the Mughal period, Lahore had been the provincial capital and even briefly, in the sixteenth century, the Imperial capital. In the eighteenth century it suffered a series of invasions and the Mughal monuments were reduced to ruins. With the British annexation of the mid-nineteenth century, new roads, canals and railways further disrupted the old settlement pattern. As a result the Mughal routeways have largely disappeared, and yet the tunnels approximate to likely Mughal roadways. *But they are not real: the tunnels exist only in people's imagination.*

It seems that the tunnel stories began to circulate in the mid-seventeenth century, as the power of Lahore waned. Over time the stories changed and only places that are still visible today are included. The asymmetry between stories told at important Mughal centres and those from lesser sites seems to reflect the original unequal power relations between the centre and the margins. It has been suggested that 'The tunnel stories represent a genre of popular criticism. Things that were (and still are) impossible on the surface, can take place underground' (Wescoat *et al.* 1991: 14). It is a muted form of criticism – no material empowerment, but some psychological advantage.

The third case study is somewhat more confrontational. In the 1970s and 1980s, the Peruvian government wanted to create a nature reserve at Lake Titicaca. It would have involved the control of reed beds that had been owned and used by the local peasant communities for centuries (Orlove 1991). State bureaucrats drew a series of maps that played down the number and location of lake-side settlements, emphasised the island settlements that were to become tourist attractions, and omitted an area of contention. The focus was, as usual, on boundaries and administrative organisation. A sequence of maps charted the progress of the development.

The peasants also drew maps in order to put *their* case to the bureaucrats. They used the same approximate orientation, same distinction of land and water. They appended names to settlement locations. But their maps were not to scale, did not include towns, and exaggerated the proximity of settlements. Their maps moved between the conventional over-view and a ground view: houses and mountains were shown vertically (Orlove 1991). The maps, faithful to indigenous perceptions, showed the natural features that cradled and protected the settlements. Each settlement was crowned with a small Peruvian flag, thus coopting the official insignia of power.

The bureaucrats and the peasants talked past each other. The bureaucratic maps were primarily for consumption by other bureaucrats; the peasants' maps were mulled over within their own communities. The maps were exchanged, but neither side 'saw' the other's map. For the bureaucrats, the peasants' maps were mere sketches. Nonetheless, though based on different conceptions – or misconceptions – the peasants had done as asked, they had provided 'documentation', and perhaps their maps had some tenuous effect. At any rate, the bureaucrats did not put their plans into action, and the peasants continued to exploit their reed beds. As Orlove puts it, this interaction hardly matches up to Foucault's vision of a world 'of subjects . . . incarcerated, disciplined, and imprisoned within spaces of social control' (Orlove 1991: 29). The maps, the way in which they were 'drawn' and 'drawn on', suggest a greater degree of incoherence within the system. This encounter bespeaks both interstitial resistance and mutual incomprehension.

In the two final case studies, the resistance is more overt. When, in 1885, the Germans colonised New Ireland, off the northeast coast of Papua New Guinea, they broke up the indigenous Malangan settlements and territories and moved the population down to the coast and onto the plantations (Kuchler 1993). The indigenous people then began to make very fine three-dimensional wooden funerary sculptures.[8] The Germans assumed that they were traditional funerary markers, analogous to grave-stones. They admired them greatly, encouraged their production, bought them, and put them in museums. They entirely failed to understand that these 'traditional' pieces were in fact three-dimensional 'maps' and were part of the dynamic of land appropriation and transmission. Unwittingly they encouraged the subversion of their own mapped universe of political boundaries and property relations.

In the making of Malangan sculptures, it is the process rather than the end product that is important: the making of the sculpture at the death of an existing holder, the brief display and the competition to win the rights to reproduce the Malangan sculpture. The destruction of the sculptures is important because it allows a re-creation the next time round. When Suzanne Kuchler tried to map, in conventional western terms, the settlements and pathways, she was told she was wasting her time. The settlements and pathways would change:

> after every mortuary ceremony which witnesses sculptural production and the reallocation of land, the surface appearance of the land is restructured according to a map laid down in memory.
>
> (Kuchler 1993: 91)

If Kuchler *had* made the map she would have defined 'permanence' where the Malangans recognised transience and changeability, and she would have created precisely the sort of powerful representation that the German occupiers desired, one of fixed boundaries, a record of land-ownership and of social relations *imposed upon* a landscape rather than *implicated in* the landscape. As it was, she saw something that the Germans had failed to see: a way of mapping that permitted continuity in the face of colonisation and fragmentation.

My final example of resistance concerns Australian Aboriginal land claims. Here I am concerned not with their indigenous maps but with their attempts to work against the grain of the western map.

Western colonisers did not recognise the Aboriginal occupation of Australia, although, on occasion, their place-names acknowledge bloody and unequal encounters. For them, Australia was *terra incognita*, an empty land. Slowly the map filled with the history of white exploration, domination and settlement. Large tracts of new territory were given grandiose names that suggested that they were extensions of Europe; mountains and rivers were named after explorers; place names recorded settlers and their activities. The Aboriginal people, herded onto mission stations or ranches, went unrecorded, though their presence shadowed the white people's place names (Morphy 1993; Strang 1997).

In recent years, as Aboriginal people have begun to press their land claims, the western map has both inhibited and, to some extent, enhanced their activities. The Aboriginal people have had to demonstrate a familiarity with the land, they have to 'behave as if dispossession had never happened. . . . There is no room [to] draw attention to the simultaneous experience of familiarity and unfamiliarity with land' (Gelder and Jacobs 1995). The white map contains places and lines of communication and boundaries. The Aboriginal people, with a quite different notion of territory, cannot draw equivalent boundary lines.[9] The Land Claim bureaucrats, while they recognise only sacred places, do not recognise sacred songlines. The continent-wide network of ancestral pathways that connect the sacred sites is, quite literally, ruled out of court. On the other hand, government acceptance of the significance of sacred sites has had unforeseen consequences. Aboriginal sacred sites are often associated with places where people die (Morphy 1993). Children inherit death names, and the Government accepts that Aboriginal named inheritance constitutes a claim on the land. But then, wonderful irony, it turns out that because of the forced movement of Aboriginal people to the missions and ranches, the *greatest* concentration of Aboriginal sacred sites is precisely around these 'white' places (Morphy 1993). And so, after all, the unrecorded shadows at the white ranches do have indigenous names, and alternative and increasingly powerful maps are being created.

The (so far, limited) Aboriginal successes are worth celebrating. But there is a price to pay for turning the colonisers' maps back on themselves: the fight is on white terrain, uses white terms, white conventions.[10]

Many of the ways through which Aboriginals understand their relationship to the land go unacknowledged; information has to be provided that was once sacred and not publicly available; knowledge that was gender- or age-specific loses its specificity. But then again, and here we circle back to Benjamin and his staff officers' map, more and more Aboriginal groups have requisitioned the Western Ordnance Survey maps *entirely for their own purposes*. They use them to create their own cultural maps. The people of Kowanyama on the Cape York Peninsula of Far North Queensland used a conventional map to locate

> the Dreaming tracks, the stories, the poison places and who belonged where . . . meeting places and such like. The result [is] a precise European-style map containing wholly Aboriginal information about the country.
>
> (Strang 1997: 223)

Indigenous maps

The Inuit are adept map-makers, but rarely bother (Lewis 1979). An Inuit elder tells the geographer that he had made detailed hunting maps from memory, but then he threw them away (Rundstrom, cited in Wood 1993: 147). The recapitulation was important, not the material object.

Without navigational instruments, Micronesian sea navigators steer their outrigger sailing canoes over distances of 300, 400, 500 miles, often out of sight of land for long distances. They sail, they say, 'by the shape of the sky'. They map the stars (Downs and Stea 1977: 153). In fact they use a combination of techniques 'including dead reckoning, following the stars at night, and making use of detailed knowledge of conditions encountered at sea – wave-patterns, bird movements, cloud formations, winds etc.' (Gell 1985: 283). The knowledge is passed on through long apprenticeships with master navigators, on land, by word of mouth and using models made of sticks and shells or pebbles (Frake 1985). It is woven into a mythology in which the stars take on the role of people and animals, and objects and events are built into the structure of the star course.

The Inuit track animals, the Micronesians track the night skies, the Western Apache track people. They 'shoot them' with stories, they 'stalk them' with places. The Western Apache also, like the Inuit, remark that 'Whitemen need paper maps: we have maps in our minds' (Basso 1983: 25). They have elaborate place names – 'where the water flows inward underneath a cottonwood tree' is one of the shorter ones. Their historical stories are anchored spatially. The stories have a moral, and people who have behaved 'wrongly', who violate Apache standards, become the subject of a moral tale. They are 'shot with an arrow'. If they take it to heart, then the place of the story acts as a constant reminder, it stalks them.

In all these cases the world is mapped both through lived experience and abstractly, but rarely takes material form. But there are also examples of indigenous people who do objectify their knowledge; who create maps as an inalienable part of their identity, and as part of their political and social strategies. Territory is not the only form of 'property'; maps are a form of cultural property to which people have differing access and by which they are differentially empowered. In Australia, the Aboriginal Yolngu bark paintings, the *daragu* boards, and the Walbiri sand paintings are sacred and secret repositories of clan knowledge. These paintings, because they are inalienable, have no autonomy, and are intimately bound up in ritual and ceremony, are constantly reworked in the present.

Past and present elide. The topographical detail – dune, hill, lake, shoreline – is the site of memory. Where Benjamin's spatial maps reflect a western sense of personal autonomy, these are the memories of ancestral wanderings that are also contemporary songlines, ancestral exits and entrances that are also contemporary sacred places. Ancestral activity is recreated and maintained by human action. And the representations are integral to the maintenance. In the western context, the map appears neutral, appears to legitimate hierarchies of place, boundaries and perspectives as abstract knowledge, not bound to particular perceptions of social relations. In Aboriginal society, this divide between nature and culture, something 'out there' as opposed to something socially and culturally constructed, is, quite literally, inconceivable.

Conclusions

These are local knowledges – sometimes, but not always, forged in hostile encounters. And even when forged, they are not entirely dependent upon the encounter – they have a life of their own.

They are, to use a word that I have so far avoided, *indexical*: they are 'indexed' on people's sense of their own history, their own social relationships.

The western map is equally indexical, but pretends not to be. As Turnbull (1989: 42) puts it:

> In the western tradition the way to imbue a claim with authority
> is to attempt to eradicate all signs of its local, contingent, social
> and individual production.

In the western map, history is recorded. But it is over and done with. In many of these alternative maps, history is present and future. Benjamin regarded everything he chose to recall of his past as prophetic of the future because the memory collapses time. The Cumbales of Colombia envision history as *in front* of the observer and as *working back* from the observer. It is in front because the people live the consequences today and can change them (Rappaport 1988).

That, optimistically, could be the message of the maps. The western map is the reality, the technology, the metaphor of global capital penetration. The alternative maps are equally the reality, technology and metaphor of local resistance. The results are as variable as the people and situations involved.

Notes

1 'Accuracy', Wood (1993: 78) points out, 'is not a measure that stands *outside our culture* by which other cultures may be evaluated, but it is a concept from our own culture which may be irrelevant in another'.

2 In Shakespeare's *Twelfth Night*, Maria, extolling Malvolio's appearance, says: 'He does smile his face into more lines than is in the new map with the augmentation of the Indies'.

3 Hastrup (1985), in the context of medieval Iceland, notes that the Icelandic people employed both proximate orientation – based on celestial observations – and 'pregnant' or social orientation based on land travel.

4 Brian Friel's play *Translations* (1981) is all about the English cartographic intrusion into Ireland: the power of the renaming of places and spaces.

5 Blunt and Rose (1994: 16) point out the paradox that

> the 'others' of the master subject are marginalised and ignored in the
> gaze at space, but are also given their own places: the slum, the ghetto,
> the harem, the colony, the closet, the inner city, the Third World, the
> private. The places haunt the imagination of the master subject.

6 Although the memories are intensely personal, they also constantly open out towards the larger body politic. So Adriane, the prostitute, leads Benjamin across 'the threshold of class'. 'Whole networks of streets', he surmises, 'were opened up under the auspices of prostitution' (Benjamin 1985: 301). This particular male and class geography has a female counterpart. Edholm (1993) has mapped the contrasting Parisian worlds of Baudelaire, the boulevard *flâneur*, and Valadon, the working-class artist and model who inhabited the tenemented backstreets.

7 Battaglia, walking with her informant Soter through the village of Sabarl (an island off the southern tip of Papua New Guinea), catches this sense of memory contained in place and activity:

The present structure of the village permitted the experience of a jumble of times brought forward to the present of the story we were walking.... Soter used boundary markers, present and absent, as 'memory stations'. The absent space carried the memory of the once present tree and the events that surrounded its removal or replacement. What was no longer on the spot carried the meaning of what now was.... Sabarl remembrance worked this way, through latent images and 'active absences'.

(Battaglia 1990: 25)

8 Kuchler (1993: 103) stresses that the Malangan carvings are a direct result of the tensions surrounding land transmission in the wake of German resettlement and of the associated rising death toll and decreasing birth-rate: 'sculpting provided the framework for the institutionalisation of land, labour, and loyalty which could no longer be adequately addressed by social organisation'.

9 When Aboriginal people talk of 'their' country, they define it in terms of sites rather than stretches of country. However, as they move from one point to the next, 'the site name is expanded to blur with the next ... no clear-cut boundaries are recognised'. It is the significant areas within a particular stretch of territory that define the territorial range (Berndt 1976: 136-7).

10 So too on Sabarl (the island off Papua New Guinea), Battaglia, *on the insistence of the village spokesperson*, creates out of 'Soter's spiralling associative leaps, his back-tracking corrections, and the like', a western-style linear narrative (Battaglia 1990: 25).

Acknowledgement

A shorter version of this chapter appeared in Clifford and King (1996).

References

Basso, K.H. 1983. 'Stalking with stories': names, places and moral narratives among the Western Apache. In *Text, Play and Story*, E. Brunner (ed.), 19-55. Illinois: Waveland Press Inc.

Battaglia, D. 1990. *On the Bones of the Serpent: person, memory and mortality in Sabarl Island society*. Chicago: Chicago University Press.

Benjamin, W. 1985. *One Way Street and Other Writings*. London: Verso.

Berndt, R.M. 1976. Territoriality and the problem of demarcating socio-cultural space. In *Tribes and Boundaries in Australia*, N. Peterson (ed.), 133-61. Canberra: Australian Institute of Aboriginal Studies.

Blunt, A. and G. Rose 1994. Introduction: women's colonial and postcolonial geographies. In *Writing Women and Space: colonial and postcolonial geographies*, A. Blunt and G. Rose (eds), 1-25. New York: The Guildford Press.

Certeau, M. 1984. *The Practice of Everyday Life*. Berkeley: University of California Press.

Clifford, S. and A. King (eds) 1996. *From Place to PLACE*. London: Common Ground.

Cobbett, W. 1987. *Rural Rides*. Harmondsworth: Penguin.

Cosgrove, D. 1984. *Social Formation and Symbolic Landscape*. London: Croom Helm.

Crouch, D. and D. Matless 1996. Refiguring geography: parish maps of Common Ground. *Transactions of the Institute of British Geographers* 21, 236-55.

Davis, M. 1990. *City of Quartz*. London: Verso.

Downs, R.M. and D. Stea 1977. *Maps in Mind: reflections on cognitive mapping.* New York: Harper & Row.

Edholm, F. 1993. The view from below: Paris in the 1880s. In *Landscape: politics and perspectives,* B. Bender (ed.), 139–68. Oxford: Berg.

Foucault, M. 1978. *The History of Sexuality: an introduction.* New York: Random House.

Foucault, M. 1994. Two lectures. In *Culture/Power/History,* N.B. Dirks, G. Eley and S.B. Ortner (eds), 200–21. Princeton, N.J.: Princeton University Press.

Frake, C.O. 1985. Cognitive maps of time and tide among medieval seafarers. *Man* 20, 254–70.

Friel, B. 1981. *Translations.* London: Faber & Faber.

Gelder, K. and J.M. Jacobs 1995. Uncanny Australia. *Ecumene* 2, 171–83.

Gell, A. 1985. How to read a map: remarks on the practical logic of navigation. *Man* 20, 271–86.

Giddens, A. 1985. Time, space and regionalisation. In *Social Relations and Spatial Structures,* D. Gregory and J. Urry (eds), 265–95. London: Macmillan.

Gow, P. 1995. Land, people and paper in western Amazon. In *The Anthropology of Landscape,* E. Hirsch and M. O'Hanlon (eds), 43–62. Oxford: Oxford University Press.

Gramsci, A. 1971. *Prison Notebooks.* New York: International Publishers.

Hammond, J.L. and B. Hammond 1948. *The Village Labourer.* London: Guild Books.

Harley, J.B. 1988. Maps, knowledge and power. In *The Iconography of Landscape,* D. Cosgrove and S. Daniels (eds), 277–314. Cambridge: Cambridge University Press.

Harley, J.B. 1992a. Deconstructing the map. In *Writing Worlds: discourse, text and metaphor in the representation of landscape,* T.J. Barnes and J.S. Duncan (eds), 231–47. London: Routledge.

Harley, J.B. 1992b. Rereading the maps of the Columbian encounter. *Annals of the Association of American Geographers* 82/3, 522–42.

Harvey, D. 1989. *The Condition of Postmodernity.* Oxford: Basil Blackwell.

Hastrup, K. 1985. *Culture and History in Medieval Iceland.* Oxford: Clarendon Press.

Helgerson, R. 1986. The land speaks: cartography, chorography, and subversion in Renaissance England. *Representations* 16, 51–85.

Kuchler, S. 1993. Landscape as memory: the mapping of process and its representation in a Melanesian society. In *Landscape: politics and perspectives,* B. Bender (ed.), 85–106. Oxford: Berg.

Lefebvre, H. 1991. *The Production of Space.* Oxford: Basil Blackwell.

Lewis, G.M. 1979. The indigenous maps and mapping of North American Indians. *Map Collector* 9, 25–31.

Monmonier, M. 1991. *How to Lie with Maps.* Chicago: University of Chicago Press.

Morphy, H. 1993. Colonialism, history and the construction of place: the politics of landscape in northern Australia. In *Landscape: politics and perspectives,* B. Bender (ed.), 205–43. Oxford: Berg.

Orlove, B.S. 1991. Mapping reeds and reading maps. *American Ethnologist* 18, 3–38.

Pred, A. 1990. *Making Histories and Constructing Human Geographies.* Boulder, Colorado: Westview Press.

Rappaport, J. 1988. History and everyday life in the Colombian Andes. *Man* 23, 718–39.

Rose, G. 1993. *Feminist Geography.* Cambridge: Polity Press.

Salmond, A. 1992. Theoretical landscapes: on cross-cultural conceptions of knowledge. In *Semantic Anthropology,* D. Parkin (ed.), 65–87. London: Academic Press.

Soja, E. 1989. *Postmodern Geographies.* London: Verso.

Sontag, S. 1983. *A Susan Sontag Reader.* Harmondsworth: Penguin.

Strang, V. 1997. *Uncommon Ground.* Oxford: Berg.

Tilley, C. 1994. *The Phenomenology of Landscape.* Oxford: Berg.

Turnbull, D. 1989. *Maps are Territories. Science is an Atlas. A portfolio of exhibits.* Geelong, Victoria: Deakin University Press.
Wescoat, J.L., M. Brand and N. Mir 1991. Gardens, roads and legendary tunnels: the underground memory of Mughal Lahore. *Journal of Historical Geography* 17, 1–17.
Wood, D. 1993. *The Power of Maps.* London: Routledge.
Young, R. 1990. *White Mythologies: writing history and the West.* London: Routledge.

4   Social landscapes in Irish prehistory

Gabriel Cooney

> He had used the place up, converted it to experiences and
> memories that made up the person he was.
>
> His mind was a jumble of contradictory thoughts and feel-
> ings; an inner landscape equivalent to the one all around him.
>
> (Dibdin 1994: 43)

Introduction

Landscape, as the heading of a recent overview on social landscapes (Gosden
and Head 1994) put it, is a usefully ambiguous concept. A distinction is
frequently made between physical and cultural or social landscapes, but
from a human perspective it could be argued that the primary way in which
we should view landscapes is as social phenomena. We perceive, understand
and create the landscape around us through the filter of our social and
cultural background and milieu (Evans 1981: 8; Tilley 1994: 25–6; Schama
1995: 12). Individuals and groups from different cultures may see the same
landscape in a very different light. Thus, for example, in the eighteenth
century there were competing perceptions of the Irish landscape (Cooney
1997: 32). The traditional Gaelic perception was based on oral traditions, on
the landscape as embodying the long history and genealogy of families and
events. By contrast the Ascendency, landowners who had come to Ireland
from Britain as part of the process of colonisation and land redistribution,
saw the potential of the physical aspects of the Irish landscape but they saw
it as dehumanised, bare, with rocks and trees. They were also very concerned
to demonstrate their place and power in this landscape, as Foster (1988: 192)
put it, 'only recently won and insecurely held'.

Bringing the question of perception forward to the present, O'Connor
(1993) has argued that the colonial image of Ireland as an empty landscape
awaiting development has strong resonances in the present-day tourist image
of Ireland as an uncrowded, green and pleasant land, a timeless land where
visitors from more frenetic lifestyles and landscapes can come for rest and
relaxation. This timeless Celtic Fringe on the periphery of a fast-lane Europe
is, of course, in itself a socially invented mythic landscape whose background
is in the development of a taste for sublime (wild, uncultured) and romantic
landscapes allied to the invention of 'the Celt' in the course of the eighteenth
century (Leerssen 1994: 6), and in this sense there may well be a link between
the colonial and romantic views of the Irish landscape. It was also an image
that was put to great effect in the development of a national identity through

the nineteenth century (Graham and Proudfoot 1993: 5), in the idea that the Irish rural landscape could be seen as the epitome of a timeless continuity of the past and the way in which the past and present can be viewed as contemporaneous (McDonagh 1983).

The complexity of perceptions of the Irish landscape over the last couple of centuries that has been touched upon here is a reminder of how difficult it is to understand landscapes as perceived by societies in the more distant, prehistoric past. Approaching the problem of how anthropologists understand other societies, Geertz, using a concept developed by Kohut, suggests that what is needed is an understanding of what are *experience-near* concepts for other people – how they see and define the world – and to place and understand these in connection with *experience-distant* concepts that theorists use to analyse and understand the general features of social life (Geertz 1983: 57–8). It seems that this is an appropriate way of looking at social landscapes – we cannot hope to think like a prehistoric person did about their landscape but we can reconstruct an overview of what the elements of that landscape may have been and then try to understand what they meant for the people who were carrying this landscape round in their heads.

Landscapes from the outside: the extent of prehistoric settlement

The impact of prehistoric settlement on the Irish landscape was much more widespread than has been previously suggested. Examination of the overall pattern of distribution of monuments and artefacts indicates that there were very few areas of Ireland that did not witness prehistoric activity. Analysis of regional or local sequences suggests activity through the major periods in prehistory, but what does change is the character of the evidence (see Stout and Stout's 1992 study of the spatial patterning of prehistoric and early historic sites in the Dublin area) (Figure 4.1). This raises the question of the degree and nature of continuity in this evidence.

The reliance on pollen analysis to suggest the character and effect of prehistoric farming and vegetational history has led to a perception and presentation of the evidence of the settlement landscape as representing phases of farming expansion alternating with regeneration of the forest cover (e.g. Weir 1995). The prominence of this view in the literature has led to simplistic formulations of the character of the prehistoric landscape when interpreted by, for example, historical geographers (e.g. Smyth 1993: 404; Whelan 1994: 63). However, the difficulties of interpretation of the pollen record in landscape terms (e.g. Edwards 1979, 1982) should make us very wary of accepting a reconstruction of the course of human impact on the environment that, by definition, is based on derived rather than direct landscape evidence. It is clear that palynological interpretation is also influenced by views put forward in the archaeological literature, leading to the danger

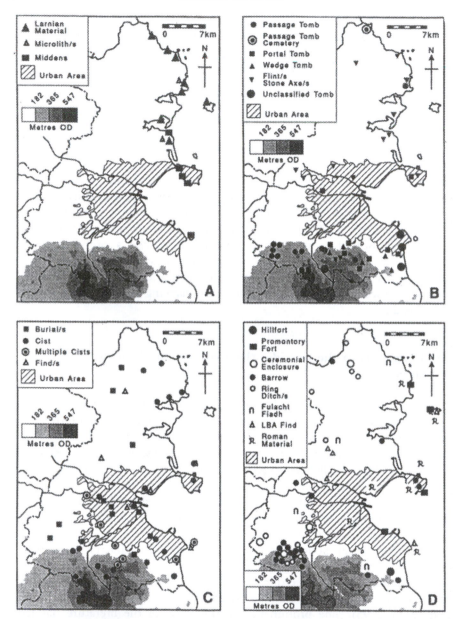

Figure 4.1 Spatial patterning of prehistoric and early historic sites in the Dublin area;
A Mesolithic, B Neolithic, C Earlier Bronze Age, D Later Bronze Age and Iron Age
(from Stout and Stout 1992).

of a circular argument. Thus until recently any apparent decrease in archaeological evidence was frequently read as representing an equivalent reduction
in the extent and intensity of human settlement and as indicative of increasing
economic difficulties (see Woodman 1992: 297). Gaps in the archaeological

record for particular timespans, such as the late prehistoric so-called 'dark age' between 600–300 BC, were seen to indicate periods of agricultural adversity, usually attributed to climatic deterioration or environmental stress, and the pollen evidence was both slotted into this framework and used to support it.

But perhaps more at issue are two aspects of the way in which we as archaeologists look at prehistoric human activity in the landscape. First, there is the question of our ability to detect human activity when there are no large-scale, high-profile monuments or easily datable artefacts. One obvious example is the sparsity of megalithic tombs dating to the Neolithic in the southern half of Ireland – an area that is now known to have been extensively settled during the Neolithic period. Another example is the recently realised potential of estuarine landscapes in later prehistory (e.g. O'Sullivan 1995), areas that had previously not featured in archaeological research strategies. Ironically the great wealth of surviving prehistoric monuments in Ireland has tended to lead to a devalued view of other types of archaeological information, such as lithic scatters and the distribution and context of metalwork. Second, there is the tendency to assume that the human response to environmental change can be isolated from other aspects of life. For example, the growing emphasis on bogs, rivers and lakes from the Neolithic through the Bronze Age and into the Iron Age as places of deposition of metalwork and other material could be a response to a deteriorating and wetter climate, but it also has to be seen as a trend in social behaviour that stretches over two millennia, as a complement to activity on dry land such as burial practice and in the context of the nature and value of the material placed in wetland contexts (Cooney and Grogan 1994).

People, pathways and places

The complementary character of activity in dry and wetland contexts referred to above is a reminder that prehistoric settlement in the landscape did not take the form of neutral dots on a distribution map but was a complex system with many components. In this context, the recent experience-distant emphasis on understanding the archaeological record in terms of the movement of people along pathways focused on locales in the landscape that may in some cases have come to be marked monumentally is very important (e.g. Bradley 1993; Tilley 1994). The background to this trend in interpretation can be seen in Ingold's (1986: 130ff) influential ideas on the concept of tenure and the emphasis in current archaeological writing in Britain on the continuity of the world view of hunter-gatherers and early farmers. The mesolithic and neolithic landscape is seen as one in which mobility was the binding thread, linking places of social and religious significance, such as megalithic structures (see Thomas 1991). It is argued that it was up to 2,000 years later, in the second millennium BC, that a place-bound landscape perspective developed with greater emphasis on community and household

identity expressed in the division, bounding and control of the land (e.g.
Barrett 1994: 147; Chapter 2, this volume).

In Ireland there is, by contrast, very good evidence to indicate that division
and control of the landscape, surviving in the form of field boundaries, was a
feature of life from the Neolithic period onwards. It would appear then that
significant differences mark the development of people's relationship with
the landscape in prehistoric Ireland and Britain. In this chapter it is suggested
that both pathways and places are important, and that in Ireland there does
not appear to be a chronological trend towards a greater emphasis on place
and belonging in later prehistory as has been recently suggested for Britain.
Indeed we can point to both the evidence of the importance of paths and
pathways in later Irish prehistory and the importance of places in earlier
prehistory. As noted above, there is in Ireland significant evidence for the
presence of field boundaries from the fourth millennium BC, during
the Neolithic. While this could, of course, still have been the result of a very
gradual change in land-use practice, it is accompanied by evidence for substantial houses from early in the fourth millennium (e.g. Simpson 1995) and
long-term clearance of forested areas for agricultural purposes (see discussion
in Cooney and Grogan 1994: 36–42). Viewed alongside the construction and
use of megalithic tombs, the occurrence of evidence of sedentary settlement
and land division suggests the early development in Ireland of a landscape based
on place and belonging (Cooney 1991). In neolithic complexes like Céide and
Rathlackan, Co. Mayo, all of these elements occur together (Caulfield 1983,
1988; Byrne 1994).

From this time on it would appear that the house was at the core of
settlement and life; the areas used for farming, gathering and hunting on a
daily basis would have been the most familiar parts of the landscape. But
locations visited less frequently, for example sites where raw materials for
stone or metal tool production were available or sacred sites and places such
as cemeteries, would also have been seen as important. It is not difficult to
imagine that people may have perceived these everyday and less often visited
locales in quite different ways and it may be relevant perhaps to view this
in terms of both a contrast but also a complementarity between a tame,
domesticated landscape and a wild, untamed world (e.g. Hodder 1990;
McMann 1994: 526).

The movement of materials from their source point to where they were
used, deposited or discarded would have brought a different sense of landscape and places; this was one in which elements were transported and
reassembled and could then serve to bring together and link in the mind's
eye places that were physically distant, to domesticate the wild and to link
people. One example that has been recently explored is the question of the
sources of the constructional and decorative stones for the major megalithic
tombs in the Boyne Valley cemetery, Co. Meath. Regarding the construction of Knowth, McCabe and Nevin (in Eogan 1986: 113–14) suggest that
the large greywacke (sandstone) slabs were quarried and probably came from
a number of quarries, at least 3–5 km away to the north and east of the site.

Mitchell (1992) has indicated the probable sources of the decorative stones concentrated on the exterior of the cairns and in settings and spreads at the entrances to the tombs at Newgrange and Knowth. The white quartz would have come from the area of the Dublin/Wicklow mountains, at least 40 km away to the south, while the richest source of the rounded granodiorite and granite cobbles and oval banded siltstones appears to have been a stretch of the northern shore of Dundalk Bay, about 35 km to the northeast.

The way in which these stones were deployed is a graphic reminder of the need to consider the landscape at a variety of different scales and perceptions, from the intimacy of human activity in the ceremonies at sacred sites to the wider landscape within which people lived and moved and brought the raw materials for the megalithic tombs. In turn, the tombs were very often deliberately aligned and orientated within the landscape. In the case of passage tombs, for example, the placement of the entrance to the tombs in cemeteries establishes connections with landmarks, other monuments and celestial phenomena (see Eogan 1986; Cooney 1990; McMann 1994; Bergh 1995). If sacred places, like megalithic tomb cemeteries, are seen as locales that were arenas for social continuity and transformation, then in a similar way it seems very likely that prominent places in the landscape, associated for example with rock sources, would also have been invested with meaning and been the focus of stories (Tilley 1994: 32–3). They would have acted as mnemonic pegs on which stories and traditional teaching hung. As Tacon (1994: 125) has put it, 'Landscapes were populated with spirits . . . everywhere humans went they bonded with landscapes and made them culturally alive, exciting places to live'. It seems probable that stone would also have been symbolically charged, particularly quartz because of its colour and iridescence (Tacon 1991: 198). The extraction of stone from the earth and its incorporation into human structures would have invested the architecture with the power of the land, and thus the natural became social.

A sense of place

The accumulation of evidence from different periods in particular locations suggests that people had a very strong sense of place in prehistoric Ireland. Of course this could be seen as mere coincidence or the result of settlement inertia, but as a pattern of human behaviour that frequently recurs in the archaeological record it does seem more likely that it implies a sense of belonging and continuity, built upon human experience and cultural identity. Hunter-gatherer communities, because of a perceived emphasis on their mobility, are often viewed as being more concerned with movement over the landscape than with living in, and having a sense of belonging to, particular places. On the other hand, hunter-gatherers would have needed to have a highly developed landscape sense to map mentally and to utilise the range of natural resources that they relied on as a food base. In the case of Australia, the idea of symbolic classification of the landscape is common amongst Aboriginal groups. This was based both on the land and on the history of its use and could have involved marking the landscape (Gosden and Head 1994: 115).

In the context of Ireland, where Woodman (1985) has argued for a degree of sedentary settlement in the Early Mesolithic, it is possible to suggest that we should see hunter-gatherers as being concerned not only about path-ways and routeways – be they of a physical or spiritual nature – but also with places. The recent emphasis in Britain on demonstrating the degree of continuity between the lifestyle and perception of landscape between hunter-gatherers and early farmers has been at least partially based on the problem of identifying permanent places of settlement in the landscape (e.g. Bewley 1994); it is worth reiterating that this has not been the case in Ireland. Here, during the Neolithic, we can readily recognise the importance of places as the landscape was altered and transformed, for both mundane and sacred purposes. Changes in the land were brought about through the creation of field boundaries around settlements, and megalithic tombs are the best examples we have of deliberately created sacred places. In both cases, bounding and division of the landscape are involved, but so also is the concept of orientation and provision for movement, stressing that these are comple-mentary and not opposed activities.

One aspect of megalithic tombs that had long-term significance was the intention of their builders to create permanent structures, monuments that would remain in the landscape, even if they would prove open to different interpretations by later generations as the original purpose of the construc-tion faded into antiquity. Bradley (1993) has shown how many monuments are located at places that may already have been viewed as special. Repeti-tive patterns of tomb-siting and -orientation suggest that people had specific ideas about the placement of, and approach to, these sites (see Thomas 1990).

It is in megalithic tomb cemeteries that we can recognise for the first time the concept of a deliberately created ritual or ceremonial landscape. In some cases these landscapes remain a focus of activity, and there is frequently the addition of later structures such as earthen enclosures, stone circles, cemetery mounds and barrows. The different form of these human additions to the landscape indicates changing perceptions between the present and the past and the role of the dead and the ancestors. As archaeologists we have the challenge of trying to understand this record from the palimpsest of evidence left behind, and our standard analytic device is to peel off the sediments of activity one by one – the experience-distant approach. The reality is that a number of images of the past may be drawn upon by people at any one time to give it meaning. In oral history and folklore, the past would have been explained in mythic terms by people living and creating the archaeological record – the experience-near lived reality.

Looking at the landscape at Loughcrew, Co. Meath (Figure 4.2), we see a terrain dominated by a striking elongated ridge orientated southwest to north-east. This ridge lies on the interface between the catchment areas of the Boyne/Blackwater and Shannon river systems. The most prominent archaeo-logical feature is the passage tomb cemetery with large focal hill-top cairns (Sites

D, L, T, Y) along the ridge and smaller sites clustered around them. The Irish name of the place, Sliabh na Caillighe, the hill of the witch or hag, directly refers to these cairns, as they are seen in oral tradition as stones dropped from her apron (Figure 4.3) as she hopped from west to east across the flat summits on the ridge before falling and dying as she jumped towards another hill. An unusually shaped kerbstone of the largest tomb (Cairn T) on the central hill top is referred to as the Hag's Chair. We could see this story as an origin myth, as a way of explaining very prominent features in the landscape and also as a mnemonic device to aid the passing on of information on place names.

When Eugene Conwell documented Loughcrew as an archaeological complex in the 1860s he thought that it could be equated with the pagan cemetery of Tailteann mentioned in the early Irish literature, and he proposed that Cairn T was the tomb of Ollamh Fodhla, a legendary king and law-giver. While today this association can be dismissed as fanciful, it has to be seen in the context of the importance of Ollamh Fodhla as an iconographic figure of great importance for Irish nationalism in the nineteenth century (Hutchinson 1987: 58). During this period, Ollamh Fodhla was seen as the founder of the nation in ancient antiquity. He was, for example, given a central place in the decorative design of a major public building (the Four Courts) in Dublin by the architect James Gandon in the late eighteenth century (Sheehy 1980: 14) and he was one of the heroic figures shown on the banners and membership cards of the Repeal movement in the 1840s (see, for example, Owens 1994).

Loughcrew is best known archaeologically as a passage tomb cemetery, but in order to put that cemetery in context we have to bring into focus other

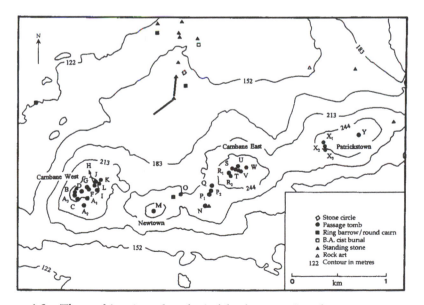

Figure 4.2 The prehistoric archaeological landscape at Loughcrew.

Figure 4.3 A child's drawing from the 1930s depicting the origin myth of Loughcrew (from McMann 1993).

aspects of the archaeological record. In the lithic material collected from the area in the late nineteenth and early twentieth century by Edward Crofton Rotherham (Figure 4.4), a local landowner and antiquarian who also investigated several of the tombs on Loughcrew, there is both mesolithic material and a substantial quantity of neolithic material, some in the form of distinct scatters suggesting settlement below and perhaps particularly to the south and east of the cemetery (Cooney and Dillon forthcoming). Hence we must see Loughcrew in terms of a striking range of hills that were already known in the Mesolithic and whose significance would have been enhanced and more widely known because of its position on the interface between the catchment areas of the Boyne and Shannon river systems. The development of the cemetery clearly suggests substantial clearance of the forest cover of the hills and surrounding area, as the ideas of visibility and procession between tombs within the cemetery would require open ground. The human perception of the place would have varied depending on location in relation to the site, from distant landmark with the major cairns as distinctive features to close encounters where the interplay between the landscape and the siting of the cairns created a range of different settings for the ceremonies that would have been carried out at and around the tombs (Cooney 1990; Thomas 1992; McMann 1994). It would appear that there was significant settlement activity in the vicinity of the cemetery; the use of local and non-local materials can be seen both in the tomb construction and in the stone axes from Rotherham's lithic collection which contains a substantial number of porcellanite axes, coming from sources in the northeast of the country.

In the Bronze Age it would appear that there was both a continued use and veneration of what were now ancient monuments, with the insertion of pottery and presumably burials into the tombs and also the development of a new outdoor ceremonial focus on a lower shoulder of ground to the north of the ridge at Ballyvalley, with a stone circle, standing stones, cairns and a few examples of rock art, including the capstone of a cist (see Moore 1987), all within sight of the ridge and its cairns to the south which formed the backdrop for this complex. A further important element in this complex is in the form of a cursus that has recently been recognised (Newman 1995a). The tombs, if we can judge by much more recent oral and literary tradition, became mythic and ambiguous, places where the real world and the

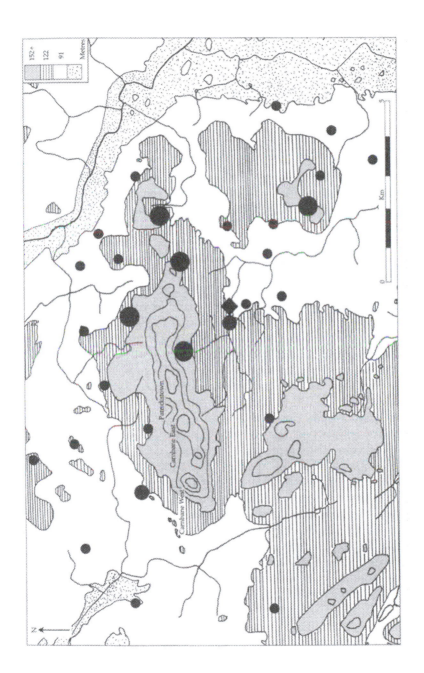

Figure 4.4 The quantity and distribution of lithic artefacts per townland in the Rotherhain collection from around Loughcrew (small dots 1–10, medium 11–20, large dots more than 20; the lozenge marks the Rotherham residence).

other world collided. Their continuing or renewed power in late prehistory is illustrated by the very large deposit of bone plaques with La Tène decoration in Cairn H (Raftery 1983: 235–8), one of the passage tombs on the westernmost of the three hills. Loughcrew, as McMann (1993: 14) has put it, is a place with many histories.

The landscape as context of activity

The discussion of Loughcrew above focused primarily on the interpretation of, and layers of meaning in, built features added to an already impressive landscape. For much of Irish prehistory, however, people's ceremonial links with the past and the landscape are not so transparent but are often hidden or at least not very visible. Of course, megalithic tombs are resonant with this tension between interior and exterior worlds (McMann 1994: 542), but subsequently, alongside the continuing focus on artificially created places such as tombs, earthen enclosures and barrow cemeteries, natural features such as rivers, bogs and lakes become increasingly important as a formal context for the occurrence of archaeological material, particularly from the beginning of the Early Bronze Age. It should be noted that this depositional activity is contemporary with evidence for bounding, land division and settlement. Mitchell (1989: 97–9), for example, has noted that on Valencia Island off the Iveragh Peninsula in Co. Kerry in the southwest of Ireland, a late bronze age sword found on the mineral soil surface below peat was within 1.5 km of a contemporary field wall system to the west (Figure 4.5) and that the pollen record from the island also indicates late bronze age agricultural activity. In the hummocky terrain of the northeastern midlands, where there is a range of glacial depositional landforms, earlier bronze age burials occur in what are the higher and drier parts of this lowland terrain. The known findspots of contemporary bronze age objects, such as bronze axes, on the other hand, are mostly from the lower-lying wetter areas, now infilled with peat, and they tend to concentrate on the periphery of the areas where the burials are concentrated. In other areas, particularly southwest Ireland, we can see an association between field boundaries and ceremonial behaviour in the form of a number of megalithic monument types such as stone circles, stone rows or alignments, four-poster monuments, boulder-burials and radial-stone cairns and enclosures. At Cashelkeelty, Co. Kerry, two stone circles, an alignment and field boundaries were located on a level terrace. Here it is suggested that the focus of activity may have switched from agricultural to ceremonial use (Lynch 1981: 72–3), although it is possible that the agricultural and ceremonial landscape may have coincided. Based on corpora studies of these megalithic monuments by Ó Nualláin (1978, 1984, 1988), Walsh (1993) discussed a number of complexes where the types occur together and suggested that they had separate ceremonial or ritual functions, that their siting in the landscape is very deliberate and that they would have been used repetitively.

In the Bronze Age we therefore have evidence of a complex use of the

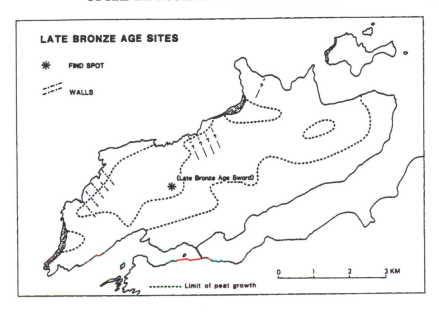

Figure 4.5 Relationship between findspot of late bronze age sword and field walls on Valencia Island (from Mitchell 1989).

landscape that incorporated fields, deposition in wet areas, and these and other marginal areas may have been the focus of ceremonial monuments, for example the stone circle complex in southwest Ireland and barrow cemeteries in north Munster (Cooney and Grogan 1994: 131). This indicates the complementarity of the domestic and sacred landscape and the probability that there were defined paths of movement between the two that would have served both to emphasise the differences between them and also literally to link them. People were still creating sacred sites, apparently of local importance and very often with a relatively small input of labour, but they were also linking themselves to permanent, natural places, particularly through the deposition of objects. Many of these natural places may always have been regarded as sacred. Either the human attitude towards them changed, allowing and calling for the deposition of material, or perhaps it is simply the case that material that is more archaeologically visible was deposited from the beginnings of the Bronze Age. There are indeed definite instances of the deposition of stone axes and pottery in bogs during the Neolithic.

One way of looking at the increased emphasis on formal artefact deposition is to see it as a complement to, or replacement of, elaborate deposition in a mortuary context (Cooney and Grogan 1994: 133ff). A link between formal burial and deposition is that they were both carried out at specific locations, and there are, of course, instances where a monument built first to contain human remains may later become the locale for deposition, because of its special character (see O'Brien 1993: 68–9). Whilst the use of cemetery areas over prolonged stretches of time has long been recognised, the repetitive deposition of objects at specific places on the River Erne, the River Shannon and the River Bann from the Neolithic onwards has come under much less scrutiny. Lakes such as Lough Gur and bogs, some of which may have been lakes at the time, saw repeated episodes of deposition, as at Lagore and Ballinderry (Hencken 1942, 1950). Indeed the question has been raised as to whether the large late bronze age assemblages from bogs, such as at Dowris or the Bog of Cullen, should be regarded as examples of this kind of prolonged deposition rather than as a single event (Eogan 1983: 11).

One of the most interesting aspects of the archaeological landscape centred on the large enclosure at Emain Macha (e.g. Warner 1994), regarded as the royal site of the kingdom of Ulster in early Irish literature, is that this practice of deposition in water is incorporated into the spatial organisation of the complex. Loughnashade, a natural lake, lies below and to the northeast of Emain Macha, and iron age material was placed in the lake (Raftery 1987). The King's Stables (Lynn 1977) is an artificially created pool lying to the northeast of the trivallate hillfort at Haughey's Fort (Mallory 1995) to the west-northwest of Emain Macha, with late bronze age dates, and here late bronze age material was deposited in the pool. We appear to be looking at a deliberate alignment of a pathway from major high-status enclosures to places of formal deposition (Cooney and Grogan 1991). Mallory (1994: 190–1) has noted that there is a very significant chrono-logical distinction between the use of the pool and the lake, while on the other hand Warner (1994: 170) has pointed out that a double linear ditch separates Haughey's Fort–King's Stables from Emain Macha–Loughnashade, suggesting that they were seen as distinct. Processions or movement along these pathways cannot be set in isolation from the level of control and division of the surrounding landscape. Weir (1994: 176) has pointed out that in the Late Bronze Age period the area around Emain Macha appears to have been subject to continuous occupation and farming, with grassland and cereal pollen represented, suggesting that a mixed farming system was carried on, presumably within a bounded landscape. At this time there was a much more defined sense of territory and boundary than in earlier social systems in Ireland. Expressions of communal effort and power were closely linked at least to the concept, if not the physical actuality, of defence and offence. This is suggested by the hillfort defences, the swords, spears and shields, and we can link them to the construction of impressive earthworks in what appear to be boundary areas, such as the Dorsey (Lynn 1982, 1989, 1991). Aitchison's (1993) thesis that the latter should be treated as a sacred enclosure with a wetland element, fulfilling a similar function to Emain Macha, rather than as a frontier fortification provides further support for the line of argument being made here. The effect of movement or procession towards a place of ceremony and/or deposition would have been heightened by the contrast with the surrounding landscape, and this might also have been reflec-tive of the social contrast between those who were free to move across the land to carry out ceremonial deposition and warfare, and those who were bound to it.

Attention has also been drawn to the similarities between the earthen embanked enclosures of the Late Neolithic and the large enclosures at the late prehistoric/historic royal sites of Emain Macha, Tara and Dún Ailinne to suggest a possibility of continuity (e.g. Wailes 1982: 21). Simpson (1989) has speculated that the enclosing bank and ditch at Emain Macha might itself belong to the earlier tradition and date back to the final stages of the Neolithic. At a practical level we might discount any direct continuity between these earlier and later prehistoric earthworks and other structures and think instead of two major phases of monumental construction for the enclosure of, and as an arena for, ceremonial and other activity. At the level of ideology, however, it seems feasible to think of social elites emphasising their power and permanence by deliberately imitating the form or, in some instances, reusing places that had already been in the landscape for a millennium (Robertson 1992: 30). Recent discoveries of timber circles at various scales and dates in the Late Neolithic and Bronze Age at Knowth (Eogan and Roche 1994), Raffin (Newman 1993) and Ballynahatty (Hartwell 1994) provide examples of a thread of continuity underlying the more archaeologically visible expression of this idea in the third and first millennia BC (see discussion of timber circle dates in Gibson 1994: 200–4). What they have in common is a circular form that focuses attention on a central point and the care that is taken in the creation of the interior space of the monument, contrasting with the excluded exterior, from where people process. In this light we can also point to the link with activities at other circular sites such as barrows and stone circles.

This emphasis on the circular form of sacred places throughout the Bronze Age can be seen then as the background to the emergence of larger-scale circular monuments in later prehistory. However, while the above discussion has emphasised the continuity in the 'sacred geography' of the circular form in later Irish prehistory, of course monuments and places have a meaning within their immediate setting, sites can be used by people in varying ways in different contexts and morphological similarity cannot be read as implying identical purpose (e.g. Harding 1991: 149–50). It is interesting to note that the discussion surrounding the identity of neolithic rectangular timber structures as houses or ceremonial places does not seem to have arisen in the case of circular Bronze Age houses, which are after all much closer to their sacred surrogates. Perhaps we should also be re-examining our ideas about the separation of the sacred and profane in the bronze age landscape.

Transforming the landscape

In discussing social landscapes in Irish prehistory, a broad chronological sweep has been used – an experience-distant view. For people on the ground, however, the experience-near reality of time was probably different; as Ingold (1993: 157) has put it, events encompassed both past experience and portents for the future, time and looking back were intimately bound up in carrying

Figure 4.6 The standing stone at Garraunbaun, Co. Galway, from the south. (Photo: author.)

forward the process of life. If we take this perspective to the study of the landscape, then we can see the relevance of the theme of transformation or, if you like, continuity within change. As has been argued above in the case of sacred circularity, continuity at the ideological level can be accommodated within a changed world view. Continuity of place may be the essential ingredient, particularly in a world of narrative tradition where connections with the landscape are regarded as history. This can operate both at the mundane, everyday level and at the level of the larger events and places that influenced the development of society.

As an example of the former, Robinson (1994: 27–9) has explored the changing meaning of a white quartz standing stone at Garraunbaun, in Connemara, Co. Galway (Figure 4.6), whose picture now adorns the front cover of the archaeological inventory of the region (Gosling 1993). It is set in a prominent hill-top location overlooking a harbour. The Irish name of the townland (a small administrative land unit) is An Gearrán Bán, or the white horse. The story to explain the name is that the stone represents (and looks like the rear of) a mythical white horse that had come from a nearby lake. As Robinson (1994: 28–9) puts it, it is 'an ancient, perhaps totemic, white horse of stone, which has been ridden over the four thousand years of its existence by various meanings we can only guess at'.

As an example of larger-scale landscape transformation, we could consider the palimpsests of prehistoric sites that mark the place of royal sites in Ireland, places like Tara, Rathcroghan and Emain Macha. The later prehistoric activity on these sites has been seen as the foundation of their importance in the early historic period, but there is evidence for activity spanning the period from at least the Neolithic onwards (e.g. for Tara see Bhreathnach 1994, 1995; Newman 1994, 1995b). More broadly there is a correlation between the location of important later prehistoric sites and earlier prehistoric activity. Most commonly this involves a hill-top enclosure around an earlier burial mound. In itself this is a good landscape metaphor for a changing focus of ceremonial activity in Irish pre-history. It is also of interest in the light of Lynn's (1992) suggestion that the stones of the cairn covering the iron age 'Forty Metre' structure at Emain Macha may be derived from another monument and be a deliberate echo of an ancient form. By making a cairn, the builders in the first century BC were projecting themselves into the past as well as making something new.

It may be appropriate to end with one of Ireland's best known literary landscapes, that reflected in the Táin Bó Cúailnge, the tale centred on Cú Chulainn's single-handed defence of Ulster against the armies of Queen Medb (Maeve) of Connacht. The late prehistoric period is supposedly the setting of the Táin, but the tale appears also to reflect the politics and propaganda of early historic Ireland (Mallory 1992: 153; Ó hUiginn 1992). What is beyond doubt is the importance of place and place names in the story. Kinsella (1969: xiii–xiv) has noted that certain incidents have been invented specifi-cally to account for a place name, and the tale is embedded in the landscape. This would appear to fit into the category of the landscape acting as memory (see Bender 1993: 11; Chapter 3, this volume), defining a sense of place – the experience-near reality – full of multivalent and ambiguous meanings. In trying to read off and understand the landscape from a distance, the challenge is to recognise the complexity and mutiple layers of meaning contained within a landscape in which in the present day more people would still recognise and name a large hill-top kerbed cairn on Knocknarea in Co. Sligo as the burial place of the mythic Queen Medb of Connacht mentioned above rather than as the focal point of a large megalithic cemetery, predating the Táin and its characters by a few thousand years!

References

Aitchison, N.B. 1993. The Dorsey: a reinterpretation of an iron age enclosure in south Armagh. *Proceedings of the Prehistoric Society* 59, 285–301.

Barrett, J.C. 1994. *Fragments from Antiquity: an archaeology of social life in Britain 2900–1200 BC*. Oxford: Blackwell.

Bender, B. 1993. Introduction: landscape – meaning and action. In *Landscape: poli-tics and perspectives*, B. Bender (ed.), 1–17. Oxford: Berg.

Bergh, S. 1995. *Landscape of the Monuments: a study of the passage tombs in the Cúil Irra region, Co. Sligo, Ireland*. Stockholm: Riksantikvarieambetet.

Bewley, R. 1994. *Prehistoric Settlements*. London: Batsford.

Bhreathnach, E. 1994. Tara: the literary and historical perspective interim report. *Discovery Programme Reports* 1, 94–103.

Bhreathnach, E. 1995. The topography of Tara: the documentary evidence. *Discovery Programme Reports* 2, 68–76.

Bradley, R. 1993. *Altering the Earth*. Edinburgh: Society of Antiquaries of Scotland.

Byrne, G. 1994. Rathlackan, court tomb with associated pre-bog settlement. In *Excavations 1993*, I. Bennett (ed.), 61–2. Dublin: Organisation of Irish Archaeologists.

Caulfield, S. 1983. The neolithic settlement of north Connacht. In *Landscape Archaeology in Ireland*, T. Reeves-Smith and F. Hamond (eds), 195–215. Oxford: British Archaeological Reports.

Caulfield, S. 1988. *Céide Fields and Belderrig Guide*. Killala: Morrigan.

Cooney, G. 1990. The place of megalithic tomb cemeteries in Ireland. *Antiquity* 64, 741–53.

Cooney, G. 1991. Irish neolithic landscapes and landuse systems: the implications of field systems. *Rural History* 2, 123–39.

Cooney, G. 1997. Sacred and secular neolithic landscapes in Ireland. In *Sacred Sites, Sacred Places*, D.L. Carmichael, J. Hubert, B. Reeves and A. Schanche (eds), 32–43. London: Routledge.

Cooney, G. and F. Dillon Forthcoming. *The Kevin (Rotherham) Collection: a lithic and landscape analysis*.

Cooney, G. and E. Grogan 1991. An archaeological solution to the 'Irish' problem? *Emania* 9, 33–43.

Cooney, G. and E. Grogan 1994. *Irish Prehistory: a social perspective*. Dublin: Wordwell.

Dibdin, M. 1994. *Dead Lagoon*. London: Faber & Faber.

Edwards, K.J. 1979. Palynological and temporal inference in the context of prehistory with special reference to the evidence from lake and peat deposits. *Journal of Archaeological Science* 6, 255–70.

Edwards, K.J. 1982. Man, space and the woodland edge – speculation on the detection and interpretation of human impact on pollen profiles. In *Archaeological Aspects of Woodland Ecology*, S. Limbrey and M. Bell (eds), 5–22. Oxford: British Archaeological Reports.

Eogan, G. 1983. *Hoards of the Irish Later Bronze Age*. Dublin: University College, Dublin.

Eogan, G. 1986. *Knowth and the Passage Tombs of Ireland*. London: Thames & Hudson.

Eogan, G. and H. Roche 1994. A grooved ware wooden structure at Knowth, Boyne Valley, Ireland. *Antiquity* 68, 322–30.

Evans, E.E. 1981. *The Personality of Ireland*. Belfast: Blackstaff.

Foster, R.F. 1988. *Modern Ireland 1600–1972*. London: Allen Lane.

Geertz, C. 1983. *Local Knowledge*. New York: Basic Books.

Gibson, A. 1994. Excavations at the Sam-y-bryn-caled cursus complex, Welshpool, Powys, and the timber circles of Great Britain and Ireland. *Proceedings of the Prehistoric Society*, 60, 143–223.

Gosden, C. and L. Head 1994. Landscape – a usefully ambiguous concept. In *Social Landscapes*, L. Head, C. Gosden and J.P. White (eds), 113–16. Sydney: Archaeology in Oceania.

Gosling, P. 1993. *Archaeological Inventory of County Galway: Volume I – West Galway*. Dublin: Stationery Office.

Graham, B.J. and L.J. Proudfoot 1993. *An Historical Geography of Ireland*. London: Academic Press.

Harding, J. 1991. Using the unique as the typical: monuments and the ritual landscape. In *Sacred and Profane*, P. Garwood, D. Jennings, R. Skeates and J. Toms (eds), 141–51. Oxford: Oxford University Committee for Archaeology.

Hartwell, B. 1994. Late neolithic ceremonies. *Archaeology Ireland* 30, 10–13.

Hencken, H.O'N. 1942. Ballinderry crannog No. 2. *Proceedings of the Royal Irish Academy* 47C, 1–76.

Hencken, H.O'N. 1950. Lagore crannog: an Irish royal residence of the 7th to 10th centuries A.D. *Proceedings of the Royal Irish Academy* 53C, 1–247.

Hodder, I. 1990. *The Domestication of Europe*. Oxford: Blackwell.

Hutchinson, J. 1987. *The Dynamics of Cultural Nationalism*. London: Allen & Unwin.

Ingold, T. 1986. *The Appropriation of Nature: essays on human ecology and social relationships*. Manchester: Manchester University Press.

Ingold, T. 1993. The temporality of the landscape. *World Archaeology* 25, 152–74.

Kinsella, T. 1969. *The Táin*. Oxford: Oxford University Press.

Leerssen, J. 1994. The Western mirage: on the Celtic chronotope in the European imagination. In *Decoding the Landscape*, T. Collins (ed.), 1–11. Galway: University College, Galway.

Lynch, A. 1981. *Man and Environment in South-west Ireland, 4000 BC–AD 800*. Oxford: British Archaeological Reports.

Lynn, C.J. 1977. Trial excavations of the Kings Stables, Tray Townland, County Armagh. *Ulster Journal of Archaeology* 40, 42–62.

Lynn, C.J. 1982. The Dorsey and other linear earthworks. In *Studies on Early Ireland*, B. Scott (ed.), 121–8. Belfast: Association of Young Irish Archaeologists.

Lynn, C.J. 1989. An interpretation of the Dorsey. *Emania* 6, 5–10.

Lynn, C. J. 1991. Further research on the Dorsey. Supplementary note to reprint of H.G. Tempest 1930 The Dorsey. *Co. Louth Archaeological and Historical Journal* 6, 187–240.

Lynn, C.J. 1992 The iron mound in Navan Fort: a physical realization of Celtic religious beliefs? *Emania* 10, 33–57.

MacDonagh, O. 1983. *States of Mind: a study of Anglo-Irish conflict 1780–1980*. London: Allen & Unwin.

McMann, J. 1993. *Loughcrew: the cairns*. Oldcastle: After Hour Books.

McMann, J. 1994. Forms of power: dimensions of an Irish megalithic landscape. *Antiquity* 68, 525–44.

Mallory, J.P. 1992. The World of Cú Chulainn: The Archaeology of Táin Bó Cúailnge. In *Aspects of the Táin*, J.P. Mallory (ed.), 103–59. Belfast: December Publications.

Mallory, J.P. 1994. The other twin: Haughey's Fort. In *Ulidia*, J.P. Mallory and G. Stockman (eds), 187–92. Belfast: December Publications.

Mallory, J.P. 1995. Haughey's Fort – Macha's other twin? *Archaeology Ireland* 31, 28–30.

Mitchell, F. 1989. *Man and Environment in Valencia Island*. Dublin: Royal Irish Academy.

Mitchell, F. 1992. Notes on some non-local cobbles at the entrances to the passage-graves at Newgrange and Knowth, County Meath. *Journal of the Royal Society of Antiquaries of Ireland* 122, 128–45.

Moore, M.J. 1987. *Archaeological Inventory of County Meath*. Dublin: Stationery Office.

Newman, C. 1993. The show's not over until the fat lady sings. *Archaeology Ireland* 26, 8–9.

Newman, C. 1994. The Tara Survey: interim report. *Discovery Programme Reports* 1, 70–93.

Newman, C. 1995a. A cursus at Loughcrew, Co. Meath. *Archaeology Ireland* 34, 19–21.

Newman, C. 1995b. The Tara Survey: interim report. *Discovery Programme Reports* 2, 62–7.

O'Brien, W. 1993. Aspects of wedge tomb chronology. In *Past Perceptions: the prehistoric archaeology of south-west Ireland*, E. Shee Twohig and M. Ronayne (eds), 63–74. Cork: Cork University Press.

O'Connor, B. 1993. Myths and mirrors: tourist images and national identity. In *Tourism in Ireland: a critical analysis*, B. O'Connor and M. Cronin (eds), 68–85. Cork: Cork University Press.

Ó hUiginn, R. 1992. The background and development of Táin Bó Cúailnge. In *Aspects of the Táin*, J.P. Mallory (ed.), 29–67. Belfast: December Publications.

Ó Nualláin, S. 1978. Boulder-burials. *Proceedings of the Royal Irish Academy* 78C, 75–114.

Ó Nualláin, S. 1984. A survey of stone circles in Cork and Kerry. *Proceedings of the Royal Irish Academy* 84C, 1–77.

Ó Nualláin, S. 1988. Stone rows in the south of Ireland. *Proceedings of the Royal Irish Academy* 88C, 179–256.

O'Sullivan, A. 1995. Marshlanders. *Archaeology Ireland* 31, 8–11.

Owens, G. 1994. Hedge school of politics, O'Connell's monster meetings. *History Ireland* 2, 35–40.

Raftery, B. 1983. *A Catalogue of Irish Iron Age Antiquities*. Marburg: Veröffentlichung des Vorgeschichtlichen Seminars Marburg.

Raftery, B. 1987. The Loughnashade horns. *Emania* 2, 21–4.

Robertson, D.A. 1992. The Navan forty metre structure: some observations regarding the social context of an iron age monument. *Emania* 10, 25–32.

Robinson, T. 1994. A Connemara fractal. In *Decoding the Landscape*, T. Collins (ed.), 12–29. Galway: University College, Galway.

Schama, S. 1995. *Landscape and Memory*. London: HarperCollins.

Sheehy, J. 1980. *The Rediscovery of Ireland's Past: the Celtic revival 1830–1930*. London: Thames & Hudson.

Simpson, D.D.A. 1989. Neolithic Navan? *Emania* 6, 31–3.

Simpson, D.D.A. 1995. The neolithic settlement site at Baliygalley, Co. Antrim. In *Annus Archaeologiae*, E. Grogan and C. Mount (eds), 37–44. Dublin: Organisation of Irish Archaeologists.

Smyth, W.J. 1993. The making of Ireland: agendas and perspectives in cultural geography. In *An Historical Geography of Ireland*, B.J. Graham and L.J. Proudfoot (eds), 399–438. London: Academic Press.

Stout, G. and M. Stout 1992. Patterns in the past: County Dublin 5000 BC – 1000 AD. In *Dublin: from prehistory to present*, F.H.A. Aalen and K. Whelan (eds), 5–25. Dublin: Geography Publications.

Tacon, P.S.C. 1991. The power of stone: symbolic aspects of stone use and tool development in western Arnhem Land, Australia. *Antiquity* 65, 192–207.

Tacon, P.S.C. 1994. Socialising landscapes: the long-term implications of signs, symbols and marks on the land. In *Social Landscapes*, L. Head, C. Gosden and J.P. White (eds), 117–29. Sydney: Archaeology in Oceania.

Thomas, J. 1990. Monuments from the inside: the case of the Irish megalithic tombs. *World Archaeology* 22, 168–78.

Thomas, J. 1991. *Rethinking the Neolithic*. Cambridge: Cambridge University Press.

Thomas, J. 1992. Monuments, movement and the context of megalithic art. In *Vessels for the Ancestors*, N. Sharples and A. Sheridan (eds), 143–55. Edinburgh: Edinburgh University Press.

Tilley, C. 1994. *A Phenomenology of Landscape*. Oxford: Berg.

Wailes, B. 1982. The Irish 'royal sites' in history and archaeology. *Cambridge Medieval Celtic Studies* 3, 1–29.

Walsh, P. 1993. In circle and row: bronze age ceremonial monuments. In *Past Perceptions: the prehistoric archaeology of south-west Ireland*, E. Shee Twohig and M. Ronayne (eds), 101–13. Cork: Cork University Press.

Warner, R.B. 1994. The Navan archaeological complex: a summary. In *Ulidia*, J.P. Mallory and G. Stockman (eds), 165–70. Belfast: December Publications.

Weir, D.A. 1994. The environment of Emain Macha. In *Ulidia*, J.P. Mallory and G. Stockman (eds), 171–9. Belfast: December Publications.

Weir, D.A. 1995. A palynological study of landscape and agricultural development in County Louth from the second millennium BC to the first millennium AD. Final report. *Discovery Programme Reports* 2, 77–126.

Whelan, K. 1994. Settlement patterns in the west of Ireland in the pre-Famine period. In *Decoding the Landscape*, T. Collins (ed.), 60–78. Galway: University College, Galway.

Woodman, P.C. 1985. Mobility in the Mesolithic of northwestern Europe: an alternative explanation. In *Prehistoric Hunter-Gatherers: the emergence of cultural complexity*, T.D. Price and J.A. Brown (eds), 325–39. London: Academic Press.

Woodman, P.C. 1992. Filling in the spaces in Irish prehistory. *Antiquity* 66, 295–314.

5 Small-scale communities and the landscape of Swaledale (North Yorkshire, UK)

Andrew Fleming

The practice of landscape archaeology has a long tradition in the United Kingdom. This is a country where people have been enclosing and subdividing the land for well over 4,000 years, and where many aspects of social, economic and political history have found some form of archaeological expression in the landscape. Historical changes have frequently resulted in the modification and adaptation of earlier landscape features, rather than their wholesale destruction. So landscape archaeologists have worked on many spatial relationships and chronological sequences, and in illustrating their work they have been able to display air photographs and site plans of enviable quality. Britain's complex geology and history have also helped to provide a remarkably wide variety of regional contrasts in a small area.

In theory, the study of cultural landscapes through time and space, using the discipline of landscape archaeology, ought to create some of the best-integrated historical accounts that it is possible to write at the level of the locality or the region. In practice, however, the landscape archaeologist is often side-tracked, tempted into focusing on one period or a particular kind of site; moreover, the conditions of his or her employment may well mean that 'research' must concentrate on threatened sites or areas. In Britain, landscape archaeology is too readily seen as the servant of planning and development processes, rather than as the dominant integrative strategy for regional and local history and prehistory. Within our university system, landscape archaeology is rarely taught as a mainstream component of the course, despite its obvious practical advantages in encouraging students to think like archaeologists while carrying out non-destructive practical work. Too readily, academics see landscape archaeology as a grouping of techniques for carrying out off-site archaeology such as field-walking, surveying and the use of Geographical Information Systems (GIS).

To a large extent, landscape archaeologists have only themselves to blame for this state of affairs, since we have largely allowed ourselves to see landscape archaeology as a technical matter, developing our observational and presentational skills, embracing new technical aids, treating the landscape as a kind of code (the breaking of which provides considerable satisfaction). At one level this is completely understandable; the landscape, particularly an old, composite cultural landscape of the type so frequently found in Britain, is after all full of intriguing puzzles to be solved. But the approach has tended to mean that landscape archaeologists have not been very willing to address theoretical questions, still less to take over the theoretical high ground, and in consequence we lay ourselves open to criticism, ill-founded or otherwise (e.g. Thomas 1993: 25–6).

In this chapter I do not suggest that landscape archaeology should be subordinate to any one school of grand theory. Instead, I intend to describe my own work in Swaledale, an upland valley in North Yorkshire (northern England). In doing so, I wish to suggest that a strong theoretical perspective may be developed by working in a text-aided period, but at the same time using a prehistorian's approach. The historian and the prehistorian tend to approach the history of landscape in rather different ways. The historian, working outwards from the documents, is inclined to view the land in terms of ownership, transfer of property, rents and taxes, agricultural improvements and estate management. The land becomes a commodity and an instrument of political and social control. Such an approach is not, of course, politically innocent, still less politically neutral. From a right-wing point of view, the history of the land becomes a question of management and organisation; seen from the left, it will be a history of increasing deprivation of rights and intensifying exploitation, albeit confronted by varying degrees of resistance. That excellent introduction to English landscape history by Williamson and Bellamy (1987) was described by one reviewer as 'an exercise in designer socialism'.

The landscape archaeologist trained as a prehistorian, on the other hand, is more likely to think of land as divided among anonymous social groupings, 'communities' for want of a better word. There is, almost inevitably, an emphasis on how the *community* manages its land, how a pattern of land use develops that utilises the resources available within its boundaries, and the extent to which social hierarchy, demographic change or external control are influencing people's land-use strategies and introducing internal, destabilising forces of change. For the landscape archaeologist, then, the English medieval and post-medieval landscape becomes the workscape, as seen by a community of farmers; for the historian, it becomes a field of legal rights and properties, the world as recorded by clerks. For the archaeologist, the social and political hierarchy of the Middle Ages seems all too well delineated, as an essentially predatory organisation; for the historian, the landscape seems a ready source of photographic illustration for a world in which the only real evidence is to be found in documents.

There is, of course, rich scope for productive dialogue in this contrast of approaches; it should certainly be possible to create a narrative around the theme of 'domination and resistance', a tapestry into which are woven the essential cognitive threads. Essentially it is the landscape that appears as a challenging presence before our eyes, a tangible, historically rich artefact.

If the objectives and personalities of the now-dead people of the past are not entirely unknown to us, they seem nonetheless interchangeable and trivial beside the more collective forces that have shaped the land and its capacity to form the world of action and agency. From this perspective the land is neither commodity nor scenery; it is the essential field on which many strands of history are brought together.

Swaledale (Figure 5.1) is an upland valley in North Yorkshire some 30 km in length, set among hills of sedimentary sandstones and limestones that occasionally reach about 700 m above sea level. It is the classic landscape of the Yorkshire Dales; small, walled fields on the valley sides produce grass and hay for sheep and cattle; above about 350 m heather-covered moorlands (upland heath) are used for grazing sheep and rearing grouse for shooting as game. The landscape of small fields and barns, roofed and walled with stone, is symbolically important in Yorkshire; in its evocation of 'traditional life', it represents the county's pride in its history, its landscape, and its people's self-proclaimed virtues of hard work, thrift, hospitality and independence. In reality, the landscape of walls and barns is only 300 or 400 hundred years old, and it is not at all clear that the small family farm has been notably autonomous and independent until relatively recently. In constant dialogue with the agrarian history of Swaledale we find the history of mining and smelting lead, an industry that expanded massively and collapsed equally dramatically in the nineteenth century. The lead production industry, as so often in Britain, tends to be studied separately, with the humans treated largely as the servants of technological progress and financial operations.

Figure 5.1 Swaledale: the village of Muker (Norse, 'the narrow cultivated land') surrounded by characteristic walls and barns.

Working in a text-aided period, we have not only documents but also place names. These are invaluable; we work with an archaeology of names. The place names of Swaledale tell us of an 'ethnic' history of the valley (Fleming 1994, 1997a). They tell us that the 'British' speakers of Old Welsh, evidently present in considerable numbers at the end of the Roman period (around AD 400), were joined c. AD 600 by 'Anglians' arriving from the east; evidently their Old English speech soon became dominant. Then, in the tenth century, Norse speakers came into the head of the valley from the west, not very long before the Norman Conquest brought the valley within the feudal system, around AD 1100. Fortunately, many of the names of localities and of parcels of land (after these were enclosed by walls or hedges) have survived to be marked on old maps. Even more fortunately, they often incorporate statements about land use or indicate to which community the land belongs. Often, the existence of two or three alternative names for the same land will reveal the time depth of its history. Thus 'Kearton or Feetham Cow Pasture' (it is always 'or' rather than 'and') refers to a settlement with an English name and a nearby settlement with a Norse name. Likewise, 'the manor of Healaugh *alias* Reeth *alias* Swaledale' refers, respectively, to a) the name of the feudal manor founded c. 1100; b) the name of the 'vill' mentioned in Domesday Book in 1086, which was the Old English name of the most important centre of agrarian production, into whose wood pasture zone Healaugh was inserted; and c) the Norse name for the area later taken over by the feudal manor. In the twelfth century we find the medieval surnames 'de Swale' and 'de Swaledale'. The Norse had evidently renamed an English polity, which had been named after the river. People, polity and valley-based folk territory took the same river name, as was quite common in early 'English' history. The two surnames commemorate this hybrid history. Swale is an English name, meaning 'the torrential (river)', which is an accurate description of the behaviour of the river in question. So we find in the archaeology of Swaledale names a process with which we have become familiar from archaeologists' studies of ceremonial monuments: the new is grafted onto the old.

As I have already pointed out, medieval Swaledale had a relatively complex history of immigration. It would be interesting to work out whether there were differences between 'English' and 'Norse' approaches to land occupancy. At present, all that can be said on this question is that in the area where Norse names are predominant, towards the head of the dale, traditional surnames were patronymics – Alderson, Hodgson, Clarkson, etc., and there were outlying grazing zones, *saetr*, which often took their names from individuals – Ravenseat from Hrafn, Gunnersett (now Gunnerside) from Gunnar, and so on. Further east, surnames tended to come from places – Harker from Herthay (now Harkerside), Kearton, Raw (from Low Row, formerly The Wra), etc. In other words, the 'English' tradition, at any rate in the later Middle Ages, was about belonging to a place, while the 'Norse' tradition was more about belonging to a family. This recalls the classic study by Cole and Wolf (1974) about two contrasting traditions of inheritance and attitudes to land-holding in neighbouring north Italian communities. But the Swaledale situation may be less a matter of ethnicity than of population density and immigration history. If the 'English' area had a complex immigration history (relating to lead-mining?) and quite a dense population (which might be suggested by its relatively large area of late medieval and Romano–British arable land), land claims based on township occupancy may have been more convenient or customary than those based on real or fictive kinship links. Further west, in an area wooded enough in the later Middle Ages to be designated a forest (that is, a hunting reserve), kin relationships mediated through exchanges of livestock may have been more important than adherence to closely defined group territories.

However this may be, the tradition of access to land for all members of the land-holding community has been a strong one in Swaledale; common rights are still exercised today on most of the moors and a small number of daleside cow pastures, about 20,000 ha in all. The tenacity with which such rights have been maintained may have been complemented by the attitudes of absentee landlords who were mainly interested in hunting opportunities and the income from lead-mining. Sixteenth-century court cases in which the 'tenants' of Swaledale defended their traditional rights against the 'owners' of the land apparently resulted in walls being built to define the cow pastures belonging to the different townships from the moors above them where livestock were grazed in summer. Some of the walls do look like continuously patched-up sixteenth-century constructions, though others have been built by professionals in the early nineteenth century. The building and maintenance of the walls was the responsibility of the commoners, who made conspicuous butt–joints at intervals to indicate the boundaries of sections that different individuals had to maintain. Quite recently one group of commoners has painted different sets of initials beside these butt–joints (e.g. Figure 5.2).

History and archaeology combine to illustrate the 'zonal' pattern of land use characteristic of land-sharing communities. In each township, it is possible to work out where wood pasture survived longest (Fleming 1997b). Sometimes this may be deduced from the presence of a group of pollarded trees in a common cow pasture (pollards are trees that have their branches and foliage periodically lopped at just above head height; they are characteristic features of old English wood pastures). Wood pasture may be inferred sometimes from the irregular outlines of fields cut piecemeal from woodland, sometimes from a group of woodland names, or sometimes from the existence of a deer park that can only have been made from the greater part of a community's woodland. Occasionally, woodland is part of a cow pasture at the present day. At Healaugh there are several fields called Thirns – High Thirns, Low Thirns, Little Thirns, etc. – all of which were clearly once part of a big wood called Thirns (Thorns) Wood. The same principle extends to other types of land use. Thus Reeth had a large arable zone called North Field, and two communal pastures or meadows called Sleets and Mill Holme.

Figure 5.2 Swaledale: the stone wall separating the daleside common cow pasture and the moorland summer pasture has vertical divisions that indicate shared responsibilities for maintenance; note the recently painted initials.

Muker had three 'ings' or meadows – Gun Ing, Long Ing and Foal Ing – the latter being quite a common name in Swaledale, along with Horse Pasture. The name Calver (the calves' *gehaeg*, or hedged enclosure) occurs at least twice in Swaledale. Sometimes, then, zones were designated for particular categories of livestock, and presumably the community as a whole could make economies of scale by hiring individuals for herding duties. Calvert (calf-herd) is still a common name in Swaledale, and the name Wetherhird was recorded in the Middle Ages. Individuals also took on management responsibilities for the community as a whole, and surnames remind us that there were Medwards (who looked after the meadows) as well as Barnwards, Haywards and Pounders (the latter taking care of the pound, the walled enclosure in which stray animals were 'impounded'); there may well have been Woodwards too. This is entirely understandable; recent commons theorists have stressed the long-term importance of good commons management – which usually means that individuals should be properly recompensed for taking on monitoring and arbitration duties (e.g. Ostrom 1990).

The tenacity with which collective resources have been retained is well illustrated by the locations of footpaths. Swaledale has many footpaths, now designated and maintained as public rights of way in the Yorkshire Dales National Park, although their distribution and density vary from area to area. It is said that some of them owe their continuing existence to the late survival of mail deliveries on horseback. Most of the footpaths perpetuate older routes, some of them medieval. It can be shown that small settlements now 'bypassed' by post-medieval roads tend to have footpaths still running through them, and continuing through the fields, even when this means that footpath and modern road run parallel to one another, separated by only 50 m or so, and that stiles have to be built and maintained across numerous field-walls. Moreover, the creation of deer parks did not usually extinguish former rights of way.

As I have argued elsewhere (Fleming 1998a), one cannot assume static and uniform conditions within traditions of collective land management. In Swaledale, it seems that a 'co-operative' phase gave way to a more 'competitive' phase of commons managment; that is to say, management objectives shifted, under pressure, from a relatively benign, facilitating structure of collective organisation to a system that attempted to subject competitive aspirations to the discipline of the well-regulated commons. In the landscape, we can see formerly open ings and pastures being subdivided on coaxial principles into strips known as dales ('shares'); and we can also see irregular walled 'intakes' on the common cow pastures, presumably made by agreement, by individuals or families. The task of relating each township's pattern of land enclosure and subdivision to its demographic and familial history has yet to be undertaken. Partible inheritance was traditional here, and historians have tended to regard it as a maladapted system, resulting in continuous fragmentation of holdings, its destructive effects only partially redeemed by attempts at reamalgamation (e.g. Fieldhouse and Jennings 1978: 135–40). However, this is not the effect that partible inheritance produced in the southern Alps (Cole and Wolf 1974: Chapter 8). The Swaledale documents, which sometimes recorded individuals as inheriting a share of a building or parcel of land as small as one forty-second part, cannot really be referring to the daily use of property, as Fieldhouse and Jennings (1978: 138) effectively admit.

These issues have been explored further in my recent book on the landscape history of Swaledale (Fleming 1998b). We are now poised to make further enquiries. We know the boundaries and some of the internal characteristics of the 'townships', as these communities came to be known, and we may use this knowledge to initiate a programme of palaeobotanical work, to try to generate a physical history that takes us beyond the written documents. And we may make further enquiries of the documents, in order to clarify individual township histories and relate them to the surrounding landscape. The rise and fall of systems of commons management within small-scale communities is, of course, only one issue for landscape archaeologists. But I believe that it is a vital one, with ramifications for many parts of the world – not simply the world of the past that is studied by archaeologists, but the present world too. After all, we are all commoners of planet Earth; we forget this at our peril.

References

Cole, J.W. and E.R. Wolf 1974. *The Hidden Frontier: ecology and ethnicity in an Alpine valley*. London: Academic Press.

Fieldhouse, R. and B. Jennings 1978. *A history of Richmond and Swaledale*. Chichester: Phillimore.

Fleming, A. 1994. Swadal, Swar (and Erechwydd?): early medieval polities in Upper Swaledale. *Landscape History* 16, 17–30.

Fleming, A. 1997a. Patterns of names, patterns of places. *Archaeological Dialogues* 4, 199–214.

Fleming, A. 1997b. Towards a history of wood pasture in Swaledale (North Yorkshire). *Landscape History* 19, 31–47.

Fleming, A. 1998a. The changing commons: the case of Swaledale (England). In *Property in Economy in Context*, A. Gilman and R. Hunt (eds) 187–214. Lanham, Maryland: University Press of America.

Fleming, A. 1998b. *Swaledale: valley of the wild river*. Edinburgh: Edinburgh University Press.

Ostrom, E. 1990. *Governing the Commons: the evolution of institutions for collective action*. Cambridge: Cambridge University Press.

Thomas, J. 1993. The politics of vision and the archaeologies of landscape. In *Landscape: politics and perspectives*, B. Bender (ed.), 19–48. Providence: Berg.

Williamson, T. and L. Bellamy, 1987. *Property and Landscape*. London: George Philip.

6   *A historical interactive landscape in the heart of Europe: the case of Bohemia*

JAROMÍR BENEŠ AND MAREK ZVELEBIL

Theorising landscapes

The 1990s have seen a resurgence of interest in landscape archaeology. Traditionally, archaeological investigations of landscapes took the form of aerial photography or of investigations of field systems and standing monuments within the landscape (e.g. Fox 1932; Caulfield 1978; Riley 1980; Cooney 1983; Reeves-Smyth and Hammond 1983; Fleming 1985, 1988; Cooney and Grogan 1994). More recently, the growing awareness of the limitations of site-oriented archaeology (e.g. Foley 1981; Dunnell and Dacey 1983; Reeves-Smyth and Hammond 1983; Rossignol and Wandsnider 1992) has resulted in the development and application of field surveys in order to collect information about human behaviour beyond the notional limit of an archaeological site (Dunnell 1992). At the same time, others have attempted to interpret historical and prehistoric landscapes in terms of social relations, relations of power, identity and appropriation, and as a reflection of our own modern beliefs (e.g. Fleming 1990; Cooney 1991; Bender 1992; Chapman 1993; Ingold 1993; Tilley 1994). The integration of these approaches is instrumental in the development of landscape archaeology.

So what is Landscape Archaeology? And how do we define landscape? Perhaps we should first make a distinction between 'scenery', to which we can all react aesthetically, and 'landscape', examined with a trained eye (Allison 1976). Next comes a much debated distinction between cultural and natural landscapes, a point much stressed in earlier writings (Fox 1932; Haggett et al. 1977), but which by now has lost much of its meaning. In contrast, Vidal de la Blanche (1902) sees *landscape itself* as an imprint left by the image of its people. Others still see landscape as text waiting to be deciphered (Tilley 1991) and as 'a setting in which locales occur in dialectical relation to which meanings are created, reproduced and transformed' (Tilley 1994: 25). Operationally, landscape could be defined as a set of real-world features, natural and cultural, which give character and diversity to Earth's surface (Roberts 1987). Yet the reading of landscape is in the eye of the beholder, and contingent on the personal view, the spatial scale and the time span adopted by the observer (Ingold 1993). (One of us, Beneš, defines the landscape as a geographical space that can be comprehended by an individual or a group of inter-related individuals, the functional and structural links of which can be understood and described within a space so defined.)

In our view, landscape archaeology goes beyond other spatially oriented conceptual and analytical frameworks (e.g. Clarke 1972; Hodder and Orton 1976; Hodder 1978; Foley 1981; Dunnell and Dacey 1983; Neustupný 1986; Kuna 1991; Rossignol and Wandsnider 1992) in two important aspects. First, landscape archaeology looks at the spatial relationships *between* archaeological residues in order to infer the past use of the landscape. Archaeological landscapes can then be defined as a past surface within a defined span of time, which is subject to antecedent features and successive modifications. A past landscape surface can be buried, eroded or modified by successive human activities or geomorphological processes. In landscape archaeology we are dealing, therefore, with both time and spatial dimensions at some hypothetical regional scale. The material residues of the time dimension consist of sedimentary deposits; the spatial dimension is expressed by the patterned distribution of artefacts and architectural features over the landscape.

Within this framework, the emphasis is on understanding the continuous structure of the human use of the landscape, and archaeological sites are simply locations of concentrated residues of human activity, whose behavioural meaning is to be established. Landscape archaeology should be built on the premise that human behaviour does not normally occur in, or indeed *generate*, spatially and temporally discrete archaeological residues (Dunnell 1992; Zvelebil *et al.* 1992). Accordingly, in landscape archaeology, we regard the archaeological record as possessing a spatially continuous pattern within a dynamic geomorphological context. Since there are normally no empty or meaningless spaces between settlements, we cannot understand the archaeological record outside the framework of landscape archaeology.

Second, landscape is seen as a surface where cultural and natural processes of one period leave traces that in turn constrain and influence the activities of subsequent inhabitants. In other words, landscape is not a passive recipient of human activities, but a dynamic and interactive element in the evolution of past societies (Roberts 1987; Fleming 1990; Zvelebil 1994; Beneš 1995). For archaeologists this means that any attempt to understand past societies has to take into account the antecedent and successor use of the landscape occurring before and after the society under investigation. Landscape archaeology, therefore, cannot but adopt the time perspective of 'longue durée' (Braudel 1980).

These considerations lead us to suggest three levels of interpretation within landscape archaeology. These are *historical reconstruction, taphonomic reconstruction* and *historical interactive interpretation*. Each is related to a particular perception of time, and each commands a somewhat different set of assumptions and methods. Alone, each is inadequate and problematic in some way; together, they can form a sound foundation for a theoretically oriented landscape archaeology.

Historical reconstruction offers the first level of interpretation, where relationships between archaeological residues are analysed within a discrete time span. In terms of a temporal framework, this type of reconstruction corresponds to an 'ethnographic instant'.

Taphonomic reconstruction takes into account post-depositional changes that have borne upon the landscape between the time span under investigation and the present. For example, *local geomorphological processes* will ensure a different status for individual artefact scatters: no surface scatters can be treated as *in situ*. *Regional geomorphological changes* are equally important in affecting the distribution of archaeological remains. Such changes include alluviation, peat development and shoreline displacement, all of which act to obscure past archaeological landscapes. *Human activity*, although treated as a separate category, often cannot be separated from geomorphological processes in causing change in the patterning of archaeological residues, or in changing the landscape. It is this problem of recognising the difference between human agency and unaided natural change that casts doubt on the concepts of natural and cultural landscape: how many landscapes are truly 'natural'? Recently, Bender (1992) further eroded this distinction by arguing for the *conceptual* indivisibility of cultural and natural.

Taphonomic reconstruction, then, aims at understanding the development of the landscape through time, and at the interpretation of human relationships in the landscape of different periods mediated through the subsequent post-depositional changes. In terms of temporal framework, taphonomic reconstruction would correspond to 'processual' time.

The historical interactive approach builds on the first two levels of reconstruction. Here, landscape is seen as a surface where cultural and natural processes of one period leave traces that in turn constrain and influence the activities of subsequent inhabitants. In other words, landscape is not a passive recipient of human activities, but an active element in the evolution of a society using it. In terms of temporal frameworks, the interactive landscape is broadly analogous to the 'longue durée' concept developed by Braudel and his school (1980), which has seen much recent debate in archaeology (Knapp 1992).

We would like to develop here the concepts of landscape antecedent and landscape successor as a means of structuring our understanding of the interactive landscape (Roberts 1987; Zvelebil 1994; Beneš 1995). Landscape antecedent is an anthropogenic feature developed at least partly through human agency that can be shown to constrain or otherwise direct the subsequent use of the same space. Conversely, landscape successor is an anthropogenic feature that can be shown to arise from, or be a consequence of, an earlier human use of a particular area.

The three levels of interpretation outlined above are focused on different sectors of the time-scale (Figure 6.1). None of these corresponds fully to personal, substantive perceptions of time. The awareness of different concepts of time, and the understanding of their expression through the material culture and in the landscape, can advance our understanding of past societies (Bradley 1991; Clark 1992; Zvelebil 1993; Gosden 1994; Vasicek 1994).

Time is a continuous phenomenon, packaged into different conceptual frameworks for the benefit of self-orientation, communication and comprehension. A fundamental distinction can be made between regular and measured time on the one hand, and personal, substantial time on the other (Bourdieu 1977; Bradley 1991). As Leach (1990: 227) noted, 'Time, as we experience it, is continuous; it contains no discrete "events". The events are put there by reflection on the past.' The substantial time can be further subdivided into secular and ritual; the former, according to Bloch (1977: 290), is associated with 'the systems by which we know the world', the latter, ritual and mythological, with 'systems by which we hide it'.

The fact that regular time can be subdivided into smaller units is pertinent to archaeology, whether for measurement (i.e. calendar time) or to reflect the duration of either discrete events (i.e. episodal time) or continuous processes, such as taphonomic changes affecting the archaeological record (i.e. processual time, see Binford 1981; Schiffer 1983; Wandsnider 1987). These relationships are illustrated in Figure 6.1. Our own, western society operates mostly within the framework of regular time; it is this time perspective that we use to comprehend and communicate our understanding of the past.

Such perceptions and definitions of time do not, on the whole, correspond to temporal divisions afforded on the basis of archaeological data. Conventionally, archaeological evidence can be divided into periods on the basis of geological strata or the occurrence of type fossils in cultural material, aided more recently by radiometric dating. In making the connection between human behaviour and conventional chronological schemes, archaeologists usually make the assumption that the boundaries of such schemes are signatures of cultural and/or behavioural change. For example, the geologically defined boundary between the Pleistocene and Holocene is often held to indicate cultural change; the boundary between the Mesolithic and Neolithic, culturally defined by the occurrence of a set of new technological traits (polished stone tools, pottery and large-bladed chipped stone technology), is held to indicate a shift to food production and a change in ideology (Thomas 1996; Zvelebil 1996, in press). Although we shall continue to use such frameworks, the links between changes in human behaviour and chronological frameworks ought to be demonstrated rather than assumed.

The separation of the process of interpretation into three levels, advocated here, has the benefit of making explicit the problem of bridging the chronological gap between what is archaeologically imposed and what is behaviourally desired; it may also go some way towards its resolution. Within the episodic perspective, the archaeological record consists of differentially

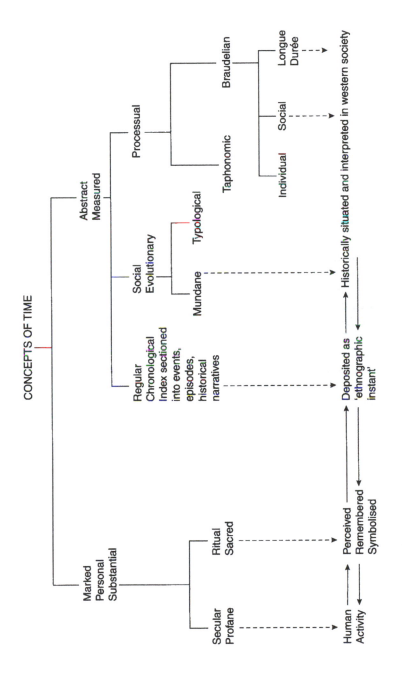

Figure 6.1 Concepts of time and the archaeological record.

preserved episodes of human behaviour, 'ethnographic instants' through time. In the taphonomic perspective, the archaeological record is regarded as undergoing a continuous interaction between natural factors and human agency, a process that it is necessary to understand in order to comprehend the episodes of human behaviour that occurred in the past. Finally, within the framework of 'longue durée', the interactive nature of human activity, past and present, can be structured and ordered chronologically outside the conventional chronological frameworks, so beloved by archaeology, yet without losing the chronological resolution of the archaeological data. Space, and landscape in particular, replaces chronology as the organising principle.

Landscapes in action: the case of northern Bohemia

We now illustrate the application of some of these frameworks in the case of landscape-oriented research in northern Bohemia.[1] The principal aims of the research are to develop a programme of long-term landscape reconstruction in northern Bohemia, and to gain understanding of the evolution of cultural landscape and of the social transformation associated with it. The time span under investigation extends from the Mesolithic to the present. The research area consists of two transects extending from the Ore Mountains on the Czech–German border, across the basin of Labe to the foothills of the Bohemian–Moravian Uplands; giving us a comprehensive range of habitats and landscape types (Figure 6.2). The project consists of field survey, sub-surface testing, aerial photography, evaluation of large-scale rescue excavations, and analyses of cartographic, archival and historical sources, and of palaeoenvironmental reconstruction based principally on pollen analysis. After five years of fieldwork, this research has been yielding an enormous amount of information, most of which is yet to be analysed. But since we are investigating such a long time span, the historical interaction between landscapes of different periods is already becoming evident, even though at the moment we are able to recognise this on a local, rather than regional, scale.

Enculturation of the landscape

It is our view that the Czech idea of the structure of the rural landscape is a rather feminine, enclosing one. As a simple abstraction, it consists of the cultivated core around the settlement, enclosed by woodland and wilderness. The role of the forest in this picture, although alien, is not necessarily threatening: rather it provides a reassuring boundary to the cultured social world, a background of otherness, and a temporary haven from social control. This basic division into culture and nature, symbolised in Bohemia by the village with its fields and the forest, is reflected in literature and in painting. In some respects, it mirrors real divisions in the Czech countryside, which traditionally consists of patterns of fields enclosed by woodland. Even at a macro-scale, this is true: in terms of relief, Bohemia can be visualised as

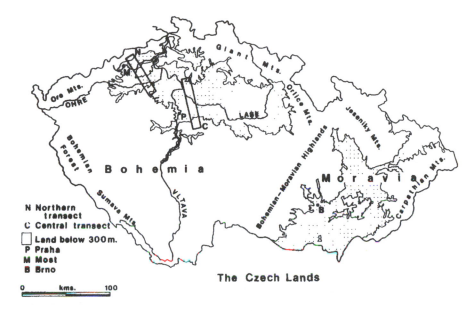

Figure 6.2 The location of the Ancient Landscape Reconstruction Project's transects in Bohemia.

a satellite dish, slightly tilted to the north, with the central lowland of the Labe river, the 'old settlement area', cosily nesting in the midst of uplands and mountains that are traditionally believed to have been a forest-covered wilderness until medieval times. So pervasive is this belief that the archaeological research traditionally avoided this 'empty' upland zone and many archaeologists still express surprise when anything dating to the Stone Age is found within it. It is a matter of speculation how far into the past this view had extended, or whether, like archaeology, the landscape of Bohemia has been shaped at least partly to reflect these subliminal notions; but the recursive role of ideology and the perception of the landscape in the composition of its structure is clear.

The structure of prehistoric landscapes can be comprehended on different scales. At the smallest scale, we are concerned with individual households, and relationships between households or household clusters and the surrounding space. The next level concerns community areas or site territories, which can be divided into specific zones such as habitation zones, ritual zones, fields and pasture. Within and beyond community areas we find field boundaries, land divisions and focal places serving several communities. All this we would consider micro-scale. Beyond, at the regional scale, we might find regional patterns of land use, settlement distribution and regional centres. Finally, at the macro-regional scale, we find an expanding and contracting pattern of settlement within Bohemia as a whole, with at least five periods of expansion from the central lowland: the Later Neolithic (3800–3200 BC),

Later Eneolithic (2400–2200 BC), Bronze Age (1650–750 BC), Halstatt and La Tène Iron Age (750–50 BC) and Early and Late Medieval (AD 600–1400). We would like to focus here on small-scale developments.

At a micro-scale, landscape evolution is reflected in changing vegetation and shifting regimes of erosion and accumulation, attested mainly by pollen analysis, geomorphological studies, aerial photography and historical sources. In the northwest transect, the key pollen sequence at Komorany Lake shows an early anthropogenic interference coeval with the funnel beaker eneolithic settlement of the area, indicating small clearings in the broadleaf dominated woodland. At this time, we get the first evidence of cereal pollen. The anthropogenic interference continues through the Bronze Age, revealed by marked fluctuations in the relative values of arable and pastoral indicators. From the Late Iron Age period, and more dramatically in the Medieval period, there is an increase in agricultural land and in deforestation. Although we need more comparative data, we can speculatively suggest that the initial clearance, whether still Mesolithic or Neolithic, acted as a landscape antecedent attracting later settlement because of reduced labour demands and increased food resources for man and beast in these more open, sub-climax conditions compared to those in mature forests. It is important to note that in most diagrams to date, the initial major clearance is followed not by full regeneration, but by a more open landscape consisting of a mosaic of biotopes. The continual maintenance of fields and pastures in the course of agricultural prehistory is suggested by an increasing number of case studies (Kuna and Slabina 1987; Smrž 1987, 1991; Beneš 1991a, 1991b).

The pollen evidence (such as there is) from the lowland sites indicates progressive landscape enculturation from the Eneolithic (the funnel beaker horizon). In the uplands small-scale clearances are first evidenced from the Middle Bronze Age (c.1650 BC), and their development is less continuous. But the progressive deforestation of the country is also recorded in the increase of erosion and accumulation from a number of profiles both within and outside our research area. At a macro-scale, we appear to have four phases of erosional activity, dating to the end of the Eneolithic, Late Bronze Age, Late Iron Age and Late Medieval period.

In the alluvial and colluvial contexts, there are many new examples of holocene soil river accumulation and slope erosion arising from human and natural interference (Figure 6.3) (Beneš 1995). Even though alluvial and colluvial processes are related, there are great differences between them, particularly in their relative strengths and their long-term effect on associated sedimentary material.

The archaeological situations in alluvial environments are a potential resource of extraordinary value. The Labe (Elbe), the largest Bohemian river, shows this clearly at the Borek site (Dreslerová 1995), where a rescue excavation was undertaken on the river terrace bank. A set of settlement features was discovered here, four of which were dated to the Late Roman period, while eight belonged to Early Medieval times. These structures lay under 50 cm of topsoil. Four metres below these contexts, a layer with neolithic and eneolithic finds was dredged. The finds included neolithic linear pottery (6300–6100 BP) and several hundred sherds of the eneolithic Michelsberg Culture (c. 5100 BP), most probably lying in situ. The depth of alluvial material that accumulated between the Eneolithic and Roman/Early Medieval periods indicates the great strength of alluviation since the Eneolithic period.

The history of the aggradation activity of larger rivers in the Czech landscape is also regionally specific: for example, investigations at Caloun's Garden in České Budějovice (the bank of the Vltava river, Budweis) recorded aggradation activity between the Early Bronze Age and the thirteenth century. At some point during this time, the burying of the early bronze age horizons began, but whether the buried material is in a primary or secondary position is still open to question. The extent of the settlement layer is at least 25×8 m, which may be too large an area for randomly moved material (Beneš 1995).

In the case of Počedlice (on the river bank of the Ohře, northwest Bohemia), settlement traces from the Roman Iron Age have been observed over a large area, under thick fluvial sediments. A section through this material revealed a set of thin red layers that indicate gradual sedimentation. Another question of interest is whether Roman iron age finds in black sediment are in a primary or secondary location when found beneath alluvium: a large number of Roman iron age finds and an extensive black layer favours the former possibility.

The examples mentioned above point to the gradual 'enculturation' of holocene river valleys through alluviation and aggradation as an originally more articulated landscape was slowly rounded and levelled out as a result of human action. The watercourses of larger rivers frequently changed, shaping new oxbows and meanders (Rúžičková and Zeman 1994) or returning to earlier channels.

Compared to the alluvium, colluvial slope sediments usually represent more easily comprehended geoarchaeological events. For example, the site of Kamenný Újezd (in the northern part of Central Bohemia) showed direct evidence of slope erosion and accumulation: the findspot with final eneolithic (corded ware) sherds lies on a moderate slope only a few metres from a steeper incline, and is covered by coniferous woodland. The study of a terrace section recorded a thick sediment, consisting of a mixture of black earths and removed loams. Erosional events took place here during and after the Final Eneolithic (after c. 4300 BP). The valley of Vranský Potok is bordered by a steep incline. Butler (1993) has documented post-glacial sediments in this location 5 m in thickness, which could play a key role in regional landscape reconstruction. The landscape of this part of Bohemia has been used continuously for arable agriculture. The depth of the sherd-bearing layer is evidence of considerable prehistoric erosion.

Other clear cases of eneolithic erosion occur when the fill of final eneolithic graves contains sherds from earlier eneolithic sites. An extraordinary example is provided by the case of the porcelainite jasper hill at Tušimice (Neustupný 1987), where clear post-eneolithic erosion was determined through an examination of the infill of corded ware graves. Similar evidence was obtained by Vencl (1992) at Dolní Počernice near Prague, where a large site of the Middle Eneolithic culture (5000–4800 BP) was defined by field-walking. A large-scale rescue action followed, during which arable land was mechanically removed and the last traces of a thin middle eneolithic cultural layer were discovered. Again, most of the ceramic material from this period was, however, identified only in the final eneolithic corded ware graves. At Hrdlovka (northwest Bohemia), the fill of a corded ware grave contained material from the eneolithic globular amphora culture (4800–4700 BP), even though the slope at the location was only 1° (Beneš and Dobeš 1992). We can conclude from the foregoing, then, that at the end of the Eneolithic period, stronger erosional activity became prevalent in the Bohemian landscape.

During the Bronze Age, there is further evidence for increase in erosional activity. For example, at Hrdlovka, a long, broad ridge contained a large quantity of final bronze age (3000–2800 BP) sherd material. The displaced loam layers on a slope south of the nearby site of Liptice belong to a similar period. In Semec (northwest Bohemia), the lower part of a long slope contained a notable accumulation layer: the late bronze age material was concentrated at a depth of c. 140–170 cm, whilst beneath, at a depth of 280 cm, holocene material containing no ceramics was identified. From the central Vltava region (southern central Bohemia), a series of examples of accumulation and erosion were identified by Smejtek (1994). Near the village of Hrímezdice, for example, the colluvial sediments displaced from higher positions on a steep valley slope covered a site containing earlier materials, which were also displaced by colluviation during an erosional event, both dating to the Bronze Age. The archaeological evidence of the late bronze age human erosional impact on the Bohemian landscape is additionally supported by the malacozoological record (Ložek 1981).

The next important group of accumulated sediments is connected to the beginning of the Early Roman Iron Age. The erosional pattern of this period was analysed at Milzany (northwest Bohemia) by Neustupný (1987). The slope erosion occurred here immediately before the onset of the Roman Iron Age (c. 2000 BP). Similar observations were described from other sites of northwest Bohemia (Beneš 1995).

Later in the Holocene period, then, several erosional episodes precipitated by human actions played a role in transforming and 'enculturating' the landscape: first in the Eneolithic, and then in the Final Bronze Age, at the end of the Roman Iron Age, and at the end of the Medieval (Figure 6.3). In some cases, secondary removal by modern ploughing cannot be excluded, but there are many reasons for believing that erosional processes can be associated with the more remote past. It is significant that these main episodes of erosion are coeval with two other developments: the onset of colder,

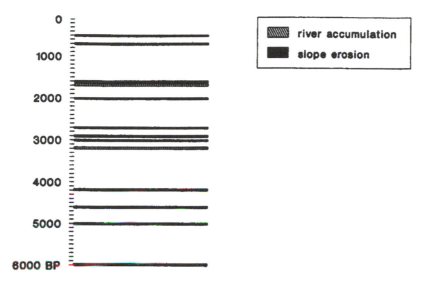

Figure 6.3 A general chronology of erosion and accumulation processes in the Bohemian landscape (after Beneš 1995).

wetter climatic conditions and the prosecution of more intensive arable land use and forest clearance.

Such a pattern of landscape transformation from wild to cultured is in agreement with the growth in settlement, attested from the Neolithic onwards. The patterns recorded by our project rely partly on field surveys and partly on large-scale rescue digs carried out by Beneš in the area affected by surface coal-mining. Figure 6.4 shows the evolution of the settlement in Bílina ecozone in the Neolithic, Early Bronze Age, La Tène and Medieval. It is surprising how little the distribution, structure and density of settlements have changed at the regional scale: a clear case of the continuation of antecedent patterns.

This picture masks more subtle changes at smaller spatial (e.g. Kuna and Adelsbergerová 1995) and temporal scales. The areas of prehistoric settlements, evident to us within one time slice of a processual time-scale, are in fact palimpsests of settlement activity over several centuries. We assume that we are dealing with the record of activity of a single or at most two or three farmsteads, whereas the medieval villages are concentrations of a greater number of social and economic units (Beneš 1986; Beneš and Koutecký 1987; Kuna 1991).

Nevertheless, the field survey carried out and analysed to date tends to support the notion of settlement stability and expansion from the existing core areas, rather than indicating a major shift in the settlement pattern. Taking the area of České Středohoří as an example, the neolithic settlement is characterised by a dense but isolated pattern of settlement cells. A localised

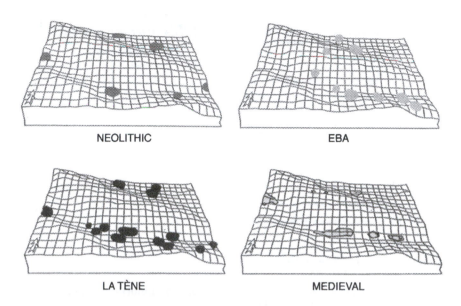

Figure 6.4 The Bilina basin in northwest Bohemia, showing the distribution of burial and settlement sites within an area totally excavated by large-scale excavations. 1: Neolithic; 2: Early Bronze Age; 3: La Tène Iron Age; 4: Medieval (after Beneš and Brůna 1994).

shift in the land use can be observed in the Eneolithic, reflecting the incorporation of lighter soils under cultivation, brought about by the introduction of the plough. Following this adjustment, a stable settlement network continues to expand through a 'budding off' process and the generation of daughter settlements during the Bronze Age, reaching its apex in the period between 900 and 750 BC. By this time, the first detrimental effects of extensive cultivation become evident in increased erosion and colluviation (Beneš 1995; Smejtek 1994). At this juncture, we can see the agricultural landscape imposing a *negative constraint* on the further evolution of settlement: in response to the impoverishment of the old farming areas, there is an increase in settlement relocation, fragmentation into dispersed farmsteads and penetration of upland zones. The network of dispersed farmsteads continued through the Halstatt Iron Age, but in the La Tène, there is a tendency again towards greater clustering. The resulting pattern of dispersed hamlets or similar clusters formed the basic structure of the agricultural landscape until the Late Medieval, when the transformation into a medieval village pattern occurred.

The end result of the enculturation of the Bohemian landscape is graphically represented for the first time in the maps of the Emperor Joseph II, commissioned principally to keep the Prussians out of Austria (of which Bohemia was then a part). These maps date to the end of the eighteenth century, and represent the greatest extent of settlement before the impact of the Industrial Revolution 100 years later. We must emphasise two major points: first, the forested areas were smaller then than they are today, and second, the natural drainage network of streams and rivers was far more extensive then. Planned reforestation of the last 200 years has masked the extent of the open countryside during medieval and early modern times. Our pollen research near Říčany indicates that clearance and open landscape in what is woodland today existed even in the pre-Medieval period, and that those upland areas traditionally regarded as wilderness may have been cultivated, at least marginally, before the Medieval period. The loss of the hydrological network through drainage, on the other hand, masks areas suitable for settlement until the end of the eighteenth century. Together with more open landscape, then, we can envisage more dispersed settlement with greater density of hamlets located in areas that are dry woodlands or upland fields today. Although this suggestion needs rigorous testing, our preliminary field survey results tend to support this impression.

Land division and field systems

In contrast to Britain, the direct study of prehistoric field systems has not even been attempted, and there are no remains above ground suggesting that field division predates the Medieval period. The late development of field division is in agreement with historical sources, recording a slow shift from a communal infield/outfield system to a three-field system in the Late Medieval period (AD 1200–1400). Individual farmstead subdivisions within the three-field system are evident only from this period, the remains of which can be identified in some landscapes. Such traditional field systems (*pluziny*) were closely tied to the immediate surroundings of medieval villages. Further afield, more recent and rationalised land divisions were established in the eighteenth and nineteenth centuries.

Most of these land divisions were deliberately obliterated by the communist regime installed in 1948. Only upland fields of low fertility, and small garden plots and holdings immediately surrounding the village, escaped collectivisation. For example, in the Central Bohemian Mountains, field-dividing hedges were ploughed out only in lower, more fertile elevations, where personal holdings combined into a collective field. In this way, the socialist field system was superimposed on the traditional one in a deliberate enactment of social revolution upon the landscape, and as a deliberate negation of the symbols of private property and land ownership. The landscape antecedents, in this case, provoked a reaction far beyond the economic, rational need.

With the collapse of communism in 1989, many land holdings were offered back to the original owners; the legal ownership of these holdings survived by now only as entries in 'landholding books', and not in the landscape itself. However, such written records now assumed the function of a landscape antecedent: of mental maps encoding a more complex, structured order. So at present, we can encounter in the Czech countryside the paradoxical situation where, in the midst of enormous fields, farmers are staking out the outlines of their narrow, traditional holdings. Is this not a glaring example of a landscape successor pattern in the making?

Burials as territorial markers

It is now generally recognised that burials such as megalithic tombs fulfilled the role of territorial markers in prehistoric landscape. For example, the changing role of Stonehenge as the focus of a ritual, mortuary landscape was discussed by Bradley (1991) and Bender (1992). A similar function must have been fulfilled by other forms of burial, such as barrows and cemeteries, which would have been marked in some ways as specific burial zones. The burial itself can be comprehended as an 'ethnographic instant', while its siting in the landscape defined the role of the area for the future.

In northwest Bohemia, especially within the Bilina ecozone in the northwest transect, corded ware cemeteries were the subject of a long-term investigation by Neustupný (1973, 1982) and others as a consequence of a large-scale removal of arable soils in the course of surface mining activities.

Corded ware interments are usually perceived as flat inhumations, either freely scattered through the landscape, or concentrated into small clusters. We now know that corded ware burials were covered by a barrow (evidenced by a circumferential ditch or a bank) denoting a burial zone. The existence of these features is also suggested by the regular spacing of corded ware burials at a distance of 8–16 m. Such demarcation is absent from the Bohemian landscape today: as in other intensively cultivated areas such as Denmark, surface burial architecture has been obliterated by the subsequent agricultural activities.

It is, however, becoming increasingly clear that the demarcation of the landscape as a burial zone survived the corded ware culture and became, in fact, a long-term feature of the landscape. At Břeštany, corded ware burials abut later cremation burials dating to the younger Bronze Age (Koutecký 1986). At Lomský potok, the distribution of older bronze age burials of the Únětice culture is linked in a clear, non-random relationship to the corded ware burials. Figure 6.5 shows the spatial association between the corded ware, bell beaker and Únětice graves. The spatial contingency of the younger graves on the older pattern seems clear.

We have some grounds for saying, then, that in the Lomský potok area, the division of the landscape already in existence in the corded ware times continued to be respected during both the older and younger Bronze Age. The division of the area by the corded ware groups acted as the landscape antecedent for later successor use of the same area by the bronze age communities, whose settlement and burial areas, in *elaboration* of the earlier use, created the landscape successors, the ideological and material expressions of an older division of the landscape.

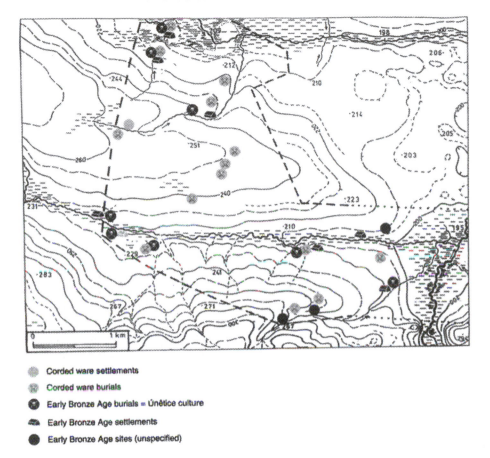

Corded ware settlements

Corded ware burials

Early Bronze Age burials = Únětice culture

Early Bronze Age settlements

Early Bronze Age sites (unspecified)

Figure 6.5 The drainage basin of Lomský potok, northwest Bohemia.

Focal places in the landscape

Focal or central places in the landscape serve to fulfil a number of central social functions for surrounding communities. The concept and its operation has been extensively researched both in geography (Haggett et al. 1977) and in archaeology (e.g. Clarke 1972; Hodder and Orton 1976). Focal places are often situated in defensive locations and they tend to be enclosed by features suggesting fortification. However, in our view, the significance of such 'fortifications' may often have been more symbolic than practical and intended primarily to mark out symbolically an area of special significance.

Focal places occur in both lowland and upland situations. In Bohemia, the following can be considered as focal places:

1 Neolithic 'rondels' (ditched banked enclosures) and eneolithic fortified settlements.

2 Fortified as well as non-fortified hill-top settlements with traces of ritual activities occurring from the Early Bronze Age onwards.
3 Hillforts and lowland fenced/palisaded/fortified enclosures added in the La Tène period, in some cases to pre-existing, earlier enclosures.
4 Market centres, religious complexes, forts and castles replacing the earlier focal places in the Medieval period.

In our view, focal places acted as landscape antecedents only partly for historical reasons. While farming settlement areas were utilised continuously for several millennia, the siting and structure of focal places were responsive to changing social demands.

Locational continuity or relocation of focal places can apparently be explained in three ways. First, landscape relief imposed limits on the range of possibilities for the siting of focal places. Second, the structure of social organisation was reflected in the organisation of the settlement. But third, at a more subtle level, the focal places can also reflect the changing or continuing ideologies of the population, the land-use patterns mediated by the mental maps of the users, and the traditions of land use passed from one generation to another as landscape antecedent: a 'habitus' (Bourdieu 1977) in the landscape.

We do not intend to argue that a focal place was always located in a dominant position within the landscape. The first farmers of Central Europe, the linear and stroke ware groups, built palisaded enclosures known as 'rondels' such as Vochov near Plzeň (Pilsen), or Bylany in central Bohemia (Midgley et al. 1993). Although we are not certain of their precise function, we regard them as the earliest examples of focal places in Bohemia.

During the Eneolithic, the increase in social ranking was reflected in a more hierarchical development of the settlement structure. The location of focal places shifted to elevated positions, without abandoning the primary function of such sites as settlements. Within our research area, the hill-top settlement of Vrany can serve as a good example. In addition to the ditch-and-bank enclosure, lunar symbols and a ceramic drum found in association with one of the houses suggest internal stratification within the settlement.

Within northwest Bohemia as a whole, a great majority of focal places have been used repeatedly. A typical example is the hillfort at Levousy, which was fortified twice, once in the Earlier Bronze Age and again in the Early Medieval period. The locality itself, however, was also occupied in the Neolithic, the Eneolithic, and in the Later Bronze Age. Other localities, such as Černovice or Hradec, were occupied almost continuously (Smrž 1991).

While the Eneolithic is characterised mostly by hill-top settlements without palisades, fortifications marked by ditches, banks and palisades increased in the course of the Bronze Age and culminated in the hillforts of the La Tène period. In addition to architecturally complex sites, such as the Stradonice hillfort, we also see the development of ritual square enclosures in the open landscape (*Viereckenschanze*). Some La Tène hillforts contained stone buildings

(*Závist*) or religious structures, marking in a more monumental way the role of focal places with particular emphasis on the ideological. This symbolic elaboration continued in the Early Medieval period with the advent of Christianity. In addition to building early medieval chapels/churches in the ancient seats of tribal chiefs – a clear case of the appropriation of the new ideology by the ruling elite – early medieval churches also marked other focal places, such as market locations or monasteries, thereby adding to their multi-functional role.

The evolution of focal places continues during the Medieval period. The villages and towns of the Late Medieval period indicate a marked increase in the density, clustering and hierarchisation of the settlement pattern. The Christian church can usually be found in the midst of the nucleated settle-ment clusters. Some medieval churches are erected in an exceptionally dominating position to symbolise additional, more inclusive, roles. For example, St Vitus' cathedral in Prague has become a symbol of the conti-nuity of the Bohemian Crown and Czech statehood. The cathedral was founded on the site not only of two earlier Christian churches but also of a pagan ritual structure. The cathedral, then, as a landscape successor within a major focal place of the region, represents a contradiction or negation of earlier beliefs, as well as the development of the Christian faith and its bond to secular power.

Conclusion

We have tried to show how landscape antecedents and successors operate within an interactive historical landscape. More specifically, we have also tried to show how they can operate in a number of dialectical relationships to each other in terms of opposition, contradiction, negation, continuation and elaboration. For example, the use of the later neolithic landscapes was constrained by the deleterious effects of their earlier use, thereby creating conditions that acted in contradiction to the pressure for further growth of agricultural settlement. The uprooting of field boundaries and other markers of private property in the modern socialist period presented a symbolic as well as practical negation of personal ownership of the landscape. In contrast, continuation and elaboration of existing patterns can be observed in the long-term use of burial zones and focal places, and in the subdivision of the landscape into ritual and profane areas, although the more specific meaning of such long-term use was transformed within each cultural context, as is apparent from the reuse of pre-Christian ritual centres for the promotion of Christianity. These structural relationships provide the basis for a more specific interpretation of the evolution of landscape in time and for under-standing social change. They also provide an alternative to our conventional typological chronologies: an alternative whose chronological points of refer-ence are embedded within the landscape.

Note

1 'Ancient Landscape Reconstruction in Northern Bohemia' is a joint research programme set up by the Department of Archaeology and Prehistory, University of Sheffield, and the Institute of Archaeology in Prague.

Acknowledgements

This chapter is an extended and elaborated version of a paper presented by Zvelebil and Beneš at the CITEE 2 conference in Newcastle in March 1994, and published originally in the proceedings of the conference in *Colloquenda Pontica* 30. We are grateful to John Chapman and Paul Dolukhanov, the organisers of the conference, for inviting us to contribute, and to John Chapman and Robert Layton for their helpful editorial interventions. Jaromír Beneš thanks the British Council for the financial support provided towards the cost of his visit to Newcastle.

References

Allison, K. 1976. *The East Riding of Yorkshire*. London: Hodder & Stoughton.
Bender, B. 1992. Theorising landscape, and the prehistoric landscapes of Stonehenge. *Man* 27, 735–55.
Beneš, J. 1986. Das Knovizer Gehoft in Liptice. In *Die Urnenfelderkulturen Mitteleuropas*, J. Beneš (ed.), 231–5. Praha: Institute of Archaeology.
Beneš, J. 1991a. Benutzung der Korrelationskarten beim Studium der Siedlungskontinuitat und – diskontinuitat am Beispiel in der Mikroregion Lomský Potok in Nordwest-Bohmen. *Veröffentlichungen des Museums fur Ur- und Fruhgeschichte Potsdam* 25, 55–64.
Beneš, J. 1991b. The Lomský potok project: investigation of prehistoric settlements of a micro-region with large-scale soil transfers. *Archaeology in Bohemia 1986–1990*, 178–84.
Beneš, J. 1995. Erosion and accumulation processes in the late holocene of Bohemia, in relation to prehistoric and mediaeval landscape occupation. In *Whither Archaeology? A volume dedicated to E. Neustupný*. M. Kuna and V. Venclová (eds), 133–44. Praha: Institute of Archaeology.
Beneš, J. and V. Brůna 1994. Má krajina pamet? In *Archeologie a Krajinná Ekologie*, J. Beneš and V. Brůna (eds), 37–46. Most: Nadace Projekt Sever.
Beneš, J. and M. Dobes 1992. Eine schnurkeramische Grabergruppe und ein Objekt der Kugelamphorenkultur aus Hrdlovka (NW Bohmen). *Praehistorica* 19, 67–79.
Beneš, J. and D. Koutecký 1987. Die Erforschung der Mikroregion Lomsky potok – Probleme und Perspectiven. In *Archaeologische Rettungstaetigkeit in den Braunkohlengebieten*, E. Cerna (ed.), 31–8. Praha: Institute of Archaeology.
Binford, L.R. 1981. *Bones, Ancient Men and Modern Myths*. New York: Academic Press.
Bloch, M. 1977. The past and the present in the present. *Man* 12, 278–92.
Bourdieu, P. 1977. *Outline of a Theory of Practice*. Cambridge: Cambridge University Press.
Bradley, R. 1991. Ritual, time and history. *World Archaeology* 23, 209–19.
Braudel, F. 1980. *On History*. London: Weidenfeld & Nicolson.
Butler, S. 1993. A strategy for lowland palynology in Bohemia, *Památky Archeologické* 84, 102–10.
Caulfield, S. 1978. Neolithic fields: the Irish evidence. In *Early Land Allotment*, H.C. Bowen and P.J. Fowler (eds), 137–44. Oxford: British Archaeological Reports.

Chapman, J. 1993. Social power in the Iron Gates Mesolithic. In *Cultural Transformations and Interactions in Eastern Europe*, J. Chapman and P.M. Dolukhanov (eds), 61–106. London: Avebury.

Clark, G. 1992. *Space, Time and Man*. Cambridge: Cambridge University Press.

Clarke, D.L. 1972. Models and paradigms in contemporary archaeology. In *Models in Archaeology*, D.L. Clarke (ed.), 1–60. London: Methuen.

Cooney, G. 1983. Megalithic tombs in their environmental setting, a settlement perspective. In *Landscape Archaeology in Ireland*, T. Reeves-Smyth and F. Hamond (eds), 179–94. Oxford: British Archaeological Reports.

Cooney, G. 1991. Irish neolithic landscapes and land use systems: the implications of field systems. *Rural History* 2, 123–39.

Cooney, G. and E. Grogan 1994. *Irish Prehistory: a social perspective*. Wordwell: Dublin.

Dreslerová, D. 1995. The prehistory of the middle Labe (Elbe) floodplain in the light of archaeological finds. *Památky Archeologické* 86, 105–45.

Dunnell, R.C. 1992. The notion of site. In *Space, Time and Archaeological Landscapes*, J. Rossignol and L. Wandsnider (eds), 21–42. New York: Plenum Press.

Dunnell, R.C. and W.S. Dacey 1983. The siteless survey: a regional scale data collection strategy. *Advances in Archaeological Method and Theory* 6, 267–87.

Fleming, A. 1985. Land tenure, productivity and field systems. In *Beyond Domestication in Prehistoric Europe*, G. Barker and C. Gamble (eds), 129–46. London: Academic Press.

Fleming, A. 1988. *The Dartmoor Reaves*. London: Batsford.

Fleming, A. 1990. Landscape archaeology, prehistory and rural studies. *Rural History* 1, 5–15.

Foley, R. 1981. A model of regional archaeological structure. *Proceedings of the Prehistoric Society* 47, 1–17.

Fox, C. 1932. *The Personality of Britain*. Cardiff: University of Wales.

Gosden, C. 1994. *Social Being and Time*. Blackwell: Oxford.

Haggett, P., A.D. Cliff and A. Frey 1977. *Locational Models in Geography*. London: Edward Arnold.

Hodder, I. (ed.) 1978. *The Spatial Organisation of Culture*. London: Duckworth.

Hodder, I. and C. Orton 1976. *Spatial Analysis in Archaeology*. Cambridge: Cambridge University Press.

Ingold, T. 1993. The temporality of the landscape. *World Archaeology* 25, 152–74.

Knapp, A. (ed.) 1992. *Archaeology, Annales and Ethnohistory*. Cambridge: Cambridge University Press.

Koutecký, D. 1986. *Knovízské pohřebiste v Břestanech, okr. Teplice. Das Knoviser Grabfeld in Brestany*. Praha: Universita Karlova.

Kuna, M. 1991. The structuring of prehistoric landscape. *Antiquity* 65, 332–47.

Kuna, M. and D. Adelsbergerová 1995. Prehistoric location preferences: an application of GIS to the Vinorsky potok project, the Czech Republic. In *Archaeology and Geographical Information Systems: a European perspective*, G. Lock and Z. Stancic (eds), 117–31. London: Taylor & Francis.

Kuna, M. and X. Slabina 1987. Zur Problematik der Siedlungsareale. In *Archeologische Rettungstatiegkeit in den Braunkohlengebiten*, B. Cerna (ed.), 31–8. Praha: Institute of Archaeology.

Leach, E. 1990. Aryan invasions over four millennia. In *Culture Through Time: anthropological approaches*, E. Ohnuki-Tierney (ed.), 227–45. Stanford: Stanford University Press.

Ložek, V. 1981. Zmeny krajiny v souvislosti s osídlením ve svetle malakologickych poznatkú – Der Landschaftswandeln in Beziehung zur Besiedlung im Lichte malakologischer Befunde. *Archeologické Rozhledy* 33, 176–88.

Midgley, M.S., I. Pavlu, J. Rulf and M. Zapotocka 1993. Fortified settlements or ceremonial sites: new evidence from Bylany, Czechoslovakia. *Antiquity* 67, 91–5.

Neustupný, E. 1973. Factors determining the variability of the corded ware culture. In *The Explanation of Culture Change*, C. Renfrew (ed.), 725–30. London: Duckworth.

Neustupný, E. 1982. Prehistoric migrations by infiltration. *Archeologicky Rozhledy* 34, 278–93.

Neustupný, E. 1986. Sídelní areály prevekých zemědelců [Settlement areas of prehistoric farmers]. *Památky Archeologické* 77, 226–34.

Neustupný, E. 1987. Pravek eroze a akumulace v oblasti Luzického potoka [Prehistoric erosion and accumulation in the Luzice brook basin]. *Archeologické Rozhledy* 39, 629–43.

Reeves-Smyth, T. and F. Hammond (eds) 1983. *Landscape Archaeology in Ireland*. Oxford: British Archaeological Reports.

Riley, D.N. 1980. *Early Landscapes from the Air*. Sheffield: University of Sheffield.

Roberts, B.K. 1987. Landscape archaeology. In *Landscape and Culture*, J.M. Wagstaff (ed.), 26–37. Oxford: Blackwell.

Rossignol, J. and L. Wandsnider (eds) 1992. *Space, Time and Archaeological Landscapes*. New York: Plenum Press.

Rúžičková, E. and A. Zeman (eds) 1994. *Holocene Flood Plain of the Labe River: contemporary state of research in the Czech Republic*. Prague: Academy of Sciences CR.

Schiffer, M.B. 1983. Towards the identification of formation processes. *American Antiquity* 48, 675–706.

Smejtek, L. 1994. Zmeny přírodniho prostředí a vývoj mladobronzové sídelní struktury v mikroregionu Hrimezdickeho potoka. In *Archeologie a Krajinna Ekologie*, J. Beneš and V. Brůna (eds), 84–93. Most: Nadace Projekt Sever.

Smrž, Z. 1987. Vyvoj a struktura osidleni v mikroregionu Luzickeho potoka na Kadansku [The development and structure of settlement in the microregion of the Luzicky stream in the Kadan area]. *Archeologické Rozhledy* 39, 601–21.

Smrž, Z. 1991. Vysinne lokality mladsi doby kamenné az raneho stredoveku v severozapadnich Cechach – Hohenlokalitaten in der Zeitspanne von der jungeren Steinzeit bis zum fruhen Mittelalter im nordwestlichen Teil Bohmens. *Archeologické Rozhledy* 43, 63–89.

Thomas, J. 1996. The cultural context of the first use of domesticates in continental Central and Northwest Europe. In *The Origins and Spread of Agriculture and Pastoralism in Eurasia*, D.R. Harris (ed.), 310–23. London: UCL Press.

Tilley, C. 1991. *Material Culture and Text: the art of ambiguity*. London: Routledge.

Tilley, C. 1994. *A Phenomenology of Landscape*. Oxford: Berg.

Vasicek, Z. 1994. *L'Archéologie, L'Histoire, Le Passé*. Sceaux: Kronos.

Vencl, S. 1992. Záchranny vyzkum v Praze 9 – Dolních Pocernicích v roce 1982 [Salvage excavation at Prague 9 – Dolní Pocernice in 1982]. *Archeologické Rozhledy* 44, 29–65.

Vidal de la Blanche, P. 1902. Les conditions géographiques des faits sociaux. *Annales de Géographie* 11, 13–23.

Wandsnider, L. 1987. Natural formation process experimentation and archaeological analysis. In *Natural Formation Process and the Archaeological Record*, D.T. Nash and M.D. Petraglia (eds), 150–85. Oxford: British Archaeological Reports.

Zvelebil, M. 1981. *From Forager to Farmer in the Boreal Zone: reconstructing economic patterns through catchment analysis in prehistoric Finland*. Oxford: British Archaeological Reports.

Zvelebil, M. 1993. Concepts of time and 'presencing' the Mesolithic. *Archaeological Review from Cambridge* 12, 51–70.

Zvelebil, M. 1994. Koncept krajiny, sance archeologie. In *Archeologie a Krajinna Ekologie*, J. Beneš and V. Bruna (eds), 20–37. Most: Nadace Projekt Sever.

Zvelebil, M. 1996. The agricultural frontier and the transition to farming in the circum-Baltic region. In *The Origins and Spread of Agriculture and Pastoralism in Eurasia*, D.R. Harris (ed.), 323–46. London: UCL Press.

Zvelebil, M. In press. What's in a name: the Mesolithic, the Neolithic and social change at the Mesolithic–Neolithic transition. In *Understanding the Neolithic of North-West Europe*, M. Edmonds and C. Richards (eds), 1–35. Glasgow: Cruithne Press.

Zvelebil, M., S.W. Green and M.G. Macklin 1992. Archaeological landscapes, lithic scatters and human behaviour. In *Space, Time and Archaeological Landscapes*, J. Rossignol and L. Wandsnider (eds), 193–226. New York: Plenum Press.

7   *Is landscape history possible? Or, how can we study the desertion of farms?*

Mats Widgren

Introduction

In this chapter, two different approaches to landscape studies are contrasted: a 'science' approach, which seeks to explain the development of human landscapes on the basis of general ecological principles, in which the evolutionary development of agro-ecosystems is seen to explain landscape change, and a 'social theory' approach, which interprets human landscapes mainly as social constructs. Researchers using the 'science' approach have often demonstrated a lack of understanding of social processes, while some of the 'social theorists' have tended to downgrade landscape studies with the argument that social processes cannot be 'read' from the morphology of landscapes.

This general problem of landscape research is exemplified here through the problem of explaining the desertion of medieval farms. In the fourteenth and fifteenth centuries AD, a large number of farms in the Nordic countries were deserted. The period was one of recession in much of northern Europe.

The focus of the particular project described in this chapter is a small estate in the Southern Swedish Uplands, where several deserted farms have been located. The researchers concerned with this project are seeking to understand the ecological and social conditions under which it was possible for a peasant family to survive on these small units. The farm areas can be shown to have played different roles over time, depending on a complex interplay of farming systems, political developments and estate organisation which eventually contributed to their desertion.

Is landscape history possible?

The present interest in landscape archaeology in European countries has clear connections with the growing concern for historical landscapes and environmental questions in planning. In an English context this external may be a rather recent one, and may be received with delight by landscape archaeologists. In the Scandinavian context, however, the interest has reached a level at which I am no longer fully convinced that the increasing demand from outside is only for the better for academic landscape studies. The present ideological and political role of landscape values and landscape management in European countries also raises some fundamental questions about the social and ideological role of landscape history. I argue that much of today's debate on the relevance and possibilities of landscape studies can in fact be reduced to arguments about two dichotomies that have long troubled and inspired students of European landscape history. These two pairs of opposites still play a central role in landscape studies. I also argue that they give some clues to the present problems in landscape studies as they relate to the present external demand.

The extent to which researchers have managed to handle the *nature:culture* perspective has been essential for landscape studies since the days of nineteenth-century geographers like Ratzel and Vidal de la Blache. As is shown clearly in the debate on land degradation in the Third World, we still have not resolved (either theoretically or empirically) the problem of differentiating the natural from the social factors responsible for environmental change. Landscape studies have also to deal with the *form:process* dichotomy. This opposition was not explicitly addressed as a central problem in landscape studies until the 1960s, but long before this it had been an implicit concern of fields such as geomorphology or settlement studies. In some periods, the difficulties in handling these opposites led many scholars to see landscape studies as a *cul-de-sac*. How many landscape researchers have been accused of an obsession with form and classification, or of being environmentally deterministic in their explanations?

Form versus process

In the early history of agrarian landscape studies in Europe, the concern was with static form, neglecting the processes of change. The areal differentiation of pre-industrial agrarian landscapes in Europe was seen as being shaped once and for all at the time of the Great Migrations, with the result that ethnicity was considered to be of decisive importance in explanations of settlement patterns and agrarian structures (Meitzen [1895], 1963). This approach remained unchallenged until the 1940s and 1950s, when researchers such as Müller–Wille and Krenzlin introduced an evolutionary perspective into the studies of settlement forms. The classificatory and morphological approach to settlement forms and field shapes was then combined with the explicit aim of explaining process and change. In Krenzlin's model, the forms in the agrarian landscape were seen as reflecting separate stages in the historical development of farming societies. By this morphogenetic approach, the problem of form *versus* process was solved with a simple and very attractive model that strongly influenced landscape research in the decades to come (Krenzlin 1958).

Owing to the influence of quantitative and formal approaches in human geography, the issues of form and process were later explicitly addressed in the studies of agrarian landscapes and field systems. The principle of equifinality, 'that very different processes can result in very similar forms' (Baker and Butlin 1973: 628), as well as the difficulty of applying a quantitative analysis to studies of field systems, undermined, or seemed to undermine, much of the previous work of the morphogenetic school. Baker (1975: 21) expressed his scepticism in these words:

> What have been termed morphogenetic studies of cultural landscapes frequently infer the processes which might have operated principally from the study of morphology of the forms, ignoring the circularity of the argument which interprets landscape features in terms of themselves.

Tools such as systems analysis and simulation were seen as possible bridges between form and process. As Baker (1988) has shown, this 'modern' approach to landscape studies never really had any important impact upon studies of the development of the European agrarian landscape.

The critique of positivist approaches and spatial analysis in human geography made the added distinction between the spatial and the social somewhat akin to the debate over form and process (Olsson 1974). Both 'modern' studies of spatial organisation and the more 'traditional' morphogenetic studies of rural landscapes often demonstrate a neglect of social theory, as if classes, power and social relations did not exist. The critique of this spatial separatism had the result that much research attention in historical geography was turned towards a mainly non-spatial, non-landscape type of social history. Landscape history was left to the 'traditionalists'. The problem of form *versus* process was considered insoluble. Landscape forms were left aside, while historical geographers turned their attention to the social processes *behind* spatial change.

An opposite tendency can be seen in the more recent 'postmodern' approaches, which deal with landscape as ideology and symbol, or with landscape as a social and cultural construct (Cosgrove and Daniels 1988). As has been pointed out, an emphasis on the meaning of forms and human artefacts in the landscape diminishes concern with understanding processes of change (e.g. Hirsch 1995: 5, 22, citing Ingold 1993). It is the ideological and symbolic meaning of landscape forms that is analysed rather than landscape as a part of an everyday practice and process. This tendency coincides with the trend in present landscape management in many countries in Europe, where agrarian landscapes are seen, managed and subsidised as 'frozen scenery', looked at from the outside by tourists and city people. The landscape concept is taken by such researchers in the current English sense as emanating from a genre of painting, rather than from the original German (and Scandinavian) sense which had much closer connections with 'land' and 'territory'. As Olwig (1996b) has recently shown, the German landscape concept had not in fact originally referred only to a territorial unit, but also to the social order and the natural conditions within such a unit.

Nature versus culture; ecological versus social theory

In traditional geography, the claim to understand the interdependence between man and nature was made as a matter of course. The quantitative revolution in geography complicated this picture. Although it initiated the present split between human and physical geography, there remained an often expressed and cherished belief in the unity of science. Systems theory was advocated as a concept uniting natural and cultural systems.

The ecosystem concept provided not only a rigorous method for describing and comparing different agro-ecosystems in space and time (cf. Bayliss-Smith 1982) but also a way of building further on the evolutionary models provided by the morphogenetic researchers. This later development was perhaps characteristic of Scandinavian landscape archaeologists and scientists, who drew indirectly on the German school of cultural landscape studies and combined their work with the evolutionary ideas of Ester Boserup. The development of human landscapes could be seen to reflect subsequent stages of more intensified human interference in natural ecosystems. Such models have also provided a basis for much interesting and relevant research into landscape history (Welinder 1975; Berglund 1991).

These models can, however, be criticized for being environmentally deterministic, since they can account only for the development of relations between humans and nature, and not for how relations within human society govern the development of agro-ecosystems (cf. Welinder 1988). The shortcomings have been explicit when, for example, they concern short-term landscape changes and desertion processes, both of which have been beyond the explanatory power of such models of change.

The main shortcomings of these models can thus be understood in terms of the nature:culture dichotomy. Agro-ecosystems cannot be understood in isolation from their social context and only 'rearrange' themselves through the actions of men and women. The critique that was directed at traditional landscape research and spatial separatism by the social theory school can as easily be applied to the ecosystems approach.

The nature:culture dichotomy has led many human geographers to question the possibility of analysing natural and social systems within the same theoretical framework, since these two types of system differ in their characters (e.g. Asheim 1990). Such an approach obviously excludes from analysis the very basis for our survival: the production of food. Olwig (1996a) has challenged this view by analysing how the geographical concept of nature developed historically.

The subject matter of landscape history eliminates all the easy choices within these two dichotomies. Landscape is form, but it is also an ongoing process, as well as the result of previous processes. Therefore it cannot be treated exclusively as either process or form. Any research on landscape has to grapple with the interrelationships between form and process. Landscapes can be interpreted and analysed from the cultural perspective, but landscape is also land, a resource for producing food, and a basis of power. If we are to understand landscape history, the ecological, social and cultural contexts of landscapes must all be taken into account. The challenge to research in landscape history is, as I see it, to deal with this complex of problems. Landscape is, on the one hand, a form, which at a given moment and in a given context can be represented in a landscape painting or recorded and interpreted in satellite imagery. On the other hand, landscapes can only be understood as continual processes, flows of energy and matter, thoughts and actions. The *raison d'être* for landscape history therefore lies in the more or less successful manoeuvring between form and process, and between ecology and culture. Exploiting the dialectic rather than avoiding one or other of the 'sides' seems the best way forward.

Is it possible to survive on a deserted farm?

Giving equal weighting to ecological and social analysis in landscape research underlies the particular project on which the remaining, empirical, part of this chapter is based.[1]

In the fourteenth and fifteenth centuries AD, a process of farm desertion took place in Scandinavia, as in numerous parts of Europe. Many were small and were from an ecological viewpoint operating within narrow margins, either because of their marginal location climatically or because of their small cultivated area. Previous research on the medieval desertion of farms in the Nordic countries has mainly been carried out by historians, with the result that written sources and related source-criticism have predominated in both methods and results. The scale of the investigations has, furthermore, not permitted the drawing of conclusions as to the development of actual settlements, only statistical averages over larger areas. As a result, causative factors have been dealt with on only a very generalised scale (Gissel et al. 1981).

Our study of the development of settlement and land use in a small area covers a longer period of time. Instead of asking why settlements were deserted, we ask why settlement occurred at all. Under what ecological and social conditions was it possible for peasant families to survive on these small units?

Historians usually work on aggregated data at a *regional* level. We have done likewise but, in addition, we have also pursued archaeological, historical and landscape studies at the level of *domain* – that area, under one owner in the Late Medieval period, that included the demesne and tenant farms. In addition, we have also worked at the most detailed level of the *resource area* of individual holdings that were later deserted.

It became clear that the deserted farms could not be seen as individual, self-contained units. They also played a role in the local social and economic systems, and were linked to neighbours, landlords and the state in different ways. These ideas on the relationship between single settlement units and the wider social structure were inspired by Odner's (1972) ecological and social analysis of peripheral settlements in Norway during the Migration Period. There are two ways in which the dependence of a farm on a wider social structure may become manifest in the agro-ecosystem. If the farm is a part of a larger structure, this may transform the judgements of risk that would have applied if it had been self-contained. Cereal production can be sustained in climatically marginal areas if, in cases of crop failure, a social fund guarantees the continuing existence of a farm. When such a farm was abandoned – as a result of years of bad harvests – it is therefore not sufficient simply to say that natural climatic factors have been the decisive reason. Desertion may also have been caused by changes in the social structure that had previously guaranteed its existence. The farm might also have had a specialised function within a re-distributive system. If cattle-rearing, hunting, fishing or crafts were the basic pursuits of the farm within this system, such a farm's supply of cereals might have been guaranteed from elsewhere. In order to understand the settlement, one must therefore reconstruct the processes that these systems operated before, during and after the period when the farms were in use.

In the Medieval period the study area consisted of two small manors, Lägersnäs and Kalvsved, and their adjoining tenant farms in Askeryd parish in the Southern Swedish Uplands (about 40 sq. km of land, most of which was woodland). In the late fourteenth century these two manors, including tenant farms, mills and fishing rights, were donated to the convents in Vadstena and Vreta. The records resulting from this donation permit a detailed recon-struction of the tenant farms. In the sixteenth century, five of the eighteen tenant farms were deserted, most of them permanently, and never resettled. Initially the only evidence for this desertion consisted of records in *terriers* (court rolls). The actual locations of the deserted farms were not known.

Surveying

The identification of the medieval farms on the ground resulted from a combi-nation of analysis of the documentary evidence, archaeological reconnaissance, detailed surveys, analyses of seventeenth- and eighteenth-century maps, and archaeological excavations.

Fieldwork started with detailed planning and phosphate mapping of one of the medieval farms. Archaeological excavations were then carried out to confirm that the settlements and fields were medieval in date. Our knowledge of features gained at that stage then formed the basis for a more extensive survey, covering the whole former estate as well as its former tenant farms. One immediate aim was to find traces of the medieval deserted farms, but the wider aim was to ensure that the survey would form the basis for an analysis of settlement and land use during the periods preceding and following the time of maximum settlement during the Late Middle Ages.

This interdisciplinary work in the field resulted in the rapid identification of all the sites known from the historical records, most of which were situated in woodlands or pastures. Not only were the areas of the deserted farms recognised, but also details of the field systems and houses (the latter identified by the heaped debris of collapsed central ovens, a type of ancient monument until then not known from Sweden).

Two factors were decisive for this successful identification of the medieval settlements. One was the interdisciplinary work, in which documentary records and landscape evidence were constantly cross-checked. The other factor was the *retrogressive approach* to landscape studies. A time-specific cross-section of landscape cannot be singled out unless the whole landscape history is taken into account. In a way, one could say that the successful identification of medieval remains depends on the possibilities of identifying also prehistoric, early-modern and recent features on the ground. Furthermore, the more recent documentary and cartographic evidence often gave clear indications of medieval settlements and land uses. Our initial emphasis on land and land use rather than on sites turned out to be the key to understanding the sites themselves. That research phase was followed by more detailed, problem-oriented excavations and sampling.

As a result, three medieval deserted farms, and their remaining field systems, have been mapped. Excavations have been carried out in settlements and fields. Ecological interpretation has been based on analyses of macro-fossils from settlements, and of pollen from mires close to the settlements and in abandoned fields.

Agro-ecosystems over time

On the basis of our analyses of an area of about 10 ha dating from the first millennium AD to the nineteenth century, we can say that a small medieval farm area might have seen the following agro-ecosystemic phases:

Phase A: Extensive farming in a large field system

During the Viking period (AD 800 to 1050), the area formed part of a larger field system which consisted of strip parcels of a kind known from other parts of southern Sweden and dated to the first millennium AD. Judging from the height of lynchets, and from other signs of cultivation, cultivation could have been either extensive and/or of short duration. So far, pollen analysis has not yet determined the type of farming. The evidence suggests that a large area was used in some kind of extensive farming system, most probably a kind of grass fallow, or possibly a bush fallow with coppices. Circulation of nutrients would have been mainly based on the rotation of grasses or bushes, although manuring could also have played a part. It is not possible to reach any conclusions regarding either the size of a holding or the location of settlements in the area.

Phase B: Medieval single farm

That a farm was established in the area, probably in the thirteenth century, can be concluded from building remains dated by archaeological excavation to the fourteenth century. Fields with high lynchets were situated close to the farm; contrary to expectation, pollen analyses have not confirmed that the establishment of such a small farm in the formerly extensively used field system would have been accompanied by intensified tilling on a small, manured infield plot. Furthermore, close analysis of the cultivated acreage of one of the more isolated farms of this period indicated that a rather extensive farming arrangement, in which an arable phase in the rotation alternated with long periods of grass fallow, might still have been in use. Any difference between phases A and B in the functioning of the agro-ecosystems could have been minor.

Phase C: Hay meadow for neighbouring farms

Following desertion, most abandoned farms were used by neighbouring tenant farms for pasture or meadow. Use of the deserted farmland was a prerequisite for the changes in field layout connected with the introduction of a three-field system. The farm area thus lost its 'independent' role to the production of winter fodder as a part of a larger field system. A major restructuring of the agro-ecosystem took place, which accounts for the spatial and land-use differences between phases B and C.

Social and tenurial development

Realisation that the establishment of small farms in the thirteenth century was not connected with any major changes in the basic agro-ecosystem is crucial for our understanding of the process. We now have to turn to the role that the territory played in the social system governed by tenurial relations: the shift from phase A to phase B was associated with the growth of the Swedish nobility during the thirteenth century. The first documented owner of this estate (during the fourteenth century) was Gustaf Arvidsson, who belonged to a family that had close links with the royal family. Arvidsson also played an important regional and national political role, and he and his son (who inherited the estate) both spent a considerable amount of time travelling between Sweden, Finland and Germany. The estate with which we are concerned was a small one as compared with other parts of Arvidsson's property, and we are forced to conclude that it formed a base of operations by which it was possible to provision a large company of followers and to entertain guests. It was in this context that a number of small tenant farms were established during the thirteenth century. All were of similar size, and shared nomenclature types with a male name or a type of occupation as the first part and -torp or related expressions as their endings: Värn-arp, Dags-torp, Rös-torp, Svart-arp, Gås-arp. It is possible that the toponymical element -torp originally meant 'tenant farm', and certainly its distribution in Sweden closely mirrors the distribution of the nobility (Brink et al. 1994: 142).

It is known from other sources that in Scandinavia in this period there were different types of small-holding tenants who paid their rents through day labour: *colonis* and *inquillini*. The emergence of such a category of tenants has been attributed to the reorganisation of demesne farming in the thirteenth century, possibly associated with the end of slave labour on large demesnes (Karras 1988: 90). Recently, Rahmqvist (1996) has produced detailed evidence for a parallel process in central Sweden. This process most probably represented a structural change whereby a system of day labourers or tenants was created to support the manor with food, labour, hunting, fishing and crafts, clearly associated with the short periods of provisioning and luxury consumption required by travelling gentry.

In the late thirteenth century, the whole estate was donated to the convents of Vadstena and Vreta. Small tenants were instructed only to obey the new owners, and even demesne land was split up into new tenant farms. Rents were no longer paid in labour, but in butter. Tenurial relations were changed and farms were withdrawn from the local social organisation, as rents had to be paid to a far-away nunnery. In the fifteenth century, five of the smallest farms were abandoned; this could have been triggered by outbreaks of plague in the 1420s and 1460s (Bååth 1983), but in any case these farms were never resettled. They remained abandoned and later on came to be used by other farms as hay meadows. After this structural change in tenurial relations, a recolonisation was no longer possible. In the subsequent agro-ecosystem, much of the abandoned land found a new role as meadow. From seventeenth-century maps, we know that the three-field system was consistently used in the area. Throughout much of this region, several of the abandoned farms were used either as the third field in a three-field system or as meadow-land to compensate for the cultivation of former hay-meadows which were turned into one of the fields in the three-field system. The abandonment of farms can thus be seen as one of the prerequisites in this region for the introduction of the three-field system. The reduction of pressure on land, as well as the increasing demand for winter-grown rye – a demand that is documented in instructions from one of the owning convents – can both be seen as factors lying behind the observed changes in field layout. Furthermore, it is possible that the decrease in population might have promoted the introduction of an autumn-sown crop, which itself would have distributed labour more evenly over the year.

Note

1 The project, which is directed by Professor Hans Andersson (medieval archae-ology), includes researchers of history, human geography, plant ecology and quaternary biology. Most took part in the interdisciplinary Ystad Project at Lund University (see Berglund 1991), and their experience has played an important role in the present project. This chapter makes use of unpublished material produced by Hans Andersson, Ingmar Billberg, Käthe Bååth, Pär Connelid, Kerstin Sundberg and the author.

Acknowledgement

This research was funded by the Swedish Council for Research in the Humanities and Social Sciences.

References

Asheim, B.T. 1990. *Norsk kultur-/samfunnsgeografisk forskning i ett nordisk perspektiv.* Oslo: University of Oslo.

Bååth, K. 1983. *Öde sedan stora döden var . . . : bebyggelse och befolkning i Norra Vedbo under senmedeltid och 1500-tal (Deserted since the Great (Black) Death . . . : settlement and population in Norra Vedbo during the late Middle Ages and the 16th century).* Lund: CWK Gleerup.

Baker, A. 1975. *Historical Geography and Geographic Change.* Basingstoke: Macmillan.

Baker, A. 1988. Historical geography and the study of the European rural landscape. *Geografiska Annaler, Series B* 70, 5–16.

Baker, A. and R. Butlin (eds) 1973. *Studies of Field Systems in the British Isles.* Cambridge: Cambridge University Press.

Bayliss-Smith, T. 1982 *The Ecology of Agricultural Systems.* Cambridge: Cambridge University Press.

Berglund, B. (ed.) 1991. The cultural landscape during 6000 years in southern Sweden. *Ecological Bulletin* 41.

Brink, S., O. Korhonen and M. Wahlberg 1994. Place names. In *Cultural Heritage and Preservation*, K.G. Selinge (ed.), 134–46. Stockholm: National Atlas of Sweden.

Cosgrove, D. and S. Daniels (eds) 1988. *The Iconography of Landscape.* Cambridge: Cambridge University Press.

Gissel, S., E. Jutikalla, E. Österberg, J. Sandnes and B. Teitsson 1981. *Desertion and Land Colonisation in the Nordic Countries c. 1300–1600.* Stockholm: Almqvist & Wiksell.

Hirsch, E. 1995. Landscape: between place and space. In *The Anthropology of Landscape*, E. Hirsch and M. O'Hanlon (eds), 1–30. Oxford: Clarendon Press.

Ingold, T. 1993 The temporality of landscape. *World Archaeology* 25, 152–74.

Karras, R.M. 1988. *Slavery and Society in Medieval Scandinavia.* New Haven: Yale University Press.

Krenzlin, A.-L. 1958. Blockfluhr, Langstreifenfluhr und Gewannfluhr als Funktion agrarischer Nutzungssysteme in Deutschland. *Berichte zur deutsche Landeskunde* 20, 250–66.

Meitzen, A. [1895] 1963. *Seidlung und Agrarwesen der Westgermanen und Ostgermanen, der Kelter, Finnen und Slawen.* Aalen: Scientia.

Odner, K. 1972. Ethno-historic and ecological settings for economic and social models of an iron age society: Valldalen, Norway. In *Models in Archaeology*, D.L. Clarke (ed.), 623–51. London: Methuen.

Olsson, G. 1974. The dialectics of spatial analysis. *Antipode* 6, 50–61.

Olwig, K.R. 1996a. Nature – mapping the 'ghostly' traces of a concept. In *Concepts in Human Geography*, C. Earl, K. Mathewson and M.S. Kenzer (eds), 63–9. Savage, Md.: Rowman & Littlefield.

Olwig, K. 1996b. Recovering the substantive nature of landscape. *Annals of the Association of American Geographers* 86, 630–53.

Rahmqvist, S. 1996. Sätesgård och gods. De medeltida frälsegodsens framväxt mot bakgrund av Upplands bebyggelsehistoria. *Upplands fornminnesförenings tidskrift* 53, Uppsala.

Welinder, S. 1975. *Prehistoric Agriculture in Eastern Middle Sweden.* Lund: Gleerups.

Welinder, S. 1988. The landscape of prehistoric man. *Memoranda Soc. Fauna Flora Fennica* 64. 50.

8   *The historic environment, historic landscapes, and space–time–action models in landscape archaeology*

Timothy Darvill

Introduction

In recent years, the idea of landscape has become increasingly important in archaeology, not just from an academic point of view but also in relation to the protection and management of sites and areas.[1] Terms such as 'the historic environment' and 'historic landscapes' are widely used with almost reckless abandon, and seemingly attached to almost every research design or report on the archaeology of a chosen area. As so often happens, an intractable term that defies close definition and lacks consensual understanding is among the most widely used. And why not? Everyone knows what the landscape is when they are surrounded by it, even if packaging it for academic analysis is more difficult.

In this chapter I argue that archaeologists interested in the matter of landscape have focused for too long on physical and structural dimensions rather than on metaphysical and social aspects. The term 'landscape' is not a synonym for the countryside, but rather something far more powerful which amounts to a generic term for the expression of particular ways of seeing the world – specialised experiences of time and place. The idea of landscape in this sense is not restricted to the emergent capitalist world of western Europe which found the need to recoin the term in the sixteenth century AD (Bender 1993: 1). The concept of landscape embraces much more widely applicable themes about relationships between people, the realm of ideas and values, and the worlds that they have created for themselves to live in. These things are matters of universal relevance and interest.

I first summarise two traditional approaches to the archaeology of landscape then reflect critically on them in the light of socially based perspectives of the past. I then develop a contextual approach to the archaeology of landscape in which emphasis is placed on the coeval structuration of social action and the social categorisation and structuring of time and space.[2] I show how this approach can be applied to the archaeological record of the later third millennium BC in the area around Stonehenge, Wiltshire, where a cosmologically founded fourfold partitioning of space provides the basic framework for the contemporary landscape.

Archaeology and the landscape

Landscapes as 'objects'

Traditionally, archaeologists have viewed the landscape as a physical phenomenon that is essentially of human construction: an object or artefact that can be measured, quantified and understood in functionalist or positivist terms just like a ceramic vessel or a flint axe. Counting the number of sites in an area and relating them to each other and to the terrain in which they lie has become an increasingly sophisticated task, often involving the use of many different strands of evidence: for example, cropmarks on aerial photographs, earthworks mapped by field survey, depictions on ancient maps, and the texts of historic documents.

Understanding the landscape as an artefact has mainly involved looking at 'man–land' relationships in locational or economic terms, emphasising the way in which people have individually or collectively moulded and shaped the physical appearance of the landscape and, conversely, the ways in which the landscape has affected human activities.

Treating the landscape as artefact (Evans *et al.* 1975; Limbrey and Evans 1978) develops the work of Cyril Fox, whose book *The Personality of Britain* so eloquently expounded the ways in which the physical geography of the British Isles influenced early populations (Fox 1933). Treating the landscape as an object has drawn attention to just how much archaeology there is in the countryside; ancient features seem to be scattered everywhere. In those places where archaeological remains are especially abundant, and where a good deal of what was created in the past survives, opportunities for a second approach to the archaeology of landscape presents itself: landscapes as 'subjects'.

Landscapes as 'subjects'

Treating landscapes as subjects involves reconstructing earlier states of existence, creating an image of a landscape as it might have appeared at some defined stage in its past. A tract of modern countryside becomes a study area that is regressed through the consideration of all possible relevant dimensions and disciplines. The descriptive technologies of mapping and reconstruction-drawing provide familiar devices to communicate these ideas, as they are used widely by later twentieth-century western societies to record modern landscapes. By selectively excluding earlier and later elements of the archaeological record, a sort of quasi-historical map of an area can be built up to show the disposition of sites and monuments as they might have been arranged at a particular time. Success generally depends on having enough recorded elements or components to fit together into a pattern: such patterns emerge through the spatial juxtaposition and stratigraphic interconnection of components.

An increasingly important element of this approach is the matter of environmental reconstruction. In this sphere, attempts have been made, often quite successfully, to chart the way in which a piece of countryside has evolved in terms of its changing vegetation, soil cover, fauna and climate. These can also be reconstructed and communicated through mapping and depiction.

The physical manifestation of landscapes rich in archaeology, and well researched in terms of their environment, means that now and again the past can almost be conjured up from the ground and brought to life; this amounts to what is sometimes called the 'historic environment' or a 'historic landscape'. In such places, it is argued, one is momentarily taken back into history: imagining what it was like in the eighteenth century when a magnificent ornamental park was set out; or standing in a village flanked by an open field system in the eleventh century AD; or roaming over the freshly constructed mound of a neolithic barrow beside a causewayed enclosure in the fourth millennium BC. But these images and feelings are nothing to do with the Neolithic, or the Medieval period, or the eighteenth century: what is being experienced is in the present and is based upon a perceptual framework that is entirely the product of our own socialisation and background.

Critique of traditional archaeological approaches to landscape

Treating landscapes as objects or subjects for reconstruction has helped the development of archaeological approaches to landscape, but neither does justice to what, if examined closely, the idea of landscape is really about. Five particular problems can be identified.

The first problem is the continued emphasis on defined sites and monuments. Many landscape studies in archaeology take the form of inventories: lists, maps and plans of individual monuments. It is widely recognised, however, that the environment or lifespace that is relevant to any community is much more extensive than the sort of loci that are most clearly visible archaeologically. People did not exist only within the confines of definable sites and monuments, they occupied territories and regions that had integrity, structure and symbolic meaning (e.g. Foley 1981; Hodder 1982). Archaeological interest focuses on not just what happens within sites but also what is going on, in social terms, on larger spatial scales.

The second problem is caused by areas without archaeological remains. The elements that articulate spatial and stratigraphic relationships between areas of dense archaeology may sometimes be extremely subtle; natural features such as rivers, lakes, rock outcrops, and even apparently empty spaces may be as important in the understanding of a landscape as barrows, tracks or any other visible and familiar man–made feature. Apparently empty spaces can be 'constructed' and categorised and can, in social terms, sometimes be the most significant (cf. Hubert 1994).

The emphasis placed on the primacy of the physical dimensions of landscape, essentially those things that can be appreciated visually, causes a further problem. Stimuli from other senses, and the feelings that they generate, are also significant in experiencing landscape: smells, sounds, textures, tastes, atmosphere. Mental images and constructs are much more important than commonly realised. These may be generated through memories of actual experiences or through secondary perception and the transformation of received images. As Schama (1995) admirably demonstrates, such mental constructs do not physically exist and can never actually be found in reality quite as visualised in the mind, yet they constitute the images that serve to represent what has been or can be experienced.

The fourth reason for concern is the lack of attention given to the social dimensions of landscape, to the basis of social action. Landscapes are essentially social, not physical, constructions. As Daniels and Cosgrove (1988: 1) put it: 'a landscape is a cultural image, a pictorial way of representing, structuring, or symbolizing surroundings'. The creation of a landscape involves the application of value systems to the categorisation, appreciation, negotiation and understanding of the spaces encountered by people as individuals, groups or whole communities. Taken to its logical extreme, there can by definition be no such thing as a 'natural landscape'; the very concept of what is 'natural' in contradistinction to what is 'not natural' is a cultural construct susceptible to redefinition at any time. As soon as something is categorised as a natural landscape, it ceases to be so because, at that moment, it has been brought into the realm of the social. Axiomatic to recognising the socially constructed nature of landscape is the appreciation that different value systems may be applied sequentially, or in parallel, to the categorisation, appreciation and renegotiation of any landscape. This constested nature of landscapes has been usefully explored by Bender (1992).

The final issue is that of process. It is sometimes assumed that the normal state for a landscape, as indeed for society generally, is a stable one. This is a view born of the translation of systems theory and steady-state modelling from the field of electronics to the social sciences. It can be argued, however, that in fact the normal state for landscapes is one of constant change, and in particular change at many different levels and at many different rates. This is one reason why no two experiences of a landscape can ever be the same. Something will always be different: perhaps something as simple as the light or the weather, or perhaps a shift in value sets and the social categories applied to what is encountered. Here the balance between physical existence and social categories is particularly important because social constructs can blind people to physical change that would be clear to an outsider. Thus a hillside that was once covered in woodland may continue to be treated, in social terms, as a wooded place even though the trees have gone. The old order will be perpetuated through such devices as myths, legends and place names, which in turn serve to stimulate memories and mental images at odds with what is observed.

These problems with the archaeological treatment of landscapes suggest that the very notion of landscape as something created and physically definable, an essentially empirical concept, traps us intellectually and prevents the wider analysis of spatial relations, social relations, social process and temporal sequence. Instead of seeing landscape as an object or a subject, perhaps we should see it as a formal and classificatory concept similar to Werlen's notion of space: 'a frame of reference for the physical components of actions and a grammalogue for problems and possibilities related to the performance of action in the physical world' (Werlen 1993: 3). Landscape in this sense becomes the socially constituted structure or web of values, categories and understandings that is imposed by a society on its surroundings at any one time – the very context of social existence.

Landscape as 'context'

There are three theoretical aspects that need to be considered in connection with the development of an archaeological approach to landscape as 'context': the conception of space, the conception of time, and the constitution and archaeological manifestation of social action.

Space

The space that can be experienced by individuals and social groups is quite different from the kind of space discussed by physical scientists. The conceptualisation, partitioning, bounding, defining and valuing of social space is the product of individual and collective socialisation and the expansion of mental as well as physical horizons. Tuan (1977) attempts to understand what is experienced through all the human senses during the development of a comprehension of space at different stages of life. He concludes that an understanding of place is essential for survival; the symbolism of place and the attachments formed by what happens in a place are crucially important. During early childhood, space is generally small scale and essentially domestic, but during later childhood and adolescence, space becomes differently conceptualised. By adulthood, an understanding of space that is shared with other members of the community is completely formed. Such understanding, however, is not really about distance or physical geography so much as about the compartmentalisation of space according to socially defined categories.

This partitioning is known as 'regionalisation', and it refers to the zoning of space according to attributed meaning. At its most generalised, regionalisation takes place in relation to routinised social practices such that certain things occur only at certain times in particular places, both timing and location being determined by social structure. By reference to socially defined categories it is possible to see space as a framework that develops into zones such as front and back, dark and light, clean and dirty, sacred and profane. The basis for the various classifications that exist is often embedded in a symbolic code or belief system, as seen for example in the cosmological ordering of space or its conceptualisation with reference to the human body, the body of a totemic beast, or the movements of celestial bodies.

Time

Time, like space, is often assumed to be theoretically unproblematic, but Bailey (1987) has argued for a duality within time, on the one hand as objective process and on the other as subjective representation. In the former an event or happening defines a duration and, when such events are chained or contingent, an order or structure. This contrasts with time as represented by concepts or units that are related to social context. As with the conceptualisation of space, time is often structured to reflect symbolic codes and beliefs and may again be tied to cosmological order.

Social action

Time and space together relate to the third element, social action. Originally articulated in the late nineteenth century by Max Weber (cf. Cohen 1968: 96) and others, the idea of social action has been developed and extended during the present century (e.g. Parsons 1951; Parsons and Shils 1951) and remains a key element of sociological theory even if its understanding is now vastly different from that of its early advocates (Giddens 1984). At its most simple, action can be seen as intentional attempts to affect or prevent change in the world. The question of intentionality is what sets action apart from the more normatively constituted concept of behaviour; with social action intentionality is prescribed within socially defined boundaries. Thus actions involve society rather than individuals alone simply because no one can stand free of social relations.

The accomplishment of social action is archaeologically manifest as material culture. The landscape itself is, however, not a passive object representing the cumulative sum of actions, but rather a set of structures and devices that, as long as they exist as socially meaningful entities, are active as agents in the prosecution of social action.

Space, time and social action provide the essential elements of a potentially powerful model of landscape applicable in the present and explorable in the past through archaeology. In it the landscape does not physically exist, although some aspects of it have visible physical expression. Rather landscape is a time-dependent, spatially referenced, socially constituted template or perspective of the world that is held in common by individuals and groups and which is applied in a variety of ways to the domain in which they find themselves.

Time–space–action models in archaeology and beyond

Time–space–action models have not yet found extensive application in archaeology. In other disciplines, the idea of landscape, although not always expressed as such, is frequently dealt with as a social or representational phenomenon. The very word 'landscape' finds its origins in artistic representation and was introduced into English from the Dutch *landskap*. For many years the word continued to refer only to pictures. Indeed, as Howard (1991: 1) has pointed out, in Britain landscapes are almost invariably imagined in elevation in a way that is close to the word's artistic origins.

In the field of human geography, ideas of time and space have been of interest for some decades, through the question of aesthetics and 'natural beauty' (Cosgrove 1989; Howard 1991: 15). Of some interest to archaeologists and sociologists is the work of Torsen Hägerstand and what has become known as 'time-geography' (Hägerstand 1975). The means of integration is, however, mechanistic and favours time and space over the contribution of social action. Giddens (1984: 116–19) has strongly criticised this approach for treating individuals independently of social settings. He argued for greater attention to overall context.

Numerous anthropological studies illuminate the way in which space is conceptualised and subdivided in a range of societies so as to produce socially meaningful places and landscapes. They also highlight the way in which material culture relates to concepts of space and place. Studies such as those of the Trobriand Islanders by Glass (1988) and the Pirá-Paraná Indians of Colombia by Hugh-Jones (1979) amplify aspects of the cross-cultural links between space, place, landscape and social action that are particularly relevant to archaeological analysis.

The categorisation of space is generally systematic and the rules that inform the understanding of each category are often founded in a received cosmology (e.g. Wheatley 1971 on ancient Chinese cities; Coe 1993: 174–90 on Mayan ceremonial centres; and Bauval and Gilbert 1994, on the pyramids at Giza). Such studies make it unsurprising that equations can be made between interpretative schemes or cosmologies and structure in the archaeological evidence. Hodder has advocated (1987) that they be considered an integral and essential part of archaeological inquiry.

It has also been argued that the categorisation of space is often 'nested' so that the same structures can be identified at several different levels, as interpretative schemes impinge on almost every aspect of life. Thus, for example, patterning in the subdivision, arrangement and meaning of space may, at the same time, be found in the decorative schemes applied to material culture, the arrangement of spaces and disposition of activities in the home, the layout of a settlement, and patterns of behaviour in the landscape as a whole. This means that if patterns can be detected strongly at one level they may also be applicable at others.

Inevitably, certain limitations inherent in the nature of archaeological data have to be taken into account when applying time–space–action models to ancient landscapes. Although individual actions and momentary events can sometimes be glimpsed, more common is evidence of repetitious action and patterning in the material culture that facilitates such actions. Equally, Bailey

(1987) has argued that the temporal index used by archaeology is not the same as that used by other social scientists because archaeology is concerned with the long term rather than the short term. The spatial categories most visible in the archaeological record are likewise those fixed by material culture through the physical structuring of space, for example in provisions to control and manipulate movement through it.

Landscape and the social use of space: Stonehenge

The Stonehenge landscape (RCHME 1979; Richards 1990; Cleal *et al.* 1995) can be viewed as an object, the most recent reshaping of its form being the construction of special tourist facilities at Stonehenge itself and the changes in the agricultural regime by the National Trust, who now own much of the farmland around the site. The Stonehenge landscape has also been treated as a subject. Four main phases to its evolution can be identified and summary maps of arrangements at each have been prepared to show what might be termed a succession of 'relict cultural landscapes' (Richards 1990: Figs 157–60; Darvill *et al.* 1993; cf. Fairclough this volume Chapter 9).

Not one of these approaches extends beyond the descriptive analysis of the archaeological remains in the Stonehenge area. To explore the broader issues of landscape as context, I take the situation in the later Neolithic/Beaker period, around 2600–2000 BC. This period is conventionally equated with Atkinson's Phase II at Stonehenge itself (Atkinson 1979: 72), or Phase 3.i in the revised chronology of the site (Cleal *et al.* 1995: 167ff).

During this period, Stonehenge itself was undergoing a period of reconstruction with the introduction of the first stone settings (the bluestone circles) in the centre of the site, replacing whatever wooden features had stood there before in a manner reminiscent of the structural sequence at many similar sites (Darvill 1987: 94). The visual appearance of the Phase 3.i setting remains speculative, although the presence of a number of cut and shaped bluestones around the site hints that it may have been more spectacular than its archaeological footprint suggests. A lintelled structure is certainly possible, and the tongued and grooved stones may suggest an elaborate focal screen of some sort. Recent work has cast doubt on the geometrical regularity of the bluestone circle as originally proposed by Atkinson, concluding that it may have been set out as a semi-circle or even a three-sided open rectangular arrangement with rounded ends (Cleal *et al.* 1995: 188). It is, however, clear that the putative entrance was elaborated with a line of up to five stones, whereas the remainder of the circuit is marked by pairs of stones. The entrance follows the midsummer sunrise axis, an alignment that had first been defined at the site during Phase 2 (*c.* 2900–2600 BC).

Stonehenge was not the only site receiving attention at this time. Much else was happening in the surrounding landscape, and Stonehenge became the focus of a tightly clustered ring of sites (Figure 8.1).

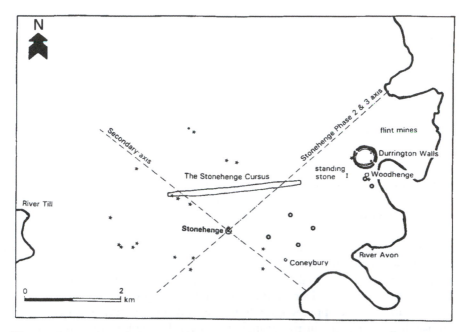

Figure 8.1 Map of the Stonehenge area, Wiltshire, showing a notional fourfold sectoring of the landscape. Solid stars indicate beaker burials.

The Stonehenge Cursus was built about 1 km north of Stonehenge in about 2700 BC and continued in use for some centuries.[3] Its 3 km extent makes it one of the longer cursus in Britain. The two ends are intervisible on the ground, but because its central section crosses a shallow valley, the ends are not always visible from within. At the east end is an earlier long barrow. The cursus is not straight, but subdivisible into three straight segments set slightly off-line to one another (Stone 1948; Christie 1963).[4] A standing stone (the Cuckoo Stone) projects the line of the cursus eastwards. This stone was removed from its original position in relatively modern times. Beyond this again, on the same alignment, is Woodhenge, probably established around the middle of the third millennium BC (Cunnington 1929; Wainwright and Evans 1979).

North of Woodhenge is Durrington Walls, a massive henge-enclosure 490 by 468 m with opposed entrances to the northwest and southwest. The southeastern entrance opens to the River Avon. Radiocarbon dates suggest that the enclosure was first constructed in 2800–2400 BC. Of more or less the same date is Coneybury Henge to the southeast of Stonehenge. This small henge is 40 m along its greatest axis (Richards 1990: 109–58). Other monuments in the area include pits containing grooved ware, and burial monuments associated with beaker pottery. Some flint mines are known to the northwest of Durrington Walls, and are also probably of this period.

A number of the monuments just mentioned incorporate within their structure a regular alignment towards the northeastern skyline. The precise descriptive geometry of these structures is far less important than the regularity of their orientation and the fact that the orientation itself can be related to the rising position on the skyline of the midsummer sun. Woodhenge, Coneybury and Stonehenge show this arrangement very clearly.

However, the midsummer sunrise axis is not the only axis visible. There are four key positions in the solar cycle: midsummer sunrise and sunset, and midwinter sunrise and sunset. The angle between midsummer sunrise and midwinter sunrise is about 80°, the same as between midwinter sunset and midsummer sunset (Hoyle 1972: 25–7). The midsummer sunrise has the same alignment as the midwinter sunset, even though the two events happen opposite each other on the skyline as visible from the centre of the circle; the same applies to the midwinter sunrise and the midsummer sunset. Thus the primary, and dominant, axis at Stonehenge is the southwest to northeast line reflected in the orientation of the entrance. The secondary axis, roughly southeast to northwest is hard to identify because of the rather partial plan of the Phase 3.i settings. However, there are two unusual features belonging to this phase, WA3654 to the northwest and WA2321 to the southeast. Both are large stoneholes, and WA2321 at least stands immediately outside the defined line of the bluestone setting; the same may apply to W3654. The axis created by these two features bisects the main axis at 80° near the notional centre of the bluestone setting (see Cleal *et al.* 1995: Fig. 80). This second alignment is well represented at Durrington Walls, where it is marked by the alignment of the two entrances into the enclosure.

This simple solar scheme, more or less in the form of a cross with a primary and secondary axis, can be projected onto the landscape outwards from Stonehenge to create two potentially significant axes defining four quarters. It is not suggested that this arrangement was itself actually marked in the countryside around Stonehenge; the partitioning of space was more akin to a cognitive map that was known to those who created the landscape. However, one direct manifestation may be represented in the way that the projected alignments intersect the line of the cursus at the places where its width changes slightly: it is narrower at the ends compared with the central part.

This linear quadruple partitioning of space also finds expression in the distribution of monuments and artefacts. The eastern sector contains sites (Durrington Walls and Coneybury Henge) whose artefactual remains suggest feasting. Table 8.1 shows that over 85 per cent of grooved ware findspots lie in the eastern sector, while 62 per cent of beaker pottery findspots lie in the north and west sectors. Peterborough pottery is widely scattered through all the sectors. The highest proportion of beaker age burials (58 per cent) lie in the western sector (Table 8.2), while henges and henge enclosures are found only in the eastern and southern sectors. Flint-mining and extensive flint-knapping are known only from the eastern and southern sectors.

Individual sites around Stonehenge also perpetuate one or other of the significant solar axes. As already noted, Durrington Walls has the southeast

Table 8.1 Findspots of principal late neolithic/early bronze age ceramics

	North	East	South	West
Peterborough pottery	4	5	8	6
Grooved ware	0	12	2	0
Beaker pottery	7	4	8	13

Table 8.2 Incidence of selected monument classes

	North	East	South	West
Henges	0	2	0	0
Henge-enclosure	0	1	0	0
Flint mines	0	1	0	0
Beaker burials	1	2	2	7

to northwest axis, while Coneybury has a midsummer sunrise axis adjusted to accommodate the different configuration of hills. Both Stonehenge and Durrington Walls are known to have beaker age burials on the outside of their boundaries (Evans 1984), interestingly both to the right of anyone approaching the entrance from the outside (cf. Figure 8.1). At Woodhenge, a human burial marks the centre of the site where the two axes notionally cross (Cunnington 1929). An analysis of the spatial distribution of finds from the postholes that formed the timber structure within Woodhenge revealed a high incidence of pig bones, and the presence of carved chalk cups in the eastern sector suggests feasting (Pollard 1992). The eastern sector also seems to have attracted the deposition of items such as scrapers, knives, arrowheads and bone pins in the Southern Circle at Durrington Walls (Richards and Thomas 1984: 202).

A common set of arrangements and alignments seems to have significance in the landscape as a whole, in the layout and design of sites of the period, and in the motifs used for the decoration of some objects.

An interest in solar events seems to be common to all these patterns, and provides the only uncontested astronomical alignments at Stonehenge itself. However, solar cosmology also occurs in non-beaker contexts. Richards (1993) has examined its implications with reference to a range of dwellings, sacred structures, henges and tombs in Orkney. He found a high correspondence between architectural form and a putative central place of the sun in the lives of the communities who built the structures. In Ireland, the developed passage graves of the Boyne Valley embody solar alignments: Newgrange, for example, was constructed so that the midwinter sunrise illuminated the central chamber (O'Kelly 1982: 122–5).

Archaeologically it is impossible to get at the stories and myths that lie behind the solar cosmologies, even though the main element is visible. The farthest we can go is perhaps the development of patterns of association from the disposition of monuments in the landscape and objects in the monuments. In this case, two sectors, the eastern and western, seem especially significant. We may speculate that the eastern sector was strongly associated with sunrise, new beginnings, life, light, fertility, feasting, water and the earth, whilst the western sector was linked with sunset, endings, death and darkness. Table 8.3 provides a provisional summary of these associations in schematic form. Movement between and within different areas may, at certain times at least, have been strictly controlled. The Stonehenge Cursus has a very interesting position in this landscape as it runs through the western, northern and eastern sectors. Its terminals lie firmly in the east and west sectors, but, as already noted, there are subtle changes in its alignment at exactly the points where the principal axes partitioning the landscape pass through it. Seen in the context of a social landscape, the cursus may be construed as a defined route between two key sectors: perhaps even a pathway for the soul from life to death.

Conclusions

Exploring the social dimensions of landscape opens up many new and exciting possibilities for the archaeological analysis of the social use of space. The question remaining is how such approaches relate to the understanding, conservation and management of archaeological remains, and to the definition of meaningful landscape units. There are two main aspects to this question: the academic and the practical.

In academic terms, it is now widely recognised that the traditional functionalist position based only on the consideration of 'man–land relationships'

Table 8.3 Provisional late neolithic cosmological scheme

	(NORTH) Earth Cold	
(WEST) Sunset Death Burial places Darkness Winter Fire	Sun Hearth Transformation	(EAST) Sunrise Life Settlements Light Summer Water Feasting
	(SOUTH) Sky Warm	

is inadequate, and that more sophisticated social models are needed for further interpretation. A space–time–action model such as that outlined here provides one starting point for new kinds of investigation. It is recognised that the picture of the Stonehenge landscape is still imperfect and that there is much analysis still to be undertaken. The focus should move from a preoccupation with the distribution of archaeological features and structures towards using such information as the starting point for exploring the distribution of actions and the way in which individuals and groups dealt with encounters and experiences.

   In practical terms, there are two main points. First, in order to preserve and manage the archaeological resource, it is necessary to think simultaneously on two scales. At the level of individual sites and monuments, existing measures for their definition and protection are probably already adequate. But there is a larger question that should be addressed which concerns the definition of academically justifiable units relevant to the understanding of past communities in relation to the idea of landscape as context. Second, whatever units are eventually arrived at, and bearing in mind that these will not be the same in area or form between periods or regions, their definition will depend on the recognition of archaeological patterning. This is unlikely to bear any resemblance to land use or islands of preservation favoured for the protection and management of other aspects of landscape. Indeed, in order to achieve worthwhile approaches to conservation and management in this sphere, theoretical approaches to the social use of space and the practicalities of modern management must come together.

Notes

1 Since this chapter was written, a number of studies have been published which illustrate a range of related approaches to ancient landscapes and suggest that a number of researchers have been independently exploring alternative perspectives on the analysis of ancient landscapes. Tilley (1994), for example, utilises phenomenology; Thomas (1993) explores the hermeneutics of space with reference to megalithic tombs; while Richards (Richards 1993; Parker Pearson and Richards 1994) emphasises the structuring or ordering of space through cosmological schemes.

2 For a more complete account of landscape structuration in all four of the phases referred to here, see Darvill (1997).

3 One radiocarbon date is available: 2878–2502 BC (2150 ± 90 BC OxA-1403).

4 The alignment of the cursus west-southwest to east-northeast means that on the equinox in March and September the sunrise and sunset can be viewed along its length; but, since the idea of the equinox is generally considered to be a recent observational phenomenon, it is here disregarded as being of significance for prehistoric patterning.

References

Atkinson, R.J.C. 1979. *Stonehenge*. Harmondsworth: Penguin.

Bailey, G. 1987. Breaking the time barrier. *Archaeological Review from Cambridge* 6, 5–20.

Bauval, R. and A. Gilbert 1994. *The Orion Mystery*. London: Heinemann.

Bender, B. 1992. Theorising landscapes, and the prehistoric landscape of Stonehenge. *Man* 27, 735–55.

Bender, B. 1993. Introduction: landscape: meaning and action. In *Landscape: politics and perspectives*, B. Bender (ed.), 1–18. Oxford: Berg.

Christie, P.M. 1963. The Stonehenge Cursus. *Wiltshire Archaeological Magazine* 58, 370–82.

Cleal, R.M.J., K.E. Walker and R. Montague 1995. *Stonehenge in its Landscape: twentieth-century excavations*. London: English Heritage.

Coe, M. 1993. *The Maya*. London: Thames & Hudson.

Cohen, P.S. 1968. *Modern Social Theory*. London: Heinemann.

Cosgrove, D. 1989. Geography is everywhere: culture and symbolism in human landscapes. In *Horizons in Human Geography*, D. Gregory and R. Walfred (eds), 118–35. London: Macmillan.

Cunnington, M.E. 1929. *Woodhenge: a description of the site as revealed by excavations carried out there by Mr and Mrs B.H. Cunnington, 1926–7–8*. Devizes: George Simpson.

Daniels, S. and D. Cosgrove 1988. Introduction: iconography and landscape. In *The Iconograpy of Landscape*, D. Cosgrove and S. Daniels (eds), 1–10. Cambridge: Cambridge University Press.

Darvill, T. 1987. *Prehistoric Britain*. London: Batsford.

Darvill, T. 1997. Ever increasing circles: the sacred geography of Stonehenge and its landscape. In *Science and Stonehenge*, B. Cunliffe and C. Renfrew (eds), 167–202. London: British Academy and Royal Society.

Darvill, T., C. Gerrard and B. Startin 1993. Identifying and protecting historic landscapes. *Antiquity* 67, 563–74.

Evans, J.G. 1984. Stonehenge – the environment in the Late Neolithic and Early Bronze Age and a beaker-age burial. *Wiltshire Archaeological Magazine* 78, 7–30.

Evans, J.G., S. Limbrey and H. Cleere (eds) 1975. *The Effect of Man on the Landscape: the highland zone*. London: Council for British Archaeology.

Foley, R. 1981. Off-site archaeology: an alternative approach for the short-sighted. In *Pattern of the Past: studies in honour of David Clarke*, I. Hodder, G. Isaac and N. Hammond (eds), 157–84. Cambridge: Cambridge University Press.

Fox, C. 1933. *The Personality of Britain: its influence on inhabitant and invader in prehistoric and early historic times*. Cardiff: National Museum of Wales.

Giddens, A. 1984. *The Constitution of Society*. Cambridge: Polity Press.

Glass, P. 1988. Trobriand symbolic geography. *Man* 23, 56–76.

Hägerstand, T. 1975. Space, time and human conditions. In *Dynamic Allocation of Urban Space*, A. Karlqvist (ed.), 3–14. Farnborough: Saxon House.

Hodder, I. 1982. *Symbols in Action*. Cambridge: Cambridge University Press.

Hodder, I. 1987. Converging traditions: the search for symbolic meanings in archaeology and geography. In *Landscape and Culture*, M. Wagstaff (ed.), 134–45. Oxford: Blackwell.

Howard, P. 1991. *Landscapes: the artists' vision*. London: Routledge.

Hoyle, F. 1972. *From Stonehenge to Modern Cosmology*. San Francisco: W.H. Freeman.

Hubert, J. 1994. Sacred beliefs and beliefs in sacredness. In *Sacred Sites, Sacred Places*, D.L. Carmichael, J. Hubert, B. Reeves and A. Schanche (eds), 9–19. London: Routledge.

Hugh-Jones, C. 1979. *From the Milk River: spatial and temporal processes in Northwest Amazonia*. Cambridge: Cambridge University Press.

Limbrey, S. and J.G. Evans (eds) 1978. *The Effect of Man on the Landscape: the lowland zone*. London: Council for British Archaeology.

O'Kelly, M.J. 1982. *Newgrange: archaeology, art and legend*. London: Thames & Hudson.

Parker Pearson, M. and C. Richards 1994. Ordering the world: perceptions of architecture, space and time. In *Architecture and Order: approaches to social space*, M. Parker Pearson and C. Richards (eds), 1–37. London: Routledge.

Parsons, T. 1951. *The Social System*. London: Routledge & Kegan Paul.

Parsons, T. and E.A. Shils (eds) 1951. *Toward a General Theory of Action*. New York: Harvard University Press.

RCHME 1979. *Stonehenge and its Environs: monuments and land use*. Edinburgh: Edinburgh University Press.

Richards, C. 1993. Monumental choreography: architecture and spatial representation in late neolithic Orkney. In *Interpretative Archaeology*, C. Tilley (ed.), 143–78. Oxford: Berg.

Richards, C. and J. Thomas 1984. Ritual activity and structured deposition in later neolithic Wessex. In *Neolithic Studies: a review of some current research*, R. Bradley and J. Gardiner (eds), 189–218. Oxford: British Archaeological Reports.

Richards, J. 1990. *The Stonehenge Environs Project*. London: English Heritage.

Schama, S. 1995. *Landscapes and Memory*. London: HarperCollins.

Stone, J.F.S. 1948. The Stonehenge Cursus and its affinities. *Archaeological Journal* 104, 7–19.

Thomas, J. 1993. The hermeneutics of megalithic space. In *Interpretative Archaeology*, C. Tilley (ed.), 73–98. Oxford: Berg.

Tilley, C. 1994. *A Phenomenology of Landscape: places, paths and monuments*. Oxford: Berg.

Tuan, Y.F. 1977. *Space and Place*. Minneapolis: University of Minnesota Press.

Wainwright, G.J. and J.G. Evans 1979. The Woodhenge excavations. In *Mount Pleasant, Dorset: excavations 1970–1971*, G.J. Wainwright (ed.), 71–4. London: Thames & Hudson.

Werlen, B. 1993. *Society, Action and Space: an alternative human geography*. London: Routledge.

Wheatley, P. 1971. *The Pivot of the Four Quarters: a preliminary enquiry into the origins and character of the ancient Chinese city*. Edinburgh: Edinburgh University Press.

9   *Protecting time and space: understanding historic landscape for conservation in England*

GRAHAM FAIRCLOUGH

Introduction

The work that this chapter describes was carried out within the framework of conservation and archaeological heritage management, as part of a widening of English Heritage's responsibilities for the conservation, preservation and improved public enjoyment of the historic environment. Our approach started from a need to understand the dynamics and historic development of the present-day countryside, rather than necessarily to understand better the detailed functioning and appearance of landscapes in the past. Its objective was to develop methods of understanding the current landscape in archaeological terms and of assessing its historical value, in order to guide the myriad day-to-day decisions that continually change the face of the land. Some of these decisions are those of farmers, foresters and agriculturalists, others are taken by local government as part of the land-use planning system, still others by national or European government. Assessment methods need to be able to influence all of these.

The approach I describe is therefore rooted in the practicalities of land management at a strategic level (see Fairclough 1995). Whilst academic research or historical understanding were not its first aims, there has throughout been a concern to ensure that archaeological perspectives underpin the work. In this it differs from other very well-developed methods of landscape assessment in England that focus on issues such as an area's ecology and its role as habitat, its scenic quality and visual character, sometimes in terms defined by artistic sensibility or present-day cultural perception (e.g. Countryside Commission 1993). All of these approaches have value. Some are referred to later and many of their techniques can be adapted for historic landscape.

The assessment of historic landscape character, however, needs to be based on its own distinctive techniques, and for this archaeology offers one of the best perspectives. The full chronological sweep of English landscape formation and the complete breadth of the social, economic and political systems and processes represented can perhaps be explored only through archaeology.

Historical documents have a part to play, though only for relatively recent periods and with a disproportionate bias toward the modelling of the landscape by the aristocracy or the State and Church in one of their several forms. Place-name evidence has its separate role, too. This again is restricted to historic periods, even if slightly less recent, but at least it introduces a view of landscape formation that is closer than the documentary evidence to the economic base of society, reflecting, for example, basic patterns of land use or culture.

Philosophy and definition

The English landscape is nowhere completely natural. Even fields or moorland can be shown to display the changing forces of human action, whether through ancient soil-impoverishment or the creation of new soils, or through more recent industrial activity. There are very few areas that are now not in sight of some type of built structure, if only an isolated farmhouse or field wall. Only geology may be unchanged, and even the impact of this has sometimes been over-ridden by cultural imperatives.

The landscape is, then, an artefact, a human product, and its evolution is visible to us in its material remains. Archaeology is therefore the proper discipline for the study of its historical dimension. Archaeological method brings us to the heart of landscape history, to the social processes that created chronologically specific land use and territorially based activity. Landscape is an artefact also in the further sense that 'it' is created in perception, and is not merely an assemblage of material objects. Landscapes, whether viewed in historic terms or not, and particularly when seen as an ideational construct, can be said at one level to exist only when thought, seen or experienced (e.g. Shanks 1993: 141–3). In other words, landscape is culturally determined in two ways – because it is the product of human, i.e. cultural, decisions about land use, and because it is understood through a set of perceptions that are themselves culturally – and historically – conditioned.

The landscape has also been used to pass on messages and rules from one generation to its successors. This intergenerational role of the landscape, especially but not exclusively in pre-literate societies, ought not to be underestimated. Social or functional activities do not take place in isolation from their environment (cf. Graves 1994: 160). The 'grammar' of the landscape has been an important vehicle for guiding the way in which it has been used. The spatial structures for living that people have created, whether on the scale of buildings or landscape, are simultaneously a framework for social behaviour and its product (Fairclough 1992). Our landscape is in this sense far from 'natural': it has over time been organised in a variety of ways that have guided subsequent land-use decisions, registered and confirmed ownership and created group identity (Fairclough 1994: 68). Just as we can study past society at the level of objects or sites through its material remains, so can landscape-scale analysis allow us to understand the political and social fabric of a society, the economic relationships between people, the social negotiation of space and privilege, the allocation and division of power. Environmental and geographical determinants will have some part to play in this analysis, but our knowledge of human capacity, even in the Neolithic, to change and control the landscape should warn us of the need not to over-estimate their influence. Having said that, some human action in the past created new environmental constraints (just as they threaten to in the future). It is a mistake to assume that past cultural systems have always been sustain-able and in harmony with their environment.

Historic landscape also needs to be approached through three general concepts that establish, at least in England, most of the landscape's historical character. These are:

- historical process,
- time-depth, and
- complexity with diversity.

The first is an analytical tool for exploring explanation and causality. Histor-ical processes include the effects of modes of inheritance as well as more functional processes such as early prehistoric clearance or the subsequent long-term grazing of upland areas, the impact of industry or the effects of ideology, as when landscapes are created to validate power, status and social hierarchy. The second concept, time-depth, brings greater appreciation of the combi-nations of change and continuity that create the historic landscape, and, in the context of landscape assessment, focuses rather more on description. The third concept, complexity and diversity, must be used at both descriptive and analytical levels in order to identify historic landscape character or to char-acterise an area's historic dimension and origins. Complexity is perhaps the most significant aspect of historic landscape.

The English approach to historic landscape assessment is based on a number of assumptions about the idea of historic landscape. The first is that any part of the English landscape retains, to some degree, traces of its past, and includes the material remains that allow an archaeological understanding of that past. In other words, the whole landscape is historic and susceptible to archaeo-logical study as one of our main sources of evidence for the past. From this assumption arises a second: that any area of landscape will have a long evolu-tion, and many successive episodes or chronological horizons are likely to leave their mark on it. The historic landscape therefore needs to be read, interpreted and perceived in terms of two dimensions – of *time* (temporal change and continuity) and *space* (patterning at various scales).

Time

There are very few simple, single-phase landscapes in England. Almost all are both multi-period and multi-functional. The southwest uplands of Dartmoor or Bodmin, far from being the 'relict prehistoric landscapes' of recent archaeological myth, are complex landscapes that have passed through three or four main time-phases (early agriculture, late prehistoric animal grazing or sacred space; temporary medieval resettlement in the climactic/demographic optimum; and recent widespread reclamation and enclosure). At any of these stages agriculture, religion, politics or industry can all be read in the land-scape, and remnants of all episodes, themes and functions are still visible.

In a similar way, the large-scale enclosure landscapes of seventeenth- or eighteenth-century eastern England retain elements of earlier quite different ways of farming the land collectively, just as elsewhere (e.g. Northumber-land) medieval hamlets with fields were succeeded by large, free-standing farmsteads in the period of rationalisation in the eighteenth and nineteenth centuries. Other landscape areas demonstrate long-standing continuity, such as the anciently enclosed and long-settled areas known from at least the first millennium BC in, say, Cornwall. This is a fundamental continuity, however, and much change of detail in land use, settlement and building style has skated over its surface. This too is legible in today's countryside.

A third assumption is therefore that landscape evolution is the result of many different historical or archaeological processes. Some operate together, for example in those areas where quite distinct ways of life, such as farming and lead-mining in the Pennine hills, co-existed in the Medieval period. Here part-time and thus small-scale farmers produced distinctive settlement, land-use and field patterns. Others have operated sequentially, as different landscapes have replaced their predecessors. This complexity may be described in several ways or through several theoretical models, but all need to encompass historical processes and causes, change and development through time, and the full range of components and types that comprises the material remains of past landscapes.

Complexity can in many cases be recognised in the site-based components of the landscape. Deserted medieval villages, for example, testify simultane-ously to the cultural and social processes of three periods: those processes that created them, those processes that led to abandonment when settlement patterns, economic needs and land ownership changed, and those processes that have allowed their continued visibility in the landscape ever since. Prehis-toric burial mounds and earlier ritual sites demonstrate, in a similar way, space set aside for religious or ideological reasons, but, in spatial terms, they also give us insights into the broader territorial division of the land. Their survival is evidence for subsequent land use up to the present day.

This phenomenon, which could be termed 'transparency' (the way in which some historic land uses allow earlier landscapes to remain visible, albeit some-times in a subtly different form), is perhaps one of the least considered aspects of the archaeology of historic landscape. It is linked to the concept of time-depth but it is rarely made explicit, probably because a great deal of landscape study is period-specific and in such studies the through-time aspects of the landscape – survival, visibility and transparency – tend to be taken for granted, overlooked, or seen as interpretative challenges to be overcome on the way to reconstructing a particular episode. The term 'transparency' is used here to denote the potential for earlier chronological horizons (whether they are relict features or still-working components of the landscape, perhaps in a new use) to remain visible beneath later, different, land uses and landscape. Transparency can take several forms. Relict features of the prehistoric landscape in the English uplands (e.g. Cheviots, Dartmoor) are highly visible because later use of the land for livestock grazing is low-key, and thus transparent to the underlying field systems. Post-medieval enclosed grass farmland in Northamptonshire is transparent to the earlier medieval ridge-and-furrow open fields that are highly visible, and until recently well preserved, within them; by contrast, it is almost completely opaque without excavation to prehistoric or Roman archaeology. In this sense, ridge-and-furrow, or deserted village earthworks, are post-medieval sites – they were medieval in their living form but as landscape features they are post-medieval. The recent agricultural changes that have introduced large-scale, over-intensive ploughing are destructive of ridge-and-furrow, but it is at the same time newly transparent to even earlier sites and landscapes, even if these survive only as flint scatters and crop-marks.

The destruction of earlier phases can thus be selective. Ridge-and-furrow may be destroyed, but other elements of the medieval pattern (such as the medieval village itself, sometimes wholly or partly deserted, and its related tracks, roads and woodlands) can survive side-by-side with surviving components of the successor enclosure landscape. Equally, vestiges of ridge-and-furrow may survive only below ground, perhaps with environmental evidence. It is thus not enough to speak of the transparency of late land use as if this is a single attribute. Later landscape horizons may be transparent or opaque in varying degrees to different elements of the landscape. It is this characteristic of the historic landscape that in part at least gives rise to the metaphors of 'patchwork' and 'palimpsest'.

Successive land uses can also differ widely in their effect on archaeological and historic survival. Some recent work in Kent attempted to analyse the historic character of a sample of the county's landscape (Chadwick forthcoming). Kent is a county where, even allowing for wide local variations, both public and specialist perception tend to identify the most historic areas of the landscape as those that retain structures of the relatively recent past, the fourteenth to eighteenth centuries AD. The principal features are hedges, woodland, particular building styles and settlement types, and a few diagnostic archaeological sites. The mix of these attributes varies, but the focus is on the Later Medieval and early modern periods, and on essentially 'rural' structures. These landscapes are rarely called 'relict' (perhaps they are not deemed 'old' enough by non-specialists), and what is being recognised as historic is not past landscapes as much as the transparency of more recent landscape overlays which have allowed visible survival of earlier features. There is a tendency to regard Kent as an 'old' county purely on the basis of quite recent remains, as if the land in the fifth century AD had been a clean slate waiting for Anglo-Saxon farmers to start afresh (e.g. Everitt 1986).

Reasons for this can be found (Kent's prehistory is rich but it manifests itself only through individual sites, often below ground with little direct landscape trace), but this invisibility of Kent's earlier landscape history is largely created because much of the county's late medieval and later land use is opaque to the remains of earlier episodes. Kent's prehistoric landscape, hidden from view below later hedges and fields, is not usually labelled 'relict', which suggests that the term 'relict landscape' has been used by archaeologists not as short-hand for survival *per se*, but for the easy visibility and a particular limited form of survival of some types of archaeological data.

Paradoxically, modern arable farming in Kent has introduced a new land-scape that is opaque to the medieval enclosed landscape but which turns out to be newly transparent to earlier prehistoric landscapes. As hedges are removed and farmland, even sometimes pasture, is deep-ploughed, the familiar medieval or later landscape disappears, and a shadow of earlier landscapes becomes more visible through air photographs and other techniques, rather as bronze age burial mounds rise out of shrinking peat in the eastern Fens. This is a destructive process, both of prehistoric below-ground archaeology and obviously of enclosure landscapes, but it does highlight certain concep-tual issues. Parts of east Kent have now lost their 'historic' landscape of hedges and roads, and are no longer commonly or easily regarded as historic. Yet these are the areas of the county where the extent and scale of prehistoric settlement and landscape change can be most readily recognised and which reveal most clearly the long-term antiquity of human interaction with the Kentish environment, and the intricacies and complexity of the landscape's historical development. This leads us to think more carefully about the precise nature of what we call historic landscape: it cannot be defined purely in terms of the visible or the physical, but needs to be interpreted at a conceptual and invisible level too. 'Historic landscapes' do not exist, they are merely sets of ideas in the mind of the interpreter and the analyst. As such, processes and causes may be as important as physical features, and perception as crit-ical as definition or identification.

The complex relationship between past and present should not either be unduly simplified, as it is misleading to confuse visible survival with historic importance or even, by implication, with landscape history itself. The dichotomy of continuity and discontinuity is a dangerous oversimplification. It is reasonable to study the discontinuation of an activity or land use, as has happened throughout history, but this should not be extended to the landscape itself. ICOMOS for World Heritage proposes a distinction between 'relict' and 'continuing landscapes', but this is a false distinction because all landscapes are to one extent or another 'continuing' landscapes. As seen already, some chronological horizons of the landscape can disappear for a time (perhaps for thousands of years) only to reappear in different, perhaps impoverished and devalued but still legible, forms under later land use. It is within these complex effects of successive land use that archaeological and other forms of survival, and therefore the historic landscape itself, will exist.

The interaction can take many forms, not merely those of continuity or discontinuity. Land use can cease, but later start again in identical or similar forms; it can be cyclical, and interleaved with other land uses. It will always experience continual modification to varying degrees, up to a scale of change at which the archaeological remains might suggest discontinuity, or at which no archaeology can survive.

An approach that isolates a single-period landscape from its chronological context, perhaps by identifying the 'best' examples of a typology, will ignore time-depth, which is one of the prime attributes of the English landscape. It may well deny the deeper chronological structure of the landscape, and specifically the long-standing and unavoidable influence of previous land users and their activity. It will risk devaluing later changes in the landscape in order to highlight the oldest (or vice versa). If nothing else, the conservation of historic landscape should seek to avoid the trap of anachronistic, time-sliced repair (e.g. the removal from buildings of later fabric in order to attempt the recreation of original form). For this reason, any approach to the understanding and conservation of the historic dimension of the landscape ought to begin with the present landscape, rather than with reconstructing earlier phases. It must also always bear in mind that, now as in the past, landscapes cannot be read precisely like a building. The metaphor of landscape as artefact breaks down if it is taken too far because historic landscape above all is a conceptual construct rather than a 'real', definable, bounded, tangible 'thing'. It is a way of seeing, not an object to be recorded in any straightforward, positivist way. It cannot therefore be catalogued or listed in the same way as simpler sites or buildings, and in England at least we do not propose to prepare national lists for protection.

It was clear to English Heritage early in its recent work that a register of special areas would not meet all, or even most, of our requirements. Notably, it would not take account of local distinctiveness, nor would it enable communities to form their own informed view on value. It would not allow the flexibility of management and conservation that is necessary to reflect local circumstances and to leave room for continuity of change. Finally, as outlined above, it would underplay the great complexity and variety of the landscape for both understanding and management. Registers of selected sites are concerned with definable objects and discrete, usually small, sites; using comprehensive systems of classification, they select the 'best' sites from a known, and ultimately finite, population of sites. Landscape requires a much wider and flexible response. The landscape needs continued active management as much as protection if it is to survive in good condition. Conservation needs to be applicable at varying scales, and to be subject to current and changing practical needs. It needs to take account of the complexity and variety involved in understanding and assessing the landscape, with its infinite range of types and combinations of landscape features. It also needs to achieve co-ordination with other overlapping conservation values, in order to influence the active land use and management that are essential to conservation.

This need to understand the whole landscape in historic terms underlies English Heritage methods and is a guiding principle of the recent Council of Europe Recommendation on Cultural Landscape Areas. This recommends that policies for the conservation of the cultural landscape should be set within the context of general landscape policy, alongside visual and ecological considerations. It defines cultural landscape as the product of the combined action over time of both natural and human factors, a product that thus testifies to the past and present relationships between people and their environment and which moulds local culture and diversity. It recommends as a starting point the comprehensive analysis of the whole landscape, whether at local, regional, national or international level.

Space and scale

All the issues just described concern the temporal dimension of the landscape: time-depth, the succession of different ways of using and living on the land, and the desirability (during most periods of the past) of following well-tried traditions of social organisation and land management. This is the *palimpsest* of the landscape, a term that Maitland borrowed from palaeography to describe the record of landscape development that exists on English Ordnance Survey maps. The idea is deeply buried in popular consciousness, which regards the English landscape as an age-old but timeless, almost natural, creation. Archaeology is, of course, always concerned first and foremost with change through time. It is the concern with the passage of time, particularly over very long periods, that above all distinguishes our discipline from other social sciences and humanities.

There must always be a second dimension, however, of spatial patterning at various scales. Human society exists in space. A culture is often defined by itself and by outsiders in territorial terms. Space, its negotiation between individual and society and its social meaning, is often at the heart of the many relationships of gender, hierarchy and subsistence that create social structures. Much sophisticated analysis has been carried out on spatial patterning at site or settlement level. Landscape study should be based to an even greater extent on spatial analysis, but there are, in Britain at least, relatively few examples of well-developed practice.

Spatial analysis of historic landscape can rest on many supports or concepts. One approach to understanding historic landscape character is by reference to three ways of looking at space at landscape scale – through local (or site) articulation, territorial inter-relationship and regional patterning. Each factor can be analysed in a single area, but all three should be viewed in terms of different scales. At each scale it is also possible to take into account questions concerned with landscape's territorial dimension: the many ways in which change and continuity are combined through time, the role of historic processes and causation and, perhaps particularly at the regional scale, the way in which what we call historic landscape depends significantly on current perception. It is essential throughout to keep in mind the inherent complexity of the landscape and its origins, and the diversity of ways in which its development can now read itself into the landscape.

These three levels of analysis – articulation, territorial inter-relationship and regional pattern – can be usefully located on a scale from local to regional or, in archaeological terms, from site and feature through system and territory to regional diversity (see, for example, Darvill *et al.* 1993). On these scales, assessment or judgement will be based at site level largely on data, at the middle level on archaeological models, and towards the regional patterning end of the scale increasing emphasis will be laid in most cases on broader perceptions.

Articulation

This level of scale expresses the ways in which individual features or components of the landscape cohere to create landscape-scale complexes, both in today's landscape (taking into account palimpsest and time-depth as well as space) and in past landscapes. The latter allows succession and change to be considered, and demonstrates the ways in which one generation's landscape, though historically and culturally specific in itself, was always fitted within an inherited framework, confirming that actions are pre-conditioned socio-environmentally.

A broad view should be taken of the range of features that contribute, through this local articulation, to the overall landscape. 'Conventional' archaeological sites are most obvious, but palaeo-environmental deposits of all kinds have an explanatory role. Local patterns of historic land cover (the reservation of land for common grazing, or the creation of spiritual space) are often both one of the articulated elements and also the matrix within which that articulation can be read. The principal framework will usually be the land and field divisions of hedge, bank or wall, the connection of road and track and the scale of settlement and farmstead hierarchy. Some landscape components (such as major strategic land-use decisions on moor and heath transhumance, the upper levels of settlement hierarchy) contribute to site-level articulation in a more limited way but come to the fore at the mid-scale (territorial) level of inter-relationships between systems.

Territorial inter-relationships

A more abstract level of archaeological interpretation offers understanding of the way in which local landscape systems, i.e. locally articulated sites, interlock at a more regional level. These are the relationships that demonstrate, for example, the long-distance symbiosis of urban centres, or of central sites like long barrows or henges, with their catchment areas and hinterlands, or of satellite farmsteads around hillforts and villa estates around Roman cities, or the sophisticated market hierarchy of, say, London and East Anglia in the Late Middle Ages. Attempts by today's planners to understand what sustainable development means for the industrialised, urban world may also come to fall into this category. It also allows other land-use relationships to be explored, such as the common use of distant upland areas by lowland farming

communities, mirroring on a regional scale a parish or township's reservation of common resources for wood and grazing at the parish edge. The
dissolution of these long-distance ties can also create historically specific landscapes, when dependencies adapt from being specialised grazing areas to being
self-supporting independent townships.

Complexity is added to spatial relationships by change through time, for
example in the ebb and flow of regional economic systems in climax periods
when territories expand in response to demographic trends. There have
also been nationally imposed landscape changes that register best at this mid-
scale, not only the most recent such as twentieth-century agricultural change
and suburbanisation, sixteenth- to eighteenth-century industrialisation, or
eighteenth-century Parliamentary enclosure driven by a rationalised approach
to farming, but earlier trends too. The 'invention' of capitalism, whether in
the eighteenth, fifteenth or fourteenth century AD (or even earlier), produced
similar landscape development in quite different contexts, and these can be
noted at the mid-scale. The second-millennium BC landscape change that
can be identified through England, and which seems to reflect the invention
of individual land ownership and control, is another apparently top-down or
external cultural change that cannot easily be read at site level, but begins to
become apparent at this mid-scale.

Regional or national patterning
This third level, finally, is a term that attempts to summarise a way of reading
meaning into regional diversity. It need not exclude considerations of local
character, but its main focus is to demonstrate broad patterns over large tracts
of land. These patterns can be read in past landscape, but they are more valuable for English Heritage's purposes when considered against the backdrop
of the present-day landscape. This allows the patterning of landscape to reflect
survival and condition, which are of course conditioned by historical factors.
It also connects with ways of valuing and using the landscape that are not
primarily archaeological but are historically and culturally conditioned, such
as visual and scenic assessment, emotional and artistic attachment and concern
for the natural world.

Methods and practice

Although much archaeological research now operates in England at a landscape scale, it is principally driven by research agendas whose objectives lie
beyond the study of either landscape history or the present landscape. Few
can readily be connected to English Heritage's need for conservation-oriented
information, or can help to drive the planning system, guide land management decisions or shape and create future landscapes. To help remedy this,
our work has recently taken two complementary directions. The first is joint
work by English Heritage with the Countryside Commission to enable their

method of landscape assessment to incorporate ideas of historic landscape character, and fully to encompass the principle that the landscape is the sum of all its parts and that its value is historic or cultural just as much as scenic or ecological (Countryside Commission 1994a, 1996). The second is English Heritage's development of its own system of historic landscape assessment (Fairclough *et al.* forthcoming).

Both programmes have been based on our awareness that approaches to landscape assessment designed originally for the scenic landscape can also meet the requirement for historic landscape assessment (Countryside Commission 1993). The Countryside Commission's ideas on the historic landscape are making a significant contribution to the Countryside Character Programme (an innovative project to map landscape character at national level as a framework for more local work), and to the work of Countryside Steward-ship (a major environmental incentive programme for farmers). There are a number of other current research projects in England that are trail-blazing a more conservation-oriented approach to landscape.

Two national projects are underway, one to characterise the country's settlement patterns, the second to produce a national map of landscape character in all its aspects. The first project starts from a basic and well-accepted division of England into general zones of nucleated and dispersed settlement, but will move beyond this to define smaller, locally homogeneous zones that exhibit a specific combination of settlement type. A map has been prepared by superimposing the surviving shape of the historic settlement pattern onto base maps of topographic and geographic determinants. The work is still in progress, but it is producing zones that are defined by historic settlement trends, that also reflect at least some of the historical complexity and diversity of the landscape other than settlement type. Historically or culturally specific patterns of settlement should relate to particular types of social or economic organisation, or (in material terms) the distinctions between zones should also be visible in other ways, for example through field remains.

Settlement is but one facet of the historical dimension of the landscape. Several other aspects will be examined in a larger project that is being carried out in England by the Countryside Commission. This Countryside Character Programme aims to produce a national map of regional landscape character as the basis for subsequent more detailed local characterisation and assessment of the landscape. It has been tested in southwest England but is now being extended to the whole country (Countryside Commission 1994b).

The first stage will be a mapping exercise using about fifteen variables, many of which either reflect the pre-conditions for historical development (such as geology and topography) or are themselves based on historic or archaeological attributes of the landscape. The latter are being designed within an archaeological framework to develop simple patterning (at least in terms of the detail and level of generalisation needed to produce a national map). The variables include field and hedge patterns, basic settlement patterns, industrial history and the character of an area's industrial archaeology.

Both these projects and others, such as a national map by English Nature of 'Natural Areas', which aims to give a base for a national overview of the country's ecology, have in common a procedure that hinges on the *characterisation* of the archaeology and history of an area, whether considering the whole study area or subdivisions based on factors such as historic land use, topography and land cover. Characterisation involves the wide understanding of landscape and its development which can be gained from an analysis of the *inter-relationship* of components linked to the topography and visual aspects of an area. In historic characterisation, it is necessary to consider all periods and all aspects of past human activity. It is a process that requires data collection and analysis based firmly upon clear understanding of objectives, scope and methods; it can itself lead to definitions of current issues for management and future change, to evaluation for priorities or levels of protection, and to the formulation of management strategies. Characterisation is, in addition, the means of allowing historic and archaeological considerations to be integrated with the conservation of the natural environment through the idea of culturally defined biodiversity; it also allows easier connection with the sustainability debate by virtue of helping to define environmental carrying capacity, indicators of environmental health, condition and of change, and objectives related to both time-scale and reversibility.

Characterisation forms the central stage of the historic landscape assessment method that English Heritage's work is producing and starting to test. This has up to ten tasks or topics which in practice are normally grouped into five broad stages:

1 to ensure that the procedure is tailored to the conservation needs of agriculture, development plans etc., of the particular study by defining first both scope and method;
2 to collect appropriate data for later characterisation by establishing the context or baseline, defining components and preliminary analysis;
3 to extract an assessment of the landscape as a whole from this data by characterisation;
4 to establish the framework and priorities of politics and policy;
5 to establish a strategy for action through the formulation of recommendations.

Characterisation, as described above, is the central task of this process, essential to an understanding and appreciation of the whole landscape. The main aims are to:

- form a view of what gives today's landscape its historic character, and *why* and *how* it does so;
- take account of the processes of cultural landscape formation, and their results through time (continuity and change);
- identify the combined contribution of all elements and components to the landscape;

- understand landscape's evolution, including the succession of landscape type and form in a given area;
- recognise the inter-relationship of features visually, spatially etc., whether or not they were originally contemporary.

One vital aspect is the choice of spatial unit, because this determines matters such as the level of detail that is suitable and practical given the potential depth of archaeological data for the particular type of characterisation required. The national map referred to earlier will provide kilometre-square resolution at a national scale, followed by assessment using a closer regional or sub-regional level of detail. A county-based assessment, although it must still be of a generalised nature, is of course able to reach greater levels of detail.

A very good example of a county assessment that uses the most recently developed techniques has just been completed for Cornwall, in southwest England. The whole of the county's historic landscape has been assessed and characterised using not kilometre-squares, but individual fields and land parcels. This is a fine level of detail, but one that it has been possible to sustain by virtue of three main factors:

1 the prior existence in retrievable form of abstracted, generalised data (e.g. on place names, habitat and ecology, which can be a very responsive indicator of past land-use patterns, and of archaeological sites of every type and date recorded in the county SMR);
2 a high level of expertise among archaeologists working within the county; and
3 the decision, though mapping at the level of individual fields, nevertheless to characterise and map in terms of areas, themes and broad patterns, rather than of sites. No aspect of the primary characterisation, for example, depends on site or point-data.

The mapped historic landscape types and zones can if necessary form the basis for a more topographic division of the landscape into areas defined by historic character. Alternatively, the archaeological character of each zone, once they have been defined, can be considered in greater detail and by more interpretative means. This can be through description, cataloguing or by means of graphic ways of demonstrating the difference between zones: using, for example, the matrix developed by Lambrick (1992). Earlier attempts to develop methods for such work have identified alternative approaches. The English Heritage historic landscape project includes two experimental projects designed to find new methods (Fairclough *et al.* forthcoming). One of these projects, in County Durham in northern England, used a superficially similar technique, but with greater emphasis on land cover and farming techniques, and with a different approach to the use of expert opinion. Another approach in Oxfordshire used sample data to produce a landscape-scale interpretation of 'indicator-features' (such as types of field enclosure, managed woodland and deerparks, hillforts, villages, moats and houses) which, combined with broad-scale topographic analysis, produced historic character subdivisions of the county. Other counties are beginning to develop similar approaches, but, if a generally applicable model exists, it is unlikely that it has yet been found. One common, inevitable, aspect, however, will be the need to work on a large canvas.

It is only at the local scale that point-data, i.e. site-based information, can readily be used at the characterisation stage. Such applications of the approach will probably tend to have relatively simple, focused objectives. They might be conducted in spatial terms, to understand a single area such as a farm or estate for management purposes, or to make an environmental assessment of a site such as Stonehenge. Site-based information may also be useful in the characterisation of a single period and theme, such as for English Heritage's cataloguing of those historic battlefields that can still be interpreted or appreciated in the landscape. In the latter case, specially adapted methods of landscape appraisal were used to identify the main components of the landscape that influenced the battle, and that still survive, with the additional identification of the battlefield landscape's amenity value (a further example of how landscapes do not exist until created in perception).

A different application of techniques of historic landscape assessment, with a very real conservation and planning-linked objective, has also been tested in one of the UK's World Heritage Sites, the Roman frontier zone of Hadrian's Wall. This was part of a wide-ranging review of the management of the World Heritage Site designed to strengthen and clarify the protective measures appropriate to the Wall's status and importance. Similar work is also underway at Stonehenge and at Avebury.

The Hadrian's Wall project included two aspects that relate to the historic landscape, one drawing its data from analysis of the Roman and later sites and features that might be regarded as creating a 'Wall landscape', the other using the Wall and its components as the focus for defining visual zones, or viewscapes, that might be said to define the Wall. Both approaches sought to define a set of appropriate territories within which to set management and protection policies; both used techniques of landscape assessment.

The project first defines discrete areas of distinct landscape character (primarily based on geology and topography but recognisable too in historic terms such as patterns, settlement and historic land use). Onto this base-map is superimposed a tripartite definition of zones. The inner, or archaeological, core defines the geographical area within which the main archaeological remains exist – the 'Wall' itself. This core sits within a direct visual envelope that is the immediate setting of the Wall – those areas within which the Wall is seen and physically experienced and over whose larger landscape evolution it has exercised greatest influence. Finally, very much broader zones can be defined within which the Wall remains a real presence, but in a less direct way – long-distance vistas, for example. In protective terms, each of these zones requires a different level of control and management, but together they constitute a solid definition of that elusive term, setting. This approach has been firmly rooted in present-day perceptions and uses the surviving remains of the Wall in the present landscape as its focus. A more rewarding task archaeologically might be to attempt to reconstruct viewscapes and settings in more strictly Roman terms, and to define the core, visual envelope and larger setting in terms of the Wall in its original sense: views from or to full-height Wall and tower ramparts, or zones defined by fort or milecastle hinterlands.

Conclusion

The various aspects of English Heritage's work on historic landscape have been driven by a desire to be able to understand the landscape's historical development and character as a means to its better conservation, protection and management. We have concluded that selective approaches to designation, however well they might work for sites, are not appropriate for the whole landscape, and that conservation is likely to achieve more, including a living relationship with the present and the future, if based on a characterision of the whole landscape.

Although driven by pragmatic, conservation-led aims, our work has nonetheless taken a strongly archaeological approach, and a number of important and helpful theoretical models or approaches are emerging. We are presently at the stage of testing these more thoroughly on the ground. Since this chapter was first written towards the end of 1994, for example, English Heritage has continued to refine and develop its ideas, notably on the importance of perception rather than identification, and of ideas rather than objects, in constructing the historic landscape. These ideas will be set out in the report of the English Heritage landscape project (Fairclough *et al.* forthcoming). Work has also continued on the English Heritage settlement map, and on the Countryside Character Programme. The Cornwall project is in its second phase, working towards the publication of its results in a methodological context, and similar projects have been carried out in Avon and Derbyshire and are in planning elsewhere. This continuing work confirms that the ideas outlined earlier in this paper have sound practical applications in conservation and landscape management.

References

Chadwick, P. Forthcoming. Historic landscape pilot in Kent. In *Yesterday's Landscape, Tomorrow's World*, G.J. Fairclough, G. Lambrick and A. McNab (eds). London: English Heritage.

Council of Europe 1995. The Integrated Conservation of Cultural Landscape Areas as part of Landscape Policies. Recommendation No. R(95)9.

Countryside Commission 1993. *Landscape Assessment Guidance* (CCP423). Cheltenham: Countryside Commission.

Countryside Commission 1994a. *Views from the Past: historic landscape character in the English countryside* (Draft Consultation Paper). Cheltenham: Countryside Commission.

Countryside Commission 1994b. *The New Map of England – a celebration of the south west landscape*, CCP444. Cheltenham: Countryside Commission.

Countryside Commission 1996. *Views from the Past: historic landscape character in the English countryside*, CCWP4. Cheltenham: Countryside Commission.

Coupe, M. and G.J. Fairclough 1991. Protection for the historic and natural landscape. *Landscape Design* 201 (June), 24–30

Darvill, T. 1987. *Ancient Monuments in the Countryside*. London: English Heritage.

Darvill, T., C. Gerrard and W. Startin 1993. Identifying and protecting historic landscapes. *Antiquity* 87, 563–74.

DOE 1994a. *UK Action Plan for Biodiversity*. London: HMSO (Cmd. 2428).

DOE 1994b. *Sustainable Development: the UK strategy*. London: HMSO (Cmd. 2426).

Everitt, A. 1986. *Continuity and Colonisation: the evolution of Kentish settlement*. Leicester: Leicester University Press.

Fairclough, G.J. 1992. Meaningful constructions – spatial and functional analysis of medieval buildings. *Antiquity* 66, 348–66.

Fairclough, G.J. 1994. Landscapes from the past: only human nature. In *The Ecology and Management of Cultural Landscapes (Landscape Issues 11, 1)*, P. Selman (ed.), 64–72. Cheltenham: Department of Countryside and Landscape.

Fairclough, G.J. 1995. The sum of all its parts: an overview of the politics of integrated management in England. In *Managing Ancient Monuments: an integrated approach*, A.Q. Berry and I.W. Brown (eds), 17–28. Mold, Clywd: Clywd Archaeological Services and ACAO.

Fairclough, G.J., G. Lambrick and A. McNab (eds) Forthcoming. *Yesterday's World, Tomorrow's Landscape: the English Heritage landscape project*. London: English Heritage.

Graves, P. 1994. Flakes and ladders: what the archaeological record cannot tell us about the origins of language. *World Archaeology* 26, 2.

Lambrick, G. 1992. The importance of the cultural heritage – towards the development of a landscape integrity assessment. In *All Natural Things: archaeology and the green debate*, L. Macinnes and C.R. Wickham-Jones (eds), 105–26. Oxford: Oxbow.

Shanks, M. 1993. *Experiencing the Past*. London: Routledge.

10 The role of caste hierarchy in the spatial organisation of a village landscape in the Dry Zone of Sri Lanka

Nilu Abeyaratne

Although this chapter is strictly speaking more ethnographic than archaeological in content, I argue that the durability of cultural dispositions that I describe is sufficiently great for them to leave their imprint in the archaeological record. I attempt to identify the mechanisms that have enabled a number of cultural practices to endure over several centuries, providing useful analogies for ethno-archaeological research on settlements in Sri Lanka.

The usefulness of ethnographic studies of village settlements in Sri Lanka for settlement archaeology lies, as Eva Myrdal-Runebjer (1990, 1994a, 1994b) has pointed out, in a continuum in ecological conditions, modes of subsistence and levels of productivity and technology that have remained to some extent unchanged for generations and possibly even for centuries. In addition, the landscapes of village settlements, particularly in the Dry Zone, have been and continue to be largely constrained by the environment or the micro-ecosystems to which they belong.

The relevance of this chapter for the theme of creating landscapes lies in its focus on the role played by social power or social domination, generated in this case mainly by caste hierarchy, in the processes of spatial organisation of a village landscape. Caste is, and has been since ancient times, a ubiquitous element of social stratification and hierarchy in the Indian subcontinent and Sri Lanka. In the Sri Lankan case, the relevance of caste to archaeology can be seen in references in both literary and epigraphic sources (Codrington 1938; Panavitana 1970; Karunatilake 1988) which show that the history and transformations in the caste system in this country seem to have taken place during the accumulation of the archaeological record from at least the Early Historic period onwards (600/500 BC to AD 300). Given the dearth of published data and the lack of literary and epigraphic data for the proto-Historic period (900–600 BC), it is not yet possible to push the historical trajectory of caste in Sri Lanka any further. It is, however, highly likely, judging by the picture of a sedentary agrarian society with social stratification and craft specialisation that is emerging from archaeological excavations, that a hierarchical order not unlike that of a caste system may have existed

(Deraniyagala 1972, 1986, 1990; Coningham 1990; Allchin and Coningham 1992; Karunaratne 1994; Karunaratne and Adikari 1994).

Based on Leach's borrowing of Hutton's definition, a caste can generally be defined as an endogamous group, located within a hierarchical gradation of groups that are distinguished from each other in terms of hereditary service duties or traditional occupations, with varying degrees of purity and pollution that place restrictions on intercaste commensality. Many different Sinhalese castes, especially in the rural milieu, to this day retain varying degrees of utilitarian and/or ritual function.

The literature on caste in Sri Lanka is fairly extensive and every ethnographic study of village society has dealt with the implications of caste for social organisation and stratification. The importance of caste as a variable in the spatial location of dwellings within village sites and in some cases the existence of different caste-based hamlets is referred to, though never attributed more than passing significance, in ethnographies (e.g. Ryan 1958; Leach 1961; Yalman 1967; Brow 1978; Perera 1985).

Bulankulama, the village settlement that is the subject of this chapter, is located in the North Central Province of Sri Lanka in close proximity to the largest town in the province, Anuradhapura (Figure 10.1). Anuradhapura was the capital of Sri Lanka from the fifth century BC to the tenth century AD. Bandara Bulankulama is situated barely 1 km away from the ancient citadel of Anuradhapura and borders on the Abhayagiriya monastic complex which is one of the oldest and most important Buddhist monasteries in Sri Lanka. The site of the Bulankulama village has been identified as an ancient settlement site by a study of surface pottery that, at a cursory glance based on the Anuradhapura Citadel typology (Deraniyagala 1972), can be attributed to the Middle Historical period (AD 300–1250). A detailed exploration of this site as well as a test excavation will be carried out in the near future.

In this analysis the village of Bulankulama is considered as a 'social space'. I follow Bourdieu's framework for analysing the social world as a multidimensional space, constructed on the basis of principles of differentiation or distribution which can confer force or power on their possessors (Bourdieu 1991a, 1991b). I explore the cultural processes that contribute to the accumulation of the habitual patterns of behaviour that Bourdieu terms 'habitus', which leave their imprint upon the material record of village life.

The Bulankulama landscape possesses all the features of the archetypal Dry Zone *purana* village (village of ancient origin) as identified in both nationalist ideology and older and more recent 'ethnographic' writings (Ievers 1899; Codrington 1938; Leach 1961), with its *vava* (tank), *dagaba* (temple) and *yaya* (paddy fields). Bulankulama, however, differs in many ways from the idealised 'agricultural republics' that British administrators such as Ievers eulogised in late ninteenth-century descriptions of the North Central Province, as the British had named the area known as the Nuvarakalaviya during the Kandyan period (from the sixteenth century AD to 1815).

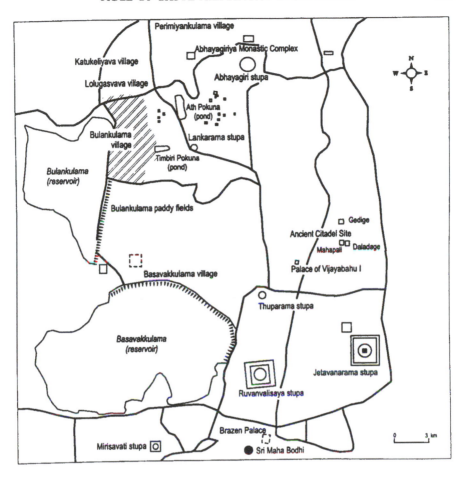

Figure 10.1   Location of Bandara Bulankulama within the sacred area of Anuradhapura.

In contrast to the archetypal village of the region, Bulankulama (Figure 10.2) today has two Buddhist temples. The Lankaramaya, which is part of the Atamastana (the eight sacred places of Anuradhapura), was built in the first century BC by King Valagamba. The chief incumbent of this temple belongs to the Siam Nikaya, which to this day offers *upasampada* (higher ordination) only to members of the *govigama* (cultivator) caste. The Lankarama *dagaba* was reconstructed and a new pinnacle placed in 1937 under the patronage of the Bulankulama family. The other temple in the village, the Tripitaka Dharmayatana, was built fairly recently on part of the Bulankulama family cemetery. This temple now belongs to the chief incumbent of a well-known temple in Colombo, the Polwatte Dharmakirtiramaya, which belongs to the multi-caste Ramanya Nikaya. This temple reflects the caste heterogeneity of the village and, according to some villagers, came into being

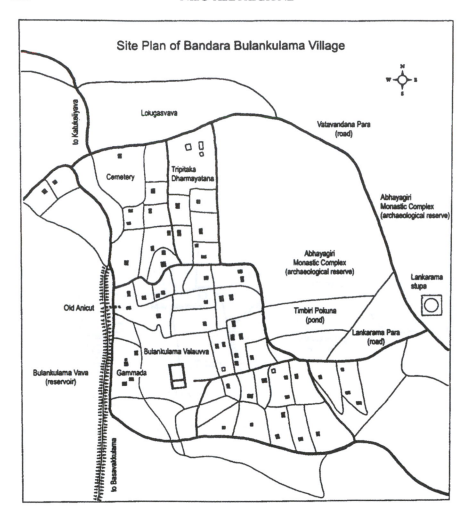

Figure 10.2   Plan of Bandara Bulankulama village.

because the lower castes were being subtly excluded from the Lankaramaya. The Lankaramaya still has members or affines of the Bulankulama family who reside in close proximity to the village among its most important *dayakayas* or lay devotees.

Bulankulama is atypical of the region in a second regard, because it is a *nindagama* or feudal holding of a *radala* (noble) lord granted by the king for services to the state. Part of the *valauvva* which, judging by its architecture, is about 300 years old and belongs to the Kandyan period, is still the residence of some members of the Suriyakumara Vannisingha Bulankulama family, who claim to be one of the oldest families in the world. They claim to be the descendants of two princes who accompanied, as its custodians, a branch of the Sacred Bo-tree that was presented by the Emperor Asoka to the king of Lanka in the third century BC. Although documentary evidence of the antiquity of this family cannot be traced back further than the sixteenth century, the trustee of the Atamastana, of which the most important is the Sacred Bo-tree shrine, is still chosen from among them. The *valauvva*, which was reputed to have comprised seven *mada-midulas* (inner courtyards) even in the early years of this century, was and to a lesser extent still is the nucleus of the village both spatially and socially. Today most of the original *valauvva* building is in a bad state of repair, with parts of it in imminent danger of collapse. However, despite a decline in their fortunes, the members of the Bulankulama family still command a degree of deference from the villagers who still use traditional terms of respect when referring to them. In addition, a major source of the family's economic capital remains intact in their continued ownership of the 22 ha of paddy land (rice fields) watered by the Bulankulama tank. Most members of the family are, however, absentee landlords whose lands are cultivated for them by sharecroppers (*anda goviyas*) from the village.

Only three families in the village, including the *vel vidane*, are guaranteed access to fields for cultivation annually as sharecroppers. A majority of the population of the village by necessity are therefore landless wage labourers, working during the cultivation season as agricultural labourers, as casual labourers at nearby Cultural Triangle Projects or, in a few cases, as permanent municipal labourers in Anuradhapura.

It is clear that, by virtue of the exhalted caste status of its inhabitants, the *valauvva* still retains its pre-eminent position in the village. The caste heterogeneity of the village has, however, greatly influenced the settlement patterns of the rest of the villagers. In the course of carrying out fieldwork, I was surprised to find that most villagers were very quick to identify themselves as outsiders and recent settlers from villages in districts situated at some distance from Anuradhapura, like Kurunegala (121 km distant), Kegalle (153 km) and Kandy (138 km). This trend was puzzling in the light of a tendency among Sinhalese villagers to identify closely with their village of origin which, along with their caste and 'house of origin' or names of ancestors who held important office from which the surnames (*vasagama* or *ge* or *gedera* name) of specially the *govi* caste are derived, is an important part of their social identity (Pieris 1958). Great pride is usually taken in being able to say that one is an original settler in a village. Many of these families in Bulankulama, however, continued to maintain close ties with their natal villages. Other members of their families often join them in taking up residence in the village, while marriage partners are invariably sought from their natal village or from neighbouring villages. Despite the availability of space towards the centre of the village, most of the newcomers have settled some distance away from the *valauvva* and the *gammada* (traditionally the central cluster of houses in the village), close to the boundaries of the village, even occupying parts of the Abhayagiriya monastic complex. A majority of these people, among whom are a few descendants of former servants of the *valauvva*, claim to be *honda minissu* (good people) of the *govigama* caste as opposed to the older settlers in the village who are low caste.

The *gammada*, which is located between the *valauvva* and the northern end of the tank bund near the paddy fields, is an important feature of Bulanku-lama. With the exception of the *valauvva*, it houses the dwellings of the oldest settlers in the village. Despite its location at the centre of the village, the *gammada* is relatively sparsely populated with only twenty out of a total village population of 232 residing within it, in four of the fifty-seven houses that make up the village. The reason is as follows. The inhabitants of the *gammada* have long been linked to the Bulankulama family as retainers or domestic servants and claim to be the illegitimate children of a grand-uncle of the present inhabitants of the *valauvva*. They belong to the *rada* or washer caste, which is located towards the bottom of the Sinhala caste hierarchy and has, apart from its utilitarian function, an important ritual role in all major life-cycle rituals where they play a vital part in purifying polluting situations and individuals (Yalman 1960). The hypergamous union between a *rada* woman and a *radala* man is quite consistent with Kandyan attitudes towards concu-binage, where sexual contact with a lower-caste individual is less damaging to a man than to a woman, who is considered internally polluted and thus endangers the purity of her kin group (see Pieris 1956; Yalman 1960). In the case of hypergamous concubinage, the caste status of offspring remains that of the low-caste mother. The attitude of the older settlers is consistent with this view as they are quite willing (especially those of the older gener-ation) to identify themselves as low-caste *rada minissu*, thereby legitimating their social domination by higher-caste individuals, especially by the Bulanku-lama family.

M. Hendrick, who at 83 is the oldest member of this community, claims that fifty years ago, there were about fifty small houses of *rada*-caste villagers clustered close together in the *gammada*. Almost all of them worked for the *valauvva* and carried out such tasks as cultivating the fields, domestic chores and fishing in the *vava*. According to Hendrick, most of these people left the village looking for better prospects elsewhere and have mostly settled in *rada* villages belonging to the same *varige* or subcaste. Hendrick's house is the oldest house in the village. It is about eighty to 100 years old and relatively large and well built for a wattle and daub structure. Hendrick said that it was built by his father for his mother, who was a servant of the *valauvva*. In keeping with their caste and the strictures of the *varige sabha* or caste council that was in operation at the time, Hendrick and his three brothers married *rada* women. Hendrick's own wife was from Nelunkkaniya, a village in the Anuradhapura district that belongs to the same *varige* as Hendrick. The villagers who are settled in greatest proximity to the *gammada* are of the same caste and related through blood and marriage to the four households in the *gammada*. The only case of cross-cousin marriage in the village was between Hendrick's daughter and a son of Pinhamy, Hendrick's brother-in-law who had come to live with his in-laws after his sister's marriage.

There has never been intermarriage within the village between those of the washer caste and other villagers. This is a clear indication of the deficiency in social capital among the older settlers and explains their desire to distance the location of their houses. The degree of social contact between the *gammada* families and other villages also seems low. On my visits to the *gammada* I have never seen any of the more recent settlers paying informal visits to these families. Even my guide and chief informant, who is of dubious but higher caste status (of the caste of *vahumpura*, cooks or jaggery palm sugar makers, but pretending to be *govigama*), claimed that she was visiting the *gammada* only because she had to show me the way.

According to several informants, all the *rada* families previously lived in the *gammada* in a row of attached rooms, disparagingly likened to the line rooms of plantation workers, which housed each nuclear family unit. Two small rooms are all that remain of this structure. These are now the home of the widow Mary Nona, who is the only member of her family who still fulfils her ritual role as a washerwoman at the puberty rituals of girls in the village and in surrounding villages. In the course of the last five to ten years, however, some members of the *gammada* families have moved out from the centre towards the periphery of the village. Senehalatha, the widow of M. Simon, the elder brother of Hendrick, lives on the other side of an abandoned paddy field that separates the *gammada* from the rest of the village. Alice, a widowed daughter of Mary's, moved out of the *gammada* partly, according to her own account, because she wanted to build a better house with a garden but mostly because living in the *gammada* with its persistent association with low caste status would affect her children's marriage prospects. Another of Mary's daughters, Gunawathi, who married an outsider of uncertain caste status, lives outside but in close proximity to the *gammada*. Somawathi, Mary's youngest daughter who married a man of good *govigama* stock, lives towards the outer edges of the village.

Due to her husband's higher caste status and his position as something of a local leader, the location of Somawathi's house was not a matter for controversy in the village. However, dissatisfaction was expressed at the movement of the other *rada* families out of the *gammada*, especially by those of considerably higher caste status, who complained of a corresponding lack of deference towards better-caste villagers. It was clear that these people approved of the former isolation or segregation of lower castes in the *gammada*. These statements, which mirror an antagonistic point of view from a position in 'social space', clearly show an enduring disposition in the need for the possessors of the social capital of higher caste status to ensure that the symbolic capital or the recognition of their status remains effective within the village.

Some other people in the village, especially those of known low or dubious caste status, often claim that caste is no longer important in their lives. Such claims are made by Sinhalese across the class spectrum and in both urban and rural settings. Such assertions are, however, often belied in practice by the low levels of interaction between high- and low-caste people. A good example of the persistence of caste ideology can be seen in the praxis associated with the *gammada* in Bulankulama in the persistent association with low caste status and the actual spatial segregation of some of the older families and the active resistance of others to this situation. All these are important indicators of the ways in which caste relations can and will continue to shape the 'social' and physical space of this village settlement. For in Bulankulama, as in other villages with a mixture of different castes (see Ryan 1958; Perera 1985), the social capital of high caste status is affirmed or denied through settlement patterns within a village landscape. In this context, attempts by people of lower caste status to overcome a very obvious sign of their lack of social capital are recent and not entirely successful.

In Bourdieu's terms, a social space can be called a field of forces or a set of objective power relations that are not reducible to the intentions of individual agents, or even to direct action between agents, to the extent that the properties chosen to construct a space confer power or capital upon their possessors (Bourdieu 1991b: 229–30). Capital or power defines the chances of profit or success in a given field, and every field and sub-field has a particular kind of capital that is current, or a power or stake in that field. The powers active in the different fields are economic capital (the ownership of property, money, means of production etc.), cultural capital (cultural knowledge which can be used as a resource of power by individuals and social groups to improve their position within the social class structure), social capital (membership in social groups and the profits that can be appropriated by the strategic use of social relations in order to improve one's position) and, lastly, symbolic capital. The latter type of power is the prestige, reputation and fame generated by the recognition and legitimisation of economic, cultural and social capital when deployed in appropriate spheres (fields) of social life (Bourdieu 1991b: 230). The efficacy of symbolic power, i.e. the misrecognition by agents of the arbitrariness of the hierarchical relations of power in which they are embedded and thus their legitimation of power and those who wield it, rests on a foundation of shared beliefs, or a common system of evaluations (Thompson 1991). The privileged position held to this day by the *govigama* (the cultivator caste), especially in the political and cultural spheres in Sinhalese society, is a good example of the effective operation of symbolic power based on a tacit acceptance of caste ideology.

This chapter has focused upon the deployment of social capital, in this case the capital that accrues from caste group membership within the 'social space' of the village. According to Bourdieu, the position of a given agent in the social space can be defined in and by the positions (s)he occupies in the different fields, i.e. their location in the distribution of the powers that are active in each field (Bourdieu 1991b: 230). The distribution of agents in the social space is determined by the overall volume of the capital they possess (measured by their effectiveness in the social world) and the composition of this capital or the relative weight of the different kinds of capital in the total set of their assets. Groups of agents occupying similar positions, being placed in similar conditions and submitting to similar types of conditioning, therefore, have every chance of holding similar dispositions (habituses) and interests, thus producing similar practices and adopting similar stances and a shared world view (Bourdieu 1991b: 231).

In trying to relate the concept of 'social space' to physical space, we can see that there is no perfect fit, but, as Bourdieu points out, almost everywhere it is possible to see a tendency towards segregation, with people close to each other in social space tending, by choice or necessity, to be close together in geographical space. However, people who are distant in social space can also encounter each other and enter into interactions in physical space. This type of interaction, which Bourdieu calls strategies of condescension, generally serves to reinforce social distance and preserve hierarchical structures. Such strategies are best seen in Bulankulama in the patron–client relations between the members of the *valauvva* who belong to the *radala* (the highest aristocratic sub-caste of the *govigama*) and other villagers from whom they differ in terms of both caste and class status.

In my use of data from Bulankulama, collected both through participant observation and in the course of structured and unstructured interviewing, I adopted a broadly hermeneutic approach that combines my observations of the spatial organisation of the village and daily social interaction between its inhabitants with interpretative statements made by various members of the different caste groups within it. Collecting information about caste is far from easy and requires great tact and subtlety.

In analysing the data collected from Bulankulama, I have focused on Bourdieu's assertion that 'sociology has to include a sociology of the perception of the social world, that is, a sociology of the construction of the world-views which themselves contribute to the construction of this world'. In relating world views or points of view to social space, Bourdieu draws attention to the existence of different or even antagonistic points of view, 'since points of view depend on the point from which they are taken, since the vision that every agent has of space depends on his or her position in that space' (Bourdieu 1990: 130).

Caste group membership can therefore be recognised as a cultural disposition with the capacity to endure for several generations and even centuries. Given the antiquity of the caste system in Sri Lanka, the identification of a spatial dimension in its operation, which is detectable at the macro-site or village level, is most helpful when one is trying to understand aspects of the social organisation of a community that inhabited a particular site in the past. However, it must be added that the caste analogy cannot be tested as long as settlement excavations in Sri Lanka are confined to test pits and no village-level site is completely excavated.

References

Allchin, F.R. and R. Coningham 1992. Anuradhapura citadel archaeological project: preliminary report on the third season of Sri Lanka–British excavations at Salgaha Watta, July–September 1991. *South Asian Studies* 8, 157–67.

Bourdieu, P. 1990. Social space and symbolic power. In *Other Words: essays towards a reflexive sociology*, M. Adamson (trans.), 123–39. Cambridge: Polity Press.

Bourdieu, P. 1991a. On symbolic power. In *Language and Symbolic Power*, J.B. Thompson (ed.), G. Raymond and M. Adamson (trans.), 163–70. Cambridge: Polity Press.

Bourdieu, P. 1991b. Social space and the genesis of classes. In *Language and Symbolic Power*, J.B. Thompson (ed.), G. Raymond and M. Adamson (trans.), 229–51. Cambridge: Polity Press.

Brow, J. 1978. *Vedda Villages of Anuradhapura: the historical anthropology of a community in Sri Lanka*. Seattle: University of Washington Press.

Codrington, H.W. 1938. *Ancient Land Tenure and Revenue in Ceylon*. Colombo: Ceylon Government Press.

Coningham, R. 1990. Anuradhapura citadel archaeology project – British sub project Anuradhapura Salgahawatta preliminary report 1989–1990. *Ancient Ceylon* 9, 23–8.

Deraniyagala, S.U. 1972. The citadel of Anuradhapura 1969: excavation in the Gedige area. *Ancient Ceylon* 2, 48–169.

Deraniyagala, S.U. 1986. Excavation in the citadel of Anuradhapura: Gedige 1984, a preliminary report. *Ancient Ceylon* 6, 39–47.

Deraniyagala, S.U. 1990. The proto- and early historic radiocarbon chronology of Sri Lanka. *Ancient Ceylon* 12, 251–92.

Ievers, R.W. 1899. *Manual of the North Central Province*. Colombo: Government Press.

Karunaratne, P. 1994. A brief report of the excavation at Ibbankatuva, a proto- and early historic settlement site. In *Further Studies in the Settlement Archaeology of the Sigiriya-Dambulla Region*, S. Bandaranayake and M. Mogren (eds), 104–9. Colombo: PGIAR.

Karunaratne, P. and G. Adikari 1994. Excavations at Aligala prehistoric site. In *Further Studies in the Settlement Archaeology of the Sigiriya-Dambulla Region*, S. Bandaranayake and M. Mogren (eds), 54–62. Colombo: PGIAR.

Karunatilake, P.V.B. 1988. Caste and social change in ancient Sri Lanka. In *Studies in the Social History of Sri Lanka*, A. Liyanagamage (ed.), 1–30. Colombo: Social Scientists' Association.

Leach, E. 1961. *Pul Eliya*. Cambridge: Cambridge University Press.

Myrdal-Runebjer, E. 1990. Ethno-archaeology to dissolve the orientalist spectre: studies of the processes of the basic field of production. *Ancient Ceylon* 9, 139–50.

Myrdal-Runebjer, E. 1994a. Premodern Sigiriya region: an ethnoarchaeological perspective. In *Further Studies in the Settlement Archaeology of the Sigiriya-Dambulla Region*, S. Bandaranayake and M. Mogren (eds), 226–37. Colombo: PGIAR.

Myrdal-Runebjer, E. 1994b. Food procurement: labour processes and environmental setting. In *Further Studies in the Settlement Archaeology of the Sigiriya-Dambulla Region*, S. Bandaranayake and M. Mogren (eds), 240–62. Colombo: PGIAR.

Paranavitana, S. 1970. *Inscriptions of Ceylon (vols 1, 2)*. Colombo: Department of Archaeology.

Perera, J. 1985. *New Dimensions of Social Stratification in Rural Sri Lanka*. Colombo: Lake House Investments Ltd.

Pieris, R. 1956. *Sinhalese Social Organisation*. Colombo: The Ceylon University Press Board.

Ryan, B. 1958. *Sinhalese Village*. Miami: University of Miami Press.

Thompson, J.B. 1991. Editor's introduction. In *Language and Symbolic Power*, J.B. Thompson (ed.), 1–31. Cambridge: Polity Press.

Wickramanayake, S.S.K. 1984. *An Historical Introduction and Some Documents Pertaining to the Nuwarawewa and Bulankulama Families.* Colombo: Department of National Archives.

Yalman, N. 1960. The flexibility of caste principles in a Kandyan community. In *Aspects of Caste in South India, Ceylon and North-West Pakistan*, E.R. Leach (ed.), 78–112. Cambridge: Cambridge University Press.

Yalman, N. 1967. *Under the Bo Tree.* Berkeley: University of California Press.

11 The anatomy of dispossession: a study in the displacement of the tribals from their traditional landscape in the Narmada Valley due to the Sardar Sarovar Project

ASHISH CHADHA

Introduction

After independence, India embarked, under the leadership of Jawaharlal Nehru, on an ambitious plan to wrench the country free of British imperialism and to assert its autonomy. Greatly impressed by Stalinist reforms in the Soviet Union, Nehru introduced similar five-year plans in order to develop and modernise the country by building huge dams, power plants, steel plants and, later, nuclear power plants. These development projects have made India one of the most powerful countries in the Third World but have caused the displacement and dislocation of about 5 million people, a number equal to the population displaced during partition of the subcontinent in 1947. The victims were never party to the planning of the projects that would render them homeless and dispossess them of a landscape that they had held for generations. Among the worst culprits were the big dams, proclaimed as 'Secular Temples' of the independent country by Nehru, of which India is the largest manufacturer in the world.

Tyre, automobile and petrochemical plants spring up with official sanction throughout the country, leading to a cultural and spiritual dislocation on a large scale. Flooding of paddy fields in rural areas of Orissa, Tamil Nadu and Andhra Pradesh, for prawn cultivation by multi-national companies, has caused an irreversible transformation of the landscape. Traditional fisher people throughout the coastal areas in India are today forced to seek new occupations because their fishing waters are now exploited by mechanised fishing boats, denying them their regular catch. Mechanised fishing boats exhaust all the catch through their faster but unsustainable fishing practices, which will eventually lead to total dispossession of the landscape of a great majority of the traditional fish workers of India. Most of the people who have been displaced due to these projects have yet to be acquainted with the benefits of development. They have not even been offered proper rehabilitation. Today in the town of Jabalpur in Madhya Pradesh, for example, once self-sustaining farmers are forced to live in slums and to pull rickshaws to earn their livelihood, after the Barghi Dam displaced them.

Other development projects have also caused dispossession. A public-sector petrochemical plant, in the Raigad district on the coastal belt of Maharashtra, for example, has polluted the atmosphere of the neighbouring tribal and non-tribal villages to such an extent that today the villagers are forced to sell their land and move into the sprawling metropolis of Bombay. With the excessive increase of tourist movement in India during the past decade, the hospitality industry has also altered the natural landscape in various parts of the country, such as the coastal state of Goa. The increasing size of urban centres is also dispossessing neighbouring tribal and non-tribal populations. The Warli tribal communities who once occupied large tracts of forested landscape near Bombay, for example, are slowly being forced to accept the urban slums and concrete jungles as their new landscape. Either their land and houses have been bought from them or they have been forcibly evicted by government bodies, builders and land developers. Similar alteration of the landscape is occurring in the heavily forested regions of the Himalayas, where excessive logging in violation of environmental and ecological codes has brought about a drastic ecological imbalance, causing the displacement of the inhabitants. Tribals inhabiting the National Reserve Forest and Protected Areas are being forcibly evicted and made to resettle outside the Protected Areas. This dispossession is carried out on the pretext that the tribals disturb the wildlife and are responsible for degradation of the landscape in which they live. Recent liberalisation of the Indian economy has greatly accelerated the transformation and dispossession of the rural landscape.

The concept of landscape is central to my discussion. I define it as a combination of land, water and forest, with which the population is culturally, physically and spiritually associated. It is the destruction of these associations that brings about a people's dispossession from their landscape. The symbiotic relationship that prevails between the population and landscape is consciously severed by the policies of the contemporary state. In order to fulfil its national objectives, the State destroys the landscape without consideration for the lives of millions who are dependent upon it for survival. In this chapter, I argue that the Government's insensitivity emanates from a colonial ideology still strongly rooted in the consciousness of the country despite half a century's independence. The Government's attitude is reinforced by the intelligentsia, among them anthropologists and archaeologists who have yet to divorce themselves from the colonial heritage in their scholarly research.

It is in the above context, primarily with regard to my experience working along with the tribal people affected by the Sardar Dam, that I ask, who are the tribals? What is their changing relationship to their landscape? I show how dispossession occurs and how the attitude of Indian anthropologists and archaeologists helps to perpetuate such dispossession.

The Sardar Dam and its impact

By the mid-1970s almost all the major rivers in India were dammed, to fulfil the objectives of providing drinking water and water for irrigation to drought-prone areas, and to generate electricity. The dams, along with pesticides and fertilisers, became a necessity in areas where intensive farming was being pursued, to usher in a Green Revolution. But the delay in the damming of the Narmada was not surprising, as agreement among the three states of Madhya Pradesh, Gujarat and Maharashtra on the distribution of the cost and benefits took around twenty years. It was not until 1978 that the awards were divided. The construction of the first dam on the Narmada, namely the Sarda Sarovar Project, consisting of a 165-m high, 1,210-m long dam and riverbed powerhouse, began only in 1987.

The Sardar Sarovar Project was among the two super dams, thirty major dams and 3,000 minor projects designed to transform the Narmada region, inhabited by around 20 million people including a large population of tribal groups. The most published and oft repeated justification offered by the project's proponents was that it would bring huge benefits in the drought-prone areas of Kutch and Saurashtra in Gujarat, by providing 40 million people with drinking water and irrigation to 1.8 million ha of land in the State. These huge benefits were contrasted to the 'sacrifice' of comparatively few people, and the land to be submerged was described as 'steep, rocky ground and degraded forest'.

While the work commenced simultaneously on both the super dams, funded by the World Bank, only the construction of Sardar Sarovar proceeded at a rapid speed. The recommendation of the Independent Review headed by Bradford Morse, international pressure and the people of the valley's resolve not to budge from their landscape, forced the World Bank to withdraw from the project in 1992. There are two aspects to the major impact of the dam: the direct impact on the people and the environmental impact. The impact on the environment directly affects the inhabitants, who, as I discuss later, have an intense relationship with their landscape. The dam will cause both direct and indirect displacement, flooding large areas and altering the surrounding landscape. According to the monitoring and evaluation team for Maharashtra,

> The Sardar Sarovar Dam is expected to impound waters to the full reservoir level of 455 feet. It will submerge 37,000 hectares (92,500 acres) of land in the three states. The canal and irrigation system aggregates to 75,000 kilometres, submerging 85,000 hectares (212,500 acres) of land. The length of the water catchment of the dam is stated to be 123 kilometres. Conservative estimates place the number of displaced at approximately 152,000 persons (about 27,000 families as per Government estimates), residing in 245 villages of these states to be affected by the submergence.

It adds:

> These figures reveal the magnitude of direct and indirect disloca-tion. No one really knows the exact magnitude of the likely

displacement in all its dimensions, and the spin off effects are yet
to be measured.

(Anon. 1992)

The emergence of popular protest movements

In the last decade, a growing awareness of the human and ecological devastation such projects cause has led to the creation of numerous people's
movements opposing them. People's movements recruit their membership
primarily among people affected, with support from other quarters of society.
There have been the movements against a missile testing range in Balipal
(Orissa) and against a dam in Silent Valley (Kerala). At the moment, two
prominent movements are continuing their struggle against an army firing
range in Netrahat (Bihar) and the Sardar Sarovar Dam (Gujarat, Maharashtra
and Madhya Pradesh) on the River Narmada in Western India. These movements take the form of a socio-political struggle by the affected people, aimed
at gaining respite. They are led by local community leaders, sometimes
working with urban activists against their immediate foe – the implementing
government agencies. Larger questions are raised pertaining to human rights,
the State's ecological ethics, the Nehruvian paradigm of development, and
involvement of the local population at the decision-making level about their
own landscape. The right to displace, and the degree of interference by the
Government in the lives of local or tribal populations who had been in existence much before the formation of the contemporary state, are both called
into question. The earlier history of resistance in some of the areas during
the colonial era has strengthened their resolve to fight for their rights.

Filing petitions against the governmental agencies, forming blockades of
arterial roads and highways, undertaking hunger strikes and courting mass arrests
are some of the most powerful strategies used by these movements. Unlike
resistance movements during the colonial era, which were more 'local riots'
and 'war-like campaigns', modern people's movements have been generally
peaceful in nature. The harshness of governmental repression of socio-political
movements in post-independence India, particularly the extreme-left, pro-
Maoist, Naxalite movement, remains fresh in the minds of local leaders.
Equally, the strategic benefits of Gandhian ideals, as they were realised in the
post-independence political movements led by Vinoba Bhave and Jaiprakash
Narayan, are too recent to disregard, particularly since the leaders of some
contemporary campaigns participated in these political movements in the mid-
1970s (see Guha 1983).

The social aims of contemporary, localised people's movements have been
evident in their region of activity. But the need to co-ordinate resistance
at the state or national level has led members of the local movements to
come together under one umbrella. The Jan Vikas Andolan (People's Development Movement) was founded in 1989, the Bharat Jan Adolan (Indian

People's Movement) in 1991 and the National Alliance of People's Movements in 1992. These organisations have enabled a number of local people's
movements to come together on a single platform, to share their experiences,
strengthen ideas and provide each other with solidarity. They are endeav-
ouring to provide an alternative to the mainstream political process, and
popular participation is intense. It was my involvement as a student activist
in Narmada Bachao Andolan (Save the Narmada Movement) against the
building of Sardar Sarovar Dam that enabled me to work with the people
who were going to be displaced and dispossessed and to oppose the construction of such a destructive dam.

Are the tribals an indigenous group?

The people who inhabited the area to be submerged consist of both tribals
living on the banks of the river where the hills and canyons of the Vind-
hyas and Satapuras ranges are fissured by a network of tributaries, and people
belonging to the dominant Hindu society situated upstream, where the river
widens. Although a considerable number of villages of the dominant society
will also be submerged, I discuss the former only because it is particularly
with them that I have worked. The country of the tribals living on the banks
of the Narmada has no motorable roads, no primary schools or health clinics.
Despite the trend immediately after partition to assimilate tribal populations
into the mainstream society, this area, due to its inaccessible terrain, has
preserved its indigenous values and outlook. The various tribal groups, Tadvi,
Vasva, Paura, Bhailala, Rattawa and Nayar, speak different languages, though
most of the men understand the official language of their respective states.
So the Tadvis in Gujarat speak Gujarati along with Bhili, whereas the Vasava
of Maharashtra speak Marathi along with Bhili. Women in these communities are, however, unable to understand the non-tribal languages, due to their
infrequent contact with outside cultures.

The constitution of India includes these populations among the 'Scheduled
Tribes' which encompass 700 different groups of people comprising a population of 60 million, living in various socio-economic conditions (Ghurye 1962).
The framers of the constitution provided these groups with special privileges
and concessions, in order to integrate them into the national life. There has
been continuous debate, particularly since 1947, over the extent to which these
tribal groups can be considered indigenous. I define *indigenous*, in the Indian
context, as a population who, prior to the *Pax Britannica*, had from time
immemorial maintained a symbiotic physical and cultural relationship with a
particular landscape, who were largely outside of the caste system of the mainstream Hindu society and who were politically independent of this system.
Though cultural and economic contact did occur between these two groups,
the indigenous one maintained its distinctive character. I distinguish my
position from that of those who argue that the mainstream Hindu society is

also indigenous by drawing attention to the fact that the tribals were the original habitants of large tracts of land in India, mainly following a hunting and gathering or pastoral subsistence pattern, with at most a chiefdom-based political system. In this respect they could be compared to the indigenous population of America and the Australian Aborigines.

There are numerous references to these tribes in Sanskrit and Hindu literature. Among the earliest, the Vedas have given a particularly complex character to their history. Throughout India they have been called *adivasi*, *admijati*, *vanyajatis*, *girijans* or *pahadia*. Most of these early terms explicitly mean the early settler, the forest settler or just the outsider. The term *adivasi*, in particular, denotes one who is an inhabitant from the earliest times and who still lives as people lived in earliest times. The other indigenous terms in use today are all of Sanskrit origin.

There has been a considerable amount of exchange between the tribal and the Hindu society. This appears to have made it difficult for historians to comprehend and differentiate between the two. Prior to British annexation, most of those now called tribal peoples were either unconscious of their ethnic identity or called themselves 'people', *vis-à-vis* outsiders, in their distinctive speech. It was the British who designated them 'tribals', to distinguish them from Hindus and Muslims, since they were considered to have 'animistic' religious beliefs. In recent times in Indian academic circles, a new theory has arisen rendering all present in the Hindu hierarchy, from Brahmins to Shudras, Ati–Shudras and the tribals as the indigenous population of India. Not surprisingly, this view comes at a time when in India, large social and political concessions are being given to the vulnerable and weaker sections of the society. Another group of scholars refuse to recognise these groups as indigenous because they have reported the usage of factory-made garments by them and the presence of pictures of Hindu gods and goddesses in their homes. The process of modernisation has indeed crept into the village market, causing the substitution of new goods for traditional material culture. Leather shoes and wooden combs have given way to plastic substitutes, just as hand-woven cloth has been substituted by the mill-made cloth. Though Sanskritisation of these tribals has a long history, the mere presence of pictures of Hindu gods or goddesses from an old calendar does not 'detribalise' these groups or make them part of the Hindu society and culture.

In post-independence India there have been several attempts to define these groups of people by listing identifying characteristics. More often than not, these lists themselves serve better to illustrate the prejudices and the presumptions of the compilers than any real distinction between tribals and non–tribals. Thus the Report of the Commissioner for Scheduled Castes and Scheduled Tribes in 1952 listed seven characteristic tribal features:

- isolation in forest and hills,
- Negrito, Australoid to Mongoloid racial stock,
- primitive tribal dialect,

- primitive occupations,
- carnivorous diet,
- naked or semi–naked attire,
- and 'love of drink and dance'.

These characterisations show a clear colonial bias, premised upon the cultural and racial inferiority of the tribal population (see Nehru 1955; Verrier 1955; Majumdar 1955). It is this colonial bias that guides the planners of the country when they go ahead with big dams like the Sardar Sarovar without taking the marginalised tribals into account. A similar bias precludes any protest from most practising anthropologists and archaeologists.

In its 1982 Operational Manual Statement, the World Bank seeks to define 'tribal people' as the object of a special policy measure in the Indian context. The comprehensive definition identifies the vulnerable nature of the group, but, consistent with its neo-colonial ideals and aims, the World Bank conveniently ignores the validity of its own definition in practice. It needed a powerful people's movement such as Narmada Bachao Andolan to force the World Bank to appoint an independent review committee to gauge the destructive nature of its own funding policies. The Operational Manual states:

> The term 'tribal people' refers here to ethnic groups typically with stable, low energy, sustained yield economic systems, as exemplified by hunter gatherers, shifting or semi permanent farmers, herders or fishermen. They exhibit in varying degree many of the following characteristics:
>
> i)   geographically isolated or semi-isolated,
> ii) unacculturated or only partially acculturated into the social norms of the dominant society,
> iii) non-monetized or partially monetized; production largely for subsistence and independent of the national economic system,
> v)   non-literate and without a written language,
> vi) linguistically distinct from the wider society,
> vii) having an economic lifestyle largely dependent on the specific natural environment,
> viii) identify closely with one particular territory,
> ix) possessing indigenous leadership, but little or no national representatives and few, if any, political rights as individuals or collectively, partly because they do not participate in the political process,
> x)   having loose tenure over their traditional lands, which for the most part is not accepted by the dominant society nor accommodated by its courts; and having weak enforcement capabilities against encroachers; even when tribal areas have been delineated.

To a large extent, the above definition embraces the specific attributes peculiar to the indigenous groups in India. These characteristics are obvious among the tribal groups in Narmada Valley. They live a highly sustainable lifestyle and depend heavily on forest produce for subsistence. Until recently they were hunter-gatherers and shifting agriculturists. Due to their geographic isolation, they have been only partially, if at all, Sanskritised or otherwise acculturated into the dominant Hindu society. The tribals in the valley who live close to the Hindu temples such as Shoolpaneshwar are relatively closer to Hindu culture than those far off from such temples. The authority of the indigenous leadership is also highly rooted in the traditional psyche and until the recent coming of non–governmental agencies they consciously avoided participation in the national political process.

Tribal communities in other parts of India can to a great extent also be called 'indigenous', and although they have contacts with the Hindu society, they have been successful in preserving their indigenous characteristics. Disregard for this difference between their culture and the dominant culture would amount to denial of the self-proclamation of the Nagas and Mizo in northeast India, who have been ruthlessly subdued by the Indian state, and the recent demands for statehood by the Stanthal and Munda tribes of the Jharkhand region in eastern India.

A changing relationship to the landscape

In the forest and hills bordering the Narmada River, tribal groups formerly sustained themselves by hunting and food-gathering. At a later period, which is difficult to date, their livelihood became dependent on shifting agriculture or *Jhum* (Ramakrishna and Patnaik 1992). This is a land-use pattern, still used in northeast India, that involves slashing the vegetation, burning the dried slash before the onset of the monsoons, raising a mixture of crops on a temporarily nutrient-rich soil for a year or two, fallowing the plot for regrowth of natural vegetation and eventually returning to the same plot for another cropping phase after a few years. *Jhum* was not just a characteristic land-use pattern, it is a way of life still practised today. It had radically affected the cultural landscape of the people whose evolving cultural life revolved around it. The rich and diverse dance and music forms of the various tribes in the valley are related to the various *Jhum* operations and performed at all festivities associated with the *Jhum* calendar. These include feasting, drinking rice beer and slaughtering pigs.

As among other tribal societies in India, the concept of sacred groves is widespread. Each village has a small patch of forest preserved in its virgin state. It was believed that deities representing various elements of nature such as sun, rain and fire resided in these sacred groves, along with the spirits of their ancestors. Each grove has a residing deity, which some of the Bhil communities in the valley still worship during various ceremonies. These groves are a direct legacy of the shifting agriculturists who comprehended the ecological paradox typical of humid tropical regions. Here the vegetation has a higher nutrient capital than the soil, necessitating the practice of slash and burn. The practice is nonetheless liable to cause the loss of rich species of tropical forests, which were therefore sanctified as sacred to protect them from destruction. The attitude of pre-British village communities toward sacred groves is reflected in the statement that the British traveller Francis Buchanan made near Karwas in northern Karanataka: 'The forests are property of the gods of the villages in which they are situated and the trees ought not to be cut without having leave from the Gauda or headman of the village . . . who were there as priest to the temple of the village God' (quoted in Gadgil and Chandran 1992).

In the nineteenth century, British administrators, who were unacquainted with the importance of such cultivation for subsistence, sought to put an end to shifting cultivation throughout India. They saw slash and burn as destructive of forests and inconsistent with orderly administration. They made shifting agriculture illegal, 'reserved' the forest, and made it a state property by establishing sources of revenue there. The forest that regenerated on areas of past cultivation, other ordinary forest and the virgin sacred groves were all treated alike, causing considerable devastation. The remnants of the colonial alteration of the landscape are still obvious and remembered by village elders. Reduced access to land coincided with population increase, gradually leading people to adopt a more intensive pattern of land use. The *Jhum* cycle (the fallow period between two successive croppings) of shifting agriculture, which was never entirely abandoned, was reduced from a twenty-year time span to less than five years. Permanent fields became a common feature of the new landscape, together with heavy reliance on domestic animals such as goats, which not only survived the worst drought conditions but were also used as meat or taken to the local market to be sold. This led to a few minor transformations of the cultural landscape too, as the tribesmen came into closer contact with the larger Hindu society. The inclusion of gods and goddesses of the Hindu pantheon, particularly Shiva, was one of the most obvious additions. Today both the tribal and the non-tribal people regard each grain of gravel from the River Narmada as the embodiment of Shiva. They remained, however, largely isolated from national life, even during the days of the Quit India Movement when the country had risen in revolt against the imperial rulers. Aurora reports that, 'In 1942 when all of British India was rocked by the struggles of nationalists, only a few people in Alirajpur knew about it. The tribals were not even remotely aware of the nationalist movement in India' (Aurora 1972).

The River Narmada has played the most important role in the tribal people's way of life and constitutes the final part of their triad of existence, the land, forest and water that encompass both the physical and the cultural landscape. For the tribals, the goddess Narmada is their divine mother who has nourished them and their ancestors and also nourishes their children. This timeless link with the river is epitomised by the symbolic importance of the river's water in all their religious rituals. Physical usage of the river other than for the normal chores is restricted to fishing, which can be carried out only by specific, traditional fish-worker groups among the tribals. Along with the river, use of forest reveals close interaction with their landscape. This is forcefully expressed in their houses, whose major components (teak for pillars and beams, bamboo for walls, baked mud tiles for roofing and various plants for ropes and storage baskets) are all harvested in the immediate neighbourhood.

Most of the permanent fields were not registered as revenue land with the local colonial authority, as the owner would have had to pay an annual tax. Any attempt by the external administration to regularise them as revenue land was fiercely resisted. The Bhils, who became famous for such resistance in the nineteenth century, created their own tribal kingdoms, taking advantage of their isolation to maintain their own cultural and economic practices. Existing landowners, along with those who were using or creating new fields, were termed 'encroachers'. Those who had possessed the landscape from a timeless past were deemed trespassers. Derecognition of tribal life made traditional land use illegal, creating the colonial foundation for the justification today of the construction of dams that deny tribal people's very right to exist. The Forest Department constituted during colonial rule and further consolidated after independence has played a significant role in changing the relationship of people towards their landscape. Forest officials reinforced the status of tribals as 'encroachers' by denying them rights to the forest and its produce. They levied fines and bribes from the encroacher as a precondition of continued access to their traditional resources and the seasonal activities of sowing and harvesting their land. These are now discharged by surrendering part of the harvest to government employees. A hostile relationship thus developed between the tribal cultivators and the same Forest Department officials who permitted illegal denudation of the forest by timber contractors from neighbouring towns. This double denial of their traditional rights has had an adverse effect on tribal morale. Until the advent of the people's movements, some believed that they would have to accept whatever the Government did.

In the last 150 years, such a process of alienation and dispossession of the landscape has occurred in almost all the tribal regions in India, and it still continues. The earlier exploitation of the colonial regime has been followed by an equally insensitive neo-colonial Government in the independent state. In some cases, complete displacement and dispossession of indigenous people has resulted.

The dislocation, an experience in an alien landscape

Tracing the ultimate dislocation of the people by the Sardar Sarovar Dam places this discussion within the realm of the politics of development, the politics of big dams, the exaggerated power and irrigation needs of the country, gross violation of the environment and, finally, the high consumption pattern of modern societies all over the world. These are issues widely discussed elsewhere and are largely beyond the scope of this discussion, except for those tribals who have been settled and rehabilitated by the Government. For these people, their relationship with a contrasting landscape of the plains, absolutely alien to their culture, has been a physically, culturally, religiously and psychologically humiliating experience for them.

Tribals taken from the first-phase submergence villages of both Maharashtra and Gujarat have been settled and rehabilitated. Some were virtually compelled to undertake this step. They saw the walls of the dam spring up before their eyes. They had to move 'voluntarily'. The Government forcibly exerted considerable pressure on others to relocate. In some cases this was accompanied by serious discrepancies in government practice, when tribal communities were shown a specific piece of land but the land allotment was cancelled after it had been sanctioned. There have also been instances where more than one person has been allocated the same piece of land. The tribals were so insecure about their newly resettled life that they continued also to occupy their land in the submergence zone.

Elimination of access to the Narmada and the produce of its adjoining forest has resulted in changed consumption patterns in the new colonies: cereals have replaced fish and meat. Daily food consumption has fallen to less than 2,000 calories per day as a direct consequence of low yields and poor employment opportunities. Where only cash can obtain the people's requirements, self-sufficiency has been reduced, creating indebtedness in a market economy. People now have to purchase items such as grains, oil, vegetables, pulses and seeds formerly harvested from the local landscape. Formerly unheard-of agricultural inputs such as fertilisers and pesticides have to be bought for their new land. Lack of cash has made wage labour a necessity, if and where it can be found. The large herds of cattle and goats symbolising possession of large tracts of land are also now threatened, as inadequate grazing land has to be shared with the local population, causing regular skirmishes between the two. Their new houses are sheds made of tin sheets which were intended as accommodation during a transitional period of six months but, after eighteen months, are becoming a permanent testimony to the drastic change they had to make. The monitoring and evaluation team for Maharashtra reports, 'These are small, hot in summer and cold in winter and cannot house cattle. The size of the plot to be given to the people is about 60 square metres, which perhaps compares with the smallest of the houses in the submerged villages (where the houses could be as large as 100 square meters)' (Alvares and Billarey 1988).

The tribals, whose relationship with their original landscape is so intense, face experiences in an alien landscape that deny their human rights to exist in a culture of their own.

An attitudinal problem

The displacement and dispossession of the rural masses has been aggravated in recent times by the proponents of development and progress. Dislodging populations has been justified by a colonial assumption that because the tribals have a culture based on a lower level of technology and quality of life, it is bound to give way to a culture with superior technology and a higher quality of life. Most organisations, both governmental and non-governmental, working with tribals reveal a messianic zeal to bring them into the main-stream of national life. Interestingly enough, however, their dance and music forms were preserved so as to exhibit them during national and international functions. Verrier writes of this trend in post-independence India:

> The ambitious programmes of the education reform and the change now being initiated by most State Governments, while bringing many economic and social benefits to the people are likely to bring an end to the older values, good and bad everywhere is apparent, this is not matched by a good interest in or respect for tribal culture. You cannot make an omelette without breaking eggs, and con-tinued existence of the tribes as tribes is regarded as of less impor-tance than the march of civilisation. This policy has already created many examples of Homo Duplex.
>
> (Verrier 1955: 19)

Unfortunately, the view that their culture is inferior to the dominant culture has permeated into academic organisations such as the Anthropological and Archaeological Surveys of India, fulfilling the colonial aims of the British and further perpetuating the ideals of detribalisation. Thus, Majumdar, one of the earliest anthropological advisers to the government, advocated:

> the only practical solution to the tribal problem in the present situa-tion would therefore lie in the integration of the tribal people in the national democratic set up in India . . . [thus] it is essential that economic and educational standards of the tribal groups should be brought on par with the rest of the people. But to achieve this objective, the different tribal cultures should be scientifically studied.
>
> (Majumdar 1955: 29)

Even today, both organisations refuse to break free from a neo-colonial time warp and acknowledge the indigenous identity of the tribals. They continue to perpetuate the assimilationist school of thought and indulge in activities that are intended to empower these illiterate 'poor' masses of people and bring them to the threshold of the modern civilisation. Viduta Joshi of the Gandhi Labour Institute in Ahmedabad asserts, commenting on the tribals of the Narmada Valley, 'I have extensively travelled in tribal areas for the last twenty years and I have observed their behaviour, I have formed an opinion that tribals want change' (Joshi 1991). This engrained pro-colonial and messianic conviction amongst the intelligentsia, particularly the anthropologists and archaeologists of the state-owned bodies and certain university departments in India, is partly responsible for the dispossession of these tribals. By perpetuating an ideological edifice that considers the tribals as inferiors who must be brought into the fold of the dominant society, they fail to accept the basic human dignity and right to cultural identity of the group they study. If this is the outlook among the intelligentsia who have frequent contact with the tribal lifestyle then other members of the mainstream society with a much narrower outlook will allow such gross violations of human rights as has occurred in the case of the Sardar Sarovar Project without a murmur.

We must be more sensitive while working with tribals. The endeavours of professional archaeologists and anthropologists should not be restricted to a purely academic description of other cultures, but should communicate to the larger world that their lifestyle is sustainable. Through our research we can demonstrate that these groups of people are highly vulnerable to the global market forces that threaten to make paupers out of once-proud human beings. It is essential to lobby in the decision-making corridors of the world and to strengthen laws to protect their rights. Our advantageous position as professionals imposes upon us the onus of conveying their concern to the larger world. We have to convince the governments of countries like India, where there are large populations of tribals in minority and highly marginalised situations, that their rights to the traditional resources have to be protected. They cannot be sacrificed in the name of 'development' and 'progress' just because many will benefit from their being further marginalised. A number of activist organisations are fighting for the rights of these people. We, as professionals, can provide solidarity to their struggle and, through our academic research, sensitise the decision-making bodies.

References

Alvares, C. and R. Billarey 1988. *Damming the Narmada*. Penang: Third World Network.

Anon. 1992. *Sardar Sarovar: report of the independent review*. Vancouver: Resource Future International.

Aurora, G.S. 1972. *Tribe-caste Class Encounters: some aspects of folk–urban relations in Alirajpur Tehsil*. Hyderabad: Administrative Staff College.

Gadgil, M. and S. Chandran 1992. Sacred groves. In *Indigenous Vision*, G. Sen (ed.), 183–7. New Delhi: Sage Publications.

Ghurye, G.S. 1962. The scheduled tribes. New Delhi (unpublished ms).

Guha, R. 1983. *Elementary aspects of Peasants Insurgency in Colonial India*. Delhi: Oxford University Press.

Joshi, V. 1991. *Rehabilitation: a promise to keep*. Hyderabad: Administrative Staff College.

Majumdar, N.D. 1955. The tribal problem. In *The Adivasis*, 23–9. New Delhi: Ministry of Information and Broadcasting.

Nehru, J. 1955 Tribal folk. In *The Adivasis*, 1–8. New Delhi: Ministry of Information and Broadcasting.

Ramakrishna, P.S. and S. Patnaik 1992. Jhum: slash and burn cultivation. In *Indigenous Vision*, Giti Sen (ed.), 215–19. New Delhi: Sage Publications.

Shiva, V. 1992. *Ecology and Politics of Survival*. New Delhi: Sage Publications.

Verrier, E. 1955. Do we really want to keep them in a zoo? In *The Adivasis*, 23–9. New Delhi: Ministry of Information and Broadcasting.

12   Perceiving 'your' land: neighbourhood settlements and the Hauz-i Rani

SUNIL KUMAR

Introduction

This chapter is about Hauz-i Rani, a small reservoir lying on the southern fringes of New Delhi. It seeks to study the significance attached to the reservoir by neighbouring settlers, and the manner in which these disparate groups of people related to the Hauz-i Rani and each other over a period of nine centuries. The population composition and settlements in the vicinity of the reservoir have hardly remained stable since the date of the construction of the Hauz-i Rani some time in the twelfth century. There has been considerable demographic change in the region and hence the manner in which people perceive and signify the importance of their landscape has also undergone considerable transformation.

My arguments are concerned with the way in which social groups 'perceive landscape', a perception which in its cognition implies a definition, an appropriation within a system of beliefs and assumptions concerning the history and the identity of a self-defined group of people. Quite paradoxically, we have a relatively large amount of information about the 'perceptions' of these people, about themselves and others, their social relationships and organisations, their interaction with, and understanding of, their environment. What we are more ignorant about are the processes whereby these 'perceptions' were constructed, the contexts and the agents, both material and individual, that constituted them. This is hardly surprising: discursive instruments often derive their authority from their ahistoricity and their anonymity. But the very process of objectification inherent in 'knowing', the process of labelling and defining, is authoritarian in the sense that it shapes the contours of reality, problematising the possibility of diversity or multiplicity of definitions. The 'perception' of a landscape, as much as the self-perception of a social group, is deliberate in its construction and acceptance; it has historical actors, a temporal context, and it attempts to obscure internal dissent and/or marginalise challenge from groups defined as 'outsiders'.

This chapter historicises and contextualises the discourses which shaped the diverse perceptions of a local landscape. The dissimilar perceptions were not just the result of internal differences in social and ideological composition present within neighbouring groups; they were as much a product of attempts to control and resist changes that were being introduced in the nature of the settlement and land management of the area. The consequence of these transformations in the Hauz-i Rani area led to the different ways in which people understood the significance of the reservoir, and, over a period of time, fractionalised the neighbourhood into aggregations of composite communities who were opposed to each other. By the end of the twentieth century, not only were there distinctly different, but concurrent, perceptions of the Hauz-i Rani, but these perceptions had no relation to how local people had understood the importance of the reservoir in the thirteenth and fourteenth centuries.

The medieval *hauz*, a local community and the city of Delhi

The Hauz-i Rani, the 'Queen's reservoir', was constructed some time in the twelfth century by a queen or a princess, a *rani* about whom we possess no further information. In fact, it is only by accident that we can at all glean episodes from the early history of the Hauz-i Rani. There were other reservoirs in the Delhi plain from the same time period, but most of them have not been remembered. The Hauz-i Rani was first mentioned in the Persian chronicle of Minhaj-i Siraj Juzjani (completed AD 1260) only because the city constructed by the early Sultans of Delhi was in its immediate neighbourhood. In the early thirteenth century the city's major entrance, the Budaun gate, was about 300 m to the west, and faced the *hauz*. As a result, people entering the city on one of its major thoroughfares from the Bagh-i Jud in the north inevitably passed by its banks. According to Juzjani, there was a vast plain next to the *hauz* that was sometimes used as an army encampment, or *lashkargah*. This area was also used for large ceremonial occasions when, presumably, the space in the city proved deficient (Juzjani 1963–4: 81–2). It was near the *hauz* on 28 October 1242, in the reign of Sultan Ala' al-Din Masud (1242–6), that Sultan Iltutmish's military slaves wrought a terrible punishment upon their political competitors (Juzjani 1963–4: 27, 469). In Ala' al-Din Khalaji's reign (1296–1316), it could not have been far from the Hauz-i Rani that the Sultan set up his major markets. The Sultanate historian Ziya' al-Din Barani noted that these bazaars were located in the vicinity of the Budaun gate which we know was close to the *hauz* (Barani 1860–2: 309).

The incidental nature of the information concerning the reservoir notwithstanding, its locale and proximity to the expanding capital of the Delhi Sultans suggest that the Hauz-i Rani did not occupy a desolate or secluded spot in the Delhi region. In fact, during the Tughluqid period (1320–1414), the area around the Hauz-i Rani saw considerable building activity. The wall of

Muhammad Shah Tughluq's (1325–51) new city of Jahanpanah passed the Hauz-i Rani about 200 m to its north. With the construction of Jahanpanah, greater efforts were made to regulate the drainage of the seasonal rivulets that meandered their way from their sources in the Aravalli Hills towards the River Jumna in the east. One of these *nalas* passed by the west and north wall of the *hauz*; another stream flowed through the area just south of the reservoir. Since it was necessary to control the flow of these streams as they crossed into the city of Jahanpanah, especially during the monsoon rains, the Satpul dam was constructed on the city wall, northeast of the *hauz*.

Through the thirteenth and into the fourteenth century, the area in and around the Hauz-i Rani underwent substantial transformation. By the early fourteenth century, this area had not only been the scene of considerable construction activity, but, as the presence of the nearby Khirki mosque suggests, it had come to possess a large enough population to warrant the construction of a sizeable mosque. The *hauz* still lay outside the Tughluqid walled city, and suburban access to Jahanpanah was provided by several gates, one of which was named after the *hauz* the darwazah-i Hauz-i Rani (Hodivala 1957: 144). We know little about the composition of the population that resided in the vicinity of the *hauz*; in all likelihood they were service-folk who either worked in the city or provided its markets with produce or artisanal products. Although associated with the material life of the capital, they were distant from its politics and unattached to the household of its elites.

What is significant, however, is that the *hauz* around which these relatively undistinguished people resided continued to be repaired well into the Tughluqid period. Today its ruined walls display the true arch which in its architectural and stylistic form can only be attributed to the fourteenth or fifteenth century (see Figure 12.1). It is doubtful if the local residents themselves possessed the means to carry out this repair work, and in all likelihood it was the Sultan or his administrative agents who made the necessary investment towards its maintenance.

The construction activity in and around the *hauz* certainly drew the attention of observers to this local landmark, a regard that also coincided with the ascription of a sacred significance to the reservoir. The hallowed character ascribed to the *hauz* was unlike the ones attached to reservoirs like Suraj Kund, constructed adjacent to a temple for ritual purposes. There is no evidence of the presence of a temple or mosque in the vicinity of the Hauz-i Rani. In fact, since the name of the *hauz*, 'the Queen's reservoir', is devoid of any religious significance, it is unlikely that the tank was associated with any deity or sacred occasion. At least to begin with, no special legend, like the one connected with the Hauz-i Shamsi and Sultan Iltutmish's vision of the Prophet Muhammad, raised the stature of the 'Queen's reservoir'. Yet the *hauz* was special because of the unique cultural role that was attached to water in the life of medieval people.

Water was not a plentiful commodity in the central Islamic lands, nor for that matter was it commonly available in the south Delhi plain in the Middle

Figure 12.1 The west wall of the *hauz* photographed in 1984. The remnants of the 'Tughluqid arches' are visible here.

Ages. Its presence was a source of comment, and the Persian term for cultivation, *abadani*, or the terms *abad* and *abadi* which meant increasing population and prosperity in a town or district, were derived from the same Persian root, *ab* (water). The benefactors who made water easily available in the community were singled out for social esteem, and when any great man won social applause because of his altruistic concern for the welfare of his community, it was said that 'the drops of rain were entrusted by God in his care' (Fakhr-i Mudabbir 1976: 16; Ringgren 1959: 737–47). In the Middle Ages, water was regarded as the hub of life, of prosperity, a gift given by God. A *hauz* was special because, amongst its other nourishing qualities, it was an indication that God continued to care by providing capable shepherds for his folk. By the early fourteenth century these sentiments had also started influencing the manner in which local residents regarded the Hauz-i Rani. Thanks to constant maintenance, it was not merely an exceptionally pleasant place to repair to from the bustle of the town, but it was also a place where one could be close to one's Maker. There was some discordance, however, about the identification of the 'shepherd' who was associated with the *hauz*.

By the fourteenth century, many local residents came to believe that it was the famous Chishti mystic saint Nizam al-Din Auliya (who died in 1325) whose association with the *hauz* lent significance to the 'Queen's reservoir'.[1]

On 26 November 1315, Nizam al-Din told how he came to establish his hospice, *khanqah*, in Ghiyaspur, at that time a small village about 5 km north of the *hauz*. The *sufi* saint was tired of living in the crowded old town of Delhi and was searching for alternative residences without much success. It was while he was praying for guidance at the Hauz-i Rani that he received a divine message to go to Ghiyaspur. The *sufi* saint's reported experiences at the banks of the *hauz* provided the reservoir with a special and venerable status (Sijzi 1990: 242; Khurd 1978: 120). Proof that the waters of the area possessed a special merit was further provided by Nizam al-Din's spiritual successor, Nasir al-Din Chiragh (who died in 1356), who performed his prayer ablutions in the stream adjacent to the Hauz-i Rani, and read his prayers in the nearby Satpul dam. Together with the veneration that both these *Auliya*, or 'Friends of God', acquired amongst their congregations in Delhi during the fourteenth century, the areas associated with their unique spiritual experiences also gained regard as sacred territories. By the fourteenth century many people residing in the vicinity of the Hauz-i Rani no longer regarded the reservoir as a simple *hauz*; it was the site of a mysterious miracle. Since their habitation was associated with the experiences of a charismatic, holy figure, a 'saint' who was close to God and empowered by Him to perform miracles, it also distinguished the residents of the *hauz* as his special disciples.

The association with the *sufi* saints also served to distance the local residents from the overweening authority and discourse of the Delhi Sultans. As the 'Friends of God', the *sufi* saints did not recognise any temporal authority. Next to the Prophets themselves, they were the special individuals chosen by God to preserve harmony and stability within the Muslim community (Kumar forthcoming). By contrast, the Delhi Sultans claimed that they were the ones who preserved the laws of Islam (*Shariat*), the social regulations that allowed individuals the opportunity to live their lives according to the Qur'anic inspiration. Sultan Ala' al-Din Khalaji's inscriptions on the Delhi congregational mosque stated, for example, that he was the 'reviver of the [Muslim] community, the elevator of the banners of the Muslim Holy Law (*Shariat*), the strengthener of the foundations and roots of the Muslim religion' (Yazdani 1917–18: 28).

One way the Sultan and his agents could strengthen Islam was by carefully supervising pietistic practices considered to be contrary to the interpretation of the *Shariat* as defined by the jurists. *Sufis*, with their emphasis upon an inner, intuitive understanding of the Holy law and obligations due to their Maker, felt the rigours of this discipline and its stress on appropriate, socially cognisable behaviour particularly keenly (Kumar 1992: 197–235, forthcoming). The construction of charitable institutions, schools and mosques was not intended merely to impress subjects of the altruistic and pious conduct of their rulers; these were also places of congregational worship and religious education where Muslims were socialised to accept the jurists' interpretation of the *Shariat* and suffer a policing of their conduct to remove 'error' in their ritual practice. There was, however, considerable resistance to this coercion, some kinds more dramatic and public than others (Kumar forthcoming). But it is important to recognise that the Hauz-i Rani residents were not rebels; their everyday life was inexorably tied to that of the Sultanate capital. What they sought to preserve, instead, was a degree of autonomy, a space that their *sufi* patron saints created for them.

Another way in which the Delhi Sultans claimed that they were strengthening the 'roots of Islam' was by attempting to destroy the foundations of idolatry and all evidence of infidel worship in their territory. There was the occasional public and dramatic statement of piety when Hindu and Jain temples in the region of Delhi were destroyed, and in the discourse of the court chronicles of the Sultans it was suggested that the righteous wrath of the 'protectors of Islam' sought to erase all signs of Hindu habitation from the region of the capital (Kumar forthcoming). The presence of the Hauz-i Rani, however, questioned this 'official' representation of the virtuous deeds of the Delhi Sultans. As the name Hauz-i Rani itself signifies, not merely were old, pre-Sultanate habitations still in existence in the vicinity of Delhi well into the fourteenth century, but the memories of their infidel patron-constructors continued to be perpetuated in their names. Nizam al-Din Auliya himself provided the information that Hauz-i Rani lay within the premises of a garden called the *bagh-i Jasrath*, the 'garden of Jasrath' who was, as his name clarifies, certainly a Hindu (Sijzi 1990: 242).[2] A stone's throw from the court, and its vaunted claims concerning the consecration of newly conquered lands through the destruction of the symbols of infidel profanity, resided a community of Muslims who were apparently unconcerned by the pre-Muslim history of their habitat. Indeed, when the local population wanted to articulate their sentiments concerning the sacredness of the Hauz-i Rani, despite the disfavour of the court towards *sufis*, they associated the reservoir with the miraculous life of their spiritual master Nizam al-Din Auliya. Rather than the *hauz*'s continued links with a 'Hindu past', it was the connection with the Delhi Sultans that was a concern to the area's residents.

The qualities ascribed to the Hauz-i Rani in the fourteenth century can be understood only in the context of its complicated relationship with the capital of the Delhi Sultanate. On the one hand, the reservoir and its population remained geographically outside the city, and, through a tenuous association with Nizam al-Din Auliya, lent itself both importance and some autonomy from the influence of the imperial city. On the other hand, the residents in the vicinity of the *hauz* were sustained by the economic life of the capital. They either worked in the town, or produced goods which were retailed in its markets. Despite all their efforts to the contrary, the prosperity of the *hauz* was materially tied to the rhythms of the neighbouring capital. The uneasy association with the powerful agencies resident in the capital implied a simultaneous attempt on the part of the suburban community to maintain its ties with Delhi, while creating a distance from the court by seeking a distinct, alternate identity.

This close association with the capital also implied that any change in the fortunes of Delhi also had a direct impact upon the Hauz-i Rani and its neighbours. This was apparent between the sixteenth and the twentieth centuries when there was a demographic shift in the population settlements in the Delhi plain (Kumar 1993). The imperial capital had already shifted away from the Delhi region during the reign of Ibrahim Lodi (1517–26), and during the sixteenth century some of its elite population also sought greener pastures away from the old capital. The older Sultanate capitals like Jahanpanah were in palpable decline, and the fifteenth- and sixteenth-century imperial residences situated in the north of the Delhi plain, Firuzabad, Dinpanah and Salimgarh, manifested only occasional flashes of a past glory (Koch 1995). The loss of markets and material support for the residents around the Hauz-i Rani was nothing short of devastating, but equally disastrous was the emergence of the hospice of Nizam al-Din Auliya as the primary sacred area associated with the saint's charisma, the major pilgrimage site in the plain of Delhi. With the popularity of the grave shrine, the *sufi* saint's association with the Hauz-i Rani carried little appreciable significance. The construction of the city of Shah Jahanabad in the northern segment of the Delhi plain, and the transfer of the Mughal capital in 1648 to that town, further transformed the region around the old *hauz* into a backwater.

Even when the last of the Mughal emperors, and some notables from the city of Shah Jahanabad, started establishing residences in south Delhi in the early nineteenth century, their hunting lodges or summer homes were located mainly to the west of Hauz-i Rani, in the Mehrauli area. Hauz-i Rani remained unaffected by the change in the fortunes of Mehrauli, and, while it continued to figure as a 'reservoir' on nineteenth-century British land-survey maps of the Delhi plain, the Gazetteer of the Delhi district admitted that by 1883-4 the *hauz* was no more than a seasonal swamp with its lands occupied by a mango grove (Anon. [1883–4] 1988; Fanshawe [1902] 1991: Map 8).

The gradual silting and ruin of the *hauz* by the nineteenth century does not mean that the area of the reservoir lost all significance to the local Muslim residents. A village called Hauz Rani was established near the reservoir, on the ruined walls of the Jahanpanah fort. Some time in the nineteenth century the banks of the 'Queen's reservoir' started to be used by the villagers as a graveyard. The choice of the area as a graveyard might have been motivated by considerations of convenient accessibility to the village, and, perhaps, by the presence of a grove of trees, incongruous in the midst of the flat, monotonous farmland, reminiscent of the garden of paradise (Figure 12.2). It is doubtful if in the nineteenth century, the memory of the *hauz*'s special significance derived from the *sufi* saints was at all alive. Instead, in the history that was ascribed to the area at this time, the tank was no longer a sacred place imbued by the *barakat* or the grace of the mystic saints; it was merely a graveyard where some of the esteemed members of the village were buried. Together with the other changes that had occurred in the old city of Delhi by the nineteenth century, the *hauz* of the Hauz-i Rani had also become unimportant in the popular imagination of its residents.

Figure 12.2 Remnants of the east wall of the *hauz* photographed in 1984. Immediately beyond the wall, and in the grove of trees, is a part of the graveyard of the Hauz Rani villagers. Note that these are unbuilt graves identified merely as mounds of earth. Beyond the graveyard is the pedestrian path that connected Hauz-i Rani with the suburb of Saket.

Sports in the 'Queen's reservoir'

When I first wandered through this area in 1975, the city had again started intruding into the area of the Hauz-i Rani. Building of the first houses in the neighbouring suburb of Saket had begun and the Delhi Development Authority (DDA) had already notified and appropriated most of the fields belonging to the residents of Shai*kh* Sara'i and Hauz Rani villages. In the transfer of land ownership, little attention had been paid to the *hauz* In the process of notification, the DDA had taken over half of the reservoir. The remaining half was left with the villagers as their graveyard and common property. In the master plan for Saket, the area of the *hauz* in the possession of the DDA was ear-marked for a sports complex. But even before the construction work could start, the DDA destroyed the southern wall of the reservoir by digging a storm water drain, or *pucca nala*, at the site of the original seasonal streams that had meandered their way from the Aravalli Hills through the Satpul dam into the River Jumna.

The response of the Hauz Rani villagers to the intrusion of the DDA was by and large supportive. Some of the larger landlords did complain about the compensation paid to them for the lands notified by the Government, but the majority saw in the recent developments signs of 'progress'. While most of the residents of the village were aware of the presence of an old reservoir near their graveyard, they could only talk positively of the *pucca nala* that had destroyed a part of the Hauz-i Rani. The new drainage system ensured that the old silted streams no longer flooded the village every other monsoon.

The 1970s and 1980s were years of dynamic transformation for the village of Hauz Rani. As construction in the suburb of Saket and adjoining Pushp Vihar gathered speed, Hauz Rani emerged as their satellite, providing commercial services to the building industry. Many of the older residents of the village worked as plumbers, electricians, welders, carpenters, masons and daily wage labourers for their new neighbours. There was some transfer of property as Hindus and Jains set up their supply and repair stores at the fringes of the village facing Saket. Together with the change in a lifestyle dependent upon a salaried or contractual relationship with an employer resident outside the social world of the village, the intrusion of the rhythms and comportment of a city lifestyle marked a difficult period as the village made the transition into a suburb of New Delhi.

Greater earnings went hand in hand with lower self-esteem as Hauz Rani residents recognised their status within a social hierarchy where the professional and business classes of the neighbouring residential areas were far and away the more privileged group. The economic disparity was further accentuated by the confessional divide that characterised the distinctions between the suburbs. The majority of the people living in Saket, Malaviya Nagar and Pushp Vihar were Hindu, followed by Sikh, Jain and, finally, a minuscule Christian and Muslim population. In Hauz Rani, only the newer residents on the peripheries of the village were Hindu, Sikh or Jain; the core remained Muslim. The 'inner–outer' geographical distribution of communities within Hauz Rani mirrored the manner in which the Muslim residents of the village sought to deal with the outside world. In their relationships with an 'outside' world, Hauz Rani Muslims presented a non–denominational, almost 'professional' face. It was only as you entered the 'inner regions' of the village that the significance of the mosque, the *maulvi* preacher, the pictures of the *kaba* in cigarette and barber saloons, the pavement *kabab* vendors with their meat delicacies, and the butchers selling buffalo meat, manifested the presence of an alternate world.

One should not, however, make too much of a case for the class and confessional divide between the neighbouring suburbs at this time, or the fact that the Hauz Rani village possessed an 'inner' face, an alternate world. Although largely Muslim, the confessional bond did not create the sense of a united community among the residents of the village. Despite sharing a common cultural and religious heritage, social relationships within the village and with members outside were also influenced and separated by a wide range of material considerations. Nor was the Hauz Rani village a closed or defensive realm during the 1970s and 1980s. There were significant breaches that muted the divisions between the village and the adjoining neighbourhood

of Saket. The parched lands of what had once been a part of the old
Hauz-i Rani reservoir were important in this context.

Although the DDA had constructed a 'sports complex' on their portion
of the *hauz*, at this stage of development it constituted three large fields
without any barriers distinguishing the open spaces, the *maidans*, from the
village burial, and common grounds. Saket residents and the Hauz Rani
villagers moved freely throughout the area. In fact, in a fit of rare sensitivity,
the DDA constructed a paved pedestrian path and bridge which passed through
a grove of trees near the village common ground and connected Saket with
Hauz Rani. The absence of barriers between the two neighbourhoods was
apparent in that children from Saket played football every evening, ten to
fifteen a side, with their peers from Hauz Rani. The very absence of a structured sports regime allowed for an unregulated fraternising between the
residents of the two neighbourhoods. The people of Saket were unaware of
the presence of a *hauz* in their vicinity and only some of the older Hauz
Rani villagers reflected about the history of their graveyard. As far as one
could make out, the lands of the old Hauz-i Rani reservoir had lost their
history and effectively become desacralised. It had also become one of those
rare areas where, at least for some time, people forgot their class, ethnic and
confessional differences.

The DDA was directly responsible for demarcating and developing this
secular lung in an area witnessing the introduction of class and sectarian
distinctions. But this was only by accident; their actual intentions for the
Hauz Rani area were clarified in 1990 when the interim sports complex was
razed and supplanted by a more elaborate version.

In the place of the accessible, open *maidans* left free for unstructured
activities, the new Saket Sports Complex was open only to members for
squash, badminton, tennis, table-tennis, cricket, jogging, basketball, aerobics,
yoga and horse-riding. The Hauz Rani villagers' competence hardly extended
into these exalted realms, and by default, if nothing else, the new Sports
Complex was not visualised as catering for the poorer segment of the area's
population. When I queried the DDA engineers about their plans for the
development of this area, they were very forthright in establishing the connection between the Sports Complex and the neighbourhood of Saket, with its
upper-middle-class residential profile. Even if it had been constructed on only
half of the bed of the old *hauz*; the orientation of the Sports Complex was
certainly not towards the Hauz Rani village.

The class bias that was evident in the construction of the new Sports
Complex was, however, only incidental to its overall conceptualisation. The
real problem for the DDA was posed by the fact that it was in the vicinity of
a 'low-class' Muslim village and its graveyard. Here 'class' was understood in
more than its economic sense and encompassed the host of Muslim practices
that the Hindu engineers of the DDA found abhorrent. Not the least of these
was the practice of burial or, more prosaically, the practice of indiscriminate
interring of corpses. As it was rather colourfully explained to me, burial was

not merely unhygienic because it attracted maggots and other sundry vermin but, since these were largely unbuilt graves covered with earth, people were forever stumbling onto them. It was a filthy, unhygienic practice, and as a guard at the Sports Complex explained to me, 'No matter how deep you buried a corpse, its odour nevertheless permeated the region.' People who observed this ritual were not merely unclean; they did not accept the norms of society as the Hindus or the DDA engineers understood them. Amongst the other cultural values ascribed to the Muslim residents of Hauz Rani by the planners of the Sports Complex (and I presume that these were believed to be more general qualities shared by the entire community) were hysteria, unruliness, pilfering, and a communal sentiment that made fraternising impossible.

If the Saket Sports Complex was to be a successful DDA project, its development thus had to include plans whereby it could be insulated from the hostile environment posed by the Muslim village. The remedy lay in zoning the areas where the villagers were permitted entry. This was now restricted by stone and barbed-wire walls to include only the approach to the half of the *hauz* that fell within the common property and graveyard of the village. The Sports Complex itself was enclosed by towering walls and reoriented towards a solitary entrance approached from Saket. The pedestrian pathway connecting the two neighbourhoods was also fenced in and secured by two gates which were patrolled at night.

If the DDA sought to divide and insulate the two communities, the reactions of the villagers only accentuated the distance and mistrust that pervaded the area of the Hauz Rani. Despite the fact that the area of the Sports Complex had been land legally notified by the DDA, the sudden and obtrusive denial of access to land and freedom was ascribed a more nefarious and long-term design. The villagers were convinced that the Government intended eventually to expel them from their common property and graveyard as well. They became acutely aware of their minority community status and sought to defend their lands. This implied a systematic destruction of the half of the *hauz* that fell into the territory of the Hauz Rani village. Its walls were pillaged to build goat and buffalo pens, and all paths into the area were barricaded with thorn and bristle bushes.

The villagers sought further protection by constructing a sacred history linking the lands of Hauz Rani with their ancestors. Ironically, it was not the history of the *hauz* that the villagers chose to embellish but that of the graveyard, which was now regarded as a sacred place where in ancient times the progenitors of the current villagers, all *Sayyids* or descendants of the Prophet Muhammad, were buried. Placards were placed around the graveyard emphasising its historicity as an ancient burial ground, *qadim qabristan*. With one stroke not merely had the villagers claimed rights to these lands from antiquity, but, as *Sayyids*, they were by extension related to the Prophet. Only the ignorant could call them 'low class' now.

The response of the Hauz Rani villagers to the DDA challenge also provoked a public articulation of their Muslim identity. Mosques were renovated and repainted and children enrolled in schools of religious instruction. In a disarming conversation between a preacher and a small congregation that I eavesdropped upon in a mosque, I managed to savour the 'facts' of Indian history taught to the children of the area. The *imam* explained to his audience that there had occasionally been governments (*hukumat*) in the past that had denigrated Islam and heaped injustice upon God's chosen community. There was, for example, the apostate Mughal emperor Akbar (1556–1606), and in modern times there was the current Hindu government, but God would give to each of them His chosen retribution at the Day of Judgement. Clearly the heroes of the Hauz Rani villagers were no longer those of the Indian republic.

Across the great divide, the response of the Saket residents to the Sports Complex differed completely from the villagers. There was immediate support for the building activity introduced in their vicinity by the DDA. On the one hand, the proximity of such an elite facility to Saket was appreciated for its positive impact in improving the profile of the neighbourhood amongst the New Delhi suburbs. It was assumed that rental rates in Saket could now be legitimately inflated. On the other hand, Saket property owners were also pleased by the security precautions. They had not quite forgotten the trauma of the 1984 riots after Mrs Gandhi's assassination, when (what were assumed to be) lumpen mobs had looted Sikh business and domestic establishments. At that time, neighbourhood vigilante groups had patrolled the streets against a faceless enemy, but they had been sure that the adversary was poor and desperate, and that he had targeted not just Sikh but all middle-class homes. By 1990, many of the Saket householders had provided an address, if not a face, to the enemy; they knew that he resided in Hauz Rani. After a burglary in Saket's 'M' block, so sure had the victims been of the provenance of the thieves that, in their rage, they had sought to sever links with the village by demolishing the bridge leading to the pedestrian path connecting the two neighbourhoods. Their worst suspicions were confirmed when the DDA also identified the Muslim villagers as a threat, and they applauded the security measures that distanced the two realms. The harmonious fraternisation that had occurred between neighbourhoods in the *maidans* of the Hauz Rani just a few years before suddenly seemed a lifetime away.

This was far from the intention behind the construction of the Saket Sports Complex. It was conceived and designed as a recreational facility to encourage physical fitness and competitive sports, all positive sentiments. Within its limited context, it was a wonderful complex which, it could be argued, successfully accomplished its goals. Nor had the engineers of the DDA intended to introduce a communal polarisation between the Saket and Hauz Rani neighbourhoods. In fact, the Saket Sports Complex was a very 'secular' institution, and its definitions of 'secularism' originated from the constitution of India no less. Its brochure clarified the fact that, as a facility constructed by the Government for the public, the Saket Sports Complex sought to 'induce . . . [a] spirit of mutual help and goodwill among citizens of Delhi' and membership was open to all individuals without respect to caste or creed. The only qualification was a prior sports record and the ability to pay the membership fees. Nevertheless, as we have noticed, these declarations of secular principles hardly served to promote 'goodwill' within the Hauz-i Rani region.

It needs to be remembered, however, that there was a phase of 'development' when in fact the DDA had successfully bridged gaps between class and sectarian differences which had started to manifest themselves in this area. The open fields of the 'interim' sports complex provided the liminal space which eased the differences between communities, presenting an opportunity to strangers to establish acquaintances outside their familiar social realms. The free access and unstructured nature of the leisure activities placed no premium on class or confessional differences. For the moment, people were accepted as individuals and not as extensions of their separate social worlds. On the contrary, the process of fraternisation provided the opportunity for doubting the validity of the many inherited, clichéd sentiments about unfamiliar people. Not merely was this sports complex secular and democratic, but it could also have proved to be an agent for neutralising a potential communal polarisation between neighbourhoods.

The problem, of course, lay in the fact that this sports complex was still perceived to be 'undeveloped'. It was unable to maximise its potential since it lacked the 'structure' of a formal sports arena. If the 'openness' of the original complex was its weakness, the prescribed 'limits' and 'discipline' of the new one were its strengths. The new sports complex promised limited membership, discipline in dress and conduct of members, coaching, and facilities where the rules of the game would be followed. This was an exclusive world available only to the familiar. The old cohabitants were suddenly relegated by the DDA to the other side of the boundary as foreigners and threats. The liminality of the *maidans* was lost and the newly resplendent sports complex presented an unmistakable class and confessional bias.

The ritual genuflection to secular sentiments was certainly present in the brochure of the Saket Sports Complex, and its construction had received the patronage of the Congress-I and the Janata Dal, all self-proclaimed secular political parties. This secularism had meant precious little to the DDA engineers, whose class and community biases distanced the neighbouring Muslim villagers from the Hauz Rani. As a final mockery of the secular spirit, the DDA chose to approach a Muslim, the Janata Dal Home Minister, Mufti Mohammad Sayeed, to inaugurate the sports complex and legitimise all their actions. By contrast the perception of the villagers regarding the changes occurring within the *hauz* area differed completely. They looked beyond the secular platitudes of the DDA Sports Complex brochure, and the Muslim chief guest; in reflecting upon the changes in their own lives they saw instead, a triumph of the Hindu *hukumat*.

Conclusion: a diachronic study of landscapes and perceptions

Within the discipline of history we should perhaps be grateful to the French historiographical school of the 'Annales' for their emphasis on the study of ecological conditions as determinants in the material organisation of, and interaction between, social groups. The 'Annales' historians understood landscapes as a part of a larger environment which influenced social organisations (Duby 1984; Braudel 1986). By contrast, landscape archaeologists study the cognitive processes whereby societies understand and make sense of their landscapes. In the latter case, it is the character of the social 'organisms' that shapes the nature of their perceptions of their landscape (Layton 1995).

Where the 'Annales' historiography and the practitioners of landscape archaeology tend to agree, however, is the motionless immensity of the landscape. For the 'Annales', the landscape hardly undergoes any transformation over historical time; it is, therefore, an ideal point of departure for a study which emphasises the *longue durée*. The landscape archaeologists' perceptions of landscape come perilously close to cultural anthropology, where the study of culture, and its social underpinnings, is carried out without any care for its temporal location.

The skills with which historians and archaeologists are able to study the cognitive categories of subaltern groups today reflects the methodological sophistication with which the 'textually silenced' groups have been rendered articulate. Yet, as in the case of cultural anthropologists, the synchronic study of the marginal or the primitive by landscape archaeologists carries with it the danger of assuming that the 'primitive' or the 'marginal' lacked a history. This is dangerously close to assuming that their resilience to change was a product of their 'backwardness'. If it is problematic to suggest that processes of change are foreign to traditional and 'primitive' societies, it is equally difficult to argue for the presence of a simple, undifferentiated society. To assume 'a' cognitive perception for a whole group of people is to suggest a remarkable internal stability and homogeneity within a society – a society unprovoked by internal dissent, distant and devoid of any reaction to changes in its neighbourhood. A group of people may possess many perceptions of their landscape, a plurality which may sometimes be muted by a hegemonic discourse. But this discourse has its own tensions and fractures, and the historian or the archaeologist can go beyond it to discover the silenced voices. We need to be more sensitive to this dialectic in our endeavour to understand the complexity in the composition of different societies over time and space.

Through my study of the Hauz-i Rani I have described the differing perceptions of a local habitat present amongst people who shared a neighbourhood. Concurrently I have provided a historical context for these different perceptions and the manner in which they came to be contesting definitions of the same region. In our efforts to move towards a richer, more nuanced understanding of human societies and the manner in which they have interacted with and understood their habitations, it is my submission that we need to pay greater attention to historical processes, agencies and contestation.

Notes

1 Unlike Christianity and its institutionalised forms of canonisation of saints, the recognition of a saint, *wali*, in Islam was the result of a social consensus concerning the exceptionally pietistic qualities of an individual. Several participants were involved in the creation of this 'social consensus', not least of all the aspirant himself, but it also included disciples who embellished and popularised the qualities of their master. Nizam al-Din, in particular, was extremely fortunate to have amongst his disciples writers of the calibre of Amir Hasan Sijzi, Amir Khusrau and Ziya' al-Din Barani, whose writings spread the virtues of their teacher to a huge audience beyond the limits of his immediate congregation in Delhi. On the question of 'sainthood' in Islam, see Currie (1989), and on the 'process' of disseminating the charisma of a saint see Eaton (1984), Lawrence (1986) and Kumar (forthcoming).

2 In Hindu myth, Jasrath/Dasrath was an ancient king of Ayodhya, better known as the father of Rama, the celebrated hero of the epic *Ramayana*. The *bagh-i Jasrath* was probably an orchard or a grove of trees rather than the formal Mughal *chahar bagh*, the walled-in garden, or the Victorian gardens popular in India today.

References

Anon. [1883–4] 1988. *A Gazetteer of Delhi*. Gurgaon: Vintage Books.

Barani, Zia' al-Din. 1860–2. *Ta'rikh-i Firuz Shahi*. S.A. Khan (ed.). Calcutta: Bibliotheca Indica.

Braudel, F. 1986. *The Mediterranean and the Mediterranean World in the Age of Philip II*. London: Fontana Press.

Currie, P.M. 1989. *The Shrine and Cult of Muin al-Din Chishti of Ajmer*. Delhi: Oxford University Press.

Duby, G. 1984. *The Early Growth of the European Economy: warriors and peasants from the seventh to the twelfth century*. Ithaca: Cornell University Press.

Eaton, R.M. 1984. The political and religious authority of the shrine of Baba Farid. In *Moral Conduct and Authority*, B. Metcalf (ed.), 333–56. Berkeley: University of California Press.

Fakhr al-Mudabbir. 1976. *Adab al-Mulk wa Kifayat al-Mamluk*. M.S. Maulawi (ed.). Teheran: Haidari.

Fanshawe, H.C. [1902] 1991. *Delhi Past and Present*. Gurgaon: Vintage Books.

Hodivala, S.H. 1957. *Studies in Indo-Muslim History: a critical commentary on Elliot and Dowson's History of India as told by its own historians, vol. 2*. Bombay: Popular Book Depot.

Juzjani, Minhaj al Din Siraj. 1963–4. *Tabaqat-i Nasiri* Vols 1 and 2. Hayy Habibi (ed.). Kabul: Anjuman-i Tarikh-i Afghanistan.

Khurd, A. 1978. *Siyar al-Awliya*. S.M. Ghuri (ed.). Lahore: Marqaz-i Tahqiqat-i Farsi Iran wa Pakistan.

Koch, E. 1995. The Delhi of the Mughals prior to Shahjahanabad as reflected in the patterns of Imperial visits. In *Art and Culture*, A.J. Qaisar and S.P. Verma (eds), 3–20. Jaipur: Publication Scheme.

Kumar, S. 1992. The emergence of the Delhi Sultanate. Unpublished Ph.D. thesis, Duke University.

Kumar, S. 1993. Making sacred history or everyone his own historian: a study of the village of Saidlajab. *The India Magazine of her People and Culture* 13, 47–55.

Kumar, S. Forthcoming. Defining and contesting territory: the Delhi Masjid-i Jami in the thirteenth century (Manuscript).

Lawrence, B.B. 1986. The earliest Chishtiya and Shaikh Nizam ud-din Awliya. In *Delhi through the Ages: essays in urban history, culture and society*, R.E. Frykenberg (ed.), 104–28. Delhi: Oxford University Press.

Layton, R. 1995. Relating to the country in the western desert. In *The Anthropology of Landscape: perspectives on place and space*, E. Hirsch and M. O'Hanlon (eds), 210–31. Oxford: Clarendon Press.

Ringgren, H. 1959. Some religious aspects of the caliphate. In *The Sacral Kingship*, 737–48. Leiden: E.J. Brill.

Sijzi, Amir Hasan 1990. *Fawaid al-Fuad*. Hasan Sani Nizami Dihlawi (ed.). Delhi: Urdu Academy.

Yazdani, G. 1917–18. Inscriptions of the Khalji Sultans of Delhi and their contemporaries in Bengal. *Epigraphia Indo-Moslemica*, 8–42.

13 In the shadow of New Delhi: understanding the landscape through village eyes

NAYANJOT LAHIRI
AND UPINDER SINGH

Introduction

This chapter investigates village-level perceptions of the physical and archaeological landscape of a segment of the Faridabad district, in the Indian state
of Haryana. This area, the Ballabgarh *tehsil*,[1] shares its border with Delhi, the
Union Capital. Under the British government in India it used to form a part
of the Delhi district. In addition to its geographical proximity, it has been
perceived as having a history broadly identical to that of Delhi. Volume 1
of the *Imperial Gazetteer of India* (Gazetteer 1991: 281) is representative of
this view:

> The history of the District is the history of Delhi city, of which
> it has from time immemorial formed a dependency. Even the
> towns of . . . Ballabgarh and Faridabad hardly possess local histo-
> ries of their own, apart from the city, in and around which are
> all its great antiquities.

Our village-to-village survey (Lahiri et al. 1996) revealed many unknown
and unreported archaeological relics that suggest a cultural trajectory that in
fact departs in many ways from that of Delhi. Ballabgarh is rapidly industri-
alising and the signs of her past are fast disintegrating. Nonetheless, rural
Ballabgarh, containing as it does such population groups as the animal-grazing
Gujars, Jat, Rajput and Meo agriculturists, snake-catchers or charmers called
Saperas and Gaur Brahmins, offers a variegated human landscape.

This chapter springs from the assumption that the ways in which peasant
and other social groups view their physical environment and the traces of
earlier habitations it contains are just as integral to the reconstruction of the
settlement history and landscape archaeology of a region as are the usual
archaeological approaches. An integrated approach to a micro-segment such
as Ballabgarh should ideally use the images of spaces and location held by
groups living in towns and cities along with those of village people. There
are two reasons why we focus here exclusively on rural perceptions. The

villages of Ballabgarh still form the locales for the habitations of a large section
of the *tehsil*'s old population groups, and our archaeological observations
(together with the limited documentary historical sources) suggest that certain
features of the rural ethnographic present have a pre-modern reality.

Two aspects of these rural perceptions and representations will be analysed.
The first relates to the physiographic duality of Ballabgarh and village perceptions of it. The second theme is concerned with the archaeological relics of
that zone and with the straightforward and unusual ways in which these are
understood and, in some cases, transformed through a filter of socio-religious
beliefs and memories. In both cases, we highlight and historicise the disjunc-
tion between scholastic observation and ground-level perception. We believe
that this has implications for, and requires acknowledgement by, geographers
and archaeologists. Our approach will help in producing a perspective of the
landscape that is more meaningful than the flat presentation of its formal and
physical attributes.

The physical landscape and rural perceptions

Ballabgarh has two geographical faces (Figure 13.1). It is a land of hills and
plains. The hills (locally called *pahadi*) are the northern-most outliers of the
ancient Aravallis, a mountain range that originates in Gujarat and cuts across
Rajasthan along an axis aligned north-northeast before reaching Haryana and
terminating at Delhi. In Ballabgarh, the hills are not especially high. Gujari-
wala Johar, at 318 m above sea level, is possibly one of the highest points.
In recent decades, the hills have also been extensively quarried. Despite this,
the *pahadi* still has a breadth of several kilometres, forming a compact rocky
plateau between Surajkund and Sirohi. Its harsh character, with unconsoli-
dated rocks and ravines and a sparse scrubby vegetation, imparts a specific
geographical identity to the western edge of Ballabgarh. The vegetation is
made up of species such as *kikar* (*Acacia arabica*), *karil* (*Capparis aphylla*) and
ber (*Zizyphus nummularia*), although the tree cover around temple complexes
can be visibly different. Tree species known locally as *gugal, gaund kathira,
parsendhu, gular, khirni, imli, aam, kadamba, khajur* and *jamun* are encountered
in the Parsaun ravine where Parasara rsi's *taposthana* (meditation spot) stands.
A spectacular sacred forest of *dhau* or *dhoy* trees, spread over several acres
and supported by three villages, still flourishes around Gudariya Baba's shrine
at Mangar. In the midst of a thorny, scrub vegetation, these forest patches
illustrate the limited but important ways in which the perceptions and ecological wisdom of rural inhabitants and temple priests have helped to sustain a
variegated floristic composition. Various streams, regarded as insignificant in
geographical parlance because they are supposed to be seasonal and not perennial, emanate from the hills at different points. We understand that there
is some water flowing in many of them even during the summer months of
May and June. Moreover, these streams were considered important by local

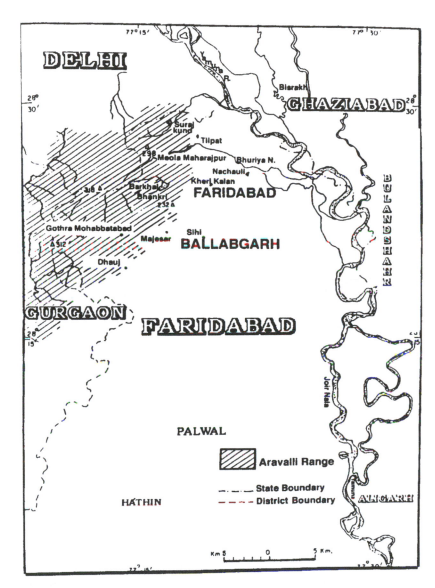

Figure 13.1 Major settlements mentioned in the text.

inhabitants in the past and still are today. A number of old mounds and villages are found in precisely those areas that form part of their catchment zones (Lahiri et al. 1996). Altogether, there are about fifteen sites (some dating back to 500 BC) around the drainage zones of the hill channels. This distribution pattern cannot be regarded as fortuitous. Several historical shrines or cult spots have also clustered around the drainage channels. Flowing south-eastwards, their configuration can be clearly visualised from the detailed list provided in the first *Gazetteer of Delhi* (Gazetteer [1883–4] 1988: 5–6). One of them, the Bhuriya *nala*, is a tributary of the Yamuna river and can be encountered in the general vicinity of many of the surveyed villages in the riverine plain.

Lying beyond the rocky contours of the Aravalli to the east is the other face of Ballabgarh. This is the plains area, which extends to the Yamuna river. The plains consist of an older and higher alluvium (*bhangar*) stretching longitudinally and flanked on the eastern edge by a much narrower strip (*khadar*) which forms the active flood plain of the river. The *khadar-bhangar* demarcation line has, however, been a shifting one because the Yamuna waters have steadily moved eastwards. Today, the river forms the eastern margin of the *tehsil*, forming the line of demarcation between this part of Haryana and the state of Uttar Pradesh. The Ballabgarh hills also stand aloof from this eastward-flowing river. That this was not always so has been demonstrated in the Landsat MSS imagery of geologists (Grover and Bakliwal 1984: 151–3). Two major phases in the history of the Yamuna can be traced. Prior to about 2000 BC, the river flowed 100 km west of Delhi and traversed Gurgaon and Faridabad before entering the southern Haryana plains. Scores of stone age sites in the hills bear testimony to this system of Yamuna palaeochannels which must have been extraordinarily important while they survived (see Chakrabarti and Lahiri 1987; Sharma 1993).

In the second phase, dated to about 4,000 years ago, the river ceased to flow through the hills and migrated to its present course, flowing within the Delhi limits and rounding the Agra canal weir at Okhla before entering Haryana. Even within the Ballabgarh plains, it has steadily shifted its course and was once decidedly more westerly in its upper course than it is today. In 1910–11, for instance, a channel of the Yamuna river meandered past the villages of Kabulpur Kalan, Kabulpur Kadar and Chirsi (Anon. 1912). Chirsi is mentioned in the late nineteenth century as a ferry point. Today, these villages lie a couple of kilometres to the west of the river. The creation of the Okhla barrage, which has regulated the discharge of water into the Yamuna to less than 200 cusecs in summer and about 4,100 cusecs during the monsoons, has also made the river more domesticated.

Interestingly enough, the delineation of *khadar* and *bhangar* land by rural residents does not follow the present geographical situation but is rather based on historical memory. At many villages where the flood waters of the Yamuna have not been sighted for decades, villagers still point to fields that they claim lie in the *khadar* zone. They also point to the old bed of the river through which the Bhuriya *nala* now flows, not as the channel of the latter stream but as the old Yamuna. These perceptions underline the durability of the remembered past when the river undoubtedly did flow past their villages in spate and used to flood their fields. Such memories provide us with important clues for investigating the old course of the river. Villagers in the active *khadar* of the present Yamuna flood plain have similarly and on many occasions noted a *bhangar* component in their village, generally identified with the place where the village houses and structures stand. Because of a steady continuity of settlement over centuries, many such places are several metres high, forming typical archaeological mounds. It is unlikely that the river would submerge such spots, and thus the villagers' characterisation is entirely logical.

On the whole, Ballabgarh is an area of remarkable physiographic variegation. In an objective, dispassionate sense, there is very little doubt that the hills with their drainage channels appear to enclose a strikingly different world to the perennially watered plains of the Yamuna river. Superficially, this difference seems to have been strengthened by the larger dependence in the hill villages on pastoralism in contrast to the agricultural settlements of the plains. The stereotyped folklore that is found in nineteenth-century British records concerning communities like the hill Gujars and Meos also depicts them as thieving, cattle-stealing, groups (Rose [1883] 1990: 308), quite unlike the hard-working, cultivating groups of the lowlands.

Our field investigations have, however, revealed the important point that this geographic variation has not generated a perceptual barrier. Among rural groups in both segments, the land that is regarded as their own is defined as much by the Aravalli hills, and their various aspects, as by the Yamuna and its plains. A context made up of shared historical features and common elements in their respective cultural patterns may help to explain why cognitive barriers have not been significantly inserted into the clearly visible physiographic duality of Ballabgarh.

An important element of group identity in Ballabgarh is provided by the various clans to which different population groups belong, among them the Gujar, Meo, Rajput and Jat. There are other groups that cannot be designated as clans. The Brahims, 'degenerate' because they cultivate Brahmins called Tagas, Saperas, menials and untouchables are such groups. With the exception of the untouchables, about whom we were able to collect very little information, the other groups, like the major clans, identify with related caste and occupational groups in this zone. It is significant that the different population groups are evenly distributed. There is no major community that is found exclusively in one type of physiographic setting. The presence of the Gujars in the hills can be documented from the tenth and eleventh centuries onwards. Anangpur, Mangar and Gothra Mohabbatabad are among the old villages with substantial Gujar populations. There are, at the same time, plains Gujar villages such as Aitmadpur, Tilauri Khadar and Salharawak. We know that the Gujar presence here is medieval because it is documented in the records of the *Bhats* (traditional genealogists) of this rural community. The distribution of Brahmins, the highest social group in terms of caste hierarchy, is similar. Tilpat is a plains village with a large number of Brahmins whose presence there is mentioned in the sixteenth-century treatise of Abul Faz'l (Allami 1949: 284). Similarly, in the foothill area, Dabwa village was settled by Gaur Brahmins 550 years ago. Moreover, some of these communities sought integration with each other through various clan institutions. The villages with significant Meo populations in Ballabgarh are, for example, linked by collateral kinship and descent, through an institution called *Chaurasi*. One such grouping has its central platform at Dhauj (Shamsh 1983: 20). Among the villages that belong to it, there is an even number of hill and foothill settlements (Silokhri, Dhauj, Sirohi, Alampur, Khori) and plains villages (Madalpur, Fatehpur, Tikri Khera, Zakupur, Ladhiyapur). Many families also have land-holdings in both hills and the plains section. A family from the foothill village of Meola Maharajpur cultivates a segment that it owns in Dungarpur in the plains, just as an old resident family in Khanpur until recently had holdings in the vicinity of Khanpur, near the *pahadi* and in the *khadar* area east of the Yamuna. This system of land-holding is evocative of a pre-modern pattern in Ballabgarh. In the report of the land revenue settlement carried on in 1872–3 (Maconachie 1882: 72–9), there are several instances mentioned of superior land proprietors who were not resident in the villages where they held lands. The superior proprietor of the agricultural land of Phaphundah, for instance, was Ganga Bakhsh Jat, a resident of Sihi village. At Tajupur, the superior proprietors were from three villages: Kheri Kalan, Sherpur and Karaoli. The links between the hills and the plains extend into the geography of matrimonial alliances as well.

Another element that may help to explain why the hills and the plains are not perceived as bounded cultural worlds relates to the shared interaction of the two zones even prior to their recent history. The archaeological evidence relating to settlement distribution permits the area-wise and period-wise reconstruction shown in Table 13.1.

The geographical spread of settlements in pre-modern Ballabgarh is evident enough. As is obvious, from the Kushana-Gupta phases of occupation, the number of sites that are located outside the riverine strip are evenly balanced with those near the Yamuna. More significantly, a majority of those in the higher plains area (Bajri, the Pali colony of Pir, Kheri Gujran, Madalpur and Qureshipur) are actually in the western segment which is close to the hills. There are also settlements in the Aravalli zone itself which are found on the hills, hill bases and the plateau areas. Dorji, for instance, is in an interior

Table 13.1 Numbers of sites in the Faridabad district (Ballabgarh *tehsil*)

Period	Riverine plains	Higher plains	Hill zone
Late Harappan and painted grey ware (*1500–550* BC)	6	3	0
North black polished ware and Early Historic (*550 BC–1 AD*)	4	2	1
Kushana-Gupta (*1st–6th centuries* AD)	11	8	5
Post-Gupta (*Several phases; Medieval to 18th century* AD)	24	18	10

plateau among the hills above Dhauj, while the occupational remains at Pali Bas are spread along a high hill slope. Badri Khar stands in the immediate base area of the hills while Meola Maharajpur, slightly east of the rugged upland, overlies a few Aravalli ripples that soon merge into the plains. This distribution pattern also continues into the medieval phase.

Similar developmental trajectories do not, of course, suggest that the people of the hills and the plains were necessarily in close political and social contact. In fact, even in the Early Historic period, agriculture in and around the hills must have been much less significant than it was on the riparian plains of the Yamuna. At the same time, the hills here possess significant non-agricultural resources, and there is evidence to show that the plains settlements not only used these resources for various purposes in their normal day-to-day lives but also preferred the hills for ritual and political reasons. First, they provided a substantial raw-material source close to the minerally poor Yamuna plains. Quartzite, sandstone, slate, mica and crystal are some of the known resources (Gazetteer [1883–4] 1988: 16–17). There are numerous iron-ore nodules around Parasaun, and *silajit* (a rock-based medicinal substance) is found in the Mohabbatabad area. From the perspective of historical settlements, our field report's inventory of artefactual and structural relics (Lahiri et al. 1996) suggests that these resources formed part of the intercourse from the hills and it is likely that the return traffic included pottery and grain, among other items.

To these economic resources, the locational and political advantages of the uplands may also be added. On the western side they provide access to human groups from Rajasthan who have been an enduring feature of Ballabgarh's history. Many Gujars, Rajputs, Meos and Brahims, among others, state that their ancestral village was in that western state. Geographically, such movements from the dry, thirsty, Aravalli areas of Rajasthan into the alluvial plains make eminent sense because the Yamuna river, forming the eastern edge of Ballabgarh, is one of the major perennial rivers that is easily approachable from there. The accessible routes from Rajasthan across and around the Ballabgarh hills and the many topographic features that the former shares with this stretch of the Aravallis (among other things, they both have a common geographical base) are also well known. It is much more significant that the links with Rajasthan, recorded through origin traditions and myths, are an integral element of the cognitive world of rural Ballabgarh and are constantly kept in circulation. This is done by various means, in which the Bhat community plays a central role. Most of the Bhats hail from Rajasthan and are described as 'expert historians' in a recent volume on Haryana (Sharma and Bhatia 1994: 76). Genealogists by occupation, they have for several centuries meticulously noted the genealogies, births, deaths and movements of the Ballabgarh communities that patronise them. This community is nomadic, moving from village to village, and at most places there are recitations of the origin myths of their various patrons. Through such discourses, the past or pasts of village communities are inserted into their cultural present. These pasts, geographically

speaking, generally begin with migrations from the western Aravalli terrain, and
with movements from place to place, before the family or groups of families
settled in the Ballabgarh *tehsil*. Culturally there is much in this micro-segment
that has both its origins and canonical setting in the hills. Rural notions of the
landscape carry the marks of that fact.

Important shrines of interlocal worship are also located in the Ballabgarh
Aravallis and beyond them both in the western areas of Gurgaon and in
Rajasthan. In Ballabgarh itself, important religious shrines include the Siddha
Baba complex at Satkund, Parasara rsi's *taposthana* at Parasaun, Uddalakamuni's
taposthana in the Mohabbatabad hills and Dadi Piplasan's shrine at Dhauj.
Most of these are old cult centres. The Satkund complex would date to the
tenth or eleventh century AD when the Surajkund, a ritual tank fed by
the waters of Satkund, was constructed. Parasara rsi's *taposthana* (Figure 13.2)
and the Dhauj shrine, with its Sultanate period structure, are also medieval;
while Uddalakamuni's *taposthana* is marked by a fourth- or fifth-century AD

Figure 13.2 Medieval structure at Parasaun.

ekamukhalinga (phallic emblem with the face of God Siva carved on it) and a twelfth-century inscription. That they continued to provide a focus for the religious life of Ballabgarh is evident from the first *Gazetteer of Delhi* (Gazetteer [1883–4] 1988: 59). The Yamuna was supposed to be an important sacred river, whose banks were considered as providing an ideal locale for the performance of elaborate Vedic sacrificial sessions called *sattra* rituals (Roy 1993: 7, 9), but this has, interestingly, been ignored in the interlocal shrine geography of this stretch of the river. The elements that may explain this shrine distribution and its implications for reconstructing religious geography on the basis of textual images and traditions are worth investigating in detail (for a critique of textually constituted religious geography see Lahiri 1996). A socio-religious coherence has come to be attached to the hills, and shrines that appear remote even by present standards have thus enjoyed an adequate patronage. This is mainly because the Ballabgarh hills and plains are peopled by groups who are completely at home in such sequestered locales. There are also many similar shrines in Gurgaon and Rajasthan. A number of communities journey annually into the hills that continue beyond and west and southwest of Ballabgarh, in the process renegotiating their cultural links with that terrain.

Finally, many population groups used the hills as a political base and a refuge during periods of trouble. The distribution of medieval fortifications from Anangpala's *Qila* (fort) in the Surajkund hills to Kot, the stronghold of a Raja Gopala Singh, and even further in the Meo-inhabited Sirohi village, is strikingly suggestive of this. Various histories compiled during the centuries following the establishment of the Delhi Sultanate (thirteenth century AD onwards) also allude to the hills being a stronghold of recalcitrant communities. In the Tabakat-i Nasiri, for instance, the author Juzjani's patron Nasiru-d din Mahmud is not mentioned as pacifying people or areas in the Ballabgarh plains. Many of his nobles seemed, in fact, to have owned fiefs and gardens adjacent to the Yamuna (Elliot and Dowson 1869: 356–7). On the other hand, in the fifteenth year of Sultan Nasiru-d din Mahmud's reign (Hijra 658; i.e. AD 1260), Juzjani records that the distinguished noble, Ulugh Khan, had to be sent 'to the hills of Delhi to chastise the rebel inhabitants of Mewat and to intimidate their Deo' (Elliot and Dowson 1869: 359). These hills are obviously those that were located to the south of the royal capital and must have included the Aravalli area that now forms part of western Ballabgarh. Incidentally, the perception of the hills as providing a refuge zone has continued into the present. As recently as 1946–7, many Muslims from plains villages took shelter there during episodes of communal violence.

Ballabgarh's visible surface, on which the hills form a distinct and separate geophysical facet from the plains, thus loses its meaning when it is enveloped in the social and cultural frames of reference through which the villagers have inscribed their notion of landscape. Regardless of their own physical location, they consider the Aravallis and the Yamuna plains to be markers of their lived environment. We have tried to show some of the historical and cultural factors that have helped in producing this view of the landscape.

The archaeological landscape and rural perceptions

The archaeological landscape in Ballabgarh is understood both in ways readily comprehended within modern archaeological thinking and in more exotic ways. Mounds are generally understood as being sites of former settlements, an understanding that may be contextualised in terms of the lived experiences of rural residents where movement of villages has been common enough. Even in the last fifty years or so, the habitation areas of different rural groups have shifted. Among the reasons mentioned by villagers for such shifts are natural causes such as 'bad' water leading to infertility (Tilauri Khadar and Kheri Gujran), epidemics (Sehatpur) and inundation by Yamuna flood waters (Dadsia). Other factors relate to socio-political events which include medieval population movements (as in Meola Maharajpur, where the Meos were uprooted by a Gujar community) and the more recent partition of India and Pakistan. The partition period is locally called *marshalla*, a corruption of the term 'martial law',[2] and several village sites (such as Agwanpur ka kheda and Baselwah) were abandoned in those violent years. Taken over in many such cases by acacia-dominated forest clumps, the palpable desolation still evident at such abandoned settlements is heightened when the extensive presence of medieval structures with Islamic features in Ballabgarh's old villages is contrasted with the very small number of Muslims who live there.

There are also ancient sites where structural remains and artefacts are perceived through traditional socio-religious associations and beliefs. At Dhauj, the Meo inhabitants recount an old tradition about the quartzite structure on the western edge of the village that dates to the thirteenth–fifteenth centuries AD. Originally domed and locally called the Dera, it is considered as being the overnight handiwork of a Jinn, a class of spirits that is regarded as belonging to the malevolent dead. Among other things, Jinns have no bones in their arms, only four fingers and no thumb (Rose [1883] 1990: 207). Similarly, local legend associates the village of Bishrakh with the father of Ravana. Ravana is the mythical transgressor in the Ramayana, the most popular epic of India, and is generally associated with the peninsular parts of the Indian subcontinent. Here, however, a spot thickly covered with medieval potsherds is pointed out as the place where Ravana was born. The village is situated on a mound with occupation layers that extend back to the painted grey ware phase (1000 BC) and continue into the Medieval period. From such deposits a large number of stone Siva *lingas* (phallic emblems of Siva) have been recovered, some of which can be seen in the open-air village shrine (Figure 13.3), along with a decapitated Nandi (the vehicle of Siva) bull - sculpture. Taken together, these seem to be the remnants of a medieval Siva

Figure 13.3   Village shrine with sculpture at Bishrakh.

temple. Since Ravana is popularly represented as a Siva devotee, these Siva-related relics are treated as material evidence for the presence of the mythical villain here. In Brahmanical tradition, Bishrakh would be geographically located in Kuru land, a segment that was 'Aryanised' quite early, unlike Ravana's kingdom of Lanka and the epic geography that has traditionally situated Ravana in peninsular India. Unintimidated by such traditions, villagers proudly proclaim a spot in their village as Ravana's *janma bhumi* (birthplace)! The 'miraculous' powers invested in iron slag from the old village mound of Sihi, which have been discussed elsewhere (Lahiri 1995: 129–30), provide another example of the ways in which local beliefs transform the meanings that archaeologists would read into artefacts of past cultures.

Sculptural relics are similarly, more often than not, divested of their original contextual associations. At Mawai, Hathin and Kheri Kalan, for example, motley collections of early medieval sculptural fragments recovered from the old mound or mounds of the village are placed in folk village shrines (*grama sthanas*) and worshipped as manifestations of the inhabited, socially domesticated land and village. In some villages, as at Gharora, single architectural fragments are similarly worshipped (Figure 13.4). The sculptural fragments attest to the existence of Brahmanical and Jaina temples in Ballabgarh between the seventh and thirteenth centuries AD. These probably perished during the foundation of the Sultanate of Delhi. For rural residents and outside observers.

Figure 13.4 Architectural fragment from an old temple at Gharora.

they strikingly evoke the way in which Sultanate authority was articulated through the desecration of sacred spaces of the conquered populace. These archaeological remnants of ancient 'high culture' are still dramatically visible, but are situated in the arena of folk worship. They are, moreover, worshipped as representational forms of deities that bear no resemblance to their original iconic form. Ganesha, for instance, is worshipped on a mother-goddess shrine, while Vishnu has been regarded as the Devi (another goddess). At the local level, these examples speak volumes for the reception of images and the irrelevance of traditional scriptural sanctions that strictly forbid any worship of broken or mutilated images.

One may also tentatively suggest a reason for structural and artefactual elements being read in such unusual ways. To understand this, we must return briefly to the history of the zone. As is evident from its archaeological sequence, Ballabgarh has a long history (see Table 13.1). The distribution of settlements suggests that, since the Historical period, there has been a steady continuity at or around most of them, which has led to the formation of substantial mounds in many such locales. It is also fairly evident, however, that there were constant readjustments of population groups and demographic mobility between these stable locations. We are fortunate to have documentation of this in the genealogies of the old communities of the area which have been maintained by the Bhats. At Tilpat village (identified with

Tilaprastha of the Mahabharata tradition that goes back to the latter part of the first millennium BC) there is, for instance, a 30-m high mound. Limited excavations have established a 1000 BC cultural stratum there (Lal 1954–5: 141). One is also certain, on the basis of an archaeological reconnaissance carried out in 1994, that Tilpat remained largely inhabited well into the Medieval period. The old family trees of resident Brahmins, who constituted a substantial segment of the medieval village population, however, go back to only the early sixteenth century or thereabouts. The family tree of the late Pandit Nathu Singh Girdawar is a case in point. Traced back to AD 1525, to a person called Mukha, the family tree from AD 1525 till 1950 has been compiled by the present family members in the form of a flow chart. It is understandable, then, that such residents would not view various archaeological indicators of the past or pasts of their habitation area in terms of their own community history or histories, or with reference to the meanings that orthodox academic scholarship invests in them. Instead they view them through the prism of their traditional beliefs and, in the process, alter the meanings that archaeologists would read into them.

Conclusion

Landscapes do not merely exist, they are made. Life histories and folk memories help in constituting them. In Ballabgarh, rural perceptions are grounded in such elements, which do not simply and mimetically reproduce the form and physical attributes of Ballabgarh's natural and archaeological landscape. On the contrary, they actively transform what is given in the topography and archaeology. In doing so they undermine certain 'logical' categories of meaning that are used to depict this land, just as they challenge the established prescriptions and prohibitions contained in the dominant Brahmanical 'Great Tradition'.

Notes

1 A *tehsil* is an administrative sub-division of a district. Two settlements that are mentioned in this chapter in fact lie outside the administrative boundaries of the district: Khanpur lies on the northwestern border of Faridabad and Bishrakh is situated east of the Yamuna but within the National Capital zone.
2 We owe this identification to Gyanendra Pandey, our colleague in Delhi University and a historian of modern India.

Acknowledgements

The memories and observations of Ballabgarh's rural inhabitants and the unhurried, generous manner in which these were elucidated have been a moving experience personally and, professionally, a relevant departure point. We would like to thank especially Ravindar Kumar of Khanpur, Phul Singh Tunwar of Ankhir, Babu Balbirji of Chrisi, Lachmi Brahmin of Tilpat and Shivanth Singh of NOIDA.

References

Allami, Abdul Faz'l-i [n.d., sixteenth century] 1949. *Ain-i-Akbari, Vol. 2.* Translated by H.S. Jarrett, corrected and annotated by J.N. Sarkar. Calcutta: Royal Asiatic Society of Bengal.

Anon. 1912. *Topographic Sheet No. 53 H/7 Punjab and United Provinces.* Calcutta: Surveyor General of India.

Chakrabarti, D.K. and N. Lahiri 1987. A preliminary report on the Stone Age of the Union Territory of Delhi and Haryana. *Man and Environment* 11, 109–16.

Elliot, H.M. and J. Dowson 1869. *The History of India as told by its own Historians, Vol. 2.* London: Trubner & Co.

Gazetteer [1883–4] 1988. *A Gazetteer of Delhi, 1883–4.* Gurgaon: Vintage Books.

Gazetteer 1991. *Imperial Gazetteer of India Provincial Series, Punjab Volume I* (reprint). New Delhi: Atlantic Publishers and Distributors.

Grover, A.K. and P.L. Bakliwal 1984. River migration and the floods: a study of a section of Yamuna river through the remote sensing. *Man and Environment* 9, 151–3.

Lahiri, N. 1995. Indian metal and metal-related artefacts as cultural signifiers: an ethnographic perspective. *World Archaeology* 27, 116–32.

Lahiri, N. 1996. Archaeological landscapes and textual images: a study of the sacred geography of late medieval Ballabgarh. *World Archaeology* 28, 244–64.

Lahiri, N., U. Singh and T. Uberoi 1996. Preliminary field report on the archaeology of Faridabad: the Ballabgarh Tehsil. *Man and Environment* 21, 32–57.

Lal, B.B. 1954–5. Excavations at Hastinapura and other explorations in the upper Ganga and Sutlej basins 1950–2. *Ancient India* 10–11, 5–151.

Maconachie, R. 1882. *Final Report on the Settlement of Land Revenue in the Delhi District.* Lahore: Victoria Press.

Rose, H.A. [1883] 1990. *Glossary of the Tribes and Castes of the Punjab and North-West Frontier Province, Vol. I.* New Delhi Madras: Asian Educational Services.

Roy, K. 1993. In which part of South Asia did the early brahmanical tradition (1st millennium BC) take its form? *Studies in History* 9, 1–32.

Shamsh, S. 1983. *Meos of India: their customs and laws.* New Delhi: Deep & Deep.

Sharma, A.K. 1993. *Prehistoric Delhi and its Neighbourhood.* New Delhi: Aryan Books International.

Sharma, M.L. and A.K. Bhatia 1994. *People of India: Haryana, Vol. 23.* Delhi: Manohar.

14 Ancestors, place and people: social landscapes in Aboriginal Australia

CLAIRE SMITH

Introduction

Researchers working with Aboriginal Australians have always had to grapple with conceptions of place. This is because patterns of indigenous land use, as well as notions of personal identity, are closely linked to social constructions of the land. As Morphy (1995) points out, relationships between landscape and Aboriginal conceptions of the world have been a central theme of anthropological research since the first detailed ethnographic studies, such as those of Roth (1897), Spencer and Gillen (1899), Strehlow (1947), Warner (1969) and Kaberry (1939). This interest has been manifested in terms of territoriality and social space (e.g. Tindale 1974; Peterson 1976), trade (e.g. McBryde 1978, 1984; Turpin 1983), social networks (e.g. David and Cole 1990; McDonald in press), totemic geography (e.g. Strehlow 1970; cf. Berndt and Berndt 1989) and indigenous land rights (e.g. Coombs 1980; Tonkinson 1980; Rowse 1993).

Recently, this enduring theme has emerged in the disciplines of anthropology, archaeology and cultural geography as an interest in social landscapes (e.g. Gosden 1989; Bender 1993, Chapter 3 this volume; Head *et al.* 1994; Fullagar and Head Chapter 22 this volume). From this perspective, not only have the landscapes in which people live been shaped *by* human action, but they also shape human action. Social landscapes are both 'transformed' and 'transforming' (Gosden and Head 1994: 114). They are multi-layered in a process characterised by Byrne (1993: 7) as 'sedimentation . . . the old being sedimented below the new in the minds of individuals' and multi-faceted in that they are subject to a plethora of meanings depending on the particular historically and politically situated position of the interpreter (cf. Smith 1994: 263). Ballard (1994: 145) suggests that 'the promise of a social landscape approach lies in the scope it offers for working with a series of overlapping constructs, different landscapes of meaning that address a variety of perspectives'.

Head (1993: 487) distinguishes two major challenges for archaeologists interested in landscape as social expression: making hunter-gatherer social structures materially visible and disentangling the relevant time-scales. This chapter aims to make an indigenous social structure materially visible by outlining some of the ways in which Aboriginal people in northern Australia conceive of place, with particular consideration of how the social identities of ancestors, people and place are constructed in relation to each other.

The study area

The main study area is the Barunga region of northern Australia. Population centres within the region are located on land that is identified with the Jawoyn and Ngarrbun language groups (Figure 14.1). The communities of Barunga, Beswick (also known as Wugularr) and Manyallaluk (also known as Eva Valley) are located on the lands of the Bagula clan of the Jawoyn people. The main language groups living in these community centres are those of the Jawoyn, Mangarrai, Mara, Myilly, Ngarrbun and Rembarrnga. The township of Bulman (also known as Gulig Gulig) and the outstations of Weemol and Gropulyu are located on Ngarrbun land and are inhabited mostly by Myilly, Ngarrbun and Rembarrnga people.[1] These communities vary in population size from around 400 people at the major townships to only twenty people at outstation communities. In this chapter I use the term 'Barunga people' and 'Barunga region' when referring to the people or region as a whole.

A map of the lands according to language groups is shown in Figure 14.1. Aboriginal languages in the region are the first languages of most older people, but generally are not spoken by middle-aged and younger people. The *lingua franca* for the region is Kriol, which is an Aboriginal creole English spoken by more than 15,000 people in the north of Australia (see Sandefur and Sandefur 1982). In the Barunga region, Kriol is the first language of younger people who are also proficient in English. The schools teach a bilingual programme of Kriol and English, and local Aboriginal teachers and teacher-aids assist with the implementation of this programme.

The Barunga population is highly mobile. Most people spend parts of the year in at least two of the community centres within the region and all people have a range of personal ties to several areas. Many of the people living in the southern group of communities (Barunga, Beswick and Manyallaluk) are not Jawoyn people even though they are living on Jawoyn land. These people have ties to the residential communities within which they live as well as the customary lands of their own language groups. Also, they spend part of the year visiting the northern group of communities (Bulman, Weemol and Gropulyu). Both Jawoyn and non-Jawoyn people move freely within the southern group of communities.

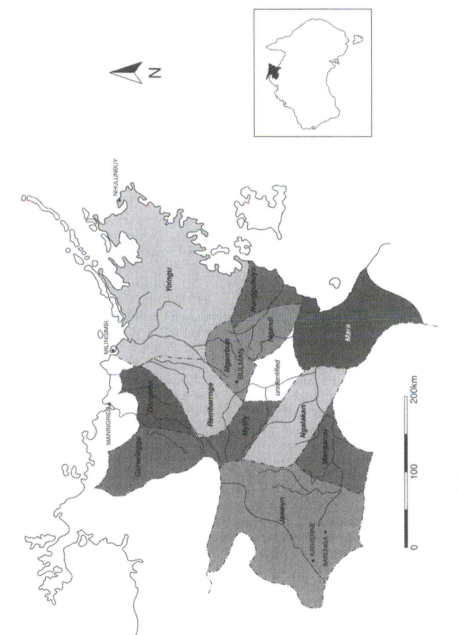

Figure 14.1 Location of relevant language groups.

Colonial history

The contact period in the Barunga region has been brief in comparison to other parts of Australia. In this region, Aboriginal socio-cultural practices have been relatively uninformed by colonial interactions and they are distinctly different from those of non-Aboriginal people. Aboriginal people in parts of northern Australia were protected from some of the worst effects of European settlement simply because the colonial frontier did not reach their lands until the mid-twentieth century. The Aboriginal Land Rights (Northern Territory) Act 1976 provided the means by which Aboriginal people in the Northern Territory were able to gain secure title to much of their land, previously of reserve status. As Morphy (1995) points out, this security of title was obtained before some Aboriginal people in the north fully realised that they were threatened with loss of their land. A significant number of Aboriginal people in central Arnhem Land were still living a fundamentally nomadic life in the 1950s and some of the older people in the Barunga region can remember seeing a white person for the first time when they were young children. The contact period in northern Australia, though short, was violent. In the pastoral district of the Victoria River, located around 300 km east of Barunga, Rose (1992: 7) suggests a population depletion of up to 95 per cent.[2] This is comparable to Keen's (1980: 171) estimate that population loss in the Alligator River region was around 97 per cent.

It is difficult to assess whether the Barunga region sustained a similar level of loss. Much of the worst violence was associated with the strategies used by pastoralists for making land 'suitable' for their activities (Rose 1992: 9; see also Merlan 1978). The first pastoral lease to encompass the country around Barunga and Beswick was that of Fisher, Lyons and Co., which was taken out in 1881, but intensive pastoral activity did not occur in this region until earlier this century (see Maddock 1965: 5, 1969). Aboriginal people who lived around the townships of Barunga and Beswick would have been fairly vulnerable to pastoralist violence. However, those living in central Arnhem Land would have been protected to a certain extent since this area was gazetted as an Aboriginal reserve which limited non-indigenous use of the land (but see Forrest 1985: 3)

Contact has had differing degrees of influence on different aspects of Barunga society. The economic base has changed radically and Barunga people are now part of a European-style market economy. The staple diet of European foods, such as flour and tea, is supplemented by occasional, high-status 'bush foods', such as bush turkey, turtle and kangaroo. Contemporary social structures, however, are fundamentally different to those of non-Aboriginal societies. These structures have been less subject to radical change not only because of the relatively short period of colonial influence but also because Aboriginal people in the region are committed to their continuance. Indigenous culture and values are highly prized, and a common derogatory term given by Barunga people to other Aboriginal people who have acted poorly is that they've 'got no culture'. In short, Barunga people incorporate non-Aboriginal foods into their diet as this suits them, but see little or no merit in adopting non-Aboriginal social structures.

Conceptions of place in northern Australia

There are a number of ways in which social identities of people and places are articulated in the Barunga region. The principal bases for social affiliation to place are language group, moiety, clan, nomenclature and, more recently, residential community.[3] The socialised landscapes of the present have their genesis in the Dreaming, the creation era during which ancestral beings travelled throughout the land, creating its topographic features through their actions. Thus, every facet of the landscape became imbued with ancestral associations.

Arguing for the subordination of time to space in the Yolngu society from the neighbouring region of northeast Arnhem Land, Morphy suggests that interaction with the landscape is part of the process whereby the Dreaming is reproduced as part of the cultural structure of contemporary Aboriginal society:

> The ancestral beings, fixed in the land, become a timeless reference point outside the politics of daily life to which the emotions of the living can be attached. To become this reference point the ancestral journeying had in effect to be frozen for ever at a particular point in the action, so that part of the action became timeless. Place has precedence over time in Yolngu ontogeny. Time was created through the transformation of ancestral beings into place, the place being for ever the mnemonic of the event. They 'sat down' and, however briefly they stayed, they became part of the place for ever. In Yolngu terms they turned into the place. . . . The flow of action was fixed for ever by the very fact of its transmission to landscape; it becomes a structure that exists outside the ancestral world.
>
> (Morphy 1995: 188, 189)

In the Barunga region, social identity is constructed and reconstructed in relationship to place and ancestral associations, as people live in and move through their landscapes. An integral part of the process of growing up is that of each community member learning their unique complex of relationships to place. As people move through their lands, not only do they learn about relationships between place and their ancestors, they also learn about themselves and their particular rights and responsibilities in this land-based scheme of existence. As Rowley (1986: 86) points out, the separation of land, kinship, inheritance and religion in Australian Aboriginal societies is simply a western intellectual exercise. Moreover, this sense of being bound to land is a major force behind the mobility of the Barunga population.

In the cosmos of Barunga people the flow of power is from inherently powerful ancestral beings to the land, imbued with a potency given to it by the actions of past people and ancestors; and to living people, who have the facility to call upon the power and authority that is inherent in both the land and ancestral beings. This is the foundation for Aboriginal conceptualisation of the contemporary landscapes as redolent with meaning, inherently powerful and potentially dangerous. Rock-art sites are often a focus of such power (e.g. Layton 1992: 38). Vinnicombe notes that in the Kimberley region west of Barunga, certain paintings are 'regarded not as dead illustrations of mythical events but as a living power with direct relevance to the present' (Vinnicombe 1982: 5). From this perspective, traversing the land is something that needs to be constantly negotiated; it is necessary that people be aware of how they are interacting with, and how their actions may impinge upon, what are essentially living landscapes, landscapes capable of retribution for misdeeds as well as munificence.

Many of the principles for negotiating such landscapes are related to the ways in which the social identities of people are articulated with those of place. One of the primary ways in which Aboriginal people in northern Australia relate to land is through their language group. Both people and land are identified with a particular language group. This is one of the first forms of information that is given about new people and new land. Language affiliation is acquired by having parents of a particular language group, which in turn is affiliated to a specific area of country. Since 'Jawoynness', 'Ngarrbunness' and so forth can only be acquired as a birthright, people who are affiliated with a particular language group are necessarily the direct descendants of forebears who also belonged to that language group. In other words, ethnic identity is projected from territory onto the people affiliated with it through direct inheritance from parents (cf. Merlan and Rumsey 1982: 6). People may be given a choice of language group affiliation if their parents come from different language groups, that is, they can choose to follow either the father or mother. However, identification seems to be imposed largely by parents, since primary language affiliation is securely recognised by adolescence.

There are both pragmatic and political influences on this matter. At a pragmatic level is choice of residence. For instance, the marriage of Lily Willika of the Ngarrbun language group and Charlie Mangga, a Jawoyn man, produced six children, all of whom are now adults. All grew up on Jawoyn land and all identify as Jawoyn people, rather than Ngarrbun. While their father's language group gave them a right to primary affiliation as Jawoyn, it is likely that they were inclined towards assuming Jawoyn identity because they were born and raised on Jawoyn land. Apart from practical concerns, there are political considerations that need to be taken into account in such matters, such as the political strength and economic power of the Jawoyn Association and the absence of a comparable Ngarrbun Association.

The second way in which Aboriginal people in southern Arnhem Land conceive of place is through the social division of moiety. During the Dreaming, ancestral beings assigned everything in the world – people, animals, plants and places – to either the Dhuwa or Yirritja moiety. As Morphy (1995) points out, this created a 'checker-board-like pattern' of alternating opposite moiety units, into which groups of people are affiliated. Moieties also alternate between generations of mother and child. For example, a mother of Dhuwa moiety will have children of Yirritja moiety.

Each moiety is associated with particular colours and proportions, as illustrated in Figure 14.2. The Dhuwa moiety is associated with dark colours, such as black and red, while the Yirritja moiety is associated with light colours, such as white and yellow. Similarly, the Dhuwa moiety is associated with shortness and the Yirritja moiety with tallness. Thus, the short-necked turtle is of Dhuwa moiety and the long-necked turtle is of Yirritja moiety. Core associations such as these allow Aboriginal people to identify the moiety of animals, plants and objects in the world around them forming the landscapes they live in and pass through.

A core theme of northern Aboriginal society that is related to this moiety division is the relationship between owner, *Gidjan*, and custodian, *Junggayi*. This reciprocal custodial relationship operates at many levels. For instance, all Dhuwa people are custodians of Yirritja land and ceremonies while all Yirritja people are custodians of Dhuwa land and ceremonies. The renewal of rock paintings is also subject to the *Junggayi* relationship between moieties. Only Yirritja people are permitted to renew (repaint) rock paintings on Dhuwa land and only Dhuwa people can renew rock paintings on Yirritja land. In terms of renewing rock paintings, moiety has precedence over language group. For example, in the Barunga region, where there are few Jawoyn people of sufficient age and knowledge to have a right to renew paintings, this custodial responsibility has passed to Ngarrbun people of the

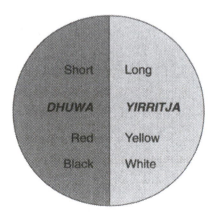

Figure 14.2 Relationships between moieties, colours and dimensions.

correct moiety rather than being taken on by Jawoyn people of the incorrect moiety. It is more important that paintings be renewed by people of the opposite moiety to the land than it is that they be renewed by people from the same language group as the land. Renewed paintings combine both Dhuwa and Yirritja colours, usually as red infill with white detailing or white infill with red detailing. This conforms to a general principle that Dhuwa and Yirritja should be 'in company'.

The third way in which social identity articulates with land is through clan. Clan relates to both language group and moiety, since a person's clan is determined by affiliation to particular tracts of country. Therefore, people of a particular clan belong to the same language group and moiety. Clan, known as *dawaro*, is inherited patrilineally. Maddock (1982: 94), who conducted extensive research in this region during the 1960s and 1970s, comments that land is the common ground, so to speak, between the human members of the clan and the ancestral powers that gave the land its form. Clan territories are covered by pathways taken by ancestral beings during the Dreaming, the physical features of the land being attributed to their actions (see Maddock 1982).

The rubric of clan has, however, endured less well than other facets of personal identity relating to land; information relating to clan is not as well known as other aspects of social identity. For example, children and younger people are often unaware of their clan affiliation though they may know the moiety, sub-section and language groups to which they belong. In addition, information about the clan affiliation of adults can often be obtained only directly from the person involved. This contrasts with the observation of Maddock (1982: 36) that 'the significance of clan and clan species for personal identity [among Dalabon (Ngarrbun) and neighbouring peoples] is suggested by the practice of speaking of or to a person by the name of his clan or its species'. Such a practice is extremely rare in contemporary Barunga society.

This raises the question of why the social identifier of clan in particular has proven vulnerable to dissolution. The answer perhaps lies in the specificity of clan in relation to relatively small and defined tracts of land and to historical problems involved in visiting these areas. The establishment of community centres in southern Arnhem Land from the 1940s onwards encouraged Aboriginal people to move away from their customary lands further north, and it became virtually impossible for many of them to visit their clan lands. This problem is long-standing and Maddock (1971) comments that some of the young men who accompanied him on his trips into central Arnhem Land were visiting their clan lands for the first time. The interesting issue is how the contemporary resettlement of central Arnhem Land through the outstation movement, combined with the greater availability of four-wheel drive vehicles, will affect the use of clan lands and the use of clan as a social identifier. While it is theoretically possible that there will be a resurgence in the use of clan as a social identifier for individual people, this is unlikely as it has been out of general usage for too long. As Rowley (1986: 86) remarks, it requires only one generation of disruption to interrupt the handing on of cultural knowledge.

The fourth way in which the social identities of people and place are integrated is through nomenclature. Often, the personal names of Aboriginal people are the same as those used for tracts of land that are owned and associated with particular creation stories and ancestral beings. These are not the names of clans, though they are associated with particular groupings of clan lands. The use of these personal names has significance beyond the individual since it evokes specific places and ancestral associations. Personal names form one element of a triadic relationship in northern Aboriginal societies that articulates the social identities of ancestors, place and people.

This relationship may be the genesis for the opinion that it is dangerous to use a person's name after they are dead, as that sound customarily also connects to place and ancestral associations. In a world imbued with 'living power' (cf. Vinnicombe 1982: 5), naming the deceased can be dangerous. Continuation and reformulation of this custom is intimated in strict adherence to the principle in contemporary situations, even if the person was known primarily by a European name that does not have direct connections to place and ancestors. If somebody called Rhonda died, for example, all people within her main sphere of social interaction who are called Rhonda would cease using that name and take on another. Subsequently, if a person using the newly adopted name died, these people would adopt a further, different name. After a suitable period, they might choose to revert to their original name. Through this process, individuals can be known by many different names during their lifetimes. An attempt to circumvent this to a certain extent may be implicit in the contemporary use of non-conventional names for children, such as 'Jessila', rather than 'Jessica'. This also may be why children of the same generation within the same community tend to be given different names.

Finally, it is possible to distinguish the emergence of a new way of conceiving of place in northern Australia, through the personal identification that comes with place of residence, or community. In the past, people resided on their own lands, though they regularly visited their neighbours in order to participate in joint social activities, such as ceremonies. Residential stability usually brought about an inherent compatibility between place of residence and affiliation to territory through clan and language group. However, the migration of Aboriginal people from central Arnhem Land to the southern group of communities during the 1940s untied the nexus between place of residence and territorial affiliation through clan and language group. This allowed room for the emergence of a different type of connection to land through affiliation to community.

The notion of residential community as a way of conceiving of place can be perceived in community T-shirts worn throughout the region. Most Aboriginal communities in northern Australia have shops that sell T-shirts with the name of the community (e.g. Barunga, Beswick, Gulig Gulig). One young Aboriginal person commented that he liked his own T-shirt because he was 'proud of Barunga'. Another remarked that 'wearing that T-shirt shows that you live at Barunga'. The information that Aboriginal people transmit through wearing the T-shirt is affiliation to residential community. This is in general contrast to the use of such T-shirts by non-Aboriginal Australians, who tend to use this form of portable art to communicate information about places they have visited, or sub-groups to which they are affiliated, rather than the community in which they permanently reside.

An emergent identification with place according to residential community can also be perceived in the art of the region. Figure 14.3 depicts the percentage of major art forms that were produced in each community in a recent study of 321 art objects by Smith (1994) and shows clear clustering in art forms according to the community in which artists spent the majority of their time. For example, all seventy-four examples of the five forms of carving (fish, crocodile, bird, snake and human figure) were produced only in the Beswick community. Thus, an informed outside person could identify the creator of a carving with this community centre. However, this does not mean that only artists who live at Beswick have a right to produce carvings; given the mobility of people within the Barunga complex of communities, such a proscription would be unworkable. Barunga people explain this patterning as due to a relative lack of suitable tools in other community centres. In addition, I suggest that this patterning is a result of mutual stylistic influence among people who reside in close proximity to one another and a reluctance by Barunga people from outside of this community centre to appropriate the stylistic forms associated with the Beswick group of artists.

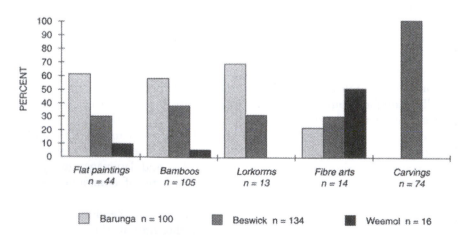

Figure 14.3 Distribution of art forms according to community.

Figure 14.3 shows that 50 per cent of fibre arts come from the outstation community of Weemol, even though the art from this community comprises less than 9 per cent of the database of Smith's study. A dialectical relationship between structure and social action can be perceived here in the fact that people who are interested in distinctly Aboriginal ways of living are attracted to the structures that exist in outstation communities. The social actions of these people, including their decisions relating to art production, tend in turn to reinforce the customarily oriented aspects of those structures. The emphasis on fibre arts at Weemol is the practical manifestation of this process. Further, the production of these art forms tends to strengthen the indigenous values of the communities in which they are produced, not least because they are the visual manifestation of these values.

Discussion

This chapter has so far focused on a particular case study in northern Australia but now considers some of the similarities and differences between Aboriginal relationships to land in northern and southern Australia. Aboriginal people in southern Australia do not derive their personal identities from the land in the same way as people from northern Australia, but they do have distinctly Aboriginal ways of using and conceiving of the land. This accords with Keefe's (1988, 1992) distinction between 'Aboriginality as resistance', which is construed in terms of difference, and 'Aboriginality as persistence', which is construed in terms of direct links to the pre-colonial past. In both northern and southern Australia, Aboriginal people have a strong sense of personal and corporate identity as separate from the non-Aboriginal, albeit multi-cultural, population.

The colonial histories of Aboriginal Australia vary according to the timing of initial contact and the resultant pressures of colonisation. This has implications for contemporary relationships to land. As Morphy (1991: 3) points out, the longer the colonial period, the more the present is determined by colonial interactions. In areas such as the Barunga region where contact occurred relatively late, the differences between contemporary Aboriginal and non-Aboriginal conceptualisations and use of place are very clear. In areas of southern Australia, especially those that were colonised within the 100 years of European settlement, the effects of colonisation caused major disjunctions with the pre-colonial past. Nevertheless, in these areas fundamental differences between Aboriginal and non-Aboriginal conceptualisations and use of place also exist.

Aboriginal people in southern Australia use the land in different ways to non-Aboriginal Australians. In many regions, Aboriginal relationships to place are established through regular visits to woodland and forest areas to teach children about native foods and medicines, as well as through the transference of oral and mythological histories concerning place (e.g. Smith 1993).

Where feasible, this is carried out on the hereditary lands of the people involved. These processes are culturally specific and thus not available to – or generally sought by – people of non-Aboriginal descent. One Aboriginal person described the difference between Aboriginal and non-Aboriginal relationships to land in southern Australia as non-Aboriginal people living 'on top of the land' and Aboriginal people living 'in the land'.

As with the north, the contemporary landscapes of southern Australia are imbued with Aboriginal spiritual values, and land-use patterns are mediated accordingly. Mythological histories of the land are transferred across generations, and mythological sites can be of educational or economic, as well as spiritual, significance. Sites such as Tooloom Falls in the Urbenville area of northeast New South Wales have been gazetted as Aboriginal Places on the basis of their cultural significance to Aboriginal people (Smith 1993). Tooloom Falls are a popular tourist attraction and it is notable that Aboriginal people did not have them gazetted in order to protect them from visits by the public. Rather, they wished 'the site protected from vandalism and destruction so that it could continue to fulfil its very important function of educating Aboriginal children in their heritage, beliefs and legends' (Haigh 1980: 83).

Certain mythological sites in southern landscapes are identified as being both potent and dangerous. For instance, Dome Mountain, another mythological site in the Urbenville area, is avoided by adult men, as this area is thought to be dangerous to them, even though the precise nature of the significance of the site has been lost (Collins 1991). Thus, the contemporary landscape in southern Australia – like that in northern Australia – is conceptualised by Aboriginal people as being both inherently powerful and potentially hazardous.

Aboriginal people from both northern and southern Australia decipher the landscapes they visit from a distinctly Aboriginal perspective. Morphy (1995) recounts a visit to southern Australia by Narritjin Maymuru, a Yolngu man from northern Australia. Narritjin interpreted the surrounding landscape in terms of the mythological principles he had learnt in northeast Arnhem Land. He stated that they were in Dhuwa moiety country, citing as proof a number of physical features in the landscape, such as the shape of the lake.

Ruby Langford, an Aboriginal woman from southern Australia, likewise experienced her first visit to Uluru (formerly known to Euro-Australians as Ayers Rock) in central Australia from a distinctly Aboriginal viewpoint. Langford recalls how greatly she was impressed by the 'spirit' of the rock:

> We came closer and closer and I could feel the goosebumps and the skin tightening on the back of my neck. Everyone was quiet. It made me think of our tribal beginnings and this to me was like the beginning of our time and culture.
>
> (Langford 1988: 234)

As Rowse (1993: 86) points out, this type of 'spiritual' interpretation is not something that features in ethnographic accounts of Uluru (e.g. Layton 1986, 1995). This difference may be due partly to the different modes of discourse used by academics and Aboriginal people, and some non-Aboriginal people certainly have metaphysical interpretations of geographic features such as Uluru. Nevertheless, these are fundamentally different from those of Aboriginal people whose descent and cultural heritage is so inextricably tied to Australian land. Nor should we anticipate that Aboriginal and non-Aboriginal people will react to the landscape in similar ways. Clearly, each individual brings their own personal history to bear on their interactions with the world around them. Aboriginal people from northern and southern Australia have a common, though varying, 'spiritual' approach to the interpretation of visited landscapes, and this is different to the ways in which non-Aboriginal people generally interpret the same features. For many Aboriginal people, contemporary landscapes are imbued with ancestral power and presence.

The existence of distinctly Aboriginal relationships to land in all parts of Australia has been recognised in both state and federal legislation. Initially, this was through the passage of a series of Aboriginal Land Rights Acts during the 1970s and 1980s, each of which is specific to a particular state or territory. The underlying premise of this legislation is that Aboriginal relationships to land are fundamentally different to those of non-Aboriginal people (cf. Morphy 1993: 230). More recently, recognition of Aboriginal sovereignty at the time of contact was made in the 1992 High Court decision for Torres Strait Islander Eddie Mabo (see Coe 1992). The Mabo decision rejected the doctrine of *terra nullius* that had provided the legal basis for the British acquisition of Australian land, equating settlement with sovereignty (Reynolds 1989: 67–8; Coe 1992: 71). The Mabo decision recognised that Aboriginal and Torres Strait Islander people held a form of native title over the lands of Australia at the time of contact.

The Federal Native Title Act 1993 formally recognised native rights and interests in Australian land and waters. This Act established the National Native Title Tribunal and gave the Federal Court jurisdiction in matters pertaining to native title. The first mainland native title agreement to be resolved by this tribunal resulted in the Dunghutti people of Crescent Head on the NSW north coast being awarded an initial compensation package of $738,000. Another 408 claims remain unresolved (*The Australian*, 10 October 1996). One of the ways in which Aboriginal people in southern Australia assert their hereditary rights to land bounded by a neighbouring group of people, and which has the potential to become subject to dispute, is through their knowledge of the Aboriginal language names and mythological histories for particular locales.

From an Aboriginal perspective, this recent legislation has merely caused land to be recognised in both Aboriginal and non-Aboriginal law as Aboriginal land. In neither northern nor southern Australia do Aboriginal people ever appear to have considered the land to be owned legitimately by anyone other than themselves, though they have recognised various constraints upon their movement over and use of the land during periods when it has been appropriated for European purposes (e.g. Rose 1991; Ryan 1995; Goodall 1996). Once the periods of direct confrontation and physical conflict had passed, there arose in many parts of Aboriginal Australia a culture of resistance that acted to subvert the oppressive facets of British colonialism (e.g. Morris 1988), particularly those relating to land. An important aspect of this resistance was the retention of cultural knowledge about the surrounding landscape.[4] Moreover,

> In fact, as the archival records show, there have been frequent south-eastern Aboriginal expressions of their rights to and need for land, beginning at least as early as the mid nineteenth century. These demands have been based on assertions of both traditional rights and the right to compensation for dispossession.
>
> (Goodall 1996: xvii)

Relatedness to place is a core theme within Australian Aboriginal societies. While the main focus of this chapter has been how Aboriginal people in northern Australia construct their personal identities in relation to a socialised landscape, Aboriginal people in southern Australia also interpret and use the land in ways that are distinctly Aboriginal. Aboriginal ways of relating to place exist in a variety of forms throughout Australia, varying according to the historically situated strategies of individuals and groups. These exist in spite of, and in some cases in response to, the pressures arising from European colonisation. The common thread is an enduring sense of Aboriginality as inextricably linked to place, and the mediation of land-use patterns in terms of spiritually powerful and dangerous places. In both northern and southern Australia, Aboriginal people live in socially mediated, and mediating, landscapes.

Notes

1   Outstations are located on hereditary lands in very remote areas. These communities usually consist of two or three houses that are lived in by extended families who have particular ties to the land in that area. For historical background on this contemporary movement towards living in small communities on heriditary lands, see Meehan and Jones (1980).
2   Rose (1992: 7) estimates that the Aboriginal population decreased from around 4–5,000 in 1883 to 187 in 1939, when the first available census was prepared by the Victoria River District Station.
3   This list is comprehensive but not exhaustive. In particular, ways of relating to the land in terms of place of conception, birth and death are not discussed in this chapter. For information on these latter issues in other regions of Australia, see Morphy 1993 and Layton 1995.
4   Layton (1995: 210) identifies four strategies used by Aboriginal people in the Western Desert to sustain identity: recollections of childhood, the assertion of ownership rights over places, the continued performance of ritual, and transmission of knowledge. In my view, it is only the continued performance of ritual that is not used throughout Aboriginal Australia.

Acknowledgements

This chapter arises from a joint presentation by myself and Christine Lovell-Jones at WAC 3 in New Delhi. I thank Christine for much productive debate on the issues discussed, and Bob Layton for encouraging me to pursue this topic. Figure 14.2 was conceived in discussion with Heather Burke and Becky Morphy, both of whom commented on drafts of this chapter. Lisa Meekison and Danielle Davis also made very useful comments. All figures were originally drawn by Heather Burke. The fieldwork at Barunga was conducted collaboratively with Gary Jackson who, as always, helped me turn fleeting notions into published ideas.

References

Ballard, C. 1994. The centre cannot hold: trade networks and sacred geography in the Papua New Guinea Highlands. *Archaeology in Oceania* 29, 130–48.

Bender, B. 1993. *Landscape: politics and perspectives*. Oxford: Berg.

Berndt, R.M. and C. Berndt 1989. *The Speaking Land*. Ringwood, Victoria: Penguin.

Byrne, D. 1993. The past of others: archaeological heritage management in Thailand and Australia. Unpublished Ph.D. thesis, Australian National University.

Coe, P. 1992. Statement on behalf of the National Aboriginal and Islander Legal Services Secretariat. In *UN Working Group on Indigenous Populations: tenth session. The Australian Contribution*, 69–71. Geneva, Switzerland: ATSIC.

Collins, J. 1991. *Report on the archaeological survey of the Duck Creek environmental impact statement area, northern New South Wales*. Report to the Forestry Commission of New South Wales.

Coombs, H.C. 1980. Implications of land rights. In *Northern Australia: options and implications*, R. Jones (ed.), 120–9. Canberra: Australian National University.

David, B. and N. Cole 1990. Rock art and inter-regional interaction in northeastern Australian prehistory. *Antiquity* 64, 788–806.

Forrest, P. 1985. An outline of the history of Beswick Station and related areas. Unpublished ms, Northern Land Council, Darwin.

Goodall, H. 1996. *From Invasion to Embassy: land in Aboriginal politics in New South Wales, 1770–1972*. Sydney: Allen & Unwin.

Gosden, C. 1989. Prehistoric social landscapes in the Arawe Islands, West New Britain Province, Papua New Guinea. *Archaeology in Oceania* 24, 45–58.

Gosden, C. and L. Head 1994. Landscape – a usefully ambiguous concept. *Archaeology in Oceania* 29, 113–16.

Haigh, C. 1980. Some special Aboriginal sites. In *The Aborigines of New South Wales*, C. Haigh and W. Goldstein (eds), 81–3. Sydney: National Parks and Wildlife Service, New South Wales.

Head, L. 1993. Unearthing prehistoric cultural landscapes: a view from Australia. *Transactions of the Institute of British Geography* 18, 481–99.

Head, L., C. Gosden and J. Peter White (eds) 1994. Social landscapes. Special issue of *Archaeology in Oceania* 29.

Kaberry, P. 1939. *Aboriginal Woman: sacred and profane*. London: Routledge.

Keefe, K. 1988. Aboriginality: resistance and persistence. *Australian Aboriginal Studies* 1, 67–81.

Keefe, K. 1992. *From the Centre to the City*. Canberra: Aboriginal Studies Press.

Keen, I. 1980. Alligator Rivers Stage II land claim. Unpublished ms, Northern Land Council, Darwin.

Langford, R. 1988. *Don't Take Your Love to Town*. Ringwood, Victoria: Penguin.

Layton, R. 1986. *Uluru: an Aboriginal history of Ayers Rock*. Canberra: Aboriginal Studies Press.

Layton, R. 1992. *Australian Rock Art: a new synthesis*. Cambridge: Cambridge University Press.

Layton, R. 1995. Relating to the country in the western desert. In *Between Place and Space*, E. Hirsch and M. O'Hanlon (eds), 210–31. Oxford: Oxford University Press.

McBryde, I. 1978. Wil-im-ee Mooring: or, where do axes come from? *Mankind* 2, 354–82.

McBryde, I. 1984. Exchange in southeastern Australia: an ethnohistorical perspective. *Aboriginal History* 8, 132–53.

McDonald, J. In press. Material and social context: influence on information exchange networks in prehistoric Sydney. In *Style, Semiotics and Social Strategy*, C. Smith, and B. Meehan (eds). Cambridge: Cambridge University Press.

Maddock, K. 1965. Report on field work in the Northern Territory 1964–1965. Unpublished report to the Australian Institute of Aboriginal Studies, Canberra.

Maddock, K. 1969. The Jabuduruwa: a study of the structure of rite and myth in an Australian Aboriginal religious cult on the Beswick Reserve, Northern Territory. Unpublished Ph.D thesis, University of Sydney.

Maddock, K. 1971. Imagery and social structure. *Anthropological Forum* 11, 444–63.

Maddock, K. 1982. *The Australian Aborigines*. Ringwood, Victoria: Penguin Books.

Meehan, B. and R. Jones 1980. The outstation movement and hints of a white backlash. In *Northern Australia: options and implications*, R. Jones (ed.), 131–57. Canberra: Australian National University.

Merlan, F. 1978. Making people quiet in the pastoral north: reminiscences of Elsey station. *Aboriginal History* 2, 70–106.

Merlan, F. and A. Rumsey 1982. The Jawoyn (Katherine Area) land claim. Unpublished ms, Northern Land Council, Darwin.

Morphy, H. 1991. *Ancestral Connections: art and an Aboriginal system of knowledge*. Chicago: University of Chicago Press.

Morphy, H. 1993. The politics of landscape in northern Australia. In *Landscape: politics and perspectives*, B. Bender (ed.), 205–43. Oxford: Berg.

Morphy, H. 1995. Landscape and the reproduction of the ancestral past. In *Between Place and Space*, E. Hirsch and M. O'Hanlon (eds), 184–209. Oxford: Oxford University Press.

Morris, B. 1988. Dhan-gadi resistance to assimilation. In *Being Black*, I. Keen (ed.), 33–63. Canberra: Aboriginal Studies Press.

Peterson, N. 1976. *Tribes and Boundaries in Australia*. Canberra: Australian Institute of Aboriginal Studies.

Reynolds, H. 1989. *Dispossession: black Australians and white invaders*. Sydney: Allen & Unwin.

Rose, D.B. 1991. *Hidden Histories*. Canberra: Aboriginal Studies Press.

Rose, D.B. 1992. *Dingo Makes Us Human: life and land in an Australian Aboriginal culture*. Cambridge: Cambridge University Press.

Roth, W.E. 1897. *Ecological Studies among the North-west-central Queensland Aborigines*. Brisbane: Government Printer.

Rowley, C.D. 1986. *Recovery: the politics of Aboriginal reform*. Ringwood, Victoria: Penguin Books.

Rowse, T. 1993. *After Mabo: interpreting indigenous traditions*. Melbourne: Melbourne University Press.

Ryan, L. 1995 *Aboriginal Tasmanians*. Sydney: Allen & Unwin.

Sandefur, J.R. and J.L. Sandefur 1982. *An Introduction to Conversational Kriol*. Darwin: Summer Institute of Linguistics, Australian Aborigines Branch.

Smith, C. 1993. *An Archaeological Investigation of the Urbenville Management Area, Northern New South Wales*. Report to the Forestry Commission of New South Wales.

Smith, C. 1994. Situating style: an ethnoarchaeological study of social and material context in an Australian Aboriginal artistic system. Unpublished Ph.D thesis, University of New England, Armidale, Australia.

Spencer, B. and F. Gillen 1899. *Native Tribes of Central Australia*. London: Macmillan.

Strehlow, T.G.H. 1947. *Aranda Traditions*. Melbourne: Melbourne University Press.

Strehlow, T.G.H. 1970. Geography and the totemic landscape in central Australia: a functional study. In *Australian Aboriginal Anthropology*, R.M. Berndt (ed.), 92–129. Nedlands: University of Western Australia.

Tindale, N. 1974. *Aboriginal Tribes of Australia*. Los Angeles: University of California Press.

Tonkinson, R. 1980. The cultural roots of Aboriginal land rights. In *Northern Australia: options and implications*, R. Jones (ed.), 111–20. Canberra: Australian National University.

Turpin, T. 1983. The social and economic significance of the movement of edge-ground hatchets in Australia. *Journal of Australian Studies* 12, 45–52.

Vinnicombe, P. 1982. Common ground in South Africa and Australia. *The South African Archaeological Society Newsletter* 5, 1–5.

Warner, L. 1969. *A Black Civilization: a social study of an Australian tribe*. Gloucester: Peter Smith.

15   Competing perceptions of landscape in Kowanyama, North Queensland

Veronica Strang

This chapter is based on recent ethnographic research carried out with Aboriginal groups and the white Australian cattle farmers who live on the western coast of the Cape York Peninsula in Far North Queensland (Strang 1994). Living on the same land, these two groups of people have constructed entirely different relationships with their shared environment, seeing it, experiencing it and valuing it in wholly different ways. This chapter considers how they have arrived at such dissimilar relationships with the environment, and explores the cultural mechanisms through which perception and evaluation of the land is inculcated in each group.

Their respective environmental interactions are examined through the theoretical framework of the concept of landscape. Although this concept has tended, with a traditionally European focus, to present landscape as 'art', it expands quite readily to encompass other visions of the land. It has proven useful both in the analysis of Aboriginal relations to country, and in examining the broader social and economic environmental interactions of the white community in North Queensland. The concept of landscape is founded on the assumption that human landscapes are culturally constructed. As Bender has pointed out: 'landscapes are created by people – through their experience and engagement with the world around them' (1993: 1). One might say, equally, that 'people are created by landscapes', by the social and cultural meaning invested in the seen and unseen environment. The human environmental relationship is thus presented as a dynamic interaction between the individual, the socio-cultural environment and the land itself.

Within this interaction, a central theme is the creation of value: as meaning is invested in each part of the human environment, so too is value. As Munn (1986) and Hirsch and O'Hanlon (1995) have described, value creation is integral to cultural interpretation of the environment. It is the location of value, where and how it is invested and expressed, that defines the characteristics of the environmental relationship. This chapter argues that various cultural factors encourage or discourage the location of value in the land, creating widely differing levels of affective concern for the local environment and its resources. With the concept of landscape as a common idiom, a range of cultural forms are cast as organisational structures, as processes of sociali-sation and as sources of symbolic imagery, all of which contribute to specifically cultural perceptions of the landscape. The chapter further suggests that each cultural form informs the others, so that there is commonality and coherence to the patterns of values contained in all of them. Thus each form, whether it is law, cosmology, economic mode or art, has characteristics and values that recur persistently in all the forms of that particular culture. This gives each cultural group a particular 'mode' of interaction with the envi-ronment, defined by the values that it has developed (and continues to develop) over time.

For the purpose of this analysis, it has been very useful to make a compar-ison of two highly contrasting 'modes' of interaction with the land. This study was carried out in 1992 and 1993 in the Aboriginal community of Kowanyama, and on the cattle stations in the surrounding area. Kowanyama is situated on the western plains of the Cape York Peninsula, close to the Gulf of Carpentaria and many hours by dirt road from the more heavily populated east coast. Until recently, Far North Queensland was regarded as one of the most remote areas of Australia. The population is still very small: the only sizeable groups are in the coastal Aboriginal communities, and most of the rest of the land is given over to vast cattle stations, or to national parks. It is quite a harsh environment. The coastal plains are largely composed of savannah grassland, with areas of scrub and thin forest; it is flat, open country that floods in the wet season and parches in the dry.

In Kowanyama, approximately 1,000 people live in the village which for most of this century was an Anglican mission. The land granted to the community covers about 2,500 sq. km, and the population consists of three main language groups whose traditional country extends well beyond the confines of this area: the Yir Yoront to the north, the Kunjen to the east and the Kokobera to the south.

For more than 40,000 years, prior to the invasion of white settlers, Aborig-inal groups sustained a hunter-gatherer lifestyle. Within a variety of climatic and ecological changes, they underwent shifts in population levels and spatial organisation, and made numerous socio-cultural and technological adaptations (see Allen and O'Connell 1995).

The colonial history of Australia is well known: during the last century the Aboriginal groups in this part of Queensland, like so many others, have been subjected to extreme and disruptive changes. However, their culture has proved to be both conservative and resilient; the current population still preserves many elements of the 'custom way', as they call it, and values have tended to resist and question the imposed technological and political changes. So although Aboriginal society is currently integrating many different ideas and values, its traditional values and beliefs are still central and pervasive.

In discussing Aboriginal people and land, it is almost inevitable that one begins by talking about spiritual matters. For the people in Kowanyama, as with Aboriginal people in other parts of Australia, physical and economic interaction with the environment is never wholly divorced from emotional and spiritual interaction. Most people are now familiar with the cosmological constructs of the Dreamtime (e.g. Morphy 1991; Strang 1994), but it is worth underlining a few of its most influential elements with regard to the investment of value in the land. One of the most important of these is that, in a traditional Aboriginal cosmology, time is presented as being cyclical rather than linear.

The Dreamtime (usually called 'the storytime' or 'the old days' in Kowanyama) is held to be a separate period 'long ago'. Recent history is generally thought of as going back about three generations. There is little concept of linear past or, for that matter, linear future, because, according to traditional beliefs, although the Dreamtime is long ago, it is also held to exist in the present because the ancestral beings remain within the landscape, and because the purpose of being here is to relive their lives. In this way, past, present and future are seen as a continuous cyclical renewal of ancestral lives. This offers what could almost be described as a lateral vision of time, with other dimensions and periods of existence placed alongside the present, and framed often in spatial rather than temporal terms (see Swain 1993; Chase 1994; Clunies-Ross 1994; Strang 1994; Williams and Mununggur 1994).

The 'storytime' was a creative period. The ancestral beings emerged from particular places, and acted upon an empty landscape to create all the features of the land and all the parts of the natural world. They then 'sat down', which is to say they returned into the earth, where they remained as a source of spiritual power for all time. The brolga ancestor,[1] for example, ended up in the Coleman River as a large rock in the water; the two girls drowned by a giant catfish became date palm trees on the edge of the waterhole. Each part of the landscape is therefore a unique ancestral creation, unlike any other place, and the continued presence of the ancestral forces creates a sentient landscape that is both physically and spiritually responsive to human action.

Places where specific mythical events occurred are particularly powerful, and the land is full of such 'poison places', as they are called in this part of Australia. As in other areas, these are often subject to taboos, or provide sources of power that can be stimulated through increase rituals to release resources into the environment (see Morton 1987). It is the responsibility of the traditional owners of the country to care for these places and ensure that the proper laws and rituals are observed.

The spiritual force with which the landscape is imbued casts it as the source of all life. The people in Kowanyama have maintained traditional beliefs about death and rebirth as a circular process that reflects the ancestral cycle. As Myers (1986) has described, this entails movement from one plane of being, the Dreaming, which is regarded as invisible and internal, held within the country, to 'becoming visible', moving out onto this plane, then, at the end of life, returning into the land to be reabsorbed into the Dreaming. When a woman becomes pregnant, it is said that a spirit child has 'jumped up' from a baby spirit site (i.e. from a place of potency), and when a person dies their spirit is returned symbolically to that place, its home, to 'sit down' again, as the ancestors did.[2]

In traditional terms, these levels of existence are not distinct: people are their country, and it is considered normal to identify with parts of the country as if they were interchangeable with self: 'this rock here, this is my father, this tree here is my mother' (see Layton 1995: 219–20).

Thus Aboriginal cosmology presents each part of the landscape as unique, and imbues it with spiritual presence. It casts the land as the source of all life, creates unbreakable ties between people and country, and offers each individual a permanent 'home' place that is the cornerstone of her or his personal identity.

As well as providing an explanation of the world, Aboriginal cosmology is also a system of law, and indeed is often referred to as The Law. A particular moral order is implicit in all of the ancestral stories, along with a socio-economic blueprint for Aboriginal society.

In Kowanyama, as in many other parts of Australia, land and personal identity are passed on together through a system of patrilineal descent (e.g. Peterson 1972; Peterson and Langton 1983; Morphy 1990). Each ancestral being, on returning into the land, became a totemic figure for a particular clan group, and each clan collectively owns the land associated with that ancestral being 'for all time'. So membership of a clan group provides both personal identity and inalienable title to an area of country and its resources.

The Law gives each clan the responsibility to care for its country through rituals, proper use of resources and traditional methods of environmental management (for example, keeping the country 'clean' with a regular fire regime). It also provides marriage laws that maintain a network of kin groups organised in geographic terms. This conflation of kin and country is perhaps the single most important aspect of Aboriginal life, which is nicely illustrated by the fact that even when forced to live within a mission village, the language groups in Kowanyama have still placed themselves spatially as they would in any large camp, according to the direction in which their country lies. The lateral network of kin groups creates uncentralised and fairly egalitarian social relations that, being constructed around particular geographic foci, are relatively unboundaried.

At a more pragmatic level, in traditional economic life the land was also the source of all sustenance. All food and medicines and nearly all materials for artefacts were drawn from the immediate environment. The careful division of land into clans and tracts of country linked in an exchange network provided a way of managing resources that was extremely effective and eminently sustainable. Surviving, with the most simple and renewable technology, in this quite harsh environment also required an intimacy of knowledge about the land, a wealth of bush lore that even today remains enormously rich and detailed.

In this traditional way of life, every aspect of existence is tightly focused on specific areas of land. This focus is supported by processes of socialisation equally directed towards the immediate environment. For example, much of the vast lexicon of bush lore required for economic success is contained in the ancestral stories which, as well as providing a spiritual, moral and social framework, are also full of details of animal behaviour, botanical information and descriptions of traditional ways of hunting and gathering. Thus Aboriginal Law can be seen to be holistic, containing a template for an entire (traditional) way of life and providing for each aspect of existence. Whether seen as mythology or history, it provides for the current population a very powerful image of Aboriginal life as something permanently rooted to the land.

In theory, and, to some degree, still in practice, this body of knowledge is maintained through continuous association with the same area of land, generation after generation, and through a system of education in which the elders are responsible for making sure that the younger people are given appropriate spiritual and practical information at each stage of their lives.

In the modern community, alongside the state education taught at the local school, much of the educational focus is still on traditional cultural forms. People in Kowanyama spend an enormous amount of time discussing the intricacies of their kin networks, polishing and refining their knowledge of these relationships, and reaffirming them. Rituals and artistic forms of expression are similarly centred on spiritual and social connection with the land, and the Aboriginal languages that are still spoken remain heavily reliant on local classifications. For example, the Kunjen calendar is based entirely on local seasonal events, so the crocodile eggs are ready to eat 'when that tea tree is flowering'; wallabies are fattest 'when the cotton trees are in flower'; 'plenty of grasshoppers' mean it is the 'time for hunting plain turkeys'.

Kunjen seasonal categories

Urrf =	Raining hard (in the middle of the wet season).
Arryul =	Fat wallaby time/cotton tree flowering time.
Uy udnam =	Fat fish time/*Udnam albar* (fat fish after the Wet when the leaves come down/when there are many dragonflies) (January–March).
Albar =	When the leaves come down (after the wet season).
Uk-igay angan =	Tea tree and beefwood flowering time/crocodile egg time (August).
Inh-agnggoy arriyjanerr =	Flying fox, time for eating (September).

This kind of seasonal classification, based on geographically specific criteria and the equally specific inter-relationships between the various elements of the environment and between people and the environment, is characteristic of any Aboriginal group.

For the Aboriginal groups in Kowanyama, the landscape is thus invested with meaning and value at every cultural level: it holds the ancestral beings, the spiritual forces and a moral order; it is the repository for social organisation and for group and individual identity; because people return to the land when they die, it holds the memories of their being and their attachment to others; it is personalised, held to be conscious and capable of both sustenance and malevolence; it is also psychic space, vulnerable to intrusion and violation by strangers. Thus it is a self-contained environmental relationship in which religious and emotional ties to land are equally social and economic: the land mediates every cultural form, and provides the major medium for complex symbolic expression.

Despite half a century of cattle-station and missionary life, the people in Kowanyama have maintained many of their traditional practices. They still hunt and fish, and until fairly recently many of them managed to remain on their own land by working for the cattle stations that had taken it over. They still regard their traditional country as belonging to them because, according to Aboriginal Law, it is not alienable, and their common goal in life is to reclaim as much of it as they can, or at least to regain some measure of control over it.

This goal is fiercely opposed by the white population on the surrounding cattle stations, who have constructed a very different kind of environmental relationship with the same land.

The earliest cattle stations in this region were established to support government outposts on Cape York following the Jardine brothers' exploration of the peninsula's interior in the 1860s. Many more stations appeared in response to the demand for local supplies of beef during the Palmer River and subsequent gold rushes of the 1870s. The stations therefore were, and to some extent still are, as much a method of colonising and controlling land as an economic pursuit.

The settlers came from an urban, technologically complex environment into what they saw as a hostile and dangerous wilderness, populated by savages and dangerous animals; for them, the new land was something to be tamed and controlled. The ensuing colonisation of the peninsula was extremely violent, and so many Aboriginal people were killed in the process that the Churches hastened to open missions along the Gulf coast in an attempt to provide some haven from this virtual genocide. The survivors were either brought onto the cattle stations as a source of cheap labour, or pushed off their land and into the mission communities.

When the gold rushes receded, the stations dotted across the peninsula were left behind, remaining for many years as a kind of 'frozen frontier'. Like outback communities in many parts of the world (e.g. Riviere 1972), this small subculture has maintained many of the characteristics of the early settlement of the area.

Because, in terms of grazing, the carrying capacity of the land is very low, the average cattle station on Cape York has to be between 2,500 and 5,000 sq. km in area in order to be viable. The homesteads are therefore widely scattered across the landscape. Most of these vast properties are owned by Queensland's self-styled landed gentry who live further south or on the east coast, leaving the land to be managed by others. Each station has a population of between ten and twenty people, the majority of whom come from farming communities in other parts of Queensland. It is an isolated and far from easy life, and people move frequently, the lower-echelon employees shifting every year or so, and even the managers rarely staying on one property for long. Though the cattle people are a relatively tight-knit subculture within Australian society, they are nevertheless tied firmly into the mainstream. They come from more developed and urbanised environments and return to them regularly for holidays, for other work and, eventually, to retire.

In this 'remote area', the spatial layout of the cattle station homesteads reflects the adversarial nature of the relationship that the settlers created with the land and its inhabitants (Figure 15.1). At each homestead the main house is invariably cast as a sanctuary, placed at the heart of a series of barriers between it and 'the bush', with rings of fences, trees, gardens, other buildings and yet more fences shielding it from the dusty run 'outside'. This spatial pattern is consistently reflected in cattle stations in many parts of Australia (e.g. Stevens 1974).

The overt control, enclosure and division of space is characteristic of the process of colonisation. On taking over the land, the Europeans' first actions were to contain it with fences, and to impose a foreign technological and economic order on it. Even today, the 'improvements' (which are usually demanded by a cattle station lease) generally refer to the building of new fence-lines and enclosures, or to the introduction of new technological methods of manipulating and managing the land and resources (Figure 15.2). Implicitly, this activity and imposition of control provides the rationale for dispossessing the Aboriginal people, who are said to 'do nothing' with the land.

The physical boundaries imposed on the landscape are reflected in the cattle stations' socio-spatial organisation. The pastoralists' intensely hierarchical and segmented social relations offer a sharp contrast to the unboundaried and relatively egalitarian socio-spatial organisation of the indigenous people. On the cattle stations, each level in the hierarchy and its relative status is clearly defined, from the owner of the station right down to the cowboy gardener. In spatial terms, the apex of this pyramid is placed at the most central part of the homestead, with the people at its base banished to the outer reaches. Thus the manager and his family inhabit the central space, which is generally accessible only to them and their guests. Usually nearby, under the managerial wing, is the girls' dormitory, used by any governess or female camp cook. Then, usually outside or at the edge of the garden perimeter, is the head stockman's quarters and further out by the cattle yards are the 'boys' quarters' which were, until recently, occupied by only the white stockmen. Finally, well away from the

Figure 15.1 The pastoralists maintain an adversarial frontier-style relationship with the land and its resources.

Figure 15.2 The pastoralists' interaction with the land, and their control of it, is heavily mediated by technology.

centre and usually down by the house lagoon outside all of the house fences, are the old Aboriginal quarters. These are now rarely inhabited. Since legislation in the 1960s forced station managers to pay all workers a fixed minimum wage, the large Aboriginal communities that used to live on each property have been pushed out to the mission reserves. In the current political climate, stations are either bringing in just a few Aboriginal stockmen to live in the team quarters or, more often, not employing them at all.

In economic terms, since the local market created by the gold diggers disappeared, the cattle properties have been barely viable financially, although the growing tourist industry and development on the east coast may change this. Essentially, pastoralism is a system of production from elsewhere that has been imposed on this environment. It is not self-sufficient but, like the pastoralists' social forms, is tied into the wider economy. Viability for a station currently depends on carrying between 12,000 and 20,000 head of cattle, and 'turning off' (sending to the meatworks) a reasonable percentage of these every year.

The economic mode of the pastoralists is quite straightforward: each property is divided into large long-term paddocks and much smaller holding paddocks, serviced by dams, bores, roads and yards. Throughout the dry season there is a systematic process of finding the scattered cattle, mustering them, taking them to the yards to be sorted, creaming off those to be trucked out to the meatworks, and redistributing the rest. This work is done largely on horseback, with the support of four-wheel-drive vehicles and helicopters. A large percentage of stock work takes place in the yards: spaying or castrating cattle, 'tipping' their horns, branding them and cutting identifying marks in their ears, injecting them against TB, and dipping them in a tank to rid them of ticks. There is also some work breaking in new horses (Figure 15.1), looking after the rest of the herd and keeping the saddles and bridles in good repair. Another major task for many stockmen is maintaining the hundreds of kilometres of fencing on each property, mending gates and yards and fixing the station's trucks and graders.

The economic activity that is the central element in the pastoralists' interaction with the landscape is thus not directed towards the natural environment, but is focused instead upon the various elements imposed on it. Each interaction with the landscape is mediated by some form of technology: movement around the property is invariably either on horseback or in a vehicle, presenting the landscape as a passing panorama; each aspect of stock work involves one sort of technology or another. The various parts of the local environment are cast as resources to support these activities.

This suggests a primarily managerial view of the land, based on European ideas about controlling it and moulding it to fit commercial expectations. It is intensely practical: the vital daily issues are whether there is enough water in each paddock; whether the boundary fences are sound; whether the old grass should be burned off to provide new green shoots for the cattle and horses; and whether the old utility truck can be kept going for another season.

These issues and their financial implications are the major concerns, and it is the commercial value of the landscape that dominates.

In this view, the land and all stock placed on it are commodities to be sold 'when the price is right'. The pastoralists have very clear ideas about what land is for: it is for 'grazing', for 'raising cattle and horses' and 'to be used productively'. In their terms, 'productivity' is measured by the criteria of a market economy, although as Layton indicates (pers. comm.; cf. Peters et al. 1989), it is quite likely that hunting and gathering actually harvest a greater biomass than ranching. As Altman (1987) points out, in traditional Aboriginal life, 'productivity' would be assessed according to very different criteria, incorporating much wider issues of social exchange.

The commoditisation of the environment and its resources is unsurprising against the background of the pastoralists' other cultural forms, including a religious cosmology in which Man is deemed to have 'dominion' over the earth, with responsibility to make it 'fruitful', and a world view dominated by scientific thought that frames the environment in generic, quantitative and material terms.

Similarly, the secular law that supports this vision is based on the right to individual ownership of land, and a well-established view of land as property that can always be exchanged and alienated. The other major feature of modern Australian law is that it is wholly secular and completely separated from any spiritual aspects of white Australian culture. Dealings with land have in general been regarded not as religious or explicitly moral responsibilities, but rather as expressions of legal rights and economic imperatives. More recently, the law has begun to encompass greater responsibility for environmental protection. Although generally directed towards issues of liability, this could be said to imply a degree of moral responsibility.

The various cultural forms through which the pastoralists are more directly socialised into their particular beliefs and values are equally detached from the landscape in which they live. Their educational system is focused on a standardised and generic curriculum unrelated to the local environment except in the most abstract terms. The language in which it is taught is generic, employing categories shared by every 'western' community on the planet. Their visual representations such as maps are also generalised and reliant on universal rather than locally meaningful codes, dividing the landscape into quantified and measured units characterised only by their resources.

The pastoralists' socialisation through action and experience is similarly focused on technical skills and imposed elements, with the landscape as little more than a stage on which to act. Once they begin work on the cattle properties, they are offered clearly defined roles: stockman; manager; mechanic; cook. Their identities are built on these professional activities, rather than on their personal geographic origins or kin groups. And their professional activities are, without exception, focused on non-indigenous elements that they have imposed on the landscape, and which could, quite easily, be picked up and carried to any similar area of land elsewhere.

At a symbolic level, their history provides images of early 'battlers' who fought to 'subdue' the land less than a century ago. An adversarial view of nature, and the normalisation of nomadic movement around the globe, are the major themes in their historical narrative. The pastoralists are encouraged to live up to and perpetuate this romantic image of life in 'the outback' in order to preserve an important element of the national identity. Such a self-image is hardly compatible with a connective or nurturing view of nature.

Thus the Aboriginal groups on Cape York and the white pastoralists on the cattle stations have widely differing perceptions of the landscape and very different modes of interaction with the environment. These are constructed through historical momentum and a range of cultural forms that, inculcated in each generation, perpetuate culturally specific patterns of value location.

None of the pastoralists' major cultural forms, neither their economic mode, their spiritual beliefs, their secular law nor their social organisation, is conducive to the creation of attachment to land or to the location of affective value in the land. The various processes of socialisation that they experience are similarly discouraging in this respect, providing only generalised and abstract categories with which to interpret or describe the environment.

These are logical cultural forms for a highly mobile society, but they do not bode well for the creation of a close and affective environmental relationship. With land reduced to the status of temporary and alienable property, it is difficult for the pastoralists to invest it with spiritual or emotional value, to develop sentimental ties to it or to cast specific places as the foundation of personal identity. The geographic mobility and size of the population are obstacles to any long-term sense of belonging to a definable place or community. Constant change means continual encompassment of the new, and a focus on mass-produced and disposable technology contributes to a sense that little is unique or permanent.

This is not to say that no pastoralists care about the land: some of them care deeply, especially those whose families have held property in the area for several generations, providing a much greater sense of permanence. However, the majority of people on the cattle stations care more about land in the abstract, rather than building attachment to a specific landscape. Their sentiment is flexible in its location, and their local environment is readily interchangeable with others. Value is only loosely applied in a romantic ideal-isation of landscape, aesthetic concepts of nature, and a generalised concern for the health of the resources.

For the Aboriginal population, the converse is true: the immediate landscape is always specific and unique, and every traditional cultural form supports the investment of value in the land. The land is used sustainably, not just in economic and physical terms, but in providing emotional and intellectual suste-nance; it is a symbolic medium for every aspect of existence, and the common ground for all discourse. The land is inalienable, and therefore provides conti-nuity and stability. It is encompassed only on a small scale and in one place, and with intimacy and immediacy; so the environment is known, familiar and nurturing rather than threatening. It mediates social forms that are similarly stable and manageable in scale, and provides a firm foundation for identity. It places spiritual being well within reach, and contains the cycles of death and rebirth. These elements combine to allow Aboriginal people to construct complex, qualitative and, above all, long-term environmental relations. They can invest themselves in the land and identify successfully with their immediate physical environment, thus enjoying a deep sense of connection and belonging.

Many of the dominant characteristics of Aboriginal culture depend on considerable continuity and stability. This brings us back to the question as to why some cultural groups develop a greater level of environmental concern than others, why they favour affective values and locate these kinds of values in the land. I suggest that the major difference between affective values and other kinds of value is one of depth: affective values are highly complex and largely concerned with qualitative issues. They are rarely constructed quickly, being formed over time in a complex interaction. It is clear that the stability and continuity of traditional Aboriginal life permit more holistic and self-contained cultural forms, and provide a situation that is not only sympathetic to the development of affective values but also encourages, indeed depends on, their location in the landscape.

The pastoralists' cultural forms, on the other hand, do not create a sympathetic context for the construction of affective value or the location of these kinds of value within the landscape. Indeed, rather than encouraging people to have a deep concern for their immediate environment, their cultural forms make it quite difficult for them to do so.

Given their completely different patterns of value location, it is unsurprising that the relationship between these two cultural groups has been characterised by deep conflict and opposition.

Notes

1   The brolga is a large grey bird, a species of crane indigenous to the coastal plains.
2   Similar beliefs in the nearby Edward River community have been discussed by Taylor (1984).

References

Allen, J. and J.F. O'Connell (eds) 1995. Transitions: Pleistocene to Holocene in Australia and Papua New Guinea. *Antiquity* 69.

Altman, J. 1987. *Hunter Gatherers Today: an Aboriginal economy in North Australia.* Canberra: Aboriginal Studies Press.

Bender, B. (ed.) 1993. *Landscape, Politics and Perspectives.* Oxford: Berg.

Chase, A.K. 1994. Perceptions of the past among North Queensland Aboriginal people: the intrusion of Europeans and consequent social change. In *Who Needs the Past? Indigenous values and archaeology*, R. Layton (ed.), 169–79. London: Routledge.

Clunies-Ross, M. 1994. Holding on to emblems: Australian Aboriginal performances and the transmission of oral traditions. In *Who Needs the Past? Indigenous values and archaeology*, R. Layton (ed.), 162–8. London: Routledge.

Hirsch, E. and M. O'Hanlon 1995. *The Anthropology of Landscape: perspectives on space and place*. Oxford: Oxford University Press.

Layton, R. 1995. Relating to the country in the Western Desert. In *The Anthropology of Landscape: perspectives on space and place*, E. Hirsch and M. O'Hanlon (eds), 210–31. Oxford: Oxford University Press.

Morphy, H. 1990. Myth, totemism and the creation of clans. *Oceania* 60, 312–28.

Morphy, H. 1991. *Ancestral Connections: art and an Aboriginal system of knowledge*. Chicago: Chicago University Press.

Morton, J. 1987. The effectiveness of totemism: increase rituals and resource control in central Australia. *Man* 22, 453–74.

Munn, N. 1986. *The Fame of Gawa: a symbolic study of value transformation in a Massim Papua New Guinea society*. Cambridge: Cambridge University Press.

Myers, F.R. 1986. *Pintupi Country, Pintupi Self*. Canberra: Aboriginal Studies Press.

Peters, C.M., A.H. Gentry and R.O. Mendelsohn 1989. Valuation of an Amazonian rainforest. *Nature* 339: 655–6.

Peterson, N. 1972. Totemism yesterday: sentiment and local organisation among the Australian Aborigines. *Man* 7, 12–32.

Peterson, N. and M. Langton (eds) 1983. *Aborigines, Land and Land Rights*. Canberra: Australian Institute of Aboriginal Studies.

Riviere, P. 1972. *The Forgotten Frontier: ranchers of North Brazil*. New York: Holt, Rinehart & Winston.

Stevens, F. 1974. *Aborigines in the Northern Cattle Industry*. Canberra: Australian National University Press.

Strang, V. 1994. Uncommon ground: concepts of landscape and human environmental relations in Far North Queensland. Unpublished D.Phil. thesis, Oxford University.

Swain, T. 1993. *A Place for Strangers: towards a history of Australian Aboriginal being*. Cambridge: Cambridge University Press.

Taylor, J. 1984. Of acts and axes: an ethnography of socio-cultural change in an Aboriginal community, Cape York Peninsula. Unpublished Ph.D. thesis, James Cook University.

Williams, N. and D. Mununggur 1994. Understanding Yolngu signs of the past. In *Who Needs the Past? Indigenous values and archaeology*, R. Layton (ed.), 70–83. London: Routledge.

16 The Alawa totemic landscape: ecology, religion and politics

ROBERT LAYTON

Traditionally hunters and gatherers, the Alawa people of northern Australia have been subject to a century of colonisation by pastoralists who brought a cattle-ranching economy to the region. Alawa land use has left a variety of archaeologically visible traces: camp sites with their associated debris of food and stone artefacts, rock paintings, stone arrangements and modification of the plant cover through controlled burning. The distribution of rock art in relation to ecology has been discussed elsewhere (Layton 1989). Pickering (1994) has examined the social landscape of another Gulf Country people, the Garawa, whose country lies about 250 km to the east of the Alawa. Pickering shows how traditional Garawa camp sites have a seasonal patterning. Camps on the Robinson River could be occupied throughout the year, while those on tributary creeks were not normally occupied during the hot, stormy season that precedes the monsoon. Garawa and Alawa land use is, however, mediated by a complex cultural system, much of which is archaeologically invisible. This chapter describes how this system is sustained, considering both traditional procedures and the response to colonial domination, in order to exemplify how cultural practice orders the creation of material residues.

Although Alawa often converse in Kriol, middle-aged and elderly people remain fluent in the Alawa language. Traditional hunting and gathering practices remain important to the Alawa, and they have been so successful in retaining their traditional system of land tenure that, thanks to the Cox River and Hodgson Downs land claims on two former pastoral leases, much of their traditional country is now Aboriginal freehold. Other parts of Alawa country are occupied by the Nutwood Downs and Hodgson River pastoral leases.

Some aspects of the Alawa totemic landscape have already been described in a paper based on fieldwork for the Cox River land claim (Layton 1989). This chapter provides more details, and is supported by further fieldwork for the Hodgson Downs land claim (see also Layton 1997). The Alawa landscape is represented in legends that provide a model for the allocation of rights and responsibilities toward the land among the living. The chapter begins by considering the texts of some Alawa legends.[1]

Four Alawa legends

Yargala (the male Plains Kangaroo)

Yargala travelled many hundreds of kilometres. He entered Hodgson Downs near Waranmilyi (Campbell Spring), where he was attacked by two dogs that were pursuing him. He travelled down Lilirrganyan Creek (known to Euro-Australians as L.D. Creek) until reaching the lagoon at Lilirrganyan, where he left a grindstone that had become too heavy for him to carry. Yargala was ill, and coughed up spit which became red ochre at Danggalaraba, downstream from Lilirrganyan. This red ochre is regularly used by Alawa for painting barks and other artefacts. At Milin, a small hill, Yargala was turned away by the Bush Turkey, a female ancestor who was incubating her eggs nearby. Yargala went south to the lagoon at Waran lower down Lilirrganyan Creek and, as he rested there, he heard the Water Goanna singing at Minyerri, a large lagoon on the main Hodgson River. Yargala was spurred forward by the sound but on reaching Iwujan became so sick that he had to crawl the remainder of the way to Minyerri, where he met up with the Goanna. Yargala addressed Goanna as Gugu ('Granny', or mother's mother) and asked her to find him a wife. Goanna only offered him an elderly woman. Yargala was so cross that he spat out his Bad Cold Sickness, which remains embedded in the rock platform next to the lagoon at Minyerri.

After leaving Minyerri, Yargala travelled to Arragarrir, on the Hodgson River flood plain, then to the spring at Budanene, where he was again attacked by dogs, who pulled him down and eviscerated him. Nonetheless, he continued to Maldinji, then Wilambilar, where he crossed the Hodgson River. When he came to the river at Wilambilar he started digging for water. The river was dry but he uncovered a soakage in the river bed that is still there. The Kangaroo had a sleep, and left his spear thrower at his camp. It became the large Leichhardt tree which still stands conspicuously among the trees fringing the river channel at Wilambilar. On the far side of the river, he sang about the Ti trees standing on Windiri Plain. Yargala travelled eastward across the plain and up into the hills beyond. At Marangalngalngamba, where Yargala crossed a watershed, he stood erect on his hind legs to see the lower country stretching away to the east and spoke the Mara language for the first time. As he continued east toward Yalmirrirr (Lancewood Knob), lightning struck the lagoon at Ajajil, awakening another, female Kangaroo who ran north. The two met up at Yalmirrir and travelled on together toward the sea. At Maralirri, a clay pan on the eastern border of Hodgson Downs, Yargala met Dudugulinji the Devil-devil who, despite his dangerous character, finally provided Yargala with a young wife.

Wadabir, the Black (Water) Goanna

Wadabir, the Goanna whom Yargala the Plains Kangaroo met at Minyerri, grew up at Galalgalalarrganya, a spring at the foot of a hill on the eastern edge of the Hodgson River flood plain (the name Galalgalalarrganya translates as 'she grew up'). She left her eggs here, now transformed to stone, and travelled up the eastern side of the Hodgson River flood plain toward Minyerri. At Arandar she dug a lagoon. At Lalamurindi, another lagoon, she camped. At Buranjina she created a large paperbark tree on the bank of the river, but did not stop. At Arngu, where there is a once-large lagoon that is now silting up, Wadabir created gum trees. On a flat plain near the lagoon called Ujumuru, Wadabir met up with the Devil-devil and Bush Turkey. The three of them danced together, creating a ceremony now performed by their human descendants. At Ujumuru, Goanna heard a family of Dogs 'singing out' from their home at Mirin-nambiri. She composed a song for the Dogs before continuing up the Hodgson River. At Bidbibnanyadan, Wadabir lay down to rest, then continued upstream until reaching a Leichhardt tree. The old Alawa name for this site has been forgotten, and it is now known simply as Dubulwar (the name of the Leichhardt tree, *Nauclea orientalis*). This particular tree marks the point where Wadabir left the main river channel and returned to the east bank. At Urlubundu, a billabong east of the main river channel, Wadabir lay down to rest again, but was disturbed by the sound of dogs approaching. She jumped up and raced for the safety of the river along a small channel called Gedegede-arrganya, whose name refers to the rustling of the long, dry grass as the Goanna ran through. The old white gum trees standing on the bank of Minyerri lagoon are the waiting Dogs, who set on the Goanna as she reached the water's edge and killed her. A rock beneath the water's surface called Mambuji marks the place where she died. The Dogs took her body to a nearby billabong named Dirwanjirr-ngadanya, where they cooked and ate it.

Ganyila (Dogs)

Mirin-nambiri is a low hill just east of the Hodgson River flood plain. It is pitted with small caves made by a female Dog who made several attempts to dig a shelter in which to give birth to her puppies. The place she finally selected is a remarkable tunnel that runs right through the hill. After giving birth, the mother Dog hunted on Arngu plain to find food for her puppies. Goanna heard them singing out as she passed. When the puppies were fully grown, a fight broke out between the bitch and the puppies' father, who was now old and infected with scabies. In one man's words, 'all the puppies got stuck into that old dog' (Bandiyan). They drove him away. He walked upstream to the billabong called Mirinjinene where he found a good place to rest. Unfortunately, he had chosen the camp of two River Pigeons, who drove him away again when they returned from hunting. The unfortunate Dog could only travel a short distance before dying. A large boulder visible in the Hodgson River during drought is his body. The puppies travelled eastward onto land that is now within the Maryfield pastoral lease.

Bush Turkey)

...ina was a non-travelling figure. She had her nest at Warigundu, a small round hill on the plain west of the Hodgson River. Jambirina was looking for food for her babies when she heard Yargala the Plains Kangaroo coughing, as he travelled down Lilirrganyan Creek. Jambirina went over to Milin to tell Yargala, 'Don't come here, it's my part of the country, because I've got babies'.

Subsistence

The environment

Hodgson Downs is situated in the Gulf Country of the Northern Territory, within the monsoon climatic zone, and is dominated by open savannah woodland vegetation (cf. Pickering 1994: 153). Grassland dominates the river flood plains while dense lancewood groves grow on some of the steeper hill slopes.

The former Hodgson Downs pastoral lease is traversed by the Hodgson River, which flows from south to north across a blacksoil flood plain. To the west are steep hills where, after rain, creeks tributary to the Hodgson flow through rocky gorges. Permanent springs and rock pools also lie within the hills. Just beyond the northern boundary of Hodgson Downs, the river swings eastward across a broadening flood plain. Lower hills form a watershed that runs from south to north across the centre of the former pastoral lease. The eastern half of Hodgson Downs is drained by smaller creeks that flow north towards the lower reaches of the Hodgson River, often petering out into clay pans and ephemeral lagoons. In the Dry Season, the Hodgson River contracts to permanent lagoons, while in the Wet Season, it floods the surrounding black soil to a depth of 1–2 m. A few semi-permanent waterholes exist in the clay pan country of the eastern claim area. In the hills, springs continue to flow for several months after the Wet Season, feeding permanent lagoons.

A detailed terminology for describing the landscape and the food species that live within it exists in the Alawa language. Table 16.1 lists the useful species that were pointed out to me during work for the two land claims. While it is only a sample of the useful species known to the Alawa (it overlaps with the list of plants in Wightman *et al.* 1991 but includes species not listed by those authors), a count of the useful species in each main habitat shows that lagoons and their banks are the richest in useful species (20 species of animal, 19 species of plant) followed by the woodland that grows on blacksoil and gravel ridge country (8 species of animal, 11 species of plant). Fewer useful species are found in cliff country (4 species of animal, 3 species of plant) (cf. Pickering 1994: 153–4). Water is not only intrinsically important for human survival; permanent reservoirs of water also support the majority of subsistence resources.

Ancestors and ecology

If the routes of ancestral beings are plotted on a topographic map they can be seen to follow rivers, creeks or valleys during their travel (see Figure 16.1). Often they create springs or dig wells in their search for water. When an ancestral being crosses dry rocky country, (s)he does not normally stop. Yargala travelled down the route of Lilirrganyan Creek to the point where it runs into swampy ground and merges with the main Hodgson River. The only point at which he threatened to leave the creek is where he was chased back by Jambirina the Bush Turkey. After travelling a short distance up the Hodgson River, Yargala turned east and followed creeks that drain into the Hodgson River across Windiri Plain. Reaching the head of these creeks, he stood up on the watershed and looked down on the plains and clay pans that occupy the eastern side of Hodgson Downs before travelling down Dirinyinji (Mason Gorge) Creek. Wadabir, the Black Goanna, travelled up the Hodgson River, creating many of the permanent lagoons between her birthplace and Minyerri, site of the Station homestead and modern residence of the Alawa community. The same pattern can be seen in the routes of other ancestral beings. The Munga-Munga ('Wild Women') travelled up the Hodgson River, taking a route slightly to the west of the Goanna. One pair of Warradbunggu (Pythons) came down Awulngu (Paisley) Creek, which drains the south-eastern corner of Hodgson Downs, stopped on the Hodgson River at Muwalalan (Cork Hole), then turned up Midiri (Kempsey) Creek. A second pair of Pythons travelled across the low-lying clay pans in the northeast corner of Hodgson Downs.

Ritual practices relate directly to ecology in two ways. There are a number of places created by ancestral beings where their creative power can be released by rubbing or striking the rock. A second, and more general, reason given for performing ceremonies that commemorate the ancestors' travels is to renew the fertility they created. Ceremonies are performed 'to keep the country alive' because, as Bandiyan put it, 'Ceremony is our life'.

People and the land

Ecology and estates

Rights to, and responsibilities for looking after, the land are held by groups of living people. The areas of land held by such groups are frequently referred to in the anthropological literature as 'estates' (following Stanner 1965). Alawa refer to them as 'countries' (*ninda*). Countries are essentially clusters of sites rather than bounded areas of land. The groups holding these estates are associated with four semi-moieties. The Murungun and Mambali semi-moieties together comprise one unnamed moiety, while the other consists of the Budal and Guyal semi-moieties.

Table 16.1   Some food species associated with principal ecological zones

Ulbul (lagoon)	
bijerri	file snake
bijiwar	'long arm' crayfish (*Cherax sp.?*)
bulunbulun	spoonbill (*Platalea sp.*)
dadajara	freshwater crocodile (*Crocodylus johnstoni*)
garag-garag	diving duck
garinji	jabiru (*Xenorhynchus asiaticus*)
gedageda	fish with red tail
gumergun	short-necked turtle with white stripe on side of head
jabarda	short-necked turtle
jangbada	long-necked turtle (*Chelodina novaeguineae*)
malabangu	freshwater mussel
wadabir	black or water goanna
mawurugu	perch
melindiwar	catfish
mijinggar	'short arm' crayfish (*Cherax sp.?*)
milin-nguwarra	pelican (*Pelecanus conspicillatus*)
nalana	black duck (*Anas superciliosa*)
wagujiri	barramundi (*Lates calcarifer*)
wanguburu	bream (*Hephaestus fulignosus*)
yirrandi	small barramundi (Note that the barramundi is bisexual. There are several Alawa words for different stages of the barramundi's life cycle.)
aldin	flower of lily (*Nyphaea violacea*)
barana	stem of lily (also called jow-jow in 'baby talk')
ganaiya	lily root
yalbun	lily seed (arrguli is another word for same lily)

on sandbank beside lagoon	
andun	wild 'potato'
burulu	pandanus (*Pandanus spiralis*); seeds are edible
dinggulili	conkerberry (*Carissa lanceolata*)
diwarlunggar	wild 'onion'
dubulwar	Leichhardt Tree (*Nauclea orientalis*). Edible fruit.
guningiji	black 'plum' (*Vitex glabrata*)
janambar	paperbark (*Melaleuca viridiflora*). Bark used to make coolamons for carrying fruit, and baby's cradle.
jurruy	a grass; bush "Vicks"; you can rub it on to clear nose and throat.
jarrlma	wild yam
marabala	grevillea with honey-bearing flowers (*Grevillea* (=wigun) *pteridofolia*)
nalanggar	white gum (*Eucalyptus papuana?*). Leaves are chewed to cure headaches.
ruwana	pandanus sp., prob. *Pandanus aquaticus*
Uninggara	fig tree (*Ficus racimosa*)
wirimal	paperbark (*Melaleuca leucadendra*). Bark used to make blankets and to wrap around food cooked in earth-oven.
yarragaga	black 'currant'
yanambul	paperbark (Wightman et al. identify yanambul as the name for young specimens of wirimal (their williman). New leaves can be boiled to extract sap to cure bad cough.)

Table 16.1 Some food species associated with principal ecological zones (continued)

yurulanyan	white 'currant' (*Flueggea virosa*)
yuwalama	Livistona palm sp.

Lirrimunja (Ironstone ridge) and Urai (Blacksoil)

anamuru, awunji	nests of two species of wild bee
galmarara	yellow goanna (*Varanus gouldi*)
ganda–uru	plains kangaroo, female (*Macropus rufus*)
jambirina	bush turkey (*Ardeotis australis*)
jinaliri	emu (*Dromaius novaehollandiae*)
nungguludu	sandridge goanna (*Varanus sp.*)
wanjimbu	nest of wild bee species that nests in the ground
yargala	plains kangaroo, male (*Macropus rufus*)
banarr	emu tucker tree (*Owenia vernicosa*). Sticks boiled in water to extract sap: good for sore eyes. Poles used in Lorgun ceremony.
dumbuyumbu	sandalwood (*Santalum lanceolatum*). Edible fruit; bark boiled in water to cure sore eyes and throats.
guniniji	black 'plum' (*Vitex glabrata*)
gurrjada	woolybutt tree (*Eucalyptus miniata*)
janambara	paperbark (*Melaleuca viridiflora*). Bark used to make coolamons for carrying fruit, and baby's cradle.
jingulili	conkerberry (*Carissa lanceolata*)
malbamba	ironwood (*Erythrophleum chlorostachys*). Gum used to haft axes.
marabala	grevillea with honey-bearing flowers (*Grevillea* (=wigun) *pteridofolia*)
malunngalnyin	(*Petalostigma pubescens*)
winygirr	corkwood. Used to make coolamons.
yanburraburra	cassava leaf (*Cochlospermum gillivraei*). Edible roots.
yurlmuru	green 'plum' (*Buchanania obovata*). Can be preserved with red ochre.

Ngayiwurr (cliff country)

girimbu	rock kangaroo, male (*Petrogale sp.*)
nalunji	rock kangaroo, female
wangugu	rock wallaby (*Petrogale sp.*)
mululbiri	porcupine
ngaldanda (or wanda)	tree with peach-like fruit
umana	spinifex (*Triodia micrstachya*); wax boiled in water to make medicine to cure coughs and colds. Also grows on rock platforms near lagoons.
wurawi	thin-leaved spinifex

Dirinyin (rock pools) and ngajal (springs)

mawurugu	perch
ngaladara	rifle fish (*Toxotes chatareus*)
yalara	wattle (prob. *Acacia leptocarpa*). Good for spear shafts.

Botanical names are taken from Brock 1993; Wightman *et al.* 1991.

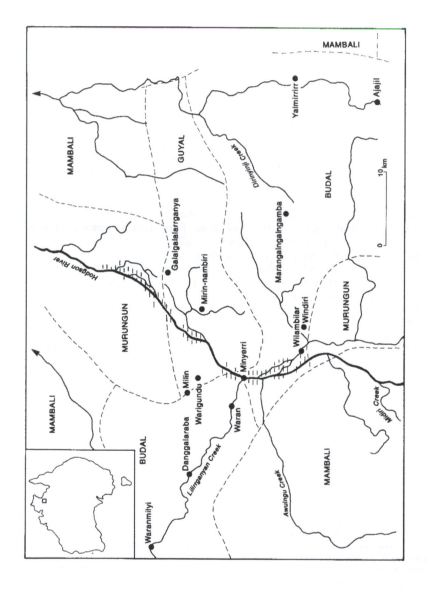

Figure 16.1 Hodgson Downs: creeks, places and estate boundaries.

Major rivers are divided into blocs generally belonging to countries of alternating moieties. Each extends back along tributary creeks, often ending in a watershed (cf. Layton 1989: 3; Pickering 1994: 156). On rivers and creeks, estate boundaries are typically precisely defined and a sacred tree, rock or water hole created by an ancestral being will be known to mark the 'last place' in a given estate. Away from major water courses, boundaries are less well defined but tend to correspond to watersheds. The focus of countries is, however, on central points rather than margins. It is the tracks (*manggan*) taken by the heroic beings that determine their foci. Each ancestral hero belongs to a particular semi-moiety. Yargala is Budal; Wadabir, Jambirina and Ganjila are Guyal. The country held by a single group may comprise more than one area of land, linked by the travels of particular heroes.

The Hodgson River flood plain is dominated by two Murungun estates, one at the northern end of Hodgson Downs, one at the southern end. They are linked by the route of the Munga-Munga women, one of the principal Murungun legends.

The hilly country to the west of the Hodgson River contains two estates. The Mambali estate, centred on Awulngu (Paisley) Creek, occupies the southwest corner of Hodgson Downs. Parts of this estate are situated on Maryfield and Hodgson River Stations. North of the Mambali Awulngu estate lies the Budal country which includes Waranmilyi (Campbell Spring) and Lilirrganyan Creek but extends east to include sites associated with Garrinji (the Jabiru) around Mt Irvine. A substantial portion of this country is situated within Elsey Station, west of Hodgson Downs.

The eastern half of Hodgson Downs contains an entire Guyal country, and almost all of a second Budal country. The Guyal country focused on Minyerri (Wapal) extends from the west bank of the Hodgson near the settlement across to clay pans east of Galpuwurrunanya (Mt Eliza), spanning the hills that form the central watershed. Small creeks draining northwest into the Hodgson north of the settlement belong to this country. To the south lies the Budal country focused on Lirijal Creek. The boundary between the two follows the watershed and escarpment formed by a line of hills running SW–NE and bounding the Hodgson River flood plain. The track of Yargala, the male Plains Kangaroo, runs through both Budal countries on the claim area, linking the two across the settlement. (See Figure 16.1, and compare Layton 1989: Fig. 18.1. Guyal from Minyerri is referred to by the synonym Guyal from Wapal in Layton 1989.)

Some Dreamings in the claim area are non-travelling (e.g. Jambirina, the Guyal Bush Turkey); some travelled relatively short distances (e.g. Guyal Wadabir Goanna and the 'Top' Mambali Warradbunggu Pythons associated with Awulngu Creek); while others, such as Yargala, the Budal Plains Kangaroo and the Murungun Munga-Munga Sisters, travelled long distances. Only a small portion of each such long-distance track lies within the claim area and some have figured in other claims (for Cox River see Layton 1980,

for the Yutpundji-Djindiwirritj land claim see Morphy and Morphy 1981
and for the Elsey land claim see Merlan 1993).

Inheritance of rights and responsibilities

Membership of semi-moieties is transmitted from father to child. Marriage is
forbidden between Budal and Guyal, constituting, as they do, an unnamed
patri-moiety. Marriage is likewise forbidden between Murungun and Mambali.
The preferred marriage pattern is for Budal to marry Mambali in one generation and Murungun in the next. Each generation should ideally reproduce
the marriage pattern of its grandparental generation, and the eight sub-sections
('skins') define the eight positions necessitated to bring the system through
such a two-generational cycle.

As noted above, each estate, or country, is assigned to a semi-moiety.
Those who inherit membership of the group responsible for a country through
their fathers are termed its *miniringgi*. Those who inherit membership through
their mothers or (in certain cases) father's mothers are termed *junggaiyi*, while
those who inherit membership through their mother's mothers are termed
darlnyin. Each individual will belong to three such groups, their father's,
mother's and mother's mother's, performing a different role in each group.
The roles entailed by these relationships are played, in the first instance,
toward the people, places, ceremonies and totemic beings of the actor's
father's, mother's and mother's mother's estates. In the absence of qualified
people who are genealogically affiliated to an estate, others of the same semi-
moiety will take over the role. Failure to protect sites and perform ceremonies
would put the community at risk from the creative, heroic ancestors' anger,
leading to human illness and the loss of fertility in the land.

The spiritual responsibilities of miniringgi, junggaiyi and darlnyin are discharged in five principal spheres: performance of ceremonies, access to and care
of sacred sites, observance of food prohibitions, social control of younger adults
and controlled burning of country. In each sphere, the three roles are complementary and essential to the proper maintenance of tradition. Each estate
has one man who is acknowledged to be its 'head' (most senior) junggaiyi.
Because he is normally the oldest, he will train his sons to succeed him, in case
he dies before completing the task of teaching and supervising the next generation of miniringgi. Should this occur, the children of the head junggaiyi will
perform this role toward their father's mother's estate. Normally, other junggaiyi are not permitted to transmit the role of junggaiyi to their own children.

Performing ceremonies

While ceremonies have a number of functions, including the initiation of
younger people into ceremonial practices and the commemoration of the

recently deceased, a central component of all major ceremonies is the re-enactment of events from the Creation Period in which heroic ancestors traversed the landscape, establishing sites and countries. Those local descent groups sponsoring a ceremony will determine which sites, ancestral tracks and countries are celebrated at a given performance (see Bern 1979). Each country possesses one or more painted motifs representing that country's principal ancestral heroes. These motifs are heraldic in that they provide a simple but unambiguous set of discrete, representational designs. It is only the minir-inggi who hold a country from their fathers who can normally wear/carry these motifs. If the junggaiyi consent, the design may also be worn by men whose animating spirit was found in that country, or by miniringgi of ritu-ally allied countries in the same semi-moiety. At circumcision, the first ceremony to which boys are subjected, male dancers generally wear the motifs to which their mothers are miniringgi.

The right to wear one of these designs in ceremony is regarded as a crucial index of miniringgi status toward a country. Participation in ceremony is thus the critical way in which young men are publicly presented as miniringgi to a certain estate. Such designs often make direct reference to sites on that country. While the estate's junggaiyi are also painted, they are simply covered with white pigment 'just to look good'; it is 'just paint' (ngadba).

Those who stand in the relationship of miniringgi to a ceremony ask for it to be performed, but it is the junggaiyi and darlnyin who agree on timing. Partici-pation of junggaiyi in a ceremony is essential. During performance of a ceremony, male miniringgi and junggaiyi have separate camps; the junggaiyi camp is closer to the ceremonial ground to emphasise their control over the ceremony. If the junggaiyi are out hunting during preparation for a ceremonial dance, the darlnyin can take over painting up the miniringgi. Darlnyin watch the junggaiyi as they apply totemic designs to the miniringgi. If the junggaiyi makes a mistake, the darl-nyin tells him to wash off the incorrect design and repaint it. In the legends out-lined above, heroes who stand in darlnyin relationships to each other interact when they encounter each other during their journeys. The Budal Plains Kan-garoo encounters the Guyal Turkey and Goanna. Similarly, the Mambali Quiet Snakes encounter the Murungun Munga-Munga; at one place, the Quiet Snakes broke up a fish trap the Munga-Munga had constructed in the Hodgson River.

Women discharge their miniringgi role through the observance of food prohibitions, and through their supportive role in male ceremonies. One of the most important roles of female miniringgi during men's ceremonies is to supervise the collection of the food on which the men depend. In one inter-pretation, the male junggaiyi performs his role on his mother's behalf (Gudabi).

Kinship and country

Alawa kinship terminology has the same structure as the sub-section system, i.e. that of four patrilines, but takes four rather than two generations to complete a patri-cycle. The sub-section and semi-moiety systems allow the use of kin terms between people even where no known genealogical link exists. Thus, if I am Budal, I can call any Budal man in the generation above mine *kuni*, or father. The kinship terminology is, however, egocentric. Hence, for example, if I am Budal my *gugu* (mother's mother/mother's mother's brother) will be Guyal but, if I am Mambali, (s)he will be Murungun. The semi-moiety and sub-section systems are, in contrast, socio-centric; if I am Budal (or *jabada*), I am Budal (*jabada*) to anyone, regardless of their semi-moiety affiliation.

Because countries are attributed to semi-moieties, the semi-moiety system maps kinship onto the landscape. I am miniringgi to my father's estate and junggaiyi to my mother's. The estate to which my mother's mother and her brother belonged is my 'gugu country' or 'granny country'. It is toward this estate that I will, in the first instance, play the role of darlnyin. This is why the Budal Kangaroo addressed the Guyal Goanna as 'Granny'.

As the logic of the system is traced away from the level of kinship, however, it moves from an ego-centred perspective to an increasingly objective and less context-dependent orientation. A person who is miniringgi to one Budal estate can, by extension, play that role towards other Budal estates and Dreamings. The same is true of the other semi-moieties and ritual roles. In default of miniringgi, junggaiyi or darlnyin directly affiliated to an estate by actual kinship or (if such individuals are too young to have learned the knowledge required to discharge their responsibilities) other junggaiyi, miniringgi or darlnyin will step in to ensure that sites are protected and ceremonies associated with the land are properly performed. Such people are said to 'come behind' those whose status is genealogical. They include miniringgi for other countries on the tracks of the same ancestors and junggaiyi belonging to the correct sub-section, but whose mothers come from different countries.

Conception affiliation

Animating spirits of unborn children were left at certain points in the landscape by the ancestral heroes. Each child is said to have been 'soaked in the water' in which its spirit lay prior to conception. A child's animating spirit is usually found by one or other of its parents, generally in an estate of the semi-moiety to which its father is miniringgi. If the animating spirit is not found in the estate that is its father's by patrilineal descent, the baby has the potential rights of miniringgi-ship in both its father's estate and its estate of conception, although these can be ratified only by the junggaiyi.

Conception affiliation provides a means of mapping contingencies onto an otherwise apparently inflexible system of social affiliation. Characteristically, the animating spirit uses an item of plant or animal food collected by its parents to reach the mother's womb. Since the parents must be camping on an estate to find a baby there, conception affiliation is likely to reflect residence patterns. During the periods of social upheaval created by colonialism and work in the pastoral industry described below, conception affiliation provided a means for children being born far from their parents' estates to be integrated into the community where the parents had taken up residence.

Observance of food prohibitions

Observance of food prohibitions is intimately related to the performance of ceremonies, because ceremonies were instituted by heroic beings who were at once human and animal. Thus, Jambirina (Bush Turkey) and Yargala (Plains Kangaroo) *are* Y.; Warradbunggu (Quiet Snake) *is* G.[2] In the words of one man, 'Budal can't eat Kangaroo because that's our body'.

Access to and care of sites

Ceremonies were originally performed by the heroic beings at certain places. Contemporary ceremonies are re-creations, and the actual ceremonial paraphernalia are reconstructions of the originals that survive, transformed into the features of sites of significance. A sacred site is *nyugurr* (a dear one, sacred). The most sacred of sites are those at which prototypical ceremonies were performed. Other sites were stopping places on the travels of the heroes. Trees, rocks, waterholes and other features at these sites are their artefacts, body parts and camp sites.

Miniringgi cannot approach important sacred sites. Junggaiyi care for sacred sites, 'clean them, make them look nice' (Jandai). Junggaiyi can declare sites closed to miniringgi. If a junggaiyi found the tracks (footprints) of a miniringgi going to a closed site, he would fine him. If a branch has fallen off a sacred tree, the miniringgi are required to pay a fine to the junggaiyi. Such trees are found, for example, at numerous places where the Budal Kangaroo and Guyal Goanna stopped. Traditionally payment was in honey or artefacts; today, it may be in cash or tobacco or cloth. Some men consider cash inappropriate because it will return to ordinary circulation after having discharged a ritual obligation. It may well then be handled by women and children who have no protection against the power of the ancestral beings. If a darlnyin notices damage to a sacred tree he must inform the junggaiyi. He may also alert the miniringgi and assist in paying the fine.

People are rarely allowed to fire the bush in country to which they stand in the relationship of miniringgi because, if a sacred site were accidentally damaged, they would have to pay the junggaiyi. It is therefore safer for the junggaiyi to undertake firing of the bush themselves. Old, sacred trees are particularly vulnerable to fire damage. When a *banar* ('Emu Tucker') tree near the football oval at Hodgson Downs community, associated with the Budal Plains Kangaroo, was destroyed by fire some years ago, the miniringgi were required to pay the junggaiyi. Junggaiyi may, however, consent to the miniringgi burning areas of country when it is considered safe to do so.

The performance of ceremonies is therefore key to asserting rights to land within traditional Alawa society, as Bern has documented: 'The estates are represented symbolically in performances of the rites with which they are associated, in particular dances performed by members of the owning group, and in the designs and paraphernalia they wear in these dances' (Bern 1979: 48). Alawa themselves state this clearly. 'Ceremony holds the country' (Dawson Daniels, a Mara man). 'As soon as you lose ceremony, you're finished' (Philip Watson). Contemporary Alawa culture is realised in the face of a century of colonisation and it is only the Alawa's success in maintaining it that enables the anthropologist to reconstruct how it might have been realised prior to colonisation.

Response to colonisation

Alawa country was colonised by Euro-Australian pastoralists in the final quarter of the nineteenth century. In 1856, the explorer Augustus Gregory travelled through the area. He noted that the country near Hodgson Downs had been subject to controlled burning (Gregory 1963: 161). Construction of the Overland Telegraph Line, which linked Australia to Asia and Europe, exposed Alawa country to pastoral colonisation. Its route ran through the site of the future town of Katherine. In 1871, a supply depot for the Overland Telegraph construction party was established at Roper Bar, in the country of the Alawa's neighbours the Ngalakan. For a brief time Roper Bar had a non-Aboriginal population of 300, a few of whom stayed to cater for the drovers who had started to bring cattle across from Queensland (Morphy and Morphy 1981: 8). The first lease to Hodgson Downs was issued in 1884 and the station stocked with cattle driven overland from Queensland (Merlan 1978: 79).

The destruction of waterholes and edible plants by the thousands of cattle brought to the region during the pastoral land boom of the late 1870s and 1880s brought the Alawa and their neighbours into fierce conflict with the colonial settlers. As cattle destroyed subsistence resources, Aborigines increasingly speared cattle for food. The settlers retaliated by shooting the cattle killers (see Merlan 1978; Morphy and Morphy 1984; Layton 1992).

The bloodiest massacre of the era, apparently over the death of some horses, occurred at Hodgson Downs shortly before 1903. Estimates of the number killed range between thirty and forty Alawa people, of all ages and both sexes. Accounts of this event are widely known among Alawa living at Hodgson Downs today. In 1993, August Sandy Lirriwirri recounted the event to Craig Elliott as follows:

> Just near the house [Hodgson Downs homestead, approximately 500 m north of the Minyerri community] there, back this side. That's where they got shot, there now. They got shot then, all the old fellas, lot of young people too, lot of woman was there,

kids. They [white stockmen] made a fire first and all the people was down here, down the hill here [approximately 500 m south-east of Minyerri community]. And they came up from down there, two bloke [white stockmen], and tell this mob here 'come on, we'll take you down, we got to do some work up there, build a firewood for the station', they said. And they took all this lot here down there, two bloke. And everyone was there now, kids and man, woman. Build that firewood, stack the firewood.... They couldn't get away them woman and man, they shot them all there.... And three bloke only got away from this mob here. They went to Winiki, up the top of a big hill, tell them bloke, 'we lost all the women and couple of old fella and young fella, got shot. Not any left, all gone, dead'.

According to August, Stephen Roberts's grandfather, Old Charlie Waypuldanya, was among the few who escaped. They made their way upstream to a small valley enclosed by hills on the east bank of the Hodgson called Winiki 'Pocket'. While most survivors kept away from the homestead area, Waypuldanya took revenge on the white men whom he believed to be involved in the massacre. He and his younger brothers killed eight in an ambush and took their guns, horses, ammunition, packs and saddles. Other white stockmen found the bodies at Winiki but did not pursue Old Charlie because they knew he was now well armed.

The continuing Alawa presence

There has been an Alawa community at Hodgson Downs throughout the pastoral era, but its size during the early colonial period is unknown. The recorded size of the Aboriginal population at Hodgson Downs remained at around forty to fifty people in 1937–44. Thonemann suggests that the birth rate at Hodgson Downs at this time was very low (Thonemann 1949: 127). Elkin carried out fieldwork at Hodgson Downs in 1947. His unpublished field notes include a summary of the Water Goanna legend at Minyerri. He apparently spoke with people such as 'Old Gilruth' (Giluru) and Ruby Megun who taught the present generation of elders. Men and women with Plains Kangaroo, Quiet Snake and other 'Dreamings' associated with sites in the vicinity of Hodgson Downs are shown on his genealogy.

Swain has recently reopened the debate as to why 'cargo cults' were hardly, if ever, found in colonial Australia, in view of the extent to which the traditional way of life was disrupted (Swain 1993: 217ff). He argues that there are indeed millenarian cults in Aboriginal Australia, and that their significance has not previously been appreciated by whites. He gives examples of cults from the Kimberleys and Western Desert in which motor cars and aeroplanes figure, which, he argues, enabled Aboriginal people to establish 'a

manageable association ... with the invading peoples ... one encoded in
rations, wages and work' (Swain 1993: 237). The critical factor, in Swain's
assessment, was the dislocation of people caused by the pastoral industry. As
long as people could 'stay in their place', they had no need of a cult that
transcended the traditional, place-oriented religion (Swain 1993: 242).

Since Hodgson Downs lies at the very heartland of pastoral colonisation
in the Northern Territory, it is a remarkable fact that it remains a centre for
cults that celebrate people's attachment to the land. This is precisely the third
reason that people give for performing ceremonies. Ashwood Farrell expressed
it modestly: 'the ceremony looks after the country, so we don't want to lose
our country'. August Sandy put it more forthrightly: if ceremonies were not
held, 'someone like you mob might shoot us and drive us off our land'.

It is possible that contemporary cults were devised or modified in response
to colonisation. There is no doubt that they were spreading during the colonial era. The spread of the G. is well documented (Berndt 1951: xvii–xx;
Elkin 1952: 251; Elkin 1961: 167–9; Stanner 1960: 275; Stanner 1963: 244–5;
Meggitt 1966). All of the key elements of the Gulf Country G. were seen
to be duplicated by Berndt in 1949, in a performance in northeast Arnhem
Land (Berndt 1951: 40–7). Berndt argued that the cult had spread into
northeast Arnhem Land from the Roper River (Berndt 1951: xxv). He noted
that the heroes celebrated in the Gulf Country G. are associated with a hole
in a creek 'about five miles to the east of Jumbuluju, now Hodgson Downs
Cattle Station' (Berndt 1951: 148). Elkin considers that the Y. also developed in the middle and lower Roper Valley (i.e. close to Hodgson Downs)
(Elkin 1961: 167). It spread over a wide part of the Northern Territory (Bern
1979: 48). On the other hand, these are not cargo cults. They do not look
forward to a time when indigenous people will gain control of the colonists'
resources; they reaffirm the ancestral order. Both cults were, moreover,
recorded by the earliest anthropologists to work in the Gulf Country, Spencer
and Gillen, who learned of them in 1902 (Spencer and Gillen 1904: 223),
only twenty years after the introduction of cattle-ranching. Spencer and
Gillen's account of the Alawa's southern neighbours to Nganji shows that
the cultural system is essentially unchanged. They wrote:

> Each totemic group of individuals originated as the offspring of
> one ancestral, eponymous creature who walked about the country
> making ranges, creeks, waterholes and other natural features. Wher-
> ever he performed sacred ceremonies, there he left behind him
> spirit individuals, who emanated from his body.
>
> (Spencer and Gillen 1904: 170)

Spencer and Gillen found that 'the totemic animal or plant is strictly
tabooed to the members of the totemic group' (Spencer and Gillen 1904: 326).
They observed a Y. ceremony performed by the Wambaiya, in which two
Nganji men participated, and noted that ceremonies celebrate the activities of
ancestral heroes at sites on the land: 'the one we witnessed was connected with

a snake totem called Putjatta, and was associated with a place known as Liaritji' (Spencer and Gillen 1904: 222). They record the word *mingaringi* (miniringgi) as the term for 'headman' among coastal tribes, and found the role to be transmitted patrilineally (Spencer and Gillen 1904: 23–4).

Spencer and Gillen were told that it was possible, although rare, for a child to have a 'totem' other than its father's, although they regard conception affiliation as unimportant, writing: 'with the rarest exceptions, the child belongs to its father's totem wherever it may happen to be conceived' (Spencer and Gillen 1904: 282). It is therefore possible that the role of conception affiliation in assimilating the children of men who had moved in search of work on cattle stations increased during later decades of the present century. It is equally possible that cults such as the G. and Y. developed in order to provide a regional forum for the assertion of rights to land; but, if this was the case, I surmise that they did no more than provide a context for the expression of an already well-established cultural system. McLaughlin has pointed out to me that the manner in which the travelling ancestors encounter different local ancestors within each estate they cross can be interpreted as evidence for the linking of existing local cults to new regional traditions (Dehne McLaughlin, pers. comm.). An alternative explanation is that localised ancestors serve to differentiate local groups whose countries lie on the route of the same travelling ancestor, and that they are a necessary counterpart to travelling ancestors in the cognitive system.

Stability and flexibility

Tracks and estates

To the extent that process can be reconstructed in an oral culture, the Alawa doctrine that the routes of the ancestral heroes and the sites they created are immutable appears sound. Certainly, none of the routes that I recorded while working on the Cox River land claim between 1979 and 1981 had changed in the slightest when I returned to work on the Hodgson Downs claim in 1993.

The extent of countries (in the sense of estates) is, however, flexible. Blocs of land associated with each semi-moiety are readily identified, but a single estate may consist of more than one bloc of land. Where adjacent blocs are associated with the same Dreaming, it may not always be possible to establish with clarity whether they constitute one estate or two. Indeed, estates on the same Dreaming track seem, over the time span of several decades, to resemble drops of water on a string, splitting and coalescing according to the current size of the descent group associated with them, the operation of the principles of succession, and the desire not to alienate allies in ritual by claiming exclusive responsibility for performance of ceremonies and care of sites on one section of a hero's track (see Layton 1989: 4–5 for evidence for such processes in the Cox River land claim and Merlan 1993: 9–10 for evidence from the Elsey claim).

Estates are therefore probably now largely, if not entirely, ceremonial units constructed for the purpose of maintaining Alawa title against Euro-Australian encroachment. Some, if not all, of them may be larger than the pre-colonial estates constructed as the loci of the foraging activities of local descent groups. They are probably formed by the amalgamation of such pre-colonial units to cope with population decline during the colonial era. The Budal country from Lirijal, through which Yargala, the Plains Kangaroo, travelled after leaving Minyerri, for example, incorporates an area of land on either side of Wija Creek, on the Nutwood Downs pastoral lease (see Layton 1989: Fig. 18.1). The two are linked by the track of the Budal Sandridge Goanna. Formerly, Wija Creek was the country of an elderly woman who lived at Nutwood Downs. When she died, custodianship passed to the Roberts family. The fact that Yargala changes his language from Alawa to Mara on the watershed at the centre of the Lirijal country hints at the possibility that this watershed was once a boundary between two estates.

During preparation for the Hodgson Downs claim hearings, senior members of the community were concerned that none of the young men who had succeeded their fathers as miniringgi had learned the associated ritual knowledge for a section of the Whirlwind track that crosses the plain at the northern edge of Hodgson Downs. Other men undertook to train them, 'so we can have ceremony through that country'. Responsibility for the section of the 'Bottom' Python track passing across this plain had already been taken on by the group holding Awulngu Creek.

Maintaining custodians for the landscape

If demographic accident, introduced disease, massacres or forced movement result in the drastic reduction of numbers of miniringgi associated with an estate, action will be taken by the junggaiyi to recruit others to take over the role. Those conceived on the estate will be obvious candidates. Alternatively, an estate with numerous miniringgi of the correct semi-moiety may surrender some young men to be initiated into the depleted group.

One example concerns the Murungun country at the southern end of Hodgson Downs, centred on the lagoon called Unulalda. The oldest miniringgi to this estate remembered by living Alawa were Old Tommy, also known as 'Grasshopper', and his brother Mardaguru. Some senior Alawa recall that Grasshopper's father's country was Langgabany, a Murungun estate on the neighbouring station of St Vidgeon, and that he was looking after Unulalda on behalf of future generations of miniringgi. Mardaguru is the name of a spring near Unulalda. Mardaguru had a son, but when his wife remarried she took the boy with her and he was raised on Mainoru Station in southern Arnhem Land. Toni Bauman was told, while preparing genealogies for the Hodgson Downs land claim, that Mardaguru and his son occasionally met at Katherine races, but the boy never returned to Hodgson Downs (Bauman, pers. comm.). In his old age, Grasshopper therefore chose Hodgson Wilfred, a young Murungun man whose father was miniringgi to a Murungun estate a short distance north of Hodgson Downs, to succeed him. Unfortunately, Grasshopper died before Hodgson Wilfred's training was complete. For a time it seemed that the country would be left without miniringgi, but August Sandy, a senior junggaiyi to the Murungun country from Unulalda, then in his sixties, took over the instruction of Hodgson Wilfred. Hodgson is now established as miniringgi and his children will inherit his position as they grow to adulthood.

Another case concerns the Guyal country centred on Minyerri lagoon. When I began fieldwork in the area in 1979, there were two senior miniringgi to this country, Sandy Mambuji and Hedrick Hall. A man whom I shall call Japal and his children should also have inherited this status, since it was previously held by their father and father's father. Unfortunately, Japal's father had been expelled by the junggaiyi in consequence of an offence committed during performance of a ceremony. Japal was conceived on Wija Creek. He and his sisters were, therefore, 'adopted' by the owners of the Lirijal estate, of which Wija Creek is part, and were recognised as miniringgi to Lirijal at the time of the Cox River claim (Kearney 1985: 15, 31). It was, however, always recognised by the senior members of the Lirijal estate that Japal's children might be readmitted as miniringgi to Minyerri. Unfortunately, the junggaiyi who had expelled Japal's father had died soon after the incident and could not rescind his decision. After the death of Sandy Mambuji in the early 1980s, moreover, the Minyerri estate was left without a senior miniringgi. In 1979, the son of Japal's sister was seeking consent to take on the role of junggaiyi to Minyerri with the support of Sandy Mambuji. He acceded to this position before his death and was responsible for placing a protective rectangle of stones around one of the most sacred sites near Minyerri during the mid-1980s. Nonetheless, it was not until 1994 that senior men felt secure in readmitting the now deceased Japal's children to the status of miniringgi in Minyerri country.

Conclusion

The Alawa theory of being, expressed through legend and ceremony, is very different to western theory. Nonetheless, Alawa ontology addresses the formation and maintenance of an environment largely perceptible to western scholars, and organises behaviour that leaves archaeological traces. Alawa legend tracks the creation of springs and lagoons that are essential to plant, animal and human life in the region, while Alawa ceremony both renews the creative forces within the land, and reasserts people's right to care for it. The Alawa, whose political system is egalitarian and uncentralised, visualise places in the landscape as nodes in a network of ancestral tracks created by the ancestors whose deeds are recorded in legend. When discussing the distribution of sites

on the land, I was frequently reminded to 'follow the line', i.e. not to jump
from the route of one heroic being to that of another, and to follow each route
according to the correct sequence of sites. The particular structure of Alawa
sacred sites and the ancestral tracks that link them is intimately connected with
the traditional system of resource management practised by the Alawa, both in
the way in which it maps the distribution of subsistence resources, and the way
in which it regulates access to them. Although estate boundaries can be identified along watersheds, for the Alawa it is not the boundaries of estates, but
their heartland in and around the water courses, that are the most important.
This is where archaeological debris is most densely concentrated. Social responsibilities to care for the land are allocated according to a complex kinship system
that, while precisely defining the roles of individuals, also possesses the flexibility necessary to ensure others can take over if the positions of primary responsibility are temporarily vacant. Those activities that leave archaeological
evidence – camping in areas where one is entitled to forage, burning the country, maintaining stone arrangements – are allocated through the kinship system.
The content of such practices is determined by the theory of being expressed
in legend and ritual. The strength of the Alawa adaptation is demonstrated
by the manner in which it has been upheld during a century of colonial
settlement.

Notes

1   There is insufficient space to consider variations in the ways in which these
    legends are told by their traditional owners, but the versions presented here
    include details provided on different occasions at a number of sites, since, when
    discussing the routes of legendary beings in camp, it is normal simply to list the
    names of the sites they visited. These legends remain the cultural property of the
    Alawa and only they can judge the correctness of any telling.
2   At the request of senior Alawa men, I have omitted the names of cults that
    should not be mentioned in public.

References

Bern, J. 1979. Politics in the conduct of a secret male ceremony. *Journal of Anthro-
    pological Research*, 35: 47–60.
Berndt, R. 1951. *K . . .: a study of an Australian Aboriginal religious cult.* Melbourne:
    Cheshire.
Brock, J. 1993. *Native Plants of Northern Australia.* Chatswood, NSW: Reed.
Elkin, A.P. 1952. Cave paintings in southern Arnhem Land. *Oceania* 2, 245–55.
Elkin, A.P. 1961. The Y. . . . *Oceania* 31, 166–209.
Gregory, A. 1963. *Journals of Australian Explorers, 1856.* Adelaide: Libraries Board of
    South Australia.
Kearney, W.J. 1985. *Cox River (Alawa/Ngandji) Land Claim: report by the Aboriginal
    Land Commissioner . . . .* Canberra: Australian Government Publishing Service.

Layton, R. 1980. *The Cox River (Alawa/Ngandji) Land Claim: claim book*. Darwin: Northern Land Council.

Layton, R. 1989. The political use of Australian Aboriginal body painting and its archaeological implications. In *The Meanings of Things*, I. Hodder (ed.), 1–11. London: Unwin Hyman.

Layton, R. 1992. *Australian Rock Art: a new synthesis*. Cambridge: Cambridge University Press.

Layton, R. 1997. Representing and translating people's place in the landscape of northern Australia. In *After Writing Culture*, A. James, J. Hockey and A. Dawson (eds), 122–43. London: Routledge.

Meggitt, M.J. 1966. *G. . . . among the Walbiri Aborigines of Central Australia*. Sydney: Oceania Publications.

Merlan, F. 1978. 'Making people quiet' in the pastoral north: reminiscences of Elsey Station. *Aboriginal History* 2, 71–106.

Merlan, F. 1993. *Elsey Land Claim No. 132: anthropologist's report*. Darwin: Northern Land Council.

Morphy, H. and F. Morphy 1981. *Yutpundji-Djindiwirritj Land Claim: claim book*. Darwin: Northern Land Council.

Morphy, H. and F. Morphy 1984. The 'myths' of Ngalakan history: ideology and images of the past in northern Australia. *Man* 19, 459–78.

Pickering, M. 1994. The physical landscape as a social landscape: a Garawa example. *Archaeology in Oceania* 29, 149–61.

Spencer, W.B. and F.J. Gillen 1904. *The Northern Tribes of Central Australia*. London: Macmillan.

Stanner, W.E.H. 1960. Sacramentalism, rite and myth. *Oceania* 30, 245–78.

Stanner, W.E.H. 1963. Cosmos and society made correlative. *Oceania* 33, 239–73.

Stanner, W.E.H. 1965. Aboriginal territorial organisation. *Oceania* 36, 1–26.

Swain, T. 1993. *A Place for Strangers*. Cambridge: Cambridge University Press.

Thonemann, H.E. 1949. *Tell the White Man*. Sydney: Collins.

Wightman, G.M., D.M. Jackson and L.V.L. Williams 1991. *Alawa Ethno-botany: Aboriginal plant use from Minyerri, northern Australia*. Darwin: Conservation Commission of the Northern Territory.

17 Managing the world: territorial negotiations among the Andoque people of the Colombian Amazon

MÓNICA ESPINOSA ARANGO
AND FISI ANDOQUE

Introduction

The Andoque people claim that their conception of the world is limited only to what is directly known by them: the territory, peoples, stories and myths. This territory is understood in terms of such features as peaks, hills, savannah and rocks, that are known and named by the shaman. Therefore, they have religious, ceremonial and communal significance. Each of these places has an owner, and, in that way, they are 'enchanted'. Such named places are the origin of everything that the people know: dance, work, healing, witchcraft and wickedness. Each place is identified by the mythical events that took place there.

The Andoque people do not conceive the world and the landscape as fixed in a permanent setting. They were moulded since primordial times until they obtained their current shapes. These shapes continue to be symbolically remodelled by shamanistic actions. Such remodelling takes place during the mental territorial transposition of the shaman. Through this process, the shaman (or *sabedor*) can communicate directly with such places, even though he is not physically there. He can also establish contact with the place's owners. From the *mambeadero*[1] (ceremonial ash place inside the *maloca*[2] or collective house) (Figure 17.1; and see Landaburu and Pineda 1984) the shaman controls the territory, undertakes purifications (*limpiezas*) and makes payments (*pagamentos*) together with other men of knowledge. Such experiences enable shamans to advise the community on matters such as when it is proper to eat meat or fish, how much should be eaten, where to walk, which illnesses will come and how to avoid them, and which animals may be hunted, and how to do so.

Anthropologists (Descola 1989; Århem 1990; Reichel-Dussán 1992; Van der Hammen 1992) have developed models of analysis for understanding shamanistic knowledge as well as detailed knowledge of the territory, the different components of the landscape (the symbolic topography), plants and animals. This integrated management of the territory is named 'eco-politic'

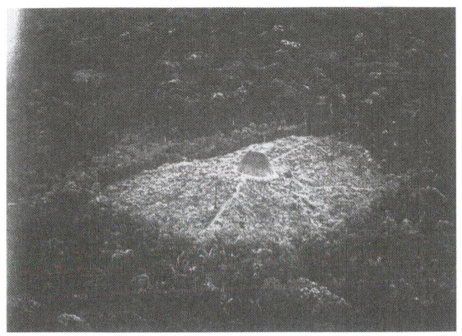

Figure 17.1 A *maloca* from the air.

(Reichel-Dussán 1992). The Andoque people have two different levels of perception of their territory: (a) the shamanistic territory, a vague entity whose symbolic management is characterised by the 'mental territorial transpositions' made by the shaman; (b) the territory of the community, which is well known by the people. In this chapter, the concept of 'mobile frontiers' is introduced in order to explain this complexity of management, particularly for the shamanistic territorial transpositions. In the cultural area of the middle Caquetá River, where the Andoque people are settled, a map of the mental territorial transpositions made by shamans of the different ethnic groups would reveal the intersections of places and the existence of overlapping borders. This mapping process shows the importance of shamanistic negotiations.

Currently, these shamans' territorial conceptions must be considered in the context of the territorial, legal and administrative reorganisation of Colombia, as well as within the socio-political changes of the ethnic groups themselves. For some anthropologists, it is premature to talk about the disappearance of this traditional knowledge, in contrast to the consolidation of a formal and legal knowledge of territory. Such knowledge is expressed through councils: *resguardos* managed by the indigenous communities, *cabildos* and *consejos* (and see Rappaport 1994: 84–5). In this chapter we focus on changes in the context of the relationships within the ethnic group, among the ethnic groups living in the area, and between them and the Colombian state. Such relationships have historically been both difficult to manage and opposed to one another.

Possessing the Amazon

The Amazon region represents about 60 per cent of the world's tropical rain forests. It extends over the lower eastern Andean lands up to the Amazon river mouth, and from the Guyana and Orinoco Basin to the north of Bolivia and the Matto Grosso in Brazil; its area is about 12 million sq. km, and the population is 23 million (Salazar 1989). Bolivia, Brazil, Ecuador, Peru, Surinam, Venezuela and Colombia have territories in the Amazon Basin. Each country has its policies and programmes, but international and national efforts follow the Amazon Cooperation Treaty's rules (Tratado de Cooperacion Amazonica TCA). This treaty proposes to develop and encourage the region's own productivity; it also deals with the sustainability of both ecosystems and human settlements (Aragón 1994; CADM 1994).

Occupation of the region has a long history. One model (Lathrap 1968) proposed that it might have started from the alluvial plains along the main rivers. Basing his view on stylistic studies of ceramic distribution, glotto-chronology, and lexicostatistics, he argued that 10,000 years ago people on the varzeas developed an incipient horticulture system related to an efficient fishing technique. The people cultivated cotton, calabash and special plants for fishing called barbasco in small gardens around the houses. They elaborated net floats, nets and substances to paralyse fish (Marcos 1988). Intense demographic pressure in the central Amazon over the alluvial plains, it was argued, might have caused a migration process to other available areas. Militarily weak small groups might have moved into interfluvial areas, transforming their horticulture–fishing systems into hunter-gatherer ones.

Both Toca do Boquirao da Pedra Furada in Brazil (c. 40,000–50,000 years BP) and Monte Verde in Chile offer new evidence for human colonisation of South America. These discoveries have forced us to modify our views of the age and characteristics of the most ancient American colonisation process (Ardila and Politis 1989).

When the Spaniards reached America in 1498, 2,000 native groups might have been living in the Amazon with a population of around 7 million (CADM 1994: 88). There were migratory movements from the Andean mountains toward the piedmont and the rain forest, and important interchanges between Andean–Amazon groups. Even though the groups who inhabited the varzea disappeared, there is useful information about them in the chronicles written by European travellers (Salazar 1989). The Portuguese who entered the Amazon from the Atlantic side found areas with a high density of population and a system of independent villages. The Spaniards who reached the Upper Amazon around the seventeenth century also found complex societies with considerable intergroup activities (Llanos and Pineda 1982; CADM 1994).

During the sixteenth to eighteenth centuries, religious missions attempted to convert the native groups to Christianity. The missionaries forced many people to live in 'towns', making for easier control and facilitating religious conversion. From 1840 until 1914, colonisation increased due to the boom in rubber extraction. The influx of new white people into the Amazon produced many impacts on both people and environment (CADM 1994; Espinosa 1995). Groups on the middle Caqueta River were decimated. According to Thomas Whiffen, a British traveller who went to the Amazon at the beginning of this century, the Andoque people numbered around 10,000. After the 'rubber boom', just eight Andoque survived and began the cultural reconstruction process. That process involved a progressive return to Gavilan's ancestral territory. The Gavilan (Eagles) clan was the leader of socio-cultural reconstruction. Ritual celebrations in new *malocas* were the basis of the return to traditional territory. During the process the people renamed the places. From that time until now, the Andoque's mythological tradition has followed the Gavilan's tradition (Guzmán 1971; Landaburu and Pineda 1984; Pineda 1985; Espinosa 1995).

After the Second World War, the Amazon entered into a new phase of foreign occupation. The main characteristic was the intense use of the soil and wood and mineral exploitation. In the Amazon today there are 400 ethnic groups with a population of about 1–2 million people (CADM 1994: 88). In the Colombian area there are 58 groups, 41 of which have less than 1,000 speakers, 33 have less than 500, and 20 have less than 200. The Andoque people belong to the latter group (Franco 1992: 158). The Amazon Cooperation Treaty created protected areas such as Natural Parks and Reserves. In 1988, the Colombian government opened the Resguardos, territorial entities belonging to the ethnic groups (Correa 1990), thereby creating a new socio-political organisation, called Cabildo, which is changing the traditional political system.

Shamanism

One of the main cultural characteristics shared by Amazon groups is shamanism (Reichel Dussán 1988). The term 'shaman' includes not only medicine men but also sorcerers; for this reason, it is either too general or too vague to be useful. In a strict sense, the word 'shaman' comes from the Tungus language spoken in Siberia (Eliade 1986). Even though the shaman is not the only person related to sacred experiences, he is the predominant one. He is the master of ecstasies and this experience is seen as a religious process. The shaman is a specialist of trance, the time during which his soul leaves his body and travels around the human world, the animals' world and the ancestors' world. The shaman can talk with dead people, with devils or with nature's spirits. The shaman can maintain his autonomy before them even if that is only possible with strong fights and sacrifices. The shaman is the specialist of human souls, he lives the religious experience with total intensity.

In the Colombian ethnographic record the concept of shamanism is both wide and complex. Reichel Dussán (1988: 131) has described it as the organized world perspective that conceives the man related to the universe and its physical and cosmic laws. Also, it conceives human beings as interconnected parts of the total ecosystem. The social and environmental patterns show an elaborate system for the short, middle and long-term. It is an adaptative process which involves humans with all their environments. Shamanism is an economic, political and spiritual discipline.

It is based on an integral world point of view. The conception about the origin and development of human beings follows a sense of unity to Nature. The people say that persons, animals and plants develop a common soul and share a vital force (Descola 1989; Århem 1990; Van der Hammen 1992; Espinosa 1994).

The shamanistic point of view influences the way in which people interact with Nature and how they seek to use resources. Human beings are not conceived as superior to, or different from, the rest of life beings. Århem (1990) terms this 'ecosophy' and describes it as a moral attitude toward Nature that changes ecological knowledge into moral values and feelings. Thus it can be said to order social actions and group behaviour.

Fisi, a shaman (sabedor)

Among the Andoque, who call themselves People of the Axe (poosíóho), there are distinctions between specialists of the human soul. Fisi Andoque says:

> The taetúo (sorcerer) is the person who gives strength to the community's heart. He resolves the group's questions and problems using psychotropic plants. The akosi síóho is the healer. Using plants and prayers he cures the mental and body illness. Finally, the po'soo, called the 'strong word man', creates all: works, dances, songs, treatments and secrets – creating and promoting a general well-being among his people.

This person, who is also a maloca's leader, can be said to give birth to everything. Through dances, rituals and sacred words he creates the world, promoting happiness and a general state of well-being. The po'soo is also called i'paaka éo, which means the famous, or the person who is named by all the people. He is also called kápúe, the person who enables others to have life, and allows them to be proper people. In Fisi's words:

> We must have a po'soo, a leader, because he is the only one who can turn the people into proper people or hóihó using the maloca, celebrations, ritual food and drinks, songs and dances. Without his protection the people are i'hooá or orphans.

In the Colombian Amazon ethnographic record, it is common to use the word sabedor to describe the man who is the guardian of traditional knowledge.

In the same way, he is the interpreter and user of that knowledge that gets wider and richer with his actions (Corredor and Torres 1989). He knows about plants and their medicinal properties; he communicates with gods and ancestors using rituals. The *sabedor* is the group's protector in both physical and social ways. There are different ceremonial paths or knowledge ways, and they determine the *sabedor*'s specialisation. That option is given by heredity.

Fisi Andoque is the first son of Yineko, the former *po'soo*. Yineko was Donekai's son, the Gavilan's *po'soo*. Fisi is the current *sabedor* and he acquired that status by heredity after a long training alongside his father. The red ritual *Charapa de Carguero* is Fisi's ceremonial path, which is related to the *pexosí* quality associated – in contradistinction to *pófio* (white, associated with calm, happiness and curative witchcraft) – with the colour red. People, lineages, myths and animals all have some of both white and red qualities. The Andoque say that senior brothers are situated within the red element, and younger brothers within white. Fisi's father is said to have been a *pofio*; Fisi himself is a *pexosí*: an element associated with strong personality, with anger, and with courage, but also with strong witchcraft (the jaguar and the hawk are both considered to be red creatures), the sun and the stars. During his life, Fisi Andoque has been developing a red career with the *Charapa de Carguero* as the central ritual, and he is seen by others to be a strong shaman.

The Andoque people belong to the group called 'People of the Center' or 'People of the Coca and Ambil'. These people inhabit the middle and lower Caqueta River, in the Colombian Amazon, and are dispersed over all the territory. However, the different groups live around the *maloca*, the supreme cultural and ritual space. Inside the *maloca*, in its turn, is the *mambeadero* or place of knowledge, a ceremonial and masculine space. The *sabedor* creates and recreates the universe accompanied by other older men there. They chew coca (*Erytroxilum coca* – and see Johns 1969: 516) and suck ambil (semi-liquid tobacco). Every day the group talks about the *mambeadero*'s tradition called *ipoíko* ('all which comes from the Father or becomes you Father'). Celebrating the rituals requires one to grow, recollect and transform the coca. For the Andoque and Uitoto people, coca is knowledge. In a similar way, to prepare and use ambil is to become wiser.

Possessing the landscape

The Andoque people define the world using the knowledge of the physical, mythical and ritual territory. Fisi says:

> We, the Andoque people, think that the world is limited to only what is directly known by us. A *sabedor* must know the names, events, and mythical protectors of the traditional sacred points on the landscape.

Comparing the landscape classifications made by the Amazon groups, it appears that they all share a common division involving two big conceptual unities: the 'aquatic world' and the 'terrestrial world'. The names of most of the topographic irregularities that shape the courses of the rivers, branches, deep parts, backwaters, lakes and jets resemble the mythological being who transformed them. The same thing happens with the hills, caves, savannahs, *rastrojos*, solid woodland or areas of monospecific plant associations such as *cananguchales*. This can be seen to be symbolic topography, with the climatic annual cycle linked to symbolic happenings. The shaman is the one in charge of purifying the space; he negotiates with the owners of the season, whether through personal intermediation (mental territorial transpositions) or through dances. He tries to create well-being, happiness and fruitfulness for the group and Nature. The meaning of 'world' includes not only the environment and landscape but also the supernatural worlds.

This world view is the basis of the group's way of life that must guide it. The notion of payment (*pagamento*), which has also been called 'watchfulness in one's mind' over territories and habitats, is essential (Reichel-Dussán 1988). *Pagamento* is a way to negotiate with Nature and its owners. The notion of 'owners' is central in the process of possessing the landscape; the Andoque people call them *noifosío oé* or 'livings from the earth'. Van der Hammen (1992: 109) considers the concept of owner as difficult to define. Nevertheless, in general 'it refers to those mythical or spirit beings who have special powers, with whom the shaman must negotiate for obtaining permission to use certain spaces or resources as well as cure illnesses'. Through this concept, the people combine a notion of space with the use of nature, and they obtain the guide to use the resources. There are various beings: spirits, owners, devils, fathers and mothers, leaders and chiefs. The notion of spirit is associated with the concept of life force which each being and object in the world possesses. The people think that there is a primordial possibility of communication between all life beings that changed when each one took on its final form. Only the shaman can establish this kind of communication between one 'life force' and another. The Shuar people from the Ecuadorian Amazon call this communication 'soul trips' (Descola 1989).

The maintenance of relationships with owners is a shamanistic task whose effectiveness varies according to the *sabedor*'s level of knowledge. Although senior men may know some simple formulae to assist in negotiatons, the shaman is the person entrusted with specialised tasks. He acquires this knowledge over long years of training with another shaman or through his father. Gradually, the new *sabedor* gets to know each place, what it is used for and when one may enter into a dialogue with the owners. In the same way, he begins to celebrate dances in the *maloca*. The rituals, songs and dances call up a positive productivity and fertility, atmosphere and fruitful alliances. While these are continuing, the shaman is negotiating with the owners, and in this way a proper way of life is achieved. 'Proper' or 'Good Way of Life' is a basic concept for the Amazon people (Espinosa 1994, 1995). Fisi Andoque describes this way of life:

A good way of life implies having a good and strong leader, good for protection of the whole group and strong for group defence. That condition makes the good life. To live in the *maloca* with dances and songs, ritual food [ambil/coca], promotes abundance, women's fertility and happiness [fundamental conditions for general well-being].

We *poosíóho* People of the Axe, and all the Indians in general, when we talk about the world we do not talk as the *duiaja*, the white men, do. When the white man talks about the world it is because he is talking about the whole world. For the Indian the world extends as far as man's knowledge. Up to where he knows. We the Andoque talk about the world as far as the territory that is ours. Up to where we know the traditional and sacred points such as Low Ridge, Hill or Lake, Savannah or Rock. Any place that has an owner, *noifosío oé*, or is bewitched. It is up to there that we speak. When we speak of the headwaters of the river it is round about the headwaters, it is not the headwaters. When we speak of the mouth of the river it is round about the mouth. But it is up to where our knowledge reaches, up to where we know the stories, the Tradition, the Mythology of our territory. That is the world.

All the tribes say centre, *dui oi*. We are the centre of the world, we are the centre of the place where we know, the place that is ours. In the same way another tribe says: we are the centre of the world. Others say the same because they are the centre of the world as far as they know the stories and the names. In this sector there are points where Dance started, where Work started, Healing, Magic, Wickedness, and thus all things that the Indians know. When the people say 'of the centre', the owners of the centre are the chiefs of a tribe. The chiefs such as the leaders, the headmen, the ones who know most.

They are in contact with all these places. They talk to the owners using secret words, mentally, they offer them coca and ambil. It is what we call *pagamento* [payment]. The *sabedor* has to know the place, what it is used for, when one can have a dialogue or make contact. If there is an illness or epidemic he has to know who defended this place before. The stories and myths contain the names of the people who occupied the place before us and made different actions for defending or purifying the spots. Then he has contact with another owner. He has his secrets with the owner. When he does a dance he has to know with whom. He manages, and creates the territory in that way.

The *pagamento* is made by the *sabedores* from the *mambeadero*. It may be when they are organizing the dance, before starting it. He senses when an epidemic is coming and he knows how to fight.

The *pagamento* is not made with all the people. It may be made with two or three people so as to set up the dialogue. When a *sabedor* senses and analyses problems that may arise, or senses something bad such as illnesses, then he goes to where another *sabedor* is, the one from the other *maloca*, or where the chief is or the council is. There he asks: What did you do before? or What do you see? There are times when one senses through dreams. He tells the dream to another. He says: look that dream means this, it means the other. The *sabedores* enter into the dialogues, and make the coca and the ambil for negotiating with the owners, whose presence is felt, not seen. It is at that moment when the points are named: Place of Weeping, Araracuara, Savannah, Axe, Red Ravine.

Those are the spots where ancient people live, people who defended them before. The myths contain the names of the people. In the *mambeadero* you talk, you make the coca and ambil and you check that they are well made. That dialogue does not take place in the view of many people or many women, but of four or two special persons only. That is the *pagamento*. This is ambil's story after the creation of coca.

Starting from the centre, the most important points for the Andoque people include: *mafosík* ['Place of Weeping'], *pópádik* [Place of *Iénapópaí*], *Araracuara* ['Place of the Ara'], *Sioyókotaí* ['chief of the animals'], *Siidufe* ['Hill of the Turkey Buzzard king'], *Maroco* Hill, *Doiansi* ['Yellow lake breeding place of the boa'], and many others. You have to identify yourself, talk to the owners, so that it does not rain, so there is not wind or lightning, so that the owners of the point should know you. From there, from the *mambeadero*, you can talk to them. First, it is up to you to visit them and introduce yourself.

That is the *pagamento*. It is made through the dialogues of the knowledge men or *sabedores* in a *mambeadero*. Following the advice of the *sabedor* who is the one who knows most, you listen. You ask: How is this?, then he answers: this is like this or not like this. And you say What has to be done? This has to be done because a bad thing is coming which may harm us. In the *maloca*, from the *mambeadero*, one may speak in the same way as my father used to: he would name the spots. He would do it for example when a sickness was coming. He would speak to the owners: you where you are over there do not let through the epidemics that are coming: divert them in another direction as it was in the creation of the world. He diverts all the evil that comes from the same wind to somewhere else. And nothing happened, there was no problem.

The knowledge of the names and owners of special places contains a secret level that is the strength derived from the *sabedor*. The people do not publicly elicit the names. Most of them are the exclusive domain of the *sabedor*. They are kept jealously and called upon only in ritual circumstances, with specific prayers. If different *sabedores* know these names, it may be an indication of a fissure in the *sabedor*'s strength. Negative action can gain entry through any such crack, thus putting in danger the *sabedor*'s position. The social and physical illnesses are interpreted like witchcraft. The *sabedor* must immediately be alert.

The *maloca* occupies an important position in this way of managing the world. Both Descola (1989) and Landaburu (1985) have shown that the open space within the collective house is the central place of speech, language and culture. Its axis is a stream or river. The individual's position in the space determines the directional indications. In the same way, rivers are the main elements of the topographic reference and constitute an integrated system of place names. The people make a speaking operation; the events and the spaces are related. You are in the headwaters of the rivers – which correspond to the west – so the things are happening there. Also, you can be in the centre, or in the mouth of the river – which corresponds to the east. This division coincides with the west–east orientation of the Amazon hydrographic system. For the Andoque people, the far east of the world is the place where all the rivers come together and, at the same time, it is the lowest place. Going into a *maloca* is going up, and leaving it is going down. An Andoque goes to, or comes from, three places: up above (headwaters), down below (mouth) and centre (inside the rain forest) (Landaburu 1985: 37).

Eco-politics and contemporary territorial management

The permanent relationships between the *maloca*s of each group, and between the *maloca*s of the large area, show that the management of space is shared and involves a joint custodianship. It is a supra-ethnic and multi-ethnic territorial management. That is why the mutual intelligibility of songs and rituals among different groups is crucial in relationships. Also, these relationships are linked to the owners' world, where there are *maloca*s. Fisi Andoque says: 'each group has a mythical born place and up from there it defines its traditional territory'. There are two territorial perception levels: (1) the territory of the group, whose limits and characteristics are known by the group, and (2) the shamanistic territory, whose boundaries are fluid and are given by symbolic management through the mental territorial transpositions of the shaman, which mark the paths of sorcery. These mental territorial transpositions have been called 'mind travelling' or 'soul trips' (Descola 1989; Reichel-Dussán 1992; Espinosa 1994). They begin in the *mambeadero*. The shamans use the coca and ambil, and, sometimes, stronger substances such as *yagé*.[3] Also, they include shamanistic recitations, many of them in a special sorcery language. This is the case of Chápune's recitations. When Van der Hammen transcribed and translated his recitations, she found thoroughly detailed knowledge of the environment (Van der Hammen 1992). Landaburu and Pineda (1984) found the same precise knowledge when they collected some of Yiñeko's recitations. Landaburu (pers. comm.) also found that shamans introduce archaisms taken from ancient Andoque language into their discourses.

The space occupied by shamanistic intercultural territories has been called 'shamanistic macrospace' and corresponds to the boundaries of each group's paths of sorcery. Its frontiers are fluid, with the consequence that the border areas may intersect with those of another shaman. Sometimes the same spot in the landscape has two names (i.e. the Andoque's name or the Nonuya's[4] name). On the basis of such ethnographic evidence, it has been proposed that the concept of mobile frontiers should refer to that overlapping process. The old men say that the ancient shamans were able to travel in jaguar form using a complex network of paths between the *malocas*. Each group has the responsibility of protecting its place of sorcery. Reichel-Dussán (1992) refers to the world view which determines the management of space, the symbolic appropriation, and the territory's boundaries as eco-politic. Eco-politics also determines the guidelines of production, management and the use of resources.

Eco-politics is in conflict with the nation's law which claims legal ownership of the subsoil, water and air, through the role of the *resguardo*, on behalf of the nation. The nation therefore has the right to use any natural resources.

In the interest of helping and supporting traditional authorities, the Amazon groups have been pressed to change their traditional political ways for newer ones. The *cabildo*, the political organisation related to each *resguardo*, has brought important changes. New alternative powers emerge beside those of the *sabedores*. For example, there is a different power possessed by the young men who know how to write and read in Spanish, as well as how to negotiate with white people using legal rules. Some groups have modified the *cabildo*'s structure in order to manage the two powers. The governor directs the *cabildo*. He is elected and he is the legal leader of the community. Besides him, the chief directs the community. Fisi Andoque is the actual chief and the traditional *sabedor*.

This new socio-political situation combining the traditional way with the new is full of potential conflicts. It is very important to manage the negotiations between the State and the ethnic groups carefully, especially to guard against conflicts between groups who share a shamanistic macrospace.

Another new development is that the public is learning the *sabedores'* knowledge. This development is crucial today because of territorial reorganisation. Old men's knowledge of ancient names and recitations are needed for discussions about such reorganisation, but the old men are frightened that their knowledge may be used in a bad way. A bad use produces social illness;

ruling power over all the things that concern common life. For, from these two things, we shall be able to understand the difference between a just and an unjust regime.

4.　Then he shows what the end of the political community or regime is, repeating what he said [I, chap. 1, n. 19]. There he determined regarding household management and a master's rule over slaves that human beings are by nature political animals, and so they desire to live with one another and not alone. Even if one in no way were to need another in order to lead a political life, there is still great benefit in sharing life in society, and this regards two things. First, life in society concerns living well, to which each contributes his share, as we perceive that one person in any society serves it in one office, and another person in another office. And so all in the society live well. Therefore, living well is most of all the end of a political community or regime, regarding all persons collectively and each person distributively.

Second, common life is also useful for life itself, as one of those sharing common life helps another to maintain life even in the face of mortal dangers. And so human beings unite with one another and preserve the political association. For even life, considered in itself apart from other things conducive to living well, is good and loveable, unless, perhaps, one is suffering very burdensome and cruel things in one's life. And this is clear from the fact that human beings, even if they should be undergoing many evils, still continue to desire to live, somehow absorbed in (i.e., strongly connected with) that desire, as if life should have in itself a solace and natural comfort.

5.　Then he distinguishes kinds of ruling, first in domestic affairs, then in political affairs [6]. Therefore, he says first that it is easy to distinguish the kinds of rule spoken of, since he has often incidentally mentioned them in public discourses (e.g., in the *Ethics*[10] and this work [II, chap. 7, nn. 1–4]). And there are two forms of ruling power in domestic affairs. One is that of a master over his slaves, and we call this despotic rule. And the same thing, namely, that a master rules over a slave, in reality benefits the one who is by nature a slave and the one who is by nature a master. Nonetheless, a master rules over a slave for his own, not the slave's, benefit, except perhaps incidentally, namely, insofar as the master's rule ceases if the slave dies.

And the second is rule over free persons (e.g., over wife, children, and the whole family), and we call this domestic rule. This rule aims to benefit the dependents, or both the head of the household and his dependents,

---

10. *Ethics* VIII, 10 (1160a31–1161a9).

but intrinsically and chiefly the dependents, as we perceive to be the case in other skills. For example, medical skill aims chiefly to benefit patients, and physical training chiefly those being trained. But benefit may also incidentally redound to those who have the skill. For one who trains youth is himself also at the same time training. He is also sometimes part of the team training, as a pilot is part of the ship's crew. Therefore, the trainer of youth and the pilot of a ship intrinsically consider the benefit of their subjects, but because they are members of the team or crew, each incidentally shares in the common benefit he procures. And similarly, the father shares in the benefit that he procures for the household.

6.   Then he distinguishes political offices according to the foregoing. He says that, since rule over free persons is chiefly directed to the benefit of subjects, it is deemed right that citizens in turn hold political offices when the latter have been established on the basis of the equality and likeness of citizens. For it then seems right that some citizens rule at one time, and others at other times. (It would be otherwise if some citizens were far to exceed others in goodness, since then it would be right that the former always rule, as he will say later.)[11]

But regarding this worthiness, the estimation of human beings varies at different times. For at the beginning, those who ruled serving others, as it were, deemed it right, as it was, that they in turn strive to benefit and serve them, and that others at other times would rule and seek the good of former rulers, as the latter themselves had previously striven for the good of others. But because of the benefits derived from goods of the community that human beings while ruling appropriated to themselves, and from the very right to rule, they later want to rule continuously, as if ruling would be healthy, and not ruling unhealthy. For human beings seem to desire ruling power in the same way that the sick desire health.

7.   Then he infers the distinction between just and unjust regimes from what he has said. For, inasmuch as ruling over free persons is directed to the benefit of subjects, it is clear that regimes in which the rulers strive for the common benefit are just regimes in accord with absolute justice. But regimes in which the rulers strive only for their own benefit are unjust and deviations from just regimes, since they are relatively, not absolutely, just, as he will say later.[12] For such rulers rule over a political community despotically, treating citizens as slaves, namely, for the rulers' own benefit. And this is contrary to justice, since the political community is an

---

11. *Politics* III, 13 (1284b25–34) and 17 (1288a15–29).
12. Ibid. III, 9 (1280a7–1281a10).

association of free persons. For slaves are not citizens, as he has said before [chap. 4, n. 2].

Chapter 6
The Kinds of Just and Unjust Regimes

Text (1279a22–1280a6)

1. With these things determined, we must consider how many and what kind of regimes there are. First, we need to consider just regimes, and perversions will indeed be evident when the just regimes have been determined.

2. And since regime and governing body mean the same thing, and governing bodies control political communities, one person, a few persons, or many persons need to be in control. Regimes in which one, a few, or many rule for the common benefit are necessarily just, but regimes in which one, a few, or the multitude rule for their own benefit are perversions. For either we should say that participants are not citizens, or they should share in the benefits.

3. And we are accustomed to calling the regime of one ruler that looks to the common benefit a kingship. And we are accustomed to calling the regime of a few rulers, but more than one, an aristocracy, whether because the best people rule, or because they look to what is best for the political community and those sharing in it. And we call the regime in which the multitude governs for the common benefit a polity, the common name for all regimes, and we do so reasonably. For one or a few persons may excel in virtue, but it is difficult for most to reach the heights of every virtue. But most may excel in military virtue in particular, and that is why the most important thing in this regime is its military power, and those who possess weapons participate in the regime.

4. And the perversions of the cited regimes are tyranny of kingship, oligarchy of aristocracy, and democracy of polity. Therefore, tyranny is one-man rule for the benefit of the ruler, oligarchy is for the benefit of the wealthy, and democracy is for the benefit of the poor. And none of these three regimes aims at the common benefit.

5.   We need to say a little bit more about the nature of each of these regimes, since there are certain questions. For one who philosophically contemplates in any way and does not look only to practicality, it is proper to state what is true about each thing and not to overlook or neglect anything. Tyranny, as I have said, is monarchical despotic rule over a political association, oligarchy is when the wealthy are in control of a regime, and democracy, conversely, is when those who do not have much property and lack means of support are in control.

6.   The first question concerns definitions. Suppose that the wealthy are a majority and in control of a political community—but there is a democracy when the people rule. Similarly, suppose that there are somewhere fewer poor people than wealthy people, and that the poor are more important and in control of a regime—but people say that there is an oligarchy when a few rule. It will not seem that we have defined regimes well.

7.   But even if one should link fewer numbers to wealth, and larger numbers to poverty, and call the former oligarchy and the latter democracy, there arises a fresh difficulty. (In an oligarchy, the few rich hold the offices, and in a democracy, the many poor hold them.) Let us assume that there are only the six previously mentioned regimes. Then what shall we now call the two just mentioned regimes, the one in which the wealthy rulers are more numerous, and the other in which the poor rulers are less numerous?

8.   Therefore, the argument seems to make clear that the number of rulers, few in oligarchies and many in democracies, is incidental, since the wealthy are everywhere few, and the poor everywhere many. Therefore, the aforementioned reasons do not explain the difference between oligarchy and democracy. Poverty and wealth are the things that distinguish democracy and oligarchy from one another. And there is necessarily oligarchy wherever the rulers, whether fewer or many, rule because of their wealth, and there is necessarily democracy wherever the poor rule. But it happens, as we have said, that the wealthy are few, and the poor many. For only a few are wealthy, but all share in freedom, and the two classes quarrel about the regime for these reasons.

Comment

1.   After Aristotle distinguished just regimes from unjust ones, he here aims to distinguish just regimes from one another, doing two things in this regard. First, he speaks about his aim. Second, he pursues what he proposes [2]. Therefore, he says first that, after he has determined the foregoing things, it remains to consider the number and kind of regimes, first about just ones, then about unjust ones.

2.   Then he distinguishes regimes, regarding which he does three things. First, he shows in what way we should understand the difference in regimes. Second, he distinguishes regimes [3]. Third, he poses an objection to the aforementioned [5]. Therefore, he says first that, since a regime is simply its governing body (i.e., the organization of the rulers in a political community), we need to distinguish regimes by their different kind of rulers. For either one, a few, or many persons rule in a political community, and this can happen in two ways in each of these three cases. It happens in one way when rulers rule for the common benefit, and then the regimes will be just. It happens in a second way when rulers rule for their own benefit, whether there be one, a few, or many rulers, and then the regimes are perversions. For we need to say that either subjects are not citizens, or that they share in the benefit of a political community in something.

3.   Then he distinguishes both kinds of regimes by their proper names, first the just regimes and then the corrupt ones [4]. Therefore, he says first that, if the regime should have a monarchy (i.e., one-man rule), we usually call it a kingship if the ruler is striving for the common benefit. And we call the regime in which a few persons, but more than one, rule for the common good an aristocracy (i.e., rule by the best people, or the best rule). Aristocracy is so called either because the best people, namely, the virtuous, rule, or because such a regime is directed to what is best for the political community and all its citizens. And we call the regime in which the multitude rules and strives for the common benefit a polity,[13] which is the common name for all regimes. It is reasonable to apply the name to this one, since we may easily find one or a few persons in a political community who far exceed others in virtue, but it is very difficult to find many people who arrive at complete virtue. Still, this happens most regarding military virtue, namely, that many excel at it. And so, in this regime, warriors and those who possess weapons rule.

4.   Then he distinguishes corruptions of the aforementioned regimes by name, saying that they are perversions of those regimes. Tyranny is a perversion of kingship, oligarchy (i.e., rule by the few) a perversion of aristocracy, and democracy (i.e., rule by the people, the common people) a perversion of polity, in which many rule because of their military virtue. And he concludes from this that tyranny is a monarchy (i.e., rule by one man) striving for the benefit of the ruler, oligarchy strives for the benefit of the wealthy, and democracy for the benefit of the poor. And none of these regimes strives for the common benefit.

---

13. See note 41 (II, chap. 16), supra, p. 169.

5.   Then he raises an objection against the aforementioned, doing three things in this regard. First, he speaks of his aim and repeats what he said before. Second, he poses a difficulty [6]. Third, he answers it [8]. Therefore, he says first that we need to discuss a little more objectively the nature of each of the aforementioned regimes, since this raises some questions. One who philosophizes in any skill, contemplating truth, as it were, and not looking only to what is practically useful, should overlook and neglect nothing but declare the truth about particulars. And he has said that tyranny is a despotic monarchy (i.e., despotic rule over a political association because it uses citizens as slaves), oligarchy when the wealthy are in control of a regime, and democracy when the poor rather than the wealthy are [4].

6.   Then he poses a difficulty. First, he presents it. Second, he rejects a certain response [7]. Therefore, he says first that the first problem regards definitions, namely, those of democracy and oligarchy, since he has said that democracy is when the poor in a political community rule, and oligarchy when the wealthy do [4]. But the word *oligarchy* denotes rule by the few, and the word *democracy* denotes rule by the people, or multitude. Therefore, assuming that the wealthy are more numerous than the poor in a political community, and that the wealthy are its rulers, it accordingly seems that there is a democracy (i.e., that the majority rule). And similarly, assuming that the poor elsewhere may be fewer than the wealthy, and that the poor are more important, are more powerful, and rule over the political community, it will accordingly follow that there is an oligarchy, since the few rule. Therefore, it does not seem that the definitions of regimes are correct, since he has said that democracy is rule by the poor, and oligarchy rule by the wealthy.

7.   Then he rejects a certain response to the difficulty. For one could say that fewness in number is linked to wealth in the definition of oligarchy, and that largeness in number is linked to poverty in the definition of democracy. That is to say, oligarchy is a regime in which the few wealthy rule, and democracy a regime in which the many poor rule. But this raises another difficulty. For if we have adequately distinguished regimes, namely, so that there is no other regime besides the aforementioned six, it will not determine under which regime the two regimes just mentioned, namely, the ones in which many wealthy or few poor persons rule, are included.

8.   Then he infers from the foregoing the solution of the difficulty, saying that the nature of the foregoing difficulty seems to make clear that a large number of rulers is incidentally related to democracies, and that a small number of rulers is incidentally related to oligarchies. For we find that the poor outnumber the wealthy. And so we use the words *democracy* and *oligarchy* as we find such regimes for the most part. But since what is incidental does not constitute a specific difference, we do not distinguish an oligarchy from a democracy, absolutely speaking, by the large or small number of rulers. Rather, poverty and wealth are what intrinsically distinguish the regimes, since the nature of one is ordered to wealth, and the nature of the other to freedom, which is the end of democracy.

And so there is necessarily an oligarchy wherever some, whether a majority or a minority, rule because of their wealth, and there is necessarily a democracy wherever the poor rule. But it is incidental that the latter are many, and the former few, since only a few are wealthy, but all share in freedom. And these two classes quarrel with one another on that account, the few wanting to be in control because of their excessive wealth, and the many wanting to prevail over the few and become their equals, as it were, because of freedom.

Index of Persons

General Index

Achaeans, 144, 148
Arcadians, 79, 84, 144, 145, 147, 150
Argives, 144, 145, 147, 150
Athens, 124, 128, 131, 174–76

Carthage, 146, 178, 194. *See also* regime(s)
citizenship, 179–85, 197–202
common property, 86–90, 95–101
common wives and sons, 86–95
craftsmen, 74–7
Crete, 5, 13, 101, 105, 144, 153, 158, 173, 176. *See also* regime(s)

De anima, 11
De coelo, 142
Delphic smiths, 5, 11
Dorian mode, 186, 189

Ethics I:8, 108; II:17, 18, 76; III:158; V:84; VI:194; VIII:40, 205; IX:93; X:3, 80

family, 66–74

household, 19–24

Larissaeans, 181, 185

Magnesians, 144, 148
Messenians, 144, 145, 147, 150
Metaphysics, 17, 33
moneymaking
    in practice, 60–66
    in theory, 48–60

Perrhaebians, 144, 148
Persian wars, 173, 175
Pharsalus, mare of, 87, 90
Phrygian mode, 186, 189
Physics, 142
political community, 4–19, 202–7
political unity, 78–86
property, 42–48

regime(s)
    Carthaginian, 166–72
    change, 185–89
    Cretan, 146, 159–66, 168, 172, 178
    of Hippodamus, 131–44
    just and unjust, 207–11
    other, 172–78
    of Phaleas, 121–31
    of Socrates: first, 101–8; second, 116–20
    Spartan, 118–19, 144–64, 166–67, 168–69, 172, 174, 178

slavery, 19–41
Sparta, 96, 99, 101, 104. *See also* regime(s)

Thebans, 145, 149, 173, 177
Thessalians, 144, 147, 148

virtue
    of a good citizen in different regimes, 197–202
    of a good man and a good citizen, 190–97

213

as the old men say, to open the pot is to open stories, and some of the knowledge is considered dangerous because its management requires a deep understanding that the young men do not possess. The young men do not have the training, or any legitimate socio-ritual position, whereby they could be seen to be authorised to decide a community's destiny. Therefore *sabedores* produce recitations in an ancient form of language that the young cannot understand.

This is a situation of potential conflict that involves both the *sabedores* and the new leaders. Those new leaders have a different knowledge that is useful for the negotiations with the State. It is a tension between participation requirements and the characteristics of the shamanistic knowledge, which is considered to be not only secret but also crucial for the support of the future of the group. In this context, knowing how to speak and write in Spanish becomes an important skill, and thus a new kind of power. It also affects the transmission of the knowledge owned by shamans because such knowledge requires a specific environment for its transmission. Today, it is not easy to find the appropriate environment.

After the constitutional change that took place in Colombia in 1991, which recognised the country as being multi-ethnic and pluri-cultural, and which gave autonomy to the territories known as *resguardos*, it is all the more essential to take into account the three levels of territorial negotiation that are at the basis of interethnic points of contact:

1 traditional processes of territorial negotiation through shamanistic management, or through the revitalisation of them (encounters among *sabedores* and sorcerers);
2 the coming together of two types of territorial negotiation: the traditional and the contemporary (the latter conducted through modern ways of negotiation such as the *cabildos* and councils);
3 territorial negotiations between the *cabildos*, the regional state and the national state.

The next years will show which type of negotiations prevails. The still awaited promulgation of the Constitutional Law of Territorial Reorganisation by Congress, which turns native territories into territorial entities similar to the administrative and political role of town councils, will be crucial for decision-making. However, already *resguardos* receive considerable funding from the national central budget and are beginning to take on the role of something like provinces; locally, leaders are standing for offices such as mayors or governors, and standing for election to municipal or provincial assemblies. In such a context, a variety of rival interests and different protagonists are bound to appear. Amazon people, particularly the Andoque people, are trying to resolve and manage the inevitable tensions. Long-term negotiations with the State will undoubtedly demand adaptation.

In spite of the constitutional call to respect diversity, Colombia has still a long way to go to build democratic and multi-cultural freedoms. Today, Fisi

Andoque continues talking about tradition in his *maloca* in the middle Caqueta River, accompanied by his allies, the coca and ambil. He is building a 'good way of life' for his people.

Notes

1   The verb 'to chew coca' (*hípie*) is *mambear*. *Mambe*, the noun, refers to the coca after the coca leaves have been collected, toasted and made into a kind of dust. This dust is mixed with ash from the dried and burnt leaves of the *yarumo* (*Cecropia sp.*) tree. Thus, *mambeaderos* are 'ash places' where men chew coca dust.
2   *Maloca* is often translated as 'collective house', the word deriving from *marooca* in the lingua franca, Neengatú, meaning 'big house'. In pre-Hispanic times, some 150 members of the same lineage would have shared the same *maloca* for both housing and ceremonial purposes. Nowadays, *maloca*s have lost any function as a domestic dwelling place; instead, they house ceremonial instruments, and are the focus for ceremonies, dance and rituals.
3   *Yagé* is Spanish for a hallucinogenic substance derived from the leaves, stems or roots of *Banisteriopsis sp.* which Andoque men take on special ritual occasions.
4   The Nonuya are another linguistic group from the middle Caquetá River.

References

Andrade, A. 1988. Desarrollo de los sistemas agrícolas tradicionales en la Amazonia. *Boletín del Museo del Oro* 21, 39–59.

Aragón, L.E. 1994. Building regional capacity for sustainable development in the Amazon. In *What Future for the Amazon Region?* Stockholm: Institute of Latin American Studies.

Ardila, G. and G. Politis 1989. Nuevos datos para un viejo problema: investigación y discusiones en torno al problamiento de América del Sur. *Boletín Museo del Oro* 23, 3–45.

Århem, K. 1990. Ecosofía Makuna. In *La selva humanizada. Ecología alternativa en el trópico húmedo colombiano*, F. Correa (ed.), 105–22. Bogotá: Instituto Colombiano de Antropología/Fondo FEN Colombia/ Fondo Editorial CEREC.

CADM. Comisión Amazónica de Desarrollo y Medio Ambiente 1994. *Amazonia sin Mitos.* Bogotá: Editorial Oveja Negra.

Correa, F. 1990. Introducción. In *La selva humanizada. Ecología alternativa en el trópico húmedo colombiano*, F. Correa (ed.), 13–34. Bogotá: Instituto Colombiano de Antropología/Fondo FEN Colombia/ Fondo Editorial CEREC.

Corredor, B. and W. Torres 1989. *Chamanismo: un arte del saber.* Bogotá: Anaconda.

Descola, P. 1989. *La Selva Culta. Simbolismo y praxis en la ecología de los Achuar.* Quito: Abya-Yala/Movimientos Laicos para América Latina.

Eliade, M. 1986. *El chamanismo y las técnicas arcaicas del éxtasis.* México: Fondo de Cultura Económica.

Espinosa, M. 1994. Informes de Investigación I, II, III del proyecto: Rituales y emociones: una nueva perspectiva del conflicto y la convivencia entre grupos amazónicos. Unpublished COLCULTURA report.

Espinosa, M. 1995. *Convivencia y poder político entre los Andoques del Amazonas.* Bogotá: Universidad Nacional de Colombia.

Franco, R. 1992. Frontera Indígena en la Amazonia colombiana. In *Amazonia Colombiana, Diversidad y Conflicto*, G. Andrade, A. Hurtado and R. Torres (eds), 154–70.

Bogotá: Comisión Nacional de Investigaciones Amazónicas CONIA/CEGA/ COLCIENCIAS.

Guzmán, M. J. 1971. Los Andokes: historia, conciencia étnica y explotación del caucho. *Universitas Humanística* 2, 53–97.

Johns, T. 1969. A chemical–ecological model of root and tuber domestication in the Andes. In *Foraging and Farming: the evolution of plant exploitation*, D.R. Harris and G.C. Hillman (eds), 504–17. London: Unwin Hyman.

Landaburu, J. 1985. El tratamiento gramatical del espacio en la lengua andoke del Amazonas. *Revista de Antropología* 1, 34–40.

Landaburu, J. and R. Pineda 1984. *Tradiciones de la Gente del Hacha. Mitología de los indios andoques del Amazonas*. Bogotá: Instituto Caro y Cuervo.

Lathrap, D. 1968. The hunting economies of the Tropical Forest Zone of South America: an attempt at historical perspective. In *Man the Hunter*, R.B. Lee and I. DeVore (eds), 23–9. New York: Aldine Press.

Llanos, H. and R. Pineda 1982. *Etnohistoria del Gran Caquetá (siglos XVI–XIX)*. Bogotá: Fundación de Investigaciones Arqueológicas del Banco de la República.

Marcos, J.G. 1988. El origen de la agricultura. In *Nueva Historia del Ecuador. Vol 1. Epoca Aborigen*, E. Ayala (ed.), 140–75. Bogotá: Funcol.

Pineda, R. 1985. Procesos de reconstrucción y violencia en el Amazonas. *Grupos Etnicos, derecho y cultura*, 183–96.

Rappaport, J. 1994. Geography and historical understanding in indigenous Colombia. In *Who Needs the Past? Indigenous values and archaeology*, R. Layton (ed.), 84–94. London: Routledge.

Reichel-Dussán, E. 1988. Asentamientos prehispánicos en la Amazonia colombiana. In *Colombia Amazónica*, 125–40. Bogotá: Universidad Nacional/FEN Colombia.

Reichel-Dussán, E. 1992. La ecopolítica en conceptos indígenas de territorio en la Amazonia colombiana. In *Antropología Jurídica. Normas formales, costumbres legales en Colombia*, E. Sánchez (ed.), 47–59. Bogotá: Sociedad Antropológica de Colombia/ Comité Internacional para el Desarrollo de los Pueblos.

Salazar, E. 1989. *Pioneros de la Selva*. Quito: Ediciones Banco Central del Ecuador.

Van der Hammen, M.C. 1992. *El manejo del mundo. Naturaleza y Sociedad entre los Yukuna de la amazonia colombiana*. Bogotá: Tropenbos Colombia.

18 The perception of landscape amongst the Q'eqchi', a group of slash-and-burn farmers in the Alta Verapaz (Guatemala)

ALMUDENA HERNANDO GONZALO

Introduction

It is very difficult to appreciate the conditions and assumptions on which we base our vision of the world. We must recall that it was only in 1913 that the first time signal was broadcast from the Eiffel Tower, enabling twenty-five nations to synchronise the official 'time' they had decided to relate to the Greenwich meridian (Kern 1983: 12–14). In 1881, the phonograph and the camera changed people's experience of the past by making it alive in the present, obliging psychologists to revise the concept of memory (Kern 1983: 37–41). The sinking of the *Titanic* in 1912 was the first disaster broadcast directly by telegraph and thus known about while it was happening on the Atlantic (Kern 1983: 64–6). The first telephone line connecting the two coasts of the United States was inaugurated in 1915 (Kern 1983: 214). Since our perception of time and space is conditioned by radical transformations that have occurred in a surprisingly brief and recent space of time, we can begin to understand why it possesses peculiarities and implications that the perceptions of other groups cannot have.

Distance is no longer time for us: in the era of the computer and internet, the present encompasses all the phenomena that are occurring simultaneously anywhere in the world. Barely 100 years ago, events that occurred anywhere other than where the observer was situated also belonged to another time: they were already in the past when news of them was received, or in the future if the observer had to move to carry them out. Space *was* time.

Time and space, the two basic means of human orientation, are being used in today's western world very differently from any other known combination (Entrikin 1991; Elías 1992: 98). Our *present* is diluted in a frenetic desire to live in the *future*. The ease of travelling and transport extends to unknown universes the space we believe ourselves to inhabit. We appropriate other people's space, incorporating 'others' into our time.

Time and space are now conceived as abstractions in themselves, without the need to give them a specific content (Entrikin 1991: 43–4). Both seem to mark the limit of possible experience that, furthermore, can be created *ex novo*: we can construct a future that reflects our desires and we can give space different contents. Both constitute, essentially, frameworks for action, for movement and transformation, for change. Since such a perception is a particularly recent characteristic of our culture, we can anticipate that other groups must have very different perceptions.

I now clarify some of my assumptions. Elías (1990b: 51) claims that the disciplines that study humans or the societies that they have created, appear to consider humans as given and fixed realities consisting of certain substances and possessing certain psychic compartments such as reason and sentiment, conscience and instincts. In fact, however, these concepts allude only to the relational functions of the human organism that are constantly changing (Elías 1990a: 51–2). Elías's contribution is to insist that the individual *is*, in part, the relations that s/he establishes, that constitute what we call society. We cannot understand the differences between societies if we do not understand that they constitute the individual differently, because society is the set of relations established by the members that comprise it. To the extent that the individual is constituted by the relationships that s/he establishes, individuals can therefore be defined as having structural characteristics in common. Socio-economic complexity simply expresses the type and complexity of the relations established by its members.

I accept the 'enchanting premise that all men [humans] are equal' (Goody 1985: 12) in their potential capacities but, in as much as they are embedded in different societies, they establish relationships of different types. In every society their emotions, sentiments and thoughts, and their functional relationships, are different. Different societies will therefore have different 'orders of rationality' or 'models of self-consciousness'. The archaeological record simply bears mute witness to a certain degree of socio-economic complexity.

In the course of the text I shall allude to the differences between 'another' kind of rationality and our own. I am aware of the apparent 'ethnocentric binarism' (Goody 1985: 18) of the resulting text, but nothing is further from my intention than to set in opposition dichotomies of the 'them/us' variety as if they were two exclusive and opposing ways of seeing the world, instead of two possible manifestations of an on-going process of shaping the order of rationality.

Space and identity

We seem to attribute immobility and profound rootedness in their ecological niches to those groups whose cultural characteristics are so clearly defined that they have attracted the attention of the ethnologists. Racially mixed groups or those that have assimilated the characteristics of other cultures, such as the 'Latinos' of Mexico, are, by contrast, seen as detached from any particular space, as a nomadic people without roots (Rosaldo 1988: 79).

Appadurai has also called attention to the association that is commonly made between the concept of 'native' and the idea of immobility, and particularly to the connotation that the latter usually has of spatial confinement. He notes that the image of the 'native' is usually so closely linked with the space in which he lives that we almost consider him a 'prisoner' of it (Appadurai 1988: 37). This interpretation has obvious moral and intellectual implications, since we seem to imagine as 'separate' those groups whose way of thinking prevents them from liberating themselves from the prison of space (Appadurai 1988: 37–8). Appadurai (1988: 38) writes, 'the link between the confinement of ideology and the idea of place is that the way of thought that confines natives is itself somehow bounded, somehow tied to the circumstantiality of place'. This provides a good point of departure for my argument about the differences between the relationships of identity and space in what are considered 'native' groups, and those that we hold ourselves.

It could be said that our relationship with space is 'contingent' (Entrikin 1991: 63), while that of so-called natives is 'necessary'. However, such a distinction does not in any way imply the latter's greater limitation or slavery to a particular way of thinking. Quite the reverse: our system of orientation and source of security, our way of thinking, makes us equally dependent on space. The difference is that our attribution of values to space displays two distinct characteristics that can be considered contradictory, whilst the so-called 'natives' do not fall victim to such a polarisation. We could say that, while we perceive ourselves at the centre of a centreless world (Entrikin 1991: 1–5; Rodman 1992: 642), they consider themselves to be the centre of a world centred on themselves (Eliade 1988: 25–55). In our case, subjective or existential experience of space is in contradiction of, and at the same time complementary to, an analytical and objectified conception of it. We maintain a 'centred view in that we are a part of place and period' while at the same time we develop 'a decentred view in that we seek to transcend the here and now' (Entrikin 1991: 1). It is precisely this dichotomy that defines the construction of modern/western identity in relation to space. And it is this polarisation that also makes it possible to explain our capacity to conceive of 'landscape' in contrast to 'nature', 'space', 'land' and 'environment'. It could be said that 'landscape' refers to symbolically constituted spaces that are conceived only through experience, while all the others refer to analytical categories in which the physical reality in which we move is objectified in one dimension or another (Ingold 1993). In this view, an understanding of the perception of landscape cannot be approached on the basis of such terminological and conceptual distinctions, because the groups themselves were unaware of them (Lévi-Strauss 1966; Clastres 1981). All space is experience, and therefore, in this sense, all 'nature' or 'land' is 'landscape'.

Where an analytical relationship with reality has not been established, all perception falls within the field of experience. Space is experienced through myth. The security that myth offers comes from the conviction that the space in which one lives is sacred, chosen by the gods. For those who live in it, it constitutes the only ordered space, the rest being relegated to chaos (Eliade 1988: 32). On the other hand, the security offered by the 'scientific' type of knowledge so esteemed in the western/modern world is associated with demands for the permanent extension of its scope. Orientation comes no longer from being in the 'Centre of the World' – chosen by the 'gods' – but from knowing the relative location of the point at which one finds oneself in relation to all the rest. This type of knowledge recognises different spaces, occupied by different species, genres, classes of things and beings. Everything is ordered and classified in accordance with a categorical logic that is gratifying for those who believe that it positions them within the whole. Furthermore, such knowledge is transmitted and consolidated by maps that reduce the possible dimensions in which the space is conceptualised so that its conceivable size can be increased. But in this way space loses its specific nature, because any area is now decentralised and demystified (Tuan 1987: 91; Eliade 1988: 27; Entrikin 1991: 47, 62).

Le Goff (1981) has discussed the interesting change in the perception of reality demonstrated by the appearance of Purgatory in the Christian view of the other world during the twelfth century AD. Until then, a schema based on the binary opposition of good/bad, Heaven/Hell, reflected, amongst other things, the hierarchy into which society was divided. Purgatory is the exact point at which a mythical perception of space meets the earliest attempts to include conceivable space (be it mythical or visible) in cartographic categories towards which a non-emotional relationship could be established. Christianity devoted itself to a vast cartographic undertaking that began by giving the time of eternity a spatial context (Le Goff 1981: 13). This was the beginning of calculation, the need to know other spaces, recourse to 'location' as a source of security, as the generator of a context in which to inscribe identity.

The space in which one lived was no longer the only conceivable one, ordained by the gods, the true World. The anthropocentric vision of reality began to give way to the less consoling conviction that the world itself was just a part of a complex and vast unit whose operation was not a function of human existence (Elías 1990a: 93). From the thirteenth century onwards, a conceptual shift began, accepting movement as a possible framework of activity. As Zumthor (1994: 61) says, 'soon the West would have penetrated a new mental universe, in which the opposite of presence would no longer be absence, but being elsewhere'.

In the sixteenth century, Galileo demonstrated that the Earth was not, in reality, the centre of the universe, and, by increasing the scale of what had been already accepted about oneself to the whole planet, he showed that the universe does not revolve around us either. Our space is not the centre of anything, for the simple reason that there are no centres in space. Space begins to be conceived as infinite, or as infinitely open (Foucault 1986: 23; Zumthor 1994: 47). 'Location' is, in effect, gradually replacing mythical 'sanctification' as a mechanism that provides security and identity. In most western societies, however, space still carries within it a sacred dimension (Foucault 1986); that is, space still forms part of the personal experience that constitutes the basis of individual personality. Colours, smells, sights and sounds that define space in our childhood thus become part of ourselves, and constitute a vital but unconscious source of security and protection.

It is this subjective and sensorial perception of space that we refer to when we talk in modern terms about 'place' or 'landscape'. This is why it is said that landscape is always personal (Tuan 1987: 157), that it is not an object, but that it is human-made (Ingold 1993: 162) and that 'place' is a condition of human experience. For that reason it cannot be understood solely in theoretical terms (Entrikin 1991: 1, 23; Ingold 1993: 155).

However, just as 'place' forms part of human experience, it is this very experience that gives meaning to 'place'. Just as identity is linked to the space where it was formed, the latter is conceived only in terms of the experience that occurred within it.

The rapid transformation of 'places' in the modern world nevertheless forces us to consider that meaning is not inherent in place, but can be attributed to different places (Entrikin 1991: 57). It is interesting to see how the most technologically 'developed' societies – those that have gone furthest in replacing a mythical with a 'scientific' perception of space – are precisely those that do all they can to 'stabilise the meanings associated with places' (Entrikin 1991: 58; cf. Tuan 1987: 196–7) through protected areas and ecological or archaeological parks.

The perception of landscape amongst the Q'eqchi'

The Q'eqchi' are one of the present-day Mayan-speaking groups (Solano 1969) who have been extending their territories, little by little, from their homeland in Alta Verapaz to neighbouring areas. Expansion is due both to the rapid demographic growth that characterises their strategy for survival and to the pressure to which they have been subjected by outside groups (Pacheco 1985: 40–1). The area chosen for this study is the municipality of Chahal, in the northwest of the Department of Alta Verapaz. This is a rugged and mountainous area, comprising the mountain ranges of Chamá and Santa Cruz, and the eastern foothills of the Cordillera de los Cuchumatanes. The soil is of poor quality and there is an abundance of caves and caverns hidden amongst the mountains and small hills.

The Q'eqchi' of Chahal constitute one of the most isolated communities of Guatemala, and can be described as having the characteristics of the 'closed corporate community' (Wolf 1968). This type of cultural configuration is the result of a defensive strategy adopted in the face of the menacing presence of the powerful western order, and consists of encapsulation within it, attempting to deny its existence by the simple mechanism of avoiding as far as possible any contact with it. The Q'eqchi' are accepted by the all-powerful western socio-political organisation with contemptuous tolerance (Elías 1990b: 249).

It might be concluded that their 'encapsulation' could induce a certain 'perception of landscape' that cannot be transferred to any other area or period. Indeed the function of land rather than kinship as a mechanism of social cohesion seems to have been the result of Spanish colonial policy, through which lands were granted under communal jurisdiction to those who originally inhabited them. This facilitated and reduced the cost of management and administration of the conquered lands, but it also provided an important instrument of personal and community identification (Wolf 1968: 297).

The Q'eqchi' therefore cannot be considered 'primitive' (cf. Wolf 1955: 454) or used to illustrate the 'contemporaneity of the non-contemporaneous' (Mercader 1993). Indeed Q'eqchi' perception of the landscape can be seen to have been the instrument of a distinctive political strategy of exploitation, precisely because of the close relationship between identity and space that defines its cultural order.

Landscape as mythical space

Q'eqchi' culture has been characterised by 'milpa' or slash-and-burn agriculture throughout the recorded past. Since this demands manual manipulation, a direct and individual relationship with each plant, this type of economic strategy implies an entire vision of the cosmos ruled by certain categories of time and space, that explains the intense emotional link with space (Medina 1990: 456).

The communities that surround the town of Chahal anthropomorphise natural phenomena and provide a mythical interpretation of the context in which 'natural' events take place. As Rodman (1992: 651) has pointed out, each human group uses its local landscape to shape myth, the two constituting the form and background of the same essential reality. In view of the multitude of small hills and valleys of Q'eqchi' territory, it is perhaps not surprising that its inhabitants believe in an essential deity, Tzuultak'á – the word combining Tzuul (Hill) and Tzak'á (Valley), although it is generally translated as 'god of the hill' (Estrada Monroy 1990: note 4).

Although they were converted to Catholicism by the Spanish conquerors. Q'eqchi' distinguish between the Catholic god and Tzuultak'á. The first is used as a source of enrichment of the ritual, an important mechanism for communicating with the sacred. They accept the Catholic priest who occasionally passes through their village, and maintain religious *cofradías* (brotherhoods) that have a well-studied social function (Wolf 1968; Rojas Lima 1988). However, although the Catholic god may have determined aspects of Q'eqchi' institutional or ritual life, he is not essential to their everyday life. This is governed by Tzuultak'á, by the Hill. That is, the landscape is sacred in itself, and just as Q'eqchi' do not differentiate an economic or political sphere within the community's life as a whole, they do not isolate space as an objectifiable, quantifiable, measurable dimension. Space, in their case, is the same as landscape.

The Q'eqchi' consider that Tzuultak'á is master of everything on and outside the earth: he provides the maize, the trees, the wild animals and the birds. To use any of these resources takes away something that belongs to him, so no Q'eqchi' would ever cut down a tree, go hunting, wound the earth by ploughing a furrow in it to sow maize, or tear out its fruit once it has grown, unless it is truly necessary and permission has been sought from the Hill by means of many rituals. If the prescribed rites are not complied with, or if they are not carried out correctly, Tzuultak'á will deny humans the use of his property and will take it back. In this way the Q'eqchi' explain failed harvests, a shortage of game, or the migration of animals. There are even times when Tzuultak'á hides animals (Pacheco 1985: 91). Tzuultak'á is not just the god to whom everything belongs, the source of all order, he is not a category separate from the manifestations of nature, but nature itself. He is the Hill. In the references that the Q'eqchi' make to the hills, it is difficult to determine the character with which they endow them. They constantly attribute human personality to the hills, although when asked to clarify this matter, they tend to equivocate.

Q'eqchi' myth attributes knowledge of maize and its cultivation to thirteen men, twelve of whom were stupid and one clever. The latter discovered that maize was kept inside the hills and found out how to release it from the hills. The old men of the community of Sebolito say: 'Now these men are the thirteen sacred hills of Alta Verapaz. . . . Although they were the only ones that fought for the maize . . . all the hills are just as brave.' Domingo Cantí of Cantutú (pers. comm.) explained that this was why, just like people, 'the hills are good and bad. . . . The hills think they own these lands. . . . Sometimes they send animals to damage the sowing' or 'if they don't want you to climb them, a snake comes out, or it's covered in water'. If people have to take their animals somewhere, 'they also ask permission of the hills where the animals are going to pass. There are (however) hills which don't allow it, and then the animal does not want to go through a pass or along a road, or it falls, for example' (Pedro Salam of Siguanjá II pers. comm.). When men go out hunting, they have first to carry out various rites at very specific times (when the animals are asleep, so they will not find out). Three days later,

> they go out hunting, at any time, because now one has done what is necessary, now one has paid: has burned copalpom. Also all those who are going to go have been named, so the hill knows. The hill always provides, but the rites have to be performed. If not, the animals don't come out, or snakes and dangerous animals appear.
>
> (Rafael Ixim of Siguanjá II pers. comm.)

The hills' behaviour appears arbitrary. Although there are declarations such as the statement by Domingo Cantí of Cantutú that 'the one that is tormented most [by the hill] is the greatest sinner', most such sentiments seem to be concessions to a foreign audience accustomed to the Christian logic of punishment and recompense, rather than to what people really believe. For a Q'eqchi', the hills are omnipotent beings to whom one must 'surrender' through rites and prayers. They are constantly prayed to and asked for forgiveness for the audacity implied in interfering in their existence by crossing a field, sowing grain or hunting an animal (Domingo Cantí of Cantutú pers. comm.).

Features of the landscape are endowed with different genders. In this respect, the Hill represents the sexual duality of the entire universe, since the Hill is considered to be masculine and the Valley feminine, but at the same time there are also Men-Hills and Women-Hills: a hill which does not produce water is male and that which does so is female (Pacheco 1988: 93). Voices and conversations are also attributed to the hills, and they are considered part of a dynamic of social relations. Any climatological or atmospheric phenomenon is interpreted within the same system; thus, the thirteen principal hills converse amongst themselves by means of thunder and lightning, while the rest use the wind (Pacheco 1985: 88). According to Pedro Salam of Siguanjá II, 'there is a hill responsible for making the rain and thunder. He starts to make it, and when the rest answer, they want to give rain elsewhere. When the rest do not answer, it only rains where he is.'

The true nature of the hills remains ambiguous. They are always discussed as if they were human but, when asked for some clarification, speakers change their vocabuary to bring them closer to the western-Catholic vision of the universe, dissociating the actual hill from the spirit that inhabits it. Thus, for example, on one occasion Rafael Izim of Siguanjá II explained to me that, 'In the past the hills behaved like people'. In fact San Pablo, one of the thirteen main hills, 'is still alive. He was responsible for the earth before the world we see now.' And they know he is still alive because

> when they come to make offerings to the hill, it brings cold weather, because it was brought by San Pablo (and he brings it every time they sow), who also lives in Xela [Quezaltenango], where there is another hill where he lives. Each time there is cold weather there it's because San Pablo is there.

The multi-faceted nature and character of the hills, and the confusion the Q'eqchi' create for our rigid classification of the world when they talk about them, is demonstrated by the following anecdote:

> In the past there wasn't a highway for going to Guatemala, and a steward made a roll of maguey traps to sell there. He climbed the hill of San Pablo and rested next to a cross that there was on the way. Then a child appeared and told him to go into the hill.

He told him to close his eyes a little bit, and when he opened them he was already inside. There was San Pablo writing a letter, which he asked him to take to Santa María Izam [another of the principal hills, in this case female]. It was an invitation for Santa Maria Izam to a lunch in honour of the sowing at eleven in the morning. So he realised that San Pablo and Santa María Izam were alive.

(Rafael Ixim of Siguanjá II pers. comm.).

Thus it can be seen that the Q'eqchi' perception of the landscape obeys completely different models of understanding from those that govern our own view of space. It could be said that a Q'eqchi' substitutes space for time to provide the setting in which the human mind liberates anxieties and complements the interpretation of its existence.

Conclusion

In my perception, the Q'eqchi' view of life is that:

1   Myth makes sense of perception of space. In consequence, 'land' or 'space' cannot be differentiated from 'landscape'.
2   Classification into inert and living matter does not make sense. The hills were humans and now they express their feelings.
3   The relationship with the landscape is essential, always giving substance to human relationships.

It is necessary to understand the cognitive and affective bases that define the models of self-consciousness of groups different from ourselves in order to evince, in some measure, our own cultural and historical reality. To recognise such 'other' systems as just one more of the possible ways of taking in the complex reality of which we form a part, we should be in a better position to study other cultures (in time or place) on a more realistic basis than has been achieved up till now.

Acknowledgements

My fieldwork (July–August 1994 and December 1995) was financed by the Complutense University of Madrid (Project PR19/94–5375/94) and I also received a *Beca Complutense del Amo* for a bibliographic study at the University of California, Los Angeles.
I thank Professors Timothy Earle and Antonio Gilman for their assistance in the USA, and Felipe Criado for his careful reading of this text and his helpful suggestions.

References

Appadurai, A. 1988. Putting hierarchy in its place. *Cultural Anthropology* 3, 36–49.

Clastres, P. 1981. *Investigaciones en Antropología Política*. Barcelona: Gedisa.

Eliade, M. 1988. *Lo sagrado y lo profano*. Barcelona: Labor/Punto Omega.

Elías, N. 1990a. *Compromiso y Distanciamiento*. Barcelona: Ediciones Península.

Elías, N. 1990b. *La sociedad de los individuos*. Barcelona: Ediciones Península/Ideas.

Elías, N. 1992. *Time: an essay*. Oxford: Basil Blackwell.

Entrikin, J.N. 1991. *The Betweenness of Place: towards a geography of modernity*. Baltimore, Md.: Johns Hopkins Universty Press.

Estrada Monroy, A. 1990. *Vida esotérica Maya-K'ekchí*. Guatemala: Ministerio de Cultura y Deportes.

Foucault, M. 1986. Of other spaces. *Diacritics*, 16, 22–7.

Goody, J. 1985. *La domesticación del pensamiento salvaje*. Madrid: Akal Editor (original edition 1977 *The Domestication of the Savage Mind*. Cambridge, Cambridge University Press).

Ingold, T. 1993. The temporality of the landscape. *World Archaeology* 25, 152–74.

Kern, S. 1983. *The Culture of Time and Space. 1880–1918*. Cambridge, Mass.: Harvard University Press.

Le Goff, J. 1981. *El nacimiento del Purgatorio*. Madrid: Taurus.

Lévi-Strauss, C. 1966. *The Savage Mind*. London, Weidenfeld & Nicolson.

Medina, A. 1990. Arqueología y etnografía en el desarrollo histórico mesoamericano. In *Etnoarqueología. Coloquio Bosch-Gimpera*, Y. Sugiura Y. and M.C. Serra P. (eds), 447–81. México: Universidad Nacional Autónoma de México.

Mercader, J. 1993. Nuestros vecinos cazadores-recolectores al borde del siglo XXI: Revisionismo y etnoarqueogéa en los estudios de caza-recolección. *Antropología* 4–5, 183–99.

Pacheco, L. 1985. *Religiosidad Maya-Kekchí alrededor del maíz*. San José, Costa Rica: Escuela Para Todos.

Pacheco, L. 1988. *Tradiciones y costumbres del pueblo Maya Kekchí. Noviazgo, matrimonio, secretos, etc*. San José, Costa Rica: Ambar.

Rodman, M.C. 1992. Empowering place: multilocality and multivocality. *American Anthropologist* 94, 640–56.

Rojas Lima, F. 1988. *La Cofradía. Reducto cultural indígena*. Guatemala: Seminario de Integración Social.

Rosaldo, R. 1988. Ideology, place, and people without culture. *Cultural Anthropology* 3, 77–87.

Solano, F. de 1969. Areas lingüísticas y población de habla indígena de Guatemala en 1772. *Revista Española de Antropología Americana* IV, 145–200.

Tuan, Y.-F. 1987. *Space and Place: the perspective of experience*. Minneapolis: University of Minnesota Press.

Wolf, E. 1955. Types of Latin American peasantry: a preliminary discussion. *American Anthropologist* 57, 452–71.

Wolf, E. 1968. Closed corporate communities in Mesoamerica and Central Java. In *Theory in Anthopology: a sourcebook*, R.A. Manners and D. Kaplan (eds), 294–300. London: Routledge & Kegan Paul.

Zumthor, P. 1994. *La medida del mundo. Representación del espacio en la Edad Media*. Madrid: Cátedra.

19 Self-determination in cultural resource management: indigenous peoples' interpretation of history and of places and landscapes

JOHN ALLISON

Today, the United States and other nations are attempting to adjust to the internal political demands of distinct societies within their boundaries. It has become clear that no single group can have control of a democratic nation without support of the other groups. The first bureaucratic response from the dominant Euro-American sub-group to challenges from other sub-groups was to develop a new vocabulary. Many politicians and social service professionals now talk about our 'multi-cultural' society or 'cultural diversity'. A new way of talking is, however, not enough. The time has come to confront hard reality and to determine the actions necessary to maintain the cultural diversity that the US government apparently values. We must ask, 'What are the primary critical constituent elements of the cultural ecology necessary to maintain and enhance these separate social systems and their cultural vitality?'

The maintenance and enhancement of languages is clearly important. Yet even groups which have adopted some version of the English language have demonstrated that other differences are also vital to maintain strong, unique cultures. One of the most obvious is the need for a legal and management framework to support education of a community's children according to their own cultural values and their own view of history. Without government, private, community and corporate support for this ecology of cultural diversity, the will of separate cultural groups to survive and grow will give way to open social conflict.

For most indigenous or 'tribal' groups, the connection to their own landscape and its features is probably rivalled only by the desire for self-determination in education of their children. It is extensively documented that the cultural life of Native Americans, in its spiritual as well as its economic aspect, is closely connected to the earth and specifically to the features and qualities of their indigenous landscape. The landscape is a necessary part of an indigenous group's sense of identity and common destiny. Without it, native people will become part of the faceless class of individuals wandering in the streets of the inner city without any identity other than that of a 'minority'. Yet such removal from the referents of the traditional landscape is part of the complex process that goes with colonial conquest such as took place in the United States, a process that is sometimes called 'enclosure'.

Around-the-Neck: the road to enclosure for the Klamath, Modoc and Yahooskin

A place name and the associated knowledge may represent a single event of great significance in the history of an indigenous society, an element that over time has become part of the society's world view. There is such a place, called 'Around-the-Neck', that is located in Klamath County, Oregon, in one of the last areas of the USA to fall to the European invasion of North America.

Bargaining with the conqueror

In August 1864, authoritative members of twenty-seven indigenous North American groups from the area that now comprises southeast Oregon, northeast California and northwest Nevada met with United States representatives at Council Grove, near Crooked Creek at the north end of Klamath Lake. It had become clear to these leaders that they must retain for their peoples a secure land base on which they would be safe from the United States army and the European-American 'settlers' who had been encroaching on their lands, abusing their resources and attacking their people for the past twenty years. Given the advantage of the European-Americans in numbers and weapons, the native leaders negotiated under duress, compromising their aboriginal land base claims for concessions in facilities and services to be provided. '[Tom Lang, who acted as interpreter for a Klamath doctor (Figure 19.1)] asserts that the Indians were induced by one of the Treaty Commissioners to compromise their claims to the north and to the south of their true holdings in order to secure a Government school in the Treaty' (Stern 1952–6).

The label 'Klamath' was applied to one cluster of these groups, although these people did not use that label and no one is certain how it originated. Another cluster of related groups speaking a language that was similar to that of the 'Klamaths' were given the name 'Modoc', which is from a Klamath word meaning 'the people to the south'. A third cluster that spoke Northern Paiute, an unrelated language, were referred to as 'Yahooskin' in the 1864 treaty. These twenty-seven groups agreed to reserve only about 5 per cent of their collective territories; and this reserved area was entirely within the aboriginal territory of the Klamaths. Thus it was called the Klamath Indian Reservation. The Modoc and Yahooskin were forced to cede their entire national territories, taking up residence on Klamath lands.

Figure 19.1 The Klamath doctor known as White Sindy.

The boundaries of the reserved territory were loosely defined by mountain peaks, referred to today as the 'peak-to-peak' boundary (Figure 19.2). In the understanding of the indigenous leaders, none of whom spoke or read English, in which the treaty was written, the boundary was not a hard line as are modern nations' boundaries but approximated to an overlapping common use area between neighbouring groups. The boundary was, moreover, never honoured by the USA, and the first surveying of the reservation boundaries was to pay more attention to the convenient, abstract lines of a contracted surveyor than to the agreed-on peaks. The differences in territory between the two interpretations were always at the expense of the indigenous peoples. In addition, the European-American 'settlers' who had moved onto the better resource lands within the reserved area were recognised by the US as having 'pre-emptive claims' over the claims of the sovereign nations to reserve these lands, and so these lands, too, were removed from the reserved area unilaterally by the USA: 2.1 million acres were eventually pared down to a reservation of 1.2 million acres.

Caught in the grip of enclosure

It was obvious from the beginning to the leaders of these twenty-seven sovereign groups that their 'sovereignty' would be subject to 'frontier justice'.

Figure 19.2 The Klamath Reservation 'peak-to-peak' boundary included Crater Lake and Mt Thielsen.

When the treaty they signed in 1864 was finally approved several years later, there had already been numerous violations of sovereignty. While the treaty was under negotiation, the US Congress granted a prime area of 44,996 ha within the northeast quarter of the proposed reservation to the State of Oregon and a private corporation, 'The Oregon Central Military Road Company' (whose board members included federal and state politicians and members of the Indian Service) in exchange for an agreement to build a road through the Reservation. Most was given to the California and Oregon Land Company in 1906 for finally building a road through the north end of the Reservation. The land is currently in the ownership of an international timber corporation. It includes much of Yamsay Mountain, 'the home of the North Wind', currently being nominated to the National Register of Historic Places as a Traditional Cultural Property of the Klamath Tribes.

Those observing the first ten years of confinement of the twenty-seven groups to the Klamath Indian Reservation, which then comprised less than half of what they had reserved, reflected the need of these people to go beyond the definition of the boundary imposed by the USA. When, for example, the resources of the Klamath River and Klamath Lake are depleted by pollution, drought or other natural disaster such as volcanic eruption, or as the seasons change, the people travel outside the Reservation to such places as Lost River where they once could harvest and dry tons of Kumals, or sun-dried giant mullet (Figure 19.3). When the big deer congregate in the Silver Lake/Christmas Valley during the winter, the people can follow their

Figure 19.3   A Klamath man angling with a willow pole, 1925.

herds into that area where lighter snows allow the deer to continue browsing, and where rabbits are abundant. When the huckleberries are ripe, whole families move to camps near the huckleberry patches, regardless of Reservation boundaries.

Some of the favourite seasonal camping places are across the crest of the Cascade Mountain Range which forms part of the 'peak-to-peak' boundary specified by their spokesmen in the treaty around the upper reaches of the Rogue River. Here the men can join with the locals fishing for salmon or trout in the Rogue while the women and youngsters spend a month gathering and preserving berries and renewing relations with friendly families from all over southern Oregon and northern California.

The social attractions and spiritual medicine to be found in a particular place are at least as important as the amount of harvest or distance travelled. Near good fishing and the huckleberries and blackberries on Union Creek are the two towering rock columns known as Rabbit Ears, on the top of which people practise spiritual training.

These uses were never intensive, as would require management such as practised in a National Park, although a particular camp might seem like a large crowd in a small area. Some activities, such as spiritual quests, might best be carried out miles from the next human being.

There are, therefore, many reasons why these peoples could not survive within the confines of the US government's definitions of their boundaries, even when population numbers were much reduced by disease and war. For the first fifty years they continued to go to Lost River, Lakeview, Clear Lake, Goose Lake, Silver Lake, Fort Rock Valley, Summer Lake and Chewaucan Marsh, Surprise Valley, Susanville, Canyonville, Yreka, the Dalles, the California Coast and Alturas, all of which are outside the Reservation. They travelled across a radius of several hundred kilometres to maintain social and other network connections, yet always centred their lives in the winter villages they considered home, in the landscape where they were created.

The Klamaths acted as though there was consistency among all the treaties with indigenous peoples in western North America. Unlike the Stevens' treaties signed with the Columbia River peoples, however, Huntington's 'Klamath Tribes' treaty did not explicitly reserve a right to harvest necessary resources and maintain necessary social connections at their 'usual and accustomed places'. The 'reserved lands' became a military concentration camp which was known as the 'rez'. Gradually the requirement for a pass to leave the Reservation became a hard rule, enforced with weapons. The increasingly 'private' ceded lands of their old towns, with their cemeteries and their communal natural 'gardens', their fruit and nut orchards, the herds of deer and elk in their pastures, and flocks of water fowl in their ponds became more and more remote and dangerous to 'trespass' into. They now had to produce a pass signed by the US Indian Agent if they were found beyond the reserved lands, and found themselves staring into the barrel of a gun while they provided the pass.

Modoc Point, a peninsula into Klamath Lake, was effectively the Modocs' concentration camp. It was located on the site of an ancient Klamath settlement, whose residents had been removed to another group's area to make room for the Modocs. One can understand that the Modocs had never felt welcome, being forced into a Klamath settlement in the heart of the Klamath homeland. Why, indeed, were they there when Modoc community representatives had already signed an agreement with an official US representative, one Major Steele, for a reservation within their own Modoc landscape, to the south, where they were created? This treaty was one of many that were never ratified by the US Congress.

Rebellion, capture and punishment

It was with the understanding resulting from these deceptions and injustices that Kientpoos (called 'Captain Jack' in the history of the Euro-Americans), with his co-leaders and their supporters, pulled out of the community at 'Modoc Point' and began a struggle to regain the land base promised to them within their own territory. The Modoc War did not immediately force the US to honour the agreement, nor has it yet achieved the Modocs' return to the area that they had reserved to themselves in their treaty through Major Steele. As one living descendant of these Modoc leaders sees it,

> After we killed that General [Canby], the United States decided that there weren't going to be any more Modocs. They hanged our leaders and shipped the rest of the trouble-makers off to Oklahoma and forced the remaining Modoc people onto the east side of the reservation with the Paiutes [Yahooskin].
>
> (Barlowe pers. comm.)

The legendary struggle of these great Modoc leaders demonstrates the intensity with which these peoples are connected to their homeland. One might say that, with their death, they drew a line in the sand. The outcome of this struggle for their aboriginal rights is yet to be settled, even though white history as taught in the schools of Klamath County, Oregon, and Modoc County, California, tries to ignore that over a thousand living people are recognised by the US federal government as being of Modoc heritage. The place of their leaders' hanging, the same place where a US army massacre of women and children occurred during the 'Bread Riot' over a decade later and the site of Old Fort Klamath, is remembered in the oral history of the Klamaths. Its name is recorded by early ethnographers as /ʔiW'qaq/. This word is translated by the authoritative linguist for Klamath/Modoc, M.A.R. Barker, as 'Around the Neck'. However, in the Oregon historical establishment, *McArthur's Oregon Place Names* translates 'Iukak' as 'within', and 'in the midst', interpreting it as a reference to a valley between mountains.

Final dispossession

In 1887, the US passed the Allotment Act which placed all the Reservation lands, except for the common lands used for grazing and hunting, in the hands of individual tribal members. When sold to non-tribal members, these allotments became the property of the individual and became part of the taxable lands of the USA.

In 1954, the US government abrogated their 1864 treaty and withdrew recognition of the Klamath Tribes as a dependent sovereign nation, a 'Federally Recognised Tribe'. Their remaining lands were purchased and became either private property or part of two National Forests. Federal recognition of the Klamath Tribes was restored in 1986, but they now had no land base. The US government had effectively legalised the theft of this sovereign nation's land, forcing even tribal members to pay land taxes to the county government. Many families have lost their homes for lack of ability to pay taxes. As one tribal consultant said, 'We were a people of the land; now we have become a landless people' (Kirk pers. comm.).

Today two historically and culturally different peoples live in their separate realities. One people, the recent colonisers, want to forget and get on with economic development of the Klamath and Modoc landscape in the European image. The other, who claim this as their Garden of Eden, the place of their Creation, remember events and retain values through their names for features of the landscape. They wish to protect (Figure 19.4) their own vision of the landscape and the values and history represented by their own place names.

Around-the-Neck is an important place for all twenty-seven groups of the Klamaths. Only one version of this history is, however, taught in public schools, and that history does not even mention the name of the place called Around-the-Neck. Instead it praises the 'heroic' deeds of such infamous Indian-killers as Kit Carson, who not only slaughtered helpless Klamath and Modoc women and children but was the main agent in rounding up

Figure 19.4 Damaged Klamath notice. The target was a painted Indian's head in feathered headdress in the centre.

and killing many thousands of Navajo people and other tribes. A giant billboard near a highway that runs through an ancient burial ground of the Klamaths causes great resentment. It is an advertisement for a bank that lends money to those who would develop this landscape for economic purposes according to their own vision. It depicts the face of an older European male. The only words on the billboard other than the banking institution's name are 'Our roots run deep.'

How archaeologists can find meaning in life

This chapter describes how I have attempted to go down a path predicated on indigenous peoples' right to self-determination in writing their history and in managing their cultural resources. It is a path that led me to conduct an ethnographic landscape inventory. Working as the tribal archaeologist for the Klamaths of the high country of eastern Oregon in the western United States, I completed one of the first attempts at such an inventory. First, I

did an exhaustive background literature search and extensive archival research
in museums and government document centres. I collected both written references to places and historical photos of places. Then I interviewed over forty
members from the three separate indigenous societies that comprise the federally recognised society known as the Klamaths. During the interview process,
I visited many of the important places and photographed them. The photos
were then used to elicit further information in further interviews and as illustrations in the final document.

This is a community of tribes who, some social scientists claim, have lost their
culture. Yet these people and the related research provided a large amount of
information about the values and uses associated with over 400 places, ranging
from small 'sites' to extensive landscape features. I consider this a mere sampling
that may give an indication of the range of classes of landscape features and sites
to which these peoples attach traditional cultural values, which are therefore
related to their cultural survival. It is important to note that, of these hundreds
of places that these people register as of great importance to them, they currently
have access to none without seeking the permission of the public agency or the
private individual who 'owns' the particular place.

The resulting document (Allison 1994), financed by a modest grant from the
National Park Service's National Historic Preservation Grants to Indian Tribes
and Alaskan Natives, provides a tool that these groups can use to assert their
sovereign cultural resource management rights to federal land management
agencies. Although these federal agencies and others control actual ownership
of their aboriginal lands and lands that they reserved in a treaty in 1864, legal
battles have shown that they retain resource rights on these former Reservation
lands that are now in US federal ownership. My document provides the kind
of leverage the tribes can use effectively to assert such rights.

A discussion of the historic context of a site such as Around-the-Neck might
now contribute to the reversal of the enclosure process. Placed in the history
curriculum of the area's school system, and working with local school districts
and county planning agencies, it could create a more enlightened relationship
between Indian and non-Indian children. Ethnographic landscape inventories
can be a useful way for all indigenous communities attempting to assert their
rights to self-determination in management of their native landscape.

Ethnographic landscape inventories are also vital to archaeologists engaged
in cultural resource management, since they work with sites and items that
probably belong to someone's cultural landscape. Such an inventory should
be compiled during the first phase of fieldwork. The ethnographic landscape
inventory links archaeology to the parent discipline of cultural anthropology.

Time, space and perceived reality

Some have called the stream of doctrine and ideology of an empire a 'great
tradition', and the cultural stream of a self-identified group of indigenous

communities a 'little tradition' (e.g. Redfield 1956). Those who lose the stream of a little tradition and become absorbed into a national culture such as the European-American society may dispute the value of preserving the landscape as valued by indigenous societies. Citizens of urban industrial society seem to lack a rooting in any specific place; they often move from place to place seeking money, property or identity. Landscape values are often reduced to economic values.

Indigenous peoples' knowledge of geography is based upon accumulated observations of generations. History, science, spirituality and aesthetics are all tied together by these peoples' oral, or recently written, bodies of local knowledge. Although such knowledge is often represented in school history texts as 'myths and legends', it goes far beyond measurements of soil chemistry, elevation and rainfall, and the recording of species of flora and fauna, observation and mapping of geology, or the dating and grouping of stone tools that guide resource management in today's government agencies. Such 'scientific' observations entail only gross, mechanically measurable phenomena that anyone could perceive and measure. In contrast to the observation of specialised professional 'scientists', indigenous knowledge is local, intensive, long-term, and based on intimate, shared experience that is dynamic, complex and recursive.

Some Lakota people of the northern plains of North America referred to the early European immigrants as 'the ones-who-are-passing-through', or *Waisichu*, while the Klamaths used a word derived from 'Boston' which is, with the clever twist of Indian humour, pronounced 'Bust-ins'. Bust-ins fail to see the values in the landscape recognised by indigenous peoples. They appear ignorant in their lack of understanding of those forces that will affect their life. Indigenous 'cultural resource' knowledge represents accumulated understandings of natural events, processes and the qualities of specific places and landscape features. These vary from one place to another; they represent solutions to problems that have worked in a particular place, a survival strategy whose evolutionary fitness within the local ecosystem is attested by a long, successful history. They are rules that guide people in annual grooming of their landscape and in their relations to all its parts.

The Bust-ins see the vulnerability of the Indian's control over the landscape from their perspective of private ownership. They want to fence and to domesticate the land after the pastoral or horticultural vision of their European ancestors, or they want to extract minerals or timber on an industrial scale, exploiting economic value-potential in the landscape. They seek personal ownership over it and the right to do with the land as they wish. Landscape becomes commodity.

The Klamaths' landscape testimony demonstrates the perception that there are linkages between significant places, places that signify an idea and associated feeling-experiences. These linkages, or pathways, provide a time-like dimension. One travels the linkages between places through what European-Americans call time. If travel between such places takes place in the tangible world, we might call these pathways 'trails' or 'roads'. Sometimes, however, indigenous peoples, in their knowledge, and resulting from shared experiences, link two places by an idea, or a person, or some event that exists at another time. The medicine of each place is unique, and yet it is of a type of medicine that occurs precisely in such type of place.

The Creator may become manifest in the form of a fox or a pine marten in two different places in the landscape, or He may have travelled from an event in one place on a tangible path to an event at another event-place (Figure 19.5), or He may have been magically transported through a dimension beyond European-American time-and-space physical reality, from one place-event to another place-event. There is a whirlpool in the Williamson River where those who seek spiritual understanding immerse themselves, lose consciousness and are supernaturally transported to a hill top about 2 km away to receive spiritual training.

The cultural nature of the roadblocks to indigenous self-determination

These separate readings and valuations of landscape represent at least two relationships to what Europeans call time and space. The identification of places on the landscape, their significance, appropriate behaviour in and toward

Figure 19.5 The place where the Creator slept after creating the earth for the Modoc people.

these cultural spaces, and the linkages between these, exist in the shared conceptual contexts of people who identify themselves collectively as a society or culture. How can individuals from one of these societies claim the knowledge and authority to write the history and designate the cultural resource values in the landscape of the other?

Ucko (1989: xvi) writes:

> I have tried to describe on several occasions how 'control' of cultural activities and especially control of the past by any group is potentially a devastatingly powerful weapon in the hands of those who are 'in power', to be used for or against those whose cultures or pasts they claim to understand or interpret.

He also proposes 'that archaeological interpretation is a subjective matter . . . that to regard archaeology as somehow constituting the only legitimate "scientific" approach to the past need(s) re-examination and possibly rejection' (Ucko 1989: xi).

The approach presented here stands in clear contrast to the way in which cultural resource management or heritage management is generally projected by the archaeological professionals who work for public land management agencies, or those who contract for public funds. History, 'prehistory' and the landscape are projected in terms of their role in the American Heritage industry, pride in knowing the archaeologists' version ('truth') of their nation's history and 'prehistory'. In this scheme, indigenous people can only hope to be peripheral proof of some supposed universal principle rooted in European epistemology.

Education in the system of local indigenous landscape names, a local school curriculum that includes the related body of knowledge and science based on many generations of indigenous, shared community experience with local cycles of change, gives priority to the interpretations by the society that is indigenous over those who are immigrant colonists of the indigenous peoples' landscape. Events are interpreted and a history is constructed in the time and space of the indigenes' own accumulated experience. This history is expressed in names and stories centred in their own native landscape. If one places an event such as took place at Around-the-Neck at the centre of modern history instead of at the periphery, what kind of history and cultural resource management results?

A setting for landscapes in the ecology of mind: a separate reality

Only recently has a recognition of the value of indigenous knowledge begun to penetrate the field of cultural resource management. There have, however, been observations throughout modern social science of the link between patterns of culture and qualities of the landscape. These range from the value to modern medicine of ethnobotanical knowledge of the medicinal properties of local plants, to indigenous peoples' overall knowledge of the carrying capacity of the regional landscape in long-term historic perspective. Local knowledge of great cycles of environmental change may emphasise both economic values and intangibles such as experiential or spiritual qualities of specific places.

Leach (1961) asserted of Pul Eliya, a village in Sri Lanka, that it is not the society that endures, but the cultural landscape, the network of places that host interlinked social functions and structures. Leach demonstrated that the village's society persists and is structured through the linked group and individual activities hosted by these places and the paths that join them. Mind, society and landscape are interdependent. The 'context' (the natural and human-influenced place) is not simply a passive backcloth to social life; it is itself a social product and is 'structured'. The people who live in it must conform to a wide range of rules and limitations simply to live there at all. The continuing entity is not Pul Eliya society, but Pul Eliya itself, the village pond, the gamgoda area, the Old Field with its complex arrangement of *baga*, *pangu* and *elapata*. Leach could as well have emphasised that the perception of this landscape is also a social product, deriving from a cultural system of representations, an ontological theory. Cultural or cognitive factors map features and relationships in the landscape and attribute values to these, creating an image of a shared reality through social processes.

While Leach and other British social anthropologists point to the aspects of culture to be found in social processes in time and space, American cultural anthropologists point to evidence of the non-tangible basis of culturally patterned behaviour. For example, Pepper (1958) supports and connects the second approach in his philosophical investigation into the sources of values, treating landscape as an artefact and locating landscape more in mind and culture than in some single reality inherent in place, making it the foremost among artefacts: the 'seat of culture'. He asserts that if you destroy or remove the artefacts, you destroy the physical basis for a culture; if one removes a people from their landscape, or alters that landscape beyond its structural meaning, the culture is put at risk (Pepper 1958).

Both these and numerous more recent, specialised studies provide a strong foundation for the field of 'environmental perception'. This approach is now overriding the more limited and narrow scientific approach to the evaluation of environmental impacts of human actions. The new ways of approaching the study of landscape also raise the question of how to weight and interrelate different cultural values perceived in a given, specific landscape. The length of time of stable residence in an area allows a prior claim for management rights based on more intimate knowledge of the dynamics of a particular place through long periods of time.

European-American archaeology and indigenous peoples' history

The notion of landscape has now entered into the mainstream of American archaeological discussion, bringing with it a body of literature that is rooted in the study of how we see the landscape, how we learn to locate ourselves in it and how landscape perception is patterned by culture. Planning cultural resource management now requires collaboration between landscape architect, indigenous people, historian, ethnographer, and both historic and prehistoric archaeologist. This requires archaeologists to defend their claim to be the principal experts in identifying and managing cultural resources.

Archaeologists have begun to grapple with problems of how to describe and explain the cultural relationships between clusters of artefacts and features that they (the archaeologists, but not necessarily the indigenous people) define as significant sites within the overall landscape. It is not difficult to sense that a link is missing between the archaeologists' perceived physical reality, their organising and explaining of a landscape of sites, and the significance of these places. What links these perceived/conceived objects and places into a system? To whom are they significant and what do they signify? Is the word 'significant' to be used only where an archaeologist recognises artefacts or features that meet one of the four criteria for listing in the National Register of Historic Places? What is the interrelation of these places and objects as they exist in the minds of the members of a given society? What is the real functional boundary of this site?

Archaeologists have begun to examine their own perception of reality in relation to other cultural traditions. They have woken up to the fact that, in writing their stories about the hypothetical past, the 'scientific' and 'objective' framework upon which they rely is itself part of a unique cultural tradition that has no special claim to global authority. It certainly does not qualify as legitimate local history (cf. Ucko 1989, cited above). American cultural anthropology relies on ethnographic and linguistic techniques for accessing values and the framework for meaning in the minds of the indigenous peoples. This cognitive approach comes directly from the root intention of cultural anthropology to develop a way for members of one society to gain an insight into the behaviour of members of a different society living in its own perceived reality. Archaeologists have, however, defined ethnoarchaeology as observation of the behaviour of the people they are studying from an outside viewpoint that they call 'objective'. They believe that they study a cultural system as an object, something that can be viewed from an external perspective, *das Ding an sich*. Very few archaeologists go so far as to study the meaning and functions of their artefacts, activity areas, sites and landscapes in the context of the cultural world view of the indigenous people who create and use these. How, after all, can an archaeologist access 'units of experience' with the tools of the physical sciences? Yet US federal law requires that agencies 'consult with the appropriate Indian Tribes' prior to project-planning activities. American archaeology must revisit its roots in the parent discipline of cultural anthropology.

Cultural resource management in the USA

Most of the laws used in cultural resource management in the USA were influenced by archaeologists, historians and architectural historians. The distinction between 'prehistory' and 'history' was central to their thinking. History, in this sense, began when Christopher Columbus 'discovered' America, 500 years ago. Historic archaeology in cultural resource management was imprinted with the framework of European-Americans' values and interests in 'historic preservation', using personal contact interviews with 'old-timers', 'early settlers', and such. This is transparently a foundation for the colonial charter, a rationalisation for claiming a 'heritage' in this 'New World' landscape. It validates modifying that landscape toward the imported European vision of a pastoral and agricultural urban society, building on a mythology concerning the magical capacity of industrial technology to dominate the 'wild' forms and forces of 'nature'. In a recent summary of historic landscape studies in a special edition of *CRM* (*Cultural Resource Management*, vol. 17), only one 'natural landscape' was presented as deserving inscription upon the National Register, and that was the area portrayed in the landscape paintings of the European-American artist Georgia O'Keefe. Although the area contains many sacred sites, the values of the landscape to indigenous society went unrecognised.

'Historic landscapes' have been construed as landscapes physically modified to satisfy the imported image of a domesticated property. Professionals make it their own when they validate a landscape's significance as part of the 'American Heritage'. Interpretive signs are erected to help the visitor see it correctly. A.J.B. Johnston has pointed out that the management of Canadian National Parks reveals a widely shared desire to educate the visiting public, usually thought to be best achieved through a presentation of 'things' such as reconstructed buildings and people in costume. If enough appropriate items can be presented, visitors will be convinced of a given site's veracity. History is seen as essentially an objectifying process, whereas, from an aboriginal perspective, intangibles are often of prime importance.

> A related challenge is to reflect the Native's view that interpreting the past is more a cultural than a curatorial question. A particular Native group may well want to talk more about their world view and less about 'things'. As Marie Battiste put it, 'We are more than arrowheads . . .'.
>
> Anthropologist Robin Ridington says that before contact with Europeans, 'technology consisted of knowledge rather than tools. It was by means of this knowledge of their ecosystems, and their ingenuity in using them to their own advantage, that Amerindians had been able to survive as well as they did with comparatively simple technology'.
>
> Lest anyone think that such knowledge was more philosophical than practical, they should recall the countless occasions when

explorers and settlers relied on Native expertise. There are, for example, accounts of surgical skill, such as when two Kutchin women perfectly repaired a broken kneecap using sinew and small caribou-bone pegs.

(Johnston 1994: 26)

The techniques for studying historical landscapes were not applied to indigenous landscapes until recently, when native peoples began to demand it. The Advisory Council on Historic Preservation responded to these demands by developing a category of historic places called 'traditional cultural property'. Not only landscape architects and architectural historians but many archaeologists consider 'historic landscapes' in terms of the European vision: formal gardens, old buildings and grounds presented as museum items appropriated as part of the great tradition that is called the American Heritage, to be managed for their value to local tourism and a nationalistic ideological education in 'history'. The idea of non-archaeologically verified traditional cultural properties has never been very popular with archaeologists nor with the European-American public. The decision to honour the Native American valuation of Mount Shasta by declaring it a historic property was recently reversed in response to European-American protests.

American archaeologists' closed system model

Archaeologists have, in general, treated indigenous societies as something of the past and not deemed the opinions and values of their living descendants valid or relevant to a history of that people's homelands. The traditional indigenous version of these peoples' own history has been relegated to a minor auxiliary role as 'mythical', or 'ethnohistory', a curiosity not to be confused with so-called objective truth. The indigenous people's version of what happened historically gains validity beyond the spoken word of the indigenous people themselves if it has been written down by an early European-American ethnographer. The Makah of the Olympic Peninsula of Washington State requested the local school district to remove certain materials from the local history text. They indicated that the tribal members who provided the information to a young graduate student ethnographer many years ago had just been joking. What she was told was not the truth. The school district rejected their attempt to provide a more genuine version for use in their children's education. In this way indigenous people are stripped of their authority.

Bringing it all back home

In the current, multi-cultural atmosphere it is important that indigenous, sovereign governments challenge archaeologists' claims to be uniquely qualified to designate areas of the indigenous Native Americans' landscape as sites, historical districts or traditional cultural properties. They should question archaeologists' ability to recognise the cultural constructs of the indigenous peoples that reside simultaneously in the tangible forms of the landscape and in the minds of the individuals in that indigenous society. Indigenous peoples should have the advantage of their own immemorial cultural tradition.

The value to archaeologists of seeking to assist indigenous people to answer questions or verify information of interest to them was recently illustrated to me in the field. It has long been anthropological folklore that mortars in bedrock and boulders all begin as shallow use-areas and get deeper with use. This also conveniently explained heavy wear on the molar teeth of excavated American skeletons induced by grit produced in the milling process. Jackson and McCarthy (1987) interviewed members of tribes that occupied both the area where I work and the area of their study, who asserted that mortars were manufactured by specialists to specific depths appropriate to the stage of acorn processing or to other materials such as light grass seeds for which a deep mortar is more efficient. They further stated that they never hit stone on stone; the pestle struck only the food material itself. In a single site, I subsequently located two examples of roughed-out troughs of mortars of different depth, on two separate granite boulders, with the debitage from the production process lying at one end of the troughs. These were the first examples of this process encountered and recognised by an American archaeologist. The Indians' information, related by Jackson and McCarthy, allowed me to 'see' the unused mortars for what they were.

The resurgence of the sovereign rights of indigenous peoples

'You don't have to be a weather man to know which way the wind blows', sang Bob Dylan, and it is not necessary for an indigenous community to send its youth to acquire European-based education and a doctoral degree in archaeology before it can manage its own cultural resources. New laws now in place in the US, and internationally, provide the basis for asserting indigenous peoples' rights.

There are precedents in the United States for litigation over water rights and other resource rights favouring claims by indigenous societies to a prior right to their aboriginal resources. Such precedence is currently being extended to cultural resources. The trend can now be expected to expand internationally:

> In my opinion, Article 27 [of the United Nations' International Covenant on Civil and Political Rights] applies to indigenous cultures that are closely linked to their land and its resources. If an indigenous people's loss of their land inevitably leads to the extinguishment of their distinct culture, the nation that took their

land has violated Article 27 of this covenant. Nations have an
obligation to protect traditional forms of economic activity on
which the cultural integrity of the indigenous people depend. . . .
The Article is ample demonstration that indigenous peoples, in
their search for self-determination, occupy the moral high ground.

(Berger 1985: 180)

The United Nations' draft Declaration on the Rights of Indigenous Peoples
is moving the world community of nations toward stronger support of indigenous peoples' right to self-determination. The Declaration contains clauses
that imply the obligation of the US to restore the Klamaths' reserved lands
and to provide them with a major role in the management of resources
throughout their aboriginal lands.

How to assert sovereignty in cultural resource management

To begin to implement these rights, an indigenous community must produce
a verbal or written consensus statement outlining its own set of definitions of
cultural resources, an inventory of the places and objects that it wants to protect within that definition, and a set of policies and procedures for protecting
them. If a community decides that a particular landscape feature or area meets
their own criteria as a site, historical district or traditional cultural property,
then it can so designate that place and declare its significance.

Refocusing cultural resource management, reversing enclosure

Employed by the Klamath, Modoc and Yahooskin peoples as their archaeologist,
I was assigned to establish a 'cultural resource management programme', the
label for describing the inventory and management activities on federal lands that
were primarily archaeological in character. I approached this assignment in my
own way, ignoring the three steps conventionally taken by archaeologists:

1   a 'Historic Overview' or compilation of existing knowledge from
    archaeological research about the known sites in the aboriginal area;
2   an additional period of survey and excavation to provide complete
    coverage of the land area; and
3   a comprehensive report of the archaeological values contained within
    the aboriginal lands, and a plan for their management.

I did not follow this sequence, first because the tribes' position was that
excavation of cultural sites is a violation of spiritual values, both because
cremated ancestors' ashes might be there and because the cultural objects left
there by the ancestors were to guide them back for rebirth; and second
because it was clear to me that the landscape, not archaeological sites,

comprised the heart of the people's own definition of their cultural resources. Archaeological values in these places are seen by the indigenous people as merely incidental to the significance of a particular place.

I interviewed forty knowledgeable tribal members, both in groups and individually. I asked them to talk about the places they valued. Later, I asked them to accompany me to some of these places and to give me further guidance on what to record. Places are valued by virtue of the land forms and such natural resources as springs, trees and other plants, wildlife and fish, together with certain intangible values of place (which I term geomantic). These intangible 'vibrations' seem to vary from one place to another. A specific mountain makes certain sounds, or has a quality to its winds; roots growing in meadows fed by the waters of a specific spring are best for drying for use in the sweat lodge. The people living in one region have different characters to those from another. These qualities determine where a specific individual would retreat to seek spiritual growth and healing. They contain the essence or seed values of the culture. As one Modoc consultant put it, 'Each place has its own medicine.' In this sense, medicine is a relationship to the energy of the place that allows one's body or spirit to balance or heal itself.

It was to record information about the cultural meaning and value of specific places that an Ethnographic Landscape Inventory was carried out, a first step in attempting to secure holistic knowledge of the landscape and the indigenous peoples' relationship to it. Their account of time is informed by experience of the natural history of the land and the sweep of events through their social history, a locally centred history and science of the universe personally experienced by people who have lived in places such as Chiloquin, Lost River, Beatty or Clear Lake from time immemorial. These are real, personal, cultural resources. It has often been pointed out that the clock and European calendar provide only one way of organising the relation of events to one another (see Layton 1989). One historian, speaking of the indigenous peoples in the Arctic, has written:

> The past and present of the northern cultures are not distinct and separate like black and white, but are joined together by history, written and remembered. . . . [I]n the south of Canada there is a widespread inclination to speak of an across-the-generations continuum, of a history that is 'cyclical' and 'holistic'.
>
> (Johnston 1994: 26)

Cultural resource management in a multi-cultural society

The materialist urban–industrial strategy is based on a very short experimentation with a technology and ideology that is untried as an adaptive strategy. To the extent that there is feedback from this adaptive strategy, the message is bleak: its impact appears to be destroying the basis for all life on the planet.

In a society such as the United States, which is struggling with both these environmental problems and a multi-cultural political commitment, the obligation to honour the indigenous traditions of landscape values and practices should be obvious. With a slightly deeper understanding of these values and practices, and with knowledge of their functions in the relationship between people and 'nature' or 'wilderness', the benefits of preserving them become apparent. They begin to reveal their value to all peoples as stored, alternative, adaptive strategies. They suggest themselves not as global but as local strategies, fit for specific regions of the Earth's surface. Such strategies can exist only in a political climate that nurtures a 'Small Is Beautiful' approach.

In the past, professional archaeologists have left to cultural anthropologists the task of encouraging or assisting indigenous communities to assert their sovereign right to self-determination. Today, however, archaeologists are awakening to the meaning of the dissolution of the Soviet Union, the developments in South Africa and Yugoslavia, and the resurgence of local sovereignty of the indigenous Native Americans signalled by such events as the uprising in the State of Chiapas in Mexico.

References

Allison, J.V. 1994. The cultural landscape of the Klamath, Modoc and Yahooskin peoples: spirit, nature, history. Report prepared for the Klamath Tribes in fulfilment of National Historic Preservation Grants to Indian Tribes and Alaskan Natives.

Berger, T.R. 1985. *Village Journey: the report of the Alaskan Native Review Commission.* New York: Hill & Wang.

Jackson, T. and H. McCarthy 1987. *Prehistoric and Ethnoarchaeological Investigations of CA-FRE-341, Big Creek Expansion Project, Powerhouse 3, Fresno County, California.* Rosemead, Cal.: Southern California Edison Company.

Johnston, A.J.B. 1994. Toward a new past: interpretation of native history within Parks Canada. *Cultural Resource Management,* 17 (9). Washington: National Parks Service, Cultural Resources.

Layton, R. (ed.) 1989. *Who Needs the Past? Indigenous values and archaeology.* London: Unwin Hyman.

Leach, E. 1961. *Pul Eliya: a village in Sri Lanka.* Cambridge: Cambridge University Press.

Pepper, S. 1958. *Sources of Value.* Berkeley: University of California Press.

Redfield, R. 1956. *Peasant Society and Culture.* Chicago: University of Chicago Press.

Stern, T. 1952–6. *Klamath Field Notebooks.* University of Oregon: University Archives.

Ucko, P.J. 1989. Forword. In *The Meanings of Things,* I. Hodder (ed.), ix–xvii. London: Routledge.

20 Traditional beliefs, sacred sites and rituals of sacrifice of the Nenets of the Gydan Peninsula in the modern context[1]

GALINA KHARYUCHI
AND LYUDMILA LIPATOVA

The Yamalo-Nenets Autonomous Region of Northern Russia, created in 1930, occupies over 750,000 sq km: it stretches 1,200 km from north to south, from the islands of the Arctic Ocean, where only moss and lichen grow, to the Siberian taiga in the south, and 1,130 km from west to east, starting in the Arctic section of the Urals. The inhabitants number approximately half a million, and of these the indigenous population accounts for some 35,000, among whom are 21,000 Nentsy, 7,300 Khanty, 1,500 Selkupy and 5,700 Komi. Some 2,500 of the representatives of these indigenous peoples lead a traditional way of life: they do not usually own flats or houses in towns or villages, but wander across hundreds of kilometres with their herds of deer, catch fish and hunt.

Within the Yamalo-Nenets Autonomous Region, the Nenets population is subdivided according to the district the people inhabit: Yamal, Ural, Forest and Basin Nentsy (which includes the Nentsy of the Gydan Peninsula). The total Nenets population of the Yamalo-Nenets Region is 21,000, which makes up two-thirds of the total Nenets population of Russia.

The Gydan Peninsula, where one of us (G.K.) works (Figure 20.1), lies to the north of the West Siberian Plain. Within the territory that comes under the jurisdiction of the Gydan Area Council there now live both Nentsy and Russian speakers: in 1992 there was a total population of 2,952 of whom 2,578 were Nentsy. In other words, this Area Council administered territory that was populated by an indigenous people.

In this territory, the incidence of oncological diseases is high (of which the most common are cancer of the oesophagus and stomach or skin cancer), particularly among those Nentsy who live on Olen (Deer) Island, situated in the Kara Sea. It is possible that local radiation levels are higher than those in other parts of the peninsula, and marked increases in the cases of such diseases were duly registered after nuclear tests had been carried out in 1961. The Nentsy do not even have a word for such illness, and refer to it as *veva khabtsy* (the bad, or the terrible, disease). This is yet another of the 'gifts' of civilisation that have befallen the Gydan Nentsy.

Figure 20.1   G. Kharyuchi during an expedition in 1994 to the Gydan Peninsula.

Today the life of the Nentsy is difficult, just as it was many years ago. What was it that helped the Nentsy in the past and still helps them to survive and, we hope, will be a source of strength in the future, which will also be hard? The secret of the spiritual resources of the Nentsy is their ability to cling tightly to the roots of their own way of life, their traditions and customs, that go back to time immemorial. These roots are very strong, because our ancestors knew how to stay alive and passed on the experience and practical skills that were acquired and have been developed over many centuries.

Until recently, the indigenous peoples of the Far North, and the nomadic tribes who lived there, were thought by many to be primitive groups untouched by the benefits of education and scientific and technical progress. The main reason for this view was the absence of objective information about these peoples, their history, their culture, their traditions and religion. Historical evidence shows, however, that they have successfully survived in the extreme conditions of the Arctic and the Far North for thousands of years, and that they were highly civilised, with their own traditional way of life, their own culture and forms of economic organisation. Most important, perhaps, is that they still retained their traditional culture, with its wealth of customs, within a special relationship with their harsh natural surroundings. The people in this part of the world protect themselves from the fierce frosts, that can go down as low as −50° C, by clothes sewn from deer-skins. In such clothes they can sit through a two- or three-day snowstorm in a snow shelter, without coming to any harm.

Their easily dismantled dwellings, or *chooms*, have evolved over the centuries, and are an essential part of their nomadic way of life (Figure 20.2). A *choom* is built of fir-wood poles between 5 and 8 m long, and was traditionally covered, in winter, with a layer of deer-skin, and in summer with specially prepared birch-bark (Figure 20.3). Nowadays, the *chooms* are often covered over with tarpaulin in the summer or suede or worn-out deer-skins in the winter. They are easy to assemble and usually take 40–50 minutes to dismantle, but can take as little as 20 minutes. Everything that has been offered to the Nenets people to replace the *choom* has proved inappropriate, whether it be mobile dwellings or tents, either because they are too cumbersome, unable to withstand the winds and frosts, or wear out too quickly.

Transport across the tundra is by sledge, an environmentally clean mode of transport that does not damage the tundra in either summer or winter. Moreover, the sledges themselves are often works of art.

In April 1992, a conference was held in the town of Salekhard, in order to prepare a plan for the socio-economic development of the indigenous peoples of the Yamalo-Nenets Autonomous Region for the period up to the year 2000.[2] The plan was elaborated by representatives of the indigenous peoples together with authoritative scientific experts and their supporters. Plans were also drawn up for the legal defence of the people of the Far North, for the protection of the traditional areas of their agricultural activity, for the future development of the schools in Yamal, and for improved health care. The Yamal Laboratory for Ethnography and Ethnolinguistics also drew

Figure 20.2 G. Kharyuchi outside her *choom*, setting off into the tundra.

Figure 20.3 Summer *chooms* in the Gydan Peninsula.

up a plan to promote the culture of the peoples within our region. This plan was based on acceptance of the fact that the culture of the northern peoples, which is the result of development that goes back thousands of years, reflects a civilisation on a par with all others, although it has a distinctive nature of its own.

The most important precondition for the preservation and promotion of the civilisation of the northern peoples is the preservation of their land. The plan for cultural development included the following declaration:

> To elaborate and implement a special status for sites that are to be protected as special reserves, as centres designed to promote the preservation of traditional culture (architectural monuments, ancient settlements, sacred sites), and to introduce appropriate measures to ensure that such protection is provided.

It was important to include the sacred sites of the indigenous peoples because, among the large number of monuments and sites of our national culture, various types of cult monuments occupy a significant place, and the study of these provides relevant material for the resolution of a number of questions concerning our ethno-cultural history.

When the so-called 'settlement' of the Far North began, the fact that the lands concerned had been settled by the ancestors of the Nentsy was ignored, in spite of the fact that, throughout those lands, many monuments bearing witness to the Nenets' past are to be found, including burials, cult sites and monoliths. Outsiders coming into the area are unaware that a stone in the tundra may in fact be a sacred monument that has been venerated for hundreds of years, and thus a sacred site may be inadvertently bulldozed if it lies in the path of a gas pipeline. Yet these sacred or holy sites, these national burials, are the essence of the spiritual culture of the Nenets, Khanty and Selkup peoples. The very concept of a 'monument' may appear inappropriate, since it suggests something frozen in time, an object from the past, whereas in this context the sacred sites or burial places concerned are living sites. However, these sites come without doubt into the category of 'monument', since they have taken shape and evolved over a long period of time. They constitute the 'churches' of the peoples concerned, and serve to protect the deer pastures and the birds' nesting places, thus making our territories into special reserves, in that the industrial activities of humans should be of a limited nature. Observation of certain prohibitions stemming from the presence of these sacred sites is an important step towards a rational exploitation of nature.

Nowadays, industrial development is the order of the day in some areas within our region, and bulldozers are ploughing up the sacred sites and burials of the Nentsy. Although these crimes are being perpetrated before our very eyes, no one can be called to account for them, because there is no law providing protection for sacred sites. The new Law of the Yamalo-Nenets Region will, we hope, usher in proper legal protection for these monuments belonging to our spiritual culture, provided that the law is duly ratified by the new administrative bodies that have been set up since the October Rebellion.

Researchers from the Laboratory for Ethnography and Ethnolinguistics of the Yamal Peninsula are currently compiling maps of the sacred sites in the various parts of the region. The compiling of maps of those sacred sites that were created by the ancestors is undertaken to help preserve the spiritual and material culture of the people and to fulfil their duty to the ancestors – as G.K. says, 'it is the only way we can preserve our people's very existence, our unique culture'. These maps will be presented to the oil and gas executives when decisions are to be made as to what land should be set aside for drilling activities. It is hoped that the oil and gas companies can then be held responsible for the state of monuments and sacred sites.

The Nentsy who live today on the Gydan Peninsula still venerate the spirits who hold sway over nature: the sky, the sun, the earth, water and fire. Although many of the ancient beliefs are now lost, and some beliefs have undergone change or taken on new elements from the beliefs of other peoples, Christianisation did not penetrate as far as the Nentsy, and the old people only knew about the Russian God from fairytales. Nentsy living near the Urals and some of the Yamalo-Nentsy worship the Russian God as well as their own spirits, and some of the old people erect icons at their places of sacrifice, in the hope that the Russian God, who after all is a god too, might help them as well.

Throughout life, from the cradle to the grave, the Nentsy are surrounded everywhere and at all times by invisible spirits, or gods. The Supreme Being for the Nenets people is known as Noom, the Spirit of the sky and nature and the source of all life; he is a being without flesh or form and is the Creator of Earth and all that exists upon it. After creating the World, Noom refrained from any further interference, leaving that to the *Tadibtse* spirits. Nentsy do not turn very often to Noom, only on the most important occasions, whether they be very happy or very sad. Other spirits are *Yamyunya erv* (the Spirit of the earth), *Id erv* (the Spirit of water), *Tu erv* (the Spirit of fire), and *Nga* (the source of evil and the Spirit of disease and death) who, according to some sources, is the son of Noom, and according to others is the husband of Noom's wife's sister. In addition, every lake, river or small hill has its own spirit.

Deer are sacrificed to the good spirits near a sacred sledge at least once a year, during the summer solstice. Sacrifices are made to the evil spirits near the 'unclean' sledge, on which such things as floor planks, bowls, buckets, twig-baskets and women's clothes (deer-skin shoes and coats) are transported. To these spirits a dog can be sacrificed, not only deer. The meat of such deer is not eaten straightaway: the meat is first cut up and then people wait until the gods and spirits have eaten their fill.

In the month of the Great Darkness (December), a sacrifice is made near the 'nose' of the 'unclean' sledge. The Nga or evil spirit roams where the *choom*s stand, and watches to see what people have put out for him, whether they have remembered him and whether they respect the Spirit of death. Human beings have to prepare for death because death is the beginning of a new life. If a poor man is not able to kill even an old deer, he must boil up a fish or a pike's head, or kill a dog. A Nga shows its gratitude to such a family that remembers him and does not wish him ill. Yet if the Nga finds nothing, no blood, no fire at the spot where the *choom*s had been grouped, he will then follow the tracks of men, follow their scent, and things will turn out badly, especially if anything is dropped from the sledge, especially by women. Some might die and not even a shaman can come to the rescue.

Every people has its gods and its sacred sites. For the Nenets people of the Arctic Urals the principal goddess is Yamine, who is responsible to Noom for the happiness of her people. When Yamine used to wander through the world on earth, every place where she stopped and set up her *choom* became a sacred site where sacrifices were made and a model, usually wooden, of the sacred site would be placed in the sacred sledge. The most important sacred site is not far from the Kara Sea at the point where the Arctic Urals end and the tundra begins, and where the goddess Yamine ceased her wanderings for the last time. At that place there are three mountains, that are held to be the *choom*s of the goddess, stag and sacred sledge. These peaks are known as Minisei.

Within the *choom* of each Nenets family, the *myad pukhutsya* (old woman, or mistress of the *choom*) has an important role to play: she is the guardian of the family, and this role is passed down through the female line. Wooden dolls representing this goddess are still to be found in almost every *choom*. The doll is kept in the woman's half of the *choom*, usually on the pillow of the oldest woman of the family or in a bag suspended over the head of her bed. The *myad pukhutsya* dolls are usually dressed in many garments: a new coat is added as a sign of gratitude each time someone recovers from illness or on the occasion of some other happy event. For a young girl it is a great honour if her mother gives her the task of sewing a garment for the *myad pukhutsya*. Traditionally, the *myad pukhutsya* would assist women in childbirth, and nurse women and children through sickness. Now Nenets women give birth in hospitals and they are helped by midwives and doctors. When a new mother comes back to her *choom*, however, the first thing she does is to show the new member of the family to the *myad pukhutsya*, in order that the guardian of the *choom* might take the child under her protection and defend it against evil spirits. During solemn occasions she should be given a place at a table.

The subterranean guardian of the hearth is the *yamunya pukhutsya* (old underground woman) who, unlike the *myad pukhutsya* – the guardian of the family hearth above ground – is not depicted in material form. She guards fire, the source of life for the clan, the tribe and the people. For the Nentsy, as indeed for all peoples of the Far North, fire is sacred. When a fire is burning, men should not curse or use foul language, and the place where the fire is burning, and indeed the earth everywhere, should not be touched with a knife. The most terrible curse is held to be when a knife 'cuts through' flame, a large fire or simply the earth.

There exists a custom in which people talk with Fire, in their thoughts. Before an important event, people listen to Fire, because it can impart good news to them, or warn them of disaster. There are special signs in this connection that are known to everyone who lives in the tundra.

From their earliest years, children take part in rituals. A boy, together with his father, takes care of the sacred sledge (*Khekhe khan*) on which are kept the cult objects (made from wood and metal) belonging to the clan and family. The sacred sledge always stands behind the *choom*. A youth would be entrusted with the task of conveying this sledge from place to place when the family is on the move; it is borne by two deer, specially sanctified for this purpose before the Supreme God, Noom. The boy will travel with adults to the sacred site where sacrifices will be offered. Young girls, however, are allowed to visit a sacred site only when they reach a certain age.

The Nentsy bring sacrifices to their numerous spirits, on which the success or failure of their various undertakings depends. It is held that prosperity and health are totally in the hands of the spirits: they send down disease to people, they protect (or, conversely, shatter) the family hearth; they can set a marriage off on the right (or wrong) track, and can ensure that birth takes place smoothly.

In ancient times, a deer of a particular breed was sacrificed to each spirit that was of significance in the life of the Nentsy. A grey-white stag would be sacrificed to Noom and a spotted deer with a white blaze to the Spirit of the sun. A brown doe would be sacrificed to *ilebyam pertya* (the protector of the deer themselves), a dark deer to the guardian Spirit of fire, and various other deer to different diseases, for example to smallpox and to Siberian Ulcer (the most dangerous threat to the health and well-being of the deer-breeder). Not all the spirits have special animals sacrificed to them by the Nentsy of today because, thanks to modern medicine, many terrible diseases no longer threaten danger. Nowadays, even without any special veterinary training, the deer-breeders are able to vaccinate their animals themselves.

Sacrifices – some involving blood and some bloodless – are made to all the spirits, and when necessary a specially sanctified deer or a deer of a particular breed is sacrificed. Sacrifice (*khan*) can be made not only to call upon the spirits for their help when a member of the family has been struck down by disease, but also in honour of the arrival of a special guest or of children returning from boarding school.

Sacrifices are offered only on rare occasions, when it is considered absolutely essential, to the sun, the moon, thunder, lightning and the wind.

In summer, after heavy thunder and lightning, a sacrifice of a *padvy ty* (spotted deer) has to be offered. One year, in G.K.'s camp (which consisted of five *chooms*), after heavy thunder had been followed by rain, and lightning had been flashing, she and her mother covered up everything that was red inside and outside the *choom*. During thunder, no one must light a fire, because then a *choom* might be struck by lightning. It was very frightening, and G.K.'s father spent the whole night outside with the deer. The next day the weather was wonderful, and no people or animals had suffered from the thunder or the lightning. It was decided that a deer of a spotted breed should be sacrificed (it was still during the period of the culling of deer). One of the family heads decided to sacrifice a brown deer (possibly because he had no more appropriate animal), and as it was being led to the place of sacrifice it dislocated its leg. The old men said that this meant that the Spirit of thunder did not accept the sacrifice.

Sacrifices were offered to the Spirit of water, *Id erv*, in the spring, after or during the time when the ice began to melt. During this sacrifice, some of the sacrificial blood has to be poured into the water. The skull of the deer, placed on a stick, would be erected on the sea-shore. Earlier, a fish that had been caught the day before the sacrifice would have been placed at the foot of the stick in a flat position as if it were swimming along. The neck of the fawn to be sacrificed would be rubbed with this same fish. This was how the Nentsy offered sacrifice to the Spirit of the water, so that he would not be angry and not 'take up' anyone to be with him.

Veneration of these spirits was a natural part of life for the Nentsy, whose main economic occupations had been breeding deer, fishing and hunting since time immemorial, and whose whole life had been bound up with nature, as were their cult practices.

Special mention should be made of the sacred sites known as *khebidya ya*. Each family had deer that were associated with a specific sacred site or ancestral shrine. In those places, idols known as *khekhe*, *syadei* or *yalya pya* were set up – anthropomorphic depictions fashioned by hand, or simply stones of unusual shape, near where antlers and skulls of deer used for sacrifice (or the skulls of sea-creatures) would be laid out.

In the past, there were sacred sites for specific clans or tribes. Now these have lost their previous significance because there are no longer any clans in the strict sense of the word: families simply move freely around from place to place in search of the best available pastures. What were once sacred places of a specific clan are now places of pilgrimage for all the Nentsy living in the vicinity. The largest and most important of these are Manto-neva (the head of an Enets person (see the Entsy, below)), *Sote ya* (the Large Hill, the cult site of the Vengo clan), *Khoi pya* or *Yaroto* (the lake of the Yar clan) and *Labangane* (the Crumbling Cape).

Representatives of a Samoyed group known as the Entsy (the Nentsy refer to them as Manto) still live on Olen (Deer) Lake in the north of the peninsula, to the east of it near the border with the Krasnoyarsk Region, and in the Taimyr Peninsula (where place names are linked with this particular ethnic group). The two most significant sites in this region are Manto-Yara and Manto-neva. There is an ancient legend regarding these sites:

> Nenets tribes have lived in these harsh places since time immemorial. They had rich pastures, and the rivers and lakes were full of fish. One day, however, people of another tribe came to these parts, speaking a different language and dressed in unfamiliar clothes. These were people of the Manto tribe. They began to drive out the Nentsy, to take away their deer and seize their pastures. There was no deliverance from them. The Nentsy assembled, grouping together in camps, and waged war against the Manto invaders.
>
> In the Month of Small Darkness a large detachment of Nentsy moved through the snowy tundra on their skis [they held themselves to be less conspicuous on skis]. Their *chooms* were erected on a high place, on the bank of a large river covered in ice. Feeling confident of their strength the Manto had not even appointed night watchmen, and the detachment of Nentsy attacked their camp, taking their enemy unawares. Many Manto and many Nentsy died in the battle that ensued. The site of the battle gradually turned into a huge mound. As time went by nature transformed the place into a high sandy hill. At the spot where the last camp of the Manto had stood, the hill bears the name Manto-Yara. After the battle the leader of the Manto camp could not be found. A young huntsman from the detachment of the Nentsy offered to search for him. He was armed with nothing

but a bow and a few arrows. He found the tracks of his enemy on the ice covering the strait, leading towards the mainland. For three days the young Nenets followed in the tracks of the leader of the Manto. After finding the route the leader of the Manto had taken, the young Nenets decided to confront his enemy face to face. He walked round a tall sandy hill strewn with snow, on which the man he was seeking lay resting. It was here that the last of the Manto perished. From that time this hill has been known as Manto-neva. Every year at the time when they move north, the Nentsy offer sacrifices at this sacred site; the Nentsy and the Entsy from Taimyr both come to this place.

This legend shows how certain religious ideas of the Nentsy took shape and evolved; it also reflects other historical processes that have taken place within this territory, such as military confrontations and migrations of local groups of the population.

Another cult site is that known as *Khekhe khan sote ya* (Large Hill of the Holy Sledge), situated 23 km to the southeast of the village. According to another legend:

A large column of Nentsy was moving through the tundra from north to south. The day was clear and those at the front of the long solemn procession had already reached the hills that marked the watershed. Suddenly the sky grew dark and a strong wind blew up making the snow whirl, and everything around them appeared dark and threatening. People began to appeal to Noom to deliver them, sacrificing to him a deer as white as the whirling snowstorm. Yet the storm raged on and Noom did not listen to the people's prayers. The deer in the column were exhausted and began to bump into the sledges. The strict orderliness of the column was disrupted and the belongings tied on to the sledges were scattered through the tundra. The people did not have the strength to go on either.

An old Nenets, the head of the threatened tribe, unhitched the sacred sledge of his clan from the deer who had been pulling it, and started to drag it himself towards the north from whence the strong snowstorm was blowing. He was an old man and the task was a heavy one. Suddenly from out of the snowstorm emerged his youngest grandson. The two of them pulled the sacred sledge on to a large hill, and as they watched, the hill began to loom skywards, raising the sacred sledge as it went. When it had risen to a certain level, the hill appeared to freeze over. At the same moment the weather changed drastically, and it felt as if there had never been any wind or blizzard. Like so many partridges, people began to shake free from their snowy captivity. After rounding up some of the deer and their possessions they made a sacrifice of three thoroughbred stags. The heads of the sacrificial deer were raised aloft on the hill together with the sacred sledge. The column moved on and for a long time the people looked back at their sacred sledge.

Ever since those times, the Nentsy have sacrificed deer on that hill, and antlers of those fine stalwarts of the north have surrounded the hill on all sides. In the spring, on their way to the village, people would stop at *Khekhe khan sote ya*, a senior man would climb to the top of the hill and place a *khangor* (bloodless sacrifice) there – a pinch of tobacco or a piece of bread. The spirit of the place would be asked for protection on the way back to the *choom*. The old people used to say that at one time there really had been a sledge there.

Near the fishing grounds of Mochui-Sale is the sacred site of *Sote ya tyortalva*, and opposite them, on the other side of the Yuratsk Inlet, there is a particularly holy place called *Sote ya*. It consists of an enormous pile of antlers and deer and polar bear skulls. A little lower down, at a height of 50 m, is a sacred site known as *Myad pukhutsya khebidya ya*, which was erected in honour of the (female) custodian of the tribe and family. When men offer sacrifices to *Sote ya*, the women stay at their own sacred site. They enact a ceremony in honour of the mother, or protectress, and cook the meat of the sacrificed deer. The cult sites are visited only by men, and there are only a few sacred sites for women. The fact that the main sacred sites are visited only by men is explained not merely by the need for bloody sacrifices to be carried out there, which women would not have been able to undertake, but also because the sacred sites were situated a long way from the camps. The main purpose of the ritual acts at that particular sacred site was to ensure the prosperity of the home and family.

There are many other legends that demonstrate the inextricable links between the culture of the Nenets and the landscape in which they live. One (related to L.L. by the Nenets writer, Anna Nerkagi) concerns Pike Lake (Figure 20.4): Nenets, god-like, used to be able to fly to the other world over Pike Lake which, at that time, was just a hole, and which itself was situated near to the mountain of Saura, in which the souls of the dead lived. No one had ever caught pike in Pike Lake, nor ever seen pike in the lake. The legend explains why it is nevertheless called Pike Lake.

A Nenets family lived on the shores of the lake. The father, who used to hunt and fish, had a son. The little boy, by the time he was three, loved to play on the shore of the lake and build things in the sand or collect pretty stones. One day, when his father had gone out to hunt, the little boy came out of his *choom* and began throwing stones into the lake. The lake took offence at the boy showing such lack of respect for it and hurled itself at the boy in the form of a large, sharp-toothed pike.

Figure 20.4 Pike Lake, a Nenets sacred site, in the mountains of the Arctic Urals.

When the father came back from his hunt, he could not find his son in the *choom*. For a long time he looked for him, shouted and called out after him, but everything was in vain – all he could find were large footprints leading out of the water and along the sand as if a large creature was roaming. Then the father made a doll out of the boy's long coat and placed it on the shore of the lake. In the night an enormous pike rose up out of the lake and crept along the sand towards the 'boy'. The father shot into the open jaws of the pike from his bow as it tried to seize the doll. He dragged the pike over towards him by hauling in the arrow he had shot, cut open its belly and pulled out his little boy, who was still alive.

Ever since then, the Nenets people, animals, nature and the lake have lived side by side, showing respect for each other (e.g. Figure 20.5).

In the Gydan Peninsula there is to date no active industrial development. Reconnaissance work is currently being carried out, but the gas deposits found have so far not been exploited. Most sacred sites also survived the post-1917 'campaign for atheism', but some were destroyed. A small sacred site near the village in which one of the authors (G.K.) lived was destroyed, and lost its significance. As recently as the early 1970s, people walking past the place would always show respect for it, tying pieces of red material to the antlers there and leaving behind sweets or coins. Then the geophysicists came and set up their poles on that beautiful hill, where in the summer

Figure 20.5 Deer in summer pastures near Pike Lake.

during the fishing season there would have stood between twenty and twenty-five *chooms*. The geophysicists completed their assignment and then left, leaving a pile of metal and rubbish behind them, and now no one approaches the sacred site any more.

In this part of the world, there are two very different civilisations living side by side, one that has been on our earth for over a thousand years and is represented by the Nenets, the Khanty and the Selkup peoples, and the second that reached our home when geologists, surveyors and oil and gas prospectors made their way to the Far North. We had expected that they would bring new prosperity to our part of the world, but they turned out to be ruthless and without mercy. Industrial civilisation sometimes totally ignores the people living in the tundra, particularly because being always on the move, and without any thought for the consequences of its actions, it tramples upon the ancient civilisation with its iron feet.

Notes

1   This chapter derives from two papers translated from the Russian by Katharine Judelson that were presented at WAC 3: the one by L.L. was entitled 'How the Nenets see the world' and the other by G.K. bore the same title as this chapter. The considerable editing needed to produce this chapter was undertaken by Jane Hubert.

2   In ancient times, Angal Cape in Salekhard was sacred and was a place of pilgrimage for Nentsy, Khanty and Komi Zyryane. The last rite performed in honour of the Spirit *Nasyadi salya* (Death-conquering Cape) was in 1953. Almost forty years

later, G.K. and others visited this sacred site, bringing with them three deer as a sacrifice, in accordance with the traditional customs of the three local tribes and in the name of all those who went there. As G.K. wrote, 'Once again there rang out over the tundra, and through the boundless taiga, songs of the all-seeing shamans – descendants of the ancient medicine men – to the sound of sledge bells. It was a festival to gladden heart and soul.'

21   Definition, ownership and conservation of indigenous landscapes at Salapwuk, Pohnpei, Micronesia

WILLIAM S. AYRES
AND RUFINO MAURICIO

Introduction

Landscape is a useful concept for archaeological interpretation because it represents the complex link between the natural and physical environment and culturally defined conceptions of the human place in that world. It represents a means of conceptual ordering that stresses relations (Tilley 1994: 34) and provides the places and temporality for narrative. Landscape includes identification and naming of features – or sites, landmarks and locales – and the shared understanding of their cultural significance as held by a community or cultural group. Archaeological evidence, oral and historical records in conjunction with physical sites, and the views of participants living on the land all serve as a basis for recognising and interpreting landscapes. Comprehensive, holistic landscape descriptions and analyses can be based on the intersecting perspectives of all three of these and represent an important archaeological integration.

Archaeological landscapes represent a distinct form of cultural landscape because they develop over long periods of time and they must be based on an incomplete cultural record (see, e.g. Gosden and Head 1994: 113). Basic approaches to formulating archaeological landscapes have included:

1 analysing regional site inter-relationships (a development out of settlement pattern studies);
2 studying catchment ecology (an outgrowth of settlement and ecological archaeology); and
3 developing social constructs of view, landmark integration and place.

The first is reflected in an emphasis on site distributional data (e.g. Crumley and Marquardt 1990); the second in site and non-site archaeology and site catchment analysis, for example that which integrates geomorphological data at the regional level (Rossignol and Wandsnider 1992); the third in phenomenological study of social history and historical context (e.g. Tilley 1994). This chapter examines the use of the landscape concept in archaeology, in particular as it affects archaeological methodology, the sustainability of historic preservation, and ownership of the past.

Documenting and understanding archaeological landscapes is essential for historic preservation and for cultural conservation because, without it, site 'significance' remains incomplete. Indigenous concepts, which in the Pacific Islands are most typically incorporated into oral traditions, can provide an ideological bridge between archaeological and contemporary expressions of landscape; access to this bridge may be attained through ethno-archaeology and ethno-history.

To possess or to own a landscape means to identify it systematically; it entails its intellectual creation and implies responsibility for maintaining it. 'Ownership' can range from the individual to the social group (see, e.g. Bender 1993: 3), but the most significant for archaeology is at the level of the group and culture. Central ownership issues concern rights to use both cultural and natural resources within the landscape. Ownership takes on special significance when we objectify the past through historic preservation. If landscape refers to an ideological framework, it cannot be 'owned' in a typical material property sense. The creators and perpetuators of such a framework can own it as intellectual property; however, western views of property ownership are often fundamental to historic preservation laws and programmes, so consequently questions of 'whose cultural resources' become real practical issues. Another practical concern of major archaeological interest is whether a landscape can be clearly bounded. How elements and complexes are inter-related may be more important than strict definition of physical boundaries.

As we gain more insight into the different ways of constructing landscapes, we recognise also the complexities of understanding their ownership. Inter-preting the regional archaeological record in terms of the social transformations that produced it can be accomplished by viewing social groups operating within the landscape to provide and sustain a social system (Gosden 1989). While this, perhaps, has more to do with archaeological model construction than with indigenous people's perceptions of ownership, we recognise that as local knowledge changes and diminishes, archaeological reconstruc-tions become more widely relied upon as a database for use, and reification, of traditional landscapes. Alternative constructed pasts depicting political landscapes at contrasting levels of geographical scale have become significant in political boundary controversies, for example in the contemporary Bougainville–Papua New Guinea case (Spriggs 1992). Here, these alternatives give new meaning to the term 'geopolitical landscape' and represent politi-cally contentious interpretations because they escalate ownership to a new level. Thus, how to identify and describe the landscape remains a problem clearly linked to issues of ownership. Pacific Islands provide insight into many issues of landscape definition and ownership because islanders emphasise use-rights and strict control of oral traditional delineation of landscape and because they 'transport' landscapes to remote settings by introducing many new plants and animals.

Islands offer valuable instances for investigating indigenous landscape and resource issues and for helping to formulate management strategies that in turn can provide for conservation and sustainable use of both cultural and natural resources (Beller et al. 1990). A number of world-wide conservation problems faced in sustaining natural resources and maintaining cultural identity in the tropics are highlighted in Pacific examples; here, traditional land-use methods have left both material culture remains and an archaeologically identifiable impact on the environment. Recognising that the environment and the landscape are culturally perceived – and thus that their management varies – is central to a linking of natural and cultural resources and the conservation measures built into every traditional way of life, both past and present.

Given the obvious limitations of natural materials on small, often remote islands – epitomised in the extreme by small coral atolls occupied in some cases for more than 2,000 years – cultural ecological analyses, including seascape–landscape relations, have been fundamental to interpretations of Pacific cultures. Anthropological interpretations of Pacific colonisation, adaptation and cultural evolution have focused on patterns of human control of resources and settlement ecology (e.g. Kirch 1980; Ayres et al. 1981; Shimizu 1982; Ayres and Haun 1990; Kirch and Ellison 1994).

The present natural resource situations in the Pacific are inextricably intertwined with past human uses and require specific plans for regional integration of environment and archaeology; this must include a landscape perspective. Cultural and natural conservation are viewed here as necessarily conjunctive efforts, and systematisation of the landscape concept within historic preservation provides an avenue for both islanders and archaeologists to participate in the process.

The Pohnpei resources project, Micronesia

Archaeological and historic preservation studies in Micronesia have been undertaken systematically only since the late 1970s, and so archaeological and cultural information necessary for historic preservation planning, conservation, site development and long-term public education is lacking for many major islands (Apple 1972; Ayres 1979; Cordy 1979; Hanlon 1979). It is regrettable that government management strategies have rarely connected natural and cultural resources. In an effort to help improve this situation, Micronesian governments, in cooperation with the US National Park Service, began in 1986 to undertake a Micronesia Resources Survey (MRS), a 'comprehensive inventory and study of the most unique and significant natural, historical, cultural, and recreational resources . . .' (Anonymous 1990; National Park Service n.d.).

An archaeological and cultural resources assessment project on Pohnpei Island, the capital of the newly emerged Pacific Island nation, Federated States of Micronesia (Figure 21.1), was carried out by the University of

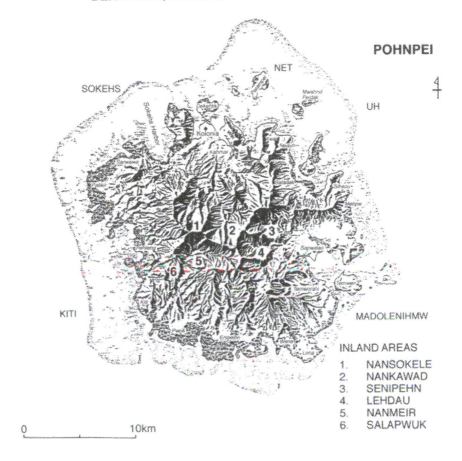

Figure 21.1   Pohnpei Island, Micronesia. Inland valleys or areas, including Salapwuk, traditionally controlled by the Sounkawad Clan are shown: 1. Nansokele; 2. Nankawad; 3. Senipehn; 4. Lehdau; 5. Nanmeir; 6. Salapwuk. (Map from US Army Corps of Engineers: Pohnpei Coastal Resources Atlas.)

Oregon to help formulate general procedures and evaluation steps applicable to all of Pohnpei as well as more broadly for the Federated States of Micronesia (FSM). Efforts were made to help train the Pohnpei Historic Preservation Office staff in field methods and to consult with community members about the importance of archaeological and cultural resource management and protection (see details in Ayres and Mauricio 1992; Ayres and Mauricio n.d.).

Pohnpei is the largest volcanic high island in Micronesia's eastern Caroline Islands, with somewhat more than 310 sq. km, and has a rugged, mountainous interior with central peaks rising to nearly 800 m above a fringing coral reef and lagoon edged with small volcanic and coral islets. Heavy rainfall of 4,650 mm annually, a high average temperature of 27° C, and rich volcanic soils support lush vegetation. The small inland community of Salapwuk in Kiti District, one of the five chiefly districts comprising the island, was selected for the field study of sites and landscapes. Because of its relative isolation, Salapwuk represents a traditional community where indigenous cultural practices, subsistence economy and knowledge of oral traditions prevail.

Past archaeological projects on Pohnpei have incorporated details from oral traditions into site interpretations and recommendations (see, e.g. Hambruch 1936; Denfeld 1979; Ayres 1985; Ayres et al. n.d.; Falgout 1987; Mauricio 1987; Mauricio 1993; Mauricio n.d.), but the Salapwuk survey required special efforts in developing this evidence because of the area's significance in the island's traditional history. We carried out our own ethnographic work in conjunction with the archaeology to develop a framework for social interaction during the fieldwork process, to acquire contemporary settlement and subsistence data, and to record traditions related to specific archaeological sites and natural features that have significance as cultural landmarks. Thus, archaeological resources are broadly defined to include not only direct evidence of past human activity, but also cultural landmarks or objects that do not necessarily preserve the results of human action. These landmarks are often natural features such as rocks, pools, ridges or even mountains that have associated oral traditions. They thus may serve as critical features of the social landscapes (Gosden 1989) that are significant for interpreting both archaeological and oral historical data.

Archaeological features on Pohnpei

Architectural ruins are found broadly throughout the tropical Pacific, and archaeological site types are diverse when variations in stone and earth constructions are taken into consideration, but most other site forms represent rather restricted forms. An understanding of stone architecture is central to almost all aspects of site and landscape analysis; the name 'Pohnpei' itself means 'upon a stone altar'. Ayres and Haun (1980; Ayres et al. 1981) have developed detailed classification coding systems for describing and analysing Pohnpeian stone architecture.

Stone architectural features comprise at least 80 per cent of Pohnpei's recorded sites. However, a variety of other physical indications of past human activity are equally important for settlement reconstruction and historic sites planning. The types distinguished are as follows: stone architectural features, earth constructions, shell middens, pottery sites, agricultural features (both stone and earth constructions), rockshelters, marine and reef sites (including fishing weirs, channels and artificial islands, especially Nan Madol), traditional landmarks, historic period sites (including Spanish, German, Japanese and US periods), and quarry sites.

The Salapwuk field project

Located in Pohnpei's southwestern interior, Salapwuk – a community of no more than 150 individuals at any one time – sits on an upland plateau over-looking the lagoon off the southwest coast. The overall research area covered approximately 600 ha, including Rasalap, Elen Pwai, Woaum Iap, Olotong and Lipwentiak adjacent to the Salapwuk plateau (Figure 21.2). Two types of terrain, flatland and slopes of up to 60 per cent or more, dominate the 339 ha of the Salapwuk plateau. Our research in Salapwuk to recover base-line archaeological data on inland Pohnpei included assessing:

1   written materials on archaeology and natural resources;
2   oral history;
3   settlement and land use; and
4   site survey data from selected areas.

Examples of all of the site types distinguished for Pohnpei, except the marine and reef sites, were found in Salapwuk. Recommendations for protection and use of prehistoric, historic and cultural materials were prepared as part of a planning and management information profile. We utilised the field study process itself to formulate general procedures and evaluation steps applicable to all of Pohnpei, as well as more broadly for Micronesia.

Contemporary Salapwuk settlement provides a living-culture occupation and land–use system that provides models for interpreting archaeological sites and landscape features as well as for defining natural locations having tradi-tional significance. However, an obstacle to interpreting patterns of early stone building within Pohnpeian society is that no ethnographically reported or modern-day construction in traditional style shows the magnitude of stone features found in Salapwuk or at major sites elsewhere. From the archaeo-logical record, particularly from the Nan Madol complex (Athens 1980; Ayres 1983; Ayres 1990), it appears that megalithic building was discontinued in the early nineteenth century AD. This cultural change leads to the necessity of inferring the function of structures from the attributes of remaining struc-tures and the few associated artefacts and, potentially, from associated oral traditions.

Site survey methods

Archaeological sites were identified by obtaining information from landowners, by walk-through survey where landowner permission was obtained, and by detailed investigation of selected sites after vegetation was cleared. Experi-ence on Pohnpei has established that the second method, the systematic, intensive, walk-through survey, is very time-consuming due to heavy vege-tation and rough terrain. To complete an intensive survey that will meet the standards of the Pohnpei Archaeological Survey conducted by the University of Oregon and those of the US National Park Service requires many person-hours per hectare; thus, the 'Salapwuk Area' had to be clearly

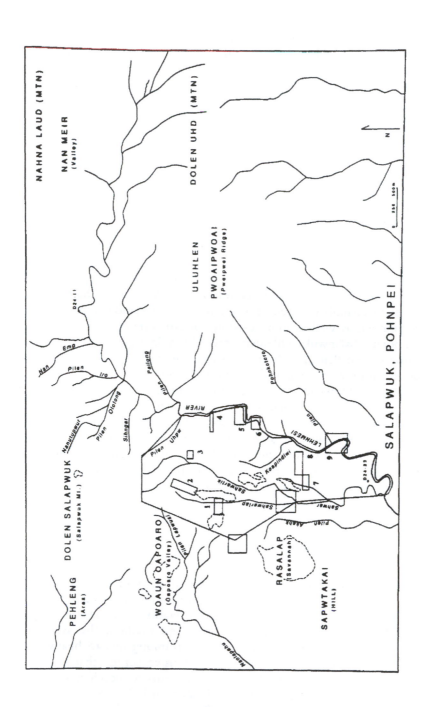

Figure 21.2 The Salapwuk Traditional Land Area showing major reconnaissance and intensive survey boundaries (1–9), Salapwuk, Pohnpei.

demarcated in terms of the local area (that is, Salapwuk section or *kousapw*) and, within this, in terms of the amount of land that could be examined first through reconnaissance and then through intensive study of selected locations (see Figure 21.2).

The significance of the Salapwuk settlement

Salapwuk is important because it is identified in oral traditions as the origin place of Pohnpei Island itself. Unusual materials representing environments not expected in the interior of a volcanic high island, such as coral and marine sand, are referenced in these local traditions. According to our informants, the Salapwuk landscape of ridges, streams, trenches, small valleys, savannahs, rocks, mounds, pools, and even trees is sacred and commemorates a deeply rooted belief system. Traditions detail clan histories, initial settlement histories, indigenous natural history concepts, and propitiation rituals to enhance the economic well-being of the entire island. The title of Soumw, a high priest of Kiti District, and the deities he worshipped are often mentioned. Narratives on the 'creation' and settlement of Salapwuk (Hambruch 1936: II, 162–4; Bernart 1977: 9) suggest that members of the Sounkawad, Lipitahn, Dipwinpahnmei and Dipwinmen clans were predominantly represented in Salapwuk during prehistoric times. Informants believe that the first legitimisation of *mwar* (the Pohnpeian chiefly title system) and its official bestowal occurred in Salapwuk.

Interactions with the contemporary Salapwuk community

To develop comprehensive historic preservation and conservation-related data, an essential step was to obtain information on the present community. Considerable time was spent on participant observation and inquiries regarding the current state of Salapwuk residents' knowledge of their environment and landscape. Contemporary settlement patterns, land-use practices, subsistence economy, traditional socio-political organisations, and belief systems related to landscapes represent a continuation of a cultural framework within which most Pohnpeians participate today. Approximately 150–200 individuals residing in eighteen households that are scattered over 350 ha of fertile valleyhead (*kahp*) land comprise Salapwuk's more permanent core. We developed a cooperative interaction with these community members, and, while this is expected of any field research situation, in Pohnpei it was essential for the training component of our work as well as for inquiring about landscapes. Household information aided in acquiring necessary details about land ownership and in better understanding the modern land-use pattern.

Discussions with the community members addressed the nature of our work and the importance of finding, recording and protecting the area's archaeological and natural resources. Inquiries from the community members varied, but two questions were asked often: Why are you doing this kind of work in Salapwuk? and What are the benefits for the Salapwuk people? Our answers referred to the project goals and the long-range educational and management benefits for the community and for Pohnpei state. A questionnaire in the Pohnpeian language was used and members of individual families helped in developing information on community social organisation and attitudes about resources. We found that opinions about archaeological sites vary greatly. Some individuals want to safeguard cultural resources because they are sacred, while others favourably anticipate economic exploitation. A few community members do not want government regulations to be imposed on their lands.

Problems in obtaining detailed oral traditions were expected because Pohnpeian custom requires some degree of secrecy that controls the revelation of such knowledge (Petersen 1993). A person not born into a Pohnpeian community does not have an automatic right to investigate or discuss certain classes of archaeological materials considered sacred in that community unless specific permission from the knowledgeable senior community members is given. Granting permission is often accompanied by instruction in the appropriate behaviours and in some cases by protective sacred formulae to be used when visiting the sites. An integral component of this belief in Pohnpei is the strong feeling and right of ownership to three equally important and complementary elements: the land on which the archaeological and cultural sites exist, the physical remains of these resources, and the knowledge and history of these resources. We obtained permission to research each of the three components and we recognised and respected this cultural belief for its capacity to promote and help develop indigenous conservation and preservation efforts. We were able to improve our understanding of local interpretations of historic properties and geographical areas, and, regulated by a constant permission-consultation process, our walk-through survey approach was successful.

Salapwuk land-use practices
The observations and inquiries in Salapwuk produced three general land-use categories that we view as essential for documenting both the physical and the settlement-subsistence landscapes (see Pickering 1994: 157). Land Use I represents all-purpose or general cultivation of areas within the vicinity of main household units. Land Use II involves cultivation of garden pockets away from the main households and the surrounding regularly cultivated areas. Land Use III refers to general cultivation of 'new land' (*sapwakapw*) that is located away from the regularly cultivated plots (*peliensapw*) and the community. This typology provides a framework that, even though simplified, represents some important venues of the evolution of the traditional land tenure system and use patterns – that is, a chronological settlement or prehistoric land-use trend – and it reflects the everyday practices that pertain to the relationship between cultivation, residency and landscape.

Soil types as one other aspect of land use were explored (Ayres and Mauricio 1992). Incorporating the indigenous understanding of soils into historic preservation considerations offers a culturally specific soil selection pattern and a system readily understandable to island landowners.

Summary of Salapwuk survey results

Many traditional and archaeological sites were recorded and these represent just a small portion of the rich cultural heritage preserved in Salapwuk. Definitions of archaeological district, site, archaeological structure, archaeological object, and two categories of the traditional, culturally significant natural entities, local landscapes or locales and objects, were developed and applied in the survey (Ayres and Mauricio 1992; Ayres and Mauricio n.d.: 132–3). Systematic, intensive survey was conducted in order to obtain samples of site frequency distribution in four well-represented environmental types on the Salapwuk plateau, including savannah, hill top, non-savannah flatlands, and slopes. Of the four environmental types selected, the savannahs were completely examined and samples were completed in other areas. Systematic walk-through was undertaken in three areas of the northern flatlands.

Forty-four prehistoric and historic sites and complexes, typically formed by clusters of earth and stone architecture, were identified and recorded in Salapwuk. An example of such complexes is the Diwien Loang site, which is associated with the priest called Soumw and is often referred to by Pohnpeians today who have not even seen it because it is believed to be crucial for maintaining the island's rich resources.

The most common sites recorded (39 per cent) are stone architectural features (house platforms, tombs, pavements and retaining walls). Thirty-four per cent of the sites are earth constructions (underground tunnels, trenches, mounds, and pits of various types including food storage pits). Shell middens and rockshelters comprise 4 per cent and traditional landmarks represent 23 per cent of the sites.

Based on site distributions in five terrain types – forested flatlands, hill tops, savannah flatlands, moderate slope terrain, and restricted flats situated on steep slopes – prehistoric inland settlement on Pohnpei was extensive. Seventy-eight per cent of the stone architectural sites were found in the flatlands and the restricted level areas on steep slopes. The earth construction sites were represented throughout the five terrain types, but 52 per cent were found in the flatland areas.

Stone architectural remains that are known and protected by the people of Salapwuk include the Pehi Sarawi site (designation PoD24–36). This isolated structure (Figure 21.3) preserves some typical Pohnpeian construction methods and building forms. More unusual is Koapinloangen Oaloahs (literally, the bottom of Heaven – west of Oaloahs), a prehistoric rectangular enclosure located centrally in the savannah of the same name; it is the largest site found thus far in Salapwuk, occupying an area of 10,000 sq. m. The enclosing walls are formed by long earth mounds (*uluhl*) rather than the more common stone construction. The east wall, typical of the overall enclosure, measures 130 m long, 5 m wide and 1.5 m high. Most of the interior is devoid of structures, with the exception of a centrally located rectangular earth mound rising up to 1 m above the surface; no artefacts were observed. Soulikin Semwei reported that this was probably used for ritual to predict

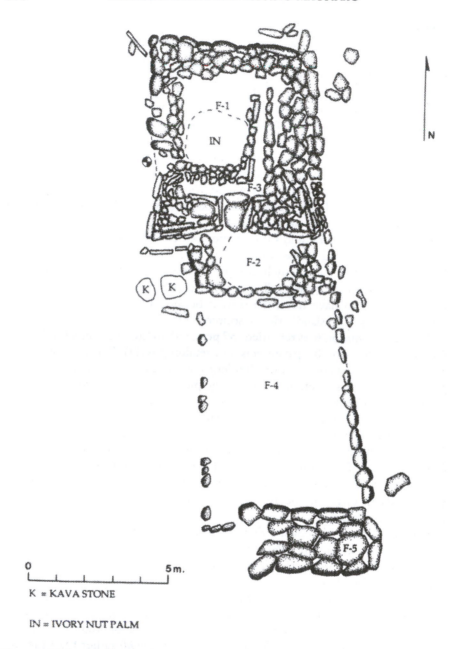

N

0   5 m.

K = KAVA STONE

IN = IVORY NUT PALM

Figure 21.3 An important ritual platform, a prehistoric site referred to as Pehi Sarawi (D24–36), Salapwuk, Pohnpei.

and control the weather. Members of the community maintain a respectful attitude toward this ritually significant site which, from its context, as seen in Figure 21.4, epitomises some of the main features of Salapwuk landscape: Salapwuk Mountain, in the background, forms part of the remote and ritually significant interior mountain core of Pohnpei, and the open fern savannah with the site shows the physical evidence of human efforts to understand and live with, or even control, the natural forces affecting the island's fertility.

Many archaeological sites and landmarks are associated with present-day residences and named land holdings. For example, Pohnmoaloawoa (D24–27) consists of a prehistoric boulder alignment and associated earth mounds and a badly disturbed house platform located north of the present Moaloawoahlap household, designated D24–28. A pit for breadfruit starch food storage and a larger, poorly preserved stone structure – partially destroyed when a recent stone fence was built – are associated with the platform.

We were allowed to record information, which was controlled by the senior male head of the Salapwuk Dipwinpehpe Clan, concerning ten traditional landmark sites. Five are large basalt boulders, four are freshwater pools (three of which were found in Lehnmesi River) and one is a waterfall. The traditional landmark sites represent key resources for defining landscapes; they fall into two general categories distinguished as Culturally Significant Natural Landscapes (CSNL) and Culturally Significant Natural Objects (CSNO). In

Figure 21.4 The Koapinloangen Oaloahs site (D24–12) is the large rectangular enclosure made by an earthen embankment to the west of the Community meeting house, Salapwuk, Pohnpei. Salapwuk Mountain (Dolen Salapwuk) is in the left background.

general, CSNL include mountains, ridges, streams, rivers or pools, reef flats, portions of lagoon, channels, prehistoric shoreline ports of entry (known as *sakar*), savannahs, valleys and waterfalls, and are equivalent to what Tilley (1994: 18) has distinguished as 'locale'. The local histories of these landmark sites commemorate significant past events that pertain to natural history concepts, prehistoric settlement, and social and ideological elements of Pohnpeian society. CSNO include natural boulders and outcrops, soil and plants. The local histories of these objects clearly indicate their specific uses (medicinal, for example) and the beliefs that are associated with them. All of these site type distinctions are considered fundamental to the process of defining sites and determining their significance. The Salapwuk sites are now considered historic properties of Pohnpei State, and historic preservation officials and members of the Historic Preservation Board, in consultation with local residents, will ultimately determine their significance for those purposes.

Landscape features summary

Some of the most significant topics in Salapwuk's landscape definition include the origin of Pohnpei itself, the richness of the island's resources, and clan origins. The concepts of island formation, with basalt rock, coral, and sand representing the coast, are found at Sokosok en Loang (D24–8), where a large stone boulder – also called Salapwuk Rock (3.0 by 2.6 by 0.75 m in size) – reportedly once had a coral clump attached to it. Another piece of brain coral now sits on top of the boulder. This is viewed locally as the place where Pohnpei rose from the sea, that is, the actual physical remains of the emergent island's volcanic rock and attached coral reef. This rock is called Sokosok en Loang (landing of Heaven) because it was on this rock that the deity, Luhk, came down and bestowed the title Soumwen Leng, the highest priestly title on the island. The people of Salapwuk take pride in their guardianship of this boulder and its significance for the origins of the Pohnpeians and their identity. Because the title Soumwen Leng was originally bestowed not by humans but by a god, it is considered the highest title of great antiquity on the island. For this reason, Salapwuk was an independent polity under the leadership of Soumw until the turn of the century.

At Lehnpoudek (D24–46) on the upper Lehnmesi River, the rocky bank of a river pool – measuring 36 by 20 m and up to 4 m deep – represents an old Pohnpei shore where prehistoric voyagers arrived. The impressions left by their canoe poles are preserved in the rock. Limwehtu, a legendary founder of Pohnpei, is associated with this pool, and the Lihm en Salapwuk (Site D24–48) is a boulder resembling the shape of a traditional canoe-bailing implement. It is a deeply weathered vesicular boulder measuring 1.2 m across that sits partially buried in the soil; it has a 70-cm wide natural depression in it (Figure 21.5). We were told that this stone represents one of the important implements used during the initial settlement of the island.

Many sites, including ones with stone architecture, relate to the role of Salapwuk's priestly leader Soumw in maintaining the island's natural life and regulating its interface with humans. Diwien Loang (D24–9) is one of Pohnpei's most important traditional sites and is associated with the island's fertility. It consists only of a small U-shaped trench in an area 12 by 15 m, but it forms a complex with other features, including stone architecture (Figure 21.6). Its two wing trenches are believed to have extended across the island to connect with other districts. A rectangular platform near the Diwien Loang trench is the remnant of Mwei Ier's house (D24–34); he was one of the Soumws. In addition, a badly disturbed platform (D24–35) approximately 10 m west of the trench is reputed to be the remains of a meeting house (*nahs*) built by one of the last Soumws. Takain Pwong (Night Rock; D24–45), representing Soumw's dwelling house, is a large boulder or outcrop located at the edge of the Lehnmesi River (Figure 21.7). It has a rockshelter of 13 by 7 m and roughly 2 m high located underneath; Soumw apparently conducted human sacrifices here with his high priests, who consumed the sacrificial victims' flesh. Another boulder located 15 m south of the 'dwelling house' represents his cookhouse.

Soumw and his priests are believed to have possessed the wisdom and power to foretell future events. This wisdom was apparently derived from their intricate knowledge of divination (*kosetipw* and *pwe*), divining through various ways of counting knots made on palm or other leaves and supernatural powers

Figure 21.5 View to the northeast of the rock called Lihm en Salapwuk, Pohnpei. This is an object and landmark site (D24–48).

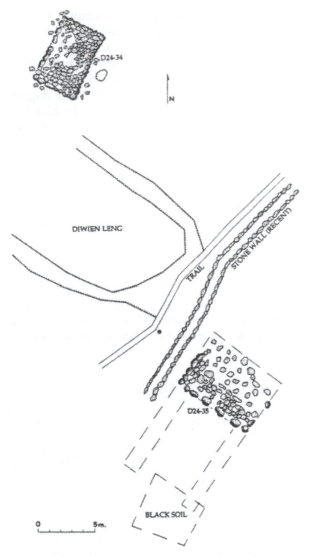

Figure 21.6 Plan view of the stone architecture and trenches at the Diwien Loang site (D24–9), Salapwuk, Pohnpei.

derived from their knowledge of powerful spells. According to oral traditions, Soumw predicted the coming of a *pwong poatoapoat* (literally, continuous darkness – possibly a solar eclipse – see Hambruch 1936: III, 316–17). In this episode, Soumw captured the night or darkness under the massive rock and it is thus named after this event. The current account is very similar to an explanation given to Hambruch (1936: III, 317) by the oral historian Luis Kehoe in the early 1900s.

Figure 21.7   View to the north up the Lehnmesi River at the Takain Pwong Site. Soumw's house is the overhang and cave to the right (D24–45), Salapwuk, Pohnpei.

Clan origins are an important element in Micronesian oral traditions (Goodenough 1986; Mauricio 1987) and these are often connected to landmarks and sites. Several sites relate to the origins of the Lipitahn Clan and in particular the deeds of its folk heroes known as Sarapwahu and Mwohnmwur. Sahwartik and Sahwarlap, high waterfalls in a deep gorge (site D24–24, a prehistoric landscape locale CSNL), are reputed to be among the great works of these legendary brothers. The Takain Roakoaroak site (D24–25) is a large boulder linked to the legendary figure Loapoango, also of the Lipitahn Clan. Two earth mounds located nearby are constructed prehistoric features. The Lipwentiak landmark site (D24–11) is a natural pool in a small river representing Lasialap Clan origins (ancestral freshwater eel).

Salapwuk's landscape significance

Salapwuk's landscape may be interpreted as replicating or embodying social and political relationships at both the local (e.g. clans) and island-wide levels. The term 'salapwuk' means 'to tie up a sennit knot', which symbolises the sacredness and secrecy of oral traditions about Mwasangap, which has to do with the richness of the land. Pohnpeians in general view Salapwuk as part of a mythical landscape and its people as the guardians of important facets of Pohnpei cultural identity and tradition. A very limited number of people, in select clans, hold much of this information today for the larger public. In one view, Salapwuk might be considered to represent ownership of all of Pohnpei by the local groups responsible for developing and perpetuating these concepts. This landscape has a strong ecological foundation because of its relationship to the physical formation of the island itself, to food production, especially plant fertility and cultivation of breadfruit, yams and kava, as well as to the island's productivity in a more general sense. Thus, Salapwuk represents something for all Pohnpeians.

While Salapwuk reflects primarily a clan and food-production-based view of the landscape, this contrasts with an island that was systematically both politically unified and dissected by a centralised chiefly system located at Nan Madol, on Pohnpei's east coast; this marks the evolution of the island's most complex chiefdom (see Ayres 1990; Mauricio n.d.): Nan Madol, with its elaborate stone architecture dominating the coral reef flat, dwarfs even the largest stone megalithic monuments found in Salapwuk (Figure 21.8). Nan Madol shows a built environment landscape – linking oral traditions, genealogy, and an archaeologically marked historical landscape – that establishes the legitimacy of ruling lines, documents hegemony, and validates traditional history. It thus serves to illustrate the social or political hierarchy and to subjugate and enculturate.

Other Pacific Islands landscapes that establish legitimacy of ruling lines and validate traditions through archaeological and historical landscapes show many parallels to the Nan Madol situation. For example, a landscape that provides a mnemonic device with permanent markers in the form of tombs was constructed in prehistoric Tonga to mark the status of rulers and of their leadership rights. According to Burley (1993), this demonstrated chiefly rights over labour and professional skills and the rights of the highest chiefs to scarce natural resources. It is less clear what the implications are for ownership; the landscape Burley describes is created and manipulated at the request of the ruling chief, but is it 'owned' by such chiefs? Its perpetuation over time suggests that it becomes larger than the individual chief or chiefly line.

Salapwuk's landscapes, like those in Tonga, replicate social or political relationships at both local level and island-wide interactions. However, because of the strong ecological significance of Salapwuk's ritual landscape, which provides for the island's fertility and productivity, this represents important values for all Pohnpeians and it is thus a landscape potentially owned or claimed by islanders beyond Salapwuk.

Preservation and conservation perspectives

Viewing culturally significant natural objects, landmarks and landscapes as cultural resources represents a preservationist perspective that has ideological

Figure 21.8 View of two massive boulders forming the northernmost portion of the Rakuh Hill retaining wall/enclosure, Site D24–15, Salapwuk, Pohnpei.

and political implications for the historical representation of Pohnpei's past. Implementing this requires that Pohnpeians specifically address the issue of which parts of their culture they wish to preserve. In North America, the process of cultural resource management, conceived in western epistemology and law, has forced Native Americans to move away from traditional resource conservation, which relied on total landscape protection and outsider exclusion, termed 'holistic conservation', to resource selection and prioritisation, termed 'cultural triage' (Stoffle and Evans 1990: 91–2). Holistic conservation responses may not provide practical and effective results when pitted against government policies and the requirements of cultural resource management and development, while, in contrast, responses reflecting the cultural triage position are reasonable and practical and increase the probability that certain resources will be protected. However, cultural triage requires an objectification of culture and its remains that forces a redefining of the past (see, e.g. Krause 1992) and heightens concerns over ownership.

The shift from the holistic-conservation to the cultural-triage perspective is evident on Pohnpei, although it is not as marked here as, for example, in the US, including Hawaii, or elsewhere in the Pacific such as on Easter Island. In Pohnpei, this shift is the result of three inter-related factors. Recent historic and cultural management on Pohnpei has been conceived and implemented within the framework of

1   pertinent US policies and laws (and since 1987 by Pohnpeian and national laws and policies),
2   western intellectual and academic traditions, and
3   relevant indigenous knowledge, responses and behaviours toward the resources in question.

The interactive network of these three elements can serve to produce a forum on cultural and historic sites issues where better understanding is reached for management procedures and policies.

In Salapwuk, the residents' inquiries reflected differing perceptions of such fundamental historic preservation concepts as 'development', 'historic and cultural properties' and 'ownership' of land and the resources on it. Other questions from the community show the need for better explanations of 'preservation and utilisation' of cultural and historic sites. When historic and cultural 'properties' were identified and explained in terms of historic 'resources', the members of the community had to wrestle with the question of whose 'properties' are being transformed into whose 'resources'. Parker and King (1989: 12–13) provide relevant definitions of the above terms or concepts for traditional properties and these need to be discussed, evaluated and, if need be, modified in accordance with Pohnpeian needs. Oral traditions (narratives) about sites, social organisation, arts, technology, subsistence and belief systems (including magical chants and herbal medicine) must be considered properties of individuals, groups (clans and lineages), communities or even districts, but this can be accomplished through triage only if such information can be safeguarded and protected by its owners.

Summary and conclusions

Salapwuk landscapes are constructed by connecting physical sites with their oral traditions and historical records, by aligning these with archaeological data, and by showing their intersection with the views of participants living on the land. It should be clear that archaeological landscapes are not isomorphic with ones maintained through oral traditions. Creating archaeological landscapes, which represent a special facet of cultural landscape, must be viewed as a long-term process because of the limited preservation of the past and long prehistoric–historic time spans.

When historic preservation and cultural resources are at issue, archaeological site 'significance' evaluations remain incomplete without considering landscape. As a result, landscape concepts are significant for archaeology and its methodologies, the sustainability of historic preservation, and ownership of the past. When objectification of the past within the context of historic preservation takes place, ownership rights to use both cultural and natural resources take on special significance. Indigenous concepts, most typically found in oral history, are essential for providing an ideological connection between the present occupants on the land – who are indispensable for sustainable site and resource conservation – and the archaeologist's landscape delineation.

Islands represent valuable cases for examining indigenous landscapes. Pacific Islanders, who have emphasised use-rights and strict control of oral historical delineation of landscape and who transported biotic landscapes to remote settings, can provide insight into many issues of landscape definition and ownership. Application of the landscape concept in historic preservation endeavours provides an avenue for both islanders and archaeologists to participate in the process.

Site survey

In Salapwuk, dissemination of information about sites and even their locations was strictly controlled, and our investigation of oral traditions and their physical counterparts in the area required adjustments in field methodology. As field archaeologists systematically recording sites, our activities had to reflect our anthropological awareness and had to respond to the community's perceptions and concerns about the sites and concepts about the past.

The significant differences of site distributions in Salapwuk's five terrain types demonstrate that assessment of archaeological resources for historic preservation purposes cannot be done independently of scientifically defined environmental concepts and parameters; however, when indigenous knowledge – such as the architectural or soil classification systems that we developed – is available, this adds an entirely new dimension for determining site significance and appropriate conservation measures. Although further systematic study of non-western conservation practices and concepts is needed, the existing Salapwuk survey provides sufficient information for archaeological site and cultural planning, conservation assessment, parks development, and other needs of the Pohnpei Historic Preservation Office and the Department of Land. The survey results improve substantially the state-wide inventory and they also provide insight into the nature of early ritual complexes that are valuable for interpreting many culturally important centres on Pohnpei, including the famous Nan Madol complex.

Although closely safeguarded in Salapwuk and throughout the island, a rich body of knowledge (oral traditions) exists about sites showing past human activity and other, non-site locations. Oral traditions are treated, in the context of our research, as cultural resources subject to conservation and preservation when development and accelerated modernisation threaten their integrity. While oral traditions are important for site conservation and for education, such uses bring into focus the question of who owns the traditions and the landscapes that are made intelligible from them.

The oral traditions about Salapwuk and the specific archaeological and natural resources in it support the conclusion that Salapwuk was transformed into a historical landscape filled with iconic representations. Bends of rivers commemorate initial settlement, boulders represent spirits or gods, savannahs represent arenas where songs and dances were stolen from the island in the ancient times. Many of these relate to the island's creation and settlement and the islanders' cosmological beliefs. In this respect, Salapwuk's landscape preserves for the Pohnpeians now and in the future important elements of Pohnpeian culture and history; it also maintains the principles of a conservation and preservation framework already built into the local culture and its history. We prefer to identify this as 'culture-based conservation' and consider it to be 'holistic', but in a somewhat broader, anthropological way compared to Stoffle and Evans (1990).

Politically, this culture-based conservation reflects a holistic conservation position that directly confronts the dilemma of preservation versus development and enables the people of Salapwuk and Pohnpei to consider appropriate steps and measures for the development and preservation of their cultural and historical resources. Both indigenous views of resource significance and conservation of cultural and environmental resources and the critical counterpart of western scientific interpretation and management are fundamental to long-term sustainable use of the tropical landscape.

The occasion of the quincentenary of Columbus's voyage to America brought heightened public awareness of the historical past because so much attention was focused on alternative interpretations of this event's significance. According to Hill (1992), this reflects a transition from a neo-colonial to a post-colonial world order that has highlighted the significance of conflicting, or alternative, ideas of how history is objectified and made significant to contemporary peoples.

In most Pacific Islands, an imported education system with its foundation in western science and democracy or egalitarianism has served to produce a new elite with differing views of traditional history (see Falgout 1992 for Pohnpei), with the consequence that cultural landscapes are becoming more complicated and are appreciated by wider, and differing, segments of the community. Micronesians are trying to use western methods and resource objectification of culture to achieve a public use of history and heritage (Krause 1992). As in all such cases, there is resultant reification; however, this is a continuing process. Thus, successful historic preservation or cultural resource management requires a broadening of meaning systems and recognition of various levels of landscape ownership.

One purpose in doing the Salapwuk project was to develop indigenous and alternative rather than just archaeological constructions of the past for accomplishing historic preservation aims. If alternative views can be developed along with the archaeologist's in cases of on-going landscape creation and use, for example, by ethnographers or by local cultural groups, these can broaden archaeological interpretation significantly.

Who owns the landscape? One way of addressing this issue is to view the landscape in terms of the politics of enactment that allows for change and correction. Pohnpei always seems to have had contested landscapes, ones that were primarily of interest to Pohnpeians. In Salapwuk, the new landscapes now interlink people at the Pohnpei local and national levels, outsiders and insiders, and archaeologists and traditional oral historians. Perhaps of necessity in the face of rapid social change and expected historic preservation needs, 'ownership' of Salapwuk landscapes has become more public, more complicated, and more openly contested because the landscape itself has taken on new meanings. We undertook an interactive project incorporating many voices in order to move towards a more integrative perspective allowing for alternative pasts.

Acknowledgements

Emensio Eperiam and his staff in the Pohnpei State Historic Preservation Office generously shared their facilities in addition to contributing valuable guidance and information. Mr Melsohr Gilmete, Mr Reti Lawrence and Mr Masao Hadley helped in the field study and shared information about oral traditions. Mr Dave Henry assisted in the field project. We especially wish to thank the members of the Salapwuk community, including in particular Soulikin Semwei (Donio Pellep), the late Oaulik Mwasangap (Pernis Washington), and Nahnkiroun Mwasangap (Kapiriel Washington).

References

Anonymous 1990. *Keepers of the Treasures: protecting historic properties and cultural traditions on Indian lands.* Washington: US Department of the Interior, Interagency Resources Division.

Apple, R. 1972. *Micronesian Parks: a proposal.* Saipan: US Dept. of the Interior, Trust Territory of the Pacific Islands.

Athens, S. 1980. *Archaeological Investigations at Nan Madol: islet maps and surface artifacts.* Guam: Pacific Studies Institute.

Ayres, W.S. 1979. Archaeological survey in Micronesia. *Current Anthropology* 20, 598–600.

Ayres, W.S. 1983. Archaeology at Nan Madol, Ponape. *Indo-Pacific Prehistory Association Bulletin* 4, 135–42.

Ayres, W.S. 1985. Micronesian prehistory: research on Ponape, Eastern Caroline Islands. In *Recent Advances in Indo-Pacific Prehistory*, V.N. Misra and P. Bellwood (eds), 399–409. New Delhi: Oxford and IBH.

Ayres, W.S. 1990. Pohnpei's position in Eastern Micronesian prehistory. *Micronesica* Supplement 2, 187–212.

Ayres, W.S. and A.E. Haun 1980. *Ponape Archaeological Survey: 1977 Research.* Saipan: Historic Preservation Office.

Ayres, W.S. and A.E. Haun 1990. Prehistoric food production in Micronesia. In *Pacific Production Systems: approaches to economic prehistory*, D. Yen and M.J.M. Mummery (eds), 211–27. Canberra: Research School of Pacific Studies, Australian National University.

Ayres, W.S. and R. Mauricio 1992. Indigenous landscapes, historic preservation and environmental conservation. In *Environment and Archaeology: proceedings of the New World Conference on Rescue Archaeology, 1992*, A.G. Pantel, K.A. Schneider and G. Loyola-Black (eds), 280–94. San Juan, P.R./Atlanta: Organization of American States and US Forest Service, Southern Region.

Ayres, W.S. and R. Mauricio n.d. *Salapwuk Archaeology: a survey of historic and cultural resources on Pohnpei, Federated States of Micronesia.* Washington: US National Park Service.

Ayres, W.S., A.E. Haun and C. Severance 1981. *Ponape Archaeological Survey: 1978 research*. Saipan: Historic Preservation Office.

Ayres, W.S., A.E. Haun and R. Mauricio n.d. *Nan Madol Archaeology: 1981 survey and excavations*. Saipan: Historic Preservation Office.

Beller, W., P. d'Ayala and P. Helm (eds) 1990. *Sustainable Development and Environmental Management of Small Islands*. Paris: UNESCO/Parthenon.

Bender, B. 1993. *Landscape: politics and perspectives*. Oxford: Berg.

Bernart, L. 1977. *The Book of Luelen*. Honolulu: University of Hawaii Press.

Burley, D. 1993. Chiefly prerogatives over critical resources: archaeology, oral traditions and symbolic landscapes in the Ha'apai Islands, Kingdom of Tonga. In *Culture and Environment: a fragile co-existence*, R. Jamieson, S. Abonyi and N. Mirau (eds), 437–43. Calgary: University of Calgary.

Cordy, R. 1979. *The Trust Territory Historic Preservation Program: its framework and projects since 1977*. Saipan, Marianas Islands: Office Report 79–1.

Crumley, C. and W.H. Marquardt 1990. Landscape: a unifying concept in regional analysis. In *Interpreting Space: GIS and archaeology*, K.M.S. Allen, S.W. Green and E.B.W. Zubrow (eds), 73–9. London: Talyor & Francis.

Denfeld, D. "C." 1979. *Field Survey of Ponape: World War II features*. Saipan: Historic Preservation Office.

Falgout, S. 1987. *Master Part of Heaven: the ethnohistory and archaeology of Wene, Pohnpei, Eastern Caroline Islands*. Micronesian Archaeological Survey Report Series No. 22. Saipan.

Falgout, S. 1992. Hierarchy vs. democracy: two strategies for the management of knowledge in Pohnpei. *Anthropology and Education Quarterly* 23, 30–43.

Goodenough, W. 1986. Sky world and this world: the place of Kachaw in Micronesian cosmology. *American Anthropologist* 88, 551–68.

Gosden, C. 1989. Prehistoric social landscapes of the Arawe Islands, West New Britain Province, Papua New Guinea. *Archaeology in Oceania* 24, 45–58.

Gosden, C. and L. Head. 1994. Landscape: a usefully ambiguous concept. *Archaeology in Oceania* 29, 113–16.

Hambruch, P. 1936. Ponape. In *Ergebnisse der Sudsee Expedition 1908–1910, II and III*, Thilenius (ed.). Hamburg: Friederichsen, DeGruyter.

Hanlon, D. 1979. *From Mesenieng to Kolonia: an archaeological survey of historic Kolonia*. Saipan: Historic Preservation Office.

Hill, J.D. 1992. Contested pasts and the practice of anthropology: overview. *American Anthropologist* 94, 819–25.

Kirch, P.V. 1980. Polynesian prehistory: cultural adaptation in island ecosystems. *American Scientist* 68, 39–48.

Kirch, P.V. and J. Ellison 1994. Paleoenvironmental evidence for human colonization of remote Oceanic islands. *Antiquity* 68, 310–21.

Krause, E.L. 1992. The looking glass of historic preservation in Micronesia: a reflection on modernization. *Human Organization* 51, 1–4.

Mauricio, R. 1987. Peopling of Pohnpei Island: migration, dispersal and settlement themes in clan narratives. *Man and Culture in Oceania* 3, 47–72.

Mauricio, R. 1993. Ideological bases for power and leadership on Pohnpei, Micronesia: perspectives from archaeology and oral history. Unpublished Ph.D. dissertation, University of Oregon, Eugene.

Mauricio, R. n.d. Ethnoarchaeological observations of Pohnpei chiefdom. Unpublished Interim Report submitted to Historic Preservation Office and Pohnpei Historic Preservation Committee. March 1986. Ms.

National Park Service n.d. *Micronesian Resources Study: protecting historic properties and cultural traditions in the Freely Associated States of Micronesia*. Washington: US National Park Service, Interagency Resources Division.

Parker, P. and T. King. 1989. Guidelines for the evaluation and documentation of traditional cultural properties. Unpublished Ms. Washington, DC: National Park Service, Interagency Resources Division.

Petersen, G. 1993. Kanengamah and Pohnpei's politics of concealment. *American Anthropologist* 95, 334–52.

Pickering, M. 1994. The physical landscape as a social landscape: a Garawa example. *Archaeology in Oceania* 29, 149–61.

Rossignol, J. and L. Wandsnider (eds) 1992. *Space, Time, and Archaeological Landscapes*. New York: Plenum.

Shimizu, A. 1982. Chiefdom and the spatial classification of the life-world: everyday life, subsistence and the political system on Ponape. In *Islanders and their Outside World*, M. Aoyagi (ed.), 153–215. Tokyo: Committee for Micronesian Research.

Spriggs, M. 1992. Alternative prehistories for Bourgainville: regional, national, or micronational. *The Contemporary Pacific* 4, 269–98.

Stoffle, R. and M. Evans. 1990. Holistic conservation and cultural triage: American Indian perspectives on cultural resources. *Human Organization* 49, 91–9.

Tilley, C. 1994. *A Phenomenology of Landscape*. Oxford/Providence: Berg.

22 Exploring the prehistory of hunter-gatherer attachments to place: an example from the Keep River area, Northern Territory, Australia

RICHARD FULLAGAR AND LESLEY HEAD

Exploring the prehistory of landscapes

Recently there has been increased interest in landscape across a number of disciplines, including anthropology, archaeology, geography and history. Despite fascination with the concepts of anthropology and geography, particularly those that situate material objects in social and symbolic contexts, archaeologists are suspicious of the extent to which such contexts can be reconstructed from archaeological evidence. Is it at all possible to discern symbolism and perception from material remains?

Such reconstruction is problematic enough for archaeologists studying monuments, villages or field systems (see, e.g. Cooney, Fairclough, Fleming and Widgren, this volume), and it is even more so for those researching hunter-gatherer societies (Head et al. 1994). Many hunter-gatherer groups, while leaving minimal archaeological remains, are known from ethnographic sources to have led rich symbolic lives and had strong attachment to particular parts of the landscape. In this chapter we explore the possibility of discerning those links in the archaeological record, and thus of examining people's attachment to place over long time-scales. We do this by comparing a particular Dreaming story from the Keep River region of northwestern Australia with the archaeological record from the Jinmium rockshelter in the same region. We argue that while the antiquity of the story can never be known, the antiquity of mapped landscapes, and of perceived links with specific places, can be traced over thousands of years.

Dimensions of landscape

Four identifiable but not mutually exclusive approaches to the concept of 'landscape' can be identified (see Head 1993 for more detailed discussion). Each of these has relevance to the ways in which we interpret prehistoric landscapes. The first is the idea of a cultural landscape being an anthropogenic transformation of the biophysical landscape. In the hunter-gatherer context of this chapter, a transformed landscape is one marked by stone quarries. Second, landscape is seen as an expression of social formations and relations. For example, the distribution of certain stone artefacts away from sources can tell us about exchange networks. A third theme is landscape as text, 'a medium to be read for the ideas, practices and contexts constituting the culture which created it' (Ley 1985: 419). Readings predicated on indigenous cultures are often very different from those derived by the scientific researcher. In the Keep River region, as the story presented below shows, prominent rocky outcrops and stone sources on the landscape are read as the evidence and manifestation of the activities of ancestral figures. The fourth theme, the appropriation and contestation of different views and parts of the landscape, arises from the competing readings identified in theme three. In this and many other regions of northern Australia, Aboriginal people and white pastoralists co-exist on and compete for the same land. An escarpment that for Aboriginal people contains sacred and significant sites has quite a different meaning and value for the pastoralist (Rose 1992; Strang, Chapter 15, this volume).

To develop a prehistory of landscape we therefore need to understand both the material expressions of these different approaches and, because they interact, the relationships between them. In this chapter we present examples where all four approaches to landscape can be applied in the material outcomes of human cultural behaviour.

Prehistoric hunter-gatherer symbolic landscapes

Observers have long contrasted the complexity of Aboriginal social and symbolic life with the simplicity of Australian material culture. More recently, it has been recognised that the features of the landscape itself can be interpreted as artefacts of Aboriginal culture. The voices of Aboriginal people in land rights debates have emphasised the fundamental role of relations to land in their way of life. Indeed Morphy (1993: 206) argues that 'Australian Aborigines made landscape a key concept in the study of their society'. Noting that the links between landscape and Aboriginal conceptions of the world have been central to studies in Australian anthropology since Spencer and Gillen, at least, Morphy argues

> it is not simply that landscape is a sign system for mythological events, as is now well understood. Rather, the landscape is the referent for much of the symbolism. Too often landscape has been seen as an intervening sign system that serves the purpose of passing on information about the ancestral past. I would like to argue that landscape is integral to the message.
>
> (Morphy 1995: 186)

There have been some attempts to discuss the prehistory of symbolic landscapes, and they are briefly reviewed here. Jones (1990) has argued that the antiquity of the Dreaming may be derived from the antiquity of rock art and its conceptual basis. In some parts of Australia this is at least 20,000–30,000 years old. Taçon (1991), on the other hand, infers changes in the belief system from changing use of particular types of stone, arguing that the symbolic power of particular types of iridescent stone only became entrenched in the belief system in western Arnhem Land within the last 3,000 years. David et al. (1994) argue that in Wardaman country the most recent phase of rock-painting associated with the Dreaming has an antiquity of 900 to 1,400 years, suggesting that the culture of the Dreaming has undergone transformations over time. While change at one level does not necessarily contradict the premise of underlying continuity, these studies illustrate some of the difficulties of inferring landscape understandings from archaeological evidence.

This is not to suggest that archaeological constructions of the past and Aboriginal Dreaming myths should be seen as equivalent and compatible; clearly they are different sorts of stories drawing on different bases of authority (Davidson 1991). There is a link, however, when relations to land have material manifestations, that is where the actions of the Dreamtime heroes are expressed in evidence that archaeologists claim to be able to interpret. Our argument here depends on establishing links between the places linked by a particular Dreaming story and the material evidence found at the site.

The study area

The study area (Figure 22.1) lies within the monsoon tallgrass area of Australia's tropical savannahs (Mott et al. 1985), with a warm dry monsoonal climate. Mean annual rainfall is 750 mm at Kununurra and nearly 900 mm closer to the coast, virtually all of it falling in the wet season between November and March (Slatyer 1970). The Keep River drains dissected sandstone hills and their associated sandy alluvial plains supporting open *Eucalyptus* woodland. The lower Keep flows through alluvial and estuarine flood plains comprising cracking clays, known locally as the 'blacksoil', to bare salty mudflats at the coast.

Murinpatha, Jaminjung and Gadgerong people have ownership rights in this area, and the right to speak for the country. Some of these people live on Marralam Outstation (a small area, now freehold, excised from the Legune and Spirit Hills pastoral leases), while others live in Kununurra, the nearest town. White land tenure in the area is dominated by pastoral leasehold, with which Aboriginal land-use aspirations co-exist and compete (for further discussion see Head and Fullagar 1991; Head 1994). Land-use pressures in the region include tourism and proposals to irrigate the blacksoil plains for intensive agriculture. Part of the study area is currently under Native Title claim.

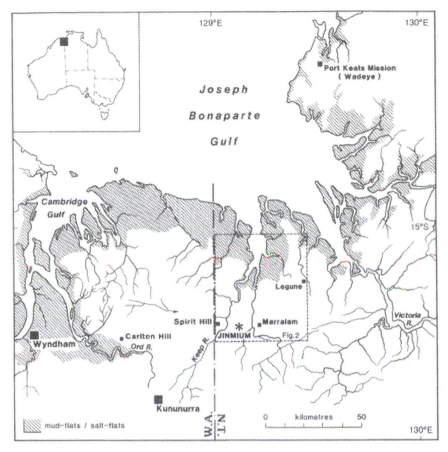

Figure 22.1 Location of the study area.

Djibigun and Jinmium, a story of attachment to place

In the East Kimberley landscape, as elsewhere in Aboriginal Australia, the naming of places and connections between places are detailed in stories and song cycles. Often, as here, the same places are mapped in several neighbouring languages. The Gadjerong story related by Paddy Carlton of Kununurra, and retold here with permission, describes a male spirit figure, Djibigun, who wanted to catch Jinmium, a female spirit being. He tracks her from west of the Keep River, through swampy ground (Figure 22.2), across Sandy Creek to the yam hills (*landani*). From there he follows her through the porcupine hills (*baranda*), red ochre hills (*djibigun*), through the stone sources at Bungyala, to Coornamu swamp (also a second ochre source). Finally he catches her at Jinmium, where she turns to stone. Djibigun turns into a little quail (*Coturnix australis*) and continues to search for her elsewhere. The quail is associated with the ochre sources.

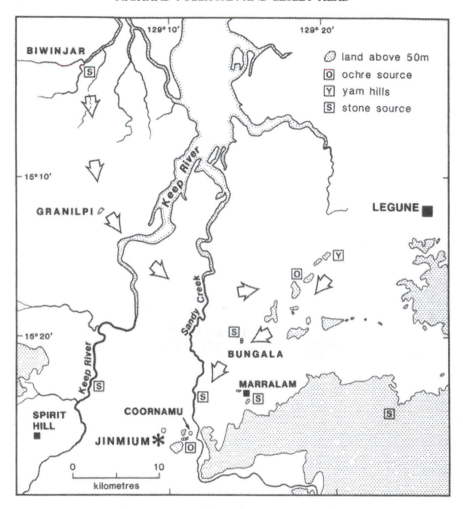

Figure 22.2   The track taken by Djibigun and Jinmium.

Evidence for the durability of details of this narrative is clearly inaccessible to archaeology. We do, however, suggest that there are at least two ways to explore the prehistory of the attachments to place that this story expresses. The first is to examine the prehistory of the named places in terms of changes in the bio-physical landscape. The second, through excavation, is to examine changes in those elements of the story that have clear archaeological manifestations – stone and ochre. We argue that the use of yams (cf. the 'yam hills') is also archaeo-logically visible, albeit less clearly, through starchy residues on stone pounding tools. The results presented here are preliminary in two respects. First, we know only the broad outline of biophysical changes in the area over the last 100,000 years or so. Second, the archaeological results come from one site only, Jinmium rockshelter. They are presented not as a regional prehistory, but as an example of discerning changes at one particular place over time.

Getting at antiquity

This chapter explores the potential of archaeology to discern changes in landscape over different time periods, ranging from the post-contact period of the last century through at least the Holocene.

The prehistory of the biophysical landscape

For most of the Pleistocene, the sea level was lower than at present, exposing large areas of the presently drowned, broad continental shelf. At the glacial maximum, the sea would have been at least 500 km distant and about 140 m lower than at present. At times of low sea level, the sandstone hills, presently small outliers (up to about 100 m elevation) of the ranges in the southeast of the study area, would have been more prominent in the landscape than at present. There is not yet any specific local evidence for late pleistocene climates and vegetation, but regional evidence suggests that dry conditions would have prevailed across the whole of northern Australia during this time (Hiscock and Kershaw 1992). Open savannah is likely to have been the dominant vegetation. Large river systems such as the ancestral Ord are likely to have been important corridors through this country.

Following the glacial maximum, the sea began to rise, reaching present levels around 6,000 BP. Warmer and wetter conditions characterised the Holocene, and much of the study area became a landscape of deposition. Intense monsoon rainfall transported sandy sediments from the ranges to the pediments and flood plains, and coastal and estuarine influences were now felt within several kilometres of the Jinmium rockshelter. Freshwater swamps, dating to 1,000–2,000 BP, would have provided water and a range of plant and animal resources.

The European pastoral period, commencing in this area in the last decades of the nineteenth century, is not marked initially by any environmental or climatic change. Reduction in resources available to hunter-gatherers occurred rather as a result of social conflict – people were dispossessed of land, their access to country was circumscribed and the opportunity to practise and transmit skills reduced. The introduction of cattle into northern Australia, and overstocking in some areas, resulted in the disappearance of many resources, both plant and animal.

Excavations at Jinmium rockshelter

Four 1 m by 1 m trenches were excavated near the Jinmium rockshelter, which has a floor area of about 8 m by 16 m, and rises about 4 m from present ground level (Fullagar et al. 1996). Six archaeological units have been identified including lower levels (units 1 and 2) and late holocene levels (units 3–6), overlain by more recent material items, probably all of post-contact age. The Jinmium chronology is based on various lines of evidence. Thermo-luminescence dates the basal occupation at earlier than 116,000 years (Fullagar et al. 1996), but single grain optically stimulated luminescence and AMS elemental carbon suggest the deposit may be younger than 11,000 years (Roberts et al. 1998). Both of these chronologies are problematic; the TL in relation to most other scenarios for the colonisation of Australia (O'Connell and Allen 1998), and the OSL/elemental carbon in relation to rock art sequencing studies which suggest that the cupules on vertical sandstone panels are likely to be at least 40,000 years old (Taçon et al. 1997). Further research into the taphonomy of the site and the relationship between the archaeo-logical and rock art stratigraphies is continuing. Precise ages for the earliest human occupation at Jinmium need not concern us here. Of significance, however, is that archaeological evidence for the region spans three techno-logically and artistically distinct periods:

1 a very recent period with a rich ethnography, European introductions such as metal and glass, and distinct rock art (e.g. Kaberry 1939; Shaw 1981, 1983, 1986; Head and Fullagar 1991; Mulvaney 1996);
2 a well-dated late holocene sequence with stone points, spanning roughly the last 3,000 years (e.g. Dortch 1977; Bradshaw 1986; Stokes 1986; Fullagar et al. 1996); and
3 an earlier period characterised by a distinct stone technology and rock art (e.g. Taçon et al. 1997; Fullagar et al. 1996).

Stone artefacts are found throughout the deposit, and bone is present only in the upper levels. Fragments of pecked sandstone similar to marks on the rockshelter wall were found in the lower levels, along with fragments of engraved mudstone. Ochre was also found in the lower levels, but occurred in higher densities during the Late Holocene.

Stone tools and plant remains

Our understanding of the relationship between the Dreaming track and the archaeological lines of evidence depends heavily on the knowledge still held and shared with us by local Aboriginal people. Since stone survives extremely well archaeologically, it is present throughout the excavation levels. Skills for flaking of stone are maintained by some local Aboriginal people. Some grinding of seeds, ochre and other materials is still carried out, but the labour-intensive grinding of starchy plant foods has not been routinely prac-tised since shop-bought carbohydrates became available. What survives best of both flaking and grinding activities is knowledge. Individual quarries, on the basis of which stone can be sourced, have been identified and mapped with Paddy Carlton and Polly Wandanga. The detailed procedures for grinding and pounding water lily (*Nymphaea gigantea*) seeds and bitter *Typhonium lillifolium* tubers into long-lasting cakes have been shown to us by, among others, Polly Wandanga and Gypsy Jinjair.

Bungyala and Barbangal are both known as sources of fine-grained rocks for the manufacture of points that were exchanged both locally and at least as far as Port Keats. Bungyala, which is on the Dreaming track (Figure 22.2), is a source of distinctive chert, silcrete and quartzites. There is extensive evidence of quarrying activity from boulders exposed above ground level. Barbangal, off the Dreaming track but nearby, provides chalcedony, which is scarce but visible near one ridge as angular fragments. Prolonged search for the main quarry, reportedly a large excavated pit, has been unsuccessful. The terrain is rugged and the Aboriginal custodians last visited this quarry over twenty years ago. The failure to relocate this quarry has been disturbing for the Aboriginal custodians.

Stone was flaked into points by men and then wrapped and carried by women and stockpiled in particular places. The tools were wrapped in paper bark and exchanged for a range of objects, including bamboo, cloth, cash, food, love magic objects and red ochre (see Falkenberg 1962: 148; Akerman and Stanton 1993: 16). Flaked stone was used by men and women for many tasks to process a range of plant and animal products. During the pastoral period, stone sources were visited regularly as groups of Aboriginal people moved around the pastoral stations, particularly during the months of the wet season when there was no employment, to carry out ceremonies and have various meetings.

In the late holocene layers of the rockshelter, grinding and pounding stones with evidence of starchy plant-processing are present. Sources of flaked stone include both Barbangal chalcedony and Bungyala cherts and quartzites. Artefact manufacture is dominated by production and repairs to unifacial and bifacial stone points. Functions include use of the points as hafted hunting spear tips (evidenced by blood residues) and as knives and scrapers for processing wood and other plant tissue. Quarry sources for the sandstone have been located in Keep River gorge, about 30 km to the south.

Pounding stones with starchy plant residues are also present in the lowest layers. Flaked stone sources are dominated by quartzites from nearby gravels and from the Bungyala source. Artefact production is based on multi-platformed cores and flakes with little retouch but clear evidence of use–wear. Tool functions already identified include plant-processing and wood-working in all layers.

The potential for tracing the use of plants generally, and yams specifically, in the archaeological record is provided by starchy residues on stone tools. This work is in its infancy. As yet it remains uncertain whether the plants processed can be identified to species level, whether starchy residues can move through sediment layers or become transferred between stone tools and sediments, and whether the chemical properties, size and morphology of starch grains contribute to their differential preservation. Starch grains recovered from the excavation fell into three broadly defined shape categories (subround, round, angular) and covered a range of sizes. Only *Dioscorea* can be identified to genus on the basis of shape alone. Nevertheless, with a combination of biogeographic assumptions together with shape and size data, it is possible to narrow the range of likely source plants.

The volume of starch in the archaeological sediments varies considerably through the fifteen spits of Pit I, and there is variability in both size and shape of starch granules with depth (Atchison 1994; Atchison and Fullagar in press). The major contribution to the total starch composition comes from the round and subround granules measuring less than 10 micrometres in diameter. Atchison has also demonstrated that a sample of stone pounding tools were a richer source of starch than the surrounding sediments, concluding then that transfer of starch from sediments to the tools was unlikely. Starch grains were found on a pounding tool from the late holocene layers of the site, and from two tools near the basal levels of the site. It is unclear which species were concerned, but starch grain size and shape suggest that several taxa may have been processed. Angular granules of 14 mm diameter were present, and these lie within the morphological range of *Dioscorea bulbifera*. More recent work by Jackes (1997) suggests that it is not yet possible to discriminate between species of *Dioscorea* on the basis of starch morphology. On these preliminary data, we argue that a range of starchy plants have been processed with stone since the site was first occupied. We cannot say conclusively whether they were yams, but yams are among the likely contenders.

Ochre and rock art

The rock art of the East Kimberley region has not yet been studied in detail, although a survey of about 50 ha has been completed for the Jinmium-Granilpi localities in the Keep River area (Taçon et al. 1997). It is this new data, together with information from nearby regional surveys (McNickle 1991; Flood et al. 1992; Welch 1993; David et al. 1994; Mulvaney 1996) as well as the ochre component of the Jinmium excavation, that allows discussion of broadscale changes.

A study by Taçon et al. (1997) of superpositioning at four site complexes in the Jinmium-Granilpi localities led to the following rock art sequence, from earlier to more recent times:

1 cupules (pecked engravings);
2 peck infill naturalistic animals;
3 purple hand stencils, Bradshaw figures and rare animals such as emu;
4 red hand stencils and hand prints, human-like figures and animals;
5 red, white, red-and-white animals and human-like figures; red, white, yellow hand stencils;
6 red sorcery figures with curvy limbs; beeswax figures;
7 white outline animals.

It is difficult to establish a secure absolute chronology that links excavated archaeological materials with rock art. Nevertheless, a framework is emerging. Age estimates of 80–150 BP for the red sorcery figures and beeswax figures in the study area (no. 6 in the sequence) are based on AMS dating of beeswax (Taçon et al. 1997). Current traditions about the red sorcery figures are related by senior Aboriginal people. Consequently, the sequence groupings 6 and 7 must relate to the contact period (beginning by the 1880s in this area). From elsewhere in northwestern Australia, Bradshaw figures have been indirectly dated by optically stimulated luminescence on mud wasp nests, with age estimates including greater than 4,000 BP (Watchman et al. 1997) up to *c.* 17,000–25,000 BP (Roberts et al. 1997). As distinct stylistic groupings (nos. 1 and 2 in the sequence), cupules and peck infill naturalistic animals are consistently older than any rock paintings executed in ochre, for which the oldest age estimate from an Australian site is *c. 39,000* years for Carpenters Gap, a site in the West Kimberley (O'Connor 1995). Cupule engravings are also found right across northern Australia and on other continents, but they are especially common in the Jinmium-Granilpi (Taçon et al. 1997). For these and other reasons, apart from thermoluminescence (TL) estimates on Jinmium sediments, Taçon et al. conclude that cupules at Jinmium and some other rock engraving sites are likely to be at least 40,000 years old in the Keep River area and elsewhere (see also Walsh 1994). Consequently, we can correlate groupings 1–3 in the Jinmium-Granilpi rock art sequence to the Pleistocene.

For the Late Holocene, Welch (1993) outlines various divisions of painting style that distinguish earlier Bradshaw figures (elongated humans in monochrome and bichrome) from later Wandjina figures (mouthless human figures in polychrome with haloes). Some elements of these Kimberley styles are present in the study area, although absolute ages are not known. Ochre of all colours is present in the Jinmium and other Keep River excavations. Red hand stencils are present on the walls at Jinmium, but this was a common practice in pastoral times and may be quite recent. Ochre (mostly red, but also white and yellow) is also present down to all but the lowest levels of the site, but is particularly abundant only in unit 3 (spits 9–11), with a radiocarbon age of $1,790 \pm 150$ BP (SUA 3036).

The most recent rock art with white outline figures depicts occasional scenes of stockmen and cattle (Mulvaney 1996). Slightly earlier in the sequence, there are links in style and form with the Lightning Brothers to the east (David et al. 1994). The presence of Bradshaw figures, earlier again in the sequence, suggests links to the east and northwest. Cupules provide a stylistic link with the rock art to the south, west and east, very early in the sequence and lie beneath Bradshaw figures at Granilpi (Taçon et al. 1997).

Pastoral contact brought a number of changes to the art of the region, including new subjects such as cows, bulls and horses. Aboriginal people continued to paint throughout the period, and can name artists and relate stories for specific paintings. There was a marked increase in the use of rockshelters in the pastoral period because people returned to the bush during the wet season, when they were laid off from station work, and they required shelter from the monsoonal rains. This resulted in increased numbers of paintings in the shelters (Mulvaney 1996). Today the ochre sources are tied into a different sort of trade network, being sold through Aboriginal art shops and providing an important source of revenue for local custodians. There is also a wide range of painted, carved and decorated objects produced for sale, particularly to the growing tourist industry.

Discussion and conclusions

Both the archaeological and landscape aspects of Jinmium show elements of continuity and change throughout the sequence. The things that are continuous are those that can be most closely linked to the story of Djibigun and Jinmium. These include the rock outcrops incorporating the yam hills, ochre hills and Bungyala stone quarry. They also include the archaeological manifestation of the use of each of those resources – Bungyala stone, ochre and starchy plant residues on tools are found throughout the Jinmium rockshelter deposit. We interpret the presence of each of these in all archaeological levels as evidence that there were connections between these places at different times in the past. We are not arguing that the Dreaming as perceived by Aboriginal people today can be traced to the Pleistocene, but we are arguing for the pleistocene antiquity of mapped landscapes, of perceived links between specific places.

To some extent, such continuities of attachment are a thread underlying all the social and ecological variation that constitutes the more traditional story of the prehistory of this area. Full glacial aridity followed by sea level rise brought massive changes in the environment of this presently near-coastal area, although we do not yet know how sudden those changes were. Stone points were introduced by about 4,000 years ago (Bowdler and O'Connor 1991), with serrated or dentate Kimberley points introduced in the last 1000 years (Akerman and Bindon 1995), and a number of changes in rock art have occurred over the period under discussion.

As we get closer to the present, the density of available evidence about peoples' perception and use of landscapes increases. The tendency has been for our explanations of the recent past to be similarly complex, while the deep past is usually interpreted in one-dimensional terms, for example accounting only for ecological factors. Our intention in this chapter has been to explore the possibility of making our interpretations of landscapes of the distant past more multi-dimensional. This cannot be attempted simply by transposing stories reflecting present-day perceptions backwards in time. What we have argued is that, by demonstrating links between those perceptions and archaeologically visible materials, which, in this case, consist of stone, ochre and starchy plants, we can begin the task of tracing changes in attachment to landscape over time.

References

Akerman, K. and P. Bindon 1995. Dentate and related stone biface points from northern Australia. The Beagle. *Records of the Museums and Art Galleries of the Northern Territory*, 12, 89–99.

Akerman, K. and J. Stanton 1993. *Riji and Jakoli: Kimberley pearlshell in Aboriginal Australia*. Darwin: Northern Territory Museum of Arts and Science.

Atchison, J. 1994. Analysis of food starch residues at the Jinmium archaeological site, Northern Territory. Unpublished BEnvSc (Hons) thesis, University of Wollongong.

Atchison, J. and R. Fullagar in press. Starch residues on pounding implements from Jinmium rock-shelter. In *A Closer Look: recent studies of Australian stone tools*, R. Fullagar (ed.). Sydney: University of Sydney.

Bowdler, S. and S. O'Connor 1991. The dating of the Australian small tool tradition, with new evidence from the Kimberley, WA. *Australian Aboriginal Studies* 1, 153–62.

Bradshaw, E. 1986. A typological analysis of five excavated stone tool assemblages, East Kimberley, Western Australia. Unpublished BA Hons thesis, University of Western Australia.

David, B., I. McNiven, V. Attenbrow, J. Flood and J. Collins 1994. Of lightning brothers and white cockatoos: dating the antiquity of signifying systems in the Northern Territory, Australia. *Antiquity* 68, 241–51.

Davidson, I. 1991. Archaeologists and Aborigines. *The Australian Journal of Anthropology* 2, 247–58.

Dortch, C.E. 1977. Early and late stone industrial phases in western Australia. In *Stone Tools as Cultural Markers: change, evolution and complexity*, R.V.S. Wright (ed.), 104–32. Canberra: Australian Institute of Aboriginal Studies.

Falkenberg, J. 1962. *Kin and Totem: group relations of Australian Aborigines in the Port Keats district*. Oslo: Allen & Unwin.

Flood, J., B. David and R. Frost 1992. Dreaming into art. Aboriginal interpretations of rock engravings: Yingalarri, Northern Territory, Australia. In *Rock Art and Ethnography*, M. Morwood and D. Hobbs (eds), 33–8. Melbourne: AURA.

Fullagar, R., D. Price and L. Head 1996. Early human occupation of northern Australia: archaeology and thermoluminescence dating of Jinmium rock-shelter, Northern Territory. *Antiquity* 70, 751–73.

Gibbons, A. 1997. Doubts over spectacular dates. *Science* 278, 220–2.

Head, L. 1993. Unearthing prehistoric cultural landscapes: a view from Australia. *Transactions of the Institute of British Geographers* 18, 481–99.

Head, L. 1994. Aborigines and pastoralism in northwestern Australia: historical and contemporary perspectives on multiple use of the rangelands. *The Rangeland Journal* 16, 167–83.

Head, L. and R. Fullagar 1991. 'We all la one land': pastoral excisions and Aboriginal resource use. *Australian Aboriginal Studies* 1991/1, 39–52.

Head, L., C. Gosden and J.P. White (eds) 1994. *Social landscapes*. Sydney: Archaeology in Oceania.

Hiscock, P. and A.P. Kershaw 1992. Palaeoenvironments and prehistory of Australia's tropical Top End. In *The Native Lands: prehistory and environmental change in Australia and the Southwest Pacific*, J.R. Dodson (ed.), 43–75. Melbourne: Longman Cheshire.

Jackes, A. 1997. Spot the difference: analyses of starch grains of the *Dioscerea* genus piloting a method in the search for differentiating and identifying features. Unpublished BEnvSci Hons thesis, University of Wollongong.

Jones, R. 1990. Hunters of the Dreaming: some ideational, economic and ecological parameters of the Australian Aboriginal production system. In *Pacific Production Systems: approaches to economic prehistory*, D.E. Yen and J.M.J. Mummery (eds), 21–53. Canberra: Department of Prehistory, Australian National University.

Kaberry, P.M. 1939. *Aboriginal Woman: sacred and profane*. London: George Routledge & Sons.

Ley, D. 1985. Cultural/humanistic geography. *Progress in Human Geography* 9, 415–23.

McNickle, H. 1991. A survey of rock art in the Victoria River District, Northern Territory. *Rock Art Research* 8, 36–46.

Morphy, H. 1993. Colonialism, history and the construction of place: the politics of landscape in northern Australia. In *Landscape: politics and perspectives*, B. Bender (ed.), 205–44. Oxford: Berg.

Morphy, H. 1995. Landscape and the reproduction of the ancestral past. In *The Anthropology of Landscape: perspectives on place and space*, E. Hirsch and M. O'Hanlon (eds), 184–209. Oxford: Clarendon.

Mott, J.J., J. Williams, M.H. Andrew and A. Gillison 1985. Australian savanna ecosystems. In *Ecology and Management of the World's Savannas*, J.C. Tothill and J.J. Mott (eds), 56–82. Canberra: Australian Academy of Science.

Mulvaney, K. 1996. What to do on a rainy day: reminiscences of Mirriuwung and Gadjerong artists. *Rock Art Research* 13, 3–20.

O'Connell, J.F. and J. Allen 1998. When did humans first arrive in Greater Australia and why is this important to know? *Evolutionary Anthropology* 6, 132–46.

O'Connor, S. 1995. Carpenters Gap Rockshelter 1: 40,000 years of Aboriginal occupation in the Napier Ranges, Kimberley, W.A. *Australian Archaeology* 40, 58–9.

Roberts, R.G., G.L. Walsh, A. Murray, J.M. Olley, R. Jones, M. Macphail, D. Bowdery, C. Tuniz, I. Naumann and M.J. Morwood 1997. Ancient mudwasps as rock painting chronometers and palaeoenvironmental archives. *Nature* 387, 696–9.

Roberts, R., M. Bird, J. Olley, R. Gallagher, E. Lawson, G. Laslett, H. Yoshida, R. Jones, R. Fullagar, G. Jacobsen and Q. Hua 1998. Optical and radiocarbon dating at Jinmium rock shelter, northern Australia. *Nature* 393, 358.

Rose, D.B. 1992. *Dingo Makes Us Human*. Cambridge: Cambridge University Press.

Shaw, B. 1981. *My Country of the Pelican Dreaming: the life of an Australian Aborigine of the Gadjerong, Grant Ngabidj, 1904–1977*. Canberra: Australian Institute of Aboriginal Studies.

Shaw, B. 1983. *Banggaiyerri: the story of Jack Sullivan*. Canberra: Australian Institute of Aboriginal Studies.

Shaw, B. 1986. *Countrymen: the life histories of four Aboriginal men*. Canberra: Australian Institute of Aboriginal Studies.

Slatyer, R.O. 1970. Climate of the Ord-Victoria area. In *Lands of the Ord-Victoria area, Western Australia and Northern Territory*, 11–61. Canberra: CSIRO.

Stokes, C. 1986. An analysis of the faunal remains from four East Kimberley rock-shelter sites, Western Australia. Unpublished BA Hons thesis, University of Western Australia.

Taçon, P.S.C. 1991. The power of stone: symbolic aspects of stone use and tool development in western Arnhem Land, Australia. *Antiquity* 65, 192–207.

Taçon, P.S.C., R. Fullagar, S. Ouzman and K. Mulvaney 1997. Cupule engravings from Jinmium-Granilpi (northern Australia): exploration of a widespread and enigmatic class of rock markings. *Antiquity* 71, 942–65.

Walsh, G. 1994. *Bradshaws: ancient rock paintings of Australia*. Geneva: Edition Limitée.

Watchman, A.L., G.L. Walsh, M.J. Morwood and C. Tuniz 1997. AMS radiocarbon age estimates for early rock paintings in the Kimberley, N.W. Australia: preliminary results. *Rock Art Research* 14, 18–26.

Welch, D. 1993. Early 'naturalistic' human figures in the Kimberley, Australia. *Rock Art Research* 10, 24–37.

23 Towards an archaeology of mimesis and rain-making in Namibian rock art

JOHN KINAHAN

Introduction

There is a lingering paradox in archaeological studies of southern African hunter-gatherers, renowned for their highly adapted way of life and the extraordinary legacy of their rock paintings at archaeological sites throughout the region. Despite considerable progress in research, the economy and ritual life of the hunter-gatherer society have remained essentially separate areas of investigation, almost always approached from different premises. The result is that southern African hunter-gatherers exemplify, on the one hand, the apotheosis of ecological knowledge, while at the same time subscribing to a complex of religious precepts that appear to contradict this very image. Although the need for a more unified view of social and environmental relations is clearly apparent, there is little to compare with the attention paid to the same general issue elsewhere (e.g. Bradley 1991; Tilley 1991; Ingold 1993).

Archaeologists in southern Africa have for several decades emphasised the technology and ecology of hunting and gathering, with detailed reconstructions of subsistence strategies in a variety of environmental contexts (e.g. Deacon 1976; Parkington 1984; Mazel 1989; Walker 1995). This interest reflects not only the preservational bias of the archaeological record, but a common view, supported by studies of surviving foragers, that adaptation is the essence of the hunting and gathering economy. Although it has yielded many valuable insights, the ecological perspective is ultimately misleading if observations on the environment are adopted as the basis for archaeological inference. The need for alternative approaches has become increasingly apparent as rock art studies reveal a pervasive and deeply held belief in the supernatural as an ideological determinant in the hunting and gathering economy (Lewis-Williams 1981, 1983; Dowson and Lewis-Williams 1994). There are few examples of research in which rock art and the conventional evidence of the archaeological record are combined within a single theoretical framework (Kinahan 1991; Yates et al. 1994; Jolly 1996; Ouzman 1996; Ouzman and Wadley 1997). One reason for this is the difficulty of establishing chronological links between paintings on the walls of overhangs and rockshelters, and the archaeological deposits that lie within them. Just as problematic, however, is the almost exclusive reliance of rock art interpretation on the authority of recent ethnography, and the fact that in rock art studies little cognisance is taken of the archaeological evidence, particularly that relating to temporal change and ecological relations (e.g. Lewis-Williams 1984, 1993). To overcome these difficulties and arrive at an integrated view, it is necessary to locate rock art in the archaeological context of hunter-gatherer economy and society. At the same time, the knowledge gained from rock art studies obviously requires that the environmental context and the archaeological record of hunter-gatherer settlement is viewed through different eyes.

Towards this general aim, I suggest that rock art may in some circumstances have served a purpose somewhat different from that which is generally supposed by current approaches to the interpretation of these complex images. The argument developed here is that rock art, particularly that relating to rain-making, represents a mimetic attempt (e.g. Taussig 1993) to establish what I shall call *concrete association* between otherwise disparate phenomena, such as rainfall, topographic features and the causative agency of animal metaphors. I propose that rock art for purposes such as rain-making was produced as a practical instrument to effect precipitation in particular places and at particular times. In contrast to the widely accepted notion that paintings were made in recollection of shamanistic experiences of the supernatural (Lewis-Williams 1988), I conclude that these paintings are more plausibly explained as a powerful act of preparation for altered consciousness; they preceded rather than followed the work of rain-making. The rock art of rain-making, which is elaborative in nature, might therefore be seen as an important and highly revealing series of thinking experiments, or a 'dialogue with nature' in the sense of Lévi-Strauss (1966: 19). As such, the art is a legacy of hunter-gatherer attempts at intervention in the rhythm of natural events, and a unique documentation of cause and effect as perceived by a people credited with an almost supernatural prescience.

The first of the following three sections introduces the environmental conditions of western Namibia, the setting of the archaeological sites to be discussed in this chapter (Figure 23.1). The second section considers the evidence of these sites against the background of conventional views based on rock art studies in southern Africa. This leads to a series of general propositions that are examined in the last section, as an attempt at a unified interpretation of the rock art and environmental context of a specialist rain-making site.

The hills and the rain

Throughout most of the year, the thornbush savannah on the edge of the Namib Desert lies still and apparently lifeless. Dust-devils in the early summer

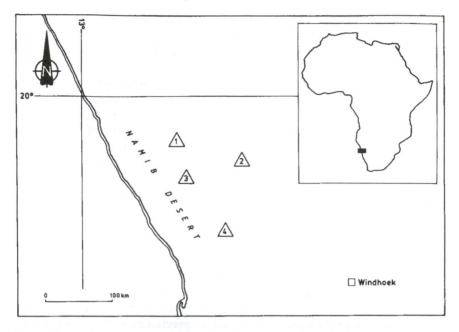

Figure 23.1 Major concentrations of rock art in western Namibia. 1 Twyfelfontein, 2 Otjohorongo, 3 Hungorob (Brandberg), 4 Spitzkoppe.

are no more or less reliable a portent than the grey haze of bushfires further east, but the expectation of rain invests meaning in everything, from the listless gaze of rock lizards nodding at the northern horizon, to the strength and shifting direction of the wind. It often happens that massed clouds, just before the storm should break, move elsewhere at the caprice of the atmosphere, or dissipate into nothing. Some years there is no rain, although a few trees and bushes may come briefly into leaf, deceived by a faint shift in humidity brought on the evening wind.

Usually, in the days before the rains begin, the sun burns more fiercely and strong winds from the north and east bring in tall white cumulus clouds. The thunderheads, steel-grey beneath, may have several showers of rain pouring from their underbellies at different points. However, showers issuing from the largest clouds very often fail to reach the ground, their enormous contents being swept repeatedly upward and into the brewing storm by the rising air mass. This spectacular development can continue over many days, with erratic cloud movements sometimes accompanied by distant lightning, as the first storms draw nearer. These are brief downpours, with the sun emerging after a few minutes to show the new moisture being drawn upward again in long fingers of vapour, seemingly as fast as it sinks into the soil.

If the rains set in for a few weeks, there is a storm almost every afternoon. The soil becomes waterlogged and the river courses, which are otherwise dry, come down in spate for a few hours, carrying dead trees and all manner of accumulated debris. Floods most quickly arise near the river source, particularly in areas with outcrops of granite which shed large volumes of water. A common feature of the desert and scrub savannah, granite hills often occur in clusters, and since they are all remnant plutonic stocks of the same Cretaceous events, they tend to be similar in many ways. Their characteristic domed shape usually represents the compressional core of an antiformal fold structure (Twidale 1988), and where the surface is broken by large fractures, these often reveal partings in the body of the granite itself. Such crevices are often convex-upward beneath topographic rises, providing deep rock-shelters in the shape of empty eye-sockets.

The relationship between the rain and the granites, especially the larger massifs, is not simply fortuitous. Within the narrow crevices of the rock, it is possible on a warm windless day to feel the current of air drawn into the hill as a result of its higher temperature and the cell of low pressure that develops around it. The rock retains this heat and the first rain clouds often gather above the hills which provide the necessary orographic lift to ensure condensation and rainfall (cf. Barry and Chorley 1976). Beside this apparent link between the hills and the rain, there is also the remarkable capacity of granite hills to retain large quantities of runoff from precipitation in crevices deep below the surface. These reservoirs fill narrow aquifers in the granite and feed tiny springs that supply animals and birds with water for months or even years between seasons of rain. Consequently, the granite hills of the desert and scrub savannah are islands of relative plenty, with a remarkable diversity of plant and animal life.

In view of its crucial importance to the survival of hunter-gatherer communities in arid parts of southern Africa, it is not surprising that there should be an abundance of folklore devoted to the rain. Such narratives contain acute observations on the weather and the unpredictability of the rain, although the explanations they offer for this evidently well-understood phenomenon do not as a rule reflect meteorological considerations (Schmidt 1979; Prins 1990; Jolly 1996). Indeed, ethnographic accounts describe the rain, in both appearance and habit, as an animal rather than a force of nature. For example, the /Xam, a Bushman group who once lived in the central parts of South Africa, referred to the dark rain clouds as the rain animal's body, to the columns of falling rain as its legs, and likened as to walking its movement across the landscape (Bleek 1933). Violent downpours were the male rain, or blood of the rain animal, as opposed to the soft, soaking, female rain which represented its milk. To another group, the !Kung Bushmen of Namibia and Botswana, these different kinds of rain left easily recognisable spoor in the sand (Thomas 1988).

The Bushmen, as Lewis-Williams (1981: 103) points out, were certainly not so credulous as to believe that the rain animal was a real creature in the mundane sense. But it was, nonetheless, a powerful and pervasive metaphor with specific ritual connotations. Certain shamans were acknowledged for their influence over the rain, the animal metaphor being extended for the purposes of rain-making into a ritual hunt, involving all the necessary cooperation, guile and weaponry, as well as the ever-present possibility of failure. In recent times, at least, the skills of rainmaker shamans from hunter-gatherer communities were much sought after by agriculturalists and pastoralists alike, since both were constantly threatened by drought and its potentially disastrous consequences (Jolly 1996). Whether rituals of rain-making were efficacious or not is less important than the fact that they represent a crucial nexus of belief and practical action. There, at least in part, lies their interest to archaeology, for the beliefs and rituals of rain-making would arguably have influenced both the subject-matter of ritual artwork and the selection of ritual sites.

Rock art and ritual

In the last two decades, systematic comparison of recent San ethnography and southern African rock art has yielded many new insights, and it is now widely accepted that the beliefs and rituals of hunter-gatherer society provide a valid framework for the interpretation of the paintings and engravings that occur throughout this region. This cognitive stance has been argued in detail elsewhere (Lewis-Williams 1981, 1982, 1983, 1993, 1995; Lewis-Williams and Loubser 1986; Lewis-Williams and Dowson 1989; Dowson and Lewis-Williams 1994), so that here it is only necessary to sketch its most relevant general features before proceeding to consider the evidence of Namibian rock art.

Among southern African hunter-gatherers, the most important and widespread ritual is the trance dance, a communal rite in which medicine people heal the sick and carry out a wide range of other related tasks. As described by Lee (1968), the trance ritual usually commences with prolonged dancing to the accompaniment of singing and clapping, contributed by the women of the community. Among some modern Bushmen, a large proportion of men and women are able to achieve trance, although few are skilled as healers and in certain groups healing is the province of ritual specialists, or shamans (Barnard 1992). The onset of trance is marked by outward symptoms including trembling, perspiration, and sometimes nasal haemorrhage, while the ensuing state of altered consciousness is frequently marked by vivid hallucinations and physical sensations, such as flying, or the ability to travel either underwater or beneath the surface of the ground. The experienced trancer construes these physiological symptoms as a form of supernatural power derived from the animal species they suggest. Animals thus serve as metaphors of the trance experience, which is associated with a small range of ritually important species. These animals recur, with some local variation, throughout the rock art of southern Africa (Lewis-Williams and Dowson 1989).

Generally, the rock art confirms the ethnographic evidence of communal participation in ritual activity. In contrast to the solitary nature of the shaman's work in other hunter-gatherer societies, the San are credited with an openness about religious experience (Lewis-Williams 1988) that is reflected in the fact that paintings were done in open rockshelters, 'not in dark subterranean caves' (Lewis-Williams and Dowson 1989: 15). There were no ritual specialists or secret rites according to this view, other than the powerful shamans who emerged in recent times as leaders of beleaguered hunter-gatherer communities (cf. Lewis-Williams 1995: 144). Although under normal circumstances the abilities of gifted individuals were acknowledged, they enjoyed no permanent rank or status. A crucial element of this conventional view is that the paintings are thought to depict the healer's recollection of the supernatural; they were shared with the community at large, and served to prepare novices for the potentially terrifying experience of trance (Lewis-Williams 1982, 1988). As Lewis-Williams (1995: 147) has argued,

> they painted while in a normal state of consciousness, recalling their vivid glimpses of the spirit world and making powerful images of those visions and of the animals that were their principle sources of potency. Probably, the very act of painting assisted in the recall, recreation and reification of otherwise transient glimpses of spiritual things. Like Wordworth's observations on poetry, San rock art should be seen as powerful emotion recollected in tranquility.

However, while the cognitive explanation as to the meaning of the rock art is well supported, this hypothesis concerning its function obviously relies on the agreement of ethnography and the evidence of rock art in those areas of southern Africa that have been studied in detail (cf. Lewis-Williams and Dowson 1989).

Namibian rock art is comparatively less well studied, although there are significant concentrations of sites in some areas, such as the higher parts of the Brandberg (Pager 1980), a spectacular granite massif deeply incised by a series of rocky ravines. In the Hungorob ravine at the Brandberg, most of the rock art sites are concentrated in the upper reaches of the ravine, where they are loosely clustered in the vicinity of a few small but reliable waterholes. Sites at the Spitzkoppe, a somewhat smaller granite inselberg complex in the same general area, exhibit a similar pattern of distribution, with large central sites located at the waterholes and smaller peripheral sites scattered about in the same general area (Figure 23.2). In both cases the central sites are spacious rockshelters with complex painted friezes. The peripheral sites are smaller, sometimes with but a single painting to attest to their use, and little or no other evidence of occupation (and see Kinahan 1990, 1991 for further details).

Excavations in the large central sites of the Hungorob and Spitzkoppe revealed evidence of repeated occupation over the last five millennia, with stone tool assemblages and faunal remains indicative of a hunting and gathering economy. The sites have major friezes of rock art depicting several aspects of the trance ritual, including men dancing to the accompaniment of clapping women, and men in various stages of trance. In both the Hungorob and Spitzkoppe site concentrations, the archaeological and related

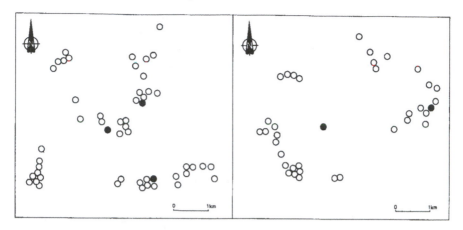

Figure 23.2 Comparative distribution patterns of rock art sites in the Hungorob (left) and Spitzkoppe (right). Solid circles are sites with eighty or more paintings.

environmental evidence points to a pattern of aggregated settlement during the dry season, followed by a period of dispersal subject to the abundance and distribution of rainfall. This hypothetical cycle has parallels among modern hunter-gatherers in the region (Barnard 1979), and it is of particular relevance that for these peoples the period of aggregation is also a time of ritual intensity (Lee 1972). The rock art at the central Hungorob and Spitzkoppe sites reflects a similar concentration of ritual activity involving the aggregated community. However, there are no obvious ethnographic parallels to help explain the more common peripheral rock art sites in the same distributions. There is no reason to suppose that paintings at these sites were any less concerned with ritual matters, for their subject-matter is generally the same. No motifs are exclusive to the larger central sites, although, having more paintings, their subject-matter does tend to be more diverse (Kinahan 1991).

Table 23.1 presents a simplified comparison of rock art from forty-four Hungorob sites and thirty-seven Spitzkoppe sites, using raw counts of paintings identifiable to species or higher taxon. Numerically, the rock art is dominated by human figures to the extent that all other subjects together comprise less than one fifth of the recorded total. The table shows the effect of this contrast on the distribution of the paintings: while human figures occurred at nearly every site, most animal subjects were restricted to one or two sites. Considerable selectivity is also apparent, although clearly it was not guided by the availability of the various species as game, and in the rock art itself the animals are often grouped without regard to their natural habits. The fact that few of the painted species are represented in the faunal remains from excavations at the sites (Kinahan 1990, 1991) also serves to show that the relationship between the hunters and their environment is not self-evident from only one of either field of evidence.

Table 23.1 Comparative frequencies of rock art subjects, Hungorob (A) and Spitzkoppe (B)

Subject	A n sites	B n sites	A count	B count	A S total	B S total
Human	42	28	158	86	494	317
Therianthrop.	3	2	3	1	5	2
Lion	3	3	1	2	3	4
Elephant	2	3	1	2	2	4
Rhinoceros	0	2	0	7	0	8
Zebra	2	2	14	1	15	2
Giraffe	11	7	6	14	28	26
Springbuck	7	2	8	1	20	2
Eland	3	3	13	2	15	4
Kudu	3	6	12	3	14	10
Hartebeest	0	1	0	1	0	1
Oryx	6	0	4	0	10	0
Ostrich	1	1	4	2	4	2
Snake	3	2	1	4	3	5
Cattle	0	3	0	7	0	10

In the rock art of the Hungorob and Spitzkoppe, human figures are often directly associated with various animal species. Moreover, there are similarities in posture that clearly indicate the metaphorical nature of the animal figures. Antelope are shown with buckled legs, as in a state of physical collapse which occurs in trance, and in some cases blood is shown issuing from the nose. Although therianthropic figures are uncommon (Table 23.1), it seems that the animals in the art are largely associated with trance experience and may therefore represent healers in a full rather than partial state of transformation. However, the way in which some of the animal species appear naturally to exemplify various stages of the trance experience and attributes of the healing process, suggests that a somewhat broader interpretation is possible. Instead of illustrating the experience of trance in recollection, painting could have been part of the active preparation for trance, as objects of contemplation. It is therefore possible that the act of painting, requiring both concentration and visual imagination, was in itself an important part of the preparation for trance.

Paintings of giraffe in the Hungorob and Spitzkoppe illustrate this alternative. In its most easily recognisable form, the giraffe is represented by its backline and head, shown in profile, with the characteristic body markings against a pale background. Very often the feet are missing, and the body is painted as an open lattice. In many cases the giraffe is indicated by the backline and profile alone, without any evidence of other paint on the rock. There are examples of disembodied giraffe heads and necks in which it is clear that the rest of the body was not painted at all, but the paintings are not for that reason incomplete. Invariably, the withers of the giraffe are shown as a slight curve of the backline at the correct proportional distance from the back of the head, thus serving as a reliable diagnostic feature. The same feature also occurs in paintings of snakes, many of which appear therefore to be transformations of giraffe, with the backline filled out and extended accordingly (Figure 23.3). Snakes are often painted as if disappearing into cracks, or into the runs of white precipitate left by rainwater streaming over the rocks. Giraffe are also sometimes found in these runs, where those painted in white are barely visible. There is no reason to believe that the surface of the rock had no coating of precipitate when the paintings were made, and the indications are that the paintings were deliberately positioned in this way. Such paintings imply an attempt to establish, through the act of their execution, a concrete association between the giraffe and the marks left by the rain.

There are clear resemblances between the form and markings of the giraffe and the initial stages of trance. The broken pattern of the giraffe pelage is highly suggestive of fractured vision in trance, and the extreme height of the animal reinforces this by apparently alluding to the feeling of attenuation in the first stages of trance. This would explain the absence of both torso and feet in some giraffe paintings. In trance, the power of the healer is said to reside in the stomach, where it is activated to rise up the spinal column (Lee 1968; Katz 1982). In the context of the other similarities between the giraffe and the symptoms of trance, the importance of the spine might therefore explain the convention of emphasising the backline in paintings of this animal. It might also explain the transformation of the backline into a serpent, such that it is worth noting the distinct similarities between the variegated body markings of the giraffe and those of the python (cf. Broadley 1983). The python is closely associated with water, and although the paintings seldom show diagnostic markings, they often depict very large snakes. The example at Snake Rock in the Hungorob is visible at a distance of nearly half a kilometre, even though much of its body is covered by a run of precipitate on the rockface (Kinahan 1991; see also Lenssen-Erz 1993: Plates 3.1, 5.3).

The obvious resemblances between these species and the early stages of trance plausibly explain their inclusion in the rock art, particularly when the conventions of their depiction are also taken into account. It is well known that positioning was important in the art and the use of natural features in

Figure 23.3 Giraffe-headed serpent with human figures, Spitzkoppe.

the rock added to the significance of some paintings (Lewis-Williams and Dowson 1990). In the context of large aggregations such as would have occurred at the central sites at the Hungorob and Spitzkoppe, these paintings would support the accepted opinion that the art served as a primer for the mysteries of trance (cf. Lewis-Williams 1982). This view could also accommodate the suggestion that the paintings were aids to mental preparation for trance, by individuals or groups within an open social setting. However, there are paintings that contradict this pattern and show that the same rock art tradition was also associated with solitary contemplation such as would be found in a more specialised tradition of shamanism, hitherto excluded from consideration in the study of southern African rock art. At the Spitzkoppe, for example, one of the peripheral rock art sites precariously overlooks the surrounding terrain from a height of nearly 100 m. The fact that it is small and difficult to reach shows that the selection of sites was not determined by convenience alone. This is but one of many isolated sites with very limited floor space, a few of which might serve to show the importance of this element, at least in the Namibian rock art.

The Mason Shelter, in the upper Brandberg some 11 km northeast of Snake Rock, has an elaborate frieze painted on the low underside of an overhanging boulder. To view the painting it is necessary to crawl under the boulder and into a confined space that receives no direct natural light. The same conditions are found at Crane Rock 15 km to the west, in another part of the mountain. The paintings at both of these sites comprise small panels in different colours, separated by bold lines, giving the effect of bounded, interlocking fields, similar to a patchwork quilt. Other examples are to be found some 60 km to the north, at the site of Twyfelfontein, where a rock outcrop at the edge of the site has a very small opening at its foot, hardly wider than a man's shoulders. The ceiling of this narrow space has painted on it a headless female kudu, barely visible in the dim light. Elsewhere on the same site is an isolated engraving of an ostrich, situated in a narrow crevice between fallen boulders, where it can be viewed only at very close range from an uncomfortable prone position. If the semi-dark confinement imposed by these sites assisted in the achievement of altered consciousness required for ritual activity, the paintings would have been executed as part of this process in which they served as a focus of concentration. Sites such as these continue to baffle rock art scholars, and of one painting in the Hungorob Ravine, Lenssen-Erz states: 'One might think that a painting of this size would deserve a splendid exposition, yet it is painted on the rather low ceiling of the shelter, visible only when entering. Besides this, figures are heavily damaged by *a waterflow cutting right through the main motif*' (my emphasis) (1993: 83). Significantly, the motif in question is a complex assemblage of snake, giraffe, feline-headed therianthrope, and dense parallel streams suggestive of falling rain.

Two general propositions are supported by the evidence presented so far. The most important concerns an apparent continuity between ritual activity and the environmental setting of these sites. Not only is there close similarity between trance experience and the habits and appearance of certain animal species, but the depiction of these in the rock art takes into account both natural features of the rock and the positioning of the site. In this way, the rock art gives the impression that it is mapped onto the physical and biotic environment of the sites. This supports the further proposition that rock art sites define a landscape mediated by ritual activity. The nature of this intervention is partly reflected in the evidence for secluded as well as public ritual. Even if the secluded sites were used in preparation for public ritual, the evidence of these sites contradicts the accepted view on the function of the rock art. In doing so, it also points to the anomalous existence of ritual specialisation in a supposedly egalitarian society.

Similarities in design, as well as the relatively fresh appearance of the artwork in the secluded Mason Shelter and Crane Rock sites, indicate approximate contemporaneity. The designs also resemble particular elements of the complex Snake Rock frieze that appear to be relatively recent, judging by their fresh appearance and superpositioning. It is therefore relevant that Snake Rock and Falls Rock Shelter were abandoned early in the present millennium when hunter-gatherers in the Hungorob adopted livestock-keeping and a different pattern of settlement. Changes in the rock art suggest the rise of specialist shamanism from within the communal healing tradition, and although the paintings are not directly datable, this development must be related to the adoption of livestock and a shift in social values. The shaman was apparently an agent of social change, and the nucleus of an emergent pastoral economy (Kinahan 1991, 1993, 1996). These changes in ritual practice and in the attendant rock art tradition would have entailed shifts in both the purpose of ritual activity and its context: while the trance dance served primarily to maintain social cohesion in the egalitarian hunting band, the specialist skills of the shaman would also have been more widely valued among neighbouring pastoral communities.

Hunting the elephant

Less hostile than the Namib, but marginal by most other standards, the thornbush savannah and mopane woodland surrounding the Otjohorongo granite massif 80 km east of the Hungorob (Figure 23.1) is traditionally an important cattle-raising area of the pastoral Herero (Köhler 1959). The trees provide nutritious browse throughout much of the year, and there are strong aquifers associated with the granite outcrops, accessible through shallow wells in the sandy river courses. Pastoral settlement is concentrated in the vicinity of these wells, while the more rugged massif with its rockshelters and small natural springs seems to have been favoured in the past by hunter-gatherer communities. The mountain is deserted now, save for a few isolated cattle-posts, but the large number of rock art sites clearly attests to its former importance. Among these sites, the largest found so far is the Rainman Shelter, named for its rich and complex rock art friezes which, together with other characteristics of the rockshelter itself, evidence its use by a specialist rain-maker shaman.

The Rainman site is situated in a major parting of the granite which is exposed by a massive fault traversing the whole of the massif. The site is different from most shelters formed in the same way, and in many respects it is unsuitable as accommodation for even a small group of people. While its location is obvious, the mouth of the shelter is screened by large boulders and thick bush, so that it is not possible to see into it from even a few metres away. Most living sites in this sort of setting have an open approach, to the extent that sites with less accessible entrances, such as the Rainman Shelter, tend not to have been used. Although relatively large at 50 m across its mouth, the Rainman site has very little even floor space under shelter. Much of the floor area is evidently a streambed that would be in spate when shelter was most required, and the remainder is either in twilight or permanent darkness, conditions that are eschewed in the selection of living sites.

The main characteristics of the site are shown in Figure 23.4, which is a cross-section along the axis of a line perpendicular to the entrance, via what appears to have been the most likely approach. In addition to the physical characteristics already described, the section shows the main archaeological features of the site. Rock paintings, of which there are more than 150 identifiable animal and human figures stretching over approximately 30 m of the shelter, were mainly concentrated just inside the dripline, either on the overhanging roof or on other rock surfaces, in open daylight. But the section also shows that some paintings occurred in deeper parts of the shelter. Some of these paintings located in the twilight part of the shelter are difficult to see, and one showing a female kudu in white can be viewed only from a prone position at a point where the roof is too low for crawling on hands and knees.

Other features shown in the section drawing include a small enclosure of rough walling, possibly used as a sleeping area, placed under a low overhang of the roof. The enclosure contained no artefacts, but a small stone mortar was found nearby, deep inside the shelter. The small hollow of the stone and its highly polished surface suggest that it was used to grind cosmetics or aromatic herbs, rather than food, and might therefore have had some ritual function. There were few other stone artefacts either inside the shelter or on the ground outside. This is in marked contrast to most living sites or major rock art sites which usually have very dense surface scatters of stone artefact debris. In the domed hollow of the shelter, there was a rough scaffolding of thorn tree poles, probably made to suspend bags and other items above the floor. The poles showed traces of blows with a steel axe, indicating a relatively recent date, and this is confirmed by a radiocarbon date of 350 ± 50 years BP (Pta-5471) for a sample of bark from one of the poles. A socketed iron point found on the floor of the shelter, and suitable for a small spear, could therefore relate to the same date. Charcoal from the smoking

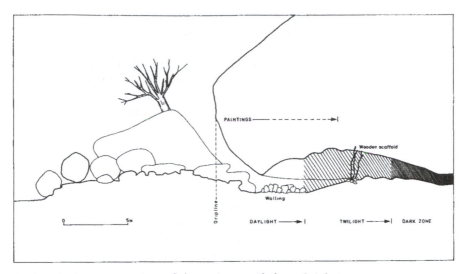

Figure 23.4   Cross-section of the Rainman Shelter, Otjohorongo.

of a bees' nest in a rock crevice nearby yielded a date of 290 ± 50 years BP (Beta-69776), and this may also refer to the same relatively recent occupation of the Rainman Shelter, with a weighted average date of 320 ± 35 years BP. Whether these dates refer to the paintings as well can only be surmised; however, the remarkably fresh appearance of many paintings in the site makes this a strong likelihood and points to the occupation of this site during recent centuries, when there would have been established pastoralist settlements in the same area (Werner 1980).

Near the far western end of the shelter is a small painted frieze that appears to depict an elephant hunt. Closer study suggests a different interpretation which in turn provides the basis for an understanding of a larger and altogether more remarkable frieze in the main part of the site. The smaller frieze, reproduced in Figure 23.5, shows three elephant apparently confronted by armed hunters. But the weapons are probably nothing more than a male secondary sexual characteristic, and other less obvious features must be considered in order to understand the purpose of the painting. For example, one of the bowmen is shown without legs, and one of his companions is shown with a hollow torso, both conventionalized symptoms of the trance state. The way in which the other humans relate to the elephant in this frieze is clearly unrealistic, as is the depiction of the elephants themselves. In the lower group, one of the human figures holds on to the trunk of the elephant, dragging it along with the aid of an assistant holding his legs: an unlikely hunting strategy in real life. Furthermore, all three elephant are shown with hollow areas in their bodies, the upper two with unrealistic hump-like elaborations on their backs. Some of these details are clarified by the large frieze, in the main part of the site, considered next. In the case of the smaller frieze it is relevant to mention that the human figures are painted as if in the act of coaxing the elephant into an area of the rock that is covered with a run of white precipitate. There are other no less suitable painting surfaces adjacent to this, so the positioning of the frieze is clearly deliberate. The frieze seems therefore to indicate an association between elephant and rainfall, mediated by ritual activity.

The main frieze at the Rainman Shelter, reproduced in Figure 23.6, is a complex work employing a variety of colours and techniques. The painting is also obviously an abstract composition, and does not immediately bring to mind any living creature or everyday event, with the exception of the line of eleven figures, identifiable as women by their long back aprons and the absence of weaponry and male sex organs. The line of women may represent a dance which involves moving in single file with extended arms. Above the women and facing toward them is a figure wearing decoration below the knees, probably for the purposes of a dance. The lack of both lower legs and face in this figure probably represents physical symptoms of the trance state. Below and to the right of this figure is a hollow human torso, with

Figure 23.5   Elephant and human figures, Rainman Shelter, Otjohorongo.

the same hook-shaped head. This figure is adjacent to an amorphous shape painted in precisely the same shade as the other figures so far described. In both colour and technique, these figures are so similar that they must form a single composition, superimposed on the rather faded painting still visible below the line of dancers.

Despite the absence of detail, the animal beneath the dancers is very clearly an elephant, or part of one. Close examination of the rock failed to locate any trace of the rest of its body, and it appears that only the belly and forelegs were painted. This is relevant because the trailing fringes in front of and behind the elephant legs were apparently painted at the same time, being similar in their degree of fading. The painting appears to have consisted of only these elements, representing the rain as the legs and underbelly of the elephant. Between the solid columns of the legs, the rain falls straight down on either side of what appears to be a bolt of lightning, shown as a meandering line with hachures at regular intervals. This must represent the centre of the rainstorm. At other points, there are similar fringes, but they are shorter and do not fall as straight. These in fact resemble fairly accurately the way in which isolated downpours seem to end before reaching the ground, with a slight curve to one side or the other indicating the force of the wind. The painting thus shows a number of easily observable features of a typical rainstorm, but conflates them with analogous characteristics of the elephant. Here, as in the case of the smaller frieze examined earlier, there is an association between the elephant, rain and ritual activity, in this case represented by the superimposed dancers.

The smaller fringes of falling rain in the right side of the frieze show that this is a single composition with a unifying theme, rather than the chance combination of different elements. This unity is important for the major reason that the frieze shows very clear evidence of being painted in several episodes. Field examination suggests that the elephant belly and legs with their fringes of rain were painted first. Next to be added were the dancers and the amorphous shape already described. Then, if it is assumed that similar but distinguishable versions of the same colours probably reflect different batches of paint and episodes of painting, the smaller amorphous shapes with fringes of rain belong to a third episode of painting. While there is no evidence that these were created at a different time from the complex of patches immediately above, there are clear traces of overpainting which suggest that this part of the frieze was elaborated on several occasions. For example, some of the bold lines within the complex are the same colour as a background layer which has been covered with a layer of chalky white paint within some of the patches. The chalky white paint appears very fresh and may represent the last of at least four episodes of painting, each a separate rain-making event.

To summarise the observations from the Rainman Shelter, it is clear from the setting and physical characteristics of the site that it would have been unsuitable to accommodate even a small group of people. The occupation

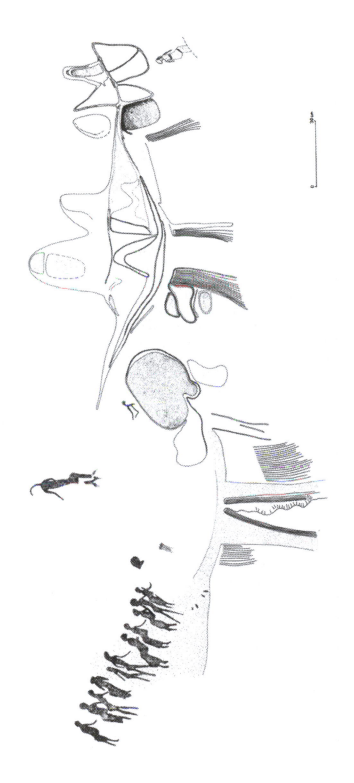

Figure 23.6 Rain animal and human figures, Rainman Shelter, Otjohorongo.

evidence confirms that the site was used during recent centuries, as reflected by the radiocarbon dating and other associations. The paintings at the site appear relatively fresh, and given that there are no indications of more intensive occupation in the past it seems reasonable to conclude that the paintings and the other evidence date to within the last few centuries, when there was established pastoral settlement in the same area. Two lines of evidence point to a relationship between the site and neighbouring pastoral communities. One is the presence of iron, both in the form of the socketed point and in the chop marks on the scaffolding. The other is the apparent use of the site for rain-making in a specialist context rather than that of communal ritual. The most likely hypothesis is that a specialist shaman used the site to make rain at the request of local pastoralists.

In suggesting specialist, possibly individual, ritual activity at this site, it is necessary to deal with the apparently contradictory evidence of communal ritual activity in the paintings. The smaller frieze shows several men attempting to coax an elephant into the run of white precipitate. In the larger frieze, the dance involves a number of women in the conventional supporting role associated with trance. Although there is a solitary figure at the extreme right of the frieze, indicating an individual in the context of the main composition, there are a further fifty-two women painted in a continuous line to the right, and not reproduced in Figure 23.6. However, considering the nature of the site and its specialised function, there are grounds to argue that human groups in the rock art are an artistic, ritual device and that they are not intended as a record of attendance. The human group is in this sense as metaphorical as the animals associated with the same ritual event. In this context, the human groups at this site underline the association between dry season aggregation and ritual, implying that communal participation may have been a powerful ingredient in rain-making rituals prior to the rise of specialist shamanism, retained thereafter as an element of the rock art.

While it is possible to object that the positioning of the first frieze in relation to the run of white precipitate is coincidental, the association between elephant and rain is difficult to refute in the second frieze. There are also similarities in the depiction of the elephants that strengthen this view. The hollow areas in the bodies of the elephants in the first frieze are paralleled in the second. Also, the hump-like elaborations in the first frieze resemble the patchwork effect in the second frieze, not as recognisable elaborations of the elephant, but rather as amorphous, interlocking shapes. Although these are probably part of the apparent analogy between elephant and rain, and it is tempting to interpret these shapes as clouds, there is no particular resemblance. On the other hand, the shapes do recall in technique the antelope torsos that occur on this and many other sites, one very good example being the female kudu at Twyfelfontein, discussed in the previous section.

The patchwork composition in the main frieze at the Rainman Shelter recalls similar paintings at Snake Rock in the Hungorob, both in general effect and in their apparent recency. The Rainman evidence also adds weight to the argument for ritual specialisation outside the context of communal life. While the evidence suggests that this is attributable to a shift in ritual practice during the last millennium, the basis of these changes must lie in the communal healing tradition that preceded the introduction of livestock to this region. The similarities with the Mason Shelter and Crane Rock also apply, along with some of the observations about them in the previous section. In common with the latter sites, the Rainman Shelter is a hidden site with some paintings in twilight and evidently used as a place of ritual seclusion. Considering the physical characteristics of the Rainman site in this context, it is tempting to speculate that the site itself seems to share some of the pool of suggestive characteristics that underlie the analogy between elephant and rain. The cool depths of the shelter in the dark and narrow parting of the rock evoke the same sensations as being under water. Furthermore, the partings of the rock appear to breathe in the heat of the day, a phenomenon associated with the rising of warm air. The fact that rain clouds often gather about such hills would merely reinforce this apparent link. Partings in the granite are good aquifers, so that, like clouds, the rock sheds water which leaves runs of precipitate. The runs resemble not only the rain itself, but also the way in which it is depicted in the rock art. Finally, the domed appearance and clustered distribution of the granites are themselves redolent of elephants, and it is unlikely that this resemblance, or the elephant's dependence on water, would have escaped the net of the shaman's mental *bricolage*. In this sense, the hills and the rain were also an elephant, interlocking parts of a continuity between ritual life, subsistence and environment.

Discussion

Rain-making, as a special skill of San medicine people, has been widely recognised in southern African rock art since the earliest stages of its study (cf. Lewis-Williams 1981). Indeed, ethnographic accounts of /Xam rain-making have been verified by archaeological research which identified rain animal motifs in the rock art of the area concerned, where it was distributed on the landscape according to specific folklore accounts of the rain (Deacon 1988). However, the metaphorical nature of these and all other paintings has led to their explanation as part of the ritual concern with the promotion of social harmony, rather than as practical attempts to influence the weather (Lewis-Williams 1982). This general interpretation of the rock art has been criticised as overly functionalist (Groenfeldt 1982), although no alternative view has developed to take into account both the social role of the healer and the environmental perceptions implied by the art.

   Although there are no ethnographic references to Namibian rock art, it clearly belongs to the same cultural tradition as the rest of southern African art. This means that while the cognitive approach is directly relevant, observations from Namibian rock art may be used to test some of its premises, particularly those based on empirical field data. Applying the cognitive approach to the Hungorob and Spitzkoppe sites confirms the ritual content of the rock art, but it leaves unanswered some questions raised by archaeological investigations at the same sites. Attempting to answer these questions inevitably leads to a reappraisal of not only the archaeological evidence but also the cognitive approach to Namibian rock art.

The first difficulty encountered by this study has been seen to be the need to explain the presence of small, peripheral rock art sites in the vicinity of putative aggregation sites. The aggregation sites could be explained as foci of concentrated dry-season residence that also served as ritual centres, according to the notion of ritual as a communal activity. Shifts in settlement over the last five millennia might explain the general pattern of site distribution, but cannot account for the occurrence of secluded sites which point to the existence of specialised shamanism within the same tradition. Although the use of secluded sites appears to be the result of a change in ritual activity during the last millennium, this seems to have arisen from an established relationship between the rock art, ritual and the environmental setting. Thus, animals were co-opted into the symbolic repertoire of the art for reasons of their supernatural potency, evoked by their physical appearance which served as visual cues for ritual trance. The same principles seem to apply in the positioning of paintings in the sites themselves and in the selection of sites for ritual and rock art purposes. In this way, ritual and rock art permeate the environment of hunter–gatherer settlement in a way that suggests an unbroken continuity between subsistence and ritual activity.

Just as hunting and the technology of subsistence obviously held strong symbolic value, the rock art and ritual activity also held some technological and practical significance. If the secluded sites are considered in this context, it appears that they were important not only for their symbolic access to the environment of animal metaphors, such as through rock crevices, but also for their use as places of sensory deprivation to aid the achievement of trance. They were also important as rock art sites, and these examples very strongly imply that the art was not a recollection of trance, as argued by Lewis-Williams (1988), but a powerful act in itself (cf. Ingold 1993). This permits a different perspective on the rock art of the Rainman Shelter, where seclusion, thematic unity, and evidence of repeated elaboration in the same frieze combine to suggest that the paintings were done in order to make rain. The paintings were therefore practical instruments rather than documents of past experience, and their production a fundamentally poetic process (see Swiderski 1995), based on the mimesis (see Taussig 1993) of natural phenomena and the causative relations between them. For this reason, the perspective gained from the Namibian sites is doubly important, for it identifies the rock art as part of what might be seen as an experimental intervention in natural processes, and an attempt to establish concrete and beneficial associations between otherwise disparate phenomena. Rain-making should therefore be seen as part of the same process of intellectual engagement that brought the perfection of arrow poisons, knowledge of plant foods and deep insights into animal behaviour, to name but a few of the widely acknowledged achievements of southern African hunter-gatherers.

The development of specialised rain-making adds a further dimension to the Later Stone Age archaeological sequence in Namibia. Based on detailed research in the Hungorob, I have elsewhere proposed that shamanism arose from the communal healing tradition as a specific response to the introduction of pastoralism (Kinahan 1991, 1993). This is in contrast to the ideological continuity argued by Lewis-Williams (1984) which I have criticised as unable to accommodate archaeological evidence for social and economic change (Kinahan 1994). However, my suggestion that shamanism was a short-lived institution in the establishment of pastoralism is apparently contradicted by the evidence of the Rainman Shelter. From this site it appears that specialised rain-making survived as a permutation of the hunter-gatherer rock art tradition alongside established pastoralism in the same area. By this time the hunting economy may well have collapsed, leaving only a few itinerant shamans. This would raise the interesting possibility of defining the areas in which these specialists practised, on the basis of idiosyncrasies of style and technique in painting. It is my expectation, based on the arguments set out above, that if the works of individual artist-shamans could be identified, they would exhibit great variety in form and content. Rather than the richness of an elaborate but static tradition of ritual art, this variety would reflect the continuous dialogue between the shaman and the forces of nature.

Acknowledgements

Fieldwork at Otjohorongo was supported by a generous grant from the Commercial Bank of Namibia, and attendance at WAC 3 in New Delhi was made possible by a grant to the Namibia Archaeological Trust by the Swedish Agency for Research Cooperation with Developing Countries.

References

Barnard, A. 1979. Kalahari Bushman settlement patterns. In *Social and Ecological Systems*, P.C. Burnham and R.F. Ellen (eds), 131–44. London: Academic Press.
Barnard, A. 1992. *Hunters and Herders of Southern Africa: a comparative ethnography of the Khoisan peoples*. Cambridge: Cambridge University Press.
Barry, R.G. and R.J. Chorley 1976. *Atmosphere, Weather and Climate* (3rd Edition). London: Methuen.
Bleek, D.F. 1933. Beliefs and customs of the /Xam Bushmen, Part VI, rain-making. *Bantu Studies* 7, 375–92.
Bradley, R. 1991. Rock art and the perception of landscape. *Cambridge Archaeological Journal* 1, 77–101.
Broadley, D.G. (ed.) 1983. *FitzSimon's Snakes of Southern Africa*. Johannesburg: Delta.

Deacon, H.J. 1976. *Where Hunters Gathered: a study of Holocene stone age people in the eastern Cape*. South African Archaeological Society Monograph Series No. 1.

Deacon, J. 1988. The power of a place in understanding southern San rock engravings. *World Archaeology* 20, 129–40.

Dowson, T.A. and J.D. Lewis-Williams 1994. *Contested Images: diversity in southern African rock art research*. Johannesburg: Witwatersrand University Press.

Groenfeldt, D. 1982. Comment on J.D. Lewis-Williams. *Current Anthropology* 23, 441.

Ingold, T. 1993. The temporality of the landscape. *World Archaeology* 25, 152–74.

Jolly, P. 1996. Symbiotic interaction between Black farmers and southeastern San. *Current Anthropology* 37, 277–306.

Katz, R. 1982. *Boiling Energy: community healing among the Kalahari !Kung*. Cambridge, Mass.: Harvard University Press.

Kinahan, J. 1990. Four thousand years at the Spitzkoppe: changes in settlement and landuse on the edge of the Namib Desert. *Cimbebasia* 12, 1–14.

Kinahan, J. 1991. *Pastoral Nomads of the Central Namib Desert: the people history forgot*. Windhoek: Namibia Archaeological Trust.

Kinahan, J. 1993. The rise and fall of nomadic pastoralism in the central Namib Desert. In *The Archaeology of Africa: food, metals and towns*, T. Shaw, P. Sinclair, B. Andah and A. Okpoko (eds), 372–85. London: Routledge.

Kinahan, J. 1994. Theory, practice and criticism in the history of Namibian archaeology. In *Theory in Archaeology: a world perspective*, P.J. Ucko (ed.), 76–95. London: Routledge.

Kinahan, J. 1996. Alternative views on the acquisition of livestock by hunter-gatherers in southern Africa: a rejoinder to Smith, Yates and Jacobson. *South African Archaeological Bulletin* 51: 106–8.

Köhler, O. 1959. *A study of Omaruru District, South West Africa*. Pretoria: Government Printer.

Lee, R.B. 1968. The sociology of !Kung Bushman trance performance. In *Trance and Possession States*, R. Prince (ed.), 35–54. Montreal: R.M. Bucke Memorial Society.

Lee, R.B. 1972. The intensification of social life among the !Kung Bushmen. In *Population Growth: anthropological implications*, B. Spooner (ed.), 343–50. Cambridge, Mass.: M.I.T. Press.

Lenssen-Erz, T. 1993. *The Rockpaintings of the Upper Brandberg, Part II, Hungorob Gorge*, by H. Pager. Köln: Heinrich Barth Institute.

Lévi-Strauss, C. 1966. *The Savage Mind*. London: Weidenfeld & Nicolson.

Lewis-Williams, J.D. 1981. *Believing and Seeing: symbolic meanings in southern San rock paintings*. London: Academic Press.

Lewis-Williams, J.D. 1982. The economic and social context of southern San rock art. *Current Anthropology* 23, 429–49.

Lewis-Williams, J.D. 1983. Introductory essay: science and rock art. In *New Approaches to Southern African Rock Art*, J.D. Lewis-Williams (ed.), 3–13. South African Archaeological Society Goodwin Series 4.

Lewis-Williams, J.D. 1984. Ideological continuities in prehistoric southern Africa: the evidence of rock art. In *Past and Present in Hunter-gatherer Studies*, C. Schrire (ed.), 225–52. Orlando: Academic Press.

Lewis-Williams, J.D. 1988. *Reality and Non-reality in San Rock Art*. Institute for the Study of Man in Africa: Raymond Dart Lecture 25.

Lewis-Williams, J.D. 1993. Southern African archaeology in the 1990s. *South African Archaeological Bulletin* 48, 45–50.

Lewis-Williams, J.D. 1995. Modelling the production and consumption of rock art. *South African Archaeological Bulletin* 50, 143–54.

Lewis-Williams, J.D. and T.A. Dowson 1989. *Images of Power: understanding Bushman rock art.* Johannesburg: Southern.

Lewis-Williams, J.D. and T.A. Dowson 1990. Through the veil: San rock paintings and the rock face. *South African Archaeological Bulletin* 45, 5–16.

Lewis-Williams, J.D. and J. Loubser 1986. Deceptive appearances: a critique of southern African rock art studies. *Advances in World Archaeology* 5, 253–89.

Mazel, A. 1989. People making history: the last ten thousand years of hunter-gatherer communities in the Thukela Basin. *Natal Museum Journal of the Humanities* 1, 1–168.

Ouzman, S. 1996. Thaba Sione: place of rhinoceroses and rock art. *African Studies* 55, 31–59.

Ouzman, S. and L. Wadley 1997. A history in paint and stone from Rose Cottage Cave, South Africa. *Antiquity* 71, 386–404.

Pager, H. 1980. Felsbildforschung am Brandberg in Namibia. *Beitrage zur Allgemeinen und Vergleichenden Archaeologie* 2, 351–7.

Parkington, J.E. 1984. Changing views of the later Stone Age of South Africa. *Advances in World Archaeology* 3, 89–142.

Prins, F.E. 1990. Southern Bushman descendants in the Transkei: rock art and rain-making. *South African Journal of Ethnology* 13, 110–16.

Schmidt, S. 1979. The rain bull of the South African Bushmen. *African Studies* 38, 201–24.

Swiderski, R.M. 1995. *Eldoret: an African poetics of technology.* Tucson: University of Arizona Press.

Taussig, M. 1993. *Mimesis and Alterity: a particular history of the senses.* London: Routledge.

Thomas, E. 1988. *The Harmless People.* Cape Town: David Phillip.

Tilley, C. 1991. *Material Culture and Text: the art of ambiguity.* London: Routledge.

Twidale, C.R. 1988. Granite landscapes. In *The Geomorphology of Southern Africa*, B.P. Moon and G.F. Dardis (eds), 198–230. Johannesburg: Southern.

Walker, N.J. 1995. *Late Pleistocene and Holocene Hunter-gatherers of the Matopos: an archaeological study of change and continuity in Zimbabwe.* Uppsala: Societas Archaeologica Upsaliensis.

Werner, W. 1980. An exploratory investigation into the mode of production of the Herero in pre-colonial Namibia to ca. 1870. Unpublished B.Soc.Sci. (Honours) thesis, University of Cape Town.

Yates, R., A. Manhire and J.E. Parkington 1994. Rock painting and history in the south-western Cape. In *Contested Images: diversity in southern African rock art research*, T.A. Dowson and J.D. Lewis-Williams (eds), 29–60. Johannesburg: Witwatersrand University Press.

24 The representation of Sámi cultural identity in the cultural landscapes of northern Sweden: the use and misuse of archaeological knowledge

INGA-MARIA MULK
AND TIM BAYLISS-SMITH

Introduction

In this chapter we consider the ways in which the culture of the Sámi (or Saami, formerly known as Lapps) is being represented in the landscapes of the interior of northern Sweden, in the province known as Lappland. Our main focus is on the area occupied by the Sámi along the Lule river valley and its lakes and catchment, within what was once the Lule Lappmark administrative region and is today the county of Norrbotten. However, we also use examples from elsewhere in the Sámi region, 'Sámeatnam' or 'Sápmi' as it is coming to be known. Sápmi is defined as the area of present-day Sámi settlement in the northern parts of Norway, Sweden and Finland and the adjacent Kola peninsula of Russia. Archaeologists are now convinced that modern Sápmi covers a less extensive area than was previously occupied by the Sámi. It is thought that the distribution of asbestos ware in the first millennium BC indicates the former area of Sámi settlement (Carpelan 1979; Jorgensen and Olsen 1988). However, for present purposes we restrict our attention to the region of acknowledged Sámi self-identity at the present day (Figure 24.1).

The Lule river has two main tributaries, the Stora and Lilla Luleälv, with catchments that extend nearly 300 km inland from their confluence near the town of Jokkmokk. Both rivers have their headwaters in the Scandes mountains along the present-day border with Norway (Figure 24.1). The upper parts of their valleys are in a mountains/foothills zone that is mainly occupied by lakes. Below Jokkmokk the combined Lule river flows a further 150 km across forested lowlands, reaching the Gulf of Bothnia at Luleå. The Arctic Circle passes through Jokkmokk, but the area is not as climatically severe as its latitude might suggest, thanks to the effect of maritime air masses from the Atlantic. Nevertheless, the main lakes are frozen for at least six months of the year and there is six to eight months of snow cover. In the mountains, the vegetation is an alpine tundra above about 700 m. Below this is a sub-alpine zone of birch forest, merging into the pine-spruce-birch forests

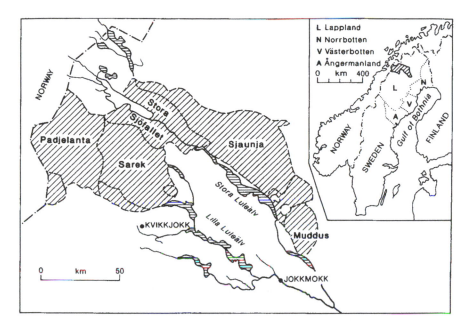

Figure 24.1 Lule River, upper valley in northern Sweden, showing the boundaries of various national parks which constitute Laponia World Heritage Area.

of the northern boreal forest zone below about 500 m. The main subsistence resources in prehistoric times were reindeer, elk, beaver and small game animals, and fish from the lakes and rivers.

The historical sources for Lappland are sparse or non-existent until after AD 1600, when the area of Sámi settlement starts to be incorporated within the Swedish state. Initially the colonisation process involved Swedish farmers spreading inland from the coast. Towards the end of the 1500s, the Lutheran church began to establish missionary outposts among the Sámi, and the Swedish crown then imposed taxation on the Sámi living in the lappmark regions of the interior (Hultblad 1968). In 1700, the Sámi population of Lule Lappmark amounted to about 3,500 persons, compared to a Swedish population of about 17,500 (Rydving 1993: 42).

Archaeological evidence shows that initial settlement of the inland region occurred as the ice retreated 8–9,000 years ago. The evidence suggests the presence from earliest times of a complex hunter-fisher-gatherer society living mostly along the lakes and rivers. Hunting pits for trapping elk and reindeer date back 5,000 years; there is also evidence for food storage and interaction with surrounding areas (Bergman and Mulk 1992; Bergman 1995; Forsberg 1996).

Trading in furs was increasingly important for Sámi hunting society in prehistoric times up to *c.* AD 1600. In the seventeenth century, the hunting culture was replaced by intensive reindeer pastoralism. For the Mountain

Sámi, reindeer-herding involved seasonal movements between the Scandes mountains and the boreal forest zone. The Forest Sámi in the lower valley regions lived a more sedentary lifestyle based on fishing and reindeer husbandry (Manker 1960, 1963; Mulk 1994a). The first record of a Sámi farmer in Lule Lappmark is not until 1738, but by the mid-nineteenth century increasing numbers had become sedentary and lived off farming, fishing or paid employment (Hultblad 1968; Lundmark 1982; Rydving 1993).

Who owns the Sámi landscape?

The rights of the Sámi to ownership of the land that they used began to change after the 1760s (Korpijaakko 1985; Kvist 1991, 1992). Sámi land that had formerly been treated by the Swedish state as if it were freehold farmland began to be regarded as land belonging to the Swedish crown, with the Sámi as tenants. The right of Sámis to inherit land was rejected by a Norrbotten court in 1827: from this point on, Sámi land rights were regarded only as a right of usufruct. This removal of ownership rights and increasing agricultural colonisation led to persistent conflicts between Sámi reindeer-herders and Swedish farmers, a situation exacerbated after the 1870s by the growing importance of commercial forestry. By an Act of 1886 the reindeer-grazing area where Sámi had usufruct rights was reduced in order to exclude some of the disputed areas, through a redrawing of the Odlingsgränsen or boundary of agricultural settlement. Grazing and other rights were restricted to the inhabitants of lappbyar, which today are the samebyar or Sámi villages. The rights of Sámi fishing or farming communities were not acknowledged at all by the 1886 Act (Beach 1981; Ruong 1982).

Those who, particularly after 1850, chose or were forced to establish new ways of life in farming, fishing, forestry, or urban/professional activities therefore tended to lose some aspects of their Sámi identity. There is no doubt that this process was encouraged by the official policies of the Swedish state which, to this day, has not sanctioned the use of the Sámi language for civil or legal purposes. In 1993, the Sámi still within samebyar lost the exclusive right to hunt elk and small game in the state forests and mountain areas inland of the Odlingsgränsen, so that this area is now in danger of becoming as overhunted as the rest of Norrbotten. By this action the Swedish state removed one of the few remaining ways through which the Sámi retained collective control over the resources of their land. The reindeer herders still retain their grazing and associated rights, but there are some bureaucrats in Stockholm and Brussels who now argue that in the European Union of the future even this concession is an anachronism.

We can see from this brief outline that the legal status of the Sámi in relation to their cultural landscape has undergone many changes. What had been ownership rights and then limited use rights have been reduced by the state to a dwindling set of privileges, available only to a limited number within a particular occupational group. After 1886, Sámi ethnicity came to be regarded as practically synonymous with the practice of reindeer-herding. Abandoning that occupation meant that a person no longer belonged to a Sámi village organisation (*lappby*), which in turn meant that he or she lost the rights granted by the state to herd reindeer, construct dwellings in state forests, hunt and fish, etc.

The narrow economic interpretation of Sámi ethnicity is part of what Kvist (1992: 70) calls 'the non-policy of assimilation'. It was accompanied in the twentieth century by a paternalistic policy of segregation for the remaining nomads, who were provided with a separate welfare administration, schools, etc., and a special police force to administer the reindeer-grazing acts. Aspects of both policies were still in force until the 1970s. Throughout the modern period, the Swedish government has shown that it is no longer prepared to grant the Sámi any rights that would diminish the claims of farming, forestry and, more recently, water regulation for hydro-electricity.

In these ways, non-herding Sámi have been obliged to relinquish an important part of their cultural identity. In Sweden today there remain only about 900 active reindeer herders within *samebyar*, supporting a population of about 2,500, whereas the total population that claims a Sámi cultural identity is at least 17,000 (Beach 1981: 5). It is not surprising that the net effect has been an erosion of Sámi ethnicity. For example, in 1975 40 per cent of the non-herding Sámi population in Sweden could not speak the Sámi language and 65 per cent could not read it (Kvist 1992: 70). In other ways, though, Sámi cultural identity remains very strong, and indeed most Sámi believe that it is stronger today than it was twenty years ago.

The purpose of this chapter is to explore the role of archaeology in the construction of this cultural identity. We do this first by examining the notion of cultural landscape as it is applies to Lappland today. Second, we consider the ways in which Sámi ethnicity has been represented in the prehistoric landscapes that archaeologists can reconstruct. Third, we consider some of the ways in which the past is being incorporated by the Sámi themselves and by others in the construction of cultural landscapes as an aspect of heritage, and to serve the interests and needs of different groups in modern society.

Constructing the Sámi cultural landscape today

In recent years the concept of cultural landscape, or *kulturlandskap*, has become quite widespread in the literature of North America, Britain and Scandinavia. It is therefore important to establish the meaning of this term. Some writers consider a landscape to be cultural merely because it shows signs of having been modified by agricultural activities, leading to a full domestication of both nature and culture. It can be argued that an environment becomes less and less 'natural' under the cumulative impact of human activities, and that therefore it becomes more and more 'cultural'. However, we prefer to use more neutral words such as 'ecosystem', 'environment' or 'surroundings' to describe this human-modified environment, its vegetation, land use, settlements, etc. Such things can be listed and scientifically analysed so as to provide a kind of total landscape inventory, but such an inventory does not, in our view, constitute a cultural landscape in the full sense.

We prefer to use the term 'cultural landscape' in a more precise way. Cultures exist in people's heads, not on the ground, but the activities that are shaped by culturally constructed meanings take place in the real world, and impact upon that world. The environment in which people live is therefore simultaneously their 'landscape', in other words one aspect of the system of shared meanings ('culture') that they construct, and also a real world of hills, forests and buildings.

Before considering the landscapes constructed by Sámi cultures in the past, it is worth considering different constructions of present-day cultural landscapes, and what ideological role such constructions might play. Duncan and Duncan (1988: 123) have argued that 'one of the most important roles that landscape plays in the social process is ideological, supporting a set of ideas and values, unquestioned assumptions about the way a society is, or should be organised'. The organisation of society obviously includes the practice of archaeology, and the knowledge that is generated by archaeologists should not be thought of as something that is outside the social process (Olsen 1991). The dominant images through which a region like Lappland is represented can therefore provide an important starting point for our analysis, showing us the unquestioned assumptions that dominate discourse about the Sámi.

Eagleton (1983) has shown that it is one of the functions of ideology to 'naturalise' social reality, and to make it seem as innocent and unchangeable as Nature itself. Through ideology, culture is thus converted into nature, and becomes purged of ambiguity and alternative possibility. Duncan and Duncan (1988: 123) use this insight to argue that landscapes are texts that are read by different cultures according to their own ingrained ideological frameworks of interpretation. Virtually any landscape can be read as a text in which social or political relations are inscribed, and naive readings of the landscape can commit the error of 'naturalising' these social and political relations.

If the way in which a cultural landscape is portrayed is an ideological construct, then assumptions about the role of the Sámi can be revealed in the prevailing images of the landscapes of northern Scandinavia. Popular literature can thus provide for us a window on the predominant ideology. We use three examples to show typical constructions of the landscapes of Lappland. One is taken from an international publication, the second from a prestigious university project within Sweden, and the third from a local source in Norbotten.

For its international readership, Time-Life Books commissioned a book entitled *Lapland*, which was translated into many languages and published around the world within the Time-Life series *The World's Wild Places*. The text fully acknowledges 'Lapland' as the homeland of the Sámi, but the coverage focuses very much on the 'traditional' reindeer husbandry of the Sámi as a dying art, amidst the backdrop of an exotic flora and fauna and the 'awesome landscapes' of this 'northern wilderness' (Marsden 1976). In accounts such as these the cultural landcape of northern Sweden is constructed as a wild place that has been lightly touched by the reindeer-herding activities of a vanishing people.

We would expect a more sophisticated conceptualisation of the landscape concept to emerge from academic writing, particularly in a prestigious project such as *Sveriges Nationalatlas* published by the Institute of Cultural Geography at Stockholm University. Volume 13 of the atlas, *Kulturlandskapet och bebyggelsen*, is a magnificent and comprehensive treatment of Swedish cultural landscapes past and present. However, it is striking how reluctant most authors are to confront the issue of cultural diversity. In particular, the role of the Sámi in constructing the landscapes of northern Sweden is notable for its absence. It is assumed that environmental modification on a scale sufficient for the creation of a *kulturlandskap* can be defined only by the presence of agriculture. The entire prehistory of the Sámi is rendered invisible by this negative definition of their landscape.

To give one example, in a map showing the regional classification of cultural landscapes *c.* AD 1750, the characteristics of a vast area described as 'the North Norrland Inland and Lappmark region' are summarised as follows: 'lacking proper agricultural settlement before 1700, and with a spread of new settlements between 1700 and 1750' (Sporrong 1994: 32, translated). No comment is provided for the equally vast Mountain Region, presumably because this region is not regarded as having been a cultural landscape at all in 1750 bcause it lacked any agricultural possibilities. Everywhere the emphasis is on the spread of farming and sedentary settlement, and their impact on the environment. For instance, the cultural landscape of Arjeplog in Pite Lappmark is defined only by its colonisation in the nineteenth century. In the Lule river valley to the north, the spread of farming from medieval times onwards is the main focus. The Sámi are mentioned only in connection with the onset of reindeer pastoralism, and no ethnic identity at all is ascribed to earlier hunting cultures (Baudou 1994: 23).

For an example of the construction of cultural landscapes at a local scale we need go no further than Jokkmokk, an important centre in northern Sweden's inland region. Jokkmokk's tourist brochure is translated into four languages, and it comments on its surrounding landscape as follows:

> Miles and miles of forest and marsh. That is how the inner part of the north can be described as well as being a source of recreation and industrial raw materials. ... Our firm right of public access allows us possibilities as well as responsibilities of free usage. Remember that the land constitutes a cultural landscape where people have lived and worked for generations.
>
> (Turism i Jokkmokk AB 1995: 2)

Specifying the cultural identity of the various people who have lived in, worked and modified such a landscape is not seen as a relevant question, when the focus is on the possibilities of the forests or lakes in relation to present-day 'mainstream' activities such as tourism, hydro-electricity and timber production.

Three concepts of cultural landscape

In academic writings over the last thirty years, the cultural-landscape concept has been explored within both natural-science and social-science traditions, and this has given rise to a diverse range of meanings for the term. We can distinguish between three rather different concepts of cultural landscape:

1　the environment as modified by the cumulative effect of human activities;
2　the landscape produced by a particular culture in a particular period, and what survives of it at the present day; and
3　the cultural meanings associated with a landscape, and the metaphors, symbols and artefacts through which these meanings are expressed.

The first concept is essentially no different from any realistic notion of ecosystem; the second concept we might summarise as being the material form of the cultural landscape; while the third is a cognitive landscape, or what was called in an older literature 'the cognized environment' (Rappaport 1968: 237–41). Each of these three ways of conceptualising a cultural landscape is now considered in turn.

The environment as modified by humans

For ecologists, palynologists and many geographers, regions like northern Sweden can be viewed as a series of interacting natural ecosystems and landforms most of which have been modified to some degree, and over a long period, by human activities. This approach was well illustrated in the symposium held at the University of Bergen and published as *The Cultural Landscape – Past, Present and Future* (Birks *et al.* 1988). Those contributing to this book fully recognised the implications of the mass of evidence emerging from the study of pollen, lake sediments and prehistory, which showed that everywhere in Europe vegetation and soils have experienced some degree of human impact. By the 1980s it was also obvious from field observations that changes were under way in apparently 'natural' meadows, mires and forests, following the abandonment of pre-industrial land-use practices:

> In the end it was recognised that even in Scandinavia a virgin landscape was a fiction. With some small and doubtful exceptions all vegetation types were created or modified by man. . . . Instead of conceiving of the Scandinavian landscape as a vast 'natural' area

with small cultivated patches, the idea developed that the whole
fjord or the whole valley is one great cultivation effect.

(Faegri 1988: 1–2)

From this there emerged the idea of 'the cultural landscape' as an object for
study, or even for conservation using our knowledge of the processes and
technologies that produced this environment in the first place.

As an example, the vegetation of the boreal forests of northern Sweden
can be seen as an ecosystem subtly modified by humans over a long period.
Human influences include changes in the frequency of forest fires, changes
in grazing pressure by reindeer and other animals, and *svedjebruk* or slash-
and-burn cultivation (Engelmark 1976; Zackrisson 1977; Tvengsberg 1985;
Aronsson 1991; Segerström 1996). These forests are therefore partly natural
and partly anthropogenic. In this sense, as with almost all places on Earth,
northern Sweden as a landscape is very much the product of culture as well
as nature.

A problem with this modified-environment approach is that the explanations offered, whether for change or for stability, tend to be extremely
generalised. The analysis takes little or no account of the identity of the actual
'cultures' that are responsible for the observed or reconstructed environmental
relationships. Climatic change or soil exhaustion is often invoked to account
for 'stress'. Human agency is diminished, and the point of view of the reindeer,
the pine tree or even the diatom receives as much emphasis as the perceptions of the hunter, the forester or the fisherman. Explanation seldom ventures
beyond the assumption that 'new technology' or 'population pressure' results
in an inevitable 'ecological impact' (e.g. Berglund 1988).

The landscape of a particular culture

The need for a different concept of 'cultural landscape' has arisen from the
limitations of the modified-ecosystem concept of environmental science. A
failure to problematise the notion of culture is understandable in a tourist
brochure. It is also not surprising when the object of study is the severe
ecological impact of an activity such as mining, colonisation for agriculture,
forestry or water regulation for hydro-electric power. The power of agencies within the modern industrial state to transform the environment so greatly
exceeds what came before, that the cultural origins of such impacts appear
to be self-evident. For example, the reasons for the State having such control
over land-use decisions in northern Sweden would not be regarded by an
ecologist as something worth studying. The answers to such questions are to
be found not in the northern lakes, forests and mountains but in Stockholm.
Meanwhile the impacts themselves demand urgent study.

Problems arise when this attitude is applied to protected areas like the Sarek,
Padjelanta and Stora Sjöfallet national parks in the mountain zone of the Lule
river system (see Figure 24.1). Because gross impacts from industrial society
have been avoided in such places, it is all too easy to assume that they are

'un-cultural landscapes'. For tourists from the south, nature conservation and wilderness are what are valued in these protected areas. Such an assumption is exploited in the rhetoric of tourist brochures. Jokkmokk, for example, presents itself to visitors in a brochure in four languages entitled *Jokkmokk – Wilderness Country*:

> You will find the forests and mountains attractive during all the seasons. Spring with snowmobiling and cross-country skiing in gleaming white sunlit surroundings. Summer with its open heavens. Autumn with its fantastic golds, reds and oranges as well as hunting and berry picking. Winter with its cold blue light and, of course, ice fishing. . . . Undisturbed nature is a human right. . . . The municipality of Jokkmokk accommodates large tracts of national parks and reserves . . . which form a huge wilderness area. Large expanses are needed to give an adequate shelter to wildlife.
>
> (Turism i Jokkmokk AB 1995: 1)

For the most famous of the national parks, Sarek, the meaning of 'wilderness' is explained in another free booklet entitled *Sarek, Myth and Reality*:

> Sarek is a magnificent untouched alpine area with sharp peaks and glaciers. . . . Sarek is a wilderness without roads. The central sections of the national park are many kilometres from inhabited areas. There are no tourist facilities established, no trails or cabins here. . . . [However] during the tourist season it is hardly desolate in Sarek. Around 2,000 people hike in the area during the summer months. . . . Wilderness implies only untouched nature in its original state.
>
> (Swedish Environmental Protection Agency 1995: 1–2)

The maintenance plans for the park are explicit that 'this unique untouched environment is to be preserved intact' (Swedish Environmental Protection Agency 1995: 3), and that no tourist cabins have been or will be provided. It therefore comes as a surprise to be told later on in this publication that reindeer husbandry is still practised in Sarek, although 'the few Lapp huts which exist in the area are more or less ruins. Only the one at Tielmaskaite is usable' (Swedish Environmental Protection Agency 1995: 6).

Untouched except by somebody's reindeer, and by 'Lapp [Sámi] ruins'? Is Sarek, or is it not, an 'untouched wilderness'? What we see here is a reluctant acknowledgement that Sarek is simultaneously two kinds of cultural landscape. It can be constructed by tourism promoters as an 'un-cultural' landscape of wilderness and a playground for adventure-seekers, backpackers, glaciologists and bird-watchers. But in fact it is also a cultural landscape of Sámi livelihood, settlement and symbolic meaning.

This duality first had to be confronted in the early 1900s, when Sarek and Stora Sjöfallet were originally proposed by the Swedish government as national parks even though large areas were used by the Mountain Sámi for summer pastures. It was politically feasible for the State to establish these parks only when guarantees were given that none of the use rights of members of *samebyar* would be in any way affected. This is in contrast to the state hydro-electricity company Vattenfall, which was given an almost unrestricted freedom to build dams and control the flow of rivers, and as a result has inundated former settlements and cultural sites and has degraded fisheries on a large scale. The national parks, however, despite being presented to tourists as areas of wilderness, have always had incorporated into their regulations the maintenance of full access rights for the reindeer herders. Sarek and Stora Sjöfallet came into being in 1909 (but had some areas removed for use by Vattenfall in the 1920s); Muddus was established in 1942, and Padjelanta in 1962.

In 1996, the Swedish government proposed to join together these national parks and some smaller areas to form one large World Heritage Area ('Laponia'), for listing by UNESCO. The government agency responsible, Naturvårdsverket (Natural Environmental Protection Agency), first promoted this idea because of the area's outstanding natural landscape and plants and animals, but Naturvårdsverket quickly realised that UNESCO's new 1994 policy to allow cultural landscapes to be included for World Heritage listing provided an opportunity for Laponia to be put forward both as an outstanding sub-Arctic wilderness and also as a cultural landscape of Sámi historic sites and present-day livelihood.

All of Laponia does indeed have cultural meaning for the Sámi. It is a cultural landscape both in the functional sense and because of its historic and cultural sites. Its functional role stems from the importance of the mountain pastures in the seasonal economy of the reindeer herders, and the significance of rights to hunt and fish in the mountain lakes and rivers. In the Sarek mountains in particular there also exist many traces of a Sámi cultural presence in the past, such as old settlement sites, earthworks showing former dwellings, hearths, cooking and food storage pits and graves. There are pitfall traps and other hunting sites, barrier fences, herding fences and other evidence for reindeer pastoralism. There are traces of rock carvings, Dreaming spots, landmarks that feature in myths, sacred mountains and sacrificial sites (Mulk 1994a). Laponia has a historical, sacred and symbolic significance that goes beyond its present-day contribution to Sámi livelihood.

The definition of Laponia as a cultural landscape for the Sámi has become an integral part of the case made for it to be given World Heritage listing, alongside the spectacular natural landscape of essentially untouched mountain peaks, glaciers and wetlands, pine forests and distinctive flora and fauna. In the past, the imposition of national boundaries, the regulation of lakes and rivers, and other legal restrictions have eroded Sámi rights. However, the Swedish government's submission to UNESCO makes it clear that in Laponia the remaining Sámi rights will be fully recognised. It is agreed that the new regulations for the World Heritage Area will not lead to any curtailment of the rights already accorded under the Reindeer Husbandry Act with respect to pasturage, felling, fishing, and hunting of animals other than the brown bear, lynx, wolf, wolverine, elk and eagles. The Sámi will continue to be allowed to work and live there, and to bring dogs and snow-mobiles with them in order to herd reindeer (Statens naturvårdsverk 1995: 21).

The Laponian World Heritage Area provides a good example of how the term 'cultural landscape' is now commonly used to describe those features of an environment that need to be understood in cultural terms. This landscape is material – it is 'out there' rather than in people's heads – but to understand it we need to appreciate the way in which particular communities, past and present, have encoded their cultural values on the land in settlements, landmarks, boundaries and sacred places. Rather than focusing on particular 'sites', we need to see the whole picture. As Bergman (1991: 66) has argued, 'by focussing on the totality of the Saami landscape, rather than its particularities, hidden structures are made visible'.

The cognitive landscape and its cultural meanings

From anthropology and cultural geography has emerged a different way to see landscape, an emic rather than an etic view, and one that is well summarised by the culture historian Simon Schama:

> Although we are accustomed to separate nature and human perception into two realms, they are, in fact, indivisible. Before it can ever be a repose for the senses, landscape is the work of the mind. Its scenery is built up as much from strata of memory as from layers of rock. . . . Landscapes are culture before they are nature; constructs of the imagination projected onto wood and water and rock.
>
> (Schama 1995: 6–7, 61)

He recalls how as a small child in a Hebrew school in London, he stuck green leaves on to a paper tree on his classroom wall, each leaf representing sixpence raised for a reforestation project in Israel. The children supposed that the trees were cedars which were planted to recreate the fragrance of Solomon's temple (in reality they were probably eucalypts planted to stabilise sand dunes). As Schama remarks, 'if a child's vision of nature can already be loaded with complicating memories, myths and meanings, how much more elaborately wrought is the frame through which our adult eyes survey the landscape' (Schama 1995: 6).

This example introduces a very different idea of cultural landscape from the human-modified-environment concept of the natural sciences. Nor is it the same concept as the landscape of surviving activities and cultural remains that is used by most archaeologists. Schama builds upon the writings of cultural geographers like Cosgrove, Daniels and Duncan, in seeing the landscape as the set of perceptions that exist within a particular culture, rather than what actually exists 'out there'. Following Duncan (1995: 415), we can define culture as an interconnected series of communicative codes, and we can see landscape as one of many signifying systems through which social and political values are communicated. The cognised environment ('landscape') is something that people construct out of the rhythms of their daily lives and from their imaginations and memories. A cultural landscape can thus be redefined as the way in which a people's surroundings are represented, structured and symbolised (Cosgrove 1984; Daniels and Cosgrove 1988; Duncan and Duncan 1988; Duncan 1990).

This landscape of cultural meanings can be studied from the traces that might survive in material form, in mountains, trees, houses, hunting pits, graves and landmarks. However, its origins must be sought in the minds and the memories of the people who lived in those houses or who dug those pits and graves. Groups of people will normally share a collective vision of how their world should be structured in names, metaphors and symbols. Where such a collective consensus can be identified it can be described as something shared by those who have a common 'ethnicity', or a shared 'cultural identity'.

The shared symbols, metaphors and meanings that people construct in their surroundings will take on a different significance for them according to their way of life and mode of subsistence. For example, hunter–gatherers and pastoral nomads may occupy the same physical space, but they will tend to perceive their surroundings differently. For hunter–gatherers, the relations of production are tied to territories or significant sites, whereas for nomadic pastoralists, productive relations are largely independent of place, being vested in their mobile pastoral capital – in other words, their herds. Thus pastoralists will normally have a concept of territory that is geared to the acquisition of pasture to allow livestock production, compared to hunter–gatherers who will seek to establish symbolic links between their community and particular places in order to guarantee consumption (Ingold 1980; Cribb 1991: 21).

Ingold (1987) has further argued that the perceptions of agriculturalists will differ from those of either hunter–gatherers or pastoralists. What agriculture achieves through the practical operations of clearing the ground and tilling the earth is an ownership of land and its separation from the wider landscape:

> Hunters and gatherers appropriate the land by holding the objects or features that originally contain it; agriculturalists appropriate the land by disconnecting it from those features so that it may be harnessed in the construction of an artificial, substitute environment.
>
> (Ingold 1987: 154)

Hunter–gatherers see the land as the source of a mystical power that brings into being the people 'holding' that land. Ritual attention focuses on the places in the landscape where the power is thought to reside, giving rise to a form of animism rather than a cult of the earth (Ingold 1987: 154–7).

Change from one way of life to another may therefore involve much more than the mere adoption of a new technology. It requires a reordering of the symbolic categories through which a culture distinguishes the domesticated sphere (termed 'domus' by Hodder 1990) from the wild, undomesticated and uncultural landscapes that lie outside (Hodder's 'agrios'). In southern Scandinavia, Hodder has argued that the adoption of agriculture by hunting-gathering-fishing communities was delayed for at least 1,300 years because of an incompatibility in symbolic categories between Ertebölle culture and the neolithic ways of life that had developed further south. Agriculture failed to spread into southern Scandinavia not for climatic reasons or because farming was regarded as an inferior economy, but because of a rejection by Ertebölle society of the symbolic and social role of the Danubian 'domus' without which the transition to farming could not be successfully accomplished. Once certain transformations had taken place in central Europe in the way in which the cultural landscape was organised, then agriculture became more compatible with Ertebölle principles (Hodder 1990: 182).

There is therefore a multitude of ways in which people, differentially engaged and differentially empowered, perceive, appropriate and contest their landscapes. Way of life, age and gender will all affect the construction of an individual's perceived environment (Bender 1993: 17). A person from a community that has lived and worked in a place for generations will construct meanings in a different way from someone who is visiting from elsewhere. Among outsiders, an archaeologist will probably see cultural landscapes very differently from the average tourist. And the archaeologists themselves can disagree, as we can show from the example of cultural landscape reconstruction in northern Scandinavia.

Problems in reconstructing the cultural landscapes of northern Sweden

For the archaeologist, it is the third definition of the cultural landscape that is the most exciting but at the same time the most problematic. Even if a 'cognitive archaeology of the ancient mind' (Renfrew 1994) should be our ultimate goal, the road towards it is hard to follow. We can catch only glimpses of the cognitive landscapes of the past. The actual artefacts that make one cultural landscape distinct from another constitute one guide towards uncovering their hidden meanings. The other guide, but one that is not always available, is ethnographic analogy. Here one needs extreme care to avoid drawing false parallels from selected evidence. Tilley (1994), for example, selects ethnographic evidence that seems to show that in Aboriginal and Melanesian societies, every prominent feature in the landscape is related to myth. He therefore argues that the location of mesolithic and neolithic sites in Britain requires an interpretation in similar terms. Landscape is indeed myth, but we would argue that it is also many other things.

The problems of reconstructing cultural landscapes of the past are fully demonstrated by the case of northern Sweden. It is now generally accepted that the nomadic pastoralist society of Sámi reindeer-herding is comparatively recent. In its traditional form, before the onset of road transport, snow-mobiles and radio communications, this way of life was quite well documented, but its origins in northern Sweden cannot be traced using historical sources further back than about AD 1600 (Hultblad 1968; Lundmark 1982). Reindeer domestication itself took place much earlier, and tame reindeer must have played an important role in the earlier hunting society for transport and as decoys (Mulk 1994a). However, there are many other aspects of that earlier society that remain hidden from us because of the sweeping changes that followed the onset of full-scale, intensive pastoralism, the adoption of Christianity, and Swedish colonisation.

To uncover the cognitive landscapes of Sámi prehistory, which in effect means the period from the end of the Ice Age until about AD 1600, we are therefore obliged to seek meanings by an imaginative integration of the evidence. The archaeological evidence, such as the distribution of settlements, reindeer-hunting pits, and the patterns of seasonal mobility that can be inferred, all needs to be viewed in its spatial and ecological context. We must also use the ethnographic evidence from what is known of pre-Christian Sámi religion, ritual, myth and social organisation, and from the surviving forms of ancient Sámi practices such as handicrafts, hunting and fishing. With caution we can extrapolate from the structural features of hunting societies in broadly similar environments elsewhere in the world, for example the Nganasans of northern Siberia and the caribou-hunting Indians and Inuit of North America (Mulk 1994b, 1996). In this way we believe that some progress can be made towards constructing the cognitive landscapes of past societies, in addition to identifying each landscape's material form as a culturally specific modification of ecological space.

The landscape as gendered and politicised

Finally, and before we confront the specific problems of reconstructing Sámi cultural landscapes, we should consider another general problem. Most of the archaeologists writing about northern Scandinavia have tended to avoid questions of gender and social status. Were there fundamental divisions in prehistoric societies between men and women, or inequalities based on power and wealth? It seemed to many archaeologists unrealistic to seek answers to such questions with the data that were available. The emphasis instead was on the collective behaviour of populations, within an environment that was conceptualised in terms of resources and ecological relationships rather than as a landscape of symbolic or social meanings.

In Scandinavia, just as questions of ethnic identity were not even mentioned in most accounts, so the prehistoric cultures of the region have mostly been constructed with little or no reference to questions of gender (Engelstad 1991; Sörenson 1992). Yet in most societies, past and present, there is a marked sexual division of labour. Does this also mean that to some extent there is a gendered division of social space? If so, we should expect that the cultural landscapes that people construct, both on the ground and in their minds, are also gendered.

Other kinds of power relations, those that derive from whatever social hierarchy may exist to control land, people and resources, will also influence the construction of the landscape. Even in relatively egalitarian societies, there are persons with specialised roles. In Mongolia, for example, there are chiefs and shamans in every community, competing with each other as sources of social power. Humphrey (1995) contrasts the competing cognitive landscapes of the chiefs and shamans. The chiefly landscape is associated with the steppes and is linked to political ambition and the organisation of space in a nomadic pastoralist society. The shamanistic landscape of the forests is linked to empowerment over the mystical realms of the cosmos. The two competing visions must also be seen as symbiotic, the one implying the existence of the other: 'the two landscapes are always superimposed on each other, even if, at a given time and place, one or other is in the ascendant' (Humphrey 1995: 158). Probably when any society is analysed in detail, the generalisations that we choose to make about its 'collective' cultural landscape become difficult to sustain.

All this makes the reconstruction of cultural landscapes of the past a particularly challenging task, as the sources of information available to us are so biased. Even in the historical period, where cultural landscapes are actually depicted, bias from social class and gender presents problems. For example, it is not easy to use Renaissance Italian or seventeenth-century Dutch paintings to illustrate contemporary attitudes to the landscape. Most of the art in these societies was controlled by men who belonged to a relatively privileged elite, and it was produced in order to please patrons and for aesthetic reasons rather than to serve as a map of the collective cultural landscape (Berger 1972; Cosgrove 1984; Green 1995).

A similar problem arises in relation to archaeological 'monuments', those particularly prominent sites and artefacts that always have a high priority in heritage legislation and protection. In the context of Norway in Viking times, Lillehammer (1987, 1994a, 1994b) has pointed to a persistent bias in the presentation of heritage. In most cases the monuments selected are the objects of male wealth, power and social status, and belong exclusively to what she terms 'the landscape of prestige' (*Prestijelandskapet*). She argues that even in modern Norway there is male bias and an automatic respect for hierarchy among the archaeologists and others who administer the heritage laws. As a result, it is very easy for those in power today to overlook the underlying structures that sustained the landscapes of prestige. These structures, which she calls 'the everyday cultural landscape' (*Hverdagslandskapet*), are defined as 'the physical as well as the mental landscapes reflecting the more secular activities of the past'. In the original construction of this everyday landscape, women were as important as men, and in some cases even more so. In contrast to this almost invisible and officially neglected everyday landscape, the landscapes of prestige are well represented by the preservation of monuments, for example prominent burial mounds, large rock-carving areas, castles and churches (Lillehammer 1994a: 2–3).

In Figures 24.2 and 24.3 we attempt to present these ideas in diagrammatic form. The diagrams are based on those presented by Lillehammer (1994b: 157–9), but they have been modified to achieve the conceptual separation outlined above between the material remains of a cultural landscape such as gendered monuments, etc. (Figure 24.2), and that landscape in its cognitive form and represented in cultural meanings (names, myths, metaphors

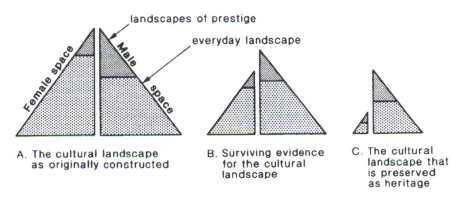

Figure 24.2 The cultural landscape in material form, gendered and divided according to its prestige or everyday purpose: (A) as originally constructed; (B) the traces of evidence that have survived; (C) the aspects typically chosen for preservation of heritage (modified from Lillehammer 1994a, 1994b).

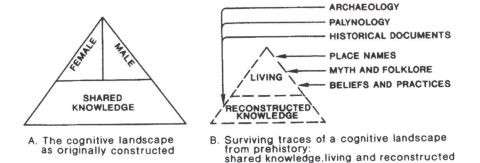

Figure 24.3 The cognitive landscape: cultural landscapes of the memory and the imagination, encoded in ritual, myth and symbolic meaning: (A) as originally constructed; and (B) in surviving or reconstructed form today.

and symbols) and what survives of them (Figure 24.3). In order to draw these
diagrams at a realistic scale, some difficult questions would have to be answered
about the ways in which actual and perceptual space was divided by gender
or status in a particular culture in the past, as well as questions about the
survival and preservation of such landscapes today.

Lillehammer's own example (1994a, 1996) was of a farming culture on
the coast of Norway in the Iron Age (c. AD 300–900). This society showed
a marked division of labour between the women who farmed and raised children and the men who were involved in fishing and in status enhancement
through ship-borne mobility and trade. The very different Sámi societies
that were living on the Norwegian coast at this time may require quite a
different conceptualisation of their cultural landscapes, and those living in the
mountains of the interior, for example in northern Sweden, still more so
(Hansen 1990).

For the coastal Sámi in northern Norway, Schanche (1995) has argued for
a division in the cultural landscape between the historical, the magical, the
sacred and the political. Both the conceptual and the material dimensions of
landscape are combined in this model, but Schanche does not attempt to
gender her landscapes, and nor does she apply this approach to the environment of any particular Sámi culture in prehistory. It is the past as imagined
in the present, or as used in the present for political purposes (for example,
to establish land rights), that gives meanings to these landscapes for the Sámi
people today.

Sámi cultural identity and sedentisation

We have argued that chiefs and commoners (in a landscape of prestige) or
men and women (in a gendered landscape) will tend to construct different
meanings for themselves in their surroundings. In the same way, the collective cultural landscape of each mode of production is likely to differ.

There is indeed evidence from northern Scandinavia that the transition
to agriculture has tended to lead to a cultural divergence between farmers
and others, which in part reflects the inevitable divergence in the cognised
environment of each group. This process can be identified between those
Sámi who continued as hunters (prior to c. AD 1500) or as reindeer herders
(c. AD 1500 to the present), and those who opted instead for a more sedentary life of cultivation and livestock husbandry. The two groups necessarily
perceived their surroundings in different ways, and so came to construct
different cultural landscapes. When this difference in perception was combined
with political pressures and economic self-interest, it led to the farmers
becoming culturally assimilated. On the coast of Norway, for example, Sámi
populations began in the Early Iron Age to adopt a farming way of life, and
what can be reconstructed of their material culture indicates that they started
to adopt, after about AD 300, many traits that signal Germanic rather than

Sámi ethnicity (Odner 1985). A similar process can be traced in the southern part of northern Sweden at about the same period. Here once again 'it was the indigenous population who chose to define themselves as Germanic', because the nature of the colonising society 'made it possible [for the indigenous communities] to express Germanic identity through exchange relations' (Odner 1985: 10).

In the interior of northern Sweden there were the beginnings of a broadly comparable process after *c.* AD 1850, among those Sámi who abandoned reindeer pastoralism and established sedentary farming-fishing-foraging economies in suitable areas around lakes and along the main river valleys. In this way, new cultural meanings were formed, based on a land-use pattern of barley cultivation, hay-making, cattle and goats (Figure 24.4). These new cultural landscapes can be seen as part of a process of cultural divergence that was actually hastened by the policies of the Swedish state, which after 1886 passed laws that defined as 'Lapps' (Sámi) only those people who continued to be nomadic reindeer pastoralists (Figure 24.5).

Figure 24.4 The cultural landscape of Sámi agriculture at Akse in Laidaure, Lilla Lule river valley, in the foothills of the Sarek mountains. It is late summer or autumn, probably in the late 1920s. The pastures around the farm yielded a crop of hay for the cattle, goats and horses. The farming community in addition gained its subsistence from hay crops from outlying meadows, from fishing in the lakes and hunting, and from relations with the reindeer-herding Sámi. At the foot of the slope below the peak of the mountain Akse is a Sámi sacrificial site that dates back to the Iron Age. In the distance can be seen the snow-covered Sarek mountains. (Photograph by Ludwig Wästfelt, Jokkmokk. Copyright: Ajtte Museum.)

Figure 24.5 A summer camp site of Mountain Sámi nomadic reindeer herders, in Padjelanta, upper Lule river valley, probably in the late 1920s. The picture shows a tent (*goahtte*) and, behind, a storage construction (*luovve*). There is also a tame reindeer used as a pack animal, and a herding dog. The scene is typical of the cultural landscape of the summer pastures, and shows traditional reindeer pastoralism in its final phase. (Photograph by Ludwig Wästfelt, Jokkmokk. Copyright: Ajtte Museum.)

The genesis of conflict in cultural landscapes

We have emphasised that the ecosystems from which people derive their livelihood and the places in which they live do not contain one fixed set of cultural meanings. We cannot specify in a single list the attributes that make up a particular cultural landscape (forests, fields, lakes, villages, churches, historical landmarks). Just as each person's perception will be subtly different, so each social group will find its own symbols and meanings in its surroundings. Conflicts may arise when two or more groups, each of which regards itself as having a distinct cultural identity, are occupying and seeking to control the same physical space.

The past is used by everyone to make sense of the present, and for most people much of their real history resides not in books but in settlements, fields, paths, monuments and place names. Symbols of the past are all about us, and help to shape our identity and make our lives meaningful in the present. Archaeology, as a prime means for identifying, conserving and interpreting these features, finds itself inevitably implicated in the meanings that people construct in their cultural landscapes. If different people are liable to construct different meanings, then the kind of information about a site that the archaeologist publicises, or perhaps chooses to suppress, can do much to influence public opinion and political debate.

The World Archaeological Congress in New Delhi in 1994 was almost brought to a halt over this question of 'who owns the past?' Specifically, the Congress had to consider under what circumstances it should prohibit public debate about the archaeological evidence for the antiquity and identity of sacred sites, whether Hindu or Muslim (Golson 1995). The Executive Committee of WAC decided to support its president, Jack Golson, in his decision to prohibit discussion of this issue, a decision forced upon WAC by threats of violence, public disorder, and the last-minute cancellation of the congress.

Conflicts in northern Sweden are unlikely to cause bloodshed or the cancellation of international meetings, but they are nonetheless deeply felt. The region has a Swedish majority population, who are numerically predominant particularly in the towns. Colonisation was small-scale and mainly agricultural until much larger numbers of settlers were attracted by mining, the construction of railways and the timber industry in the nineteenth century, and by hydro-electricity and tourism in the twentieth century. Many of the immigrants were from Finland rather than from other parts of Sweden, and Finnish-speaking peoples still constitute a substantial minority, numbering today about 30,000 people in Norrbotten and constituting a majority in the border regions of Tornedalen (Norrländsk Uppslagsbok 1995: 250).

The Sámi themselves form another minority, but are one that is less easy to define in numerical terms. In Sweden there are only about 2,500 people that are wholly dependent upon reindeer-herding as a full-time activity. Until recently, this occupation constituted the official definition of Sámi ethnicity, an imposed definition that to some extent has been adopted by the Sámi themselves. The current definition of Sami ethnicity is linguistic. It is based on a person having at least one parent or grandparent speaking the Sámi language, and on this basis there are 17,000 Sámi living in Sweden. However, the number could be much larger if the state allowed cultural self-identity to be the criterion.

There is, in addition, a substantial Sámi minority in northern Norway (around 35,000) and smaller numbers in Finland (about 5,000) and Russia (2,000). The Sámi people everywhere see themselves as the indigenous people of an extensive land, Sápmi, which they now must share with the populations of the various nation states into which they have been incorporated. This process of co-existence began at least in the Bronze Age if not before. From the south there was interaction with the farming cultures of the Germanic peoples (later Swedes and Norwegians), while from the east came important trading opportunities with Finnish peoples, Karelians and Russians. Throughout history there has been interaction between these different groups, and it has been argued that Sámi ethnicity itself arose out of this process, perhaps in the Late Bronze Age or Early Iron Age period, as an outcome of what can loosely be termed the fur trade (Odner 1983, 1985).

It would be wrong to assume that the political advantage has always been in favour of the colonists, or that their cultural identity has always tended to dominate over the Sámi identity of the indigenous population. However, in recent history the growing power of the nation states (Norway, Sweden, Russia/Soviet Union, and later Finland) has led to a process whereby many Sámi have been assimilated economically, linguistically and, to some extent, culturally.

There are now definite signs that this seemingly inexorable process of assimilation has come to an end. If continued, this process would, according to the arguments advanced in this chapter, eventually have led to a more homogeneous conception of the cultural landscape of northern Scandinavia, as happened for example in medieval England with the formation of a unified English cultural identity out of what had been, in the Early Middle Ages, a disparate interacting community of Romanised Celts, Anglo-Saxons and Vikings. In the Scandinavian case there has been a reversal of this process of homogenisation of culture, with a revival particularly in Norway and Sweden in the Sámi language, literature and music. It has led also to new Sámi political institutions in those two countries, which themselves are helping to forge a stronger Sámi identity in the new political environment of the European Union.

The representation of the Sámi archaeological heritage

It is in this context that we see a revival also in conflicts over how cultural landscapes should be represented and interpreted. It is, for example, significant that the Nordic Sámi Institute in Guovdageadnu/Kautokeino (the place name itself is contested) should specify 'cultural landscape activities' as one of its goals. As part of its programme on economic, environmental and legal rights, the Institute sponsors research into the legal system as it affects the Sámi, reindeer-herding, local history, tourism, and 'the development of methods for a systematic study of the Sámi cultural landscape' (Sámi Institutuhtta 1993: 2).

The relevance of this topic was well explained by Ole Hendrik Magga, President of the Norwegian Sámi Parliament, in his address to the ICOM 1995 conference in Stavanger. Since 1994, the Sámi Parliament has been given responsibility for the administration of all Sámi heritage sites in Norway, which are now managed by the Sámi Heritage Sites Council. Magga shows that such a responsibility could have potentially far-reaching implications, because of the way in which 'heritage' can be defined as involving not merely sites but also cultural landscapes:

> Sámi heritage sites are defined first and foremost as physical traces of Sámi life, either portable or constructed in one place. But non-physical remains too, such as place names and local traditions, are also part of this concept. Also of particular significance for this concept are the interactions with nature and the conditions determined

by nature: the collective cultural landscape. Only the preservation
of all this enables one to see the Sámi culture in a historical perspective. The Sámi cultural landscape forms an historical and cultural
framework for the Sámi people today.

(Magga 1995: 4)

Magga is emphasising here that the Sámi cultural heritage should encompass
'the collective cultural landscape' and not just sites within it. It is a point of
view entirely consistent with our evidence for how the Sámi perceive their
environment as a totality, and not as something separated into the 'natural'
and the 'cultural' (Bergman 1991; Mulk 1994b; Bergman and Mulk 1996).
However, Magga's concern is also political, and stems from his recognition
that for the Sámi nation the historical and cultural heritage should act as a
focus for the people's capacity to define themselves: 'the point is not just to
recapture one's own history, but to create one's own character and identity'
(Magga 1995: 2).

Archaeology, heritage and the museums can play an important role in
either promoting or hindering this process of using the past in order to establish a nation's cultural identity in the present. Unfortunately, however, in
culturally diverse states like those in Scandinavia, there is a long tradition of
a hegemonic relationship between the majority group (Norwegians, Swedes,
etc.) and the minority 'others' (notably the Sámi). As Olsen (1991: 213) has
argued, even to be allowed to speak and to have their voices heard, the
'others' are forced to structure their conception of the world within the
dominant discourse.

It is worth considering briefly the predominant way in which cultural identity has been appropriated in the history of Scandinavian archaeology
(Schanche and Olsen 1985; Olsen 1986; Opendal 1996). Until quite recent
times, the acquisition of ethnographic and archaeological knowledge in
Lappland was an integral part of the colonial process itself. The collection of
artefacts and skeletons, old and new, and the recording of curiosities such
as myths and vocabularies, was in a real sense the scientific parallel of the
economic and territorial conquest that incorporated these lands and peoples
of the north into the emerging nation states of Norway, Sweden and Russia.
Such knowledge was constructed and represented in ways that served to
emphasise the contrast between the societies of the 'civilised' centre and those
of the 'primitive' periphery (Opendal 1996).

Until well into the twentieth century, archaeology played its part in
justifying the dominant nations' stereotypes about Sámi culture and way of
life. At the same time, of course, much that we can now use as valuable
information was also recorded, through pioneer work in linguistics, anthropology, ethnography and archaeology. But there is no question that in much
of the older literature we see portrayed, amongst other things, an image of
the cultural landscapes of the north that is distorted to serve the interests of
the outsider. It is the lingering echoes of these images that are now being
contested by the new generation of archaeologists and intellectuals.

'Vuollerim 6000 år': the Swedification of Lappland

These are by no means dead issues, as is shown by the example of Vuollerim 6000 år (Vuollerim 6,000 Years Ago), a successful popular museum that is situated in a small town along the river valley of the Lilla Luleälv in Norrbotten, northern Sweden. The museum was established near to the site of Älvnäser, where the remains of a settlement dated to 6,000 years ago were discovered by archaeologists from Umeå University in 1983. It has now become a tourist destination along the main road that leads from southern Sweden towards Jokkmokk and the 'wilderness' landscapes of the Laponian World Heritage Area (see Figure 24.1).

The archaeology at Vuollerim relates to the well-preserved traces of houses, storage pits, ovens and cooking pits, together with tools, food remains, burnt stones, and debris from tool manufacture. It is interpreted as a winter base camp for a band of hunter-gatherers exploiting elk, beaver, small game, seals, fish and birds and using a late stone age technology (Westfal 1990: 2). These findings have been used to reconstruct the prehistoric houses, diet and way of life, in a 'living museum' widely regarded as one of Sweden's most successful projects in popularising archaeology and presenting it to young people.

There is no direct evidence for the ethnicity of the people living at Vuollerim 6,000 years ago. Aspects of the material culture of this and other sites in northern Fenno-Scandinavia are similar to contemporary cultures further east, in Finland, Karelia and northern Russia (Huggert 1996). However, many archaeologists continue to argue that material culture traits are not a reliable signifier of ethnicity in Scandinavia (Bolin 1996). It therefore becomes possible to ignore linkages to the east, and to interpret Vuollerim within the old 'hegemonic' assumption that sees in the prehistory of northern Sweden a more primitive but derivative version of cultural developments in the south.

To be fair, there are no overt claims made at Vuollerim about the cultural identity of its inhabitants 6,000 years ago. There are, nonetheless, some not-so-hidden messages about their ethnicity that are perfectly obvious in the museum's colourful information leaflet, copies of which are available in Swedish, German, French and English and can be found in practically every museum, tourist office and hotel in the north of Sweden (Figure 24.6). By portraying the prehistoric inhabitants of the Lule river as tall, blond, blue-eyed people with stereotypical Germanic features, the Vuollerim museum is complicit in the strengthening of an old archaeological myth that directly relates to the identity of the Sámi people at the present day.

Vuollerim's picture of the origins of cultures in northern Sweden is a direct parallel to the Norwegianisation of prehistory that Opendal (1996) discusses in relation to the writings of A.W. Brögger. In the 1920s and 1930s, Brögger portrayed Norwegian settlement in north Norway as being an ancient culture with its roots in the Stone Age, whereas the Sámi presence there was the result of a late immigration from an Asian homeland.

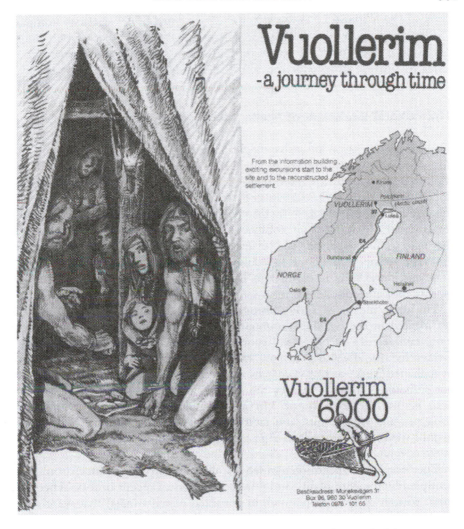

Figure 24.6 Vuollerim 6000 år: not-so-hidden messages about ethnicity.

Nationalism as strident as that of Brögger is no longer acceptable in Scandinavia, but the Vuollerim example shows how easy it is for the prehistory of the north, along with its resources, to be incorporated into the Swedish national project. Even the map that Vuollerim provides for its tourists can be seen as part of a subtle Swedification of the area's prehistory, in showing Vuollerim as being at the northernmost extremity of a communications axis (the modern E4 highway) that stretches from Malmö near Denmark to the top of the Gulf of Bothnia, but not beyond. The implication is that Vuollerim's links, past and present, are with the south, not the north or the east. It is entirely appropriate that one of the main sponsors of Vuollerim 6000 år should be Vattenfall Norrbotten, the state-owned hydo-electicity company. Vattenfall has been responsible for destroying much of the former cultural landscape of the Lule river valley through its massive dams and reservoirs, in order to provide power for the south of Sweden.

The cultural landscape of 'stallo' sites

The misappropriation of archaeological knowledge can also be seen in relation to a much later phase in prehistory, the Late Iron Age and Nordic Medieval period. For the interior of northern Sweden, this period is so poorly documented in the historical sources that its interpretation remains largely in the hands of archaeologists. In the remainder of this chapter we examine in some detail a case study of conflicting versions of the so-called 'stallo' sites that date from this period. We review a long-standing argument within Scandinavian archaeology about the cultural identity of the inhabitants of these sites, and show how resolving this issue still has implications today for some aspects of Sámi cultural identity.

The stallo sites have a long history of dispute. Briefly, the sites in question are located in the Scandes mountains in northern Sweden and the adjacent mountain regions of Norway (Figure 24.7). Each site consists of a group of former huts or dwellings defined by central hearths that are surrounded by oval-shaped banks of soil. Typically there are two to three dwellings per site, but sometimes more, and they are in rows aligned approximately east–west with an average distance of 7 m between dwellings. There are associated oven pits and storage pits, and radiocarbon dates indicate that the sites were mainly used in the Late Iron Age and early Nordic Medieval period (Mulk 1988, 1994a).

The sites have been recognised as different in appearance from those occupied by the Mountain Sámi reindeer herders of recent history. The settlement pattern of modern pastoralism consisted of tents (kåta) that were always more widely scattered than the stallo dwellings, so that each family had a surrounding area in which to gather fuel (Manker 1960: 304), and to facilitate the management of the reindeer herds, milking the animals and keeping dogs (Ruong 1982: 94). However, use of the terms 'stalo' or 'stallo' to describe the sites of non-recent settlement is rather new, and results from information provided by Sámi informants to Pettersson (1913). Stalo is a giant in Sámi myths, and Pettersson was told that the sites were 'Stalo-graves'. He understood that they were not graves but hut circles, and so attached to them the name 'Stalo-circles'. In fact, Pettersson may have misunderstood his informants, as a different Sámi term for these sites is jähna-kåterikkek, or 'sleeping berths for the giants'. In any case it is clear that the role of these places in the recent cultural landscape of the Mountain Sámi was as a reference point for part-mythical persons who featured in the oral history of the pastoralists (Mulk 1988).

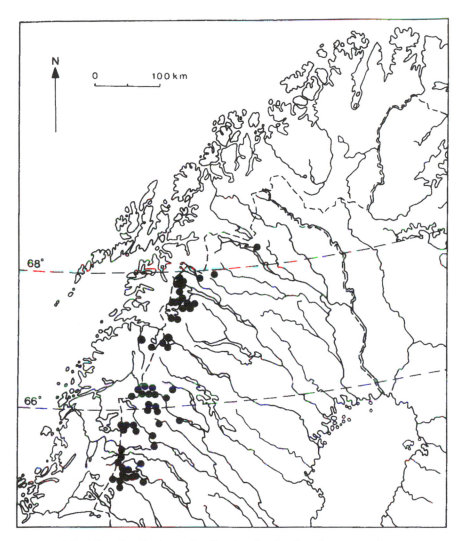

Figure 24.7 The distribution of stallo sites in the Scandes mountains.

In conformity with the assumptions then prevalent about the Sámi and
their lack of prehistory, Pettersson could not believe that the Stalo circles
were really connected to the Sámi except in their myths, and therefore
proposed that some Nordic, non-Sámi tribe had inhabited these sites. It was
a suggestion enthusiastically supported by Drake (1918), who stated that
Pettersson's 'Stalo-circles' were cultural remains from tribes of Germanic
origin. These ideas became almost entirely accepted among contemporary
culture historians.

Meanwhile a Sámi folklorist, Torkel Tomasson, was carrying out his own
excavations of a group of hut foundations, and was strongly critical of the

'Germanic' theories. He also dismissed any connection with Sámi mythic Stalo-characters. Instead he proposed that they were cultural remains from Sámi prehistory, basing his argument on their location in the zone between the birch forest and the bare mountain just like modern Sámi camps, and on their similar design, size and construction. He pointed out that an oval or rectangular form is necessary for a Sámi hut built as a bent-pole construction. Because Tomasson's ideas were published as articles in *Samefolkets egen Tidning*, 'The Sámi People's Own Newspaper' (for details see Mulk 1988), they were unread or ignored in academic circles until rescued from obscurity by Ernst Manker of the Nordic Museum in Stockholm.

Manker, himself a giant in Sámi ethnography, carried out a large-scale and integrated archaeological-ethnographic study that fully supported Tomasson's ideas (Manker 1960). He believed that the stallo sites were clearly attributable to people of Sámi origin who hunted wild reindeer but also kept domesticated reindeer as draught and pack animals. He pointed out that extensive hunting-pit systems are often found near to the stallo sites. However, Manker's work does not mark the end of the speculative phase of stallo historiography, as Manker's successor at the Nordic Museum Rolf Kjellström had his own distinctive ideas. According to him, 'stallo' means 'stalo' or 'steel', and the character Stalo is 'he who is covered with steel'. Kjellström (1983) thus explains 'stalo' as being either a name for foreign men in coats of mail, or a name for the Norwegians who introduced steel to the Sámi. He claims that the Stalo people were tax collectors, sent out by Nordic chiefs.

Sámi hunters or Sámi pastoralists?

We therefore have competing interpretations for stallo sites, some of which we can dismiss as not only fanciful but also based on the kind of assumptions that denied the Sámi their own history. The stallo dwellings were attributed to mythical giants, Germanic tribes or Norwegian tax collectors. However, in recent discussions it is entirely accepted that the stallo dwellings are of Sámi origin, and are the remains of tent structures like the *kåta* of the recent past. There is also agreement that these high-altitude settlements can have been occupied only in the summer or autumn, and that they were used by people who had control of domesticated reindeer as draught animals. On a number of other questions, however, there is sharp disagreement between Storli (1993, 1994, 1996), Mulk (1988, 1993, 1994a) and others (see discussion in Storli 1993).

What is at issue is no longer the cultural identity of those occupying stallo sites, but the more particular question of why exactly the Sámi were occupying these sites in the high mountain areas. The excavations by Kjellström (1983), Mulk (1988, 1994a) and Storli (1994) show that the habitation period of the sites extends from AD 500–1500. By AD 500 livestock husbandry (cattle, sheep and goats) was already being practised by farming communities along the coasts, both in northern Norway and along the Gulf of Bothnia in what is today northern Sweden and Finland. It is also a period when fragments of historical evidence, notably Othere's account recorded by King Alfred in England in *c.* AD 890, suggest that tame reindeer were already used for decoys, and that the people known as Finnas were paying tribute (*finneskatt*) to Norwegian chiefs on the Atlantic coast. This tribute was partly paid in furs, and was one element in an extensive fur trade that linked the Finnas (Sámi) of the inland areas of Fenno-Scandinavia with, in particular, the trading centre of Novgorod to the east. The main demand was for the squirrel's winter fur, marten fur, beaver and fox furs, as well as fur and leather products from the reindeer (Ahnlund 1946; Mulk 1996).

Most historians and archaeologists have agreed that the establishment of stallo sites should be seen as a reflection of the growing fur trade between the Sámi (Finnas) and outsiders during the Viking period, which was also a period of increasingly extensive trapping of wild reindeer. Stallo dwellings were therefore seasonal sites for reindeer hunters:

> The fur trade of the Late Iron Age and Early Medieval time . . .
> led to more intensive hunting and trapping in the forest zone in
> the winter months. There was a consequent need for the moun-
> tains to be used more intensively for food production in the brief
> summer months. This intensification process involved an expan-
> sion of hunting pit systems, a deployment of specialised hunting
> groups that included women, food storage techniques, and the use
> of tame reindeer as pack animals.
>
> (Mulk 1994a: 262)

According to this model, the onset of full reindeer pastoralism happened only after the breakup of the egalitarian society of hunting and fishing bands (*sijdda*). There is no convincing historical evidence for the existence of this new economy until the sixteenth century AD (Hultblad 1968; Lundmark 1982; Hansen 1990), while the archaeological evidence for early pastoralism is equally unconvincing (Mulk 1993, 1994a).

In disagreeing with this interpretation, Storli (1993, 1994, 1996) has persistently argued that the historical evidence has been misconstrued. She also claims to have found archaeological evidence that indicates the possibility 'that reindeer pastoralism among the Sámi could be very old, in fact older than 1000 years' (Storli 1996: 81). She dates the transition to pastoralism among the Sámi to around AD 900, and sees the establishment of stallo sites as part of a seasonal pattern of mobility by nomadic pastoralists. She envisages a direct link between the summer grazing in the mountains and the winter grazing in the coniferous forest zone to the east, where settlements showing a similar alignment of hearths have been described (Bergman 1991).

If we accept it as true, then this bold attempt to rewrite Sámi prehistory implies that the cultural landscapes of the stallo sites also need to be reconceptualised. At the micro-scale, Storli (1993: 11–13) places much emphasis on hearth stones which she considers to be markers of male space (*boassjo* stones), plus a few finds to which she attributes a female/symbolic meaning. From these she reconstructs an ordering of social space within the dwelling that she regards as similar to that claimed by Ränk (1949) and Yates (1989) for Sámi society in the historical period. At a macro-scale, she proposes that we should take note of the regular spacing of stallo dwellings along an east–west axis, and their location in mountainous areas adjacent to reindeer hunting pits which she assumes are older and belong to the former territories of the hunting groups (*sijdda*). All this evidence represents, she believes, a significant reordering of the cultural landscape:

> I find great inspiration in Henrietta Moore's (1986) theory of a spatial text. Following Moore, I will suggest that the spatial organization of the *stallo* sites was ascribed a symbolic, or metaphorical meaning, in order to legitimize pastoralist claims to exclusive rights to land areas which had previously carried the status of shared *sijdda* land.
>
> (Storli 1993: 15)

Furthermore, the paucity of settlements prior to AD 800–900 implies that the high mountains were probably not previously included in what Storli calls the 'mythological landscape' of the Sámi, their landscape of history and genealogy, before the occupation of the stallo sites. The 'strict organization of space' at these sites therefore served to establish cultural space in what had been previously 'an unknown and dangerous nature' (Storli 1993: 15).

The evidence of reindeer-hunting

This argument would be compelling if it were based on empirical evidence that was secure, but unfortunately this is far from being the case. Indeed, Storli's argument comes close to being 'a-past-as-wished-for', to adopt the phrase used by Piggott (1968: 11) to describe 'a convenient selection of the evidence . . . fitted into a predetermined intellectual or emotional pattern'. The society of reindeer pastoralists with which Storli wishes to inhabit the stallo cultural landscape is based on no direct evidence whatsoever. The historical evidence has been read by practically all scholars as indicating the presence of a Sámi hunting society in the inland regions, participating actively in the fur trade. Ecological evidence of vegetation change induced by pastoralist activities cannot be detected until a much later period. The archaeological evidence that Storli uses, like that of Manker and others, demonstrates overwhelmingly that hunting, not herding, was the primary activity in the stallo sites. For example, there are many radiocarbon dates for reindeer-hunting pits in the period *c.* AD 800–1500 (Mulk 1993, 1994a: 167).

All this evidence, which demonstrates the presence of a Sámi hunting society in the mountain zone at this time, cannot simply be ignored. Storli's idea that the stallo sites represent a symbolic ordering of space designed to convey meaning to others is not a convincing idea when used to support her argument for a cultural landscape of early pastoralism. We accept that it is necessary for archaeologists to consider symbolic meanings in the organisation of space, but to do this properly requires that we take a balanced view of the entire cultural landscape of stallo, and this must include the widespread and dramatic evidence of the reindeer-hunting pit systems.

The pitfalls dug to trap elk or wild reindeer have been mapped over extensive areas of northern Fenno-Scandinavia, and many date back to the Stone Age. However, as Mulk (1994a) has shown, it is in the late period of prehistory that this hunting technology is extended to the high mountain areas. At Kisuris, for example, there are calibrated dates indicating use of hunting pits around AD 979 ± 168 years, while at Suollakavalta another pitfall system that is immediately adjacent to a stallo site is dated to AD 983 ± 66 years (Mulk 1994a: 167). One hunting pit system near Tjärovaratj in the foothills zone, so far undated, shows the impressive scale of reindeer-hunting. Here the line of hunting pits (a double line in places) extends 1.1 km across the valley between two steep hills, Tjärovaratj and Tuolpuk, thus intercepting all the reindeer migration routes (Figure 24.8).

The hunting of wild reindeer on such a scale cannot co-exist with the management of domesticated herds, so we can be confident that the continuation of reindeer-hunting practices implies that pastoralism has not yet become established. What we are actually seeing in the period c. AD 500–1350 is an intensification of reindeer-hunting and its extension to mountain areas, in order to supply a surplus of meat and skins. This surplus was needed by Sámi communities whose economy was becoming more and more focused on hunting for the fur trade, an activity carried out from winter base camps in the forest zone.

It would, however, be wrong to consider this landscape of organised, large-scale hunting as being entirely explained in functionalist and ecological terms. Sámi hunting society was changing over this period in response to the new social relations that followed from interaction with trading partners and coastal farming communities. Mulk (1994a, 1996) has argued that these influences threatened the solidarity and egalitarian status of the Sámi *sijdda*. The new situation required strong leadership and co-ordination of the large-scale co-operative groups that had to be mobilised on a seasonal basis. Moreover, the fur trade could reward successful hunting with enhanced individual status and wealth. For both reasons we might expect a more ranked society to have emerged in the interior of northern Sweden, and the same is true of the Sámi *sijdda* in Varanger, north Norway, where large-scale reindeer-hunting also took place at this time (Odner 1992).

It is significant that in neither case can we find evidence for the emergence of a ranked society. Odner (1992: 99) suggests that there was no social stratification among the Varanger Sámi hunters until the introduction of firearms around 1700. In the case of northern Sweden, evidence for differences in

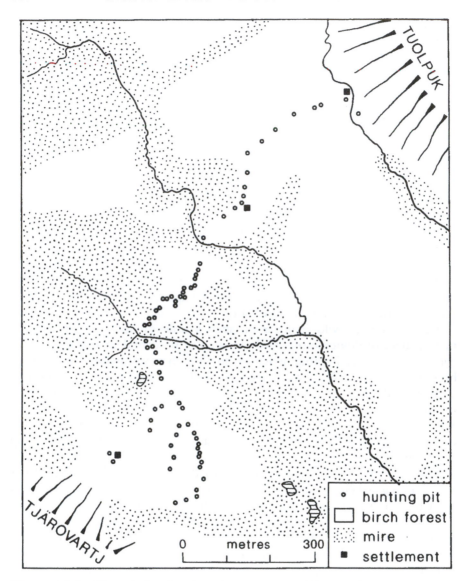

Figure 24.8 The reindeer-hunting pit systems near Tjärovaratj.

individual wealth and status begins with the onset of intensive reindeer pastoralism after 1600. Mulk (1994b, 1996) has argued that for the Mountain Sámi there were social mechanisms equivalent to the North American 'potlatch'. The destruction of prestige objects and coins by depositing them in sacrificial sites was one mechanism that served to preserve the society's egalitarian character. Another mechanism to diminish conflict between neighbouring *sijdda* might well have been the creation of visible evidence signalling territorial rights in the cultural landscape of reindeer-hunting.

In this way we can interpret the very presence of stallo sites in the mountains, the aligned arrangement of the dwellings, and the rights to collective hunting that are implied by the hunting pit systems, as together representing a symbolic landscape of acknowledged territorial rights. Similarly, the sacrificial sites that are found nearby may have served to provide spiritual protection and legitimation of those hunting rights. In this period of increasing competition for territory, we might well expect that fishing rights along lakes and rivers would also have been signalled in some visible way. The fur trade was an attractive option to the Sámi, yet it also threatened social stability. It therefore stimulated Sámi hunting society to create a new cultural landscape in the mountains that not only fulfilled a particular economic purpose, but also served to diminish the threat of conflict within and between groups.

The-past-as-wished-for

To make full sense of the stallo controversy, we have to go beyond the evidence itself and the ways in which it should best be interpreted. The alternative prehistory that has been proposed, for an early transition to reindeer pastoralism 'almost 1000 years earlier' than the usually accepted date (Storli 1996: 107), is undoubtedly a version of the past that would be very acceptable to many Sámis today, more so than the extended prehistory of hunting, foraging and fishing that the archaeological evidence actually supports. The lingering assumptions of Social Darwinism and cultural evolution still mean that for some Sámis, as for many other people in the world, a prehistory of pastoralism seems more dignified than one dominated by hunting and gathering. If the stallo sites were to be seen as a cultural landscape of early reindeer pastoralism, then Sámis who had adopted the hegemonic view of cultural evolution would feel that their cultural identity today had been significantly strengthened. Grazing rights for modern reindeer-herding might also be seen as having a stronger basis if a millennium of continuous pastoralist land-use could be established.

In other ways, too, modern Sámi cultural identity would be confirmed if we were to interpret cultural landscapes in ways that suggest that Sámi pastoral society had very ancient roots. Scandinavian society today focuses substantially, perhaps disproportionately, on reindeer-herding as a symbol of Sámi cultural identity. This is a situation in part imposed by the nation states that have equated Sámi ethnicity with reindeer pastoralism, but in part it is created by the Sámi themselves, as a nostalgic reaction to the abandonment of reindeer-herding by the majority of the Sámi people.

Storli herself hints at this hidden agenda that underlies her contribution to research. She writes of her surprise at the omission from a recent culture history of north Norway (Drivenes et al. 1994) of any suggestion that there was Sámi reindeer pastoralism before AD 1550:

Considering the political debate concerning Sámi land rights which
followed the Norwegian Government's decision of 1980 to force
through the regulation of the Alta–Kautokeino River in spite of
heavy Sámi protests, one might have expected a discussion of this
matter.

(Storli 1996: 81)

We see here an overt reference to 'the-past-as-wished-for', with archaeology
seeking to assist the Sámi with political ambitions to retain control of their
cultural landscapes in the face of the overwhelming power of the nation
state. The archaeologist can play an important role in reconstructing a cultural
landscape of 'ancient pastoralism' in a way that serves present-day Sámi
interests.

There is a further sense in which Storli's version of the stallo past reflects
what Shanks and Tilley (1987: 198) call 'the politics of truth'. Her construction of the cultural landscape of stallo sites depends heavily on the presence
of women spinning wool and the supposed existence of female domestic
space within the *kåta* dwelling to support an argument for pastoralism rather
than hunting. Both assumptions need to be questioned. It seems ludicrous to
assume that women in hunting societies were unable to obtain wool or use
a spinning whorl, when trade and the exchange of ideas with the outside
world had been a dominant theme in the prehistory of the inland regions
for thousands of years. Like Yates (1989), Storli (1993) is projecting on to
the archaeological data a gender-based model of how social life ought to be
structured that is not only a popular theme in recent archaeology, but also
reflects the strong dichotomy in concepts of gender that has dominated western
religion and thought since the Middle Ages.

In fact there is no evidence that people in Sámi hunting society did
conceptualise male/female divisions in the way Ränk (1949) and Yates (1989)
proposed for Sámi pastoralists after *c.* 1600, and as assumed by Storli for
the earlier period. Indeed, considering the extremely strong need for complementarity in gender roles to ensure survival in this arctic environment, and
in the light of historical evidence that women as well as men hunted, an
alternative conception seems just as likely.

The theoretical assumption of a gendered division of space in arctic
hunting societies has also been questioned by Bodenhorn (1993) in her
ethnography of the Inupiat on the North Slope of Alaska. In hunting and
gathering societies generally, the existence of a sexual division of labour has
often been used to assume that the cognised landscape is also fundamentally
divided into male and female categories, without much evidence for such
an assumption. In the feminist/anthropological search for the origins of
women's inequality, it would be unwise to unload on to Sámi hunting society
too many of these preconceptions, even though this might be very appropriate in the more gendered landscapes of the agrarian societies (Lillehammer
1994a).

Conclusion

This chapter has attempted to combine the perspectives of geography and archaeology, and to explore an approach to cultural landscapes that is sensitive not only to the outside (etic) perspective of ecology, resources and trade, but also to the inside (emic) view which explores landscape's hidden meanings, metaphors and symbols. We have reviewed the ways in which Sámi cultural identity has been ignored, distorted or exaggerated within the cultural landscapes of northern Sweden. We have criticised those who, we believe, construct versions of the cultural landscape in which the Sámi presence is rendered invisible simply because their ecological impact was not sufficiently drastic for their culture to be stamped on to nature in obvious and irreversible ways. We have also disagreed with interpretations that seek to project on to the past the political concerns of the present, whether they be nation-building myths, the legitimation of land rights, a feminist agenda, or the prejudices that stem from a lingering Social Darwinism that sees greater dignity in some versions of prehistory than in others. What we have not so far done in general terms is present any coherent alternative.

All prehistory is a story told in the present about the past. Does this therefore mean that no vision of the past, no reconstructed version of its cultural landscape, can ever be more than the fulfilment of a wish in the present? We reject such a view. The practice of archaeology becomes meaningless unless we can believe that some stories about the past are more truthful than others. The search for archaeological truth should be our goal even if we admit that, regrettably, it is an ideal that is always just beyond our reach because of human frailties (for example personal, political or cultural biases) that will result in any 'truth' being derived from 'facts' that are subjectively constructed and interpreted.

But subjectivity has its limits. At the end of the day we cannot 'construct' the Great Pyramids in northern Sweden, and nor can a cultural landscape of reindeer-hunting ever be 'constructed' in the Nile valley of the pharoahs. To admit that such perverse prehistories are possible, or even that they merit an equal respect if they serve a useful political purpose, requires that we should abandon any systematic attempt to match reconstruction with the material record of the past. Archaeology would degenerate into science fiction and move to the lunatic fringe.

We therefore agree with Piggott (1968) and Renfrew (1989) that 'the-past-as-wished-for' is not an adequate description of archaeology's contribution to human knowledge, even if many previous and some current versions of prehistory are tainted in this way. Nor do we believe that a prehistory from which cultural identity has been excluded is necessarily the most truthful outcome of our efforts to interpret the totality of the evidence available.

In the case of northern Sweden, somewhat perverse arguments are now being used in an effort to situate prehistoric societies within what are essentially 'uncultural' landscapes of purely social interaction. Bolin (1996: 11), for example, states that in relation to the former Yugoslavia, South Africa and the Sámi people, the desire to prove or disprove cultural identities in prehistory 'has somehow eroded the attitude to scientific relevance and criticism'. In the particular case of the Sámi he therefore rejects the idea that the material culture of the Bronze Age/Early Iron Age period in northern Fenno-Scandinavia can be used to signal ethnic identity in any way. In his opinion, 'the Saami problem and their claim to territorial rights is . . . primarily a political matter and not a (pre)historical problem' (Bolin 1996: 11).

We disagree, and propose instead that cultural identity within cultural landscapes is both a political question and a problem to be confronted by prehistorians. To suggest otherwise is to remove from people both in the past and in the present an important aspect of their identity as human beings. The challenge of cultural landscape analysis should be confronted, not avoided, to prevent this whole approach to the past from degenerating into myth, propaganda and political mischief.

References

Ahnlund, N. 1946. Norrländska skinnskatter. Saga och sed. *Kungl. Gustav Adolfs Akademiens Årsbok* 3, 32–55.

Aronsson, K.Å. 1991. *Forest Reindeer Herding AD 1–1800: an archaeological and palaeo-ecological study in northern Sweden.* Umeå: University of Umeå.

Baudou, E. 1994. Luleälvsprojektet. In *Kulturlandskapet och bebyggelsen*, S. Helmfrid (ed.), 22–5. Stockholm: Stockholm University.

Beach, H. 1981. *Reindeer-Herd Management in Transition: the case of Tuorpon Saameby in northern Sweden.* Uppsala: Acta Universitatis Upsaliensis.

Bender, B. 1993. Introduction: landscape – meaning and action. In *Landscape, Politics and Perspectives*, B. Bender (ed.), 1–17. Berg: Oxford.

Berger, J.P. 1972. *Ways of Seeing.* London: BBC/Penguin Books.

Berglund, B.E. 1988. The cultural landscape during 6,000 years in southern Sweden – an interdisciplinary study. In *The Cultural Landscape – Past, Present and Future*, H.H. Birks, H.J.B. Birks, P.E. Kaland and D. Moe (eds), 241–54. Cambridge: Cambridge University Press.

Bergman, I. 1991. Spatial structures in Saami cultural landscapes. In *Readings in Saami History, Culture and Language II*, R. Kvist (ed.), 59–68. Umeå: Umeå University.

Bergman, I. 1995. *Från Döudden till Varghalsen – en studie av kontinuitet och förändring inom ett fångstsamhälle i övre norrlands inland, 5200 f. Kr. – 400 e. Kr.* Umeå: Arkeologiska Institutionen.

Bergman, I. and I.M. Mulk 1992. Fortida bebyggelse och näringar in inland och fjäll. In *Norrbottens synliga historia, Norrbottens kulturmiljöprogram, vol. 1*, K. Lundin (ed.), 42–53. Luleå.

Bergman, I. and I.M. Mulk 1996. Det samiska landskapet. *Västerbotten* 3, 12–15.

Birks, H.H., H.J.B. Birks, P.E. Kaland and D. Moe (eds) 1988. *The Cultural Landscape – Past, Present and Future*. Cambridge: Cambridge University Press.

Bodenhorn, B. 1993. Gendered spaces, public places: public and private revisited on the North Slope of Alaska. In *Landscape, Politics and Perspectives*, B. Bender (ed.), 169–203. Oxford: Berg.

Bolin, H. 1996. Kinship, marriage and traces of social interaction. Aspects on the hunter-gatherer societies in northern Sweden during the Bronze Age and early Iron Age. *Current Swedish Archaeology* 4: 7–20.

Carpelan, C. 1979. Om asbestkeramikens historia i Fennoskandien. *Finskt Museum* 85, 5–25.

Cosgrove, D. 1984. *Social Formation and Symbolic Landscape*. London: Croom Helm.

Cribb, R. 1991. *Nomads in Archaeology*. Cambridge: Cambridge University Press.

Daniels, S. and D. Cosgrove 1988. Introduction: iconography and landscape. In *The Iconography of Landscape: essays on the symbolic representation, design and use of past environments*, D. Cosgrove and S. Daniels (eds), 1–10. Cambridge: Cambridge University Press.

Drake, S. 1918. *Västerbottenslapparna under förra hälften av 1800-talet. Etnografiska studier. Lapparna och deras land*. Uppsala: Skildringar och studier.

Drivenes, E.A., M.A. Hauan and H.A. Wold 1994. *Nord-Norges kulturhistorie, Vol. 1.* Gylendal.

Duncan, J. 1990. *The City as Text: the politics of landscape representation in the Kandyan kingdom*. Cambridge: Cambridge University Press.

Duncan, J. 1995. Landscape geography, 1993–94. *Progress in Human Geography* 19, 414–22.

Duncan, J. and N. Duncan 1988. (Re)reading the landscape. *Environment and Planning D: society and space* 6, 117–26.

Eagleton, T. 1983. *Literary Theory: an introduction*. Oxford: Blackwell.

Engelmark, R. 1976. The vegetational history of the Umeå area during the past 4,000 years. In *Early Norrland 9: palaeo-ecological investigations in coastal västerbotten, N. Sweden*, R. Engelmark, I.U. Olsson, I. Renberg and O. Zackrisson, 75–112. Stockholm: KVHAA.

Engelstad, E. 1991. Images of power and contradiction: feminist theory and post-processual archaeology. *Antiquity* 65, 502–14.

Faegri, K. 1988. Preface. In *The Cultural Landscape – Past, Present and Future*, H.H. Birks, H.J.B. Birks, P.E. Kaland and D. Moe (eds), 1–4. Cambridge: Cambridge University Press.

Forsberg, L. 1996. Forskningslinjer inom tidig samisk förhistoria. In *Arkeologi i Norr 6/7 1993/94*, L. Forsberg (ed.), 165–86. Umeå: Umeå University.

Golson, J. 1995. What went wrong with WAC 3 and an attempt to understand why. *Australian Archaeology* 41, 48–54 (reprinted in *WAC News* 3, 3–9).

Green, N. 1995. Looking at the landscape: class formation and the visual. In *The Anthropology of Landscape: perspectives on place and space*, E. Hirsch and M. O'Hanlon (eds), 31–42. Oxford: Clarendon Press.

Hansen, L.I. 1990. *Samisk fangstsamfunn og norsk h vdinge konomi*. Oslo: Novus.

Hodder, I. 1990. *The Domestication of Europe: structure and contingency in neolithic societies*. Oxford: Blackwell.

Huggert, A. 1996. Early copper finds in northern Fennoscandia. *Current Swedish Archaeology* 4, 69–82.

Hultblad, F. 1968. *Övergång fran nomadism till agrar bosättning i Jokkmokks socken*. Stockholm: Acta Lapponica.

Humphrey, C. 1995. Chiefly and shamanist landscapes in Mongolia. In *The Anthropology of Landscape: perspectives on people and space*, E. Hirsch and M. O'Hanlon (eds), 135–63. Oxford: Clarendon Press.

Ingold, T. 1980. *Hunters, Pastoralists and Ranchers*. Cambridge: Cambridge University Press.

Ingold, T. 1987. Territoriality and tenure: the appropriation of space in hunting and gathering societies. In *The Appropriation of Nature: essays on human ecology and social relations*, T. Ingold (ed.), 130–64. Manchester: Manchester University Press.

Jorgensen, R. and Olsen, B. 1988. Asbestceramiske grupper i Nord–Norge 2100 f. Kr. – 100 e. Kr. *Tromura, Kulturhistorie* 13, Tromso.

Kjellström, R. 1983. Staloproblemet i samisk historia. In *Folk og resurser i nord. Foredrag fra Trondheims-symposiet om midt-og nord-skandinavisk kultur 1982*, J. Sandnes, A. Kjelland and I. Osterlie (eds), 213–35. Trondheim: Tapir.

Korpijaakko, K. 1985. *Samerna och jordäganderätten I. Lappmannarättigheternas privaträttsliga ställning fran 1500-talet till medlet av 1700-talet.* Kautokeino: Diedut 3.

Kvist, R. 1991. Saami reindeer pastoralism as an indigenous resource management system – the case of Tuorpon and Sirkas, 1760–1860. *Arctic Anthropology* 28, 121–34.

Kvist, R. 1992. Swedish Saami policy, 1550–1990. In *Readings in Saami History, Culture and Language III*, R. Kvist (ed.), 63–78. Umeå: Umeå University.

Lillehammer, G. 1987. Looking for individuals in archaeological burial data. In *Were They All Men? An examination of sex roles in prehistoric society*, R. Bertelsen, G. Lillehammer and J.R. Naess (eds), 78–97. AmS-Varia 17, Stavanger.

Lillehammer, G. 1994a. Gendering the landscape: an environmental approach towards the understanding of the cultural landscape. Paper presented to World Archaeological Congress 3, New Delhi.

Lillehammer, G. 1994b. Forvaltning i et feministisk perspektiv. *K.A.N.: Kvinner i Arkeologi i Norge* (Tromso Museum) 17/18, 136–74.

Lillehammer, G. 1996. *Død og grav. Gravskikk på Kvassheimfeltet, Hâi Rogaland, SV Norge. Death and grave Burial rituals of the Kyassheim cemetery, Ha ir: Rogaland, SW Norway.* AmS-Skrifter 13, Arkeologisk museum i Stavanger, 1–128.

Lundmark, L. 1982. *Uppbörd, utarmning, utveckling. Det samiska samhällets övergång till rennomadism i Lule lappmark.* Lund: Arkiv avhandlingsserie.

Magga, O.H. 1995. Museums and cultural diversity: indigenous and dominant cultures. Paper presented to ICOM General Conference, Stavanger.

Manker, E. 1960. *Fångstgropar och stalotomter. Kulturlämningar från lapsk forntid.* Stockholm: Acta Lapponica.

Manker, E. 1963. *The Nomadism of the Swedish Mountain Lapps: the Siidas and their migratory routes in 1945.* Stockholm: Acta Lapponica.

Marsden, W.E. 1976. *Lapland: the world's wild places.* Amsterdam: Time–Life International.

Moore, H.L. 1986. *Space, Text and Gender: an anthropological study of the Marakwet of Kenya.* Cambridge: Cambridge University Press.

Mulk, I.M. 1988. Sirkas – ett fjällsamiskt fångstsamhälle i förändring 500–1500 e. Kr. *Bebyggelsehistorisk tidskrift* 14, 1987, 61–75. (Translated and reprinted as Sirkas – a Mountain Saami hunting society in transition. In R. Kvist (ed.) 1991. *Readings in Saami History, Culture and Language II*, 41–57. Umeå University: Center for Arctic Cultural Research.)

Mulk, I.M. 1993. Comments on Sámi Viking Age pastoralism – or the fur trade reconsidered. *Norwegian Archaeological Review* 26, 34–41.

Mulk, I.M. 1994a. *Sirkas. Ett samiskt fångstsamhälle i förändring Kr. f.-1600 e. Kr.* Umeå: Studia Archaeologica Universitatis Umensis.

Mulk, I.M. 1994b. Sacrificial places and their meaning in Saami society. In *Sacred Sites, Sacred Places*, D.L. Carmichael, J. Hubert, B. Reeves and A. Schanche (eds), 121–31. London: Routledge.

Mulk, I.M. 1996. The role of the Sámi in fur trading during the Late Iron Age and Nordic Medieval period in the light of the Sámi sacrificial sites in Lappland, northern Sweden. *Acta Borealia* 13, 47–80.

Norrländsk Upplagsbok 1995. *Norrländsk Upplagsbok. Ett Uppslagsverk om den norrländska regionen, vols 1–3.* Höganäs: Bokförlaget Bra Böcker.

Odner, K. 1983. *Finner og terfinner. Etniske prosesser i det nordlige Fenno-Skandinavia.* Oslo: Occasional Papers in Social Anthropology.

Odner, K. 1985. Sámis (Lapps, Finns and Scandinavians) in history and prehistory. *Norwegian Archaeological Review* 18, 1–35.

Odner, K. 1992. *The Varanger Saami: habitation and economy AD 1200–1900*. Oslo: Scandinavian University Press.

Olsen, B. 1986. Norwegian archaeology and the people without (pre)history. *Archaeological Review from Cambridge* 5/1, 17–36.

Olsen, B. 1991. Metropolises and satellites in archaeology: on power and asymmetry in global archaeological discourse. In *Processual and Postprocessual Archaeologies: multiple ways of knowing the past*, R.W. Preucel (ed.), 211–24. Illinois: Southern Illinois University Press.

Opendal, A. 1996. A.W. Brogger and the Norwegianization of the prehistory of North Norway. *Acta Borealia* 13, 34–46.

Pettersson, O.P. 1913. *Bidrag till kännedomen om fornminnen inom Västerbottens Lappmark*. Stockholm: ATA.

Piggott, S. 1968. *The Druids*. London: Thames & Hudson.

Ränk, G. 1949. Grundprinciper för disponeringen av utrymmet i de lappska kåtarna och gammerna. *Folkliv*, 1948–1949, 87–111.

Rappaport, R.A. 1968. *Pigs for the Ancestors: ritual in the ecology of a New Guinea people*. New Haven: Yale University Press.

Renfrew, C. 1989. Comments on archaeology into the 1990s. *Norwegian Archaeological Review* 22, 34–41.

Renfrew, C. 1994. Towards a cognitive archaeology. In *The Ancient Mind: elements of cognitive archaeology*, C. Renfrew and E.B.W. Zubrow (eds), 3–12. Cambridge: Cambridge University Press.

Ruong, I. 1982. *Samerna i historien och nutiden*. Stockholm: Bonnier Fakta.

Rydving, H. 1993. *The End of Drum-Time: religious change among the Lule Saami, 1670s-1740s*. Uppsala: Historia Religionum.

Sámi Instituhtta 1993. *Nordic Sámi Institute*. Guovdageaidnu/Kautokeino.

Schama, S. 1995. *Landscape and Memory*. London: HarperCollins.

Schanche, A. 1995. Det symbolske landskapet – landskap og identitet i samisk kultur. *Ottar* 4, 38–47.

Schanche, A. and B. Olsen 1985. Var de alle nordmenn? En etnopolitisk kritikk av norsk arkeologi. In *Arkeologi og etnisitet*, J.R. Naess (ed.), 87–99. Stavanger: Arkeologisk Museum.

Segerström, U. 1996. Naturmiljön, agriculturen och människans påverkan på vegetationen i Norra Norrland. In *Att leva vid älven. Åtta forskare om människor och resurser i Lule älvdal*, E. Baudou (ed.), 57–77. Stockholm: CEWE-Förlaget.

Shanks, M. and C. Tilley 1987. *Reconstructing Archaeology: theory and practice*. Cambridge: Cambridge University Press.

Sörensen, M.L.S. 1992. Gender archaeology and Scandinavian bronze age studies. *Norwegian Archaeological Review* 25, 23–49.

Sporrong, U. 1994. Det äldre agrarlandskapet före 1750. In *Kulturlandskapet och bebyggelsen*, S. Helmfrid (ed.), 30–5. Stockholm: Stockholm University.

Statens naturvårdsverk 1995. *Nomination by Sweden: the Lapponian World Heritage Area, precious nature, Saami culture, for inclusion in the World Heritage List – Natural Property*. Paris: UNESCO.

Storli, I. 1993. Sámi Viking Age pastoralism – or the fur trade paradigm reconsidered. *Norwegian Archaeological Review* 26, 1–20.

Storli, I. 1994. *Stallo-boplassene. Spor etter de först fjellsamer?* Oslo: Skrifter XC.

Storli, I. 1996. On the historiography of Sámi reindeer pastoralism. *Acta Borealia* 13, 81–115.

Swedish Environmental Protection Agency 1995. *Sarek, Myth and Reality: information to mountain hikers who wish to visit the national park*. Stockholm: Statens naturvårdsverk.

Tilley, C. 1994. *A Phenomenology of Landscape*. Oxford: Berg.

Turism i Jokkmokk AB 1995. *Jokkmokk – Wilderness Country*. Jokkmokk: Touristin-
formation.

Tvengsberg, P.M. 1985. Skogfinnene på Finnskogen og svedjebruket. Naering som
etnisk kjennetegn. In *Arkeologi og etnisitet*, J.-R. Naess (ed.), 57–74. Stavanger:
Arkeologisk Museum.

Westfal, U. 1990. *Vuollerim 6000 år: a story in pictures of the Bothnian stone age, based
on findings from archaeological diggings at Älvnäset, Vuollerim*. Umeå: Vattenfall
Norrbotten.

Yates, T. 1989. Habitus and social space: some suggestions about meaning in the
Sámi (Lapp) tent *c.* 1700–1900. In *The Meanings of Things: material culture and symbolic
expression*, I. Hodder (ed.), 249–62. London: Unwin-Hyman.

Zackrisson, O. 1977. Influence of forest fires on the North Swedish boreal forests.
Oikos 29. 22–32.

25   Ancestors, forests and ancient settlements: Tandroy readings of the archaeological past

MIKE PARKER PEARSON,
RAMILISONINA AND RETSIHISATSE

The region of Androy in southern Madagascar is a semi-arid zone, about 150 km north–south by 200 km east–west, of grassy plains and spiny forests, watered by unpredictable rains from December to March and baked in the heat of the long dry season, when the rivers and lakes dry up as the land becomes scorched. Androy, literally the 'land of thorns', can be divided into four regions. The south coast is a broad strip of sand dunes, both active and ancient. North of this are the largely deforested sandy plains which are the ancestral lands of many of the older clans among the Tandroy people. Further north, these flat plains are still covered by extensive forest and brush. The most northerly zone is a large stony plateau of hills and plains covered by a mosaic of forests, brush, open areas and bare rock; this region was not occupied by the Tandroy until the beginning of the nineteenth century. Tandroy daily life is hard, particularly towards the end of the dry season, and many have migrated northwards in recent years into the sparsely populated vast inland grasslands and to towns and plantations throughout Madagascar. Most Malagasy are rice cultivators, whereas the people of the dry south (the Tandroy and their neighbours the Mahafaly, the Karimbola and the Bara) are pastoralists. In contrast to the Bara who concentrate on raising cattle, Tandroy herds consist of fat-tailed sheep, goats and cattle. Subsistence crops of manioc, sweet potato, maize, ground nuts, beans, melons, onions, prickly pear and even tomatoes are grown in the cactus-edged fields that surround the dispersed villages throughout Androy.

Aspects of traditional life such as dress, domestic utensils and, in northern Androy, house-building styles have changed dramatically in the last twenty years. Yet the Tandroy way of life has been relatively unaffected, partly because of the region's isolation from the rest of Madagascar and partly because of a strong sense of identity. The south of Madagascar was the last region to be subdued by French troops in 1900. The French colonial authorities established a series of posts which have continued as markets and administrative centres since independence in 1960. However, their small populations are largely composed of outsiders from other parts of Madagascar, since most

Tandroy prefer to live in villages. In these villages and hamlets the houses are small, rectangular wooden dwellings which are conventionally burned or destroyed on the death and burial of their occupant. Like many other pastoralists, Tandroy descent is patrilineal whilst marriage is polygamous and exogamous. Husbands construct houses for each of their wives, and villages are largely composed of brothers with their families and other dependants. Seniority is traditionally expressed spatially by the placing of junior house-holds to the north of senior ones, a pattern opposite to that of most of the rest of Madagascar. The internal organisation of the house similarly contrasts with other areas by having the doorway on the north side instead of on the south end of the west side. More traditional houses still retain a door on the south end, a vestige of nineteenth-century social structure when the south-west door was the slaves' entrance.

In common with the rest of Madagascar, the Tandroy dead are com-memorated by lavish funerary rites and elaborate tombs. In contrast to the communal burial rites that are common to most other Malagasy people, however, Tandroy, Karimbola and Mahafaly monuments are erected over the graves of individuals (Figure 25.1). The competition and hierarchy embodied in asymmetrical relationships between wife-giving and wife-taking lineages are central to the exchanges of animals and food at funerals. Throughout the south, the huge rectangular stone tombs, often painted and covered with the bucrania of steers slaughtered during the funerary rites and lengthy tomb-building, line the dirt roads and occupy hillsides. Tombs are placed according to seniority, with the eldest of a family buried to the south of the others. Men's tombs are distinguished by paired standing stones ('man-stones') and they are normally placed to the east of women's tombs. The bodies of depen-dants may be buried within another's tomb, and they are placed in relation to the primary burial according to the spatial ordering of seniority and gender. Standing stones are set up as cenotaphs to commemorate those men whose bodies cannot be returned home for burial. The stone-tomb tradition is little more than a century old and is replacing burial within rectangular wooden palisades hidden in sacred forests.

Although tombs and burial places are protected by taboo, the stone tombs form visible markers of lineage and genealogy. Many people can remember the names of their ancestors going back six generations or more. This knowl-edge is largely an oral tradition. Tandroy social structure is segmentary, divided into clans that are composed of lineages and sub-lineages. Each clan has its own history of origin and ancestry, as has been meticulously researched for the Afomarolahy (Heurtebize 1986a). The founding ancestors of the Afomaro-lahy, originally Bara from the north, probably arrived in Androy at the end of the seventeenth century, since which time the clan has grown from about twenty-five people to over 200,000. Oral traditions recall the migration of the Afomarolahy into Androy, their association with the royal clan, the Andria-mañare, the establishment of their ancestral lands in northern Androy and their subsequent expansion northwards out of this area into zones largely

Figure 25.1 A typical Tandroy tomb, built in the 1970s. The body is buried prior to the construction of the walled cairn. Secondary burials may be inserted later into the cairn. The standing stones at either end indicate that this is the burial of a man and that a second male burial has been added. Cattle bucrania are placed on top of the tomb, which is decorated with paintings and a central house/coffin representation.

empty but where they came into occasional conflicts with Bara over grazing areas. The ancestral land is centred on the large lake of Andrananivo, whose mud has curative properties. Whilst the many small lakes of Androy are a significant and circumscribed resource, this one is perhaps the only one to have a central significance for a clan history.

Interpreting the material remains of the past

Our experience with the inter-relationship of archaeology and oral history can best be explored by comparing two separate contexts: that of the Andriamañare's ancient past and that of other clans' perceptions of their archaeological landscapes. Whereas each clan has an ancestral area of origin, only the Andriamañare, the descendants of the royal clan, maintain the memory of certain ancestral villages which are today the sites of sacred forests. Such places are not only prohibited to other clans but may be the cause of disagreements and tribunals over the illicit collection of wild resources within them.

Archaeology is largely an alien concept for the Tandroy as a whole, although European and Malagasy outsiders have been conducting substantial research programmes in Androy since the 1950s (Battistini *et al.* 1963; Radimilahy 1980, 1988; Emphoux 1981; Heurtebize 1986a). There continues to be a deep-seated suspicion of all outsiders, especially in the more remote areas, but archaeological teams always attempt to be sensitive to local requirements and concerns. Local people will often join in fieldwork but interest wanes after the first afternoon of fieldwalking or digging. Currently the only archaeologist of Tandroy origin is one of the authors of this chapter. Ethnographers and visitors have written extensively about Tandroy life and culture (Grandidier 1904; Defoort 1913; Decary 1921, 1930, 1933, 1952, 1962; Frère 1958; Guérin 1978; Heurtebize 1986b; Middleton 1987; Musée d'Art et d'Archéologie 1989). Georges Heurtebize and Sarah Fee have also established a major museum exhibition of Tandroy life and culture at the Berenty nature reserve in southern Madagascar.

Local awareness of the remains of the ancient past is notably at variance with an archaeological perspective. Observations of pottery and bones unearthed while digging fields are frequently made, and many people have a good knowledge of the distribution of ancient settlement sites in the vicinity of their village. Yet the explanations for and significance of such sites may vary considerably. In many parts of Androy, people may know only the location of their nineteenth-century ancestral village, even though it sits in an archaeological landscape of earlier settlements. In many cases such earlier sites are often considered to be non-Tandroy and are attributed to the Bara or other groups since moved away, even where there is independent evidence that such sites were inhabited by Tandroy.

The archaeology and oral history of the Andriamañare

The Andriamañare, once known as the Zafimanara, are the royal clan of the Tandroy. They trace their origin to a small group of immigrants, probably of Islamic descent, from the northeast coast of Madagascar who established the ruling dynasties of the Maroserana among the Mahafaly to the west and the Zafiramini of the Tanosy to the east. According to Etienne de Flacourt, the administrator of France's abortive seventeenth-century colony at Fort Dauphin, this other ruling dynasty, the Zafiramini, were already long established by the 1650s in Anosy, the southeast corner of Madagascar (1661). Migrating from the east, the Andriamañare settled on the bank of the Mandrare river, the traditional eastern frontier of Androy. According to oral traditions, they then established what has come to be their most ancient ancestral village at Anjampanorora, in the centre of the southern grass plains. Today the Temaromena branch of Andriamañare live in its vicinity together with several other clans. The second ancestral village is considered to be Montefeno, about 10 km to the west. An Andriamañare village in the vicinity of the site of Montefeno was abandoned over four generations ago and other clans now live here. The third ancestral site is on the west bank of the lower Manambovo river, further to the west. This is the ancestral land of the Tefanomboke lineage of the Andriamañare. Finally, the fourth ancestral village was established at Ambaro, in the forested northen part of the sandy plain, by Andrianjoma, the founding ancestor of the Tekonda lineage of Andriamañare. This is a brief summary of more detailed work in progress by Georges Heurtebize and Retsihisatse but it provides a framework that we have set out to document archaeologically through field prospection and excavation.

The ancestral village of Anjampanorora is covered by a sacred forest that is also a burial ground and thus cannot be entered except during funerals (Figure 25.2). There is pottery on the surface, suggestive of an ancient settlement, but it is undated. Archaeological survey in the vicinity of the forest located seven settlement scatters. The earliest probably dates to the sixteenth century. A small settlement may be dated to the later seventeenth century, but otherwise the other large sites are of nineteenth- and early twentieth-century date. What we suspect is that the sixteenth-century settlement is actually the original ancestral village whilst the subsequent seventeenth- to eighteenth-century settlement remains lie within the sacred forest. In other words, the act of commemoration of the ancestral village was focused on a later settlement site, since memory of the precise location of the earliest site had disappeared.

Montefeno is especially interesting as it was visited by a squad of French soldiers in 1649. Flacourt (1661: 263–5) described it as the 'great village' of the Tandroy (although he called them the Ampatois) and the residence of their *roandria* (chief or noble), Andrianmififarivo. In 1913, the French administrator and ethnographer E. Defoort suggested that the site of this village may have been located near the neighbouring village of Belanky, where another group of Andriamañare lived at that time. Today, the Andriamañare have gone from this place, but a sacred forest lies over most of their abandoned nineteenth-century village site. One and a half kilometres to the north, there are the remains of a large village with sixteenth-century pottery, the only one other than Anjampanorora of this early date located within the 15 km long transect surveyed in the southern sandy plains. Its name, Andavenoke ('place of cinders'), is testimony to local knowledge of its existence as an archaeological site, but it is not associated with any specific oral histories or notions of sacredness. One kilometre to the east, there is one of the many seventeenth-century settlement sites in the area, located at the centre of one of six settlement concentrations. Its ceramics are probably best dated to the later part of the seventeenth–century. Whilst most of the settlement site is cultivated, a small part is covered by a copse; at the centre of this is a sacred fig tree beneath which are buried the umbilical cords of the *roandria* of the Tekonda Andriamañare, who now live many kilometres to the north at Ambaro. The practice of burying umbilical cords of newborn babies explicitly links Tandroy lineages to the place of their origin, and indicates that the 'royal family' of the Tekonda Andriamañare trace their ancestry back to this area, where their ancestors lived prior to their migration to the north and Andrianjoma's subsequent establishment of his residence at Ambaro (Figure 25.3). In a similar vein, ancestral burial areas are retained even if they are

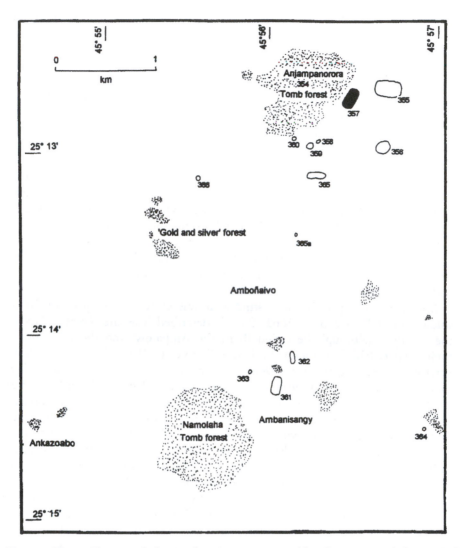

Figure 25.2 The sacred forest of Anjampanorora with adjacent sacred forests and archaeological sites (numbered). Although there is an ancient ancestral settlement within the forest, Site 357 can be dated to the sixteenth century and may be the oldest.

many miles from the village now inhabited. For example, it was only after 1978 that a group of Andriamañare who had moved northwards from Ambaro to a new village, Soalapa, in the late eighteenth or early nineteenth century moved their place of burial from Ambaro.

Certain forests and trees may be sacred or special for many reasons. Whilst woodlands in southern Androy have been reduced by more than 60 per cent since 1950 (Garrod et al. 1995) through the needs for firewood, charcoal,

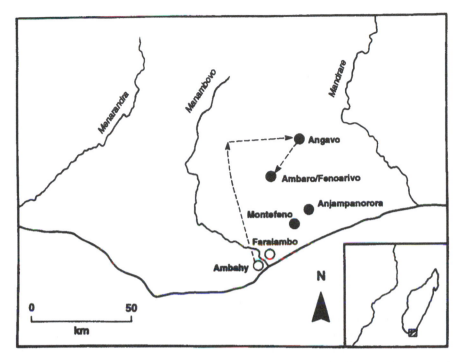

Figure 25.3 The route taken by Andrianjoma, the late seventeenth- to early eighteenth-century *roandria*, from the west bank of the Manambovo to the mountain of Vohimena to the hill of Angavo and finally to Ambaro. The filled circles are large settlements of the sixteenth, seventeenth and/or eighteenth century identified archaeologically. The open circles are ancient royal centres not yet researched archaeologically.

houses, fences and coffins and the expansion of grazing areas, many small copses and forests survive on account of their sacredness. Firewood is imported into the area and there is considerable pressure on remaining woodlands. Most of the tombs in the southern region are still constructed in traditional form: rectangular palisade enclosures hidden deep in a wood that is sacred because of the presence of the cemetery. Whilst these surviving pockets of forest cover are of considerable potential importance to outsider ecological interests and to local collectors of medicinal and magical materials, they are protected by taboo against exploitation. Occasionally, forests are taboo for other reasons; sometimes they are said to contain buried gold and silver, the heirlooms of people with no direct successors, or they contain beehives. The beehive forests, where investigated, are located on abandoned settlements. At times, forests will be shunned because they are haunted by ghosts or by *koko-lampo*, invisible spirits who make mischief but may also bring benefits such as curing the sick.

The third ancestral village of the Andriamañare at Ambahy has seventeenth-century origins. This area is considered to be the ancestral land not only of the Tefanomboke Andriamañare but also of many other clans who have since moved eastwards and northwards. For the Tekonda Andriamañare, Andrianjoma is the greatest ancestral *roandria*. He established the last royal dynasty amongst the Andriamañare and is said to have had 2,000 slaves and a large entourage of warriors. He is thought to have left Ambahy to commence his perigrination around northern Androy before settling at Ambaro. His residence at Ambaro is located in a sacred forest just east of the modern village. Our excavations of settlement areas immediately to the west of this forest have identified a large late eighteenth- to early nineteenth-century settlement which is probably later than the pottery found on a site within the forest itself. Further west again, behind the current village of Ambaro, is the later nineteenth-century settlement, in the middle of which is located the umbilical cord tree for those Tekonda Andriamañare who are not direct royal descendants. Andriamañare tradition records that Andrianjoma was invited to remain in this area by the indigenous inhabitants, the Tetreso clan, a history that the Tetreso confirm. Whilst the Tetreso know of their nineteenth-century ancestral village, we were able to locate its predecessors going back to the seventeenth and possibly sixteenth centuries.

Additional evidence, in the form of *Robert Drury's Journal*, suggests that Andrianjoma's settlement was the royal capital formerly known as Fenoarivo (Parker Pearson 1996) (Figure 25.4). Drury was one of a few survivors from an English East Indiaman's crew shipwrecked and subsequently massacred in 1703. He records that the king, Deaan Crindo (probably Andriankirindre), lived at Fenoarivo. Since names are changed after death, we have no way of knowing for certain whether Andrianjoma was the *roandria* referred to by Drury. However, Heurtebize's study of Afomarolahy and Andriamañare genealogies concludes that Andrianjoma lived at the end of the seventeenth century (Heurtebize 1986a: 180–3). The name of Fenoarivo is today associated with a royal residence of the later nineteenth century, 2 km away from the Ambaro settlement sites.

The creation of sacred forest is itself an interesting phenomenon. In the case of burial places, the forest is normally primary woodland hitherto untouched. In the case of ancient settlements, regeneration has occurred. Regeneration may be only partial, since settlements of the seventeenth to nineteenth centuries were, according to the European sources, often carved out of existing forest in order that the spiny trees would provide a natural defence. In the case of Andrianjoma's settlement, the aerial photographs from 1950 indicate that it was at that time an area of open ground with some scrub and a few trees; today the site is fairly dense woodland. According to senior elders in the modern village, the trees were planted by the ancestors when the settlement was deserted, and the forest had been there for as long as they could remember. Their account is at odds with the evidence of the aerial photographs.

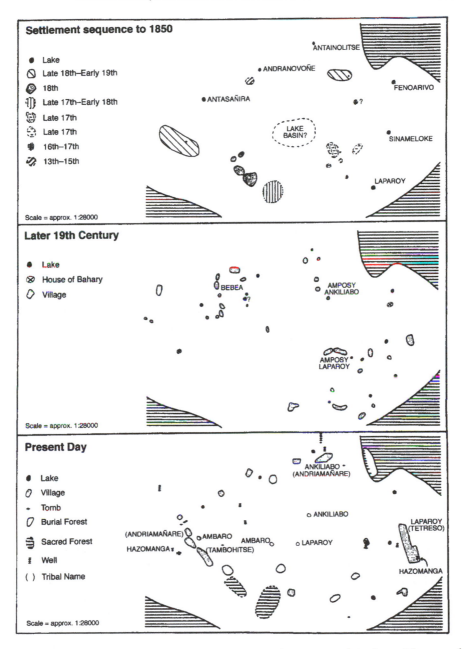

Figure 25.4 The ancient and contemporary landscape around Ambaro. The sacred forest in the central southern area is the location of Andrianjoma's capital, thought to have been called Fenoarivo.

The comparison of oral history with archaeological evidence is often difficult because each tends to work best for very different classes of evidence. Oral
history provides the best information about personal names and sequences,
while archaeology gives the most reliable evidence for places and dates. Our
respective histories, however, have indicated many points of convergence. The
oral traditions of the location of ancestral villages are supported not only by
archaeological discoveries but also by the testimony of the contemporary
observers, Flacourt and Drury. Where there are discrepancies, we may profit
by drawing conclusions about the different approaches to history. The evidence
from Anjampanorora and Montefeno suggests that precise knowledge of
the actual locations of the 400-year-old settlements has been lost. Just as
knowledge of the royal genealogies becomes uncertain before Andrianjoma, so
there is a concomitant loss of knowledge about settlements prior to the eighteenth century. The momentous events of 1703, the shipwreck and massacre,
are not recalled, nor is Drury's presence as a white slave (Drury [1729] 1890).
Whether oral history fades through time uniformly after 300–200 years, like
the disappearing wake of a ship, or whether it changes dramatically in the face
of political uncertainty, such as the coming of the French, we cannot say. It is
of course a social and political tool; whilst groups like the Andriamañare are
justly proud of their history, others of lowlier origin and ex-slave descent have
no such recourse. In a community where ancestors are an important resource
and whose honouring is the focus of so much investment, their memory and
recitation form a powerful ideological discourse.

Oral history and the people who came before

Tandroy settlement dynamics are very fluid and villages may be moved readily.
Many clan groups now live in territories at some distance from their ancestral lands. Thus Tandroy history is very much one of migration. During the
late eighteenth and early nineteenth centuries, some Tandroy clans, especially
the Renevave clans of Afomarolahy, Afomihala and Afondriambita and the
Andriamañare lineages of Tsirandrane, Temangaike, Tekonda and Tekopoke,
moved into new lands in northern Androy. Here they encountered occasional Bara cattle herders and also a variety of ancient sites, notably the *manda*
('enclosures') (Figure 25.5) and small stone burial monuments (known as
vatomita). The Tandroy generally consider these to have been built by the
Bara and many are clearly the remains of a pre-Tandroy presence in this area.
The various *vatomita* occasionally have named individuals associated with them,
such as the nineteenth-century burial of Namolora, whose name is preserved
in the name of the adjacent modern village. However, most are anonymous
and may date anywhere between the sixteenth and nineteenth centuries.
Nonetheless, they are still sacred since the remains of the dead should not
be disturbed. Ancient stone-walled enclosures are known throughout this
area at Bevotry, Amandabe, Vohidolo, Bemoke and Mandameriñe. All are

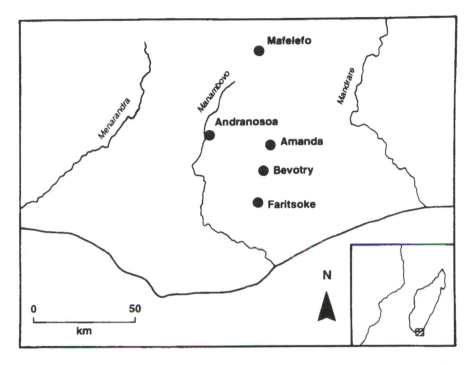

Figure 25.5 The distribution of eleventh- to thirteenth-century stone-walled enclosures (*manda*) in Androy.

explicitly associated with the Bara and all but Vohidolo are supposed to have been built and inhabited by the Bara bandit Manorotoro ('the Crusher'). One of the stories associated with him is that Manorotoro's kinsman, Laimanara, was killed in battle by the Tandroy at Andalatanosy and his corpse was returned to Bara country by a Tandroy, Berida. Though many of the Bara wished Berida dead, a wise elder persuaded them to reward him with a gift of fifty cattle. The story is frequently retold in the songs of the *beko*, the funerary singing in the days prior to burial.

Manorotoro must have lived during the nineteenth century when the Tandroy moved into this area and came into conflict with Bara groups over grazing land. Yet the enclosures date from many periods. The various *manda* at Bevotry, Vohidolo and Mandamerine are part of a complex of apparently non-defensive ceremonial enclosures of the same date as Great Zimbabwe, i.e. the eleventh to thirteenth centuries. The *manda* at Amandabe and Bemoke date to the eighteenth century and both lie on or close to the ancient limit of Androy. Bemoke is, in our opinion, almost certainly a Tandroy settlement since it is located on Angavo, a high hill, and is probably the 'town' of Deaan Afferer (Andriafara?), a member of the royal dynasty, visited on Angavo by Robert Drury around 1710.

Further south there is another eleventh- to thirteenth-century *manda* at Faritsoke. According to Sianameloke oral tradition, its north end was a cattle-corralling area and its south end was for habitation; these details are supported by the presence of sherds and bone around the southern walls. The enclosure is linked to two men, Remanaly and Fotsinay of the Sakavehe lineage of the Afondrantehake clan, who would probably have been alive in the nineteenth century. Such stories of nineteenth-century people, whether Bara or Tandroy, may well be accurate; people may well have reinhabited more ancient ruins. But there is no account of earlier people which is required to explain these sites. This is perhaps not surprising given the prehistoric antiquity of many of the enclosures. Were the builders likely to have been Bara? At two enclosures in northern Androy, Vohidolo and Andranosoa, there are long-term ceramic sequences from the eleventh to the seventeenth centuries, after which the area was abandoned until the appearance of nineteenth-century Tandroy pottery on settlement sites. Flacourt makes several references to the peoples of this northern area in the mid-seventeenth century who were not the Bara but the Machicores. He is probably referring to the Masikoro, a group who now live in western Madagascar with the Vezo, south of the Sakalava, and whose territory would seem to have massively contracted.

Similar contraction of long-term sequences of settlement has been documented in other parts of Androy. In the Tsihombe area, members of the Sanamena clan could locate the remains of the nineteenth-century settlements but not those of the eighteenth century, which were positioned 1 km to the south. Similarly, only nineteenth- to twentieth-century village sites were known about by Tanalavondrove clan members. This was also the case for the Jambe clan at Amanda in southern Karimbola. Equally, people do know of ancient sites, found during field clearance and cultivation, but these places are of little significance and are simply ascribed to peoples of before.

The contraction of history and the *post hoc* rationalisation of ancient remains as the deeds of relatively recent individuals are common features of folk histories all around the world. Some archaeologists might take a social-constructivist position, arguing that the 'reality' of 800-year-old sites perceived as nineteenth-century creations is an accepted truth for certain Tandroy clans that should not be disputed. We would wholly disagree with this approach because it implies an uncritical condescension that sacrifices historical enquiry and accuracy for the sake of not engaging with the history of others. We consider that the study of the past is an enquiry that all are involved in; new discoveries and reassessments may potentially enrich and deepen people's perspectives of their history. It is not simply a matter of varying interpretations and multiple histories but a question of accuracy. Direct conflict over ancient sacred places has happened. During the period of French colonisation, the French built a landing strip through the sacred burial forest at Tsihombe. However, their policy of desacralisation was more extensive amongst the Mahafaly, where they deliberately planned roads to cut through the sacred forests where the Maroserana dynasties were buried (Esoavelomandroso 1991: 100–1).

What is significant in the case of Androy is not that oral history should deviate from the history recoverable by archaeology and contemporary written sources, but that it varies according to subject matter. As in many societies, the remains of ancient sites are broadly unimportant. Even on the often tricky subject of origins, these ancient remains have little significance. That there may have been other Malagasy groups living in Androy in the long-distant past is not a matter of significance in making claims to land, since the origin stories of all clans involve coming into the region from elsewhere and, in some cases, displacing existing groups. Thus the lands of the ancestors, though once occupied by others, are not contested by any other ethnic group. The only context where archaeological remains are incorporated into oral histories is amongst the Andriamañare, for whom history constitutes a more important resource than for other clans. This may partly be because their power declined with the last powerful *roandria*, Bahary, on his death in about 1888. With the invasion of the French, slavery was abolished and the three-tiered system of princely clan, free clans and slaves came to an end. Today the Andriamañare retain aspects of their former status, through titles, marriage preferences, greeting formalities and ultimate control of land given to ex-slave groups, but they are largely just one clan amongst many. There may still be tensions between them and other clans with regard to land rights and the history of the granting of land titles. Perhaps one of their most important resources is the past, in terms of defining genealogical distance from other clans, access to certain land, control of certain sacred forests and access to the blessings of the most powerful ancestors. These things still matter and will continue to do so, especially with increasing interest in their culture, traditions and history. It is clear from the relatively recent forest regeneration around Andrianjoma's capital that Andriamañare perceptions of history have continued to change in the twentieth century, as the past continues to be manipulated not only in a purely ideological sense but also as a physical resource of forests, lakes and land.

Acknowledgements

The fieldwork was carried out in 1991, 1993, 1995 and 1996 by Mike Parker Pearson, Karen Godden, Ramilisonina and Retsihisatse, with Victor Razanatovo in 1993, 1995 and 1996, Jean-Luc Schwenninger and Helen Smith in 1995 and Georges Heurtebize in 1995 and 1996. We are grateful to Tsihandatse and Alphonse Tsiongaha at Ambaro, Dada at Bevotry, Tsiavehe at Androvasoa, Manandongo at Mitsoriake, Bejana at Mafelefo and especially Georges Heurtebize at Analamahery for their knowledge of oral histories. The research was made possible by Jean-Aimé Rakotoarisoa, Director of the Museum of Art and Archaeology, and has been helped by advice and help from Georges Heurtebize, John Mack, Karen Middleton, Chantal Radimilahy, Pierre Vérin and Henry Wright. The research was funded by grants from the Nuffield Foundation, the British Academy, the Natural Environment Research Council of Britain, the Society of Antiquaries of London and the National Geographic Society (grant no. 5470–95).

References

Battistini, R., Vérin, P. and Rason, R. 1963. Le site archéologique de Talaky. *Annales Malgaches* 1, 111–27.

Decary, R. 1921. Monographie du district de Tsihombe. *Bulletin Economique de Madagascar* 18, 5–38.

Decary, R. 1930. *L'Androy (extrême sud de Madagascar): essai de monographie régionale.* Vol. I. Paris: Société d'Editions Géographiques.

Decary, R. 1933. *L'Androy (extrême sud de Madagascar): essai de monographie régionale.* Vol. II. Paris: Société d'Editions Géographiques.

Decary, R. 1952. Les conditions physiques du peuplement humain de Madagascar. *Mémoires de l'Institut Scientifique de Madagascar* 1, 1–12.

Decary, R. 1962. *Le mort et les coutumes funéraires à Madagascar.* Paris: Payot.

Defoort, E. 1913. *L'Androy: essai de monographie.* Antananarivo: Bulletin Économique de Madagascar.

Drury, R. [1729] 1890. *Madagascar: or Robert Drury's Journal during fifteen years captivity on that island.* London: W. Meadows.

Emphoux, J.-P. 1981. Archéologie de l'Androy: deux sites importants: Andranosoa et le manda de Ramananga. *Omaly si Anio* 13/14, 89–98.

Esoavelomandroso, M. 1991. La forêt dans le Mahafale aux XIXe et XXe siècle. *Aombe* 3, 97–102.

Flacourt, E. de. 1661. *Histoire de la grande isle de Madagascar, composée par le sieur de Flacourt, avec un relation de ce qui s'est passé les années 1655, 1656, et 1657 non encore veue par la première impression.* Paris: Clouzier.

Frère, S. 1958. *Madagascar: panorama de l'Androy.* Paris: Aframpe.

Garrod, S., Clark, C. and Parker Pearson, M. 1995. Tombs, forests and remote sensing: landscape archaeology in the semi-arid spiny forests of southern Madagascar. *Proceedings of the 1995 Conference on Remote Sensing.* Southampton: University of Southampton.

Grandidier, G. 1904. L'extrême sud de Madagascar – les pays Mahafaly et Antandroy. *Annales Coloniales* (15 mars), 118–25.

Guérin, M. 1978. *Le défi: l'Androy et l'appel à la vie.* Fianarantsoa: Ambozontany.

Heurtebize, G. 1986a. *Histoire des Afomarolahy (extrême-sud de Madagascar).* Paris: Centre National de Recherches Scientifiques.

Heurtebize, G. 1986b. *Quelques aspects de la vie dans l'Androy.* Antananarivo: Musée d'Art et d'Archéologie.

Middleton, K. 1987. Marriages and funerals: some aspects of Karembola political symbolism (Madagascar). Unpublished DPhil thesis, University of Oxford.

Musée d'Art et d'Archéologie 1989. *Androy.* Antananarivo: Musée d'Art et d'Archéologie.

Parker Pearson, M. 1996. Re-appraising *Robert Drury's Journal* as a historical source. *History in Africa* 23: 1–23.

Radimilahy, C. 1980. Archéologie de l'Androy – contribution à la connaissance des phases de peuplement. Unpublished Mémoire de maîtrise soutenu au Département d'Histoire de l'EES Lettres. Centre d'Art et d'Archéologie, Université d'Antananarivo.

Radimilahy, C. 1988. *L'ancienne métallurgie du fer à Madagascar.* Oxford: BAR International Series 422.

26 Living with stones: people and the landscape in Erromango, Vanuatu

DAVID ROE AND JERRY TAKI

Introduction

In this chapter we describe and comment on a number of sites that have cultural importance for the people of Erromango in southern Vanuatu, an island nation in the southwest Pacific. These sites are all marked by stones, either natural or emplaced, and are significant for a wide variety of reasons.[1] An examination of the different roles that these stones play in the social and economic relationships between Erromangans and between Erromangans and their landscape is instructional for studies of archaeological landscapes in Melanesia and critical for effective cultural heritage management practice. Our review is by no means exhaustive and excludes equally important sites that have no stone features of any kind. Furthermore, our review uses categories of sites (stones and land, stones and agriculture, for example) only as a convenience and not as a reflection of any Erromangan typology of places.

The data that we draw upon was collected during a series of surveys conducted under the auspices of the Vanuatu Cultural and Historic Sites Survey (hereafter the VCHSS).[2] The VCHSS surveys on Erromango were initially prompted by relatively small-scale logging proposals in 1991. In 1993–4, additional and more extensive survey exercises were required when the timber reserves of the entire island were licensed to four major multinational companies for logging operations. These surveys provided information on site locations and their physical features, and recorded the manner in which a site was significant based in large measure upon the oral histories and commentaries of local informants (Roe 1992; Kolmas et al. 1993; Batick and Huri 1994). This information was supplemented by additional material from the published accounts of ethnographers, missionaries and other visitors (e.g. Brenchley 1873; Robertson 1902; Humphreys 1926; Woodburn 1944; Cheesman 1957) as well as earlier archaeological reconnaissances (Shutler and Shutler 1968; Groube 1972; Spriggs 1988; Spriggs and Roe 1989; Spriggs and Wickler 1989; Spriggs and Mumford 1992). The equal emphasis of the VCHSS surveys on archaeological and cultural sites differed from the earlier archaeological surveys, which had primarily targeted sites where the presence of excavatable deposits or other humanly-made features indicated the potential for the collection of purely archaeological data from the remote past. Thus, for example, the total of five sites in the 4 km stretch of coastline between Potnarvin and Potnuma that had been recorded prior to 1992 was increased by the VCHSS surveys to fifty-two. This serves to highlight the fragmentary nature of the purely archaeological record that can be recognised in the landscape, and the complexity that this record may actually represent.

In 1993, a group of indigenous fundamentalist Christians were directly responsible for the destruction or desecration of numbers of sacred stones on the island. At about the same time, the activities of one of the multi-national logging companies destroyed or damaged a number of cultural sites on the island; this included several instances of the removal of, or damage to, stones in the landscape. The loss of these stones provoked a very strong response from the communities affected. The church group was threatened with legal proceedings for alleged acts of sacrilege, theft and coercion, and a moratorium on logging operations was declared pending the renegotiation of logging concessions and the guarantee of adequate site protection measures. It can properly be claimed that this public response, and the support of the Government for it, was facilitated by the VCHSS whose surveys on the island had been directed at providing not only an inventory of sites but also an assessment and, therefore, a recognition of their significance based on essentially local criteria. The strength of the public response demonstrated the importance that stones of various kinds still have for the people of the island, despite a long history of missionisation (Miller 1981), colonial exploitation (see, e.g. Shineberg 1967) and depopulation (McArthur and Yaxley n.d.: 4).

Stones and land

With a rural economy that still depends heavily upon the subsistence production of agricultural staples, particularly yam (*Dioscorea spp.*) and taro (especially *Colocasia esculenta*), in a swidden system requiring relatively frequent movement of garden areas and settlements, it is hardly surprising that concerns over land ownership and usage are central to Melanesian social and economic systems. These concerns are heightened by the need to access and control other resources; these include, *inter alia*, timber for construction, medicinal plants, materials for weaving and artefact manufacture, pigments for ritual and exchange, stones for cooking ovens and, in coastal communities, fishing and shellfishing grounds. In Melanesia, the relationship between a group, or an individual, and a land or sea area is often made by reference to named places in the landscape and their associated stories (Roe et al. 1994). These places, which assist also in the creation of mental maps of the environment (cf. Larmour 1979), act as the evidential proof of the use rights enjoyed by a group or individual in respect of a given land or sea area.

The site of Sauhenuvalam in west Erromango consists of a single moss- and lichen-covered monolith now standing in *mori* (*Acacia spirorbis*) scrub forest. Although the full story of this site appears to have been lost, the monolith is considered to be the spear of a spirit called Poghorvi. Whatever the original purpose of its erection, the monolith now serves as a simple land boundary marker. The apparent lack of detailed documentation of the circumstances of its emplacement and those responsible for it makes it less compelling as evidence of ownership than does, for example, the stone of Noghopen Yoghorewi.

On the east coast of Erromango, an uplifted and fissured coral terrace near the Suvuva river mouth features in a lengthy origin story of Noghopen Yoghorewi and his lineage. The history commences with the arrival of Noghopen in a canoe (now a 1.5 m long coral block with a small volcanic stone cemented onto its surface) through a fissure in the coral terrace, and proceeds through a sequence of settlements and associated cemeteries and shrines that encompass the 'territory' of the lineage. The sites themselves, the chronological order in which they were established and used, and the knowledge associated with them are used to validate the group's ownership of land and the resources that it holds or to which it governs access. The association of named stones to lineage histories is commonplace, whether these begin with human ancestors, as in the case of Noghopen, or with spiritual/ animal ancestors, as at Melvi in southeast Erromango where Nompuntanep Imelvi, a group of stones in the rivermouth, indicates the arrival point of a clamshell responsible for the establishment of a nearby settlement. The location of many origin sites in coastal positions allows them also to be used for the validation of marine tenure claims.

Stones and history

In Melanesia, the 'indexing' and 'anchoring' of history through the association of narratives with named places in the landscape has been remarked by several commentators. In New Caledonia, for example, Leenhardt noted that the landscape was similar to a book of knowledge and that 'each stone has a name, a history, a life', and that with the knowledge of named places 'the landscape transposes itself into a scheme . . . in which each name is a title to a chapter' (Leenhardt 1930: 241 cited by Kahn 1990). In similar vein, Mead, discussing the importance of place names in Santa Ana in the Solomon Islands, observed that 'a rock was simply a rock if it was not named and had no story attached' but that named places were able 'to represent in concrete form the stories they symbolise' (Mead 1973: 219). Kahn (1990) and Harwood (1976) have discussed for the Trobriand Islands of Papua New Guinea the anchoring of indigenous 'mythical' history through its association with places and in particular with stones. All authors recognise two important aspects of such associations:

1   the use of places as mnemonic devices for the recall of histories, events
    and people; and
2   the use of places as validations and/or spatial representations of histor-
    ical events.

Although there are clearly time-reckoning systems of greater or lesser
complexity throughout Melanesia (see, e.g. Malinowski 1927; Austen 1939;
Panoff 1969; Prendeville 1976; Waleanisia 1989), these generally describe
yearly or seasonal cycles and lack the vocabulary that provides the ability
to place events in anything other than a short-term temporal framework.
Erromangan historical frameworks instead rely heavily on spatial referents.
Historical sequences are known, described and validated in terms of where
events took place rather than by reference to the time of their occurrence.
Places then, rather than times, become the divisions of history; but while
Erromangan histories depend upon the knowledge of 'where', they are
incomplete and cannot be accurately demonstrated without a complementary
knowledge of 'who' and 'what'. The knowledge of the individuals (human
or otherwise), families and lineages associated with particular places, and the
record of their actions at them, completes the historical description that is
initially identified by the place itself. Many Erromangan histories involve
a range of non-human beings, including some stones, who have interacted
with the human populations of the island in various ways. Human history
is, therefore, intimately bound up with and influenced by non-human actions.
Harwood and Kahn's descriptions of Trobriand sequences as 'mythical' histories partially obscures their importance, in that the categorisation of histories
as 'myth' and 'legend' implicitly denies their actuality and undermines the
veracity of purely human histories with which they are inextricably associated. Erromangan historical frameworks, therefore, make no such distinction
between 'myth' and 'reality' but, conversely, will not – or cannot – accommodate clear evidence of human use of the landscape where this is not
accompanied by supporting stories. Such evidence includes the great majority
of purely archaeological sites.

The site of Malap, for example, is remarkable for the number of engraved
rock art designs to be found there and is indisputably important archaeologically. The site lies on a beachrock exposure that appears to be a thin capping
of lava on the underlying coralline limestone. In Erromangan history, the
engraved designs of fish, anthropomorphs and geometric forms are ignored
(even though some demonstrably post-date European contact in the late
eighteenth century). A curious cup-like formation is, however, identified as
the bowl of a *nombo* spirit and features in the history of kava (a drink made
from the roots of *Piper methyisticum*, much used in ritual) and specifically in the
story of the marriage of the kava and coconut spirits. This history is important
not only as an explanation of the use of coconut shells in kava rituals, but in
its ability to demonstrate a spiritual link between two different areas of the
island through its 'anchoring' to locations in Ifo in southern Erromango and

Malap on the northwest coast. This spiritual link also serves to underwrite important secular links between the two communities.

Yam cultivation dominates the subsistence agriculture of Erromango, although there is evidence that taro was formerly more commonly grown than it is today. Many varieties of both crops are recognised and their origins generally well known. The original yam of the variety known as *pete* is located, in the form of a large basaltic boulder, at Elizabeth Bay in west Erromango, whither it had been brought for a feast from an old village site near Puniavet.

Other stones in the landscape also mark historical events: the limestone outcrop of Selnoisap was the main *siman-lo* (meeting-house) of the two chiefs Novur and Novual. Although traditional *siman-lo* are single-roomed structures, Selnoisap was unusual in that it had two rooms, one for the two chiefs and one for their people. On the northern side of the outcrop is a small fissure in which was kept the 'sacred fire' used for the preparation of certain types of food.

The stone of Vetikau, which stands at the mouth of Ifo harbour, recalls the period when the people of Tanna, the island immediately to the south of Erromango, visited southern Erromango to trade for pigments. This natural stone is named after Kauiel, a Tannese man who used the stone as a canoe mooring. Vetikau not only marks a historical event but also embodies an important social and economic inter-island relationship.

The erection of stones as memorials, or historical indicators, continues to the present. The establishment of the Presbyterian mission on Erromango met with severe opposition, including the murder of several of its missionaries and teachers (Campbell 1843; Robertson 1902). The mission station at Potnuma is marked now only by the foundations of the church and mission house and James Gordon's grave. Gordon was killed on 7 March 1872 by Nerimbao Novoyalpat and his brother Nare Yambalao, both of Nova village to the north of Potnuma. At the time of his death, Gordon was accompanied by Yomot, Soso and his servant–girl Uvoisiloki. A small stone monolith, set up by Erromangan converts, marks the place not at which Gordon was slain but to which his spilled blood ran. Published accounts of Gordon's death (Robertson 1902; Miller 1981) accord well with oral testimonies; the latter, however, rely on the evidence of the monolith, rather than the foundations and grave, to demonstrate not only their veracity but also the ferocity of the attack.

Stones for agriculture and fishing

Traditional agriculture on Erromango depended upon sound practice but required also the intervention of spiritual assistance for an assurance of success. The landscape hosts numbers of shrines associated with agriculture and the physical reminders of crop origins.

Agricultural shrines may be open to common use or be restricted to certain lineages. The site of Toruputongiwi consists of at least ten cairns of small pebbles (Figure 26.1). The largest cairn is 0.4 m in diameter and 0.1 m high, but most average 0.2 m in diameter and 0.1 m in height. The group of cairns lies adjacent to a commonly used trackway and was constructed for the purpose of securing fruitful garden harvests. There appears to have been no complex ritual associated with the site nor was access to it restricted.

This contrasts markedly with the *niepmitema* garden shrine of Raunklae in Potnarvin village, in which resides a *natmarandenogh* or *tema* spirit. It is marked by a rounded boulder, some 0.5 m in diameter (precise measurements could not be made for cultural reasons), by the side of which has been planted a red-leafed shrub – *yalimyao* – to prevent the stone from running away. The shrine is the property of a specific lineage, and knowledge of the associated rituals is restricted to its members. Strict rules of practice are applied to gardens in which the assistance of this shrine is sought – clearance procedures are well defined, it is forbidden for pregnant or menstruating women, or the husbands of such women, to work in the gardens, and pre-harvest offerings must be made to the *tema* spirit. To ignore such restrictions and regulations results not only in the failure of the garden but in affliction with tuberculosis (*tema*) for the transgressor. Shrines of this kind are treated with much respect, not only because they are regarded as being so powerful,

Figure 26.1 Jerry Taki points to one of the small cairns of pebbles at Toruputongiwi, west Erromango, which were built to ensure successful harvests of staple crops.

but also because incorrect or disrespectful use results in severe penalties. These penalties are exacerbated, in some instances, through the loss of the knowledge regarding cures for the illnesses that may result. In some cases, as apparently at Raunklae, the 'freedom' of the *tema* spirit would not only be regrettable but also potentially dangerous in this way.

Shrines specific to certain crops are also known. At the abandoned village site of Impinti are located two small stones used in yam garden magic and recognised as the property of the brothers Iau and Noghovet. The stones are named, the smaller Neitieti, the larger Ghorevnuwo, but despite their recognised efficacy and power they have not been removed from their original location by the descendants of the brothers who were the original owners. It is suspected, but was not specifically so stated by those consulted, that this results from a recognition that the village of Impinti, although abandoned by its human occupants, remains the home of the stones.

As stones can assist in agricultural practice, so they can assist in, or hinder if improperly used, other subsistence activities. Various forms of fishing are associated with powerful stones. Supplicatory offerings made to the spirits associated with the massive limestone blocks at Nomu at the mouth of the Tanwau river assured success in fishing expeditions. The larger boulder, known as Nomuikri or Nomupotnimo, provided help in inshore fishing, the smaller, Nomuilpalam, in deep-water expeditions. Like the agricultural shrine at Raunklae, the improper use of the stones, or disrespectful actions towards them, resulted in penalties – in this case sores on the soles of the feet of the offenders. Although use of the stones seems to have been restricted only to men and not to a particular kinship group, their ownership is linked to a named lineage. The desecration of such a stone thus also implies a second penalty, that resulting from the disrespect shown to its owners.

Stones, magic and illness

The human use of the environment may either be enhanced or proscribed by the actions or abilities of certain stones. The recognition that stones can act in these ways may be harnessed either for the common good or for the enhancement of one's own position through directing actions against others. This is illustrated by the stones of Umlahawai and Yowar, which are associated with thunder magic in particular and weather magic in general. Little specific data was available for these stones but it was generally agreed that the two stones could be used, by those in possession of the necessary formulae, to influence and change weather patterns, that the stones could be approached and touched only by those to whom they belonged and that, although the rituals might be more widely known than the owners might admit, the 'copyright' of the information was beyond doubt. The stones have become an economic asset for their owners in two ways. Rituals may be made at the request of others, either for their own benefit or to disadvantage competitors, and upon payment of a suitable fee. Of equal importance is the inherent threat posed by the restriction of such powerful knowledge to a small section of the community and the power that this accords to them (cf. Lindstrom 1985) and which becomes as much an item of exchange value as material objects.

Stones may, however, act independently and without regard to human agency or control and by so doing restrict or prohibit the use of certain parts of the environment. The ascription of certain diseases and afflictions to the agency of stones is common. Elephantiasis, or *seve*, stones are often associated with water sources or streams, such as the springs of Linti and the Sombo river, and thus render these water sources unavailable for human use. The stone of Wamprintavou causes sores on the soles of the feet; the stone of Ulevogh is avoided because of its association with leprosy and from which it takes its name. Less severe results arise from contact with the coralline boulders of Nombulbeh and Nompuhuri (Figure 26.2), renowned for their ability to cause baldness.

Stones, spirits and sanctions

The people of Erromango recognise that the environment in which they live and from which they derive their livelihoods is a shared one. Various kinds of spirits, especially *nombo*, simultaneously inhabit the same space as humans. They have their own histories, they own land and they may compete

Figure 26.2 At the mouth of the Melvi river near Ipota lies the large coralline boulder Nompuhuri. To touch the stone will cause baldness. Scale = 1 m.

directly for resources. Spirits also have their own stones to indicate their control and use of the environment; in some cases spirits are stones, and have many of the abilities of humans – for example, movement, procreation and speech.

At Ipota is an important complex of sites associated with the *nombo* spirit Nvatimbuap. The stone of Nahangat is one of several stones sent by Nvatimbuap to mark out his territory on the coast. These stones, sometimes referred to collectively as *naghorniauiau* ('the people who make a noise'), often lie on or at the end of earthen ridges which are the roads that the stones followed to the coast. They also include Yorwongi, Irongoi and his wife Usei Irongoi, who were responsible for identifying strangers in the area. Other areas near Ipota are identified as settlements and water sources belonging to the *nombo*. Near Tuwit, on the east coast of Erromango, the basalt boulders at Tangkolghol guard the land of the two *nombo* spirits, Tarat and Neiu, and have the power to kill trespassers or passers-by whom they do not recognise.

Stones, archaeology and heritage management

The great majority of the sites described here have no extant features in themselves that serve to distinguish them from natural (and therefore unimportant) rocks and stones in the landscape. In archaeological terms they are invisible, as their identification and interpretation depends entirely upon local knowledge. It is clear, however, and was often clearly stated, that the information recorded during the VCHSS surveys is that which can be freely given without compromising the sanctity of the site, its ownership, its economic value or the 'copyright' of the information. The significance of the sites in Erromangan cultural constructions and to the historical record of Erromango and Vanuatu lies in their association with more or less detailed histories. These histories transform the silent landscape of rocks and stones encountered in purely archaeological enquiries into a landscape in which some stones are keys to knowledge or information or have a being of their own.

The people–land relationship in Erromango is expressed partly through the knowledge of named places in the landscape (cf. Mead 1973). Stones, both natural and emplaced, and the knowledge about them serve to define a series of complex and interlocking elements of this relationship. Stones can serve as evidence of land ownership and can enhance lifestyles, they can also restrict or proscribe certain actions, and they can admit or limit access to resources. Stones serve to remind and instruct (sometimes directly). They can also demonstrate that the landscape is not only the domain of living humans; land and land use is shared with spirits of various kinds, with ancestral figures and, by extension, with 'generations yet unborn' (Zoloveke 1979: 4). Erromangans, therefore, are not only aware of the manner in which they possess and utilise the landscape but are equally aware that others share the same landscape and that in some sense the landscape possesses them.

In a book about land tenure systems of the Pacific, Arutangai (1987: 262) wrote of the Vanuatu situation:

> All ni-Vanuatu feel that land is everything – it is basic to their identity. Traditionally, land is not only the source of subsistence but the foundation of all custom. It represents life itself, both material and spiritual.

The stones of the Erromangan landscape, which define access to land and its resources, are, therefore, an essential economic resource. By acknowledging, and attempting to describe, the critical role that stones and their associated information play in the belief systems of Erromangan people, we can not only begin to appreciate better the complexity of the people–land relationship, but we can ascribe to them an economic value. Furthermore, the significance assessments provided by the VCHSS surveys in Erromango did not include the construction of site inventories formulated as ranked lists of sites from 'more important' to 'less important'. The survey and documentation methods employed clearly indicated that the physical attributes of places and their stories provide indivisible and unique units and that no place can be adequately 'represented' by any other, even when two sites may possess physically similar features.

The clear demonstration of the uniqueness of individual places and the ascription of measurable economic values to places have important implications for heritage management. Designing site protection and site-recording measures that conserve the uniqueness of sites requires the refinement of existing strategies, which emphasise the allieviation of damage to physical remains, to include appropriate ways of recording and anchoring the stories associated with particular parts of the landscape. By providing significance assessment criteria that indicate the social and economic value of stones (and other sites), we can more readily justify and influence discussions with economists, development planners, aid agencies and natural resource management authorities. This takes heritage management issues from their hitherto peripheral place to a more central arena, and allows them to be properly considered by those whose decisions will directly affect the future of Erromango's stones and the people who live with them.

Notes

1 As the oral histories associated with sites may variously have an economic value, be subject to traditional copyright or distribution restrictions and/or be essentially sacred in nature, it is often unclear whether information has been lost or is not available for general consumption. The traditional knowledge reported in this chapter has been freely provided in the foreknowledge that it will be made publicly available. It can be safely assumed that greater detail is known but has been retained.

2 The VCHSS, also known by its French and Bislama names as *Inventaire des Sites Historiques et Culturels de Vanuatu* and *Rejista Blong Olgeta Olfala Ples Blong Vanuatu*

respectively, was established in 1990 by the Government of the Republic of Vanuatu with funds and services supplied by the European Union and ORSTOM. The main objectives of the project, which has since become a division of the Ministry of Justice, Culture and Women's Affairs, were to create a national inventory of archaeological and cultural sites and to determine appropriate site significance assessment criteria and site protection procedures in a context of development planning.

Acknowledgements

The data presented in this chapter were collected in the course of a number of surveys conducted under the auspices of the VCHSS, surveys that would have been impossible without the permission, assistance and guidance of the chiefs, siteowners and people of Erromango, whose help is gratefully acknowledged.

References

Aruntangai, S. 1987. Vanuatu: overcoming the colonial legacy. In *Land Tenure in the Pacific*, R. Crocombe (ed.), 261–302. Suva: University of the South Pacific.

Austen, L. 1939. The seasonal gardening calendar of Kiriwina, Trobriand Islands. *Oceania* 9, 237–53.

Batick, J.-P. and D. Huri 1994. *Ol Damej Long Olgeta Olfala Ples We I Save Kamaot Sapos Ol I Wokem Niu Rod mo Katem Wud Long Cook Bay, Antiok mo Happy Land, Erromango*. Port Vila: Rejista Blong Olgeta Olfala Ples Blong Vanuatu (VCHSS).

Brenchley, J.L. 1873. *Jottings During the Cruise of the H.M.S. Curaçoa Among the South Sea Islands in 1865*. London: Longmans.

Campbell, J. 1843. *The Martyr of Erromango: or, The Philosophy of Mission, illustrated from the labours, death and character of the late Rev. John Williams*. London: Tyler & Reed.

Cheesman, E. 1957. *Things Worth While*. London: Hutchinson.

Groube, L. 1972. Erromango. Unpublished fieldnotes, Department of Prehistory, Research School of Pacific Studies, Australian National University.

Harwood, F. 1976. Myth, memory, and oral tradition: Cicero in the Trobriands. *American Anthropologist* 78, 783–96.

Humphreys, C.B. 1926. *The Southern New Hebrides: an ethnological record*. Cambridge: Cambridge University Press.

Kahn, M. 1990. Stone-faced ancestors: the spatial anchoring of myth in Wamira, Papua New Guinea. *Ethnology* 29, 51–66.

Kolmas, P., J.-P. Batick and D. Roe 1993. *Logging in South Erromango: the potential impact on the archaeological, historic and cultural site heritage*. Port Vila: Vanuatu Cultural and Historic Sites Survey.

Larmour, P. 1979. Customary maps. In *Land in Solomon Islands*, P. Larmour (ed.), 28–40. Suva: University of the South Pacific and the Solomon Islands Ministry of Agriculture and Lands.

Leenhardt, M. 1930. *Notes d'Ethnologie Néo-Calédoniens*. Paris: Institut d'Ethnologie.

Lindstrom, L. 1985. Doctor, lawyer, wise man, priest: big-men and knowledge in Melanesia. *Man* 19, 291–309.

McArthur, N. and J.F. Yaxley n.d. *Condominium of the New Hebrides: a report on the first census of the population 1967*. New South Wales: Government Printer.

Malinowski, B. 1927. Lunar and seasonal calendar in the Trobriands. *Journal of the Royal Anthropological Institute* 57, 203–15.

Mead, S.M. 1973. Folklore and place names in Santa Ana, Solomon Islands. *Oceania* 43, 215–37.

Miller, J.G. 1981. *Live: a history of church planting in the New Hebrides now the Republic of Vanuatu to 1880. Book Two.* Sydney: Presbyterian Church of Australia.

Panoff, M. 1969. The notion of time among the Maenge people of New Britain. *Ethnology* 8, 153–66.

Prendeville, K.F. 1976. The festival of the seventh month: a new year type festival of the Gari-speaking people, Solomon Islands. In *Powers, Plumes and Piglets*, N.C. Habel (ed.), 25–32. Bedford Park: Australian Association for the Study of Religions.

Robertson, H.A. 1902. *Erromanga: the martyr isle.* New York: A.C. Armstrong.

Roe, D. 1992. *Report No.4. Erromango: Elizabeth Bay, Potnarvin, Ipota and Ifo.* Port Vila: Vanuatu Cultural and Historic Sites Survey.

Roe, D., R. Regenvanu, F. Wadra and N. Araho 1994. Working with landscapes in Melanesia: some problems and approaches in the formulation of cultural policies. In *Culture, Kastom, Tradition: developing cultural policy in Melanesia*, L. Lindstrom and G.M. White (eds), 105–18. Suva: Institute of Pacific Studies, University of the South Pacific.

Shineberg, D. 1967. *They Came for Sandalwood: a study of the sandalwood trade in the south-west Pacific 1830–1865.* Melbourne: Melbourne University Press.

Shutler, M.E. and R. Shutler 1968. A preliminary report of archaeological exploration in the southern New Hebrides. *Asian Perspectives* 9, 157–66.

Spriggs, M. 1988. Cultural resources of the proposed Erromango Kauri reserve and adjacent areas. In *The Erromango Kauri Reserve*, B. Leaver and M. Spriggs. Rome: FAO Working Document 1, Program VCP/VAN/6755.

Spriggs, M. and W. Mumford 1992. Southern Vanuatu rock art. In *State of the Art: regional rock art studies in Australia and Melanesia*, J. McDonald and I.P. Haskovec (eds), 128–43. Melbourne: Australian Rock Art Research Association.

Spriggs, M. and D. Roe 1989. *Planning for Preservation: a general evaluation of the cultural resources of Erromango, Tafea District, Republic of Vanuatu.* Hall, ACT: National Heritage Studies.

Spriggs, M. and S. Wickler 1989. Archaeological research on Erromango: recent data on southern Melanesian prehistory. *Bulletin of the Indo-Pacific Prehistory Association* 9, 68–91.

Waleanisia, J. 1989. Time. In *Ples Blong Iumi: Solomon Islands, the past four thousand years*, H. Laracy (ed.), 47–60. Suva: Institute of Pacific Studies, University of the South Pacific.

Woodburn, M.K. 1944. *Backwash of Empire.* Melbourne: Georgian House.

Zoloveke, G. 1979. Traditional ownership and land policy. In *Land in Solomon Islands*, P. Larmour (ed.), 1–9. Suva: University of the South Pacific and the Solomon Islands Ministry of Agriculture and Lands.

27 Prehistoric human occupation in the Bass Strait region, southeast Australia: an Aboriginal and an archaeological perspective

ROBIN SIM AND DARRELL WEST

Introduction

This chapter presents recent findings from archaeological research in the Bass Strait region, interpreted from both an archaeological and an indigenous perspective. The research investigates questions concerning the use of water craft and the exploitation of island food resources by Tasmanian Aboriginal people in prehistoric times. Sim originally undertook the project for her Ph.D. research. West, a Tasmanian Aborigine working as the Aboriginal Consultant on Sim's fieldwork, chose to become involved with the research as it was clear that useful information for the Tasmanian Aboriginal community could be obtained from remains excavated by Sim.

While it was not a joint project, collaboration has taken place between the authors regarding the interpretation of results of their separate analyses of remains from the Beeton Rockshelter midden site. West's investigations provide detailed information about prehistoric Aboriginal muttonbird exploitation at the site. This evidence strongly supports the Tasmanian Aboriginal land rights claims for several Bass Strait islands, particularly islands that Tasmanian Aboriginal people currently lease from the Government for commercial muttonbirding purposes.

The question of prehistoric muttonbird exploitation was somewhat peripheral to the main focus of Sim's research, as her work was principally concerned with broader-scale questions concerning Aboriginal land-use patterns in the Bass Strait region. Although targeting of island resources is obviously integral to this research, Sim's excavations on remote Bass Strait islands were undertaken primarily to investigate the question of relict holocene Aboriginal populations on the Bass Strait islands and the use of water craft in the region in prehistoric times. Some of the cultural remains recovered from her excavations were outside the main focus of her research, and yet were of interest to the Aboriginal community. These included the muttonbird bones that might not have been investigated in such depth had West not sought to be involved in the analysis of remains from the Beeton Rockshelter site.

Involvement of Aboriginal people in archaeological research in Australia is limited generally to fieldwork activities and consultation processes; the latter are ultimately intended to give archaeologists access to Aboriginal sites and information. Circumstances usually deny Aboriginal communities the opportunity to be involved with research design or the analytical activities that occur in the post-fieldwork stage. Although there are now a small number of Aboriginal archaeology graduates, few are actively involved in research or fieldwork. Thus avenues that could provide useful and interesting information for Aboriginal communities are being overlooked and not investigated by archaeologists. This situation can be changed only by direct Aboriginal involvement in the overall archaeological process.

We are not advocating Aboriginal control of non-Aboriginal research agendas, or vice versa. The issue we address here is that of maximising useful information being obtained by archaeological activities, not the ethics of what archaeologists may be doing. In Australia, all archaeological research involving Aboriginal material is carried out only with the approval of the relevant Aboriginal people, and this situation is well accepted if not welcomed by archaeologists.

What we do advocate is that Aboriginal people are made fully aware of aspects of archaeological research apart from the fieldwork component. This will provide Aboriginal individuals and communities with the opportunity further to investigate material or information that may be of little relevance to archaeologists' research aims, but significant to Aboriginal people. The increasing number of Aboriginal graduates from archaeology courses at Australian universities should facilitate this awareness process and, we hope, ensure that some future archaeological research is primarily directed toward issues of significance to Aboriginal people.

The excavations at Beeton Rockshelter exemplify how archaeological research can provide information that is of interest to Aboriginal people. This information was, however, obtained not through an archaeologist's research, but because an Aboriginal person recognised that the site contained remains that could potentially be highly significant to the Tasmanian Aboriginal community. Moreover, West ensured that these remains would be investigated in accordance with Aboriginal objectives by obtaining funds, and access to facilities and support personnel, to enable him rather than an archaeologist to undertake the muttonbird analysis (West 1994).

Both Sim's and West's investigations and interpretations of remains from the Beeton Rockshelter are presented below. The results of this research are also examined in terms of the regional (archaeological and Aboriginal) significance of the site, with particular reference to the issues of water craft use, the nature of island occupation and resource exploitation. Sim presents the archaeological background to the Beeton Rockshelter investigations, and the role this site has played in the regional interpretation of human occupation in the Bass Strait region. West discusses the evidence for prehistoric exploitation of *yolla* or muttonbird, a potential island food resource for Aboriginal people.

An archaeological perspective (Robin Sim)

Background

When the first European explorers arrived in the Bass Strait region at the end of the eighteenth century, the more remote Bass Strait islands such as the Furneaux group and King Island were truly *terra nullius*. Moreover, no evidence such as shell middens was observed that would have suggested that these islands had been occupied or visited by Aboriginal people in past times (Flinders 1801, 1814; Baudin 1803; Peron 1802 in Micco 1971: 11; Cumpston 1973: 44–5).

The absence of human populations on the larger islands was somewhat puzzling to explorers, especially as both King and Flinders islands appeared capable of sustaining a human population: there were abundant terrestrial and marine food resources, both of these islands are each more than 1,000 sq. km in area and both have permanent fresh-water sources (Flinders 1814). The Furneaux Islands could be sighted from mainland Northeast Tasmania, where explorers encountered a population of what is estimated to be between 3,000 and 5,000 people, or possibly more (Jones 1971; Ryan 1981). It was widely believed that the remote islands of Bass Strait had never been occupied by Aboriginal people; the Tasmanian Aboriginals' ancestors were assumed to be sea-faring people from the Pacific or Indian Ocean regions who had colonised Tasmania in Late Holocene times.

Evidence of prehistoric Aboriginal occupation was subsequently discovered on several islands in the Furneaux group and also on King Island in Bass Strait (Mackay 1946; Jones 1979; Orchiston 1979a; Sim 1988, 1991; West 1990; Sim and Stuart 1991; Sim and Gait 1992). Much archaeological evidence on the islands comprised isolated or low-density scatters of stone artefacts. These finds were not surprising considering that, until about 8,500 years ago, when the post-glacial sea-level rise severed Tasmania from mainland Australia and created Bass Strait, the Bassian region would have been a vast expanse of land connecting Tasmania to mainland Australia (Chappell and Shackleton 1986; Cosgrove 1991; Chappell 1993). Moreover, there is securely dated evidence of pleistocene occupation in Tasmania, indicating that people could have been traversing overland or inhabiting the Bassian region between mainland Australia and Tasmania for more than 20,000 years (Cosgrove 1991).

The shell midden sites discovered on Flinders Island in the 1970s, and King Island in the late 1980s, are more puzzling, given the absence of Aboriginal occupation on the remote Bassian islands when Europeans arrived (Orchiston and Glenie 1978; Sim 1991). Aboriginal water craft in use in Tasmania and Victoria at the time of contact were seemingly incapable of journeying between the more remote Bass Strait islands and the Tasmanian (or Australian) mainlands.

The discovery of shell middens on Flinders Island suggested that the Furneaux islands were occupied in prehistoric times, raising the question as to why these islands were devoid of human populations when Europeans arrived. The coastal location of the middens certainly suggested that people were there at least as recently as 6,500 years ago. Were these deposited by people stranded on the islands as the post-glacial rising seas inundated the Bassian region? And if so, then what had subsequently happened to these people?

The extinct island population theory

During the 1970s, Orchiston excavated several midden sites on Flinders Island, and from the evidence at these sites concluded that Flinders Island had been inhabited by a group of Aboriginal people stranded there for several thousand years (Orchiston and Glenie 1978; Orchiston 1984). Orchiston (1979b: 135) implied that the extinction may have occurred as a result of isolation, that the Flinders Island extinction represented a microcosm of the process of cultural decline that Jones (1977, 1978) suggested was happening to the Tasmanian Aboriginal people as a result of their isolation from mainland Australia.

One of us (R.S.) believed that this interpretation was somewhat insecure, since there was at that time no securely dated evidence of human occupation in the island phase from any of the remote Bass Strait islands, and Jones's 'decline theory' was not widely accepted by archaeologists (Jones 1977, 1978; Vanderwal 1978; Allen 1979; Horton 1979; Bowdler 1980; Anderson 1981; Walters 1981). Before the Flinders Island situation became entrenched as the archetype model for the extinction of isolated human populations, it was necessary to demonstrate that people had actually inhabited these remote islands in the prehistoric island phase. And, if there was secure evidence of human occupation in the remote island period, then the nature of this occupation would require investigation to determine if people were actually living in isolation on the island, or if ephemeral or seasonal visits were being undertaken from mainland Tasmania by people using water craft. These were the principal questions addressed in this part of the research on the Bass Strait islands.

In addition to undertaking site surveys and a number of major excavations on several of the larger Bass Strait islands, more than thirty outer islands in the Furneaux group were also surveyed for middens and other prehistoric Aboriginal sites (Sim 1989, 1991, 1994). The results of these investigations indicated that, although there was evidence of pleistocene occupation in both eastern and western regions of Bass Strait, the only secure evidence of long-term occupation after isolation from mainland Tasmania was found on Flinders Island, in the Furneaux group of islands in eastern Bass Strait (Sim 1988, 1991, 1994; Sim and Thorne 1990).

Prehistoric occupation in the Furneaux islands region

On the eastern side of Bass Strait, people appeared to have continued to occupy or visit the Flinders Island area in the Furneaux group for several thousands of years after it was severed from mainland Tasmania. Five Flinders

Island midden sites were dated and all were of mid-holocene antiquity; the calibrated C14 shell dates (at 95.4 per cent probability) all fell within the period from about 5,300 to 7,200 years ago (see Table 27.1). The shell-dating clearly demonstrates that people were on Flinders Island several thousand years after the sea had reached a level similar to that of today (Orchiston and Glenie 1978; Sim 1989, 1991).

The Flinders Island shell midden sites did not contain evidence suggesting that people were swimming and diving to exploit the subtidal zone. All shell-fish species observed on the numerous Flinders Island midden sites were inter-tidal species (Sim 1994). This is consistent with the broader Tasmanian pattern where people do not appear to have been exploiting subtidal resources such as abalone and crayfish until the Late Holocene (Bowdler 1988; Sim 1989, 1994; Dunnett 1993).

Both the sequence of dates obtained from the Flinders Island midden sites and the number of midden sites around the island indicated long-term occupation of the island in the mid-Holocene. The dating results alone did not resolve the question as to whether the Flinders Island middens were deposited by a stranded island population, or if they were food refuse left by people visiting from mainland Tasmania. It is possible to reach Flinders Island by a series of island hops; each island can be easily sighted ahead and the greatest distance between any of the islands is less than 15 km.

In southwest Tasmania in recent prehistoric times, people were using water craft and deliberately voyaging to Maatsuyker Island, a return trip of more than 20 km (Roth 1899; Jones 1976; Vanderwal and Horton 1984). Thus, it is not implausible that the Flinders Island middens may have been deposited by people visiting the island some time before about 4,000 years ago, rather than by a permanent island population. Another less credible explanation is

Table 27.1 Radiocarbon shell dates from Flinders Island midden sites

SITE	C14 shell date	
	calibrated and corrected age BP	uncalibrated but corrected for marine reservoir effect
Palana	5,340, 5,460, 5,560	4,730 ± 78 BP ANU–7,400
Old Mans Head Sth	5,760, 5,820, 5,880	5,070 ± 87 BP ANU–7,405
Caves Beach	6,310, 6,380	5,560 ± 97 BP ANU–7,404
West End	6,740	5,920 ± 87 BP ANU–7,402
Boat Harbour Sth	7,170	6,250 ± 97 BP ANU–7,406

Calibration and correction following Gillespie and Polach 1979; Stuiver and Pearson 1993; Stuiver and Reimer 1993a.[1]

that people were initially stranded on the island, but after several thousand years of isolation independently developed water craft and migrated to Tasmania.

The advent of water craft was obviously a key factor in determining the nature of the mid-holocene Flinders Island occupation. Since it was highly unlikely that water craft of mid-holocene antiquity would themselves be recovered in the archaeological record, a strategy was devised to test for the use of water craft in the region. Using the hypothesis that people on Flinders Island in prehistoric times did possess water craft, and were therefore not stranded on Flinders Island, other islands in the Furneaux region were surveyed for midden sites or other holocene evidence of offshore island visits. It was also assumed that if people were using water craft to make ephemeral visits to Flinders Island, then one could similarly expect to find evidence on stop-over islands *en route* between Flinders Island and mainland Tasmania, and also on those that hosted seasonal resources such as mutton-bird or seal rookeries. All outer Furneaux islands and other islands *en route* between Flinders Island and Tasmania were surveyed for midden sites to test this hypothesis.

Only one midden site was located during systematic surveys of Swan Island and more than thirty outer islands in the Furneaux group (West 1990; Sim and Stuart 1991; Sim 1992, 1994; Sim and Gait 1992). The shell midden was located in Beeton Rockshelter on Badger Island some 10 km southwest of Flinders Island. The presence of the midden on this small offshore island suggested prehistoric visitation. Water craft with the capacity to undertake a 10 km crossing between Flinders Island and Badger Island would also almost certainly have been able to make the distance to mainland Tasmania. The discovery of a prehistoric midden site on Badger Island was therefore at first regarded as strong evidence in support of use of water craft in the Furneaux region, suggesting that the mid-holocene midden sites on Flinders Island may also have been deposited by island visitors rather than a stranded extinct population.

This was not verified by subsequent excavations at the Beeton Rockshelter site, as the most recent cultural material in the deposit was a shell midden layer dated to about 9,400 BP. The evidence indicated that Aboriginal occupation at the Beeton Rockshelter site ceased some 4,000 years earlier than on Flinders Island. Radiocarbon dates from hearth charcoal in levels underlying the midden deposit indicate that people were visiting the rockshelter as early as 20,000 or so years ago (see Table 27.2).

The Beeton Shelter shell midden layer appears to have been deposited between about 9,400 and 9,800 years ago, at a time of lower sea level when Badger Island would have been part of a greater Furneaux Island or possibly part of a northeast Tasmanian peninsula. All the Beeton Shelter shell dates fell within a span of about 400 years, suggesting a relatively short span of shellfish consumption at this site. This span reflects the period from when the migrating shoreline became close enough for marine foods to be

Table 27.2 Radiocarbon dates from shell and hearth charcoal excavated from the Beeton Rockshelter

midden shell C14 dates	
calibrated and corrected Age BP	uncalibrated but corrected for marine reservoir effect
9,650	8,700 ± 125 BP ANU-8,130
9,700, 9,850	8,794 ± 152 BP ANU-8,746
9,580, 9,620, 9,640	8,676 ± 93 BP ANU-8,748
9,670, 9,760, 9,830	8,754 ± 97 BP ANU-8,749
9,860	8,811 ± 214 BP ANU-8,747
9,440	8,441 ± 136 BP ANU-8,750

charcoal C14 dates from cultural deposit underlying midden deposit
16,250 ± 2,620 BP ANU-8,753
18,180 ±   940 BP ANU-8,751
19,300 ±   730 BP ANU-8,752

Calibration and correction following Gillespie and Polach 1979; Stuiver and Pearson 1993; Stuiver and Reimer 1993a.[1]

conveniently transported to the shelter, until the period when the sea-level rise began to threaten to sever the Beeton Rockshelter location from the greater Furneaux region.

The separation of Badger Island from the greater Furneaux landmass would have made the shelter inaccessible without water craft. The evidence unequivocally indicates abandonment of Beeton Rockshelter at this stage, suggesting that the people who were on Flinders Island for the following several thousand years did not possess water-craft technology. This interpretation is further supported by the total absence of shell middens or other evidence from the post-6,500 BP island phase on any of the outer Furneaux islands apart from Flinders Island itself (Brown 1993; Sim 1994).

The continuation of Aboriginal occupation on Flinders Island for several thousand years after the sea reached its present level, about 6,500 years ago, suggests that people retracted to the Flinders area, either because it was already established core territory, or simply because as sea levels rose it was perceivably the largest landmass available in the immediate region. This contrasts with the western region of the Bassian land bridge (the area that now constitutes King Island), as people appear to have abandoned this region with rising seas, retracting to higher land in northwest Tasmania.

The relatively early date for the midden in the Beeton Shelter deposit concurs with the general regional prehistory. The excavation and survey results together provide a consistent past land-use pattern, indicating that water craft were not in use in the mid-Holocene in the Furneaux region. These results are also consistent with the absence of evidence of water-craft use elsewhere in Tasmania prior to about 3,500 years ago (Vanderwal 1978). Thus the Beeton Rockshelter evidence strongly supports the Flinders Island middens as evidence of an isolated Aboriginal population on Flinders Island in the mid-Holocene.

Interestingly, this stranded population on Flinders Island proved to be viable for 4,000 years or more after the post-glacial sea-level rise first severed the Furneaux region from mainland Tasmania about 9,500 or more years ago. Sim is currently investigating explanations for the demise of the Flinders Island group. Preliminary results suggest that the mid-holocene extinction of the Flinders Island Aboriginal population is indirectly related to other marked changes in the mid- to late-holocene archaeological record on mainland Tasmania. The changes evident in mainland Tasmania indicate a late-holocene expansion of coastal sites into the higher-energy coastal regions of western Tasmania (Stockton 1981), and also reflect swimming and diving activity in the marine resources being exploited from this time on (Bowdler 1988). I believe that it is highly probable that these changes were a direct response to a broad climatic shift in southeast Australia some time around 4,000 years ago (Sim 1994).

Lower precipitation, or other factors heralding the beginning of the climatic shift that appears to be associated with mainland territory and resource expansions, may have been lethal to people living in the confines of the Flinders Island environment. General stress on resources, possibly caused by a relatively minor climatic change, may well have had fatal consequences for the small human population. Water in particular may have been scarce for periods and, while localised shortages could be overcome in mainland Tasmanian contexts by migration to areas with more dependable water sources, in the confines of the Flinders Island environment it well may have been fatal.

In summary, the archaeological findings indicate that there was a relict Aboriginal population isolated in the Furneaux region in the mid-Holocene by the post-glacial rise in sea levels. It appears that the population remained there in total isolation from other people for some 4,000 or 5,000 years, until they died out about 4,000 years ago. At this stage, it is considered that the ultimate demise of this population is probably attributable not to a single cause, but to a suite of changes associated with the onset of a mid- to late-holocene climatic shift.

An Aboriginal perspective (Darrell West)

The discovery of prehistoric sites on Bass Strait islands by archaeologists was very important for the Tasmanian Aboriginal people. It showed non-Aboriginal people, particularly those on Flinders Island, that Aboriginal people were in the Bass Strait region in the past. We Aboriginal people have always known this, but it generally takes scientific evidence to prove to non-Aboriginal people what we often already know. Archaeology is useful in this way, as non-Aboriginal people give credence to information they consider scientific, particularly when it is published.

Archaeology is not so useful when archaeologists do not publish information, especially when they disturb sites and remove cultural remains to get the information. It disturbs me (D.W.) when I see boxes and boxes of our cultural property sitting in laboratories in universities, and in museums, knowing that the contents of many of these boxes have probably not been studied for fifteen or twenty years or more, and most probably will never be looked at again. It also disturbs me because in the past anthropologists and archaeologists used evidence such as that in the boxes I see to suggest ideas about the Tasmanian Aboriginal people that were very offensive.

As a result, I find my relationship with archaeology and archaeologists disturbing. I understand and appreciate what archaeology involves, and respect and enjoy the friendship of nearly all the archaeologists with whom I have worked – 'some of my best friends are archaeologists'. Generally, however, there is little information in most of their research that is of direct use or interest to Aboriginal communities. Whilst we understand that archaeology is done primarily to serve academic research or cultural resource management purposes, this need not exclude Aboriginal people from using archaeology (or archaeologists) to obtain information in which we may be interested.

After working as the Tasmanian Aboriginal consultant on the Beeton Shelter excavations and Sim's other research on the Bass Strait islands, I realised that this work would be of interest to the Tasmanian Aboriginal people. Many of our people had spent some of their lives on the islands, and nearly all were directly related to people who had lived on the Furneaux islands at some stage. We have grown up with stories from the birding sheds and many of us have spent time on the muttonbird islands, working in the sheds or in the rookeries.

For many of us, muttonbirds and birding pervaded many aspects of our lives, even outside the birding season. Not only did we eat muttonbirds; we slept on muttonbird feather mattresses, whatever was wrong with us was cured with muttonbird tonic and liniment, we used muttonbird fat and oil as everyday grease, lamp oil and cooking oil. It was always there on the shelf in a glass bottle, and a barrel of salted birds stood out at the back. Birding was predominantly the domain of the Tasmanian Aboriginal community, although a few white people had birding sheds too. The school year on Flinders Island was scheduled around the muttonbirding season so that the children could go with their families to the offshore birding islands. Many families depended on their income from the birding season to carry them through leaner times during the rest of the year. Children helped around the sheds and learned how to catch and process birds. The birding islands are special places for all the families who went, and for those who still go, birding.

Muttonbirding continues, under government lease agreements, on several outer Furneaux islands. These islands have been included in land rights claims because they are of particular significance to the Aboriginal people of Tasmania, most of whom have some connection with the islands' mutton-birding industry.[2] It had been suggested that our land claims on the birding islands were motivated by the financial rewards to be gained from the birding industry, and that this was inappropriate as birding was not a 'traditional' Aboriginal practice.

We know that muttonbirds and their eggs would have been used for food by Aboriginal people long before the British arrived and supposedly showed us how to do it. However, there is very little archaeological evidence of muttonbird-catching and consumption. Before the excavation at the Beeton Shelter site, the only archaeological evidence of intensive Aboriginal mutton-birding was the remains of about forty-five birds excavated from Prion Beach Rockshelter on the south coast of Tasmania (Dunnett 1992). The discovery of quite dense muttonbird bones amongst the shellfish refuse in the midden in Beeton Shelter was therefore quite an important find for Aboriginal people.

There were many arguments about the origin of the muttonbird bones in the midden during the excavation. Sim, the archaeologist, said it was not clear if they were human food debris and suggested that muttonbirds may have been using the shelter as a rookery in past times, and mixed the shell midden deposit with bones from natural deaths in the rookeries. The midden deposit had no detectable layering or stratigraphic changes within it, so Sim thought that it was quite likely that it had been reworked by nesting birds after the shell had been originally deposited, and that some of the bird bones were food refuse from human occupation, and others from use of the site as a rookery.

Jerry Van Tets, an ornithologist and expert on muttonbirds, was also participating as a member of the excavation team. He was unsure whether the muttonbird bones were from natural deaths of birds in an extinct rookery or past human activity. As the excavation progressed, revealing numerous muttonbird bones in the midden, it was not possible to get a decisive opinion from him one way or the other as to whether there had been a rookery in the past. Basically, no one could tell during the excavation if the mutton-bird bones were part of the midden material. I strongly believed that most if not all of the muttonbird bones were part of the midden remains. Because the muttonbird question was of personal interest to me, and would be useful information for the community because of the claims on the birding islands, I sought funds to do some further research on the muttonbird remains. I received a research grant from the Australian Institute of Aboriginal and Torres Strait Islander Studies and have been undertaking the project in the Prehistory Department in the Research School of Pacific and Asian Studies at the Australian National University in Canberra.

Outlined below are the various aspects of the remains that I examined, and the methods employed. More than 5,000 muttonbird bones were recovered and these were examined and classified, wherever possible, to species and element level. Dr Van Tets identified remains from six different muttonbird species in the site, although initially I was familiar with only one – the Short-tailed Shearwater (*Puffinus tenuirostris*) now found on the Bass Strait islands. The Tasmanian Aboriginal name for this bird is *yolla*, although it is more commonly known as the muttonbird. Dr Van Tets organised a reference collection of material and instructed me in the bird species and element identifications, checking those of which I was unsure. At first I could recognise only the parts of the bird that I usually eat – although I rapidly learnt to identify less familiar elements such as the wing and foot bones.

The site

As previously discussed by Sim, the shell dates from the midden at this site show that people were using the shelter until about 9,500 years ago. The crescent-shaped shelter is located in a low-lying limestone outcrop about 200 m from the shore. It is about 20 m long and 3–5 m deep, with a sloping roof that has about 2.5 m of headroom at the front. In all there is at least 60 m of habitable space in the shelter.

Research aims

The overall aim of my research was to determine whether there was evidence of human exploitation of muttonbird at the Beeton Rockshelter site. At first it seemed that the question of muttonbird exploitation could easily be solved by dating the bird bones themselves to check if these dates correlated with the shell dated also from the midden deposit. This was not the case, as there were some major problems with the dating.

If we used conventional dating methods, it would have been necessary to combine a number of the muttonbird bones to obtain the sample size required for C14 dating. If the bones had been excavated from a stratified deposit, then this would not have presented so much of a problem, as one could assume that there was some chronological association between remains within each layer. The problem was that the midden levels of the deposit in the Beeton Rockshelter site had no such stratigraphy, and had to be subdivided artificially in (measured) layers for excavation and analysis purposes.

Even though it was nearly 0.5 m deep, the entire midden itself really represented one stratigraphic unit. The problem was that it may have been created by muttonbirds reworking existing midden material in the shelter when they nested. If this were the case, and at some stage the site had been a rookery, then it was possible that the muttonbird bones in the midden deposit were a mix of both human food refuse and bird bones from natural rookery deaths.

If midden food refuse bones were combined with considerably younger rookery bones, dating a combined muttonbird bone sample from a mixed-deposit context could potentially provide an aberrant, averaged date. It would be possible to obtain dates useful in determining the origin of the muttonbird bones only if I could get a date from bones from one individual bird, or else from single bones rather than combined samples. Since it was not possible to distinguish remains belonging to one individual, it was necessary to use AMS dating to obtain individual element dates. When my project was first conceived, the need for AMS dates was not foreseen and no funds were allocated for this purpose. Relatively late in the project, I was fortuitously afforded the opportunity of obtaining three AMS dates, and a further six bones were subsequently dated in a follow-up project (Anderson et al. 1996).

Because of the problems inherent in radiocarbon dating the muttonbird remains, the main focus of my investigation was on other (non-chronometric) aspects of the muttonbird remains which could determine their origin in the deposit. These analyses included the species range and relative proportions amongst all seabird remains, muttonbird element analysis, horizontal distribution of seabird remains, condition of the muttonbird bones and chemical analysis of midden sediments. Comparative samples for some of the analyses undertaken were provided from two prehistoric sites where secure evidence of human exploitation of muttonbirds has been described and analysed. One of these sites was the Prion Beach Shelter in southern Tasmania (Dunnett 1992), and the other was Tiwai Point in southern New Zealand (Sutton and Marshall 1980).

Muttonbird bone investigation results

The results from the distribution analysis (i.e. element bias, breakage and burning patterns, and the distribution of remains, etc.) strongly suggest that at least some component of the muttonbird bones is derived from an extinct bird rookery in the outermost area of the shelter (Table 27.3). Nonetheless, rookery deaths cannot account for the muttonbird bones found in the inner midden area, nor the presence of other seabird bones in the shelter. The range and distribution of seabird remains indicate that muttonbirds, along with a range of other seabirds, and shellfish, were being consumed in the shelter by people in past times.

Nine AMS dates from individual muttonbird bones were obtained some months after I had completed the other analyses. The ages of the dated bones spanned from about 5,000 to 10,000 years BP. Eight were more recent

Table 27.3 Distribution and relative proportions of muttonbird compared with other seabirds

Excavated square	Muttonbird g/kg of midden deposit	Muttonbird % of all seabird	Other seabird g/kg of midden deposit	Other seabird % of all seabird
D9	.5	98	.008	2
D6	.648	98	.011	2
C6	.366	79	.095	21
All squares combined	.508	94	.034	6

than the midden shell dates by several thousand years, and one was contemporaneous with the midden shell (Anderson et al. 1996). This latter date supported the conclusion from the other analyses that the muttonbird bones were at least in part attributable to people eating birds at the site, although there was also evidence that the site was also an extinct bird rookery.

Conclusion

Two aspects of prehistoric Aboriginal occupation in the Bass Strait region have been presented here:

1   an overview of the prehistory of the region spanning the last 20,000 or more years, and
2   a site-specific investigation addressing a particular behavioural aspect in a period spanning some several hundred years at the most.

It is interesting that the overview, the archaeologist's perspective, is beyond an individual's conceptual time frame, whereas the investigation by the Aboriginal person is concerned with what is chronologically almost a single event. The Aboriginal person in this instance is interested in examining an aspect of midden deposition, with a view to demonstrating the continuity of resource exploitation patterns over many thousands of years. The archaeologist is concerned with variation in land-use patterns, in terms of long-term changes taking place in a period beyond the conceptual framework of the event.

Clearly the Aboriginal and archaeological interests in this situation are divergent but not mutually exclusive. We believe we have demonstrated that, despite different agendas, it is possible for Aboriginal people and archaeologists to undertake research in a symbiotic manner. An equitable situation will, however, arise only when Aboriginal people are in a position independently to undertake research programmes should they wish to do so. In Australia we are rapidly approaching the situation where Aboriginal people could offer archaeologists opportunities to carry out academic research as part of broader projects instigated and undertaken by Aboriginal individuals and communities.

Notes

1   Radiocarbon dates quoted in this chapter that (at three standard deviations) are less than 18,000 BP have been calibrated using the Calib 3.0 programme, bidecadel calibration (Stuiver and Pearson 1993; Stuiver and Reimer 1993a). Where relevant, conventional dates are given in brackets immediately following the calibrated dates. Shell dates discussed are similarly calibrated, and these have also been corrected by −450 +/− 35 years for oceanic reservoir effects (Gillespie and Polach 1979; Head et al. 1983; Stuiver and Pearson 1993). If calibration has produced more than one possible date for the sample, all dates are given. Uncalibrated but corrected dates for shell are also given.

2   The Tasmanian Aboriginal people were successful in their land claims for the
     major muttonbirding islands in Bass Strait. Badger Island was amongst a number
     of islands and other Tasmanian Aboriginal sites to which the Aboriginal Land
     Council of Tasmania was granted freehold title in 1995. These are the first
     successful Aboriginal land claims in Tasmania.

Acknowledgements

Research projects described in this chapter were funded by the National Estate Grants
Program, the Australian Institute of Aboriginal and Torres Strait Islander Studies and
the Australian National University. The approval and assistance of the Tasmanian
Aboriginal Land Council and Tasmanian Parks and Wildlife also facilitated this
research. Rhys Jones, Atholl Anderson, Andree Rosenfeld, Mike Smith, Alan Thorne
and Isabel McBryde have supervised and advised Sim's research in Bass Strait. We
also thank the ANU Quaternary Dating Research Centre and the ANTARES AMS
dating facilities.

References

Allen, H. 1979. Left out in the cold: why the Tasmanians stopped eating fish. *The
     Artefact* 4, 1–10.
Anderson, A.J. 1981. The value of high latitude models in South Pacific archae-
     ology: a critique. *New Zealand Journal of Archaeology* 3, 143–60.
Anderson, A.J., J. Head, R. Sim and D. West 1996. Radiocarbon dates on shearwater
     bones from Beeton Shelter, Badger Island, Bass Strait. *Australian Archaeology* 42, 17–19.
Baudin, N.T. 1803. *The Journal of Post Captain Nicolas Baudin.* Adelaide: Libraries
     Board of South Australia.
Bowdler, S. 1980. Fish and culture: a Tasmanian polemic. *Mankind* 12, 334–40.
Bowdler, S. 1988. Tasmanian Aborigines in the Hunter Islands in the Holocene: island
     resource use and seasonality. In *The Archaeology of Prehistoric Coastlines*, G. Bailey
     and J. Parkington (eds), 42–52. Cambridge: Cambridge University Press.
Brown, S. 1993. Mannalargenna Cave: a pleistocene site in Bass Strait. In *Sahul in
     Review*, M. Smith, M. Spriggs and B. Fankhauser (eds), 258–74. Canberra: Depart-
     ment of Prehistory, Australian National University.
Chappell, J. 1993. Late pleistocene coasts and human migrations in the Austral region.
     In *A Community of Culture: the people and prehistory of the Pacific*, M. Spriggs,
     D.E. Yen, W. Ambrose, R. Jones, A. Thorne and A. Andrews (eds), 43–8.
     Canberra: Department of Prehistory, Australian National University.
Chappell, J. and N.J. Shackleton 1986. Oxygen isotopes and sea level. *Nature* 324,
     137–40.
Cosgrove, R. 1991. The illusion of riches. Unpublished Ph.D. thesis, La Trobe
     University, Bundoora.
Cumpston, J.S. 1973. *First Visitors to Bass Strait.* Canberra: Roebuck.
Dunnett, G. 1992. Prion Beach Rockshelter: seabirds and offshore islands in south-
     west Tasmania. *Australian Archaeology* 34, 22–8.
Dunnett, G. 1993. Diving for dinner: some implications from holocene middens for
     the role of coasts in the late Pleistocene of Tasmania. In *Sahul in Review: pleistocene
     archaeology in Australia, New Guinea and island Melanesia*, M.A. Smith, M. Spriggs and
     B. Fankhauser (eds), 247–57. Canberra: Department of Prehistory, Australian
     National University.

Flinders, M. 1801. *Observations on the coasts of Van Diemen's Land, on Bass's Strait and its islands, and on part of the coasts of New South Wales.* London: Nicol.

Flinders, M. 1814. *A voyage to Terra Australis.* London: Nicol.

Gillespie, R. and H.A. Polach 1979. The suitability of marine shells for radiocarbon dating of Australian prehistory. In *Radiocarbon Dating: Proceedings of the Ninth International Conference, 1976,* R. Berger and H. Suess (eds), 404–21. Berkeley: University of California Press.

Head, J., R. Jones and J. Allen 1983. Calculation of the 'marine reservoir effect' from the dating of shell-charcoal paired samples from an Aboriginal midden on Great Glennie Island, Bass Strait. *Australian Archaeology* 17, 99–112.

Horton, D.R. 1979. Tasmanian adaptation. *Mankind* 12, 28–34.

Jones, R. 1971. Rocky Cape and the problem of the Tasmanians. Unpublished Ph.D. thesis, Department of Anthropology, University of Sydney.

Jones, R. 1976. Tasmania: aquatic machines and off-shore islands. In *Problems in Economic and Social Archaelogy,* G. Sieveking, I.H. Longworth and K.E. Wilson (eds), 235–63. London: Duckworth.

Jones, R. 1977. The Tasmanian paradox. In *Stone Tools as Cultural Markers: change, evolution and complexity,* R.V.S. Wright (ed.), 219–24. Canberra: Australian Institute of Aboriginal Studies.

Jones, R. 1978. Why did the Tasmanians stop eating fish? In *Explorations in Ethnoarchaeology,* R. Gould (ed.), 11–47. Santa Fe: University of New Mexico Press.

Jones, R. 1979. A note on the discovery of stone tools and a stratified prehistoric site on King Island, Bass Strait. *Australian Archaeology* 9, 87–94.

Mackay, D. 1946. The Prehistory of Flinders Island. *Present Opinion* 1, 48–50.

Micco, H.M. 1971. *King Island and the Sealing Trade 1802.* Canberra: Roebuck.

Orchiston, D.W. 1979a. Pleistocene sea level changes, and the initial Aboriginal occupation of the Tasmanian region. *Modern Quaternary Research in Southeast Asia* 5, 91–103.

Orchiston, D.W. 1979b. Prehistoric man in the Bass Strait region. *See Australia* 2, 130–5.

Orchiston, D.W. 1984. Quaternary environmental changes and Aboriginal man in Bass Strait, Australia. *Man and Environment* 8: 49–60.

Orchiston, D.W. and R.C. Glenie 1978. Residual holocene populations in Bassiania: Aboriginal man at Palana, northern Flinders Island. *Australian Archaeology* 8, 127–41.

Roth, H.L. 1899. *The Aborigines of Tasmania.* London: F. King & Sons.

Ryan, L. 1981. *The Aboriginal Tasmanians.* Brisbane: University of Queensland Press.

Sim, R. 1988. King Island visited: an archaeological survey. Unpublished BA Hons thesis, La Trobe University, Bundoora.

Sim, R. 1989. Flinders Island prehistoric land-use survey. Unpublished report to the National Estate Grants Programme on behalf of the Tasmanian Archaeological Society.

Sim, R. 1990. Prehistoric sites on King Island in the Bass Strait: results of an archaeological survey. *Australian Archaeology* 31, 34–43.

Sim, R. 1991. Prehistoric archaeological investigations on King and Flinders Island, Bass Strait, Tasmania. Unpublished MA thesis, Australian National University, Canberra.

Sim, R. 1992. Beeton Shelter excavation: a prehistoric archaeological site investigation on Badger Island, the Furneaux group, Bass Strait, Tasmania. Unpublished Tasmanian Environment Centre Report for the National Estate Grants Programme.

Sim, R. 1994. Prehistoric human occupation in the King and Furneaux Island Regions, Bass Strait. In *Archaeology in the North: Proceedings of the 1993 Australian Archaeological Association Conference,* M. Sullivan, S. Brockwell and A. Webb (eds). Darwin: NARU Publications.

Sim, R. and P. Gait 1992. Southern Furneaux Islands Archaeological Survey: stage two of the prehistoric and historic archaeological site recording project in the Furneaux group, Bass Strait, Tasmania. Unpublished Tasmanian Environment Centre Report for the National Estate Grants Programme.

Sim, R. and I. Stuart 1991. The Outer Furneaux Islands Archaeological Survey: a prehistoric and historic archaeological site recording project in the Furneaux group, Bass Strait, Tasmania. Unpublished Tasmanian Environment Centre Report for the National Estate Grants Programme.

Sim, R. and A.G. Thorne 1990. Pleistocene human remains from King Island, Bass Strait. *Australian Archaeology* 31, 44–51.

Stockton, J. 1981. Radiocarbon dates for archaeological sites in Tasmania. *Australian Archaeology* 12, 97–101.

Stuiver, M. and G.W. Pearson 1993. High-precision biplacadel calibration of the radiocarbon timescale AD 1950–500 BC and 2500–6000 BC. *Radiocarbon* 35, 1–23.

Stuiver, M. and P.J. Reimer 1993a. Extended C14 database and revised calib. 3.0 C14 H calibration programme. *Radiocarbon* 35, 215–230.

Stuiver, M. and P.J. Reimer 1993b. *University of Washington Quaternary Isotope Laboratory Radiocarbon Calibration Program Rev 3.0.3.*

Sutton, D.G. and Y.M. Marshall 1980. Coastal hunting in the Subantarctic Zone. *New Zealand Journal of Archaeology* 2: 25–49.

Vanderwal, R.L. 1978. Adaptive technology in South West Tasmania. *Australian Archaeology* 8, 107–27.

Vanderwal, R.L. and D. Horton 1984. *Coastal Southwest Tasmania: the prehistory of Louisa Bay and Maatsuyker Island.* Canberra: Terra Australis.

Walters, I. 1981. Why did the Tasmanians stop eating fish: a theoretical consideration. *The Artefact* 6, 71–7.

West, D. 1990. 1989 survey for archaeological sites undertaken on Cape Barren Island. Unpublished report for Tasmanian Dept. of Parks, Wildlife and Heritage.

West, D. 1994 Prehistoric Tasmanian Aboriginal exploitation of muttonbird. A report for the Australian Institute of Aboriginal and Torres Strait Islander Studies, Canberra.

28   Cognitive maps and narrative trails: fieldwork with the Tamu-mai (Gurung) of Nepal

CHRISTOPHER EVANS

In Figure 28.1 a prominent Tamu-mai shaman, Yarjung Kromochain Tamu, video-tapes a 'Tibetan' woman's dance group while in Mustang in northern Nepal. One of the Project's co-directors, he is investigating the migration trails of his ancestors; largely forgotten, the dance lessons have been insti- gated by younger members of the community wishing to learn from aged seniors. Speaking of cultural pluralism and revitalisation, journeys, documen- tation and 'indigenous' study, this inspiring image acts as a suitable introduction to the diverse themes of this chapter.

It was as Director of the University of Cambridge's Archaeological Unit that the author was first contacted in 1993 with the aim of investigating ancestral Tamu-mai/Gurung villages in the Annapurna Himal of west-central Nepal and, in particular, the site of Kohla.[1] Acting on behalf of the Tamu Pye Lhu Sangh (hereafter TPLS), a major cultural organisation in Pokhara, this was initiated by Yarjung and Judith Pettigrew, the latter a social anthro- pologist working in the region. After much discussion and long-distance negotiation, the Kohla Project emerged with a shaman, social anthropologist and archaeologist as its respective co-directors. A train of connections arising from a legacy of Cambridge anthropology in the region, the work is effec- tively a cultural commission, initially by the TPLS and later endorsed by other Tamu-mai organisations in the Pokhara region. Its ultimate catalyst was democratisation in 1990 which gave voice to Nepal's many minorities. Permit- ting greater expression of subnational identities, this has led to the establish- ment of diverse cultural organisations and ethnic congresses; a number of these groups now also have access to magazines in which their history is amongst the themes explored by local 'lay' specialists (e.g. Tamu and Tamu 1993; see Des Chene 1996).

The Tamu-mai practise terrace rice-agriculture in 'highland' villages. Gener- ally sited between 1,000 and 2,500 m above sea level, these villages formally lie in the upper range of the 'midland' zone of Nepal (Blair 1983: 13). The Tamu-mai are a Tibetan-Burman-speaking people, the predominant group living in the Annapurna region (there are also communities in the east of

Figure 28.1   Shaman, Yarjung Kromochain Tamu, in Mustang, September 1995.

the country). There has been debate concerning their historical roots. Whilst some argue for a southern origin, certainly they themselves and most scholars would see them arriving from the north, from Tibet, China or Mongolia. Their 'indigenous' religion is shamanistic with two 'schools' of practice, and within villages today there are still as many as two to three shaman priests, with some including urban Pokhara within their parish. The role played by them is central to the maintenance of cultural identity and historical aware-ness (concerning Tamu-mai shamanism, see Messerschmidt 1976c; Mumford 1990; Pettigrew 1995; and also Allen 1974 concerning ritual journeys). During rituals they recite long oral 'texts' which narrate the itinerary of successive villages during migration southwards. Yarjung has drawn his own map of the narrative route; the settlement genealogy is inherently linear and the long scroll charts a narrow trail-corridor. Comparison concerning the standardis-ation of the oral accounts has found them to be remarkably consistent – each shaman recites the same basic migration history (Strickland 1982).

   Although, by appearance, village life remains traditional, theirs is not a 'pristine' ethnography. The Tamu-mai are amongst the main Himalayan groups from whom the Gurkhas have been raised, and widespread military service has had major ramifications in terms of foreign travel, literacy and respect for book-learning, especially amongst retired officers (see Caplan 1995 concerning the 'worldly context' of Gurkhas – 'the warrior gentlemen' – and their place in western imagination). Equally influential has been the impact of a succession of social anthropologists (e.g. Macfarlane 1976; Messerschmidt 1976a; Pignede [1966] 1993; Pettigrew 1995); awareness of being 'objects of study' has clearly prompted their own instigation of research.

Archaeologically, it is a case of working 'blind'. There has been no archaeological fieldwork in this region of Nepal and any aspect of study is a first. Although much emphasis has recently been given to historic building/ monument conservation, apart from a major initiative in the north (the Nepal-German High Mountain Project – e.g. Simons et al. 1994) and some excavation in the southern Terai, there has been little fieldwork in the country as a whole. In this context the local commissioning of the Kohla Project is all the more extraordinary. Whilst evidence would never be overlooked, the fieldwork occurs within a specific research framework – it is not a 'World Prehistory-type' exercise concerned with the earliest occupation within the Himalayas. Although traditional archaeological issues are addressed (e.g. pottery sequence, the study of highland ecology and trade), it is primarily *a community archaeological and ethno-historical project*. The concern is with how the history is created in the present and with archaeology as 'community process'. Its practice involves not just excavation/survey, but also the collection of oral histories and interviewing subsets of the community concerning their views of the past. Cognitive issues are also important, as the work involves different ways of 'seeing' the past and landscape: the shamanic, 'folkloric' and our own more disciplined approaches. The documentation of this interaction is one of the main directives of the work, and is considered as important as the tangible results themselves. This is not a matter of making a 'present' of, or bestowing, the past, and it may not be one Tamu-mai/Annapurna archaeology that is created. Perhaps foremost amongst the project's aims is the provision of material reference so that the Tamu-mai can further build and transform their own history.

'Delegation walking' lies at the core of the venture. To date, there have been two main seasons of field survey (and further reconnaissance in Manang Valley), with excavation set to commence in 1999. Marked by much ceremony and often 'parade-like', the march is something of a community event. Reminiscent of expeditions from an earlier era, all supplies and equipment must be portered-in, involving the hire of ten to twenty men. The team is accompanied by various members of the TPLS and, whilst in the field, visits are made to the sites by various seniors (and shamans) from both villages and Pokhara. There is nothing particularly unique in this, group-trekking being the only way to get around in the mountains. In fact, the starting point for the project occurred when senior members of the TPLS themselves and Pettigrew first visited Kohla in 1992 during a month-long traverse of the migration route going from the site to Manang and back to Pokhara. Such walking of the route itself serves as an act of cultural/historical reclamation. The various journeys – both informal reconnaissance and project expeditions – have now themselves their own chronology, and participation is a source of some prestige (Pettigrew 1995).

The past is never, of course, embarked upon without motivation and agenda. This, nevertheless, does not detract from the genuine emotion so evidently involved in much of the work. Much ritual and fanfare accompanies departure from, and arrivals in, Pokhara, and also the expedition's procession through villages. The presentation of artefacts evokes enthusiasm and weeping (particularly a fingerprint-impressed sherd – the 'imprint of the ancestors').

The beginning and end of these journeys has been the *Kohinbo*, the Tamu-mai cultural centre in Pokhara built in 1993 (Figure 28.2). Vaguely evocative of the Sidney Opera House, it was designed by members of the TPLS according to Tamu-mai cosmology (e.g. the zodiac) and closely resembles the moulded *Chop* rice effigy central to their religion (Figure 28.3); other such centres are now being built throughout the region. A remarkably rapid spread and invention of a *new* material cultural tradition, their knowledge of the past is essentially based on oral and textual evidence, with few direct material correlates. Whilst their commissioning of archaeology relates to a desire for physical 'presencing', its absence to date has certainly not inhibited active cultural reference.

A fieldwork itinerary

During the first season, a round trek was made of some 45 km, from 1,500 up to 3,500 m above sea level (Figure 28.4). Major settlements were surveyed

Figure 28.2 The Pokhara *Kohinbo*.

Figure 28.3 A shaman seated before the *Chop* rice effigy (during a six-hour long ritual for the expedition's departure).

in detail (including full contour-mapping), with more informal techniques employed on minor sites. Literally and conceptually the fieldwork was very much a *journey*. That the same route was traversed there and back proved a key factor in the provision of context; records made on the upward trail had to be extensively revised on the return leg.

Although exquisitely beautiful, it is a rugged landscape that can be negotiated only by steep trails. Adjacent to villages, these are often stepped and much of the time one climbs, in effect, a stairway into the mountains.[2] There are few points along the main routes level enough to invite large settlement, and, not surprisingly, these are generally where large ruins are sited. Limited off-trail visibility and exhaustion hinder reconnaissance, making this an exercise in 'linear' archaeology. The impact of severe erosion must

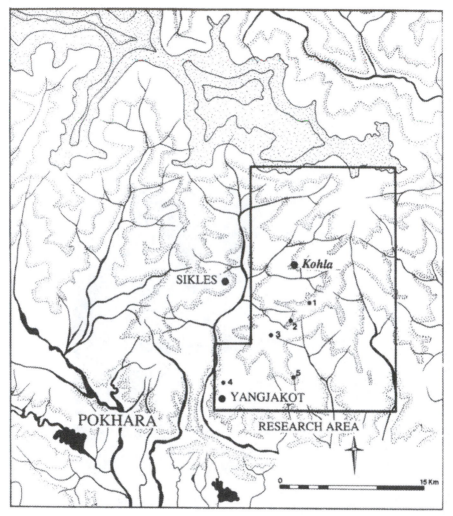

Figure 28.4 A Highland itinerary (Site 1, Chikre; 2, Khoido; 3, Karapu; 4, Kui Choh; 5, Nadr Pa).

also be taken into account when working at such altitudes.[3] Off-slope down-cutting produces reversals in vertical/chronological level. Points that have been sealed, whether by trees, paths, cairns or pastoralist shelters, are often raised by as much as a metre, with run-off water having carved away uncapped soil. These factors bias archaeological survival and survey towards substantial structural remains.

The main archaeological focus is the site of Kohla *Sombre* ('Kohla, the Three Villages') (Figure 28.5). Reported to be the last place in which the Tamu-mai lived collectively together as a people, and the residence of 'kings', it is of near-mythical status and has great emotional importance (for the

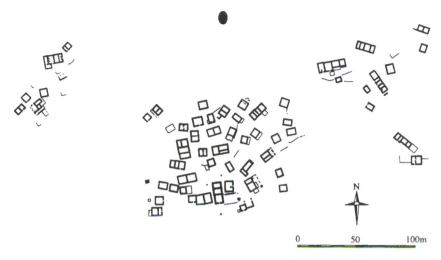

Figure 28.5 Kohla plan.

porters, their first encounter with the ruins gave rise to displays of heart-felt feeling). Subject to intense hail and thunder storms, three weeks were spent surveying this spectacular village complex which lies within a large valley/plateau just below the snow-line at *c.* 3,200 m above sea level.[4] Open on the southern side, it is otherwise surrounded by high forested ridges and is rather like a great amphitheatre. The ruins are imposing and generally stand 1–1.5 m high; 57 buildings, possibly representing some 70–80 houses, were recorded. Divided into three sectors by a stream and escarpment, it does indeed seem the site of 'The Three Villages'. The vast majority of the structures lie within the central portion, many fronting on to 'avenues', and there is obvious evidence of organised public space (e.g. stairs, yards and platform-terracing).

A number of the buildings have complex plans involving multiple cells/building ranges, yet few seem to have interior connection. While doorways were apparent in a number, extensive collapse often made recognition difficult. Individual ruins that have had value ascribed to them (various 'King's Houses') are mainly those that *appear* most impressive: one in the central village stands 2.75 m high (40 courses) and another in the western sector is 2.95 m (48 courses); the latter has triangular windows and a number of shelf recesses in its central room. Yet, although of simple 'two-cell' plan, immediately beside this western 'house' is located the highest standing building that has no such status (4 m; 62 courses). It is, moreover, the only structure in which there is definite evidence of a second storey, the upper floor level being marked by joist holes and a level string-course.

Fragments of slag were recovered, suggesting industrial activity, and a series of horizontal water-mills were located along the western stream. Much pottery was found across the northern quarter of the valley floor. An area with few old structures, many pastoralist shelters are sited there and it is possible that their construction involved the robbing of stonework.

One of the most remarkable aspects of the village site is its apparent ritually focused spatial structure. An enormous dolmen-like setting (a great capstone naturally balanced/slipped onto uprights), lying at the foot of the back-slope and opening onto the village, immediately strikes one upon entering the valley. A commanding *geological* 'presence', it is distinguished by a large shrine set within its interior. Two much smaller dolmen-/cist-like 'shrines' are located at either end of the southern edge of the village centre.[5] Although other such settings may have escaped detection, these three 'megaliths' define a triangle, whose central southern axis is marked by a large standing stone. Whilst standing stones were found on another village site (see below) and others elsewhere may have been toppled, the formality of the evidently religious architecture at Kohla is without immediate parallel.

Kohla is the highest/furthest settlement thus far identified within the main research area. Some hours' march above it are, however, the ascribed 'Cave of Nuns' and 'The Racecourse'. The former proved to be no more than a low drystone wall-enclosed overhang whose antiquity was difficult to appreciate (i.e. it may be no more than a pastoralist shelter). The latter is a narrow valley remarkably free of obstacle for some 600 m and thought to be the site of a horse-race track. While there is little basis by which to evaluate this sporting association, two apparently early structures were distinguished on the ridge-top above. Also of obvious antiquity, isolated trail-side buildings were identified at three locations below the main village site. Although apparently referred to as 'villages', these we tentatively interpreted as 'staging posts', their situation suggesting regulation of trails. Close to one was a dammed pond. An impressive drystone construction, to find a dam in such an alpine situation was, to say the least, unexpected.

Two other major ruins were identified *en route*. At Khoido, a line of three very large buildings lie on a slight ridge along the eastern edge of the valley plain, and a fourth, poorly preserved, can be distinguished at the northern foot of a central knoll. Standing 0.4–0.75 m high (four to nine courses), with the exception of the hillside building, all are very substantial with well-built drystone walls (0.8 m wide). Much pottery was present across the northern half of this hillside. This, and its platform-suggestive terraced contours, could suggest that other buildings may have once dotted its flank. An avenue-like hollow extends west from it, at whose foot the line of axis is marked by a standing stone, and a worked slab was found set atop a great boulder on the crest of the valley. Another significant geological presence, this immense rock was further marked by a recent shrine at its village-side base; a series of cairns and mounds dot the valley floor. It is the formality of this site that is striking – the eastern line of buildings and the central standing stone. Whilst reminiscent of Kohla, the sense of planning seems all the greater due to the limited number of buildings, and suggests a formality of function, perhaps in some manner administrative.

Perched high on a cliff-edge at Chikre, the other major complex, four/five buildings lie along the spine of a ridge overlooking a meadow pasture; another lies isolated, some 70 m to the west beside the main trail. Recording took place during the onset of the monsoon below and was literally undertaken in clouds.[6] The cliff-top situation of the ruins is extraordinary. It is difficult to imagine why any community would choose to live in such circumstances – defence or control must be the key. The southern end of the ridge is enclosed by a substantial drystone wall with two projecting tower-like cairns/footings, suggesting that the site was a fort.

Another possible defensive enclosure was eventually identified at Karapu, located on a peak a day's march above Yangjokot. Work on this dramatic site, situated at the junction of trails, suitably framed the results of the initial field season. As the first large ruin visited on the way up, much time was given to its recording. Apart from a major rectangular stone-walled enclosure, sited to block passage along the narrow ridgeway, many structures were identified that were thought to be subsidiary houses. Only on the downward leg, familiar with the formal attributes of the up-mountain village sites, was it recognised that most of the surrounding structures were, in fact, various types of pastoralist shelters (*phohron*). The large rectangular enclosure is an impressive ruin (11 × 14 m), with substantial, though not particularly well-made, drystone walls. Apart possibly from a 'spanable' (?roofed) internal sub-division, it was evidently open and probably another minor fortification strategically situated so as to control the trails.

After the first season's work it appeared that Karapu marked something of a divide, with the impressive drystone ruins confined to the trails above it. Accordingly, the second season was restricted to the immediate hinterland above the inhabited villages of Yangjokot and Wharchok, with a 'palace' also recorded within the terrace fields of the former.

At Kui Choh, on the crest of a high ridge immediately above Yangjokot (the peak said to be the home of a god – for single women), another cliff-edge complex was recorded. Ringed by terraces, its focus is a bi-vallate walled-enclosure of polygonal plan. Within its interior two to four slightly ovoid house platforms were identified and other possible buildings were observed. Along the western and northern sides, the outer circuit follows the line of a deep, moat-like hollow. Rather than a strictly defensive feature, this would seem to be the reduced junction of two hollow-way trails. Nevertheless, the ruins would, again, primarily seem to be those of a small fort. Although more impressive and of a different plan configuration than that at Karapu, both share comparable strategic locations – on the crests of high ridges at the junction of trails.

On the village site at Nadr Pa directly above the neighbouring village of Wharchok, houses also proved to be slight. Extending for more than 350 m along a ridge-top, the remains are denuded, suffering damage through erosion and evidently disturbed by pastoralists. Yet there is extensive evidence of village terracing and, down the eastern slope, agricultural terracing. Apart from eight *kuni* mortars (see below) and two rotary querns, much pottery was recovered, leaving no doubt that this was a major settlement. Detailed survey revealed two definite 'platformed' houses and many more potential candidates – at least thirteen, perhaps as many as twenty. The site is estimated to be perhaps 200–400 years old (large rhododendron trees grow on the walls), and a local informant from Wharchok suggested a date of 300 years for the site's abandonment.

At the southern end of the ridge lies a 'palace', a very impressive two-cell building (7 × 11.6 m). This has been much reduced and a circular hermit's cell, apparently abandoned only fifteen to twenty years ago, built within the interior. Nevertheless, at its corners the ruin still stands 1.2–1.8 m high and along its southern front 2.1 m high (39 courses).[7] Beneath a great serpentine tree rooted within the wall along the building's southern side is a stepped shrine – the place of a snake god – which is considered very sacred. Although a few short lengths of wall (and a cairn-type shrine) were observed within the immediate vicinity, this building stands isolated from the north-lying village site. Its isolation, size and relatively robust survival justify its consideration as a 'special building', possibly somewhat later in date than the village. In the light of other sites within the region, there seems no reason to dispute its designation, albeit a palace of very modest scale.

Conversely, a 'palace' surveyed within the bounds of Yangjokot itself proved suspect. Whilst quantities of pottery (and daub) present throughout the area probably attests to an earlier settlement, the so-identified ovoid building seems no more than the remains of an old hill-crown terrace field system.

The archaeology of trails

Given the lack of previous archaeological work in the area, it is impossible to say how old the remains are without scientific dating. However, the great size of the trees growing on the walls at Kohla and Khoido suggests considerable age, perhaps 500–800 years, and their actual abandonment could have been much earlier. Whilst the ruins are spectacular, they do not appear to be particularly 'complex', inasmuch as there is no evidence of deep sequences. Not mounded through settlement succession, the sites appear relatively short-lived. Such measures of complexity are, of course, only archaeological readings of the materially obvious and may have little relevance for social status of the sites. Indeed the presence of a considerable amount of pottery (which will provide a basis of inter-site settlement analysis and the study of trade), the evidence of craft specialisation and the suggestion of a planned formality of settlement could all undermine this too easily made estimation.

Whilst the survey phase is far from completed, and other sites are known within the immediate Yangjokot/Wharchok environs, coverage is sufficient to begin to identify patterns and raise key questions. From Karapu and below, the quality of the stonework is generally inferior, which is probably reflective of chronological difference (and access to building materials). The frequency of 'forts' and hill-top 'palaces' within this area also suggests a divide; they probably mark the territory of the Kaski Kings and date to after the twelfth century. In contrast, apart from the wall system at Chikre, no defensive works have been observed in the higher lands and, in particular, within the vicinity of Kohla. Their absence could suggest that the great village lay within a secure zone above any frontier or is considerably earlier than the Karapu/contemporary village-zone sites.

Supporting the attribution of kings at Kohla, the scale and formal spatial organisation of the village sites, the evidence of craft specialisation and industry (pottery, stone-working and slag), and the discovery of forts, a dam and trail-side posts all speak of a 'developed' social organisation and even possibly some manner of (proto-)state. The standard quality of drystone construction and uniform architectural style suggests that the ruins represent the remains of one group, although this is an inference that could be undermined by the cross-settlement zone distribution of pottery types (though this could be the result of up-mountain/lowland trade).

The stonework on sites above Karapu made for ready identification of ancient ruins in contrast to pastoralists' *phrohon* (some rough dressing of stone so that wall faces are flush, coursing regular and corners tight). For our Tamu-mai colleagues, one of the main type-artefacts defining settlement presence were *kuni*, large stones with deep cup depressions produced through the operation of foot-mortars during the husking of millet. Still in use in most present-day villages, two were found at Kohla and others observed at Karapu (well outside the fort) and on the trail above Yangjokot. These latter two locations are mentioned in the texts as ancient Tamu-mai villages. Yet, apart from these mortar stones and large-scale terracing at Karapu, no evidence of settlement was found at these locales. The recovery of *kuni* (unlikely to have been used by pastoralists) but not village ruins could suggest extensive robbing of stone by pastoralists.[8] As sites of seasonal encampment, a number of the ruins (including Kohla) have been severely damaged in this manner. However, not all this disturbance is necessarily recent. Many overgrown, ruinous and themselves evidently old, pastoralist shelters are present in almost all substantial up-mountain meadows and clearances. Compared with how limited such transhumant practices are in most villages today, this could indicate that stock-related migration previously involved a much larger sector of the population and could be seen to support the observations of earlier visitors to the region that the Tamu-mai (Gurung) were primarily transhumant pastoralists (e.g. Buchanan 1819).

Houses today within Tamu-mai villages, with their rectangular plan and very substantial drystone rectangular construction, have obvious similarities with the upland ruins (e.g. Blair 1983: 31–41). This contrasts with the denuded and often subovoid house platforms found on sites in their immediate hinterland. Nevertheless, this does not curtail identification with them, and it is reported that their houses previously were much less robust and built of bamboo/thatch; their present form probably relates to the 'affluence' brought by 175 years of foreign military service. If so, this shows a marked change in vernacular house tradition and makes the Tamu-mai's ready identification with the upland sites all the more intriguing, inasmuch as it presupposes a capacity for material culture change.

Shamanic knowledge essentially pertains to the migration routes and village sites as a whole; it does not detail individual structures. However, this has not impeded broader ascription of value or identification, which seems to be of two basic kinds. For ruins in the immediate hinterland of inhabited villages, it is essentially a matter of oral history – generally where something happened. It is said, for example, that the recognition of the snake god at Nadr Pa derives from when a man, whilst hunting, killed a snake, which subsequently brought disaster upon his family. Given this origin and the situation of the 'palace' (and the evocative serpentine character of the great tree growing out of the walls above the shrine), it is curious that the knowledge of the god is accredited with greater antiquity than the building.

Ascription of another type seems to occur on the higher sites above Karapu. Although there are points on the trail that are marked as having historical significance (e.g. where the Ghale king lost his leg in battle or the Cave of Nuns), these places are little frequented and generally there are few such associations. What there is tends to derive from more recent visits and relate to context – the immediate situation of individual buildings.[9] The above-mentioned King's Houses at Kohla are obvious examples. Confidently identified as such previous to formal recording, both are large and complex structures with common architectural details and share 'L'-shaped plans. In the case of the central village King's House, survey showed that this plan was actually the product of conflation with a neighbouring building. Nevertheless, it is very imposing and fronts on to what seems formal public space, where the standing stone is situated (see above; Figure 28.6). Building 'entitlement' evidently has a capacity to attract further association, allowing a ruin to take on a life of its own; in this instance, the stone has become interpreted as the tethering post for the King's horses.[10]

In scale and complexity, none of the other ruins compares with Kohla. Yet given the possibility of a specialised function for the other sites – Chikre and Khoido, respectively a fort and administrative complex – Kohla may be the only true village investigated, at least in the highlands above Karapu.[11] Although possibly qualified by the evidence of settlements missing through stone robbing/disturbance, in the light of the number of buildings present there it would be difficult to see Kohla's relationship with the other high ruins as chronologically successive (i.e. insufficient houses seem represented on these to suggest the dispersion of the Kohla populace). They and Kohla were, therefore, probably broadly contemporary, an interpretation that could be supported by the evidence of a common architectural style and post-abandonment tree-growth upon their walls (i.e. roughly comparable overgrowth).

Figure 28.6 Kohla – the 'King's House' (central village sector); note the standing stone/'tethering post' (right).

Kohla's tripartite plan bears out its association as 'The Three Villages'. Not only is this reflected in its topographic sub-division, but certain architectural traits occur only in individual 'quarters' (e.g. the narrow barracks-like ranges in the eastern). Sympathetic with the number of clan divisions amongst the Tamu-mai, the sectored and ritual organisation of the settlement is extra-ordinary, and Khoido is the only other site that seems to share in any way its quality of formal/ritual layout. That Kohla is recorded as the last place in which the Tamu-mai lived together as a people could, if taken at face value, imply that other examples of this village pattern should be found at higher stopping points along their migration route. Yet it could also be the case that part of Kohla's status relates to the fact that it was a time/place of socio-cultural coalescence, its spatial structure equally read as a 'coming together'. Only further survey above Kohla will determine whether this 'Three Village' structure is unique or the final expression of a recurrent along-route settlement type.

The shifting centre – cultural geographies

Not undertaken as a lesson for western practice, fieldwork of this kind has broader resonance. It particularly reflects upon the character and complexity of landscape, specifically the currency of the idea of there having been *a* cultural landscape. All have their *history*, and to employ such a concept presupposes cultural homogeneity rooted in (inevitable) long-term continuities. A case in point was recently reported by a traveller to Tibet, who attempted to visit the spectacular 'nomad barrows' megalithic complex at Doring discovered by Roerich in the 1920s and which he compared to Carnac (Bellezza 1995). Accurately surveyed at the time, the site could not be found. Instead, there stand today ten rows of ten prayer chortens; the megaliths have apparently been reduced to small stone cairns, which are themselves now attributed with a long antiquity relating to a guru's fight with an ogress.

Megaliths into chortens represents the past rewritten, reworked and reinvented. The complexity of landscape interaction was striking when visiting Manang in 1995. A major corridor linked with trade routes to the north (an 'axis of history'), this great alpine valley runs behind the length of the Annapurna range north of the main area of study. A landscape dotted by stuppas and exposure platforms, the contemporary villages are largely of Tibetan Buddhist affiliation and organised according to hierarchical/centralist cosmological principles – the sacredness of the village core and its bounds as opposed to their periphery, which correlates with a vertical distinction between the sacred and profane (i.e. gods in mountains/demons below; e.g. Ramble 1995).[12] Readily identifiable in its broad precepts, this is the type of straightforward nature/culture spatial modelling now frequent in structuralist reconstruction within western archaeology (inside/outside and up/down). Yet, like a hand spread across landscape, within Manang/Mustang this 'target-type' cultural patterning is overlain (underpinned) by, and co-exists with, the migration/narrative routes of other Himalayan peoples – the Tamu-mai, Thakalis and Magars – *there is not one cultural landscape but many.*

Yet it would be a mistake to see these issues of landscape organisation as a simple opposition between principles of hierarchical centring and linearity (trail narratives versus village cosmologies). This overlooks shifting topographic reference – the conceptual displacement or multiple identification of key landscape features; within a Himalayan context most obvious are various Mountains of the Dead. For Buddhist communities it is Mount Kailas, of which there are offspring in Kathmandu and elsewhere. Oble, the great basalt massif that dominates the eastern end of Manang valley, fulfils a similar role for the Tamu-mai, and it is from there that the soul flies northwards before ascending to heaven. Apparently the latter is but the last (or latest) manifestation from a more distant original northern source-mountain. It appears to mark a division in their cognitive geography: below, places/history can be roughly fixed; beyond, the landscape (and trail) has a less determined and more mythical quality. Segmenting the migration trail/narrative, this is an expansionist model of cultural landscape – the serial shifting of a significant centre. It should alert us that behind obvious topographic reference (e.g. the megalithic alignment on a peak or the demarcation of a river) may lie distant source-landscapes linked to immediate locale by geographic approximation.

Concerned with 'the ancestral', archaeology increasingly employs vaguely anthropological precepts of time/locality (e.g. the mythical, the circular) and the idea that landscape can be 'read' (e.g. Tilley 1994). But what if land-scape narrative is just that – the historical referencing of distant place? Although this concept is essentially inaccessible without 'insider' knowledge (under-mining direct one-to-one past/landscape association), and perhaps ultimately irrelevant in structuralist agendas, nevertheless to dismiss it as a possibility is to deny historicism and the fact that people(s) move.

Fieldwork with shamans – building histories

In hindsight, it is difficult to evaluate how working with shamans was envis-aged. Although the sites are emotionally evocative for them, apart from Yarjung's reaction to the eastern courtyard at Kohla (and his site-related dreams),[13] in practice there has been little indication of direct extra-sensory archaeological perception. Nevertheless, providing a framework of ancient knowledge and, as the source of past authority, the role of shamans is some-what parallel to that of archaeologists, and it is with them that the past must be negotiated. The most obvious case in point arose at Kohla, where our colleagues were much concerned with the identification of the village ceme-tery ('finding the ancestors'). Interpretation of the 'geological dolmen' and small cairns as having possible religious significance was a source of some consternation. During that time, a visit was made by a delegation of senior TPLS members accompanied by three shamans and an apprentice. Many hours were spent touring the site, when the status of the 'megaliths' was discussed at length. Resolution occurred only when the senior shaman conducted a personal ritual at the great stone, in effect validating that there was a potential for *archaeological* interpretation and 'difference'.

Working with the Tamu-mai proves intellectually challenging. Whilst there is a need to weigh the ramifications of interpretation, at no time have we felt censored or restricted. Generally, the encounter with archaeology has apparently also proven a learning experience for them. This became obvious when, on the downward trek during the first season, it struck us that, although our companions had previously visited the sites, they were not aware of, or at least could not define, the formal attributes of the 'ancient' ruins. On the way up, they had encouraged the recording of *phrohon* at Karapu, evidently thinking them houses, and when previously visiting Khoido they had not found the village complex itself.

Pending excavation, it is obviously impossible to evaluate and foolhardy to second-guess final results. Yet, thus far, where settlements are said to lie/cluster in the migration itinerary, sites do exist. Of course, it is almost invariably likely that the sources would indicate only relative location along trails. Nevertheless, there is no escaping the extraordinary character and layout of Kohla – 'The Three Villages' – and the site does seem to co-relate directly with the accounts. Lacking a documented handicraft tradition, there is little with which directly to compare the archaeology and contemporary

Tamu-mai society, apart from the shamanic sources and oral tradition. Whilst, therefore, within a framework of western science, absolute attribution may not be possible (or necessary), our local colleagues certainly have no doubt that what has been found is their cultural past. Yet there are aspects of the remains that have proven entirely unexpected for all parties (e.g. forts, a dam and 'staging posts'). These are without parallel within contemporary village life, which for obvious reasons is the main source of their interpretative analogy and determines a somewhat domestic framework. This discrepancy need not prejudice the Tamu-mai's identification with/of them – nor do they today have 'kings' such as resided at Kohla (though they do have 'king's clans'). For our Tamu-mai colleagues the past is bound in narrative – stories link the remains that leave little room for historical change. Often without direct material correlates, these associations can seem arbitrary and difficult to evaluate (e.g. 'The Cave of Nuns'). Yet, what do we do when trying to come to terms with the ruins? Inevitably focusing upon points of 'planned' formality and distinguishing distinct ritual features, we attend the attributes of 'higher civilisation' (craft specialisation/industry, defence, communication/trade and social hierarchy). Confronted with a 'new past', we all carry our respective 'homes' with us.

Complex ethical issues, of course, underlie fieldwork in these circumstances and, having elsewhere explored the arbitration of competing cultural pasts (Evans 1995), these are not ignored. Yet in such a multi-ethnic society as Nepal it is difficult to conceive of any culturally pure past – trade, migration and history would have determined diversity. Equally crucial is the question of contemporary empowerment – the degree to which monument identification relates to territorial claim. Although no 'people' apart from the Tamu-mai identify with the Kohla area, no such claim is argued in this case. In the face of any intellectual qualms, in the end one is left with the mess, emotion and contingency of life. Besides this, it is too late for we are already caught up in their history. Whether such practice is deemed 'postmodern' seems irrelevant; this is not the same late-colonial world in which Wheeler, for example, operated in India. Whilst trying to avoid the politics of exclusivity, situated in our/their time and with community, the study is inevitably 'sided' to some degree. Weighed in the balance, it is a great privilege to work (and walk) with such company.

Notes

1   More widely known by the Nepali as the Gurung, many now prefer and use only their own name, Tamu-mai; it will be employed throughout this chapter (for general background, see Macfarlane 1976; Messerschmidt 1976a; Pignede [1966] 1993).
2   Trails within the vicinity of present-day villages are regularly maintained through funds raised by performances of local 'Mothers Dance' groups, which are used to hire the labour of young men.

3 At many points the upland trails run along wash-out stream courses, and substantial lenses of charcoal could be traced for kilometres in their sections. Whilst this could be the result of lightning-struck fires, the extent/uniformity of these horizons would suggest early slash-and-burn clearance.

4 The site had previously been visited in 1972 by Messerschmidt (1976b: note 10) and sketched by Temple in 1992 (Temple 1993).

5 Although the smaller 'megaliths' had not been recognised at all by our colleagues on their previous visit, Yarjung had apparently undergone a pre-trance reaction in the area of the courtyard in which the eastern is set, which he subsequently refused to enter. Paved with slabs and enclosed on one side by a terrace wall built of massive boulders, this yard would seem a 'special place'. Whilst it is impossible to say what he responded to, given its scale, formality and off-centre situation within the village, it could have been religious/ritual space; amongst the explanations offered was that a building that backs on to it was the house of an important shaman.

6 Working with a reduced team as a number of the men had to be sent down due to altitude sickness, over a number of days the theodolite could be effectively used only between 5 and 7 a.m. – before the clouds rose.

7 One of our colleagues reported his father saying that when he visited the site in his youth (c. 50–60 years ago), arrow firing-holes were to be seen in the palace's walls. If so, they must have been very high for none survives today. A more likely explanation may be that these were for first-storey floor joists such as were observed at Kohla. If nothing else, this suggests that the building has undergone considerable damage during this century.

8 The robbing of these sites must itself reflect upon the currency of past/site recognition and suggests that it requires 'informed' appreciation (by shamans/specialists).

9 This view may be biased by the fact that, to date, ethnographic research has largely been confined to the arable village-sector of the populace. The transhumant pastoralists may well have their own landscape associations; these will be investigated in future years.

10 This association, and that of the high valley above Kohla as 'The Racecourse', suggests that horses are identified with their upland past. Ill-suited to steep mountain trails, few are kept today; one possible derivation of the name Tamu-mai is 'People of the Horse'.

11 Of the sites thus far investigated, only the long ridge-top complex at Nadr Pa has a layout/density comparable to contemporary Tamu-mai villages.

12 Extraordinary features, for example isolated trees or ruins, are often marked by prayer flags; in this way the landscape is signified (arguably 'domesticated') by cosmology and immediate mythologies.

13 Spending considerable time in the woods surrounding Kohla seeking revelation of the cemetery, Yarjung described a dream quest for a lightning 'axe'-split juniper tree. (Apparently there are three types of lightning-struck trees: that which 'boils' so that it is completely dead, the 'axe'-split and that which burns – the 'axe' is not an implement as such, but a type of black stone that the lightning leaves embedded within the trunk.) He found the tree of his dream on a cliff by 'The Racecourse', but failed to locate its 'axe'. Apart from the boulder at Khoido, sites beyond the immediate Kohla environs seem to have little ritual/evocative impact. However, after visiting 'The Cave of Nuns', Yarjung dreamt of the death of one of its early occupants; apparently evil, their spirit went 'into the cliff' (i.e. not 'north').

Acknowledgements

My debt of gratitude to fellow co-directors Judy and Yarjung is immense and, in fairness (though weighted in this instance towards archaeology), this chapter should be read as a collaboration. We, of course, are grateful to the TPLS and our many Tamu-mai colleagues, and also for the support given the project throughout by R. Boast, A. Herle, I. Hodder, A. Macfarlane, M. Rowlands and P. Vitebsky. Apart from those mentioned, this chapter has benefited from discussions with B. Cambell, N. Howard, G. Lucas, C. Ramble, A. de Sales, W. Schon, S.S. Shrestha, A. Simons and M.L.S. Sørensen.

The Cambridge Archaeological Unit field-team, D. Gibson (pottery), J. Pollard and C. Begg (graphics), should be aware of the considerable thanks owed them; text figures are the work of Begg. The fieldwork to date has been ('inspiredly') funded by the McDonald Institute of Archaeological Research and the Crowther-Benyon and Williamson Funds of the University Museum of Archaeology and Anthropology, Cambridge.

References

Allen, N. 1974. The ritual journey, a pattern underlying certain Nepalese rituals. In *Contributions to the Anthropology of Nepal*, C. von Furer-Haimendorf (ed.), 6–22. Warminster: Aris & Phillips.

Bellezza, J.V. 1995. Doring revisited. *Himal* 8, 29–32.

Blair, K.D. 1983. *4 Villages: architecture in Nepal*. Los Angeles: Craft and Folk Art Museum.

Buchanan, F. 1819. *An Account of the Kingdom of Nepal*. Edinburgh: Constable.

Caplan, L. 1995. *Warrior Gentlemen: 'Gurkhas' in the western imagination*. Oxford: Berghahn.

Des Chene, M. 1996. Ethnography in the *Janajati-yug*: lessons from reading *Rodhi* and other Tamu-mai writings. *Studies in Nepali History and Society* 1, 97–161.

Evans, C. 1995. Archaeology against the state: roots of internationalism. In *Theory in Archaeology: a world perspective*, P. Ucko (ed.), 312–26. London: Routledge.

Macfarlane, A. 1976. *Resources and Population: a study of the Gurungs of Nepal*. Cambridge: Cambridge University Press.

Messerschmidt, D.A. 1976a. *The Gurungs of Nepal: conflict and change in a village society*. Warminster: Aris & Phillips.

Messerschmidt, D.A. 1976b. Ecological change and adaptation among the Gurungs of the Nepal Himalaya. *Human Ecology* 16, 167–85.

Messerschmidt, D.A. 1976c. Ethnographic observations of Gurung shamanism in Lamjung District. In *Spirit Possession in the Nepal Himalaya*, J. Hitchcock and R. Jones (eds), 197–216. Warminster: Aris & Phillips.

Mumford, S.R. 1990. *Himalayan Dialogue: Tibetan lamas and Gurung shamans in Nepal*. Madison: University of Wisconsin Press.

Pettigrew, J. 1995. Shamanic dialogue: history representation and landscape in Nepal. Unpublished Ph.D. thesis, University of Cambridge.

Pignede, B. [1966] 1993. *The Gurungs: a Himalayan population of Nepal*. Kathmandu: Ratna Pustak Bhandar.

Ramble, C. 1995. Gaining ground: representations of territory in Bon and Tibetan popular tradition. *Tibet Journal*, 20, 83–124.

Simons, A., W. Schon and S.S. Shrestha 1994. Preliminary report on the 1992 campaign of the team of the Institute of Prehistory, University of Cologne. *Ancient Nepal* 136, 51–75.

Strickland, S.S. 1982. Beliefs, practices and legends: a study in the narrative poetry of the Gurungs of Nepal. Unpublished Ph.D. thesis, University of Cambridge.

Tamu, B.P. and Y.K. Tamu 1993. Long road to Gandaki. *Himal* 6, 27–8.

Temple, M. 1993. The ruins of an early Gurung settlement. *European Bulletin of Himalayan Research* 5, 43–8.

Tilley, C. 1994. *A Phenomenology of Landscape*. Oxford: Berg.

29   Archaeology and the evolution of cultural landscapes: towards an interdisciplinary research agenda

JAMES MCGLADE

Introduction

Recent decades have seen a steady rise in the use, exploitation and conflict within the cultural landscapes of Europe. Much of this is a consequence of the development of modern market systems, increasing land-use conflicts, and an exponential growth in mass tourism, as western society experiences an unprecedented increase both in disposable income and in leisure time. The mobility and insatiable curiosity that have accompanied this latter exercise in 'cultural' consumption must be treated, not with cynical censure, but with realistic proactive schemes. The commercial marketing of historical landscapes throughout Europe is by now an irreversible phenomenon, as is the desire to 'curate' them, as witnessed by the construction of archaeological parks, eco-museums and the creation of 'reserves'; the construction of a new species of landscape is afoot – a new partitioning (legally sanctioned by the Malta Convention) in which cultural/historical spaces are separated out from the wider context of the living landscape and packaged for consumption (Bender 1992; Kolen 1995). The real problem with such schemes is that they tend to reflect official views of the past and, more contentiously, a single knowable past (cf. Lowenthal 1985).

The relative ease with which these attitudes can be deconstructed has generated an entire academic industry over the last decade, encompassing archaeology, anthropology and geography. However, critique is of itself facile and ultimately of only academic interest unless it promotes constructive alternatives. A primary argument of this chapter is that practical alternatives can be found in the promotion of integrative planning and management structures that do not regard scientific and local knowledge structures as mutually exclusive, but promote a rapprochement between them. Only in this way will we have a realistic chance of avoiding the irreversible cultural degradation that frequently results from the isolationist decisions of management and policy makers alike.

A key aspect of the type of approach we are suggesting is that it must locate archaeological concerns at the centre of the environmental agenda and, in so doing, demonstrate the central role of history in any understanding of the cultural construction of space. Such an agenda should attempt to foster the landscape not as some passive repository of lost information, but as a dynamic arena in which interpretation and reinterpretation are seen as vital parts of the creation of cultural knowledge. Archaeology's relative lack of concern for this agenda is all the more surprising given, first, the central importance of political/ideological issues in current theory, and, second, a renewed interest in the landscape, not as a passive container for human settlement but as the active and 'contested' arena of societal reproduction.

In what follows, we shall address the problem of the role of archaeology in the construction of dynamic cultural landscapes. What this means is that archaeology must actively participate in the dominant late twentieth-century debate, i.e. the human–environment problematique. This requires a resituating of research and the construction of an appropriate conceptual framework, specifically the need for an integrated, multi-disciplinary perspective. Importantly, this is not simply a methodological issue, but is primarily a conceptual problem whose solution lies in replacing the natural-science model that pervades the current environmental discourse, with an interpretive framework that promotes pluralistic outcomes rather than the reductionist search for single solutions. An example of an integrated research framework is presented based on current research in the Empordà, northeast Spain. The final outcome of this research will not be based on a systematic description and synthesis of each of the research axes, but rather will contribute towards the construction of an interpretive, 'dialogic' method. The chapter concludes by arguing that an archaeology that does not actively seek to contribute historical knowledge to the debate on the future of cultural landscapes is in danger of becoming marginalised and excluded from the most important issues in the contemporary human–environment discourse.

Archaeology and the cultural landscape

Research in recent years has seen a progressive movement towards a more overtly social and political view of human environment relations in archaeology. Two separate strands can be detected: the first is represented by new theoretical directions in landscape archaeology (e.g. Bender 1993; Thomas 1993b; Tilley 1994), foregrounding symbolic, structural and phenomenological perspectives, and the second is identified with a rapid growth of heritage management issues, central to which is that the landscape is an arena of political discourse (e.g. Hewison 1987; Fowler 1992; Bender 1993; Ucko 1994, 1995). Taken together, these developments amount to a profound change in the way in which archaeologists are examining the past – not so much as something already 'understood' and objective, but as something that is socially constructed and hence subject to continuous reinterpretation (Stone and Molyneaux 1994). This view that landscapes are not 'neutral' but ideologically constructed is critically important if we are to arrive at any real understanding of structural change in prehistoric societies.

While it is clear from these developments that archaeology has gained a great deal from the introduction of ideas from geography and anthropology (e.g. Cosgrove 1984; Layton 1986; Daniels and Cosgrove 1988; Morphy 1991; Duncan and Ley 1993), there has been a tendency to translate these influences into a semantic, place-centred discourse that revolves around representation and experiential issues (e.g. Thomas 1993b; Tilley 1994; Lemaire 1997). What we argue here is that this recent stress on the 'identity' of landscape, and its presence as a cultural image, has been emphasised at the expense of culture process. While the hermeneutic/interpretive orientation of this work is clearly a much-needed antidote to the empiricism of conventional approaches in landscape archaeology, there is a growing tendency to see landscapes exclusively through this filter. What we suggest is that landscape archaeology is in danger of conducting its debates within a rather narrow and restricted sphere dominated by themes such as 'memory', 'gaze' and 'dwelling' – all, in a sense, reflecting current postmodern preoccupations with ideas of representation, fragmentation and the decentring of the subject. However, important contributions by both Ingold (1993) and Hirsch (1995) have stressed the static nature of such approaches, arguing that ultimately they undervalue the importance of dynamic processes in the structuring of the landscape.

Landscapes are essentially multi-dimensional constructions, the outcome of an interplay between historically determined structures and contingent processes, and it is this dynamic that must be factored into any interpretive framework. A consequence of such a view is the need to see landscapes as being the product of long-term social–natural co-evolution (McGlade 1995a). As we shall see below, from an evolutionary perspective, landscapes are also the result of 'historical path-dependence', in the sense that frequently it is the essentially arbitrary or unintended features that emerge to determine subsequent historical pathways (Arthur 1988). For this reason, landscapes can thus be conceived as nonlinear dynamical systems whose evolution is governed by abrupt transitions, and it is in this sense that they can be said to have a 'bifurcation history'. We argue here that this history can be detected archaeologically. But tracking such evolutionary discontinuities requires a new conceptual approach – one that eschews conventional models of the long term as a single, cumulative trajectory amenable to discrete chronological partitioning and concomitant chronocultural analyses.

In addition, some theoretical approaches to an archaeology of landscape are also detached from a variety of pressing contemporary concerns represented by the problems of living landscapes: contested landscapes threatened by a variety of pathologies such as degradation, pollution and the forms of social–natural impoverishment that inevitably accompany them, and whose ubiquity would seem to qualify as the signature of post-industrial society. Apart from a few exceptions (e.g. the EU Archaeomedes programme), archaeology has contributed little to this environmental debate, which has now assumed the position as the most politically sensitive issue of the late twentieth century.

The dynamics of human-modified landscapes

At root this requires a resituating of the relationships defining human–environment interaction. One of the fundamental aspects of post-processual archaeologies has been the almost total dismissal of the environment, and this has meant an undertheorised – not to say nonexistent – concept of the evolutionary aspects of human–environment relationships. In many ways, this was a predictable reaction to the deterministic emphasis that had prevailed in palaeoeconomic approaches to prehistory. Unfortunately, the resultant purging of ecological concepts in favour of the ideational aspects of social life has effectively relegated environmental dynamics to the status of epiphenomena. The influence of this theoretical shift has led to the neglect not simply of the spatio-temporal complexity of ecological dynamics, but also of the crucial co-evolutionary dynamic that underpins all social–natural interaction.

Paradoxically, archaeology's renewed interest in landscape (e.g. Bender 1993; Thomas 1993a, 1993b; Tilley 1993, 1994; Barrett 1994; Gosden 1994), especially the importance accorded to the social construction of space, has not promoted interest in such issues. There is a sense in which the new landscape archaeological studies, while presenting an important counter to normative chronocentric approaches, are dangerously close to presenting over-socialised views of the relationship between people and their environment. For example, the fashion for experiential, subject-centred studies promotes a discourse that effectively dislocates social practice from the ecological milieu within which it is embedded. Indeed, as Benton has pointed out, this 'idealist' tendency within the social sciences generally is ultimately constrained, for 'it is unable to grasp the ecological and social consequences of unacknowledged conditions of social practices in relation to nature, and their unintended or unforseen consequences' (Benton 1994: 45).

What we are arguing for is caution against any representation of cultural schemata (social, symbolic, structural) that distances itself from the temporalities of lived experience – not those simply related to bodily experience, but particularly the insertion of such experiences in natural and physical phenomena. Without such embedding, we are in danger of constructing fictive landscapes – landscapes whose only points of reference are residual networks of meaning structures. At worst, the reductionism inherent in such approaches tends to render our interpretations of social–natural dynamics incomplete and ultimately misleading.

Human ecodynamics: an alternative spatio-temporal discourse

Recent work (McGlade 1995a, in press) has sought to contribute to this debate by emphasising the way in which social–natural co-evolution is driven by nonlinear dynamical processes. The adoption of a nonlinear dynamical perspective forces a rereading of the human–environment problem: thus, human agency and decision-making are resituated within an ecological context that is at once evolutionary and contingent, and stresses the need for an alternative approach to the study of human-modified landscapes – for a non-functionalist human ecology. Towards this end, a theory of human eco-dynamics has been proposed (McGlade 1995a, 1996, in press). Simply put, a human ecodynamic approach is concerned with the dynamics of human-modified landscapes from a long-term perspective, and viewed as a nonlinear dynamical system. Human–environmental relationships are thus defined as involving the co-evolution of socio-historical and natural processes, and their time-space intersection. At a fundamental level, a human ecodynamic perspective implies that: there is no 'environment'; there is no 'ecosystem'; there are only socio-natural systems.

What we are underlining here is the fact that concepts such as 'environment' and 'ecosystem' have no single identifiable definition independent of human observation; moreover, both are social and cultural constructions embedded in contemporary attitudes and value systems. In the first place, current emphasis on the 'environment' and 'environmental issues' has effectively reified the term, giving it some objective status; the reality is, of course, that there can be no objective study of the natural environment for the very good reason that there is no 'objective' world independent of human observation. There is, for example, no *a priori*, generic 'ecosystem' possessing a set of globally identifiable attributes; there are only multiple perceptions of the natural world and these are both scale dependent and context specific.

It is important to point out here that this is not simply a rereading of landscape ecology, for this sub-discipline is devoid of any concern with the meaning structures that inhere in socially constructed landscapes. Landscape ecology, by comparison, privileges structure and function and specifically the distribution of energy, materials and species in ecosystems (Forman and Godron 1986). To further emphasise the difference between human ecology and what we have termed *human ecodynamics*, Table 29.1 presents a caricature of the main theoretical oppositions.

The drawing out of such differences is necessarily incomplete and is intended only to highlight the major shift of focus proposed by a human ecodynamic approach. In the first instance, the temporal dimension is stressed such that we contrast the normative idea of time as an abstract container of events with an alternative stress on the temporalities that articulate social–natural systems (cf. Ingold 1993; Picazo 1997; McGlade in press). This acknowledges the fact that we cannot adequately deal with questions relating to socio-natural interaction and their dynamics with reference to any 'single'

Table 29.1 Comparative theoretical concerns in human ecology and human ecodynamics

Human ecology	Human ecodynamics
Time as abstract	Time as substantive
Space as measurable	Space as socially constructed and time dependent
Linear causality	Nonlinear causality
Negative feedback (stabilising)	Positive feedback (destabilising)
Adaptation	Self-organisation
Equilibrium	Nonequilibrium
Stability	Resilience
Continuity	Discontinuity
Complexity as safeguard against perturbation	Complexity incorporates perturbation
Quantitative description (statistical)	Qualitative description (attractors, bifurcation)
Prediction	Impossibility of prediction (chaos)
Deductive, analytical	Interpretive, integrative
System	Agency (communicative action)

privileged concept of time. In other words, time cannot be relegated to the realms of the abstract, nor can there be any single unifying 'time'; rather, time is to be grasped in relation to the particular sets of biological, social, economic, political and ideological processes that articulate societal reproduction.

The conventional use of space is equally problematic, since it assumes that space as a 'physical' entity can be separated from time and expressed as an absolute value, e.g. as a bounded territory with measurable dimension. In a sense, spatially motivated archaeology and its variants such as 'settlement archaeology' assume that spatial structure is something independent from its social context; there is little appreciation that space is, in fact, not a neutral Cartesian concept that is to be understood with reference to statistical analysis, but is socially constructed (Soja 1980, 1989; Gregory and Urry 1985).

The question of causality is the next issue raised in our comparison of human–environmental systems. As we have noted above, one of the main characteristics of complex socio-natural systems is the presence of nonlinear interactions; it is these that are capable of generating complex dynamics and are implicated in system restructuring – often unanticipated. In a nonlinear system, a small change in one variable can have disproportionate and even catastrophic effects on the entire system. Tracking nonlinear causality is thus a key research question in understanding the evolution of human systems.

Intimately related to this issue is the role of feedback. Human ecology has tended to stress the notion of negative feedback, and this is said to be implicated in the maintenance of stability, or homeostatic equilibrium. This is a legacy from cybernetic approaches to culture change and is, by definition, functionalist. By contrast, it is the self-reinforcing or positive feedback properties that should concern us, for it is these that generate destabilising dynamics. Such self-reinforcing properties can push the system through a series of unstable transitions (bifurcations). Fluctuations acting on the system can cause it spontaneously to bifurcate to a new 'order' or transformation. As Prigogine and Stengers (1984) have pointed out, this type of emergent organisation occurs independently of external intervention; it is purely endogenous.

The importance of adaptation as a central thesis in human ecology carries within it an implicit teleological assumption. Human groups are thus engaged in a constant goal-directed activity; their energies are directed at adapting to the environment. The persistence of human societies is therefore seen as a measure of adaptedness. As we have shown above, this tautological relationship misrepresents the true human–environment dynamic, a dynamic that is best described in relation to self-organisation.

One of the problematic areas in interpretations of both human and natural systems concerns the question of scale. From a landscape archaeological perspective, recent research has demonstrated the function of multi-scalar temporalities that structure the semi-arid environments of the Vera Basin in southeast Spain (Courty et al. 1995; Fedoroff and Courty 1995; McGlade 1995b, 1996). The primary message of this research is that landscape structure emerges as a result of the intersection of different temporalities, ranging from the slowest processes such as tectonic movements (10^7), climatic cycles (10^5), all the way to population dynamics (10^2) and other micro-level phenomena (10^{-1}). These temporalities are characterised by differential rates of change; i.e. a spectrum can be envisaged from slow, cumulative rates represented by glacial and tectonic movements, to those soil or vegetational dynamics that display rapid turnover. Discontinuity in the system can be the result of the conjuncture of 'fast' and 'slow' variables (Holling 1986). What is critical from our perspective is that the mapping of human action and decision-making on to such phenomena is responsible for the creation of human ecodynamic structuring – an intertemporal dependence that maps the social on to the natural and the natural on to the social.

Another major difference between human ecological approaches and our human ecodynamic counterpart involves the question of complexity and its relationship to stability. The commonsense view is that increased diversity in a system generates more flexible options and hence leads to greater stability – complexity is thus a hedge against perturbation. However, it seems that increased diversity may be achieved at the cost of increasing system lag, and hence operates as a significant destabilising force. Such time delays are capable of generating wholly unpredictable outcomes and, in some cases, the complex dynamics associated with chaos. A human ecodynamic definition of complexity, therefore, is based on the principle that complexity incorporates perturbation – a definition synonymous with resilience.

A fundamental goal of many human ecological models is the notion of prediction, i.e. a 'good' model should be capable of anticipating the future. However, as we have seen, prediction as one of the basic tenets of positivist science has been undermined by recent discoveries in the natural sciences – particularly the existence of deterministic chaos in nonlinear systems (Lorenz 1963). It is, thus, important that a human ecodynamic description of events accommodates these findings, and moreover moves from an emphasis on quantitative description to the kind of qualitative description appropriate to dynamical systems (the term 'qualitative' must not be confused with its use in the social sciences, where it is defined by opposition to rigorous quantitative method). Qualitative dynamics as first defined by Poincaré (1899) is concerned with the discovery of underlying coherent structures that define the long-run behaviour of a dynamical system – i.e. bifurcation points and attractors.

Finally, in our comparative scheme, we come to the question of 'explanation'. Human ecological theory in its positivist mode of operation privileges deductive analytical 'answers' to research questions. Knowledge acquisition is resident in our ability to abstract and 'rationalise' more and more data. Such an empiricist orientation generates a false dichotomy – it perpetuates the social–natural divide, and ultimately relegates the reflexive, intentional, subjective aspects of human behaviour to epiphenomena.

Most of all, however, what we are opposing here is the idea of a systemic model of the human environment in which deterministic processes hold sway, and in which the division between nature and culture is a persistent feature of research. Landscape evolution is thus viewed as a consequence of the role of human impact on the 'natural' system. By contrast, we are promoting a co-evolutionary model in which the notion of 'environment' is replaced by what we might refer to as a process of social–natural structuration; evolution in such a system is notably governed by the play of contingent forces within a complex nonequilibrium environment. The evolution of a human ecodynamic system is thus consistent with the bifurcation behaviour that is a feature of all nonlinear complex systems (cf. McGlade 1995a, in press). Unintended consequences and discontinuous transitions constitute normal behaviour – i.e. they are perfectly 'predictable' in nonequilibrium landscapes.

A final and important point is that the construction of a human ecodynamic approach is clearly something that cannot be achieved within narrow discipinary limits, but is pluri-disciplinary in concept and requires an integrated research methodology.

Multi-disciplinarity and integrated research

It is common for archaeologists – and indeed scientists in general – to believe that integrated research is simply a question of creating an arena within which disparate disciplinary contributions can be placed alongside one another. Commonly, we have a series of studies of, for example, climate, soils, hydrology, and demographic factors that are assembled, and frequently followed by an accompanying 'synthesis'. Such a strategy can never produce a truly integrated picture, for the whole is conceived as a kind of additive jigsaw; moreover, it is essentially a methodologically driven enterprise. The development of archaeological science as a distinctive sub-discipline separated from cultural, social and ideological concerns has done much to promote the notion of inter-disciplinary research as one based on a series of specialist analyses (McGlade 1995a). We are thus in a world where knowledge acquisition is achieved through a systematic fragmentation of separate specialist observations, which subsequently become appendices to be 'incorporated' into synthetic reconstructions of the cultural environment. The continuing practice of rendering palynological, anthracological and carpological data as discrete analytical and classificatory entities, devoid of any epistemological discussion, can only retard our ambitions to move towards a mature archaeological theory.

The recent history of multi-disciplinary research is most prominent with respect to environmental issues. In this sense, it might reasonably be argued that interdisciplinary research modes are the result of crisis. In a century of crises – political, economic, social, intellectual, technological and scientific – perhaps the most prominent crisis of the past three decades has been the growing human–environment problem (Clark and Munn 1986). This has arisen particularly as a consequence of population growth, economic expansion, the increase in industrial agriculture, water and airborn pollutants, as well as growing social and natural impoverishment caused by land degradation and desertification phenomena. This situation has led to the emergence of a new politico-academic discourse, 'the environment', which currently assumes the role of the most fashionable academic pursuit (Benton and Redclift 1994). Indeed, Environmental Science now constitutes the largest single growth area in academic and non-academic spheres alike, and environmental consultancy has emerged as a lucrative by-product, with some scientists even floating companies on the stock exchange. Science has now become a multi-billion-dollar industry.

By the advent of the 1980s, it was becoming clear that the inherent complexity of environmental systems – particularly when exacerbated by anthropogenic involvement – could not be grasped by conventional disciplinary perspectives; i.e. reductionist methods of analysis were increasingly seen as being incapable of generating an understanding of the complex causalities governing both natural and social systems. The result was the emergence of 'big science': multi-disciplinary, large-scale projects, and along with them the arrival of a new breed of scientific entrepreneur – usually ex-scientists – assuming powerful organisational and administrative roles. Science was becoming big business with its own set of stars and gurus, frequently sought out by governmental and social agencies.

Notwithstanding the financial investment and organisational infrastructure that characterised these global projects dealing with climate change, sea-level rise, desertification, etc., from today's standpoint what is remarkable about this period of global, multi-disciplinary research is their failure. Thus, many of these large-budget projects have failed to generate satisfactory explanations and understandings of the array of environmental problems posed. The reasons for such failures are complex and, moreover, vary with individual context and cultural specifics. However, if a primary cause is to be profferred, it can be traced to the epistemological basis upon which multi-disciplinary science projects are founded. In many ways it is here that the failure to generate integrative knowledge is to be seen at its most obvious. The model of science used in multi-discipinary research has conventionally been based on the positivist methods that for centuries have contributed to the philosophy under-pining the natural sciences. The overtly empiricist nature of these traditions and their reductionist method are ingrained within the scientific community; their persistence is easily explicable in view of their demonstrable success in fields such as biotechnology, microbiology and genetics in generating scien-tific information and explanatory frameworks.

In spite of the fact that the natural-science paradigm is clearly inadequate with respect to social issues and particularly the problem of values, never-theless its methods continue to underwrite most mutli-disciplinary research. At root, the failure of multi-disciplinary science is a failure adequately to contextualise social action and the unintended consequences generated by complex nonlinear decision processes. An understanding of such issues requires a radically different approach, i.e. an interpretivist method that operates from a fundamentally different epistemological stance. Conventionally, integration is seen as a purely methodological issue, rather than an interpretive problem. The main criterion for a successful integrative, multi-disciplinary approach lies not in the ability of a project to generate results *per se*, but in its capacity to generate transdisciplinary knowledge, i.e. emergent knowledge.

A model for integrated interdisciplinary research

The Empordà project[1] (McGlade and Picazo 1997) is designed to contribute to such a goal, and to provide substantive social and environmental research to the debate on sustainable futures for the landscapes of the southern Euro-pean Mediterranean. Ongoing research concerns an investigation into the role of social and political power structures in directing the historical evolution of land-use conflict in the region.

The Empordà is a rich agricultural region occupying a privileged geo-graphical position, since it lies astride the main inland route linking France with Spain, but at the same time is open to the Mediterranean and largely shut off from the interior. Throughout its history, therefore, the Empordà has been an area of passage and contact, and this has generated a rich archaeological and historical record. This region, over the past 2,000 years spanning the first neolithic colonisations, through the later Iberian and Romanisation periods, presents a particularly well-developed sequence of changes in the structuring of political space, involving the operation of a variety of processes such as conquest, colonisation and migration at the hands of Greeks, Romans, feudal lords and other market entrepreneurs. Significantly, over the long term, we are confronted with a series of major structural transformations in the organisation of political space, i.e. the emergence of urbanisation, with the development of the first towns in Iberia such as the Greek city of Emporion and its Iberian counterparts, Ullastret and Mas Castellar de Pontós. Ultimately, what we have is a long-term sequence of extractive economic strategies which have sought to appropriate the land for political gain. It is in this sense that the history of the Ampurdán is the history of land-use conflict.

A primary goal of the research project currently underway is to generate a more complete understanding of the evolutionary dynamics that have structured – and continue to structure – the social–natural environments of the Empordà, spanning a period covering the last 2,500 years. Given such a synthetic objective, the study has been designed to combine a number of different disciplines, techniques and perspectives, including remote sensing and Geographic Information Systems (GIS), ecology, geomorphology, hydrology, agrarian history, archaeology, archival research, historical geography, ethnography and sociology (Figure 29.1). Thus, a central feature of the project is its desire to view the human–environment problem from an integrative long-term perspective, with a view to demonstrating the vital role that both archaeology and palaeoecology can contribute to an assessment of contemporary landscape dynamics. This is not simply a question of inserting references to cultural dynamics and the archaeological settlement of past landscapes; rather, it stresses the need to retheorise environmental phenomena as the historical product of continuous social structuring and restructuring.

Significantly, the adoption of a long-term historical perspective is intended to underline the fact that decisions made in the past form the initial conditions of what are often perceived as 'present-day' crises; in this way, problematic issues relating to agricultural production, industry and tourist expansion are situated within a perspective that views them as the latest stages in a sequence of changes brought about by the intended and unintended consequences of past economic and political decisions as well as a variety of short-term approaches to social–environmental dynamics. More specifically, the adoption of a human ecodynamic approach stresses the crucial importance of nonlinear structuring processes in the maintenance of resilience and is already providing new insights into the essential scale-dependence of the temporal and spatial dynamics that define the urban/rural problem. For example, the dynamic behaviour of the biotic and abiotic environmental variables are characterised by 'intrinsic times', and collectively they form a nested spatio-temporal hierarchy (McGlade in press).

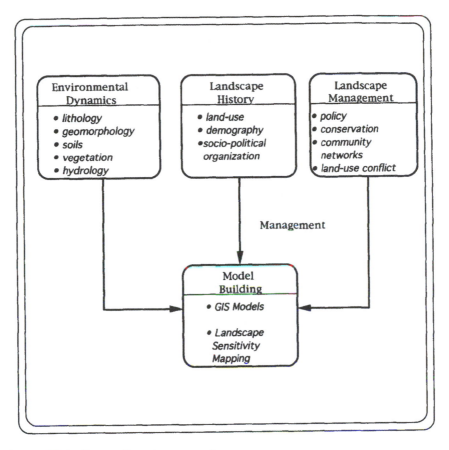

Figure 29.1 Empordà project research axes.

A major aspect of this research strategy and its relevance to the contemporary problems facing the Empordà lies in the fact that, currently, land-use strategies are characterised by short-term decision-making; there is a lack of research directed at an understanding of the nature of the long-term consequences of human modification on both the social and ecological well-being of the environment. There is thus a need to view the vulnerability and resilience that characterise the contemporary landscape within the context of a historical trajectory. The Empordà project asserts that socially viable developmental pathways for sustainable management of the cultural landscape will become clear only when we expose the complex events that collectively comprise the decision history of the socio-political landscape as the product of long-term structuring processes. Thus, the paleo-landscape is not simply a palimpsest of inert, fossilised structures, but rather represents the set of initial conditions that have provided the enabling and constraining contexts within which the contemporary landscape has been fashioned.

Methodology

The primary research objectives enumerated above are currently being implemented through two principal analytical orientations: environmental monitoring and landscape management, and dynamic modelling and Landscape Sensitivity Mapping (LSM). The interaction of these research tools is designed to provide the analytical and interpretive context within which data sets pertaining to social and environmental processes can be situated. These activities can be summarised as follows.

Environmental monitoring and landscape management

Operationally, this involves the integration of four primary research axes:

1   *Remote sensing and GIS*
    Remote sensing is being used to provide information on the present-day landscape, and is being calibrated with maps of present-day vegetation, soils and land use. In addition, the GIS houses historical and environmental information from survey work, as well as representing a realisation of the historical landscape of the region from written documents and other textual sources. Satellite imagery is also being used as a means of detecting relict water courses and irrigation networks as part of palaeo-hydrological mapping, and is being employed to aid in the detection of the fossil cadastre system of the Greco-Roman colony at Emporion.

2   *Environmental dynamics (ecology, geomorphology, hydrology, soils)*
    The reconstruction of the palaeoecology and neoecology of the area is concerned with the classification of the present-day vegetation and with reconstruction of the local landscape from fossil pollen. In concert with this, a study of the superficial water circulation and water table dynamics is underway; a secondary aim is to infer past dynamics, particularly precipitation rates, and their relevance to the settlement history of the Empordà.

3   *Historical geography (archival research, demography and historical land use)*
    This research orientation involves extensive study of the relevant social, historical and demographic materials pertaining to the evolution of the social landscape. It attempts to provide the proper context within which land-use conflict is situated – i.e. as an inevitable product of the extractive history of the landscape. An important aspect of this axis is an intensive socio-economic survey so as to provide information on the development of land-use practice and population dynamics from the Late Medieval period to the present day. As well as supplementing existing knowledge, this work provides important data for the construction of LSM as an aid in the sustainable management of the socio-political landscape.

4   *Community dynamics and social networks (local decision-making structures and contemporary land-use conflict)*
    A micro-scale study has been designed to isolate the structural organisational networks that articulate local communities in the Empordà, and to identify the linkages between social, political and ideological networks. This allows examination of the interstructural processes that determine social relations, spatial structures and decision-making, since it is these that form the structural core and give meaning to the term 'community' (Taylor 1983; Cohen 1985). More especially, it will provide data on the conflicting perceptions that are embedded in the cultural landscape and their relationship to questions of identity.

Community is viewed here not as a fixed immutable entity, but rather as a mosaic of semi-autonomous networks, shifting in size and composition over time. In addition, kinship structure and social inequalities (hereditary or otherwise) guarantee diverse affiliations and uncertain (fluctuating) membership. This variability is mediated by the existence of boundary phenomena, some of which are relatively fixed and others relatively porous. It is for this reason that not all social networks are visible; the fluidity with which certain networks structure and restructure as a function of temporary needs and decision-making contexts makes it inherently difficult to isolate single, unambiguous networks with discrete functions. However, it is to these 'fuzzy sets' that we must direct our attention if we are to make sense of the relationships linking agency with the various degrees of organisational structure that articulate social action. Any insight into how a community will respond to a variety of EU policy directives, as well as its attitude to issues of sustainability and the archaeological heritage, is vitally dependent on identifying not only these interaction networks, but the relative strengths of their connectivities.

If we are to understand the contexts within which decision-making processes occur, and the potential receptivity to external change, we must identify the agents of change, or those assuming 'gatekeeper' roles in the community, and assess their influence, for example in the management of agricultural production systems at different hierarchical levels. Thus, from a historical perspective we are interested in:

1   which forms of socio-political organisation, at both the local and regional levels, have contributed to community persistence over the long term?
2   how do tradition, risk and innovation enable or constrain societal structures?
3   how important is group identity/kinship membership in this structuring?
4   how do structures of power, domination and inequality co-exist with alternative enabling and creative forces in human agency?
5   how do social organisational networks – both overt and covert – contribute to adaptive resource management and sustainable agricultural futures?

Currently, a series of structured and semi-structured interviews are being undertaken with individuals, organisations and public institutions, with the aim of understanding the different perceptions of land-use conflict along with perceptions of the archaeological heritage and the cultural landscape generally. It is hoped that these data on the decision networks that govern rural communities may reveal some properties pertinent to an understanding of the dynamics of community organisation.

Dynamical modelling and Landscape Sensitivity Mapping (LSM)

A major challenge in this research lies in the synthesis of historical, ecological, demographic and social data sets, so as to gain new insight into structural stability and bifurcation phenomena with respect to the long-term evolution of political space in the region. A critical tool in achieving such a goal involves the operation of an integrated multi-scalar research framework, developed elsewhere (McGlade 1995b); this is designed to accommodate both qualitative and quantitative data sets at micro-, meso- and macro-scales, so as to create an environment in which a variety of different model representations can co-exist in the construction of an interpretive framework generating potential 'dialogues'. The main implication of such a strategy is that it actively precludes the possibility of interpretation and understanding as being the preserve of any single model, i.e. socio-natural systems have no intrinsic analytical scale.

The construction of a decision support tool for monitoring the susceptibilities of the landscape to changing social, political and economic circumstances is one of the primary aims of the project. This LSM functions as an integral part of a GIS, to aid in the exploration of future sustainable pathways for the landscapes of the Empordà. Practically, the task of achieving a useful definition of sustainability involves a synthesis of data on environmental, social, demographic, political, land-use and settlement history, so as to calculate a semi-quantitative measure of resilience for individual locations in the study area. This development of a more comprehensive definition of resilience is designed to reflect the social-welfare needs of the community, as well as reflecting the requirements for the maintenance of biodiversity.

More specifically, from a pragmatic perspective, it is designed to act as a decision support system useful to a large number of constituencies, for example planners, ecologists, conservationists, and those involved in environmental management in general, so as to provide a practical, interrogative tool for policy makers in the amelioration of land-use conflict in the Empordà region. It thus can provide a landscape-monitoring scheme, providing information on changing levels of biodiversity, the protection of agricultural land and the limits of tourist expansion. Ultimately, it is seen as an aid to more efficient culturally and socially aware land-use planning, and hence is of direct consequence to the management of the archaeological heritage.

The LSM is designed to integrate structural, functional, organisational and perceptual criteria that define a series of landscape states related to specific organisational scales (Table 29.2). These categories form the fundamental units

Table 29.2 Landscape Sensitivity Mapping scalar dynamics

	Biophysical	Social-political	Economic
Macro (European)	• climate regimes • Mediterranean biogeography • hydrological regimes • sea-level rise • coastal-zone morphology • perturbation dependence	• continental demographic trends • EU political administration • coastal-zone management • wetland protection • sustainability • urban–rural conflict	• 'Brussels effect' • EU subsidy • capital investment • transportation networks • Common Agricultural Policy • market dynamics
Meso (regional)	• climate trends • river catchments • biodiversity • nonlinear spatial structuring • flooding • erosion processes	• regional population trends • social relations of production • land ownership • social/cultural networks • land-use planning • regional government • nature conservation	• 'Madrid effect' • regional investment • agricultural economy • industrial economy • tourist sector • service sector • transportation
Semi-micro (comarca)	• weather patterns • soil fertility • catchment dynamics • fire/flood regimes	• comarca-level administration • land use • population dynamics • conservation issues • tourist development	• 'Barcelona effect' • migration • labour market • capital investment • service sector • pollution
Micro (local)	• weather • local erosion episodes • extreme events • localised perturbations (fire, flood, grazing) • plant dynamics • soil micromorphology	• fertility/mortality rates • municipal administration • kinship networks • tradition • history • toponomy • identity	• 'Girona effect' • local employment • local investment • tourist economy • land price • roads • canalisation/irrigation

with respect to investigating system resilience and its sensitivity to change. The basic research questions being asked are thus: what are the primary axes of change operating in the Empordà landscapes, and what are their attendant attributes (Table 29.3)?

From a methodological perspective, the data needed for the construction of the LSM have been partitioned into three areas: 1) ecological sensitivity measures, 2) economic sensitivity measures, and 3) social-cultural sensitivity measures. Currently methods are being developed to provide sensitivity evaluations for individual map cells, in conjunction with the land-use attractivity surfaces being developed in the GIS. Our aim is to seek nonreductionist methods, i.e. to construct sensitivity indices (resilience) that will retain the richness and diversity of the data sets. An accompanying set of analytical modelling methods is also being developed so as to isolate key variables that are seen to play a major role in the structuring of social and natural dynamics. These model representations are intended to capture the 'global' economic and social dynamics that articulate the relationships between demography, agricultural production, tourism and capital investment in the Empordà. A primary concern of this analysis is to reveal the nonlinear linkages between key variables at different observational scales.

Table 29.3 Primary axes of change in the Empordà landscapes and their constituent attributes

Axes of change	Attributes
Social	• relations of production • land ownership • demography
Political	• administration • regional/local government
Cultural	• recreation/leisure • conservation management
Economic	• agriculture • mass tourism • eco-tourism, etc.
Biophysical	• rainfall variability • floods • soil structure/erosion • loss of biodiversity • coastal erosion • wetland disturbance • hydrological balance, etc.

The Empordà landscape as long-term history

The primary assumption of the present research is that the landscape has a social history, and that this social history is detectable if we adopt a coherent investigative methodology. Viewed from a long-term perspective, the evolution of the landscapes of the Empordà can be conceived as a succession of human ecodynamic structures that have been articulated by specific social formations. These human ecodynamic structures are broadly defined by those changes in the natural landscape as a result of human modification, i.e. transformations in the social exploitation of nature. Research is thus focused on the manner in which these transformations are effected, with respect to changing political, economic and ideological criteria.

It is in this way that the Empordà landscapes have acquired a specific 'identity', as a consequence of social–natural evolutionary history. They represent a historical ensemble of attitudes, actions and choices, a confluence of the intended and unintended consequences of human behaviour, and it is these aspects that require our attention. Conventional descriptive approaches, by comparison, tend to equate archaeological landscapes with 'patterns of the past', i.e. the locational history of the landscape. By contrast, we are interested, not in a history of the 'occupation' of the Empordà landscape, but rather in its (re)production. This underlines the fact that space is not simply a container of human activities but, rather, a conscious creation – it is a socially constructed phenomenon.

Ultimately, we are interested in gaining insight into the structural stability of the various social–natural configurations that have characterised landscape history from its formative neolithic imprint to the socio-political structures that characterise the contemporary landscape. It is thus that we can view the long term as constituting the 'bifurcation history' of the landscape.

Landscape, power and identity

The Empordà, however, is more than a simple history of ruptures in a succession of different modes of production: it is also the locus of the enactment and the transformation of ideologies. Ultimately, the Empordà project will attempt to demonstrate that an important part of landscape dynamics can be based on the historical recovery of ideologies. It is clear that ideologies are involved in the creation both unintentionally and deliberately of the landscape not only as a system of signification, but as an expression of cultural identity. This may be manifest in three ways: 1) as a quest for order, 2) as an assertion of authority, and 3) as a project of totalisation (Baker 1989). At a practical level, the historical recovery of ideologies within the context of the Empordà involves the identification, linking and interpretation of a mass of archaeological, environmental, historical and archival documentary sources, e.g. legal codes, ecclesiastical records and even personal correspondence. Architectual forms and style thus become an important element in the cultural construction of the landscape.

Perhaps one of the most difficult aspects in pursuing past ideological systems is that the landscapes we are studying may have several different systems of symbolic representation existing simultaneously and even antagonistically. This is precisely the situation we have in the contemporary landscapes of the Empordà. However, our first task is to attempt to understand the broad structure of human occupation in the area, as a prelude to generating a series of analytical interpretations with respect to ideological criteria.

At a fundamental level, all communities are structured with respect to symbolic, material and ideological criteria, and these are manifest in sets of power relations. In order to understand better the operation of such mechanisms, and their role in the maintenance of viable social configurations in interaction with the natural world, we must locate these power structures within a historical frame of reference, i.e. within a 'social history of nature' that emphasises the action of past events and their ideological contexts in generating the present conditions within which human-modified environments have evolved.

Historical path-dependence

As was stressed at the outset, a proper understanding of the socio-spatial contexts that articulate the landscapes of the Empordà requires a long-term evolutionary perspective, situating the trajectory from the primary neolithic occupation through successive periods of Roman, medieval, industrial and post-industrial occupations of the landscape. Without such a perspective, the role of social, political and economic processes can only be imperfectly understood; i.e. the dynamical trajectory of such processes can be severely misrepresented if viewed within a short-term time-frame.

Our first point in discussing such a proposal is the designation of the communication landscape as a human ecodynamic system, in which there is a dialectical interaction between social and natural phenomena. The landscape is, thus, primarily viewed as a social construction – the product of successive structuring over millennia – rather than simply being portrayed as a geometric locational entity. From this it follows that the primary structuring of social space during the Neolithic and Bronze Age was made possible by the initial communication arteries – the rivers, roads and trackways that dissect the landscape. It is these that have dictated the initial location of settlement, and which constitute and delimit the 'possibility space' of human action and interaction.

But the landscape is more than a simple conjunction of environmental, social and economic processes – it is, above all, a historical construction, and it is in this sense that we must see landscape as having a social history in which the communication networks constitute a specific evolutionary component. This militates against interpreting the landscape as a series of chronocultural snapshots; it is thus that the conventional practice in archaeology of constructing discrete temporal units within which to discuss cultural phenomena, can actively distort the trajectory of change.

This is not to suggest that the landscape is to be viewed as the simple process of cultural accumulation moving on a simple-to-complex course. Rather, it emphasises the landscape as the locus of multiple structural transformations, which are in a significant way a consequence of enabling and constraining factors represented by the communication networks. Significantly in the Empordà, as elsewhere, once the primary road network is established, it acts as an attractor for the future development of settlement. The evolutionary importance of initial conditions in structuring processes is a fundamental property of complex dynamical systems, and such a concept has been usefully described by Arthur (1988) in terms of historical path-dependence. Arthur's examples from the world of technology and manufacturing demonstrate how the introduction of a new product or locational choice acts as a determinant for the future evolutionary trajectory of the system, creating irreversible outcomes. From our current perspective, we can see how the superimposition by the Romans of the Via Augusta produced a lock-in effect, dictating the ensuing nodal structure of the settlement pattern. Thus, the establishment of this axis of passage persists until the present day, manifest as the modern autopista route connecting the Iberian peninsula with France and the rest of Europe.

The dominance of this north–south attractor supplanted the primary east–west attractor represented by the river systems in the Empordà. This primary structural element acted as the controlling force for at least five millennia, defining the possibility space of all social, economic and political interaction. From a dynamical perspective, the transformation wrought by the imposition of the new north–south axis was not a gradual, smooth transition effected over centuries, but an abrupt discontinuity – something entirely consistent with the concept of bifurcation in the evolution of nonlinear dynamical systems (cf. McGlade and van der Leeuw 1997).

Water control and 'contested' landscapes

Another significant outcome of the project's methodology has caused us to resituate social/political conflicts that reside in the contemporary landscape; these assume a new meaning when set within the context of a long-term perspective. Thus, for example, the water-use conflicts we see in the contemporary landscape, as farmers fight with conservationists over the future of the Empordà wetlands, are not specific to the late twentieth century. Rather they form part of a recurrent human ecodynamic conflict that can be traced to the initial occupation of the landscape, and subsequently has been played out through the successive Roman and Medieval periods. For example, in the area of the River Ter during the seventeenth and eighteenth centuries, increasing inequality is evident, with a small group of families assuming economic and social power. This resulted in the drainage and appropriation of wetland areas, producing subsequent conflict between competing parties. Documentary evidence shows frequent accusations referring to the deliberate changing of the course of the River Ter.

Research to date demonstrates that the control of water resources constitutes a primary structuring thread in the fabric of the landscape. For this reason, we are currently integrating the palaeoecological, archaeological, historical and social data bases so as to provide a unique insight into the structuring of social space. The human ecodynamic methodology we are proposing here is not simply appropriate for the evolution of the Empordà landscapes, but at a wider level suggests a useful integration of theory and practice, i.e. a mode of praxis for understanding cultural landscapes generally.

Resource management: the protection of cultural landscapes

Defining resilient landscapes

Another aspect of the potential for conflict relates to archaeological heritage and to the management of cultural landscapes generally; such issues are affected by differing social, cultural and ideologically bounded perspectives (Stone and Molyneaux 1994). An additional problem is that any questions relating to sustainable futures for the cultural landscapes of Europe must inevitably confront issues such as: Sustainable for whom? Sustainable on what time-scale? Sustainable under what conditions of social welfare? In this respect, what is clear from recent research in the Argolid (Allen *et al.* 1995) and southeast Spain (McGlade *et al.* 1995) is that in order to be 'sustainable', land-use patterns must display a dynamic response to constantly changing ecological, political and socio-economic conditions; in other words, they must demonstrate resilience.

The fundamental issue facing archaeologists, planners and policy makers, therefore, is to generate an understanding of sustainable cultural landscapes. Systems need to be produced that are at once sensitive to the contextual specifics of a particular locale, and which work in concert with the natural ecological resilience of the landscape in such a way as to absorb the levels of perturbation induced by human agency as well as natural forces. The key here is that these aims must be achieved within an acceptable level of toler-ance – i.e. one that does not result in irreversible degradation and/or socio-economic impoverishment. What this means from a resource manage-ment perspective is that we need to recognise cultural landscape systems as conforming to a co-evolutionary dynamic that ideally can foster and promote a reciprocal interaction between natural and social processes that are mutu-ally beneficial.

Thus, an understanding of the structures of societal organisation and their relationship to the natural environment is a prerequisite for the construction of any policy-related issues concerning the long-term future of the archaeo-logical heritage and its relationship to the cultural landscape generally. Political, economic and ideological power structures play a fundamental role in the management of natural resources and their persistence over time.

Managing resilient landscapes

A primary feature of the proposed research methodology is that it provides a set of tools for landscape management. Conventional scenarios for resource management schemes are based on risk, impact and predictive models; they generally contain three major assumptions: 1) linear causality, 2) short-term perspectives, and 3) humans as external perturbations.

For example, remedial measures are often short-term 'technofixes' that show little understanding of the real complexities underlying the dynamics of complex social–natural systems and/or the perceptions of the actors involved. A major aspect of the future management of cultural landscapes is the need for the implementation of land-use planning directed at medium- to long-term development; unfortunately, in many parts of Europe there are few monitoring mechanisms to control speculative projects – particularly those related to tourism. In an effort to contribute research that is relevant to such a goal, we might begin by establishing the principal aims of a viable socio-environment policy for the sustainable archaeological management of the landscape, and the criteria it must reflect:

1   First, we must work towards the maintainance of a level of diversity that will support viable social configurations; this requires that human intervention in the landscape be planned with an emphasis on medium- to long-term change.

2   Second, it must be realised that homogenisation of agricultural land, as a result of policies that favour large-scale mechanisation on the grounds of efficiency for the optimal use of resources, actively works against the maintenance of ecological diversity as well as a plurality of social formations, and the archaeological heritage.

3   Third, the participation of local communities is an imperative in any policy designed to promote diversity and sustainable developmental pathways, since it stresses the importance of 'local knowledge' as a necessary adjunct to the academic focus of science-based research This is a prerequisite for the establishment of a better relationship between people and the land, particularly in fragile areas under threat either from soil degradation, or from cultural erosion at the hands of tourism.

4   Fourth, and finally, we must reiterate the importance of the inter-action between archaeological, historical and environmental studies for a more complete understanding of the long-term ecological rhythms and periodicities that structure human-modified environments. Lack of awareness and understanding of long-term socio-economic processes severely impedes the ability of policy makers to generate an accurate picture of landscape dynamics, and hence works against informed legis-lation and planning and jeopardises the maintenance and future well-being of the archaeological heritage.

In the final analysis, what we are suggesting is that historical landscapes should not be 'preserved' in a kind of cultural formaldehyde, nor should they

be conserved as objectified trophies to be curated and separated from the
larger environmental context; both of these options promote landscapes in
what is a passive voice. Rather, the archaeological heritage needs to be
presented as the locus of participatory (both intellectual and physical) action
as cultural fragments within the larger context of the complexities and contentious nature of contemporary life. These are, after all, the ingredients that
constitute the human environment as a living, evolving entity. This inevitably
means that cultural historic landscapes must be embedded in the contemporary debates on the maintenance of biodiversity and sustainability. This is
consistent with Morphy's (1988) assertion that the archaeological past is
inevitably subject to the political map of the present.

As we have seen, current archaeological approaches mean that environmental issues are treated as epiphenomena, the preserve of alternative academic
concerns. This is especially problematic since it presents current enviromental
debates as essentially separate from the social and cultural contexts discussed
by archaeologists. It is no longer productive either from a practical or intellectual perspective to maintain this false separation. The real problems of
getting to grips with the dynamics of human-modified environments – one
of the key issues for the future of archaeological research – can be profitably
approached only within a perspective that combines social, cultural and environmental knowledge. Only in this way can we make substantive inroads
towards integrated studies of cultural landscapes, and in so doing resitute
archaeology as a key element in the contemporary environmental discourse.

Note

1   The Empordà project is a multi-disciplinary EC project framed within the
    Archaeomedes Programme and funded under the auspices of the Environment
    and Climate programme (DGXII). It involves the colaboration of Spanish, Dutch
    and French universities: Universitat Pompeu Fabra (Barcelona), the Universitat
    Autonoma (Barcelona), the Universitat de Girona, the University of Amsterdam
    and the Université de Pau (France).

References

Allen, P.M., M. Lemon and R.A.F. Seaton 1995. Agricultural production and water
    quality in the Argolid valley, Greece. In *Understanding Natural and Anthropogenic
    Causes of Desertification and Land Degradation in the Mediterranean Basin (Archaeomedes
    Project)*, S.E. van der Leeuw (ed.), Chapter 8. Brussels: Directorate General XII of
    the Commission of the European Union.
Arthur, W.B. 1988. Urban systems and historical path dependence. In *Cities and their
    Vital Systems Infrastructure: past, present, and future*, J.H. Ausubel and R. Herman
    (eds), 85–97. Washington, DC: National Academy Press.
Baker, A. 1989. Introduction: on ideology and landscape. In *Ideology and Landscape
    in Historical Perspective*, A.R.H. Baker and G. Biger (eds), 1–14. Oxford: Clarendon
    Press.

Barrett, J. 1984. Fields of discourse: reconstituting a social archaeology. *Critique of Anthropology* 7, 5–16.

Bender, B. 1992. Theorising landscapes and the prehistoric landscapes of Stonehenge. *Man* 27, 735–55.

Bender, B. 1993. *Landscape: politics and perspectives.* Oxford: Berg.

Benton, T. 1994. Biology and social theory in the environmental debate. In *Social Theory and the Global Environment*, M. Redclift and T. Benton (eds), 28–50. London: Routledge.

Benton, T. and M. Redclift 1994. Introduction. In *Social Theory and the Global Environment*, M. Redclift and T. Benton (eds), 1–27. London: Routledge.

Clark, W.C. and R.E. Munn (eds) 1986. *Sustainable Development of the Biosphere.* Cambridge: Cambridge University Press.

Cohen, A.P. 1985. *The Symbolic Construction of Community.* Chichester: Ellis Horwood.

Cosgrove, D. 1984. *Social Formation and Symbolic Landscapes.* London: Croom Helm.

Courty, M.-A., N. Fedoroff, M.K. Jones, P. Castro and J. McGlade 1995. Temporalities and desertification in the Vera basin. In *Understanding Natural and Anthropogenic Causes of Desertification and Land Degradation in the Mediterranean Basin (Archaeomedes Project)*, S.E. van der Leeuw (ed.), 19–84. Brussels: Directorate General XII of the Commission of the European Union.

Daniels, S. and D. Cosgrove, 1988. Introduction: iconography and landscape. In *The Iconography of Landscape: essays on the symbolic representation, design and use of past environments*, D. Cosgrove and S. Daniels (eds), 1–22. Cambridge: Cambridge University Press.

Duncan, J. and D. Ley 1993. *Place/Culture/Representation.* London: Routledge.

Fedoroff, N. and M.-A. Courty 1995. Le role respectif des facteurs anthropiques et naturels dans la dynamique actuelle et passée des paysages méditerranéens: cas du bassin de Vera, sud-est de l'Espagne. In *L'homme et la degredation de l'environnement*, S.E. van der Leeuw (ed.), 115–42. Juan les Pins: APDCA.

Forman, R.T.T. and M. Godron 1986. *Landscape Ecology.* New York: John Wiley & Sons

Fowler, P.J. 1992. *The Past in Contemporary Society: then, now.* London: Routledge.

Gosden, C. 1994. *Social Being and Time.* Oxford: Blackwell.

Gregory, D. and J. Urry 1985. *Social Relations and Spatial Structures.* London: Macmillan.

Hewison, R. 1987. *The Heritage Industry: Britain in a climate of decline.* London: Routledge.

Hirsch, E. 1995. Landscape: between place and space. In *The Anthropology of Landscape*, E. Hirsch and M. O'Hanlon (eds), 1–30. Oxford: Clarendon Press.

Holling, C.S. 1986. The resilience of terrestrial ecosystems: local surprise and global change. In *Sustainable Development of the Biosphere*, W.C. Clark and R.E. Munn (eds), 292–316. Cambridge: Cambridge University Press.

Ingold, T. 1993. The temporality of landscape. *World Archaeology* 25, 52–74.

Kolen, J. 1995. Recreating (in) nature, visiting history: second thoughts on landscape reserves and their role in the preservation and experience of the historic environment. *Archaeological Dialogues* 2, 127–59.

Layton, R. 1986. *Uluru, an Aboriginal History of Ayers Rock.* Canberra: Australian Institute of Aboriginal Studies.

Lemaire, T. 1997. Archaeology between the invention and destruction of the landscape. *Archaeological Dialogues* 4, 24–35.

Lorenz, E. 1963. Deterministic non-periodic flow. *Journal of Atmospheric Sciences* 20, 130–41.

Lowenthal, D. 1985. *The Past is a Foreign Country.* Cambridge: Cambridge University Press.

McGlade, J. 1995a. Archaeology and the ecodynamics of human-modified landscapes. *Antiquity* 69, 113–32.

McGlade, J. 1995b. An integrative multiscalar modelling framework for human eco-dynamic research in the Vera basin, south-east Spain. In *L'homme et la degredation de l'environnement*, S.E. van der Leeuw (ed.), 357–85. Juan les Pins: APDCA.

McGlade, J. 1996. Social natural dynamics in the middle Aguas catchment: a modelling approach. In *Palaeoclimatic Reconstruction and the Dynamics of Human Settlement and Land-use in the Region of the Middle Aguas (Almeria) of the South-east Iberian Peninsula*. Brussels: DG XII, CEU.

McGlade, J. In press. The times of history: archaeology, narrative and nonlinear dynamics. In *New Approaches to Time in Archaeology*, T. Murray (ed.). London: Routledge.

McGlade, J. and S.E. van der Leeuw 1997. Introduction: archaeology and non linear dynamics: new approaches to long-term change. In *Time, Process and Structured Transformation in Archaeology*, S.E. van der Leeuw and J. McGlade (eds), 1–32. London: Routledge.

McGlade, J. and M. Picazo (eds) 1997. Human ecodynamics and land-use conflict: monitoring degradation-sensitive environments in the Empordà, north-east Spain. Archaeomedes II, First Interim Report. Brussels: DGXII, CEU.

McGlade, J., P. Castro, M.-A. Courty, N. Fedoroff and M. Jones 1995. The socio-ecology of the Vera basin: towards a dynamic reconstruction. In *Understanding Natural and Anthropogenic Causes of Desertification and Land Degradation in the Mediterranean Basin (Archaeomedes Project)*, S.E. van der Leeuw (ed.), 297–326. Brussels: Directorate General XII of the Commission of the European Union.

Morphy, H. 1988. Maintaining cosmic unity: ideology and the reproduction of Yolngu clans. In *Hunters and Gatherers: property, power and ideology*, T. Ingold, D. Riches and J. Woodburn (eds), 249–71. Oxford: Berg.

Morphy, H. 1991. *Ancestral Connections: art and an Aboriginal system of knowledge*. Chicago: University of Chicago Press.

Picazo, M. 1997. Hearth and home: the timing of maintenance activities. In *Invisible People and Processes: writing gender and childhood into European archaeology*, J. Moore and E. Scott (eds), 59–67. London: Leicester University Press.

Poincaré, H. 1899. *Les méthodes nouvelles de la mécanique céleste. Vol. 3*. Paris: Gautier-Villars.

Prigogine, I. and I. Stengers 1984. *Order out of Chaos: man's new dialogue with nature*. London: Fontana.

Soja, E. 1980. The socio-spatial dialectic. *Annals of the Association of American Geographers* 70, 207–25.

Soja, E. 1989. *The Reassertion of Space in Critical Social Theory*. New York: Chapman & Hall.

Stone, P. and B. Molyneaux (eds) 1994. *The Presented Past: heritage, museums and education*. London: Routledge.

Taylor, L.J. 1983. *Dutchmen on the Bay: the ethnohistory of a contractual community*. Philadelphia: University of Pennsylvania Press.

Thomas, J. 1993a. The politics of vision and the archaeologies of landscape. In *Landscape: politics and perspectives*, B. Bender (ed.) 19–48. Oxford: Berg.

Thomas, J. 1993b. The hermeneutics of megalithic space. In *Interpretative Archaeology*, C. Tilley (ed.), 73–98. Oxford: Berg.

Tilley, C. (ed.) 1993. *Interpretative Archaeology*. Oxford: Berg.

Tilley, C. 1994. *A Phenomenology of Landscape*. Oxford: Berg.

Ucko, P.J. 1994. Foreword. In *The Presented Past: heritage, museums and education*, P. Stone and B. Molyneaux (eds), xx–xxxiii. London: Routledge.

Ucko, P.J. 1995. Introduction: archaeological interpretation in a world context. In *Theory in Archaeology: a world perspective*, P. Ucko (ed.), 1–27. London: Routledge.

Index

Aborigines: Aboriginal and white conceptions of landscape, comparison of 7–8,
216–17; ancestors, presence of in the
landscape 193, 195, 196, 208, 211, 223,
237–8, 323; archaeological research,
involvement in 424, 430–1, 435; cargo
cults, absence of 233–4; clan membership, its role in relating people to land
209; contact period history of 192, 199,
207, 211–12, 232–3, 425; cyclical
conception of time 208–9; descent
systems of 209; Land Claims 192, 201–2,
423; landscape, competing representations
of 7–8, 216–17; landscape, its creation by
ancestors 193, 194, 208, 223; landscape,
role of in construction of social identity
193, 194; The Law, its relationship to
land 209, 210; maintenance of traditional
cultures of 210–11, 219; moiety and
conception of place 195; myth, presence
of in the landscape 193, 195, 200, 220–2,
223, 237–8, 323; place, establishment of
relationships to 199–202; powerful places
in the landscape, conception of 194, 208;
practical knowledge of landscape 209–10;
rock art of, antiquity of 324, 328;
supernatural perception of landscape 200,
207–9; supernatural, its presence in the
landscape 193, 195, 196, 200, 207–9,
237–8, 323, western maps, resistance to
39–40; *see also* Alawa; Australia; Barunga
region; Bass Strait; Dreamtime;
Gadjerong; Keep River area;
Kowanyama; Walbiri; Yolngu

Afomarolahy: Andriamañare, their
association with 398; history of
398–9, 406; *see also* Andriamañare
Africa: *see* Bushmen; Namibia
agrios: concept of 370
Alawa: ancestors, presence of in the
landscape 223, 237–8; ancestral routes,
immutability of 235–6; ancestral
routes, relationship of to water sources
223, 237–8; colonisation, response to
233–5; conception affiliation 230–1;
conflict with white settlers 232–3;
contact period history of 232–3;
countries, concept of 223; cults,
modification of in response to
colonisation 234–5; custodianship of land
236–7; estate, concept of 223; estates,
modern functions of 236; estates,
modifications in 235; food prohibitions
231; food species terminology of 222,
224–5; Ganyila, legend of 221; Hodgson
Downs, environment of 222; hunter-
gathering, maintenance of among 219;
Jambirina, legend of 222, 223, 231;
kinship terminology of 229–30; land, its
distribution amongst semi-moieties 227,
228, 230, 235; land, management of
223, 227; landscape of, creation of by
ancestors 223; landscape terminology
222, 224–5; legends of 220–2, 223, 231;
myth, presence of in the landscape
220–2, 223, 237–8; moieties,
membership of 228; moieties, spatial
distribution of 227; ritual, functions of